ECCLESIASTICAL FACTIONALISM AND RELIGIOUS CONTROVERSY IN FIFTH-CENTURY GAUL

ECCLESIASTICAL FACTIONALISM AND RELIGIOUS CONTROVERSY IN FIFTH-CENTURY GAUL

RALPH W. MATHISEN

THE CATHOLIC UNIVERSITY OF AMERICA PRESS
WASHINGTON, D.C.

Copyright © 1989
THE CATHOLIC UNIVERSITY OF AMERICA PRESS

Printed in the United States of America

LIBRARY OF CONGRESS CATALOGING-IN-PUBLICATION DATA

Mathisen, Ralph W., 1947–
   Ecclesiastical factionalism and religious controversy in fifth-century Gaul.

   Bibliography: p.
   Includes index.
   1. Gaul—Church history.   I. Title.
BR844.M34   1988   274.4'02   88-18922
ISBN 0-8132-0658-8

For Arnold H. and Barbara L. Mathisen
My Parents

CONTENTS

PREFACE

"nequivi tamen obtegere vel certamina flagitiosorum vel vitam
recte viventium"
(Gregory of Tours, *Hist. Franc.* 1 *praef.*)

Nearly all the sources for the ecclesiastical affairs of fifth-century
Gaul contain references to various forms of quarreling, conflict, and
controversy. There also appear to have been two kinds of dissension,
which differed if not in kind at least in scope: local quarreling, usually
involving a bishop's relations with his clergy and constituency, and
extra-local or regional contention, involving interactions among bishops and other influential churchmen, often acting in groups. The
purely local variety, however, which was concerned with local status,
office, and authority, seems not to have had a particularly Gallic flavor.
A recent study has suggested, rather, that local discord of this sort is
endemic in so-called traditional societies everywhere at all times, from
antiquity until the twentieth century.[1]

The following study will concentrate upon extra-local Gallic ecclesiastical strife, which does appear to have had aspects which were
peculiarly Gallic in nature and unique in the late Roman world. Examples of strictly local dissension will be discussed only insofar as they
illustrate or affect more widespread interactions among powerful Gallic potentates. Much of the collective history of the fifth-century Gallic
church, it will be suggested, can be explained from the point of view
of the activities of groups (or parties, or factions) of individuals with
similar interests, who formed, often ephemerally, alliances for the pursuit of mutually desirable goals. The result often was factional quarreling, or "factionalism," as one group contended with another.

Prosopographical methods will be employed in an attempt to identify some of these groups.[2] The activities of the individuals associated

1. See Van Dam, *Leadership.*

2. For this methodology, see Carney, "Prosopography" pp.156-179; Chastagnol, "Prosopographie" pp.1229-1235; Graham, "Limitations" pp.136-157; Mathisen, "Late Roman Prosopography" pp.1-12; Maurin, "Prosopographie" pp.824-836; Pflaum, "Réflexions" pp.318-321; and
Stone, "Prosopography" pp.46-79.

with each group will be interpreted in the context of the corporate interests of the group as a whole. The concentration on ecclesiastical controversies, moreover, necessarily means that the motives of individual churchmen, or groups of churchmen, may not always be portrayed in the best possible light. However commendable for their piety they may have been on some occasions, on others these Gauls can appear ambitious, self-centered, and downright cantankerous. Yet, it is only by examining such aspects of their natures that their activities can be fully understood.

This approach also will allow the evidence to be interpreted in the same context as it often was written, that of dissension and contention. This will portray it in a new light. Contemporary writers consistently tried to present their own point of view, and very often to obfuscate that of their opponents. Their works cannot be interpreted in isolation from the other viewpoints, prevalent at the same time, which often affected the way that an author presented his case, even if he made no mention of competing versions or opinions.

This study is not intended, moreover, to provide a narrative account of the history of the Gallic church during the fifth century: this has been done many times in the past.[3] Nor is it meant as a coherent discussion of the development of church dogma, administration, or hierarchy. It is rather an investigation of the interactions, activities, and where possible the motives of groups of Gauls whose corporate actions affected all these areas. It attempts to reconstruct the socio-religious context of contemporary sources and events. It will show that the past tendency to assume that the Gallic church acted as a single entity is untenable. There never was unity of action or organization, as group contended with group for influence and authority. There were, however, times when the Gallic bishops were more united than at other times, when groups of bishops made common cause in their pursuit of mutual objectives.

One way in which the Gallic church seems to have differed from other areas of the Roman world was in the role played by the conflict between orthodoxy and heresy. Unlike nearly every other part of the empire, disputes over orthodoxy were rarely of great moment in fifth-century Gaul. This is not to say, however, that the Gauls were not concerned about theological orthodoxy. It is simply that they were united in their definition of what was orthodox and what was heretical. Manicheism, Pelagianism, and Augustinian predestination were

---

3. Most recently in the three-volume study of Griffe, *Gaule*. A proposed fourth volume was left unfinished, although chapters from it have been published separately in the *Bulletin de littérature ecclésiastique*. For secular histories, see Bury, *L.R.E.*; Jones, *L.R.E.*; Seeck, *Untergang*; and Stein, *Geschichte*. For Gaul, see Stroheker, *Adel*.

roundly and universally condemned; other heretical beliefs were rarely even mentioned.

The fifth-century heresies with which the imperial government and church were so often concerned had scarcely any impact on Gaul. Gauls showed little interest at all in discussing them, and usually did so only when requested to from the outside, and even then only half-heartedly. They preferred to define orthodoxy for themselves, not on the basis of some outside authority. Any differences of theology or schisms that the Gauls did have, and these were very few, were solved internally and without a great deal of fuss. The late fourth-century Felician controversy was put to rest by c.400, and the debate over the nature of the soul was pursued in a genteel, drawing-room atmosphere, not in a rambunctious church council. It would appear that, if anything, heretical theologies served to unify the Gallic episcopal establishment by serving as a means of reaffirming consensus. Ritual condemnations of Pelagianism and predestination reassured Gallic ecclesiastics of their mutual orthodoxy.

Elsewhere in the empire, it has been suggested, heretical or schismatic views could serve as a cloak for nationalistic sentiment, could reflect conflicts between town and country, or could provide a means for solving irreconcilable differences in local communities.[4] Africa had its Donatists, Spain its Priscillianists, Britain eventually its Pelagians, Rome its Manichees and Novatianists, and the east its monophysites and a multitude of others. Only Gaul, it seems, lacked its own peculiar, local heresy.[5] In the midst of all the quarreling in which Gallic ecclesiastics engaged, specific accusations of heresy against specific individuals are vanishingly few.[6] As a result of their disdain for accusa-

4. See Jones, "Heresies," pp.280-298; Matthews, *Aristocracies*, pp.146-172; Myres, "Pelagius"; and Van Dam, *Leadership*.

5. This is seen, for example, in Sidonius' praise of Patiens of Lyons (*Epist.* 6.12.4) for diminishing the number of heretics, but in default of any Gallic heresy, all he could name were "Photinians," hardly a Gallic concern. The only local heresy which received any attention at all was Arianism, and this not because it threatened catholic orthodoxy, but because it was the belief of the intrusive Germans. Some Gallo-Romans may even have welcomed it as a segregating element; they showed little real concern about it, and were even rather restrained in their treatment of Gallic Arians. Sidonius mentioned Arianism only twice by name, reporting a debate between Basilius of Aix and the Goth Modaharius (*Epist.* 7.6.2), and noting that the Arians of Bourges raised no objections to the ordination of the orthodox bishop Simplicius (*Epist.* 7.8.3). Elsewhere (*Epist.* 1.2.4), Sidonius could praise the religious devotion of the Visigothic king Theoderic without mentioning that he was an Arian. See also *Carm. de prov. div.* 5.27-60; *Chron. gall. a.* 452 no.138, s.a.451 (the "infanda Arrianorum haeresis, quae se nationibus barbaris miscuit...."); Faustus, *De spiritu sancto* 1.1, 1.3, 2.2-4, *Epist.* 20/3 (perhaps to be identified with his *Contra Arrianos et Macedonianos* of Gennad. *Vir. ill.* 86) and 3/20.1, 25; 4/14.3; 7/17.20; Salv. *De. gub.* 7.9; and Vincent. *Comm.* 4,11. The *Statuta ecclesiae antiqua* (ch. 1) condemned Arian beliefs, but never even mentioned the heresy by name.

6. See Woodward, *Nationalism*, p.77. Van Dam, *Leadership* (passim), however, sees accusations of heresy as a regular aspect of the Gallic scene, although most of his evidence, as he himself recognizes (p.87), comes from North Africa and Spain.

tions of heresy, the Gauls had to find other means for resolving their own unresolvable differences.

Another way in which the Gallic church in the fifth century seems to have differed from other areas of the empire is in the relationship between monks and bishops. Unlike areas where there often was tension between monks, who frequently represented the lower orders of society, and the established church authorities, who often came from the aristocracy, Gaul had no such difficulties.[7] As of the beginning of the fifth century, rather, monastic cliques in Gaul began to coöpt the episcopate. Monks from the monasteries of Marmoutier, Lérins, and St. Victor at Marseilles became desirable episcopal candidates. At the same time, it became standard practice for bishops to found their own monasteries if there were not any already associated with their episcopal sees. The Gallic bishop-cum-abbot became a common theme. A unifying element, it seems, is that both the monks and the bishops very often came from aristocratic backgrounds. By their very nature, all shared a common concern: the maintenance of their local authority. In fifth-century Gaul, the lower classes seem generally to have been excluded from high monastic and clerical rank. The tension caused in the later fourth century by the ordination of the monk Martin as bishop of Tours vanished in the fifth, when Sidonius (*Epist.* 7.9.9–14) could opine that a monk made every bit as good a choice as bishop as a government official.

The Gallic ecclesiastical establishment also seems to have had little interest in extra-Gallic affairs of a secular nature. The secular politics of Spain and Italy attracted very little attention from Gallic ecclesiastics, and those of the east received even less.[8] With one exception, even the secular affairs of Gaul had surprisingly little obvious effect on the history of the Gallic church during the period c.425-470. The far north, of course, lost most of its contact with the rest of Gaul early in the century, and the expanding Visigothic kingdom also was removed from the mainstream of Gallo-Roman ecclesiastical life.[9] The rest of Gaul (Lugdunensis, the Rhône valley, and Provence), however, ecclesiastically remained remarkably stable during the fifth century. One does find occasional references of a generalized nature to the troubles of the times, as they served to hinder or delay the performing of normal church operations. But unlike Spain, where ecclesiastical activities

---

7. See Jones, *L.R.E.* p.932, "The eremetic and monastic movements were in some sense a rebellion against the constituted authorities of the church."

8. The lack of awareness of eastern affairs in Spain already has been noted by Thompson, *Romans* pp.146-150.

9. See Mathisen, "Aquitania."

were seriously disrupted, there is never any indication that normal operations ever were threatened in Gaul.

Even some of the most significant political events of c.425-475, such as the campaigns of Flavius Aetius (425-454), the invasion of the Huns (451), the reign of the Gallic emperor Avitus (455-456), the visits of Majorian (458-461), the revolt of Aegidius (461-464), and the offensive of Anthemius (469-471), had virtually no discernable effect on the regional interactions and activities of Gallic churchmen, and left no particular mark in ecclesiastical sources.[10] Gallic ecclesiastics seem rather to have taken these events in stride, and to have conducted business as usual.

There was, however, one important exception to the lack of impact of secular affairs. Changes in the secular power structure in Gaul at the highest levels often brought a concommitant restructuring of the Gallic episcopal establishment at the same levels. At Arles in particular, such changes could result in the expulsion, or even the murder, of the current bishop and the selection of a new one, who also would be a partisan of the new secular master. As a result, there was a tendency for the bishops of Arles, and their partisans, to be the protégés, or allies, of the most powerful secular potentates in Gaul, at least until the death of Aetius in 454. Elsewhere in Gaul, influential bishops also tried to ally themselves with the local secular authorities.

In the 460s, moreover, as Roman influence waned, it appears that Germanic potentates attempted to adopt a similar policy of involvement in the activities of the Gallo-Roman church. For the time being, however, such interference was rather restrained in nature, and the Gallic church gained even greater independence of action. Only later did the Visigoth Euric (466-484) begin to intervene more heavy-handedly in the functioning of the church in Aquitania, and this was to mark the beginning of ever greater Germanic control over the church.

With regard to extra-Gallic ecclesiastical affairs, the bishops of Gaul did have one significant interest: their relation with the bishop of Rome. The Gallic concern, however, usually was from the perspective of what he could do *for* them, not what he might do *to* them. The bishop of Rome learned that, however great his prestige and moral authority might be, he had the ability to influence Gallic affairs only to the extent that he had strong supporters there willing and able to implement his decisions. Sometimes, therefore, the Roman pontiffs

---

10. Of the many Gallic sources written c.425-475, only Salvian's *De gubernatione dei* speaks at any length about the barbarian invasions, and even this not in the context of church operations in his own time.

allied themselves with a powerful bishop of Gaul, usually the bishop of Arles, and looked at him as their Gallic "representative," although not yet their "vicar."

The Arlesian bishops, however, were very jealous of their own perquisites. They were perfectly willing to accept whatever additional status the bishop of Rome chose to grant them. This did not mean, however, that they were any the more willing to obey his orders when such orders were contrary to their own interests. Consequently, conflicts often arose between the bishops of Rome and Arles when the former gave the latter a command which he was unwilling, or unable, to carry out. The only response available to the bishop of Rome in such circumstances was to threaten to reallocate (or actually to do so) some privilege he had bestowed in the past.

All too frequently, moreover, historians have assumed that such decrees in the extant papal correspondence actually went into effect, and have failed to realize that these were merely what the pope wanted to happen. Too much emphasis often has been placed upon the relations between the bishop of Rome and the church of Gaul simply because this correspondence makes up so much of the extant evidence. Viewed in context, however, the letters indicate that contacts between Rome and Gaul were relatively infrequent, and nearly always were initiated by disaffected Gauls, who hoped to gain something in Rome which they had not been able to gain in Gaul. The bishops of Rome do not appear to have been overly concerned with Gaul.[11] Their primary concerns lay in Italy and in the east. Their dealings with Gaul seem to have been more *ad hoc* in nature, a series of responses to Gallic appeals; their only consistent aspect was the repeated assertion of papal authority in Gaul.

The bishops of Rome, therefore, normally could be expected to intervene in Gaul only when requested to do so by Gauls. This meant that the Gallic bishops, if they were averse to the pope's involvement in Gaul, could hinder it only to the the degree that they could maintain unity and consensus among themselves, and thus forestall discontented Gallic ecclesiastics from making the portentous appeal to Rome. Their natural tendencies toward factionalism, however, meant that it was never easy to reach this consensus.

Like-minded Gallic bishops had several means of promoting factional unity. One already has been mentioned: gaining the patronage of secular potentates at the highest levels of the Gallic administration. Another was by supporting their partisans as candidates for Gallic episcopates. This practice not only allowed them to obtain the most

---

11. Contrary to the conclusions of Langgärtner, *Gallienpolitik* passim.

powerful kind of the cherished local authority, it also gave them the opportunity to exercise the most visible means of ritually expressing unity and consensus, by their attendance at church councils. Here, bishops could meet, discuss any differences, and reconfirm their commitment to their mutual interests by issuing canons designed to regulate the Gallic church. Such councils also provided the opportunity for settling disputes, and therefore lessened the negative impact of factionalism. Even if councils did not always fulfil this purpose, they could at least give the outward appearance of doing so. Finally, a faction needed a powerful leader, and one such usually was the bishop of Arles, whose status occasionally was magnified by the willing cession to him of the metropolitan rights of some of his partisans.

Even if the organization of ecclesiastical factions limited dissension among their members, there always was some degree of competition among factions. On many occasions, dissension arose over questions of ecclesiastical status and authority. Some controversies involved the control of parishes, or the rights of metropolitans to ordain bishops in certain cities. Others concerned who was to be bishop of a city, and episcopal losers in such disputes ran the risk of being deposed, on real or trumped-up charges, by the partisans of an opposing faction. Sometimes these losers could be induced to take the matter no further. At other times, however, a bishop, especially a metropolitan one, who felt that his authority had been infringed upon and who was not powerful enough to obtain redress in Gaul chose to appeal his case to Rome.

Such appeals even could be viewed as the ritual means by which powerful Gallic ecclesiastics expressed irreconcilable differences. An appeal to outside authority at a time when outside authority meant very little in Gaul provided the Gauls with a safety valve which allowed them to continue to live together without irreparable damage. It was these appeals which also gave the bishop of Rome his best opportunity to exercise supervisory authority in Gaul. As a result, the popes seem to have welcomed them. In every attested case, they found in favor of the appellants. This practice would only encourage additional appeals in the future. Regardless of whether a papal decree went into effect or not, every appeal gave the bishop of Rome one more precedent attesting his Gallic authority.

The first three-quarters of the fifth century, and especially the period c.425-475, were a short period during which powerful Gallic ecclesiastics had an inordinate degree of control over their own destinies. Organized into powerful factions, they flouted the will not only of the bishop of Rome but even of secular officialdom. Their ability to do so, however, was largely a result of the political uncertainties of the times. The appearance of the barbarian kingdoms toward the end of the century brought these bishops' extensive authority and cooperation to an end. Episcopal elections came to be either pre-ordained or at least approved by the local king. Councils were summoned only under his auspices, and they united bishops only of a particular kingdom. By A.D. 500, the brief period during which Gallic ecclesiastical factions could enjoy an independent field of operation over wide regions of Gaul was over. Bishops, of course, continued to be very powerful locally, where they could become virtual petty monarchs. But in the sixth century, no bishop of Arles could presume to take part in the deposition of a bishop of Besançon, nor could the bishops of Lyons and Autun hope to attend a church council at Arles.

A few technical matters now might be mentioned. Most names of persons are left in their Latin forms, although names of well-known individuals have been Anglicized, such as, for example, Innocent, Boniface, and Celestine rather than the pedantic Innocentius, Bonifatius, and Coelestinus. Hilarus of Rome, however, and Hilarius of Narbonne remain Hilarus and Hilarius so as to avoid confusion with Hilary (Hilarius) of Arles. Modern French geographical names, where known, are usually cited. For the sake of convenience, central Gaul (i.e. Lugdunensis) will be referred to as "the north," and Provence and the lower Rhône valley as "the south." By this time, the far north (Belgica and Germania) had effectively ceased to be a part of unified Gallic ecclesiastical life. Papal letters, documents with multiple authors, and some imperial constitutions are cited by the conventional first two or three words of the text. Secondary sources are cited by author's name and short title; full references are given in the bibliography. It is the author's personal preference to quote primary source material *in extenso*, with translations, when directly relevant to the topic. Ellipses occasionally will be omitted in translations when alterations in the word order prevent their use.

This study could not have been undertaken, or completed, without extensive assistance from many institutions and individuals. Financial support has been gratefully received from the American Council of Learned Societies, the American Philosophical Society, and the University of South Carolina's Venture and Research and Productive Scholarship Funds. U.S.C.'s Computer Services Division and Humanities and Social Sciences Computing Laboratory allowed very generous use of their computer resources. The Interlibrary Loan Department of U.S.C.'s Thomas Cooper Library also has been very helpful.

A great debt is owed to scholars such as L. Duchesne, E. Griffe, and K.F. Stroheker, whose work on late Roman Gaul gave this study a firm foundation. Similarly, it would have been difficult to pursue any kind of prosopographical study without the past meticulous effort of the editors of the *Prosopography of the Later Roman Empire*, and the assistance of John R. Martindale in particular is appreciatively acknowledged. A large number of specialists, including Barry Baldwin, Timothy Barnes, Peter Brown, Thomas Burns, Frank Clover, Robert B. Eno, Martin Heinzelmann, R.A. Markus, and Robert B. Patterson, have graciously read the manuscript at various stages of completion. Their many helpful comments and criticisms have saved me from a multitude of errors and missteps, and have given me new insight into my own research. I also am very grateful for the patient assistance and guidance given me by the staff of The Catholic University of America Press, and in particular Peggy Leonard and David McGonagle, during the lengthy publication process. Finally, special thanks are due to my wife Rita, for putting up with all this for the past seven years, to my four-year-old daughter Katherine, for helping me to keep my papers arranged, and to my four-month-old son David, who occupies my lap as I write this.

Columbia, South Carolina
1 December 1987

ABBREVIATIONS

A.C.O.	E. Schwartz ed., *Acta conciliorum oecumenicorum*
A.A.S.S.	*Acta sanctorum*
Clavis	A. Gaar and E. Dekkers eds., *Clavis patrum latinorum* (2nd ed.) (Turnhout, 1962)
C.I.L. 12	O. Hirschfeld ed., *Corpus inscriptionum latinarum* 12: *Inscriptiones Galliae Narbonensis latinae* (Berlin, 1888)
C.I.L. 13	O. Hirschfeld, C. Zangenmeister, A. von Domaszewski, O. Bohn and E. Stein eds., *Corpus inscriptionum latinarum* 13: *Inscriptiones Trium Galliarum et Germaniarum latinae* (Berlin, 1899-1943)
Corp.chr.lat.	*Corpus christianorum, series latina*
C.S.E.L.	*Corpus scriptorum ecclesiasticorum latinorum*
I.L.S.	H. Dessau, *Inscriptiones latinae selectae*, Vol. 1 (Berlin, 1954)
M.G.H. A.A.	*Monumenta Germaniae historica, Auctores antiquissimi*
M.G.H. Epist.	*Monumenta Germaniae historica, Epistulae*
M.G.H.	*Monumenta Germaniae historica,*
S.R.M.	*Scriptores rerum merovingicarum*
P.G.	J.-P. Migne ed., *Patrologia graeca*
P.L.	J.-P. Migne ed., *Patrologia latina*
P.L.R.E. I	A.H.M. Jones, J.R. Martindale, J. Morris eds., *The Prosopography of the Later Roman Empire. Volume I. A.D. 260-395* (Cambridge, 1971)
P.L.R.E. II	J.R. Martindale ed., *The Prosopography of the Later Roman Empire. Volume II. A.D. 395-527* (Cambridge, 1980)
P.L.S.	*Patrologia latina, supplementum*
S.C.	*Sources chrétiennes*

INTRODUCTION
'AMICITIA' AND 'FACTIO'

During Roman times it was very common for secular aristocrats with similar outlooks and desires to form associations, or factions, in the pursuit of their common goals. Speaking of the late Republic and early Empire, Sir Ronald Syme noted, "Roman political factions were welded together, less by unity of principle than by mutual interest and by mutual services (*officia*). . . . on a favourable estimate the bond was called *amicitia*, otherwise *factio*."[1] One's own ties, of course, were described as *amicitia*, whereas the more pejorative term *factio* was applied to associations of one's rivals. This distinction was described by Sallust in a discussion of "those whom desire for the same things, hatred of the same things, and fear of the same things brings together," when he noted that "among good men, this is called *amicitia*, among the wicked it is *factio*."[2] Aristocratic associations, therefore, had positive and negative sides to them. In discussions of one's own circle of friends, the positive aspect, *amicitia*, was most heavily stressed; one never would refer to one's own circle as a *factio*.

In late Roman Gaul, the bonds of friendship were extremely important. Sidonius Apollinaris repeatedly referred to the *iura amicitiae*.[3] It also was important to have the same friends—and enemies. In a letter to a friend, after discussing the similarities of their backgrounds, Sidonius went on to note, "In addition to these things is that which is even more important and effective in strengthening friendships: in seeking out or avoiding any individual persons whatsoever, we strove

---

1. Syme, *Roman Revolution*, p.157; see also p.12 for political alliances as being *amicitia* or *factio*. See also Cicero, *De re publica* 3.23, "cum autem certi propter divitias aut genus aut aliquas opes rem publicam tenent, est factio, sed vocantur illi optimates."

2. "quos omnis eadem cupere, eadem odisse, eadem metuere in unum coegit. sed haec inter bonos amicitia, inter malos factio est" (*Bell. jurg.* 31.14-15).

3. See *Epist.* 4.7.1, 6.2.3, 7.6.1; note also the "leges amicitiae" (ibid. 4.2.2, 7.17.1). See Matthews, *Aristocracies* pp.5-10 for a discussion of "religio amicitiae" in the circle of Symmachus.

I

equally with a likeness of judgment."[4] The following study is concerned with friendships, however, only insofar as they related to the
quarrels and controversies of fifth-century Gaul. It therefore will be
more concerned with the negative side of aristocratic associations, the
factional side.

During the later Roman Empire, the word *factio* often was applied
to organized seditious activity, especially in a legal context. The juris-
consult Paul had opined that in cases of treason (*maiestas*), the accused
first should be asked "with what resources, what faction, and what
leaders he had done this."[5] In the fourth century, one law was issued
against anyone who led the barbarians "in an abominable faction,"
and another against "whoever entered an abominable faction with
the soldiers, with private persons, or with barbarians."[6]

In fifth-century Gaul, factionalism continued to be associated with
unsavory special-interest groups, and the word "faction" regularly referred to organized groups of one's opponents. Paulinus of Pella told
how in 414/415 the city of Bazas was threatened by "a servile faction,
mixed with the insane fury of a few wicked, although freeborn,
youths, armed especially for the slaughter of the nobility."[7] Eucherius
of Lyons, in a discussion of the pitfalls of the secular life, suggested in
432 that riches "arouse the eyes and spirits of the factional, and in
some way cause proscriptions themselves to appear."[8] Sidonius Apollinaris spoke of being accosted in Arles in 461 by a "mob of factious
men," the henchmen of his enemy Paeonius, and elsewhere, Victor of
Tonnena wrote of how Olybrius, the new western emperor, had been
supported "by the faction of the patrician Ricimer."[9]

In the ecclesiastical world organized factionalism also was common.
A law of Constantine, for example, stated, "We recognize that the

---

4. "quod est ad amicitias ampliandas his validius efficaciusque, in singulis quibusque per-
sonis vel expetendis aequaliter vel cavendis iudicii parilitate certavimus" (*Epist.* 3.1.1).

5. "quibus opibus, qua factione, quibus hoc auctoribus fecerit" (*Sententiae* 5.29.2).

6. *C.Th.* 7.1.1 (28 April 323), "scelerata factione"; 9.14.3 (4 September 398), against "quisquis
cum militibus, vel privatis, barbaris etiam scelestam inierit factionem aut factionis ipsius susce-
perit sacramenta vel dederit." See Wiener, *Commentary* pp.157-164, who suggests that the legal
definition of the Germanic blood feud arose originally from the Roman *factio*.

7. "factio servilis paucorum mixta furori / insano iuvenum [nequam] licet ingenuorum, /
armata in caedem specialem nobilitatis" (*Euch.* 334-336).

8. "factiosorum oculos animosque provocant, proscriptionesque ipsas quodammodo osten-
tant" (*Epist. ad Valer.*: *P.L.*50.716).

9. "turba factiosorum" (Sid.Apoll. *Epist.* 1.11.8); "factione Ricimiri patricii" (Vict. Tonn.
Chron. s.a.473: *M.G.H. A.A.* 11.188). The word *factio* was particularly favored by Fredegarius;
see *Chron.* 3.7, 3.84, 3.92, 3.89, and 4.12. Gregory of Tours, however, very rarely used this particular word, except to describe the circus factions in Constantinople (see *H.F.* 5.30), on which
see Cameron, *Circus Factions*. For the similarity between circus factions and "ecclesiastical parties," see MacMullen, *Enemies* p.178. For another use, see Brown, "Patrons" p.56 n.6, "Rival
rhetors had long been suppported by rival factions."

clerics of the catholic church are troubled by the faction of the here-tics."[10] In 367/368, Valentinian referred to the "turbulent factional-ism" which had arisen at Rome over the election of a new bishop.[11] In 381, a law was issued against heretics involved "in any factional uprising."[12] In 383 or 384, the emperor Theodosius discussed those who "through contention, with a detestable insinuation, perverted the minds of many not by faith but by faction."[13] Prosper of Aquitaine told how in 418 the Roman Constantius "suffered much at the hands of the faction of the Pelagians."[14] Hydatius reported that in 441 the bishop Sabinus was expelled from Seville by a *factio*.[15]

An apt description of later Roman factionalism is given by Isidore of Seville, who in his chapter "de quibusdam vocabulis hominum" included the following definition: "factional [man]: in the midst of quarrels, when we wish to be accepted as conspiratorial, when, truly, [we wish to be accepted as] influential and powerful, and as a member, so to speak, of a powerful faction."[16] This description contains all the key elements of factionalism as it existed in the fifth-century Gallic church, when one group strove with another for status, influence, and authority. Gallic ecclesiastical sources repeatedly refer to *opprobria* and *seditiones*, not to mention the *calumniae, contentiones, discordiae, dis-sensio, intentio, perfidia, perturbationes, praesumptio, pravitas, usurpa-tiones,* and *scandala.* Likewise, the seeking of *gratia* ("favor," "influ-ence") and *potentia* ("power," "authority") sometimes was nearly as common in the church as it was in the secular world.[17]

The desire in late Roman Gaul to associate oneself with those who had similar sentiments, so as to acquire greater, corporate, influence, was an inherent part of the aristocratic nature. Even though the par-ticipants themselves would have referred to their relationships as *ami-*

10. "haereticorum factione comperimus ecclesiae catholicae clericos ita vexari ..." (*C.Th.* 16.2.1 [31 October 313]).

11. "licet iusta videatur fuisse vindicta, quae illic turbulenter exercitam factionem coerci-tione sedavit...." (*Epist. imp.* 5: *C.S.E.L.* 35.48).

12. "si quid eruptio factiosa tentaverit" (*C.Th.* 16.5.6.3).

13. "sed circa eos non est dilata ultio, qui insidiati bonis moribus et caelestibus institutis paulisper ex contentione non fide sed factione multorum mentes detestanda insinuatione per-verterent" (*Epist. imp.* 2a: *C.S.E.L.* 35.45).

14. "factione eorundem [Pelagianorum] multa pertulit" (*Chron.* 1265 s.a.418).

15. *Chron.* 124.

16. "factiosus: inter opprobria, cum seditiosum accipi volumus, cum vero gratiosum ac po-tentem et quasi magnae factionis" (*Etym.* 10.106).

17. For the terminology, note also Paul. Pell. *Euch.* 264-265, "namque et quanta mihi per te conlata potentum / gratia praestiterit...." For ecclesiastical, and in particular episcopal, *potentia*, see *De sept. ord. eccl.* 5 (*P.L.* 30.154), which speaks of "singuli quique pro potentia episcopalis nominis, quam sibi ipsi illicite absque ecclesia vindicaverunt...."; see also Heinzelmann, *Bi-schofsherrschaft* p.123. For a suggested relationship between secular and ecclesiastical *gratia* see Myres, "Pelagius" pp.21-36. See also chapter 1 below.

citia, their activities often more properly fit the old Roman definition of *factio*. One can only note, finally, the degree to which Caesar's assessment of Gallic factionalism in the first century B.C. also could be applied to that of the fifth century A.D.: "In Gaul, not only in all the cities and in all the villages and districts, but almost even in individual homes there are factions, and the leaders of these factions are those who are thought to have the greatest influence. . . ."[18]

18. "in Gallia non solum in omnibus civitatibus atque in omnibus pagis partibusque sed paene etiam in singulis domibus factiones sunt, earumque factionum principes sunt, qui summam auctoritatem . . . iudicio habere existimantur. . . ." (*B.G.* 6.11.2-3).

CHAPTER I

THE GALLIC CHURCH
IN THE FOURTH CENTURY

THE ORIGINS OF GALLIC FACTIONALISM

THE GROWTH OF THE GALLIC EPISCOPATE

During the fourth century, the Gallic church became increasingly organized and influential.[1] In 314, the first imperial-sponsored church council was held at Arles.[2] In the middle of the century, Hilary of Poitiers was one of the leading anti-Arians and theologians of the day. As the century wore on, more and more Gallic *civitates*, even some of the very obscure, gained their own bishops.[3] This occurred, however, on a very hit-and-miss basis. There still were no established lines of authority, even though ever since the council of Nicaea it had been understood that secular provincial metropolitan sees also were to have ecclesiastical precedence as well as secular precedence.[4]

As a result, administrative anomalies existed. In southern Gaul, the church of Marseilles exercised an informal primacy based upon its antiquity; its direct authority extended all the way to Nice.[5] Circa 365, Marcellinus, the first bishop of Embrun, the metropolitan see of Alpes Maritimae, was consecrated by Aemilianus of Valence (in Viennensis) and Eusebius of Vercelli (in northern Italy), perhaps because there were no other bishops in between.[6]

---

1. See Duchesne, *Fastes* vols.1-3, passim; Franses, *Leo* pp.11-16; Gilliard, "Apostolicity"; Griffe, *Gaule* vol.1, passim; Jalland, *Leo* pp.157-159; Kidd, *Church* pp.353-354; and Langgärtner, *Gallienpolitik* pp.18-20.

2. *Corp. chr. lat.* 148.14-22. Gallic bishops attended from Marseilles, Arles, Vienne, Vaison, Orange, Nice, Apt, Rheims, Rouen, Autun, Lyons, Cologne, Javols, Bordeaux, Trier, and Eauze.

3. On urbanization in southern Gaul, see Février, *Développement* and "Origin and Growth," passim.

4. See Duchesne, *Fastes* 1.94; Griffe, *Gaule* 1.332-33; Harries, "*Notitia*"; and Jones, *L.R.E.* pp.880-882.

5. See Griffe, *Gaule* 1.337.

6. See the *Vita Marcellini* in *A.A.S.S.* April II p.751 and Greg. Tur. *Glor. conf.* 68. See also Duchesne, *Fastes* 1.290; Griffe, *Gaule* 1.305; and Lanzoni, *Diocesi* p.1047. Marcellinus supposedly

During this period Gaul also was undergoing secular administrative changes which necessarily would affect the ecclesiastical organization. From Augustus to Diocletian, there had been only four
Gallic provinces: Narbonensis, Lugdunensis, Aquitania, and Belgica
(or six, if the Germanies are considered separately).[7] The Alpine
provinces still were considered part of Italy. Diocletian increased
the total to eleven (including the two Germanies)—thirteen if the
two Alpine provinces are included. By 355, Lugdunensis had been
divided into two Lugdunenses and Maxima Sequanorum; Novempopulana had been broken off from Aquitania; Viennensis had been
taken from Narbonensis; and Belgica had been divided in two.
Shortly thereafter, probably by the time of Gratian, there were four
Lugdunenses and two Narbonenses.[8] Finally, perhaps in the 380s, the
secular *Notitia Galliarum* was drawn up. This document, which also
came to serve as the basis for Gallic ecclesiastical organization, contained no fewer than seventeen Gallic provinces (including the Alpine
ones) with their respective metropolitan sees.[9] The southern seven
(Viennensis, Narbonensis I-II, Aquitania I-II, Novempopulana, and
Alpes Maritimae) made up the diocese of Septem (initially Quinque)
Provinciae (also called Viennensis), whereas the northern ten (Lugdunensis I-IV, Belgica I-II, Germania I-II, Maxima Sequanorum, and
Alpes Graiae), comprised the diocese of Gallia. By the end of the
century, it has been suggested, most Gallic *civitates* had acquired bishops, although some would assert that this did not occur until well into
the fifth century.[10]

---

was an African who came to Gaul with two comrades, Domninus and Vincentius; the first of
these may be the contemporary bishop Domninus of Grenoble (*P.L.* 16.916, 935).

7. The Germanies seem to have been detached under Augustus, although administratively
they remained to some extent dependent upon Belgica. See Duchesne, *Fastes* 1.65-75, 91; Jullian,
Gaule vol.4 (Paris, 1920) pp.67-68; Lot, *Gaule* pp.193-204, 364-367; and Mommsen, *Provinces*
pp.82-178 and *M.G.H. A.A.* 9.955.

8. See Chastagnol, "Aquitaine" passim, and Griffe, *Gaule* 1.334-336.

9. *M.G.H. A.A.* 9.552-600. See Duchesne, *Fastes* 1.67; Harries, "*Notitia*" passim; Jones,
L.R.E. pp.712-715; Nesselhauf, "Verwaltung"; and Rivet, "Notitia Galliarum." For the Alpine
provinces, see Lambaglia, *Liguria Romana* and Prieux, *Alpes Cottiennes*. The Alpes Graiae et
Poeninae seem to have been a "double" province under a single prefect; each province had only
one *civitas* ("civitas Ceutronum id est Tarentasia" and "civitas Vallensium id est Octodoro"
respectively). The two may have alternated as metropolis, or each may have been the metropolis
of its own province (see Mommsen, *M.G.H. A.A.* 9.557-558, 598-600).

10. Late fourth: Duchesne, *Fastes* 1.76-80 and Griffe, "Paroisses rurales," "Origines" p.150,
and *Gaule* 1.365, 403, 412-413. Fifth: Harries, "*Notitia*". Harries assumes, however, that cities
which did not send bishops to the Gallic councils of 439-442 *a priori* did not have bishops. For
other reasons why such bishops may have absented themselves, see chapters 6-7 below.

The Late Roman Aristocracy and the Church [11]

One of the reasons for the expansion of the Gallic church in the fourth and early fifth centuries was the increasing attractiveness of high ecclesiastical office, which gave aristocrats in particular an opportunity to pursue local interests in the context of an influential local office.[12] As early as the 360s, Hilary of Poitiers, speaking of the afterlife, had discussed ecclesiastical office using the conventional terminology applied to the fulfillment of the traditional aristocratic responsibilities and ambitions: "In a state of leisure which is aware of its security, the happy spirit relaxes in its anticipation ... it likewise speaks out to others through the service of an imposed priesthood, expending its favors in its responsibility for public salvation."[13] This concept of the performance of duty through Christian service also was reflected in the *topos* of *militia Christi* or *militia caelestis*, in contrast to the usual *militia saecularis*.[14] Clerical, and especially episcopal, status came to be endowed with a nobility, and authority, all its own.[15] There now arose an ecclesiastical aristocracy, in which secular and ecclesiastical office both had equal places in an aristocratic cursus.[16] Episcopal dynasties even began to monopolize particular sees.[17]

11. For the late Roman aristocracy, see Arnheim, *Aristocracy* pp.18-19; Arsac, "La dignité" pp.198-243; Chastagnol, *Sénat* passim and "L'évolution" pp.305-14; Jones, *L.R.E.* p.523; Lecrivain, *Sénat* passim; Matthews, *Aristocracies* pp.1-31; Stroheker, *Adel*, p.70; and Sundwall, *Studien* passim and *Abhandlungen* pp.178-308.

12. The rise of local interests and the increasing attractiveness of ecclesiastical office to aristocrats are well known. On the former in Gaul in particular, see Brown, *World* passim; Jones, *L.R.E.* p.529; Matthews, *Aristocracies* pp.308, 320-321, 349-351; Oost, *Placidia* p.77, 147; Stein, *Geschichte* pp.409, 544; Stroheker, *Adel* pp.3, 19, 48-62; and Sundwall, *Studien* pp.8-14. Note that *C.J.* 12.1.5 even encouraged aristocrats to stay at home. For the "aristocratization" of the Gallic church, see Arnheim, *Aristocracy* pp.106, 187; Arnold, *Caesarius* pp.15-16; Beck, *Pastoral Care* pp.6ff, 21-22; Brown "Patrons" p.61 and *World* p.174; Brugière, *Littérature* p.213; Dill, *Gaul* p.220, 479 and *Last Century* p.216; Duchesne, *Fastes* 1.112-113; Griffe, *Gaule* 2.181; Heinzelmann, *Bischofsherrschaft* 12, 211ff (especially p.231) and "L'aristocratie" p.275; Loyen, *L'esprit* p.41; Matthews, *Aristocracies* p.346; Mathisen, *Ecclesiastical Aristocracy* passim; Oost, *Placidia* p.147; Pricoco, *L'isola* pp.65-73; Prinz, *Mönchtum* pp.48, 57-62 and *Stadtherrschaft* pp.8-9; Stroheker, *Adel* pp.8-9, 72-75, 92, 106ff; Wieruszowski, "Zusammensetzung" pp.1-2, 50-63; and Woodward, *Nationalism* p.77.

13. "in hoc igitur conscio securitatis suae otio mens spebus suis laeta requieverat ... tamen per ministerium imposti sacerdotii etiam ceteris praedicabat, munus suum ad officium publicae salutis extendens...." (*De trinitate* 1.14: *Corp. chr. lat.* 62.15). See also Aug. *Retract.* 1.1.1 (*C.S.E.L.* 36.11) for "Christianae vitae otium."

14. See Auer, "Militia Christi," and von Harnack, *Militia Christi*.

15. For the commonplace of the nobility of the clergy, see Sid. Apoll. *Epist.* 7.12.4; Alc. Avit. *In ordinatione episcopi* 1 (*M.G.H. A.A.* 6.2.124); and Ven. Fort. *Carm.* 1.15.32. For the status and authority of bishops, see Dill, *Gaul* pp.476-488; Heinzelmann, *Bischofsherrschaft* pp.35-36, 221; Klauser, "Bischofe" passim; Prinz, *Stadtherrschaft* passim; and Stroheker, *Adel* pp.72-73.

16. See Brown, *World* p.131, for the "double oligarchy of senators and clergymen now closely interrelated" which arose at Rome. For Gaul, see Mathisen, *Ecclesiastical Aristocracy*; and Stroheker, *Adel* p.9, for the "weltlich-kirkliche Aristokratie."

17. See Sid. Apoll. *Epist.* 4.25.2, where episcopal office is claimed on the basis of an "antiqua

With the decline of imperial authority and the decreasing number of imperial offices during the fifth century, even those who in the past might have had opportunities for such office also were compelled to retrench and pursue more local opportunities. In the 460s, Sidonius Apollinaris told how one Arvernian family had come to seek its future with the church rather than the state: "Their service has been carried out in clerical rather than Palatine company."[18]

Some Gallic writers questioned the movitations of some who sought ecclesiastical office. Circa 400, Sulpicius Severus wrote, "Now episcopates are sought through depraved ambitions."[19] Such reasons for the seeking of church office were, of course, officially frowned upon by the church hierarchy. In 418, Boniface of Rome complained about the ambitions of those who sought high church office, saying (Epist. "Exigit dilectio": P.L. 20.669ff):

This is brought about by the excessive negligence of our fellow bishops, who seek out the acclaim of the multitude, for they believe that from such a crowd they can acquire some kind of glory for themselves. Thence, here and there, the numerous supporters of such individuals are found even in those places where there is solitude, when they wish their parishes to be extended, or they bestow holy orders upon those whom they are not at all able to justify.[20]

As a result of the increasing desirability of episcopal office, partisan conflicts often could arise over elections.[21]

As elsewhere, ecclesiastical influence seeking was common in Gaul. The anonymous fifth-century author of the *De septem ordinibus ecclesiae* complained about bishops who were excessively concerned with secular affairs and influence: "There are many who, pursuing the favor of the people, do not observe the discipline of the church ... they sinfully cultivate the nobility rather than upright behavior...."[22]

---

natalium praerogativa." For episcopal dynasties, mainly in Gaul, see Brown, "Patrons" p.61; Brugière, *Littérature* p.265ff; Dill, *Gaul* pp.310-329; Heinzelmann, *Bischofsherrschaft* pp.211-232; and Wieruszowski, "Zusammensetzung" pp.50-56.

18. "militia illis in clericali potius quam in Palatino decursa comitatu" (*Epist.* 7.2.3). Dill, *Gaul* p.487, suggests that "the Christian bishop succeeded to the dignity of the chief priest of the Augustan cult in the municipal community." Wallace-Hadrill, "Gothia" p.224 sees the state "losing" recruits to the church. For the lack of desire, either real or affected, to enter state service, see Sid. Apoll. *Epist.*1.3.2, 1.4.2, 3.6.2 and *Carm.* 7.465, and Paul. Nol. *Epist.* 8.3 and 25.3.

19. "nunc episcopatus pravis ambitionibus appetuntur" (*Chron.* 2.32).

20. "facit hoc nimia remissio consacerdotum nostrorum, qui pompam multitudinis quaerunt, ut putant ex hac turba aliquid sibi dignitatis acquiri. hinc passim numerosa popularitas etiam his locis, ubi solitudo est, talium reperitur, dum paroecias extendi cupiunt, aut quibus aliud praestare non possunt, divinos ordines largiuntur."

21. See Beck, *Pastoral Care* p.15, "Cliques formed in support of one aspirant or the other...."

22. "sunt enim multi qui sequentes vota populorum, disciplinam ecclesiae non observant ... peccantes, nobilitatem potius quam mores optimos benedicunt" (*De sept. ord. eccl.* 7: P.L. 30.160); for this work, see chapter 6 below, n.77.

Circa 460, the bishop-elect Eutropius of Orange was rebuked for his initial reluctance to accept such an unprestigious post, "Because you are not received by a church overflowing with wealth, decorated with its ministers, puffed up with its privilege, restless with its retinue of nobles. . . ." [23] In a letter of 502 addressed "to the bishops of Gaul," the bishop of Rome, Symmachus, reiterated earlier prohibitions against the pursuit of episcopal ambition: "Let them neither through secular patronage, nor through a grant of any kind of exception, with illicit presumption exceed the boundaries of their allowed jurisdiction." [24]

The clerical pursuit of power and influence merely paralleled that which already was common in the secular world. In the early fifth century, the protagonist of an anonymous Gallic comedy expressed an ambition which presumably reflected some current practices: "Let me be able to despoil those who owe me nothing, to slaughter those I do not know, even to despoil and slaughter my neighbors." [25] In the middle of the century, bishop Valerianus of Cimiez could preach, "Behold, the neighborhood frequently is armed for conflict; why is this, unless because one perhaps plans to cross his boundaries and to occupy ground belonging to another?" [26] As the following discussion will show, the seeking of prestigious sees, the bestowing of ecclesiastical office upon one's supporters, and the expansion of one's ecclesiastical jurisdiction were to cause much dissension among Gallic ecclesiastics in the fifth century.

The Gallic Church and the Bishop of Rome

Before the end of the fourth century, the Gallic church seems to have had relatively little contact with the church of Rome. After the Decian persecution of c.250, the Gallic bishops informed the bishop of Rome of the actions of Marcian of Arles. Following the imperial-sponsored Council of Arles of 314, the assembled bishops forwarded a letter to Sylvester of Rome informing him of the results.[27] At the Council of Sardica in 343, the Gallic bishops gave their *pro forma* subscriptions, and one of the canons granted precedence to the see of Rome. Rather later, either Siricius or Damasus—even the individual

23. "quia te non suscepit ecclesia distensa censu, ornata ministerio, inflata privilegio, comitatu nobilium inquieta. . . ." (*VEutropi* p.56)
24. "nec per saecularia patrocinia, nec per cuiuslibet excusationis obtentum, illicita praesumptione terminos concessae potestatis excedant. . . ." (*Epist.* "Sedis apostolicae"= *Epist.arel.* 25: *M.G.H. Epist.* 3.35–36).
25. "licet spoliare ut non debentes mihi, caedere alienos, vicinos autem spoliare et caedere" (*Querolus* 15.6).
26. "ecce armatur vicinitas frequenter ad litem, unde est, nisi quod hic forte terminos transcendere, et cespitem iuris alieni cogitat occupare?" (*Serm.* 20.5).
27. Duchesne, *Fastes* 1.90 rightly points out that this letter was not of the Gallic episcopate in particular but "de tout l'épiscopat d'Occident."

is uncertain—sent to the bishops of Gaul some "Canons of the Synod of Rome" dealing with ecclesiastical practices, the sacraments, and the rights of metropolitan bishops.[28]

A more substantive involvement of the bishop of Rome in the ecclesiastical affairs of Gaul came in 385/386, when Siricius of Rome wrote to the emperor Magnus Maximus about the case of the priest Agroecius, whom Siricius accused of having been illegally ordained. The only evidence for this affair comes from Maximus' reply (*Epist. imp.* 40.2: *C.S.E.L.* 35.91):

> But as regards Agroecius, whom you claim had wrongly risen to the rank of presbyter, what can I decree more reverently on behalf of our catholic religion than that catholic bishops judge on this very matter? I shall summon a council of those who dwell either in Gaul or in the Five Provinces, so it may judge with them sitting and considering the matter.[29]

Some have seen this case as an instance of Gallic recognition of Roman authority, but it would appear that here Maximus was merely informing the bishop of Rome, perhaps as a courtesy to secure his good offices, of what he intended to do.[30]

Such evidence has been used by traditionalists to assert that even before the end of the fourth century "l'Eglise des Gaules était habituée à tourner ses regards vers Rome."[31] Only the mid-third-century example, however, shows actual contact of the Gauls by themselves with Rome.[32] Before the 380s the bishop of Rome made no obvious attempts to exercise ecclesiastical authority in Gaul: he did not order the convening of church councils, he did not become involved in the Gauls' internal affairs, and he was neither consulted nor informed about Gallic problems. The Gauls rather convened their own inter-

---

28. "Canones synodi Romanorum ad Gallos episcopos" (*P.L.* 13.1181-1194). See Griffe, *Gaule* 1.334, who suggests Siricius as the sender, perhaps c.385. Pietri, *Roma* 1.763-772, however, prefers Damasus. Gaul, in the sense of Cisalpine Gaul, also could be included as part of Italy not only in the fourth century (by Damasus: *P.L.* 13.548) but even in the fifth (Roman synod, 19 Nov. 465: Thiel, *Epistolae* p.159). In this sense, perhaps note Sozomen's report (*H.E.* 6.23) that the bishops of "Gaul" and Venetia reported to Damasus about Arian activities. For the presence of Brictio of Trier at a council at Rome c.382, see Duchesne, *Fastes* 3.36 and *A.A.S.S.* May II p.12.

29. "ceterum de Agroecio, quem indebite ad presbyterii gradum conscendisse commemoras, quid religioni nostrae catholicae possum praestare reverentius, quam ut de hoc ipso . . . catholici iudicent sacerdotes? quorum conventum . . . vel qui intra Gallias vel qui intra quinque provincias commorantur . . . constituam, ut isdem residentibus et cognoscentibus . . . iudicetur."

30. Pietri, *Roma* 2.969-970, suggests that Maximus accepted "l'interpretation romain de cette ordination illicite."

31. Griffe, *Gaule* 1.348-352, see also Pietri, *Roma* 2.967. McShane, *Romanitas* p.263, however, suggests that the Gauls "gardaient leur autonomie."

32. Even Griffe, *Gaule* 1.349-351, admits that in the fourth-century Arian controversy "nous ne voyons pas l'Eglise des Gaules consulter l'Eglise romaine," and that overall the evidence is "fragmentary."

provincial councils on their own authority, and passed canons binding on themselves.[33]

If the Gallic bishops had little contact with Rome in the fourth century, they did maintain very close ties with the church of northern Italy and the bishop of Milan, which, as the imperial capital of the time, even overshadowed Rome.[34] The bishop of the city from 374 to 397, Ambrose, himself born in Gaul where his father Marcellinus had been prefect, was able to extend his influence into Gaul.[35] When requested by Gratian in 381 to convene at Aquileia a council of bishops from his own diocese to hear the case of two accused Arians, Ambrose also admitted three official *legati Gallorum*, Constantius of Orange, Justus of Lyons, and Proculus of Marseilles, as well as three other Gallic bishops, Theodorus of Octodorum, Domninus of Grenoble, and Amantius of Nice.[36] After the council was over, he also saw to it that a special letter was addressed "to the bishops of Gaul, of the provinces of Viennensis and Narbonensis Prima and Secunda" informing them of the results.[37] It would appear, therefore, that as of the late fourth century the bishop of Rome had little authority, or interest, in Gaul, and that any Italian influence there was exercised by the bishop of Milan.[38]

UNITY AND DISUNITY: ARIANS, PRISCILLIANISTS, AND FELICIANS

The Gallic bishops, under the leadership first of Hilary of Poitiers and then of Ambrose of Milan, were generally united in their opposition to Arianism. Only a southern clique, led by Saturninus of Arles, favored the emperor Constantius II (337-361).[39] As a result of his choice of sides, Saturninus developed an unsavory reputation. He was described by Sulpicius Severus as an "impotent and factious man"

33. See *Corp. chr. lat.* 148.30-60 for texts, and Gaudemet, *Conciles*, for translations and commentary.
34. For the influence of Milan, see Duchesne, *Fastes* 1.92-93: "une telle situation était peu faite pour agréer aux papes." See also Batiffol, "Les églises" p.168; Jalland, *Church* pp.309, 333 and *Leo* pp.1-163; Langgärtner, *Gallienpolitik* pp.24, 37-39; Lanzoni, *Diocesi* pp.1017-1019; McShane, *Romanitas* pp.261-262; Palanque, "Dissensions" pp.496-497; Pietri, *Roma* 1.782-785, 2.887 ("le 'pape' de Milan"), 897-909; and Vogel, *Introduction* pp.248-250.
35. See Griffe, *Gaule* 1.342-345; Lanzoni, *Diocesi* pp.1015-1017; Palanque, *Ambroise* passim; and Pietri, *Roma* 2.897-908, 971-973.
36. *P.L.* 16.916-939 and *C.S.E.L.* 82.325ff; a total of thirty-three bishops attended. See Gottlieb, "Das Konzil" pp.287-306; Griffe, *Gaule* 1.342-343; and Hefele-Leclercq, *Conciles* 2.49-53. Duchesne, *Fastes* 1.92, does note that there was no representative of the bishop of Rome.
37. *P.L.* 16.939-940.
38. This Milanese influence has caused particular problems for traditionalists. See Duchesne, *Fastes* 1.90-93 and Griffe, *Gaule* 1.351-352.
39. See Duchesne, *Fastes* 1.90-91.

(*Chron.* 2.41, 45), and according to Jerome, Hilary of Poitiers had been exiled "by the faction of Saturninus" (*Vir. ill.* 100). The Gauls held their own meetings on Arianism, such as those attested at Arles (353), Béziers (356), and Paris (360-361).[40] They also oversaw their own discipline, as in 374 when the Council of Valence recommended the deposition of the bishop-elect Acceptus of Fréjus.[41] As of this time, however, there was not yet a strong system of ecclesiastical organization: at church councils, for example, the primate, the senior bishop by consecration, presided, not the metropolitan.[42]

During the 380s, the Gallic church became involved in a controversy which had arisen in Spain: Priscillianism.[43] Its founder, Priscillian of Avila, was accused, for example, of advocating an ostentatious asceticism and the performance of the sacraments outside the established church. Sulpicius Severus said of this period, "There followed portentous and dangerous times of our age, in which the churches were defiled and everything was disturbed by an unaccustomed evil."[44]

In 380, a council at Saragossa in Spain drew into the conflict the Gallic bishops Delphinus of Bordeaux and Phoebadius of Agen, the latter of whom presided.[45] After the emperor Gratian had been induced to issue a decree condemning "universi haeretici," Priscillian and a few supporters traveled to Rome and Milan seeking ecclesiastical support, but were rebuffed by both Damasus and Ambrose in 381 and 382.[46] They were successful, however, in gaining the support of Ambrose's enemies at the imperial court.[47] In 384 they were sum-

---

40. "frequentibus intra Gallias conciliis" (Sulp. Sev. *Chron.* 2.45). Councils: *Corp. chr. lat.* 148.30-34. The extant *acta* of a Council of Cologne held in 346 are considered suspect (ibid. 26-29). Hilary of Poitiers (*Contra Constantium* 2: *P.L.* 10.579) asserted that the Council of Béziers was organized "by the faction of their false apostles" ("per factionem eorum pseudoapostolorum").

41. *Corp. chr. lat.* 148.35-48. Acceptus was said to have made false accusations against himself in order to evade the office. For the Gallic tradition of deposing bishops, see de Leo, "Deposizioni."

42. See Jalland, *Leo* p.158. This was the system used in Africa, see Thiel, *Epistolae* pp.143-144 n.10. Kidd, *Church* p.353, suggests that the presiding Gaul was chosen on "personal grounds."

43. For Priscillianism, see Babut, *Priscillien*; d'Alès, *Priscillien*; Chadwick, *Priscillian*; Griffe, *Gaule* 1.316-329; Matthews, *Aristocracies* pp.146-172; Palanque, "Dissensions" p.491; Prinz, *Mönchtum* p.28; Rouselle, "L'affaire priscillianiste"; Van Dam, *Leadership* pp.88-117; and Vollmann, *Priscillianismus.*

44. "sequuntur tempora aetatis nostrae gravia et periculosa, quibus non usitato malo pollutae ecclesiae et perturbata omnia" (*Chron.* 2.46). For the Gallic ecclesiastical dissension after the death of Hilary of Poitiers, see Griffe, *Gaule* 1.315-316, 343.

45. Sulp. Sev. *Chron.* 2.47; Mansi 3.633 (Oct.10); Hefele-Leclercq, *Conciles* 2.66-68.

46. Gratian: Sulp. Sev. *Chron.* 2.46-48; Priscil. *Tract.* 2.50-52; Philast. *Haeres.* 33(61), 56(84); see also Langgärtner, *Gallienpolitik* p.53; Matthews, *Aristocracies* p.163; and Van Dam, *Leadership* p.101.

47. See Matthews, *Aristocracies* pp.163-169.

moned to a church council at Bordeaux, at which Priscillian chose to appeal to the emperor Magnus Maximus.[48] Two years later, therefore, a synod was convened at Trier.[49] Among those present in the city were Martin of Tours and Ambrose of Milan, as well as Priscillian's principal accuser, Ithacius of Ossonoba in Spain. The ultimate result was the execution of Priscillian and several of his followers.[50]

The role of Magnus Maximus is seen especially in his letter to Siricius, bishop of Rome, informing him of the affair (*Epist. imp.* 40: *C.S.E.L.* 35.91):

Our arrival found and discovered certain matters so contaminated and polluted by the sins of the wicked that, unless our foresight and attention had quickly brought aid, great disturbance and ruin immediately would have arisen . . . but it was then disclosed how great a crime the Manichees recently had committed, not by doubtful or uncertain rhetoric or suspicions, but by their own confession.[51]

According to the emperor, therefore, the Priscillianists were Manichees: in fact, he never referred to Priscillian or Priscillianists by name at all. He may have seen no need to try to define a new heresy when Manicheism, a previously condemned and detested one, was available.

Priscillian himself already had realized the effectiveness of such a tactic, noting, "with our names disguised, [Hydatius of Emerita] sought a rescript against pseudobishops and Manichees, and of course obtained it, because there is no one who does not feel hatred when he hears about pseudobishops and Manichees."[52] The contemporary Italian writer on heresies Philastrius of Brescia also made similar connections, it seems, referring to the "so to speak ascetics in Gaul, Spain, and Aquitania, who likewise follow the most pernicious belief of the Gnostics and Manichees."[53] And this in spite of Priscillian's own ex-

---

48. *Corp. chr. lat.* 148.46; Sulp. Sev. *Chron.* 2.49-50; Prosp. *Chron.* 1187. A few Bordelaise had become involved in the heresy, but this appears to have been the only Gallic inroad it made.

49. *Corp. chr. lat.* 148.47-48; Sulp. Sev. *Dial.* 2(3).11-13; see Matthews, *Aristocracies* pp.166-167.

50. Sulp. Sev. *Chron.* 2.50-51; Ambrose *Epist.* 24.12; Paul. *VAmbrosii* 19; and Pacatus *Pan.lat.*. 12(2).29.

51. "noster adventus ita inquinata aliqua et sceleratorum labe polluta deprehendit et repperit, ut, nisi nostra provisio atque medicina . . . his opem celeriter attulisset, ingens profecto divulsio atque perditio fuisset exorta . . . ceterum quid adhuc proxime proditum sit Manichaeos sceleris admittere, non argumentis neque suspicionibus dubiis vel incertis, sed ipsorum confessione."

52. "dissimulatis nominibus nostris, rescriptum contra pseudoepiscopos et Manichaeos petit et necessario inpetrat, quia nemo non, qui pseudoepiscopos et Manichaeos audiret, odisset. . . ." (*Tract.* 2.50: *C.S.E.L.* 18.40-41).

53. "in Gallis et Hispanis et Aquitania veluti abstinentes, qui Gnosticorum et Manicheorum particulam perniciosissimam aeque sequuntur. . . ." (*Haeres.* 56[84]: *C.S.E.L.* 38.45). See also Philast. *Haeres.* 33(61) for the Manichees, "qui et in Hispania et quinque provinciis latere dicuntur." For these as references to Priscillianists, see Matthews, *Aristocracies* p.162. See also Sulp.

plicit anathematization of Manicheism.[54] The association of Manicheism with Priscillianism was to prove common, and convenient, in the
future as well.[55]

Some Gallic bishops, such as Felix of Trier, supported this secular
interference; as the newly elected bishop of an imperial city, he may
have been hard-pressed to do otherwise. Others, however, such as
Martin of Tours, not to mention Ambrose of Milan, vehemently opposed such heavy-handed imperial intervention in the internal affairs
of the church.[56] Thus arose the so-called Felician controversy, in
which bishops of the two sides excommunicated each other.[57] Martin,
for example, "avoided sharing in the communion of the Ithacian
party," and refused to attend any further Gallic councils: "He lived
for sixteen years more; he attended no synod, he absented himself
from all assemblies of bishops."[58] This is not to say, however, that he
did not retain an interest in them, as when in the mid-390s, "a synod

---

Sev. *Chron.* 2.46, "namque tum primum infamis illa Gnosticorum haeresis intra Hispanias de-
prehensa, superstitio exitiabilis . . . ab his Priscillianus est institutus. . . . ." Augustine made a similar connection (*De haer.* 70: *P.L.* 42.44), and Prosper of Aquitaine noted specifically (*Chron.* 1171
s.a.379: *M.G.H. A.A.* 9.460), "ea tempestate Priscillianus episcopus de Gallaecia ex Manicheorum
et Gnosticorum dogmate heresim nominis sui condit."

54. *Tractatus* 1.26, 2.47: *C.S.E.L.* 18.22, 39.

55. Later imperial legislation also lumped Priscillianism and Manicheism together, see *C.
Th.* 16.5.40 (22 February 407), "we especially persecute the Manichees, or Phrygians, or Priscillianists," and *Sirm.* 12 (15 November 407), "against the Manichees or Priscillianists." Elsewhere,
the Priscillianists were equated with the Donatists (*C. Th.* 16.5.38 [2 December 405]), the "Manichees and Phrygians (who call themselves Pepyzites, or Priscillianists, or some other misleading
name)" (*C. Th.*16.5.59 [9 April 423]), and the Montanists (*C. Th.*16.5.65 [30 May 428]). Priscillianism also was related by some to Origenism, see Orosius, *Commonitorium de errore Priscillianistarum et Origenistarum* (*C.S.E.L.* 18.153), who asserted (ch.2) that "Priscillianus primum in eo
Manichaeis miserior." For similar accusations of Manicheism, see Chapter 3 below and Boshof,
"Rombeziehungen" p.105; Langgärtner, *Gallienpolitik* p.53; Pietri, *Roma* 1.446, 2.970; and Van
Dam, *Leadership* pp.85-114.

56. Martin himself had founded a monastery at Milan in the late 350s, although he soon
was hounded from the city by the Arian bishop Auxentius (Sulp. Sev. *VMartini* 6; Greg. Tur.
H.F. 10.31). For the ties between Martin and Ambrose, see van der Lof, "San Ambrosio"
pp.441-450.

57. Sulp. Sev. *Dial.* 3.12-13; *Conc. Taur.* can.6 (*Corp. chr. lat.* 148.57-58). See Griffe, *Gaule*
1.327-329; Pietri, *Roma* 2.969-976. Babut, *Saint Martin* p.156, however, suggests that the anti-
Felicians were merely "un groupe de clercs et de laïcs" who were excommunicated by Milan
and Rome and included no bishops. For rebuttal, see Palanque, "Dissensions" pp.490-491.

58. "cavit cum illa Ithacianae partis communione misceri . . . sedecim postea vixit annos;
nullam synodum adiit, ab omnibus episcoporum conventibus se removit" (Sulp. Sev. *Dial.* 3.13).
Severus' chronology seems faulty here, for if the sixteen years dated from 386, Martin would not
have died until 401/402, and other evidence places his death firmly in 397 (Duchesne, *Fastes*
2.302). Perhaps Severus was counting from the beginning of the Priscillianist controversy in 380.
Martin himself was suspected of being tainted with Priscillianism or Origenism; see Babut,
Turin pp.220-230; Brown, "Patrons" p.67; and Prinz, *Mönchtum* pp.21, 28. For Martin as an
anti-Felician, see Gaudemet, *Conciles* p.123.

of bishops was convened at Nîmes, to which he did not at all desire
to go, but he did wish to know what occurred there."[59]

The fall of Magnus Maximus in 388 and the reassertion of imperial
rule in Gaul by Theodosius seems to have brought a reaction against
Felix and his supporters, as suggested by Pacatus in his panegyric to
Theodosius in the same year (*Pan. lat.* 12[2].29):

> What more than this could the accusing bishop [sc. Ithacius] attempt? He
> was, indeed, he was also like those betrayers, who, bishops in name, or actu-
> ally henchmen, and therefore executioners, not content with having deprived
> the condemned of their paternal property, sought their blood, and took the
> lives of the defendants already made paupers . . . [60]

Hard feelings would have continued as the anti-Felicians, with the
apparent support of the imperial government, tried to reassert themselves in Gaul.

Soon thereafter, in 390, Ambrose attempted to end the controversy
by holding a synod at Milan.[61] In this, however, he was unsuccessful,
and he too adopted Martin's method for dealing with the problem, as
he noted when giving his reasons for a journey to Gaul in 392: "Nor
did I suppose that the cause of my journey was a synod of the Gallic
bishops, on account of whose constant quarreling I repeatedly had
excused myself."[62] Curiously, yet another presumptive member of this
circle, the monk Aper, an ex-secular official who was a close friend of
Martin's partisan Paulinus of Nola, had the same attitude: Paulinus
described him as "disdaining church tumults and disquieting councils."[63] Apparently, Martin and his monkish associates recognized that
at any church council they would be in the minority, and therefore
disdained to attend. It will be seen that absenting oneself from church

59. "apud Nemausum episcoporum synodus habebatur, ad quam quidem ire noluerat, sed
quid gestum esset scire cupiebat" (Sulp. Sev. *Dial.*. 2.13).

60. "quid hoc maius poterat intendere accusator sacerdos [sc. Ithacius]? fuit enim, fuit et hoc
delatorum genus, qui nominibus antistites, re vera autem satellites, atque adeo carnifices, non
contenti miseros avitis evolvisse patrimoniis, calumniabantur in sanguinem, et vitas premebant
reorum jam pauperum. . . ."

61. Amb. *Epist.* 51.6, a synod held "propter adventum Gallorum episcoporum," see Hefele-
Leclercq, *Conciles* 2.78-80. For the attendees as anti-Felicians, see Pietri, *Roma* 2.973.

62. "nec arbitrarer causam itineris mei synodum Gallorum esse episcoporum, propter quorum frequentes dissensiones crebro me excusaveram" (*De obitu Valentiniani* 25: *P.L.* 16.1367).
The attitude of Ambrose, and Martin, toward councils was echoed by Gregory of Nazianzus,
who wrote in 382 (*Epist.* 130), "My inclination is to avoid all assemblies of bishops, because I
have never seen any council come to a good end, nor turn out to be a solution of evils. On
the contrary, it usually increases them. You always find there a love of contention and love of
power . . . which defies description" (translated in B. Kidd, *Documents* p.112 no.85).

63. "ecclesiarum tumultus et concilia inquieta declinans" (*Epist.* 38.10); for Paulinus' ties to
Martin see ibid. 18.9. For Aper, see Mathisen, "Addenda" p.366.

councils was to become an even more common means of expressing dissent in fifth-century Gaul.

In his final words about the Felician controversy, Sulpicius Severus noted c.400,

And among our own people there flared up a perpetual war of discord, which, already having been pursued for fifteen years amid shameful dissent, could in no way be put to rest. And now, because everything is seen to be disturbed and confused in particular by the quarreling of bishops and on account of them everything has become corrupted by hatred or favor-seeking, by fear, inconstancy, envy, factionalism, lust, greed, arrogance, sloth, and apathy, ultimately the majority, with insane advice and unyielding eagerness, contend against the few who advise well.[64]

Evidence of these continuing quarrels is seen in the canons of the synod of Nîmes, held on 1 October, in either 394 or 396, and attended by nineteen bishops from throughout Gaul.[65] The canons began: "Because, in our desire for peace, we have come to the church of Nîmes, in order to do away with the scandals of the churches and put dissension to rest."[66] No specific mention was made here of the Felician controversy, but because no known anti-Felicians attended, and Felix of Trier did, it has been assumed that this was a council of Felicians.[67] The aforementioned refusal of Martin of Tours to attend this council also would support this interpretation.

Meanwhile, another Gallic bishop with anti-Felician ties may have found a different method of responding to the Felician controversy. Justus of Lyons, it will be recalled, had been one of the Gallic legates

---

64. "ac inter nostros perpetuum discordiarum bellum exarserat quod iam per quindecim annos foedis dissensionibus agitatum, nullo modo sopiri poterat. et nunc, cum maxime discordiis, episcoporum omnia turbari ac misceri cernerentur cunctaque per eos odio aut gratia, metu, inconstantia, invidia, factione, libidine, avaritia, arrogantia, somno, desidia depravata, postremo plures adversum paucos bene consulentes insanis consiliis et pertinacibus studiis certabant" (*Chron.* 2.51).

65. The heading reads "episcopis per Gallias et Septem Provincias salutem": the bishops, therefore, presumed to speak for the entire episcopal establishment of Gaul. Two other bishops sent representatives. The bishops' sees, unfortunately, are not given, but those who can be identified with some certainty include Aprunculus of Auch, Felix of Trier, Adelfus of Metz, Urbanus of Langres, Remigius of Aix (for his see, see note 100 below), Melanius of Troyes, and Ingenuus of Arles. For text, see *Corp. chr. lat.* 148.49-51; see also Griffe, *Gaule* 1.345-346. For the date of 394, see Duchesne, *Fastes* 1.366; Hefele-Leclercq, *Conciles* 2.91-97; Gaudemet, *Conciles* p.124; and Palanque, "Date" p.362 and "Evêchés" p.118, although in "Dissensions" p.492 he opts for 396.

66. "cum ad Nemausensem ecclesiam, ad tollenda ecclesiarum scandala discessionemque sedandam, pacis studio venissemus. . . ." (*Corp. chr. lat.* 148.50).

67. See Babut, *Turin* p.237; Gaudemet, *Conciles* p.124; Griffe, *Gaule* 1.346; and Palanque, "Premiers" p.380 n.5 and "Evêchés" p.118, who notes the absence of Proculus of Marseilles and Simplicius of Vienne (suggesting therefore that they were anti-Felicians). Pietri, *Roma* 2.976 n.4 questions why Ingenuus, if he was bishop of Arles, subscribed only in the last position: it apparently was because Ingenuus was most junior and Arles did not yet have any extraordinary status.

who attended Ambrose's council at Aquileia in 381.[68] At some time thereafter, perhaps c.390, Justus mysteriously decided to abdicate his see; his epitaph asserted that "afterwards, enflamed by the love of the anchorite life, he thirstingly sought the distant deserts of Egypt."[69] If Justus had continued to be associated with the anti-Felician Ambrose, he may have faced opposition from those with Felician sentiments at home. Such opposition perhaps was another consideration in his departure.

The Council of Turin

The Felicians were mentioned specifically around the turn of the century, when another Gallic council, apparently sponsored by anti-Felicians, was held not in Gaul, but just across the Italian border at Turin, in the province of Liguria.[70] That the council was for the benefit of the Gauls is indicated by the opening lines: "When we had gathered at the request of the bishops of the provinces of Gaul."[71] Unfortunately, the list of those attending is not extant, but it has been suggested that the bishop of Milan presided.[72] From the point of view of the Gauls, this council not only was to be the most important one held to this point, it also was to be concerned with controversies which were to affect the Gallic church throughout the fifth century. It would be the last time the prestige of Milan would overshadow that of Rome in the north.

68. See n.36 above.

69. "post anachoriticae vitae flammatus amore / longinqua Aegypti sitens deserta petivit": Le Blant, Inscriptions 1.61; VJusti: A.A.S.S. September I p.373. The vita also states that Justus departed because of some unspecified accusation, which was attributed to the "fraus grassantis inimici." See Coville, Lyon pp.441-443 and Duchesne, Fastes 2.162.

70. The current consensus of opinion favors a date of 398 for the council; see Batiffol, "Les églises" p.158ff; Corp. chr. lat. 148.52-60 (q.v. also for text); Gaudemet, Conciles pp.133-134; Griffe, "La date" pp.289-295 and Gaule 1.336-340; Langgärtner, Gallienpolitik p.21; Lumpe, "Synode" pp.7-25; McShane, Romanitas p.277; Palanque, "Dissensions" pp.481-500 and "Premiers" p.380 n.5; and Pietri, Roma 2.973-975 (who suggests either 398 or 399 and includes a long discussion of the controversy). Palanque, one of the main proponents of 398, makes much of the unsupported assumption that Siricius of Rome (384-399) was alive at the time of the council. The council earlier had been dated to circa 400 by Duchesne, Fastes 1.91; Hefele-Leclercq, Conciles 2.85 (A.D.401); Franses, Leo p.15; and Kidd, Church p.104. Babut, Turin (q.v. for earlier bibliography), argued for two councils at Turin, held c.405 and in 417, and this interpretation had a brief vogue, see Bury, L.R.E. 1.363 n.4; Jalland, Leo pp.163-166; and Stein, Geschichte p.411. Duchesne, however, calls this "absolument inacceptable" (Fastes 1.86 n.1, see also "Le concile de Turin" p.279). Supporters of 417 must propose interpolations from otherwise unknown earlier councils. The suggestion of Mommsen (M.G.H. A.A. 9.577 n.1) that the council met not at Turin but at Tours has found no supporters (see Duchesne, "Concile de Turin ou concile de Tours?" and Jalland, Leo pp.164 n.204, 166).

71. "cum ad postulationem provinciarum Galliae sacerdotum convenissemus . . ."

72. See Griffe, Gaule 1.346-347; Lanzoni, Diocesi p.1018; and Pietri, Roma 2.976-977. Triferius attended both Turin and Nîmes.

With regard to the Felician controversy (canon 6: *Corp. chr. lat.* 148.57-58):

The blessed synod further decreed that, because Gallic bishops who are in communion with Felix send legates, if anyone desires to separate himself from his communion let him be received into the fellowship of ours, according to the recently delivered letters of bishop Ambrose of venerable memory and of the bishop of the church of Rome, which were read at the council in the presence of these legates.[73]

Their sending of representatives would seem to indicate that at least some of the Felician bishops, even if they did not attend, were willing to make amends with their adversaries. The reason perhaps is to be found in the late *vita* of Felix himself, which notes that "after the twelfth year of his episcopate, therefore, he abdicated, weakened by the tedium of secular affairs."[74] Felix, therefore, may have resigned his office only shortly before the council, and as a result removed a major stumbling block to a reconciliation.

This controversy could suggest the existence of two general points of view, if not parties, in the late fourth-century Gallic church: one, of the so-called "Felicians," favored a more isolationist outlook, and preferred to conduct Gallic affairs and resolve Gallic problems internally, and the other, of the "anti-Felicians," was willing to look outside Gaul for support.[75] This pattern, of some Gallic bishops striving for Gallic independence of action, and others, often disgruntled losers in Gallic disputes, appealing to Italian authority, was to become a common feature of the fifth-century Gallic church. Furthermore, even if at Turin the bishop of Rome's opinion took second place to that of the bishop of Milan, he at last had gained the attention of the Gallic bishops.

SECULAR CONSIDERATIONS

Around the turn of the century, Gaul also was affected by important political changes. One brought the transference of the seat of the praetorian prefect of Gaul from Trier, in the far north, to Arles, on

---

73. "illud praeterea decrevit sancta synodus ut, quoniam legatos episcopi Galliarum qui Felici communicant destinarunt, ut si quis ab eius communione se voluerit sequestrare in nostrae pacis consortio suscipiatur, iuxta litteras venerabilis memoriae Ambrosii episcopi vel Romanae ecclesiae sacerdotis dudum latas, quae in concilio legatis praesentibus recitatae sunt." Ambrose died in 397.

74. "hic igitur post duodecimum episcopatus sui annum rerum saecularium affectus taedio ... renuntiavit" (*VFelicis* 9: *A.A.S.S.* March III p.622). This would place Felix' abdication in 398, which is consistent with the date usually assigned to the council. The life has been dated to the tenth century or later (Griffe, *Gaule* 1.329 n.85). See also Palanque, "Dissensions" p.485.

75. Pietri, *Roma* 2.973, suggests that the latter also looked to the emperor Theodosius I.

the Mediterranean coast, perhaps c.395, or very shortly thereafter.[76] This new importance of Arles made it not only the secular capital of imperial Gaul, but also, ultimately, one of the most important Gallic ecclesiastical centers.[77] The position of Arles was magnified still further in the early years of the fifth century, perhaps c.402/408, with the initial establishment there, under the prefect Petronius, of an annual provincial council, the *concilium septem provinciarum*.[78]

A more serious political development occurred on the last day of 406, when northern Gaul was invaded by groups of Alans, Burgundians, Suevi, and Vandals. In the next year, the situation was complicated by a rebellion of the Roman armies in Britain, culminating in the crossing of the usurper Constantine from Britain to Gaul to pursue his own imperial ambitions. Finally, a new rebellion arose in the north in 411 under another pretender, the Gallic aristocrat Jovinus.[79]

These changes not only affected the secular and ecclesiastical hierarchies of Gaul, but also tended to bring them into much closer contact with each other, a circumstance which is most visible, and best documented, at Arles. The already great secular importance of the city as of 408 was magnified by Constantine's choice of it as his capital, and its new ecclesiastical role was enhanced by his involvement in the ecclesiastical factionalism there and elsewhere in the south.[80] Before Constantine's activities in Gaul can be discussed, however, it is necessary to describe some contemporary ecclesiastical controversies, especially those involving the churches of Tours, Marseilles, and Arles, all of which were considered at the council of Turin.

76. For 395, see Griffe, *Gaule* 1.337; Nesselhauf, "Verwaltung"; Palanque, "La date" pp.359-365; Stroheker, *Adel* pp.19-20, 43; and Zeller, "Zeit" pp.91-92. A date of 407 is suggested by Chastagnol, "Le repli" pp.23-40 and Matthews, *Aristocracies* p.333 n.1 (on which see Palanque, "Du nouveau" pp.29-38). The Council of Turin must have taken place after the transfer, which would have been the only justification for the new pretensions of the bishop of Arles (see Jalland, *Leo* p.166; Palanque, "Dissensions" pp.487-490; and note 77 below), although even this is denied by Pietri, *Roma* 2.974-975. To date the transfer to 407 would require a very difficult, even later, date for Turin, in the midst of considerable secular turmoil. Franses, *Leo* p.16, suggests a date of 392 for the transfer.

77. For the increased status of Arles, see Heinzelmann, *Bischofsherrschaft* p.74ff and Matthews, *Aristocracies* pp.338-339.

78. Known only from the law "Saluberrima magnificentiae" (the so-called "Constitutio saluberrima") of 418, reestablishing the council (Haenel, *Corp. leg.* p.238); see Matthews, *Aristocracies* p.334; Oost, *Placidia* p.151; Seeck, *Regesten* p.338; and Stein, *Geschichte* pp.409-410. For Petronius' date, see *P.L.R.E. II* pp.862-863, and note the constitution's statement that the council had fallen into desuetude "vel incuria temporum, vel desidia tyrannorum." For a possible connection to the 15-year tax reassesment of 402, see Stein, *Geschichte* pp.409-410. It is unlikely that the earlier council was intended to meet at Trier: it would not have been then the "concilium septem provinciarum" because Trier was in the diocese of Gallia.

79. For the revolts, see chapter 2.

80. For Arles as Constantine's capital, see Demougeot, "Constantin" and Matthews, *Aristocracies* pp.309-313. Langgärtner, *Gallienpolitik* p.24, presumes Constantine did not arrive in Arles until 409.

Tours

At Tours, the Pannonian monk Martin had been chosen bishop c.371, in the face of strong local opposition.[81] According to Martin's biographer, Sulpicius Severus, "A few, nevertheless, and some of them bishops, impiously objected, claiming, as would be expected, that he was a contemptible person, that he was unworthy of the episcopate, that he was a man despicable in demeanor, sleazy in dress, and unkempt in hair."[82] This incident reflects the opposition among some parties in Gaul to the ordination of monks, and especially foreign ones, as bishops. Monks, however, remained popular candidates.

Martin's episcopate seems to have ended in dissension as well. According to several of Martin's biographers, Martin, near the end of his life, fell out with his presbyter Brictius, who previously had been one of his protégés. Sulpicius Severus, for example, claimed that Martin often used to say, "If Christ suffered Judas, why should I not suffer Brictius?"[83] Furthermore, Gregory of Tours said of Brictius, "But even having been endowed with the rank of presbyter, he more often afflicted the blessed man with abuse."[84] The reasons for the quarrel are unclear. It is known, however, that local and foreign factions repeatedly contended for the see of Tours.[85] If the foreigner Martin, an anti-Felician, represented one side, it may be that Brictius belonged to the local party. If so, he also may have had Felician sentiments, and this even could have been one of the causes of his estrangement from Martin. What is clear is that when Martin died in 397, it was his *inimicus* Brictius who was chosen as his successor.[86]

Nor did the matter end there, for apparently Brictius' opponents were unwilling to let him enjoy his victory, and he was faced immediately with ecclesiastical opposition of his own.[87] Soon after his election, he was attacked at the councils of Turin and elsewhere, by a certain Lazarus, who seems to have been a monk of Tours and an-

81. See Ganshof, "Election" pp.481-484, and Griffe, *Gaule* 1.281-283. For Martin, see Griffe, *Gaule* 1.271-329, and Stancliffe, *Martin*.

82. "pauci tamen, et nonnulli ex episcopis . . . impie repugnabant, dicentes scilicet: contemptibilem esse personam, indignum esse episcopatu, hominem vultu despicabilem, veste sordidum, crine deformem" (*VMartini* 9).

83. "si Christus Judam passus est, cur ego non patiar Brictione?" (*Dial.* 3.15). On this passage see Hoare, *Western Fathers* p.66. For Severus' hostility toward Brictius, see also *Dial.* 3.16: "sciat non magis ore inimici quam amici animo me locutum." See also Griffe, *Gaule* 1.296, 2.305.

84. "sed et presbyterii honore praeditus, saepius beatum virum [sc. Martinum] conviciis lacessivit" (*H.F.* 2.1).

85. See Mathisen, "Georgius" passim.

86. For the "anti-Felicians" as the minority, see Gaudemet, *Conciles* p.124. For Brictius' election, see Greg. Tur. *H.F.* 2.1, "adeptum ergo consentientibus civibus pontificatus officium."

87. See Griffe, *Gaule* 1.347, 2.305; Palanque "Dissensions" pp.494-495.

other protégé of Martin. In 417, the bishop of Rome Zosimus noted, "Lazarus has an old habit of accusing the innocent. At many councils he was found to be a devilish accuser of Brictius, our fellow bishop from the city of Tours. [Lazarus] was accused of calumny by Proculus of Marseilles at the synod in the town of Turin."[88] In another letter, Zosimus said, "But Lazarus was condemned recently at the Synod of Turin as a calumniator in the opinions of the most influential bishops after he had attacked the lifestyle of the innocent bishop Brictius with false accusations...."[89] Such accusations may have included those which Sulpicius Severus claimed Martin had made against Brictius: "He was reprimanded by Martin for keeping horses and procuring slaves: for even at that time it was claimed by many that he bought not only barbarian boys, but even good-looking girls."[90] Furthermore, given that Turin was an assembly of anti-Felicians, Lazarus also may have accused Brictius of Felicianism. The personal charges, however, probably would have been dismissed as monastic gossip, and the latter charge, if it was made, might have fallen victim to the new spirit of reconciliation.

Ultimately, this plotting against Brictius did bear fruit, for c.430 he was expelled from his see. According to Gregory of Tours, in the thirty-third year of his episcopate "there arose against him a lamentable reason for accusation": he was charged with adultery and then, after a further accusation of practicing magic arts, "They arise against him in a conspiracy ... he is dragged forth, reviled, and expelled." Brictius then made what was to become a popular Gallic response: "Coming to Rome, he reported to the pope everything which he had suffered. Remaining at the apostolic see, he often celebrated the sacrament of the mass there."[91] Ultimately, "with the authority of the pope," he returned to Tours, and reoccupied the see c.437.[92]

88. "vetus Lazaro consuetudo est innocentiam criminandi. per multa concilia in sanctum Brictium coepiscopum nostrum Turonicae civitatis diabolicus accusator inventus est. a Proculo Massiliensi in synodo Taurini oppidi sententiam calumniatoris excepit" (*Epist.* "Posteaquam a nobis" 5: *C.S.E.L.* 35.103-108). For Lazarus' Turonese origin, see chapter 2 below.

89. "sed Lazarus, dudum in Taurinensi concilio gravissimorum episcoporum sententiis pro calumniatore damnatus, cum Brictii innocentis episcopi vitam falsis objectionibus appetisset...." (*Epist.* "Cum adversus": *M.G.H. Epist.* 3.7-9).

90. "obiurgatus enim ... ab eo fuerat cur ... equos aleret, mancipia compararet: nam iam illo tempore arguebatur a multis, non solum pueros barbaros, sed etiam puellas scitis vultibus coemisse" (*Dial.* 3.15).

91. "oritur contra eum lamentabilis causa pro crimine ... insurgunt contra eum in una conspiratione ... trahitur, calumniatur, eicitur ... at Brictius episcopus Romam veniens, cuncta quae pertulerat papae refert. qui ad sedem apostolicam resedens, plerumque missarum solemnia caelebravit ibi" (*H.F.* 2.1, cf. 10.31).

92. While Brictius was gone, his immediate successor Justinianus was himself expelled and ultimately died at Vercelli in Italy: perhaps he too had gone to Rome to appeal. Only after the next bishop, Armentarius, died was Brictius able to reclaim the see (Greg. Tur. *H.F.* 2.1, 10.31).

This sequence of events, the expulsion of a Gallic bishop and his subsequent appeal to Rome, was to recur several times in the fifth century. Another repetitious pattern, which often will surface when multiple sources survive, is seen in the directly opposed perceptions of Brictius found in Zosimus on the one hand and Severus and Gregory on the other. The strong feelings associated with such dissension often resulted in irreconcilably different accounts of the events which can be attributed only to the partisanship of the authors.

Marseilles and Narbonensis Secunda

During the 390s, Proculus, the bishop of Marseilles at least from 382, was faced with problems of his own, which arose because of a dispute over who was to be the metropolitan bishop of the province of Narbonensis Secunda.[93] Proculus had been exercising this role based upon both the antiquity of his see and his personal authority. He did so even though Marseilles was not only not the metropolitan city of the civil province, but not in Narbonensis Secunda at all: it was in Viennensis, whose metropolitan city was Vienne.[94] This situation had arisen because until recently Narbonensis Secunda had in fact been part of Viennensis; only c.359/381 had it been reorganized into a separate civil province, with Aix as its metropolitan city.[95] As a result, Aix should have become at the same time the ecclesiastical metropolitan see of the province, but for the time being the powerful bishops of Marseilles were able to thwart any pretensions of the bishops of Aix, itself, apparently, but a recently founded see.[96]

It also might not have been even this simple, for one school of thought at the time argued that the division of a secular province need not necessarily result in a new ecclesiastical metropolitan see. Circa 415, for example, Innocent of Rome wrote to Alexander of Antioch (*Epist.* "Et onus et honor": *P.L.* 20.547):

It is unclear what the "auctoritas papae" was. It may have merely been an opinion that Brictius was innocent of the charges against him. If, however, it was an order that he be restored, it was not put into effect, for Brictius settled down six miles from Tours and waited for Armentarius to die.

93. Including at this time, it seems, Alpes Maritimae: see Griffe, *Gaule* 1.335 n.9, 339 n.13.

94. See Batiffol, "Les églises" p.159; Clerc, *Massalia*; de Wewer, "Massaliote" pp.71-117; Duchesne, *Fastes* 1.92, 102-104; Griffe, *Gaule* 1.336-339; Jones, *L.R.E.* pp.881-882; Langgärtner, *Gallienpolitik* p.23; and Nesselhauf, *Verwaltung* p.12. Apparently, many of the sees of Narbonensis Secunda were rather late foundations.

95. See Chastagnol, "Diocèse" pp.273-279. For a date of c.380, see Griffe, *Gaule* 1.337. Proculus' claims would have been even stronger if the inception of his episcopate antedated Aix's new status (as assumed by Langgärtner, *Gallienpolitik* p.21).

96. Duchesne, *Fastes* 1.278, does not cite a bishop of Aix until the early fifth century. See also Palanque, "Dissensions" pp.486-487.

As to what you ask, whether, when provinces have been divided by imperial decree so that there are two metropolitan cities, there ought therefore to be named two metropolitan bishops, it does not at all seem proper that the church of God should be altered according to the changeableness of worldly necessities, and that it should utilize the offices and divisions which the emperor thinks should be introduced for his own purposes.[97]

If the official view of the bishop of Rome was that changes in the state administrative structure need not affect that of the church, the ultimate view of the state was different. In the sixth century, for example, the emperor Justinian recalled what had happened to Thessalonica in the 440s: "The bishop of Thessalonica gained any preeminence he may have had not by his own authority but through the influence of the prefecture."[98] There could have been grounds, therefore, for an argument in Gaul that the bishop of Aix was not necessarily the metropolitan at all, an argument that Proculus of Marseilles could have used to justify maintaining his own position.

It was probably a result of this uncertainty over who was to be the metropolitan bishop of Narbonensis Secunda that in the 390s serious opposition from the bishops of the province, led by a certain Remigius, arose against Proculus of Marseilles.[99] Specifically, Remigius, who may have been the bishop of Aix, and three other bishops of Narbonensis Secunda (whose sees are not known), Octavius, Ursus, and Triferius, had been presuming to consecrate bishops in the province, a right which Proculus claimed as his own.[100] This controversy, too, was considered at Turin, and the very first canon noted (*Corp. chr. lat.* 148.54):

The blessed bishop Proculus of Marseilles claims that he ought to oversee the churches, in the capacity of metropolitan, which are seen to be located in

---

97. "nam quod suscitaris, utrum divisis imperiali iudicio provinciis, ut duae metropoles fiant, sic duo metropolitani episcopi debeant nominari, non e re visum est ad mobilitatem necessitatum mundanarum dei ecclesiam commutari honoresque aut divisiones perpeti, quas pro suis causis faciendas duxerit imperator."

98. "Thessalonicensis episcopus non sua auctoritate, sed sub umbra praefecturae meruit aliquam praerogativam" (*Nov. Just.* 11). See Mommsen, *M.G.H.* A.A. 9.553 n.2.

99. See Griffe, *Gaule* 1.336-339.

100. For Remigius as bishop of Aix, see Babut, *Turin* p.237, and de Manteyer, *Origines* p.44. Note, too, that Glanum, the third stop up the *Via Aurelia* from Aix, later had the name Saint-Remy [that is, Remigius] de Provence. For other suggestions, see Duchesne *Fastes* 1.102, and Palanque, "Evêchés" p.136 and "Dissensions" pp.477, 487 (Remigius bishop of Gap); Palanque, "Premiers" pp.380-383, "Evêchés" pp.118, 129 and Pietri, *Roma* 2.976 (Triferius bishop of Aix). Palanque, "Premiers" p.380, also speculates that the four bishops represented the sees of Aix, Fréjus, Apt, and Gap, and that they had consecrated a bishop of Antibes; see also Palanque, "Dissensions" pp.493-494. Those who deny Remigius was bishop of Aix do so because they suppose that the bishop of Aix was murdered during the reign of Constantine III, and Remigius was alive afterward. Discussion below (chapter 2, n.11), however, will suggest that the bishop of Aix was not killed.

Narbonensis Secunda . . . insofar as he asserts that these same churches and parishes are his own . . . but on the other hand the bishops of this same region claim otherwise, and they contend that it is not fitting for a bishop of another province to oversee [them].[101]

Ultimately, despite Proculus' irregular legal position, the bishops at the synod were unable to resist his authority, and his metropolitan status was confirmed for his lifetime, although when he died it was to revert to the bishop of Aix.

For the time being, then, the anti-Proculan faction was thwarted. Indeed, in light of the contemporary Gallic ecclesiastical affiliations, Proculus' victory at Turin probably is not surprising. All four of his opponents—Ursus, Octavius, Remigius, and Triferius—had attended the Council of Nîmes; Proculus had not. Perhaps they were Felicians whereas Proculus, who had many connections outside Gaul, apparently was not.[102] At Turin, therefore, Proculus would have been able to present his case before a favorable tribunal.

At least one of Proculus' four opponents, moreover, seems to have come to Turin himself in order to reaffirm his own local authority (*Corp. chr. lat.* 148.57):

Concerning the layman Palladius, moreover, who leveled a serious accusation against the presbyter Spanus, who accompanied them, the bishop Triferius testified that he was aware of the cause of this same accusation. . . . The authority of this council decided that this same Palladius should receive the same sentence which was imposed upon him at the time of the hearing by the bishop Triferius. . . . The blessed synod also decreed concerning the presbyter Exuperantius, who heaped many serious injuries upon his blessed bishop Triferius and provoked him with frequent abuse . . . that when this same Exuperantius either has given satisfaction, or seems to have done so, to bishop Triferius, then let him receive the sacrament of communion.[103]

These local squabbles had induced a Felician to be judged by the anti-Felicians and, presumably, to reenter communion with them. In ex-

---

101. "vir sanctus Proculus Massiliensis episcopus civitatis se tamquam metropolitanum ecclesiis quae in secunda provincia Narbonensi positae videbantur diceret praesse debere . . . siquidem assereret easdem ecclesias vel suas parrocias fuisse . . . e diverso eiusdem regionis episcopi aliud defensarent, ac sibi alterius provinciae sacerdotem praeesse [sic] non debere contenderent." See Griffe, *Gaule* 1.346-348, 2.252.

102. For Proculus as an anti-Felician, see Gaudemet, *Conciles* p.124.

103. "de Palladio autem laico qui Spano presbytero non leve crimen intenderat, inter quos episcopus Triferius eiusdem criminis causam se cognovisse testatus est, id concilii decrevit auctoritas ut idem Palladius in eadem sententia maneret qua cognitionis tempore a Triferio fuerat sacerdote mulctatus. . . . statuit quoque de Exuperantio presbytero sancta synodus qui in iniuriam sancti episcopi sui Triferii gravia et multa congesserat et frequentibus eum contumeliis provocarat . . . ut quando vel idem Exuperantius satisfecerit vel episcopo Triferio visum fuerit, tum gratiam communionis accipiat."

change, Triferius himself would have obtained powerful support for his own local authority.

Arles and Vienne

A very long-lived quarrel which had its origins at this same time involved the bishops of Arles and Vienne and concerned the exercise of their metropolitan status in Viennensis.[104] During the fourth century Vienne had been both the secular and ecclesiastical capital of the province.[105] The relocation of the seat of the praetorian prefect from Trier to Arles, which was not even a provincial capital, around the turn of the century created an anomaly: Vienne remained the metropolitan city of the secular province and even the capital of the diocese, whereas Arles became the "capital" of all Gaul. The bishop of Vienne, therefore, would have felt justified in maintaining his status as metropolitan of the province, whereas that of Arles now would have looked for increased ecclesiastical jurisdiction to match the secular status of the city.[106] The result was a continuing and festering conflict between the two bishops which would shatter any unity the Gallic church might have acquired in the fourth century.[107]

This question too was considered at Turin, and the council solomonically divided the province between the two cities (*Corp. chr. lat.* 148.56):

Indeed, in order to maintain the bond of peace, by this more useful plan it is decreed, if it is pleasing to the bishops of the aforementioned cities, that each should appropriate for himself the nearer of the cities within the province, and should visit those churches which he understands to be more near to his own town, with the result that, mindful of unanimity and concord, one might no longer disturb the other by usurping to himself that which belongs to the other.[108]

104. See Batiffol, "Les églises" p.159ff; Bury, *L.R.E.* pp.362-363; Chastagnol, "Diocèse"; Duchesne, *Fastes* 1.86-146; Griffe, *Gaule* 1.336-340; Gundlach, *Der Streit*; Hefele-Leclercq, *Conciles* 2.424-428, 1385-1386; Jones, *L.R.E.* pp.212, 889-890; Kidd, *Church* pp.353-355; Palanque, "Dissensions" pp.487-490; and Pelletier, "Vienne" pp.491-498.

105. Much later, the church of Vienne was to use this status to claim ecclesiastical jurisdiction over the entire Septem Provinciae in a forged letter supposedly written by Sylvester of Rome (*P.L.* 8.848) in the early fourth century. Its relevance to the context of the fifth-century controversies, however, is demonstrated not only by its opening words "Placuit apostolicae," an obvious plagiarism from Zosimus' letter of 417 (chapter 3 below, n.29), but also by its being addressed to Paschasius, bishop of Vienne in the 440s.

106. The suggestion that Concordius, bishop of Arles at least c.374-396, was a native of Trier (Heinzelmann, *Bischofsherrschaft* pp.70-71) may be significant in this context, for if the offices of the prefecture were withdrawn to Arles in the 390s, Concordius may have found newly arrived influential allies in his quest for greater status for his see.

107. See Mommsen, *M.G.H. A.A.* 9.553-554, "nata inde sunt litigia inter sedes duas Viennensem et Arelatensem de primatu per saecula continuata."

108. "certe ad pacis vinculum conservandum hoc consilio utiliore decretum est, ut si placet memoratarum urbium episcopis, unaquaeque de his viciniores sibi intra provinciam vindicet

The cities subordinated to each see, moreover, were left unnamed, at least in the extant canons, perhaps because only an agreement in principle could be reached, but not a decision as to which cities were "nearer" to which see.[109]

The significance of the Council of Turin cannot be overstated. Seventy years would elapse before there would again be anything approaching ecclesiastical unity and harmony in Gaul, and then only for a short time. This was to be the last time that the Gauls could discuss matters concerning the organization of their church without needing to consider the potential for appeals by disaffected Gauls to the bishop of Rome. The decisions regarding metropolitan authority in Viennensis and Narbonensis Secunda were to serve as the bases for many disputes and decisions in the fifth century. The question of jurisdiction in Viennensis in particular not only continued to be hotly debated, but the resultant quarrels were to give the bishops of Rome additional opportunities to extend their influence into Gaul.

---

civitates, atque eas ecclesias visitet quas oppidis suis proximas magis esse constiterit, ita ut memores unanimitatis atque concordiae, non alter alterum longius sibi usurpando quod est alii proprium inquietet." The "pacis vinculum" is a euphemistic reference to shared communion.

109. In the early 450s, Leo of Rome suggested that Vienne was to oversee Geneva, Grenoble, and Valence in Viennensis, as well as Tarentaise in Alpes Graiae, a decision clearly based upon Turin; see chapter 8 below, n.38, and Griffe, *Gaule* 1.339-340.

CHAPTER 2

PROCULUS, PATROCLUS,
AND PELAGIANISM

THE GALLIC CHURCH IN THE AGE
OF THE TYRANTS

The revolts of Constantine, a common soldier, in 407 and Jovinus, a Gallic aristocrat, in 411 added new elements to Gallic factionalism, both secular and ecclesiastical.[1] On the secular side, it is apparent that many Gallic aristocrats sided with the usurpers. Two natives of Lyons, for example, Apollinaris and Decimus Rusticus, were early partisans of Constantine. Apollinaris served in Spain as his praetorian prefect of Gaul. Eventually he was replaced by Rusticus (probably in 409), who had been Constantine's *magister officiorum*.[2] After the defeat of Constantine, Rusticus then joined Jovinus, whom he served in the same capacity. Jovinus also was supported by an Agroecius, his *primicerius notariorum*, and by "many nobles".[3] The only other secular Gallo-Roman supporter of Constantine who is expressly named as such is Jovius, who served as his ambassador to Honorius in 409 (Zos. 6.1.1-2). Jovius was a pagan acquaintance of Meropius Pontius Paulinus of Nola and, it seems, a native of southern Gaul; his name could suggest that he was a relative of the usurper Jovinus.[4]

As Constantine extended his influence in Gaul, imperial officials

---

1. For the revolts, see Demougeot, "Constantin"; Matthews, *Aristocracies* pp.307-316; Oost, *Placidia* pp.76-119; Seeck, *Untergang* pp.379-408; Stein, *Geschichte* pp.384-401; and Stevens, "Marcus."

2. Apollinaris: *P.L.R.E. II* p.113. Rusticus: *P.L.R.E. II* p.965. Apollinaris at times wrongly is said to have been a native of the Auvergne; he in fact came from Lyons: see Mathisen, "Addenda" p.366. For Constantine's supporters, see Matthews, *Aristocracies* p.333; Stroheker, *Adel* p.45; and Sundwall, *Studien* chap.I: "Die gallische Präfektur und das Verhältnis Galliens zum Reich" (including clerics).

3. Ren. Prof. Frig. *ap.* Greg. Tur. *H.F.* 2.9. For Agroecius' origin, see Mathisen, *Ecclesiastical Aristocracy* pp.452-455. For Jovinus' supporters, see Matthews, *Aristocracies* p.314 and Stroheker, *Adel* p.45.

4. See *P.L.R.E. II* p.622.

and Gallic loyalists would have been placed in an untenable position. Some officials, possibly Gauls, are known to have fled to Italy, including the Gallic prefect Limenius and the master of soldiers Chariobaudus, as well as Eventius, the *consularis Viennensis*, who died at Rome in 408.[5]

Very few Gauls, moreover, seem to have remained loyal to the Italian regime. The *Gallic Chronicle of 452* singled out Claudius Postumus Dardanus, Honorius' praetorian prefect of Gaul, and praised "the diligence of the vigorous man Dardanus, who alone did not capitulate to the tyrant."[6] At least one other person, however, also presumably remained loyal—Dardanus' brother Claudius Lepidus.[7] Their careers suggest not only why they did so, but also why so few others followed their example: they, unlike most Gauls, had been able to attain high office in the central administration. Dardanus was a past *consularis Viennensis*, *magister libellorum*, and *quaestor sacri palatii*. Lepidus, for his part, by c.412 had held the offices of *consularis Germaniae Primae*, *magister memoriae*, and *comes rei privatae*. Few other Gauls had such opportunities.[8]

CONSTANTINE AND THE CHURCH[9]

Once Constantine had become master of the secular affairs of Gaul, he seems to have taken charge of the ecclesiastical sphere as well, by adlecting among his supporters several influential Gallic bishops. Some, already in office, apparently took advantage of his support to

5. For Limenius and Chariobaudus, see *P.L.R.E. II*, pp.684 and 283 respectively, see also Zos. 5.32.4, and Soz. *H.E.* 9.4.7. Both may have had Gallic ties. Other contemporary Gallic Limenii include a correspondent of Salvian of Marseilles (Salv. *Epist.* 6). Chariobaudus' name would suggest he was a German, and one might note the abbot Chariobaudus who was a correspondent of Sidonius (Sid. Apoll. *Epist.* 7.16). For Eventius, see Marrou, "Eventius" pp.326-331 and *P.L.R.E. II* p.413. Other Eventii are well attested in Gaul: note an Evanthius who owned land near Tours c.400 (Sulp. Sev. *Dial.* 2.2, Paul. Pet. *VMartini* 4.96ff and Mathisen, "Addenda" p.372), an Eventius buried at Vienne during late antiquity (*C.I.L.* 12.2110), a bishop Evantius at the Council of Nîmes in 396 (*Corp. chr. lat.* 148.51), an Evanthius in office in Aquitania c.470 (Sid. Apoll. *Epist.* 5.13.1), an Evantius, or Venantius, a presbyter at Langres in 538 (*Corp. chr. lat.* 148A.127, 129), not to mention several other Venantii, a variant spelling of this name.

6. "industria viri strenui, qui solus tyranno non cessit, Dardani" (no.69, s.a.411: *M.G.H. A.A.* 9.654). For Dardanus, see Heinzelmann, *Bischofsherrschaft* p.224; Matthews, *Aristocracies* p.323; *P.L.R.E. II* pp.346-347; and Stein, *Geschichte* 1.264.

7. *P.L.R.E. II* p.675.

8. Another Gaul who also held high office at this time was Rutilius Claudius Namatianus, *magister officiorum* in 412 and *praefectus urbi* in 414 (*P.L.R.E. II* pp.770-771). He, however, apparently was in Italy during the Gallic revolts, and may have been another refugee. Curiously, he, like Dardanus and Lepidus, had the *nomen* Claudius. Rutilius' father (?Claudius) Lachanius also had held high offices at court, including *comes sacrarum largitionum*, *quaestor sacri palatii*, and *praefectus ?urbi* (*P.L.R.E. I* pp.208, 491). For the preference for Italians in such positions, see Matthews, *Aristocracies* pp.333-334.

9. See Heinzelmann, *Bischofsherrschaft* p.74 and Pietri, *Roma* 2.1003-1004.

pursue their own ambitions. Others gained office under his patronage, and would have been even more beholden to him. An entry in the *Gallic Chronicle of 452* for the year 408 indicates that Proculus of Marseilles took the opportunity offered by the changed conditions to move against his nemesis Remigius: "Proculus, bishop of Marseilles, is held in renown, and with his approval, a great investigation concerning the suspected adultery of bishop Remigius is initiated."[10] Although the chronicle does not report the results of this investigation, Remigius' fate may be inferred from a letter of Zosimus of Rome written in 417, which recalled how Lazarus, the earlier accuser of Brictius, had become bishop of Aix: "Many years later [viz. after the Council of Turin] he was made bishop by this same Proculus, with the tyrant's support. After the bishop of the city of Aix had been struck down when he objected, [Lazarus] rushed into the very sanctuary and episcopal throne which was, so to speak, sprinkled with innocent blood"[11]

The Remigius of 408 presumably is the same Remigius with whom Proculus had quarreled in the 390s, who already has been identified as the bishop of Aix. Zosimus' report of the deposition of the bishop of Aix also is consistent with Remigius being that bishop.[12] If so, Remigius' enemy Proculus finally had triumphed over him. It may be that more heavy-handed measures, "with the tyrant's support," succeeded where a trumped-up charge of adultery had failed. Nor did Proculus' reputation seem to have suffered from such activities, for c.412 Jerome could write to one of Proculus' parishoners, "You have there the blessed and most learned Proculus, who surpasses my missives with his living and present voice."[13]

Proculus of Marseilles, therefore, was another influential Gaul who

10. "Proculus Massiliensis episcopus clarus habetur. quo annuente, magna de suspecto adulterio Remedi [sic] episcopi quaestio agitatur" (*M.G.H. A.A.* 9.652). The charge of adultery, also used against Brictius, was very common: note also Greg. Tur. *Glor. conf.* 75, 92 and the Chelidonius affair (chapter 7 below). See also Pietri, *Roma* 2.1003 n.3.

11. "ab eodem Proculo fit post multos annos sacerdos tyrannici iudicii, defensore civitatis Aquensium cum contrairet adflicto, in ipsum penetrale et sacerdotale solium sanguine innocentis paene respersum irrupit" (*Epist.*" Posteaquam a nobis": *C.S.E.L.* 35.103-108). See Griffe, *Gaule* 2.253-256. The references to blood perhaps are rhetorical, or may refer to the murder of Honorius' Spanish relatives (Matthews, *Aristocracies* p.310). Duchesne, *Fastes* 1.227, assumes the bishop of Aix was actually killed. The same story of Lazarus' promotion is repeated by Zosimus in *Epist.* "Cum adversus" (*M.G.H. Epist.* 3.7-9): "sed Lazarus . . . post vero indebitum ab eodem Proculo, qui inter ceteros in synodo [sc. Taurinensi] damnationis eius assederat, sacerdotium consecutus. . . ." These passages indicate that the Council of Turin occurred some time before c.408, not in 417 (see chapter 1 above, n.70). For the bishop as the *defensor civitatis,* see Declareuil, "Les curies" p.28.

12. For other suggestions about Remigius' see, see chapter 1 above, n.100.

13. "habes istic sanctum doctissimumque pontificem Proculum, qui viva et praesenti voce nostras schedulas superet" (*Epist.* 125.20).

cooperated with Constantine. His need to have Constantine's support in his quarrel with Remigius may have been one factor which induced the wily bishop to support the usurper. It also would seem that Proculus had been forced by political necessity to change his political views. In the past, he had held "anti-Felician" sentiments regarding foreign ties, and had taken an active part in the Gallic affiliations with Milan. The appearance of Constantine, however, apparently caused him to reevaluate his outlook, and he seems to have been very successful at finding allies within Gaul. Another example of his about-face is seen in the way that he embraced his old enemy Lazarus, whom he had accused at Turin. He even consecrated him as the new bishop of Aix. The case of Proculus shows that one's factional affiliations at this time were by no means hard and fast, and could change as conditions changed.

As for Constantine, not only had he set the precedent in Gaul for secular interference in an episcopal election, he also would have gained a supporter in a metropolitan see as well. The new bishop Lazarus, however, probably was unable to exercise his *de iure* metropolitan rights, for the Council of Turin had left them in the hands of Proculus of Marseilles, another metropolitan supporter of Constantine. Nor were Aix and Marseilles the only places where Constantine had metropolitan allies. Heros, the bishop of his imperial capital, Arles, also looked to him for patronage. Zosimus said of him in the same letter in which he had reviled Lazarus, "Indeed, with regard to Heros, everything was similar: the same tyrant as a patron, the same slaughters, riots, and shackling and imprisoning of objecting priests."[14] Small matter that Heros, whatever his inclinations, probably had little choice. Like Felix of Trier, he was the bishop of an imperial capital, and would have been under close scrutiny.

These two bishops, Heros and Lazarus, both had strong ties to Tours. Lazarus, as seen above, was an accuser of Brictius of Tours, and Heros was described by Prosper as a "disciple of the blessed Martin."[15] The two, therefore, would have known each other, and their appearance in southern Gaul as protégés of Constantine is unlikely to have been mere coincidence. Unfortunately, it is not known exactly when Heros became bishop, but his close association both with his "patron" Constantine, and with Lazarus, whom Con-

14. "de Herote vero similia omnia, idem tyrannus patronus, caedes, turbae, presbyterorum contradicentium vincla atque custodiae...." ("Posteaquam a nobis": *C.S.E.L.* 35.103-108). For Heros, see Duchesne, *Fastes* 1.96-97 and Prinz, *Mönchtum* p.25.

15. "beati Martini discipulus" (*Chron.* 1247 s.a.412: *M.G.H. A.A.* 11.466); see Duchesne, *Fastes* 1.96-98, and Prinz, *Mönchtum* p.25. Given their similar careers, Lazarus too once may have been a monk of Tours, as suggested by Rousseau, *Ascetics* p.174.

stantine did make bishop, would suggest that Heros too may have obtained his episcopal office through Constantine's favor at the same time, circa 408.[16]

Confirmation of the close ties between Heros and Lazarus, as well as accusations about the trouble they caused, comes from Zosimus, who noted in 417, "Wherever there is campaigning for an episcopal see, [these two] traverse the lands and seas, nor do they overlook any source of support."[17] He also referred to them as "those who were responsible for such great machinations against their brothers and fellow bishops, those who created so much dissension in the church."[18] Heros and Lazarus, therefore, not only came from similar backgrounds, they also worked together.

By supporting these two Turonese opportunists, Constantine foreshadowed another common fifth-century practice, that of favoring outsiders as bishops of important sees.[19] Such a practice would result in a natural alliance between the patron, in this case Constantine, and the alien bishop. The latter presumably would have little local support and therefore would do what he could to remain in the good graces of his sponsor. The use of this tactic in the cases of Lazarus and Heros was attested, once again, by Zosimus: "It is apparent that these two, unknown and foreign born, appropriated episcopates in Gaul by means of improper ordinations, against the wishes of the people and clergy...."[20] If this charge is true, they could not have done so without support from somewhere.

In spite of the precedents he set concerning church-state relations in southern Gaul, Constantine's own reign was relatively brief. After achieving momentary recognition from Honorius, he was faced not only with a revolt led by his general Gerontius in Spain in 409, but

16. See Duchesne, *Fastes* 1.96-97, 255, and Griffe, *Gaule* 2.237-239, 146-147, 252-256, who dates Heros' election to late 407-early 408. Palanque, *Marseilles* p.19, presumes that Proculus of Marseilles was involved in the election of Heros as well as that of Lazarus.

17. "ubi de episcopatu ambiendo agitur, maria terraeque lustrantur nec ulla suffragia praetermittuntur" (*Epist.* "Posteaquam a nobis": *C.S.E.L.* 35.103-108).

18. "qui in fratres et coepiscopos tanta machinati sunt, qui tot tempestates ecclesiae reddiderunt" (*Epist.* "Posteaquam a nobis": *C.S.E.L.* 35.103-108).

19. It remains problematical just why Constantine supported Heros and Lazarus. Perhaps he or his associates had ties to Tours. His son the caesar Constans once had been a monk: could this have been at Tours? (see *P.L.R.E. II* p.310; Orosius 7.40.7; Marcel. *Chron.* s.a.411; and Jord. *Get.* 165, *Rom.* 324). Nonnichia, the wife of Constantine's general Gerontius, may have been related to the Nonnichii of Nantes, just west of Tours (*P.L.R.E. II* pp. 508 and 788 [as "Nunechia"]; Soz. *H.E.* 9.13.5; Olymp. no.16). Or Constantine's general Justinianus (*P.L.R.E. II* p.644; Zos. 6.2.2-3; Olymp. no.12) may have been related to the Justinianus who became bishop of Tours after Brictius was expelled in 430 (see chapter 1 above, n.92).

20. "patuit hos inobservatis, plebe cleroque contradicente, ignotos, alienigenas ordinationibus intra Gallias sacerdotia vindicasse...." (*Epist.* "Magnum pondus": *C.S.E.L.* 35.99-103). Zosimus apparently exaggerated the degree of their "foreign birth."

also with an invasion from Italy led by the general Constantius.[21] While the Italian army approached, Constantine patiently awaited the arrival of his general Edobichus, who had been sent north to recruit reinforcements among the Franks.[22] Edobichus, however, was defeated by the imperial generals Constantius and Ulfilas, and he fled to a client of his, a certain Ecdicius, who repaid the defeated general for past favors by sending his head to Constantius.[23] Then, when Ecdicius attempted to gain a reward from Constantius, the latter dismissed him, "for he did not consider the companionship of a malicious host to be good for himself and the army. And . . . the man who had dared to commit the most unholy murder of a friend and guest who was in an unfortunate situation, this man went away, as the proverb says, gaping with emptiness."[24]

This incident sheds some scanty light on the predicament in which Constantine's Gallic supporters must have found themselves when the defeat of the usurper became imminent, for surely this Ecdicius, who had been a friend of Constantine's general, would have been a partisan of the usurper. Constantius' refusal to reward Ecdicius also suggests that the latter, unlike Dardanus, had not been an open supporter of the Italian government. Perhaps it was considered sufficient that Ecdicius should escape with his life. Other supporters of Constantine, however, such as his prefect of Gaul, Decimus Rusticus, did not give up so easily, and escaped to the north to continue the fight in the train of the other Gallic usurper of this period, Jovinus (411-413).[25]

After the defeat of Edobichus, Constantine's last hope of victory was gone, and now he could only hope to survive. He arranged to surrender to Constantius on condition that his life be spared, but at the same time he also took the novel precaution of having himself ordained as a presbyter of the church of Arles, a ceremony which would have been carried out by his partisan Heros. This charade, however, was no more effective than Constantius' oath in saving him from being beheaded as soon as the city was surrendered.[26] Even though Constantine himself did not benefit from this ploy, it did serve as a precedent for the ordination into ecclesiastical, usually episcopal, orders of other deposed emperors in the future, such as Eparchius Avitus at Piacenza in 456 and Glycerius at Salona in 475.[27]

21. See note 1 above.

22. Edobichus: *P.L.R.E. II* p.386.

23. Ecdicius: *P.L.R.E. II* p.383.

24. Soz. *H.E.* 9.14.3-4, translation cited from Hartranft, *Ecclesiastical History* p.426.

25. Ren. Prof. Frig. *ap.* Greg. Tur. *H.F.* 2.9. See Matthews, *Aristocracies* pp. 313-314.

26. For Constantine's ordination and death, see Olymp. no.16, Soz. *H.E.* 9.15.1. For Heros' role, see Duchesne, *Fastes* 1.96-97 and Oost, *Placidia* p.147 n.36.

27. Avitus: *P.L.R.E. II* p.198. Glycerius: ibid. p.514, see which also for the tradition that he

The fall of Constantine in 411 was followed in 413 by that of Jovinus. The latter's attempts to secure an alliance with the Visigothic ruler Athaulf had been thwarted by the intervention of the Gallic loyalist Claudius Postumus Dardanus, who persuaded the king to support the Italian government.[28] After being besieged and surrendering to Athaulf at Valence, Jovinus, who was supposed to have been delivered to Honorius in Italy, was taken to Narbonne and executed by Dardanus, who supposedly carried out the task with his own hand. Narbonne may have been chosen because Jovinus had relatives and perhaps even his home there.[29] Dardanus also had the brothers of Jovinus, Sebastianus (also an augustus) and Sallustius, executed for good measure.[30] The pointed performance at Narbonne of the execution, apparently against the emperor's orders, not only of Jovinus but of his brothers as well would suggest that Dardanus had a very personal score to settle with Jovinus and his family.

Dardanus' extreme actions may have been one factor which alienated him from the mainstream of the Gallic aristocracy.[31] In the 460s, Sidonius Apollinaris, the grandson of Constantine's prefect, wrote to Aquilinus, the grandson of Decimus Rusticus, saying that their two forebears were alike "in that they reviled the inconstancy of Constantine, the tractability of Jovinus, the perfidy of Gerontius, individual faults in individual men, and all these faults at once in Dardanus."[32] Sidonius' negative portrayal of Constantine and Jovinus, who were supported by his and Aquilinus' ancestors, probably is a result of the usurpers' ultimate defeat and the ruin they were to bring upon their Gallo-Roman supporters, both of which assured the damnation of their memory in Gaul.

What, however, was the reason for Sidonius' treatment of Dardanus, whom he singled out as guilty not merely of a single fault, but of all of them combined? Was it merely because of Dardanus' loyalty to

---

was later made bishop of Milan in 480. Constantine's tactic may show the influence of his son, the ex-monk Constans, who already had been killed earlier in 411 (*P.L.R.E. II* p.310).

28. See Matthews, *Aristocracies* pp.314-315 and Sundwall, *Studien* pp.11-12. For the suggestion that the Visigothic puppet Attalus also may have been supported by "some of the magnates who had supported the other recent usurpers in Gaul," see Oost, *Placidia* p.130.

29. See Olymp. no.19. The grammarian and rhetor Consentius of Narbonne was married to the daughter of a Jovinus, probably the usurper: Sid. Apoll. *Carm.* 23.170ff; see Mathisen, *Ecclesiastical Aristocracy* pp.73-74 and Matthews, *Aristocracies* p.339.

30. See *P.L.R.E. II* pp. 622, 971, 983.

31. For the resultant "deep and lasting resentment" against Dardanus, see Matthews, *Aristocracies* pp.322-323. Stroheker, *Adel* p.51 sees the rejection of Dardanus as a rejection of imperial rule as well (cf. Sid. Apoll. *Carm.* 7.359).

32. "cum in Constantino inconstantiam, in Iovino facilitatem, in Gerontio perfidiam, singula in singulis omnia in Dardano crimina simul execrarentur" (*Epist.* 5.9.1).

the Italian party at a time when Sidonius' own relatives had supported the usurpers? Even if this were the case, the evidence of the *Gallic Chronicle* shows that there must have been others in Gaul who felt positively about Dardanus. Non-Gallic sources also depicted Dardanus very favorably. Jerome, for example, saluted him in 414 as "Most noble of Christians, most Christian of nobles," and Augustine addressed him as "Dardanus, more illustrious to me because of the love of Christ than because of secular rank."[33]

Dardanus' past political involvements may have been one factor which led him to his own adoption of the religious life. Not only did he correspond with Jerome and Augustine, he also retired sometime before 412 to a fortified estate in the Alps between Digne and Sisteron named Theopolis, perhaps an allusion to Augustine's "Civitas dei."[34] Dardanus, therefore, may have succeeded in the escape to the religious life which his enemy Constantine had only attempted.

The varied opinions of Dardanus would suggest a parallel between the outlooks of secular and ecclesiastical potentates. The viewpoint of Dardanus and his partisans is at least outwardly similar to that of the "anti-Felicians," in that both groups seem to have welcomed aid and contacts from outside Gaul. The supporters of the usurpers, on the other hand, preferred, like the "Felicians," to settle the affairs of Gaul internally, and to have their ties there. In both cases, furthermore, the local group seems to have been in the majority. It remains to be seen, however, whether such general similarities in outlook led to actual political affiliations among powerful *saeculares* and *ecclesiastici*.

THE EFFECTS OF THE FALL OF THE USURPERS

Jovinus and his brothers were not the only ones to be treated harshly after the fall of the usurpers. The now lost history of Renatus Profuturus Frigeridus reported, "At the same time, Decimus Rusticus, the prefect of the tyrants, Agroecius, who had been the *primicerius notariorum* of Jovinus, and many nobles were captured at Clermont by the generals of Honorius and cruelly murdered."[35] The specific

33. "Christianorum nobilissime, et nobilium Christianissime" (Hieron. *Epist.* 129.1); "Dardane inlustrior mihi in caritate Christi quam in huius saeculi dignitate" (Aug. *Epist.* 187.1).

34. Construction was assisted by his brother and by Naevia Galla, his wife. For this estate, see Chatillon, "Dardanus"; Marrou, "Un lieu" passim; and *P.L.R.E. II* p.347. See also Benoit, "La crypte" pp.69-89, and "Les chapelles" pp.129-154, which discuss a local cult of Dardanus and his family, centered at the chapel of Notre-Dame-de-Dromou.

35. "isdem diebus praefectus tyrannorum Decimus Rusticus, Agroecius ex primicerium notariorum Iovini multique nobiles apud Arvernos capti a ducibus Honorianis, crudeliter interempti sunt" (*apud* Greg. Tur. *H.F.* 2.9). Note also the *Carm. de prov. div.* 40, which, in the context of the barbarian invasions, refers to the "mors quoque primorum" in 416.

mention of the Auvergne as a focal point for the Gallic opposition is significant for two reasons.[36] First of all, it may explain the outwardly reprehensible actions of Ecdicius, for his name is one used exclusively in Gaul by the Arvernian Aviti. Such a family background would be consistent with the suggestion that he was implicated in the revolt.[37] If so, he would have had all the more reason to take drastic measures to protect himself. It also could explain Sidonius' own attitude toward Dardanus, for not only was Sidonius the son-in-law of the Arvernian emperor Avitus (455-456), but he also became bishop of Clermont.[38]

Reprisals also occurred in the ecclesiastical sphere, for at this same time Constantine's partisans Heros and Lazarus both lost their sees, although it probably was their ecclesiastical status which did protect their lives.[39] Lazarus' departure was described by Zosimus of Rome: "And thus far a shadow of the episcopacy existed in him, as long as a semblance of rule remained for the tyrant, but after the murder of his patron, [Lazarus] divested himself of this position of his own will and condemned himself by his own departure."[40] With regard to Heros, Zosimus noted in the same letter that he suffered a "like penitence of the abdication of his episcopate."[41] Elsewhere, however, Zosimus gave a slightly different view of Lazarus' departure: "But Lazarus ... having obtained an episcopate, after orders had been given for his abdication, personally removed himself from it of his own will, mindful of his own life."[42] This passage would tend to contradict Zosimus' other statement that Lazarus' departure was wholly of his own will; apparently he had been encouraged to do so by an official order, not to mention fear for his life.[43]

The tendentious nature of Zosimus' account is demonstrated, moreover, by the Gaul Prosper's account, under the year 412, of Heros' expulsion (*Chron.* 1247 s.a.412):

Heros, a saintly man and a disciple of the blessed Martin, while he was presiding as bishop over the city of Arles was expelled by the people of the

36. See Stroheker, *Adel* p.46.

37. See Mathisen, "Epistolography" pp.100-101 and *P.L.R.E. II* pp.383-385.

38. See Stevens, *Sidonius* passim. For Avitus, see chapter 8 below.

39. Proculus may narrowly have escaped expulsion: see Duchesne, *Fastes* 1.96-97, and Jalland, *Leo* p.158-159.

40. "stetitque in eo hactenus umbra sacerdotii, donec tyranno imago staret imperii, quo loco post internecionem patroni sponte se exuit et propria cessione damnavit" (*Epist.* "Posteaquam a nobis": *C.S.E.L.* 35.104).

41. "similis paenitentia de abdicatione sacerdotii" (ibid.).

42. "sed Lazarus ... sacerdotium consecutus, a quo se ipse vitae suae conscientia, datis litteris in abdicationem sui, sponte submovit" (*Epist.* "Cum adversus": *M.G.H. Epist.* 3.7-9). The use of "sui" rather than "suam" suggests that it was not his own decision.

43. For another mention of their departure, see Zos. *Epist.* "Magnum pondus," *C.S.E.L.* 35.100-101: "quibus se ipsi propria abdicavere sententia."

city, innocent, and guilty of no charge, and in his place was ordained Patroclus, the friend and protégé of Constantius, the master of soldiers, whose patronage was sought by Patroclus himself. This incident was a cause of great discord among the bishops of that region.[44]

Once again, Italian and Gallic perceptions of the same event contradict each other.

The appearance of the master of soldiers Constantius as the new imperial overseer of the affairs of Gaul, and the concommitant ordination of Patroclus as bishop of Arles, provide another example of how a change in the secular power structure resulted in a revision in the ecclesiastical hierarchy.[45] The ecclesiastical partisans of the old regime again were replaced by supporters of the new, at least in some of the most prestigious and influential sees. Just as Heros and Lazarus had been supporters of Constantine, this Patroclus was an adherent of Constantius.[46] Like them, Patroclus also may have been a non-local. His origin is unknown, although his name would suggest that he was not of an influential Gallic family, as it was rarely used in Gaul, and by no one of any importance.[47] He therefore may not have been a Gaul at all; his position as a "friend and protégé" of Constantius could suggest that he, like Constantius, was an Illyrian.[48] Nevertheless, one cannot discard the possibility that, as Constantine had done with Heros and Lazarus, Constantius had found in Patroclus a local, if obscure, Gallic ally. An indication of Patroclus' desire to please his patron is seen in the possibility that he transferred the cathedral of Arles to the city center and called it the *basilica Constantia* in the patrician's honor.[49]

44. "Heros, vir sanctus et beati Martini discipulus cum Arelatensi oppido episcopus praesideret, a populo eiusdem civitatis insons, et nulli insimulatione obnoxius, pulsus est, inque eius locum Patroclus ordinatus, amicus et familiaris Constantii magistri militum, cuius per ipsum gratia quaerebatur. quae res inter episcopos regionis illius magnarum discordiarum causa fuit." Duchesne (*Fastes* 1.98) suggests that Heros' deposition was "par aucun tribunal ecclésiastique," but there is no reason to believe that the proper ecclesiastical forms would not have been observed, even if the result was foreordained. Zosimus himself alluded to procedures which were carried out "ut error velamento aliquo tegeretur" (*Epist.* "Cum adversus": *M.G.H. Epist.* 3.7-9).

45. For Constantius, see note 1 above, and Matthews, *Aristocracies* pp.302-378; Oost, *Placidia* passim; *P.L.R.E. II* pp.321-325; Seeck, *Untergang* pp.33-65; and Stein, *Geschichte* pp.408-416.

46. See Duchesne, *Fastes* 1.96-97; Franses, *Leo* pp.17-20; Heinzelmann, *Bischofsherrschaft* p.74; Kidd, *Church* pp.103, 354; Oost, *Placidia* pp.147-148; Pietri, *Roma* 2.1004-1005; and Stein, *Geschichte* pp.410-411.

47. Only one other occurrence is attested, a recluse, presbyter, and abbot Patroclus at Bourges, probably in the sixth century (Greg. Tur. *Vit. pat.* 9.1, *H.F.* 5.10). Not a single Patroclus anywhere is listed in either volume of *P.L.R.E* after c.318.

48. Constantius was a native of Naissus (Olymp. no.39). For the Greek origin of Patroclus' name, see Levillain, "Rivalités" p.560; this would not necessarily mean, however, that he was not a Gaul.

49. See Palanque, *Diocèse d'Aix* p.19. For a possible Arlesian municipal decree in honor of Constantius, see Carpocino, "Choses" pp.48-56.

It also seems that changes occurred in other, lesser, sees. Remigius, the deposed bishop of Aix, apparently was able to regain his see after the expulsion of Lazarus.[50] Furthermore, the *Gallic Chronicle of 452*, under the year 414, reported that "Patroclus, the bishop of Arles, dared to sell episcopates in an infamous sale."[51] Regardless of whether these sees were actually "sold" or not, it would appear that Patroclus did take the opportunity to install his own, and presumably Constantius', supporters in other sees as well.

THE ROLE OF PELAGIANISM IN GALLIC FACTIONALISM

The early years of the fifth century saw the spread of the doctrine which later came to be known as "Pelagianism." This teaching had been developed by the expatriate Briton Pelagius at Rome during the years immediately before and after A.D. 400.[52] His denial of original sin and his contention that it was possible to live without sin necessarily restricted the role of divine grace, and his views soon were to be challenged by influential churchmen such as Jerome and Augustine. Several of the individuals already shown to have been deeply involved in the Gallic dissension of this time also were involved in the early stages of the Pelagian controversy.[53] Two who were strongly anti-Pelagian, for example, were the bishops Heros and Lazarus.[54] After their ejections, they preserved their previous close association by going into exile—although they may have referred to it as a pilgrimage—in the east. In 415 they dispatched a letter condemning Pelagianism to the Council of Diospolis; they also sent another to the Council of Carthage in 416.[55]

The anti-Pelagian activities of these two met with a mixed response

50. See chapter 3 below. Duchesne, *Fastes* 1.97, professes ignorance on who succeeded Lazarus, believing Remigius not to be bishop of Aix.

51. "Patroclus Arelatensis episcopus infami mercatu sacerdotia venditare ausus" (no.74; *M.G.H. A.A.*9.654).

52. For Pelagianism, see Chapman, *Papacy* pp.133-183; de Plinval, *Pélage*; Ferguson, *Pelagius*; von Harnack, *Lehrbuch* pp.165-257; Kidd, *Church* vol.3 passim; Pietri, *Roma* 1.448-452; Souter, "Pelagius' Doctrine" pp.180-182; and Wermelinger, *Pelagius*.

53. Most general discussions of Pelagianism pay only scant attention to the controversy in Gaul; see Liebeschuetz, "Pelagian Evidence" p.444: "The problem of British—and Gallic—Pelagianism remains an interesting one. It is likely that the last word has not yet been written on the subject."

54. See Griffe, *Gaule* 2.255 n.53; Hefele-Leclercq, *Conciles* 2.148-218; and Kidd, *Church* pp.87-120.

55. See Zos. *Epist.* "Magnum pondus" and "Posteaquam a nobis"; Aug. *De gest. Pel.* 2,39,62 and *Epist.* 175.1, 179.7. See also Bury, *L.R.E.* p.361; Griffe, *Gaule* 2.255; von Harnack, *Lehrbuch* pp.174-179; and Pietri, *Roma* 2.1004-1005. Despite the Gallic testimony, Pelagius was acquited. For the parallel eastern "pilgrimage" of Pelagius himself, see Brown, "Patrons" p.71.

in the west, particularly in Rome itself, where many influential
aristocrats supported Pelagius.[56] Zosimus, the initially pro-Pelagian
bishop of Rome, vitriolically attacked the two Gauls in several letters.[57] In one, written in 417, he stated, "Is it any wonder if they wish
to afflict with libelous letters a layman struggling to bear good fruit
through long servitude on behalf of God?"[58] In another, Zosimus also
tried to discredit them (*Epist.* "Magnum pondus": *C.S.E.L.* 35.100):

But when he [sc. Caelestius] was asked about them, he asserted that he never
had discussed such charges with the aforementioned individuals, nor had he
ever seen them before they had written about him. [He said that subse-
quently] he had met Lazarus briefly, and that Heros, after apologizing for
disagreeing with someone who was unknown and absent, had departed ami-
cably. Given that such a charge against an unknown individual was blind
and groundless, it was doubtless irrelevant. One might question the character
of such men, which appeared to be so conceited and inconsequential, [and
ask] whether their status and past life, at least, justified granting faith to
absent men with regard to those absent, and sufficient value to their letters
so that they would be worthy of the authority of testimony.[59]

A different portrayal of Lazarus and Heros emerges, however, from
the works of Augustine, an ardent anti-Pelagian since c.412/413, who
supported and praised their efforts.[60] In the *De gratia Christi* he suggested that it was Pelagius himself who felt personal enmity toward
the two Gauls: "Let us omit his invidious complaints against his enemies."[61] In a letter to Bishop John of Jerusalem, Augustine wished to

56. See Brown "Patrons" and "Pelagius"; Bury, *L.R.E.* pp.360-362; Ferguson, *Pelagius*;
Kidd, *Church* p.100; Morris, *Arthur* p.338ff; Oost, *Placidia* pp.149-156; Pietri, *Roma* 1.448-452
(with bibliography); and Wermelinger, *Pelagius* pp.122, 209. Included among them was the Gaul
Meropius Pontius Paulinus, bishop of Nola. Others in Rome, however, opposed Pelagianism,
and suffered for it: Prosper noted under the year 418, "At this time Constantius, a servant of
Christ, living at Rome as an ex-vicar and devotedly resisting the Pelagians on behalf of the grace
of God, endures much from their faction" (*Chron.* 1265: *M.G.H. A.A.* 9.468). See also *Praedestinatus* 88 (*P.L.* 53.618).

57. For Zosimus' Pelagian sympathies, see Kidd, *Church* p.100; Pietri, *Roma* 2.934-948; and
Wermelinger, *Pelagius* pp.134-164. For a defense of his actions, see Chapman, *Papacy* p.161ff and
Jalland, *Church* pp.287-288.

58. "mirum est si isti laicum virum [sc. Pelagium] ad bonam frugem longa erga deum
servitute nitentem, falsis litteris percellere voluerunt. . . ." (*Epist.* "Posteaquam a nobis": *C.S.E.L.*
35.104).

59. "sed cum de his interrogaretur, adseruit nullum sibi de talibus contentionibus umquam
cum antedictis fuisse sermonem, nec ante sibi, quam de se scriberent, visu fuisse compertos;
Lazarum sane in transitu cognitum; Herotem vero etiam satisfactione interposita, quod secus de
ignoto et absente sensisset, cum gratia recessisse. tam caduco ac nullo fundamine criminationis
ignotae, procul dubio e re fuit, ut [de] persona talium, quae tam ventosa et levis extiterat, quaereretur, si saltem illis loci sui ratio vitaeque constaret, ut fides absentibus in absentes debuerit
adhiberi, tantumque pondus in litteris eorum, ut auctoritatem testimonii mererentur."

60. For Augustine's early anti-Pelagian activities, see Prosper, *Contra collatorem* 1.2: *P.L.*
51.216.

61. "omittamus eius invidiosas de suis inimicis querelas. . . ." (*C.S.E.L.* 42.150).

learn what Pelagius "said in response to the objections of the Gauls."[62] Then, in the *De gestis Pelagii* he referred to "those objections against Pelagius which were read from the letter which our blessed brothers and fellow bishops, the Gauls Heros and Lazarus, sent."[63] The two Gauls apparently had been claiming episcopal status in spite of their depositions, and Augustine, in order to give greater weight to their testimony, granted it to them.[64]

In the same work Augustine gave his own version of why the two Gauls did not attend the Council of Carthage in person: "Because of the serious illness of one of them."[65] Nor was Augustine the only westerner to depict Heros favorably, for the anti-Pelagian Prosper, as noted above, somewhat later described him as a "blessed man" and "innocent." Once again, therefore, the differing perceptions of different sources discussing the same events are striking.

It now might be asked exactly where and when Heros and Lazarus acquired their anti-Pelagian sentiments. Their whereabouts between 412, when Heros was expelled from Arles, and 415, when they reappeared in Palestine, are unknown. If they went directly to the east, they would have arrived at about the same time as Pelagius, who left Africa also in 412.[66] It may be, therefore, that they did not begin to oppose Pelagius' teachings until after they too arrived in the east.[67]

It also is possible, however, that their theological leanings might have had something to do with their factional affiliations in Gaul. It has been suggested, although on slim grounds, that Constantine III was himself opposed in Britain by pro-Pelagian elements.[68] His Gallic supporters certainly included individuals, such as Heros and Lazarus, who later had anti-Pelagian sentiments. Furthermore, Proculus of Marseilles' warm reception of Lazarus when the latter returned from exile would suggest that he also was not unsympathetic to Lazarus'

---

62. "se dixit objectis respondisse Gallorum" (*Epist.* 179.7).

63. "quae de libello, quem dederunt sancti fratres et coepiscopi nostri Galli, Heros et Lazarus . . . recitata sunt objecta Pelagio. . . ." (ch.2: *C.S.E.L.* 42.52).

64. Zosimus too seems to have known of the Gauls' anomalous episcopal status, for he went so far as to declare "sacerdotali eos loco et omni communione summovimus" (*Epist.* "Magnum pondus": *C.S.E.L.* 35.99).

65. "propter gravem . . . unius eorum aegritudinem": *De gest. Pel.* 2; see also ch.62, "illis quidem absentibus, et de aegritudine unius eorum excusantibus."

66. Ferguson, *Pelagius* p.50.

67. For their initial involvement in the east, see Aug. *De gest. Pel.* 53: *P.L.* 44.350.

68. For Constantine in Britain, see Chadwick, "End" pp.9-20; Collingwood, "Evacuation" pp.74-98; Stevens, "Marcus" pp.316-347; and Thompson, "Zosimus" pp.162-167. The statement of Prosper (*Contra coll.* 21[41]: *P.L.* 51.271) that the British Pelagians of the 420s were "solum suae originis occupantes" could suggest that British Pelagianism arose very early. For possible British Pelagianism at the time of Constantine III, see Liebeschuetz, "Pelagian Evidence" pp.436-447 and Myers, "Pelagius" pp.21-36; see also Sigisbert, *Chron.* s.a.404 (*M.G.H. S.S.* 6.305). For the suggestion that the Pelagians who appear in the south in the early fifth century were

views.[69] On the other hand, the leader of the pro-Italian party in Gaul, Claudius Postumus Dardanus, is thought to have had Pelagian leanings, as suggested by the uncertainties he expressed to Augustine on the baptism of infants. The latter's response of c.417, at the height of the Pelagian controversy, is replete with his thoughts on the doctrine of grace.[70] It is just possible, therefore, that the Gallic anti-Pelagianism was at least in part another manifestation of Gallic anti-Italian sentiment; if influential Italians were going to favor Pelagianism, all the more reason for many Gauls to oppose it.

Anti-Pelagianism does seem to have served as a unifying element in Gaul. At no time during the fifth century is any Gallic bishop, or influential Gallic ecclesiastic, known to have been accused of Pelagianism by his contemporaries in Gaul. In fact, only three Gauls were ever accused by name of having any Pelagian sentiments, and two of them were in fact Augustinians. Of the first, Sulpicius Severus, Gennadius wrote in the 490s. "In his old age he was deceived by the Pelagians, and acknowledging the sin of loquacity, he kept silent until his death. . . ."[71] Severus' close friend Meropius Pontius Paulinus of Nola did have ties of his own to Pelagian circles in Italy, making Severus guilty at least by association.[72] The second, Leporius, took refuge with Augustine in Africa, and the third, Lucidus, was accused of Augustinian predestinarianism in the 470s, even though he also

---

expelled from Britain at this time, see Haslehurst, *Fastidius* p.xlv, and Morris, "Pelagian Literature" pp.26-60. It may be, however, that Pelagianism did not arise in Britain until long after Pelagius' own departure: see Thompson, *Germanus* p.21, although his statement that "Pelagius' teachings were not considered to be heretical until the Council of Carthage met in 411" applies only to Africa, and says nothing about what the response may have been in Gaul, much less in Britain. For Britain as a later Pelagian stronghold, see Chadwick, "Intellectual Contacts" pp.189-263 and Johnstone, "Vortigern" p.18.

69. As late as 412, Jerome, another anti-Pelagian, referred favorably to Proculus (*Epist.* 125). Note also that one of the Divjak letters has Lazarus carrying a letter from Jerome to Augustine (Aug. *Epist.* 19*.2). Perhaps their shared anti-Pelagianism helped to reconcile Lazarus and Proculus to each other.

70. See Aug. *Epist.* 187.22ff (*C.S.E.L.* 57.100ff). For Dardanus as a potential Pelagian, see Matthews, *Aristocracies* p.323. It also has been suggested that Augustine's anti-Pelagian letter of 416 to a certain bishop Hilarius (*Epist.* 178) was sent to Hilarius of Narbonne: see Wermelinger, *Pelagius* p.91 n.14. His only justification, however, is that "unser Hilarius ist Bischof aus Übersee," and it perhaps is more likely that the bishop Hilarius is the same as the Sicilian layman Hilarius who corresponded with Augustine in 414-415 on the same problem (Aug. *Epist.* 156-157). Wermelinger's reasoning that the earlier Hilarius was a layman and the latter one a bishop means little: transfers from the laity to the episcopate were all too common at this time.

71. "hic in senectute sua a Pelagianis deceptus, et agnoscens loquacitatis culpam, silentium usque ad mortem tenuit. . . ." (*Vir. ill.* 20). On Severus and Pelagianism, see Brown, "Patrons" p.60, and Prete, *Chronica* pp.124-126.

72. See Brown, "Patrons" and "Supporters" passim; and Lienhard, *Paulinus* pp.111-115. This evidence for Pelagianism in the neighborhood of Tours is at least consistent with Heros' and Lazarus' involvement in the controversy.

was compelled to condemn Pelagianism for good measure.[73] The association of two of these supposed Gallic Pelagians with the leading anti-Pelagian of the day makes even these accusations look rather questionable.

All in all, then, there is little evidence for widespread Pelagianism in Gaul at any time during the fifth century, and there is absolutely no evidence that it made any inroads into the Gallo-Roman ecclesiastical establishment. This is not to say, however, that accusations of Pelagianism were not to serve as rhetorical devices in Gallic ecclesiastical debates in the future.[74] Who knows, for example, what the real charge against Sulpicius Severus may have been. Like Manicheism, Pelagianism ultimately was universally condemned and detested. Affirmations of anti-Pelagian sentiments were to become in Gaul a means of establishing consensus among the often contentious Gallic bishops: it was one view upon which they all could agree. In this, the Gauls of the later fifth century were the spiritual heirs of the tyranophiles Heros and Lazarus.

Meanwhile, in Italy it was not until 418 that Pelagianism received its official condemnation.[75] Zosimus ultimately was induced, primarily by Augustine and the African bishops, to cease equivocating, and to issue a now-lost *Epistola tractoria* condemning the belief, followed by his letter "Quamvis patrum" (*C.S.E.L.* 35.115-117) of 21 March 418. Then, on 30 April 418 Honorius issued his own rescript, "Ad conturbandum," making Pelagianism a crime against the state.[76] Even though Pelagian propositions were to enjoy a brief revival in the 420s under Julianus of Eclanum, they never again were to have influential support.

RECONCILIATION AND
REORGANIZATION IN GAUL

After the imperial government's initially repressive reaction against Gallic aristocrats implicated in the revolts of 407-413, a more conciliatory stance was adopted by 416. On 1 March of that year, for example, a law was addressed to the patrician Constantius "On annulling those deeds which were committed under the tyrants or bar-

---

73. For Leporius see chapter 6, and for Lucidus, chapter 10.

74. See chapters 4, 6, and 10 below.

75. See von Harnack, *Lehrbuch* pp.184-187; Kidd, *Church* pp.110-114; Pietri, *Roma* 2.937-948; and Wermelinger, *Pelagius* pp.165-253.

76. See Haenel, *Corpus legum* pp.238-239, no.1171. This law was reissued as the edict "In Pelagium" by the prefects Palladius (Italy), Monaxius (Orient), and Agricola (Gaul) (ibid. p.239 no.1171).

barians," proclaiming a general amnesty for crimes committed during
the rebellions: "If any acts were done improperly or spitefully, let
them not be summoned before the spitefulness of an avenging law by
the crafty charges of litigants. Let them have impunity from all accusations."[77] At the same time, the punitive indemnity imposed upon
the Auvergne seems to have been lifted.[78] If Gauls from the Auvergne,
one of the focal points of the Gallic resistance, could enjoy such favor,
this policy presumably extended to other Gauls in other regions
as well.

Two years later, on 17 April 418, a further step was taken to restore
normality to the Gallic administration. The so-called "Constitutio saluberrima," addressed to the prefect of Gaul, Agricola, reinstituted the
concilium septem provinciarum, initially established c.402/408, which
had fallen into desuetude during the usurpations.[79] Although inter-
pretations of this move range from seeing it as an attempt to conciliate
the Gallo-Roman aristocracy to viewing it as an institution which only
contributed further to Gallic particularism, it must be borne in mind
that it was a product of conditions c.400, not of the rebellions of
407-413.[80] Rather than being an innovation, the council was an attempt to reconstitute the situation which had existed before 407.

The rebellions do, however, seem to have resulted in a change in
the imperial attitude toward who the holders of high offices in the
Gallic administration should be. Before 407, the praetorian prefects of
Gaul, for example, usually had been Italians, or at least non-Gauls.
This policy must have been one consideration which had induced
many Gallic aristocrats to throw in their lot with the usurpers. The
Italian government, therefore, as yet another conciliatory move, c.417
initiated a new policy of choosing Gauls almost exclusively for high
civil offices in Gaul.[81]

Even members of Gallic senatorial families which had been involved in the rebellions benefited from this new policy. The sons of

77. "si qua ... indigne invidioseque commissa sunt, ad invidiam placatarum legum a callidis
litigatorum obiectionibus non vocentur. habeant omnium criminum impunitatem" (*C. Th.*
15.14.14: "De infirmandis his, quae sub tyrannis aut barbaris gesta sunt"). See Oost, *Placidia*
pp.151-152; Stein, *Geschichte* p.409; and Stroheker, *Adel* pp.47-50.

78. Sid. Apoll. *Carm.* 7.207-214. For a connection between this reassessment and the regular
15-year census, see Oost, *Placidia* p.152, and Stein, *Geschichte* p.409.

79. See Haenel, *Corp. leg.* p.238, no.1171. On such provincial councils, see Larsen, "Provincial Assemblies" pp.209-220. On this council, see chapter 1 above, n.78.

80. Stroheker, *Adel* p.50 suggests that a "reunification" policy of c.420-425 succeeded: there
were no new revolts. Oost, *Placidia* pp.147-152, however, suggests that attempts to unify Gaul
and Rome failed. See also Carette, *Les assemblées* pp.450-463, and Matthews, *Aristocracies*
pp.334-335.

81. See MacMullen, *Enemies* pp.211-213; Matthews, *Aristocracies* pp.333-334; Nesselhauf,
"Verwaltung" p.34; Oost, *Placidia* p.77; Stroheker, *Adel* p.48ff and *Eurich* p.17; Stein, *Geschichte*
p.6; Sundwall, *Studien* p.8ff; Twyman, "Aetius" p.483; and *P.L.R.E. II, fasti* pp.1246-1247. Mat-

the rebel prefects Apollinaris and Decimus Rusticus both rose to high office, serving as *tribuni et notarii* under Honorius, before 423, and as praetorian prefect of Gaul (in 448-449) and governor of a Gallic province (at an earlier date) respectively.[82] The Agricola who was prefect of Gaul for the second time in 418 and consul in 421 was a relative, probably the father, of the Arvernian Eparchius Avitus, who became emperor in 455 and who had a son also named Agricola.[83] Indeed, it was the young Avitus himself who, presumably with the aid of his father, obtained the aforementioned tax relief for the Auvergne.[84]

The imperial conciliation of Gaul also would have been facilitated by the official Italian condemnation of Pelagianism in 418. In fact, it may be no coincidence that Honorius' decrees condemning Pelagianism and reestablishing an administrative structure for Gaul were issued only thirteen days apart.[85] The appointment of the master of soldiers Constantius, a staunch anti-Pelagian, as the administrator of Gaul also would have helped to remove any religious incompatibilities between the central administration in Italy and the influential anti-Pelagian party in Gaul.[86]

The first decades of the fifth century saw a great increase in the secular involvement in Gallic ecclesiastical factionalism. Changes in the secular power structure now tended to bring concurrent alterations in the ecclesiastical hierarchy, at least in the most influential sees. Magnus Maximus had overseen the election of Felix of Trier, and at Arles, Constantine had supported Heros, and Constantius, Patroclus. On every such occasion, moreover, imperial support of a powerful bishop had been the cause of great dissension among the Gallic bishops. This secular involvement in the Gallic church could not but have a stifling effect. As long as the imperial government maintained a strong presence in Gaul, it would be difficult for Gallic ecclesiastics to be truly independent.

---

thews' statement that "it is impossible to show that a single praetorian prefect was other than a member of the Gallic upper classes" may overstate the case: Auxiliaris (chapters 5 and 7 below) very probably was an Italian.

82. See Sid. Apoll. *Epist.* 5.9.2, 8.6.5 and *P.L.R.E. II* pp.113, 965.

83. Prefect: Haenel, *Corp. leg.* p.238 no.1171, Sid. Apoll. *Carm.* 15.150-153 (as grandfather of Magnus of Narbonne), see *P.L.R.E. II* pp.36-37. Avitus: *P.L.R.E. II* pp.196-198; his son: ibid. p.37.

84. So it may be that Ecdicius' murder of Edobichus, if the former were in fact related to the Arvernian Aviti (above, note 37), did in fact receive its eventual reward.

85. Seeck, *Regesten* p.338.

86. Note Constantius' decree "Quae quum praeteritae" (Haenel, *Corp. leg.* p.240 no.1174 = *P.L.* 48.404) condemning Pelagianism. See also Chastagnol, "Volusien" pp.241-245; Oost, *Placidia* pp.150, 156-159; and Stein, *Geschichte* 1.412-413.

CHAPTER 3

THE GALLIC CHURCH AND THE
BISHOP OF ROME

THE ASSERTION OF PAPAL AUTHORITY[1]

By the early part of the fifth century, bishops of Rome such as Innocent had begun to assert their authority to a greater extent than they had in the past.[2] Toward the end of the fourth century, for example, they took advantage of ecclesiastical dissension in the east to create a papal "vicariate" of Illyricum.[3]

In the west, however, the Roman pontiffs were initially not so successful. In Italy, Milan continued to go its own way. Equally troublesome was the continued independent stand of the churches of North Africa, which resulted in the especially embarrassing "Apiarius affair."[4] After the priest Apiarius had been excommunicated in Africa, he had appealed to Zosimus of Rome, who, favoring Apiarius, had ordered the case to be retried. The resultant African synod of 419, however, not only apprehended Zosimus trying to use canons wrongly attributed to Nicaea, but also responded that such appeals to Rome should have no validity. The Africans ultimately informed Celestine in 424-425 (*Corp. chr. lat.* 149.170-171),

We very much entreat you not to admit easily to your presence those who come from here, and that you not wish any more to receive into communion

1. See Gmelin, *Auctoritas*; and Langgärtner, *Gallienpolitik* passim.
2. On Innocent, see Demougeot, "Interventions" and Gebhardt, *Bedeutung*; and for Roman expansion to 431, see Pietri, *Roma* 2.887-966.
3. See Bardy et. al., *Eglise* pp.255-256, 263-264; Greenslad, "Illyrian Churches"; MacDonald, "Vicariate"; McShane, *Romanitas* p.281ff; and Pietri, *Roma* 1.776-789. For the letters of Innocent of Rome entrusting the churches of Macedonia-Dacia to Anysius of Thessalonica "nostra vice," see Silva-Tarouca, *Collectio* nos.4-5. In 412, Innocent claimed to have chosen Rufus of Thessalonica as his "vicar" based on his merit; unmentioned factors would have been the apostolic foundation of the see and its status as the seat of the praetorian prefect of Illyricum (see *P.L.* 20.552, and MacDonald, "Vicariate" p.482).
4. See Bardy et. al., *Eglise* p.257; Chapman, *Papacy* pp.184-209; Kidd, *Church* pp.392-393; and Marschall, *Karthago und Rom*. For traditional minimizing of this affair, see Jalland, *Church* pp.288-291.

those whom we have excommunicated, because Your Venerableness should note that this was established by the Council of Nicaea. For if it appears that this should be avoided in the case of the lower clergy and laymen, by how much more should one wish to observe this in the case of bishops, so that those suspended from communion in their own provinces not seem to be restored to communion precipitately or unworthily by Your Sanctity.[5]

Another of the canons of the council of 424, it seems, was "that no one dare to appeal to the church of Rome."[6] In Africa, then, the organized church openly flouted the claims of the church of Rome to overall authority.[7]

The early years of the fifth century also saw increased efforts of the bishops of Rome, and particularly Innocent, to extend their influence in Gaul.[8] Innocent's first known involvement in the ecclesiastical affairs of Gaul seems to have come when Victricius of Rouen, an old partisan of Martin of Tours (Sulp. Sev. *Dial.* 3.2), was charged with unorthodoxy. Victricius' friend Paulinus of Nola wrote to him "about the multitude of opponents, because wicked witnesses have arisen against you."[9] The only charge Paulinus mentioned, however, was that of "Apollinarianism," hardly a concern in Gaul.[10] This accusation perhaps was a sham, and may have concealed some other charge, just as Manicheism had served as a blind for Priscillianism. Victricius ultimately went to Rome in the early years of the fifth century and appealed to Innocent, who duly attested to his orthodoxy.[11] While in Rome Victricius also seems to have taken part in hearings before the emperor Honorius about *curiales* in the clergy.[12]

5. "impendio deprecamur ut deinceps ad vestras aures hinc venientes non facilius admittatis, nec a nobis excommunicatos in communione ultra velitis excipere; quia hoc etiam Nicaeno concilio definitum facile advertat venerabilitas tua. nam etsi de inferioribus clericis vel de laicis videtur ibi praecaveri, quanto magis hoc de episcopis voluit observari, ne in sua provincia a communione suspensi a tua sanctitate praepropere vel indebite videantur communioni restitui."

6. "Ut nullus ad Romanam ecclesiam audeat appellare," cited in the *acta* of the Council of Carthage of 525 (*Corp. chr. lat.* 149.266). For the date, see Munier, "Canon." Apparently earlier editors of the council found the passage so offensive that they deleted it.

7. Augustine often is misquoted as having said "Roma locuta est: causa finita est" at the end of the Pelagian controversy, and this passage is cited as evidence that the Africans did in fact recognize the authority, as well as the primacy, of Rome. The full citation, however, is "iam enim de hac causa duo concilia [i.e. in Africa] missa sunt ad sedem apostolicam; inde etiam rescripta venerunt; causa finita est" (*Serm.* 131.10: *P.L.* 38.734). See Adam, "Causa finita est" and Kidd, *Church* p.102.

8. See Griffe, *Gaule* 1.351-352; McShane, *Romanitas* p.276; Pietri, *Roma* 2.978-1000; and Turner, "Arles and Rome" pp.242-247.

9. "de multitudine adversantium . . . quoniam insurrexerunt in te testes iniqui" (*Epist.* 37.4). See Pietri, *Roma* 2.983 and Walsh, *Letters* pp.336-337.

10. *Epist.* 37.6.

11. Paul. Nol. *Epist.* 37.1, "qui ad urbem per tanta terrarum spatia perveneras," see also 37.4-7 for Victricius' hearing before Innocent.

12. Innoc. *Epist.* "Etsi tibi" 12: "imperatore praesente . . . ipse nobiscum positus agnovisti." Any resultant legislation is not extant.

It is not clear who Victricius' opponents were. Like many of the anti-Felicians discussed above, he did have foreign connections: not only did he appeal to Rome, he also traveled to Britain at the very time when unrest there was soon to lead to the revolts of 406-407.[13] He also was friendly with the leading anti-Felician, Martin of Tours. It may be that Victricius' accusers were bishops who held Felician sentiments. That Victricius' problems were related to the Felician controversy has been inferred from Innocent's concluding comment to him: "Ambition will cease, dissension will be calmed, heresies and schisms will not arise, the devil will have no opportunity to rage, unanimity will remain, and iniquity, overcome, will be trampled."[14] If this were the case, it would demonstrate, again, the tendency of the anti-Felicians to seek support outside Gaul and, conversely, the preference of the Felicians for more local ties.

Victricius' appeal to Rome was one of the earliest of many such appeals by disgruntled Gallic ecclesiastics. Innocent used the opportunity not only to pronounce judgment on Victricius' orthodoxy, but also to assert his authority over the entire Gallic church. In 404 he forwarded to Victricius a long list of ecclesiastical *regula*.[15] In a discussion of "accusations or strife among clerics," he noted, "If greater accusations appear in your midst, after episcopal judgment they should be referred to the apostolic see, as the synod decreed."[16] Even though this mild claim to act as a higher court of appeal seems not to have been pursued at this time, it ultimately became the primary means by which the bishop of Rome was to establish and exercise his influence in Gaul. Innocent also ordered, "Nor is it permitted to anyone to flit to another province without the prior consent of the church of Rome," which has been seen as a weak attempt to limit the influence of the bishop of Milan in Gaul.[17]

At about the same time, Innocent forwarded a similar letter to Exsuperius of Toulouse, in which he complimented him because he

13. For this journey, see Victric. *De laude sanctorum*, *praef.* and Borius, *Germain* p.80.

14. "cessabit ambitio, dissensio conquiescet, haereses et schismata non emergent, locum non accipiet diabolus saeviendi, manebit unanimitas, iniquitas superata calcabitur" (*Epist.* "Etsi tibi" 14: *P.L.* 20.468-481). See Palanque, "Dissensions" pp.491-493.

15. *Epist.* "Etsi tibi": *P.L.* 20.468-481; see Griffe, *Gaule* 1.306-310 and Pietri, *Roma* 2.982-991.

16. "causae vel contentiones inter clericos ... si maiores causae in medium fuerint devolutae, ad sedem apostolicam, sicut synodus statuit ... post iudicium episcopale referantur" ("Etsi tibi" 3: *P.L.* 20.472-473).

17. "nec alicui liceat sine praeiudicio tamen Romanae ecclesiae ... ad alias provincias convolare" (ibid.). See Griffe, *Gaule* 1.352; Pietri, *Roma* 2.982-991; and Duchesne, *Fastes* 1.94-96, who suggests (p.95) that Innocent could not have had much of an effect "avec cette démonstration timide."

"chose to consult the apostolic see about what view he should uphold in doubtful matters rather than asserting in individual cases whatever seemed best to him, with a presumptuous usurpation."[18] Innocent also went out of his way to condemn "Novatianism," which never had been of great moment in Gaul.[19] This perhaps concealed an attack on the Priscillianism which had had a vogue in Exsuperius' neighborhood.[20] Exsuperius was another Gallic prelate who, like those with anti-Felician sentiments, sought foreign contacts. He was particularly close to Jerome, who in 406 dedicated to him his *Commentary on Zachariah*.[21]

Perhaps in this context also belongs a passage of Paulinus of Nola cited only by Gregory of Tours:

If indeed you today look at bishops worthy of the Lord such as Exsuperius of Toulouse, or Simplicius of Vienne, or Amandus of Bordeaux, or Diogenianus of Albi, or Dynamius of Angoulême, or Venerandus of Clermont, or Alethius of Cahors, or now Pegasius of Périgueux, you will immediately see them to be, however great the evils of this age, most worthy guardians of all faith and religion.[22]

It is not known under what circumstances Paulinus compiled this list of noteworthy Gallic bishops. Given his own inclinations and affiliations, it may include those who shared his anti-Felician views on foreign ties: Simplicius, as has been suggested, was an anti-Felician, and Exsuperius did have foreign ties.

Victricius and Exsuperius, and others, represent a segment of the Gallic episcopate which continued to look outside Gaul for support, and even for guidance. In doing so, they had the same outlook as the anti-Felician party of a decade earlier. This is not to say, however, that they belonged to an organized group. Victricius and Exsuperius are not known to have had any contact. Nevertheless, there were some loose connections, even if only by association, among Gallic ecclesiastics with this kind of outlook. Churchmen such as Paulinus of Nola,

---

18. "ad sedem apostolicam referre maluit quid deberet de rebus dubiis custodire potius quam usurpatione praesumpta quae sibi viderentur de singulis obtinere": *Epist*. "Consulenti tibi" *praef.*: *P.L.* 20.495–496; see Di Capua, *Ritmo Prosaico* pp.193-196; and Griffe, *Gaule* 2.267-268.

19. *Epist*. "Consulenti tibi" 2.

20. See Pietri, *Roma* 2.993 n.1. Novatianism did continue to be a minor concern in Rome; see chapter 7 below.

21. *P.L.* 25.1415–1542.

22. "si enim hodie videas dignos domino sacerdotes, vel Exsuperium Tolosae, vel Simplicium Viennae, vel Amandum Burdigalae, vel Diogenianum Albigae, vel Dynamium Ecolisnae, vel Venerandum Arvernis, vel Alethium Cadurcis, vel nunc Pegasium Petrocoris, utcumque se habent saeculi mala, videbis profecto dignissimos totius fidei religionisque custodes." Paul. Nol. *Epist*. 48 *apud* Greg. Tur. *H.F.* 2.13: *C.S.E.L.* 29.389-390. The fragment is dated only to post 401, for example, by Walsh, *Paulinus* 2.357.

Sulpicius Severus, Victricius, and Exsuperius all had ties to the circle of Martin of Tours. Even if the Felician and anti-Felician parties, such as they were, disappeared soon after the Council of Turin, the points of view which each party represented continued to cause dissension among the ranks of the Gallic clergy. There still were those who preferred to handle Gallic affairs internally, and those who felt the need to seek outside support, advice, and intervention.

The individual who would be most likely to benefit from any appeals for outside support was the bishop of Rome. Innocent already had shown himself to be responsive. Other than these two letters, however, the bishop of Rome still had little direct contact with the Gallic church for the first decade and a half of the fifth century.[23] He still had in Gaul little real influence of any sort, however great may have been his prestige. He seems only to have responded to stimuli, and few Gauls looked to him either as a leader or as a judge.[24] Nevertheless, he always was available, and any dissatisfied Gauls had the opportunity of appealing to him, piously asserting that they were referring their case "in particular to the one established in the apostolic see, who is free from all ambition."[25]

ZOSIMUS AND GAUL[26]

It was not until after the imperial reorganization of 416 that Innocent's successor Zosimus also moved to establish his own ecclesiastical authority in Gaul. He attempted to revise the Gallic church hierarchy in order to make it not only more centralized but also more dependent upon him. Like both Constantine III and Constantius, Zosimus rec-

23. For a possible early ruling on the see of Narbonne, see note 68 below. There also would appear to have been at least one Gallic appeal to Rome at this time about Maximus of Valence (note 81 below).

24. See Pietri, *Roma* 2.1005. For Innocent's intervention in Spain, see *Epist.* "Saepe me": *P.L.*20.485ff.

25. "illo praesertim in sede apostolica constituto apud quem vacat omnis ambitio" (Aug. *Epist.* 22*.7.3).

26. For Zosimus and Gaul, see Jalland, *Leo* pp.159-164; Pietri, *Roma* 2.1000-1021; and Silva-Tarouca, *Nuovi studi* p.384. Zosimus' episcopacy usually has been seen as a disaster; see Duchesne, *Histoire* 3.228; Franses, *Leo* pp.17-20; and Kidd, *Church* 103; but for a more favorable view, see Jalland, *Church* p.286ff. The evidence for these events comes primarily from the *Epistulae arelatenses*, a collection of the correspondence between Rome and Arles put together by Sapaudus of Arles in the 550s to support the claims to precedence of his see: see Di Capua, *Ritmo Prosaico* pp.206-209; Gundlach, *M.G.H. Epist.* 3.4; and Silva-Tarouca, "Nuovi studi" pp.382-386. Unfortunately, Gundlach chose to print in his edition barbarisms and solecisms, even when contrary to the manuscript evidence. These readings sometimes can interfere seriously with the sense of a passage. The quotations below occasionally will prefer more grammatical renderings, such as those which appear in the editions of the *Patrologia latina* and Sirmond.

ognized the increasing importance of the city of Arles. He therefore focused his attention upon its bishop, Patroclus.[27] The close ties of these two would have been a result, in part, of the remarkable, though apparently fortuitous, coincidence that Patroclus, the client of Constantius, seems to have been in Rome when Zosimus was elected in March of 417.[28]

Only four days after Zosimus' ordination, he issued the letter "Placuit apostolicae" (M.G.H. Epist. 3.5-6 [22 March]), which was intended to alter drastically the ecclesiastical structure of southern Gaul. Stating (ch.2), "In the ordination of bishops, let him have the authority," Zosimus assigned to Patroclus extraordinary metropolitan rights in the Tres Provinciae of Viennensis, and Narbonensis Prima and Secunda (including, it seems, Alpes Maritimae).[29] This turn of events occurred so soon after Zosimus' election that it has been suggested that there was a quid pro quo involved, and that the new powers were at least in part granted in exchange for Patroclus-cum-Constantius' support in the election.[30]

Justification for this innovation was offered on several grounds. Zosimus, of course, had to make the customary appeal to "vetus privilegium," which was based upon the pious fiction that a certain St. Trophimus had been sent from Rome to evangelize Arles, and by implication much of Gaul, in the second century.[31] But Zosimus also

27. On Zosimus and Patroclus, see Chapman, Papacy p.186 (where Zosimus is "duped . . . by the lies of Patroclus"); Duchesne, Histoire 3.228 (Zosimus as "un personnage assez suspect"); Jones, L.R.E. pp.212, 889 (Zosimus as Patroclus' "dupe"); and Kidd, Church pp.103-104 (where Zosimus' first "blunder" was the "favour he showed to Patroclus . . . an adventurer").

28. See Zos. Epist. "Quid de Proculi" (M.G.H. Epist. 3.10-11): "cum meo interesses examini," and Epist. "Cum et in" (M.G.H. Epist. 3.12): "in praesenti cognoveris"; see also Langgärtner, Gallienpolitik p.26, who presumes that Patroclus was in Rome to complain about Hilarius of Narbonne's exercise of metropolitan authority; and Pietri, Roma p.1005-1006.

29. "in ordinandis sacerdotibus teneat auctoritatem." See Babut, Turin p.33; Batiffol, "Les églises" p.156ff; Bury, L.R.E.1.363-364; Duchesne, Fastes 1.86ff; Gilliard, "Apostolicity"; Griffe, Gaule 2.146-164; Heinzelmann, Bischofsherrschaft p.75; Oost, Placidia p.149; and Stein, Geschichte 1.411. Duchesne, Fastes 1.87 n.1, supposes that Alpes Maritimae would have been included as part of Narbonensis II, and Kidd, Church p.104, that "four provinces" were involved. Langgärtner, Gallienpolitik p.32, assumes that "Viennensis" included the entire pre-Diocletianic province of Narbonensis. In later times Narbonensis I-II and Alpes Maritimae sometimes were referred to as Viennensis II, III, and IV respectively, and Alpes Graiae was even called Viennensis V (Notitia galliarum: M.G.H. A.A. 598-611). Such appellations could imply that these provinces also belonged under the jurisdiction of the metropolitan of "Viennensis."

30. See Duchesne, Fastes 1.98; Kidd, Church p.354; and Oost, Placidia pp.147-150.

31. Griffe, Gaule 2.148, calls the appeal to tradition a "chose curieuse"; such appeals were in fact standard practice in such cases. On the legend, see Gilliard, "Apostolicity" pp.17-33; Duchesne, Fastes 1.121-122, 253-254; Griffe, Gaule 2.161; Jalland, "The Trophimus Saga," Leo pp.168-170; Langgärtner, Gallienpolitik pp.42-45; and Levillain, "Saint Trophime." Van Dam, Leadership pp.169-170, suggests that such local cults were not yet an important factor, noting that Vienne, an even more ancient foundation, did not yet advertise its own patron.

referred to a strictly personal relationship between himself and Patroclus when he claimed that the change had been made "in consideration of his special merits."[32] Other reasons were left unmentioned, but
one would have been to bring the ecclesiastical structure of southern
Gaul into line with the new secular administrative structure.[33] Another of Zosimus' motives may have been to secure a counterweight
to the Gallic influence of the bishop of Milan.[34]

Such a decree would have benefited both Patroclus and Zosimus.
The former, whose ambitious nature never has been in doubt, gained
something immediately useful: ecclesiastical primacy in southern
Gaul. Zosimus, on the other hand, obtained implicit recognition of his
possession of the highest ecclesiastical authority in Gaul, and a precedent which could be cited in the future by his successors. Whatever
the ultimate success or failure of his reorganization of Gaul, he was
the first Roman pontiff to be able to claim any real ability to regulate
the ecclesiastical affairs of Gaul.

Nor was extraordinary metropolitan status the only benefit Patroclus gained from Zosimus' decree. Zosimus also attempted to make
the bishop of Arles the Gallic representative of the bishop of Rome by
introducing the requirement that any Gallic ecclesiastics, even bishops,
visiting Rome must first obtain *litterae formatae* from the bishop of
Arles.[35] Such a requirement perhaps reflects the realization that one
of the greatest problems Patroclus might face in exercising his authority would be the tendency of disgruntled Gallic ecclesiastics to appeal
to Rome.[36]

It is anachronistic, however, to speak of Patroclus, as often is done,
as a "papal vicar."[37] Zosimus himself never used the word; indeed its
first use was by the Gauls themselves in a servile letter to Leo of Rome

32. "meritorum eius specialiter contemplatione" (*Epist.* "Placuit apostolicae": *M.G.H.
Epist.* 3.5-6).

33. See Duchesne, *Fastes* 1.122-128; Griffe, *Gaule* 2.161; and Jalland, *Leo* p.132.

34. See Duchesne, *Fastes* 1.95-96, 124-125; Kidd, *Church* pp.354-355; and Lanzoni, *Diocesi*
p.1019. Zosimus seems to have raised the status of Arles for many of the same reasons that
Innocent raised that of Thessalonica (above, note 3).

35. See Duchesne, *Fastes* 1.87; Griffe, *Gaule* 2.151; and Langgärtner, *Gallienpolitik* pp.29-31.

36. Jalland, *Leo* p.161, sees the requirement as an attempt to slow the flight of Gallic clerics
to Italy "in search of more secure and perhaps more lucrative employment." If this were the
case, little evidence of such flight at this time survives. In the 440s, Prosper of Aquitaine did
move to Rome, but he seems to have had other reasons for doing so (see chapter 6 below).

37. On the so-called papal vicariate of Gaul, see Bardy et. al., *Eglise* p.248ff; and Kidd,
Church pp.104,354. It is questioned, however, by Jalland, *Leo* pp.160-164, who asserts that it is
"inaccurate and misleading to speak of a papal vicariate in Gaul created by Zosimus." One
might as well speak of a "vicariate of Auxerre" on the grounds of Prosper's claim that Celestine
sent Germanus of Auxerre to Britain "vice sua" (*Chron.* 1301 s.a.429). For the vicariate of Arles
created by Pelagius of Rome in the 550s, see *Epist. arel.* 50-52: *M.G.H. Epist.* 3.73-76. For the
technical use of the late Roman word "vicarius" or "vice" ("in place of") see Alc. Avit. *Epist.* 35;
C. Th. 9.34.3; Paul. Pet. *VMartini.* 5.798; and Rutil. Namat. *De red.* 1.501.

in 449/450.[38] Nevertheless, Zosimus may have been trying to contrive a relation between himself and Patroclus similar to that which already had been established between the bishops of Rome and Thessalonica.[39]

Finally, Zosimus also showed Patroclus a more material sign of his favor, decreeing (*Epist.* "Placuit apostolicae": *M.G.H. Epist.* 3.5-6),

We certainly warn everyone that each should be content with his own boundaries and territories: in this regard, we warn you lest any further complaints be referred to us. Indeed, the church of Arles provides an example: it desires that the parishes Citharista and Gargaria, located in its own territory, be granted legally to itself, so that no bishop will presume any further to injure another bishop. . . . Therefore, let [Arles] possess with an inviolate authority any parishes that it had in antiquity, in whatever territories, even beyond its own provinces.[40]

Zosimus, therefore, granted Patroclus the right to lay claim not only to two parishes in particular, but also to any others he coveted. Patroclus' sweeping powers were only potentially limited by a postscript: problems in implementation were to be referred to Patroclus himself, "unless the seriousness of the case demands my own consideration."[41] Only as an afterthought did Zosimus remember to reserve to himself the right of final appeal.

Seven extant letters written by Zosimus after his decree show how it was received in Gaul, and to what extent it actually went into effect. Five of the letters are dated between 22 September and 3 October 417; the other two date from March of the following year. All seven referred in some way to the lack of adherence to Zosimus' commands.[42]

The decree met so much resistance that in September of 417 Zosimus responded by assembling a council in Rome attended by Patro-

38. *Epist.* "Memores quantum" (*M.G.H. Epist.* 3.19): "sibi [Arelato] apostolicae sedis vice mandata." See chapter 8 below for the Gallic motivations for this letter.

39. For the similarity, see Bardy et al., *Eglise* 4.248; Duchesne, *Histoire* 3.230; Franses, *Leo* p.19ff; and Langgärtner, *Gallienpolitik* pp.32-33 (who applies the titulature of "primate of Gaul," or "apostolic vicar").

40. "omnes sane admonemus, ut quique finibus territoriisque suis contenti sint . . . de qua re, ne ad nos querela ulterius redeat, admonemus. dedit enim exemplum Arelatensis ecclesia; quae sibi Citharista et Gargarium parochias in territorio suo sitas incorporari iure desiderat, ne de cetero ullus sacerdos in alterius sacerdotis praesumat iniuriam . . . idcirco quascumque parochias in quibuslibet territoriis, etiam extra provincias suas, ut antiquitus habuit, intemerata auctoritate possideat." Gundlach shows no alternate readings for "provincias," although this reading does seem extreme; it would have given Patroclus license to appropriate parishes anywhere in Gaul, a very unlikely possibility. It might be better to accept Sirmond's reading of "parochias."

41. "nisi magnitudo causae etiam nostrum requirat examen." Such cases would be analogous to the "maiores causae" of Innocent's *Epist.* "Etsi tibi" to Victricius of Rouen.

42. See Kidd, *Church* pp.104, 355; Langgärtner, *Gallienpolitik* pp.46-50; Levillain, "Rivalités" p.559; McShane, *Romanitas* p.277; Morrison, *Tradition* p.79. Duchesne, *Fastes* 1.106-108 (see also pp.87-88, 95-112) notes that "un tel décret, si manifestement contraire à l'usage, ne pouvait manquer de provoquer la contradiction des interéssés."

clus.[43] Problems which were considered included the repeated failure of Gauls to obtain the required *litterae formatae* from Patroclus, and Zosimus' complaint "that some individuals from every sort of secular service betake themselves to the church and with a kind of leap seize the highest position in religion."[44] The council also gave its *pro forma* approval to the extended authority of Arles, which Zosimus now asserted had been "observed up to the present time, by the testimony of many bishops in the proceedings held in my presence."[45]

The main stumbling block in Gaul was that the decree would deprive the metropolitan bishops of three provinces, Proculus of Marseilles, Simplicius of Vienne, and Hilarius of Narbonne, of their existing rights. Proculus in particular resisted. In "Quid de Proculi" (*M.G.H. Epist.* 3.10 [26 September]), for example, Zosimus wrote to Patroclus, "Your Conscientiousness knows what I think about the condemnation of Proculus, for you were present at my investigation, nor shall the authority of our acts or writings conceal from you those decisions which we have sent throughout the different lands about his condemnation."[46] Proculus himself, moreover, had pointedly ignored not only Zosimus' decree, but also his demand that he attend the council, as Zosimus complained in the letter "Multa contra veterem" (*M.G.H. Epist.* 3.11 [29 September]):

Proculus has been apprehended usurping many things contrary to established practice by illegally carrying out ordinations of certain individuals, which matters recently were discussed in a well-attended hearing, although he himself, whom we awaited for a long time, treated haughtily the truce we offered when he disdained to attend.[47]

---

43. The date is inferred from the dates of the resultant letters. The council also considered, for the second time that month, the case of the Pelagian Caelestius (see Kidd, *Church* pp.105-108). The simultaneity of these two discussions presumably explains the references to Proculus and Lazarus in Zosimus' *Epist.* "Posteaquam a nobis" (*C.S.E.L.* 35.104 [21 September 417]) to the African bishops.

44. "quia nonnulli ex quacumque militia se ad ecclesiam conferentes statim saltu quodam summatem locum religionis affectant": *Epist.* "Quid de Proculi" (*M.G.H. Epist.* 3.10-11 [26 September]).

45. "custoditum usque in proximum tempus, gestis apud nos habitis multorum consacerdotum testimoniis": *Epist.* "Mirati admodum" (*M.G.H. Epist.* 3.9-10).

46. "quid de Proculi damnatione censuerim, tenet conscientia tua, cum meo interesses examini, nec te gestorum nostrorum auctoritas latet, vel scriptorum, quae de ipsius damnatione per terrarum diversa [loca] direximus." This *examen* seems to have taken place recently, for the letter "Multa contra veterem" (*M.G.H. Epist.* 3.11), written at about the same time, describes it as having occurred "proxime." Patroclus, then, may have made another trip to Rome in his attempt to secure support against Proculus.

47. "multa contra veterem formam Proculus usurpasse detectus est in ordinationibus nonnullorum indebite celebrandis, quas proxime numerosa cognitione discussimus: licet ipse diu expectatus fastidiose ferat sibi indutias attributas cum venire dissimulet" The reading of Sirmond, "ferens sibi indutias attributas convenire dissimulet," does not seem to make quite as much sense.

In order to justify his removal of Proculus' metropolitan status, Zosimus now had to come to terms with an obvious objection, hitherto ignored, to his original decree: Proculus had specifically been granted metropolitan status in Narbonensis Secunda by the Council of Turin. In "Quid de Proculi" Zosimus therefore asserted that "Proculus crept into this rank, furtively usurped at an improper synod."[48] Zosimus repeated his attempted invalidation of the Council of Turin in the letter "Multa contra veterem" (*M.G.H. Epist.* 3.11 [29 September]), addressed to the bishops of Viennensis and the two Narbonenses:

But his presumption has angered us in particular because he thought that something against the interest of the apostolic see ought to be tricked out of the Council of Turin, when [in reality] something far different was being considered, in order that the deception of this council which he had perpetrated would obtain for him the right to ordain bishops, as if he were a metropolitan, in the province of Narbonensis Secunda.[49]

Zosimus went on to state (ibid.),

He indecently attempted (and should have been cut off at the very beginning) to extort from the bishops, who were carrying on a council for fixed reasons, that which, contrary to the statutes of the fathers and reverence for St. Trophimus . . . not even the authority of this see could yield or change.[50]

By attempting to invalidate this canon of Turin, Zosimus would have been claiming authority not only over individual Gallic bishops, but also over Gallic councils.[51]

Proculus' continued ordinations, about which Zosimus so bitterly complained, seem to have been intended by Proculus to negate another of Zosimus' decrees of the previous March. The two parishes of Citharista and Gargaria, which Zosimus had authorized Patroclus to appropriate, seem at the time to have been under the ecclesiastical jurisdiction of Marseilles.[52] Proculus was not about to surrender them

48. "in quem furtive locum per indebitam synodum Proculus usurpatum irrepserat" (*Epist.* "Quid de Proculi": *M.G.H. Epist.* 3.10-11 [26 September]).

49. "attamen illa praesumptio nos admodum movit, quod in synodo Taurinensi, cum longe aliud ageretur, in apostolicae sedis iniuriam subripiendum putavit, ut sibi concilii illius emendicata praestaret obreptio ordinandorum sacerdotum, veluti metropolitano, in Narbonensi Secunda provincia potestatem"

50. "indecens ausus, et in ipso vestibulo resecandus, hoc ab episcopis ob certas causas concilium agitantibus extorquere, quod contra statuta patrum et sancti Trophimi reverentiam . . . concedere vel mutare ne huius quidem sedis possit auctoritas." For similar arguments, see *Epist.* "Mirati admodum": *M.G.H. Epist.* 3.9-10.

51. Langgärtner, *Gallienpolitik* pp.39-40, sees in Zosimus' rejection of Turin an attempt to counteract the influence of Milan.

52. See Batiffol, "Les églises" pp.161-162; Duchesne, *Fastes* 1.98 (where the parishes are identified with Ceyreste and Saint-Jean-de-Garguier); Griffe, *Gaule* 1.408-109; Gundlach, *M.G.H. Epist.* 3.6 n.1 (where Citharista is in the ecclesiastical diocese of Toulon and Gargaria in that of Fréjus); Jullian, *Gaule* 6.45, 313 n.9 (where Gargaria, Citharista, and Toulon form a band

passively. He responded by raising them to the status of episcopal sees and ordaining two of his partisans, Ursus and Tuentius, as their bishops, as reported by Zosimus in a letter of 22 September 417 addressed "To the bishops of Africa, Gaul, and Spain."[53] Zosimus first discussed the inadvisability of failing to adhere to established ecclesiastical procedure, and went on to attack the character of the new bishops ("Cum adversus": *M.G.H. Epist.* 3.7-9):

But no less has been done by Ursus and Tuentius, of whom one [sc. Tuentius], after being cured by the diligent medication of this see, was unable to achieve the heathfulness of an atoned-for error, and the other [sc. Ursus], having been dismissed a few years earlier when an accusation was raised, as the reports of the citizens attested, or rather instructed, when they had been heaped up, indeed has accepted the rank of bishop from the very same person by whom he had been condemned before . . . [This person] wished to adhere neither to his own sentence regarding Ursus, nor to that of others regarding Tuentius.[54]

A later section of this letter expanded upon the faults of Tuentius:

And would that in Tuentius only a depraved character were visible, and not the Priscillianist superstition as well, upon which the humanity and pity of this see recently wished to take counsel in him, so that he would remain more emended in other things. If he had wished more diligently to recognize this kindness, granted to him nearly beyond custom, it would have been fitting for him to repent that earlier sin, and not to have hastened in a rash rush to the episcopate. . . .[55]

---

separating Marseilles from Aix); Langgärtner, *Gallienpolitik* pp.27-28; and Palanque, *Marseilles* pp.17-19. In Pliny *H.N.* 3.35 Citharista is identified as a *portus* on the Massiliote coast. In the Middle Ages, both parishes were back under Marseilles.

53. The ordinations of these two must have occurred after Zosimus' letter of March 417, for he surely would have mentioned such an irregularity if he had known of it then. Moreover, the decree of March applied only to ordinations made *posthac*. That the two new episcopal sees were Citharista and Gargaria is suggested by Zosimus' complaint (*Epist.* "Cum adversus": *M.G.H. Epist.* 3.8), "quid his tot tantisque improba usurpatione posthabitis addi potest, nisi . . . ut territoriis indebitis ad Arelatensem civitatem antiquitus pertinentibus locarentur?" Several other Ursi are attested in Gaul, including one who traveled from Victricius of Rouen to Paulinus of Nola in the late 390s (Paul. Nol. *Epist.* 18); an abbot who founded Martin-style monasteries (Greg. Tur. *Vit. pat.* 18); and a client of Ruricius of Limoges (Rur. *Epist.* 2.12). The name Tuentius is otherwise unknown in Gaul.

54. "sed nihil minus ab Urso et Tuentio quorum unus [Tuentius] assidua sedis huius medicina curatus, ad emendati erroris pervenire non potuit sanitatem: alter [Ursus] vero ante aliquot annos obiecta criminatione submotus, sicut civium scripta testantur, vel ingesta docuerunt, etiam ab eo ipso gradum summi sacerdotis accepit, a quo fuerat ante damnatus . . . nec velit aliorum de Tuentio, nec suam de Urso tenere sententiam." For "sed nihil minus" see Sirmond; Gundlach reads "sed nihil mirum."

55. "atque utinam in Tuentio pravi tantum mores non etiam Priscilliana superstitio patuissent: quae sedis huius dudum humanitas et misericordia in hoc illo consulere voluit, ut emendatior de cetero permaneret. quod beneficium, sibi paene praeter exemplum praestitum, si dili-

Tuentius, therefore, somehow had been implicated in the earlier Priscillianist controversy, perhaps as an adherent of the anti-Felician school.[56] If so, he and Proculus would have shared at least this outlook. Like other disaffected Gauls, he then had appealed to Rome and, like Victricius, had been kindly received.

Ursus at some time had been expelled, or deposed, by Proculus, apparently from clerical office. If he had been a bishop, he perhaps is to be identified with the bishop Ursus who had challenged Proculus' metropolitan rights at the Council of Turin.[57] This would mean that Proculus had been able to revenge himself upon at least two of the bishops who had opposed him at Turin: Ursus and Remigius. Proculus' eventual reconciliation with Ursus would be another example of his ability to change with the times.

Proculus already had had a similar reconciliation with Lazarus, his candidate c.408 for the see of Aix. This very Lazarus, who perhaps returned to Gaul as a result of the amnesty of 416, was personally involved in Proculus' irregular ordinations.[58] Zosimus complained (*Epist.* "Cum adversus"),

> Not even the fellow provincial bishops were canvasssed, so that the impropriety would be concealed by some cloak of legality, although Lazarus [was consulted]. . . . It truly was incongruous that [Lazarus], unfitted for the episcopate, deposed on his own confession, ordained a bishop just the same, with the metropolitan [sc. Patroclus] disregarded.[59]

Although Zosimus made much of the supposed impropriety of Lazarus' involvement, as recently as 417 Augustine had referred to Lazarus (*De gest. Pel.* 1) as his *coepiscopus*. The party of Proculus may not have recognized Lazarus' deposition at all. Lazarus may have continued to act as a bishop, perhaps in a see in Narbonensis II found for him by his patron Proculus. Lazarus' performance of the ordination

---

gentius observare voluisset, erroris illum anteacti oportuit poenitere, non ita praecipiti impetu ad sacerdotium festinare. . . ."

56. It is unknown under what circumstances his case was referred to Rome. The charge of Priscillianism may be related to the accusation at about the same time of Manicheism against Maximus of Valence (see n.81 below). If the charge referred to the controversy of the 380s, it would have been ancient indeed.

57. See chapter 1 above, n.100.

58. Palanque (*Marseilles* p.22) asserts that "sans doute" Lazarus had returned to Gaul with Cassian of Marseilles.

59. "nec saltem comprovinciales episcopi corrogantur, ut error velamento aliquo tegeretur: sed Lazarus . . . re vera incongruum fuit, ut illicitus sacerdotio, omisso metropolitano, sua confessione spoliatus sacerdotem pariter ordinaret." Later in the same letter, Zosimus also noted "et Lazarus in consortio illicitae ordinationis adscitus." As an additional illegality, Zosimus also asserted it was "ne dies quidem legitimus ordinationis," and "nec saltem diei custodita sollemnitas."

must have been done with Proculus' approval, and probably *vice Proculi*. It may have been justified on the grounds of Lazarus' earlier status as bishop of the metropolitan see of Aix.

Zosimus concluded his consideration of this case by ordering the excommunication of both Ursus and Tuentius:

> Wherefore, dearest brothers, we have sent letters to Your Sanctity and throughout the entire world in order that you realize that Tuentius and Ursus are not to be received into the communion of the church, from which they are totally anathematized, in any ecclesiastical office whatsoever. Indeed, they are said to be mountebanks, as we have been informed by the sentences which they received in different regions, promulgated in their condemnation by sacerdotal authority.[60]

In spite of this sentence, it appears that Tuentius, at least, could not be dislodged, for in Celestine of Rome's letter to the Gallic bishops in 431, he commented, "Concerning these [laymen] much already has been said at that time when we wrote in answer to the letter of brother Tuentius. . . ."[61] If this were the same Tuentius, still in office circa the late 420s, it would indicate that once again the will of the bishop of Rome had been flouted in Gaul.[62]

Other bishops, too, were concerned in the controversy over parishes. This ruling soon was followed by another, involving another of Proculus' nemeses, Remigius of Aix. He, it will be recalled, had been deposed at the instigation of Proculus in 408 and replaced by Proculus' protégé Lazarus, who in turn was expelled after the fall of Constantine, when Remigius was able to regain his see. Remigius, like Proclus, apparently was taking advantage of Zosimus' antipathy toward the bishop of Marseilles to protect his own interests.[63] On 3 October

---

60. "qua de re ad sanctitatem vestram, et per totum orbem ... scripta direximus, fratres carissimi, ne Tuentium et Ursum in communione ecclesiae, in quocumque ecclesiastico gradu, a qua in totum anathematizati sunt, suscipiendos esse ducatis. dicuntur enim circumlatores esse, quod nos ex sententiis agnovimus in eorum damnatione sacerdotali auctoritate probatis, quas in diversis regionibus exceperunt." For "communione" Gundlach reads "commune." Was the letter also addressed to the bishops of Africa and Spain because Zosimus suspected that, à la Heros and Lazarus, Ursus and Tuentius might flee thence?

61. "super his [laicis] multa iam dicta sunt eo tempore, quo ad fratris Tuentii dedimus scripta responsum. . . ." ("Apostolici verba": *P.L.* 50.529-530).

62. Duchesne, *Fastes* 1.99-100, assumes that the two actually were expelled and that Arles resumed control of the parishes. There is no reason, however, to presume that the shift in jurisdiction occurred immediately. It probably dates, rather, to a time when the bishop of Arles had much greater authority vis-à-vis the bishop of Marseilles, perhaps in the early sixth century. On 6 November 513, Symmachus of Rome, in a letter to the Gallic bishops, wrote "alias vero parochias vel dioeceses cunctas privilegio et honore suo Arelatensis episcopatus sub temporum continuatione defendat" ("Sedis apostolicae": Thiel, *Epistolae* no.14 pp.722-723). Such a decree would have been pointless if Arles already had recovered its lost territory. Soon afterward Citharista is in fact attested as being under the jurisdiction of Arles (*VCaesarii* 2.17).

63. Duchesne, *Fastes* 1.106-108 presumes that the bishop of of Aix was "à la dévotion de Patrocle." Both, at least, would have felt animosity toward Proculus.

417, Zosimus responded to a letter of Remigius: "Although we recently put forth rulings that no one should think that parishes could be held in the territory of another, we nevertheless wish Your Worship to recover for yourself those churches which you complain have been appropriated by Proculus, Domninus, and others. . . ."[64]

Just what parishes was Remigius supposed to reclaim? It has been suggested that they were full-fledged *civitates* which hitherto had lacked bishops, but there is no precedent for such a usage of the word *parociae*.[65] It might be more likely that Proculus had done with these parishes what he had done with Citharista and Gargaria: raised them to the status of episcopal sees. One of them might even have been granted to his protégé Lazarus, who may have seen it as a stepping-stone back to his old see of Aix. It also may be that Patroclus of Arles was one of the "others" who were claiming Remigius' parishes. Perhaps he was trying to regain some of the territory which his city had lost to Aix in Diocletian's reorganization, just as he had done with regard to Marseilles.[66]

Nor was Proculus the only powerful Gallic bishop to oppose the attempt to grant Patroclus extended metropolitan authority. He was joined by the two others whom the ruling would disenfranchise, Hilarius of Narbonne and Simplicius of Vienne, both of whom complained to Zosimus about the innovation. In his letter "Mirati admodum" (*M.G.H. Epist.* 3.9-10 [29 September]), addressed to Hilarius himself, Zosimus responded to Hilarius' complaint:

We were absolutely amazed when your letter was read because, although you wish your assertion and desires to be taken into account, you have ignored true faith and colored your report with a certain tinge of integrity, asserting that it is improper for bishops to be ordained by another in an alien province, when in point of fact you ought, at least, to cite not what seems best to you personally, but what past custom sanctions.[67]

64. "licet proxime scripta dederimus . . . ne quis parrocias in alterius territorio civitatis crederet retinendas, tamen . . . eas de quibus quereris ecclesias per Proculum et Domninum ceterosque detineri . . . dilectionem tuam ad se volumus revocare. . . ." ("Licet proxime": Duchesne, *Fastes* 1.101-102 n.2). Domninus' see is unknown; it presumably adjoined Aix. See Di Capua, *Ritmo Prosaico* pp.205-206; and Duchesne, *Fastes* 1.101-102 n.2, who concludes only that Remigius' see was in Narbonensis Secunda.

65. Griffe, *Gaule* 1.406-407. As of the Council of Turin, at least four cities of Narbonensis Secunda did have bishops.

66. For the Diocletianic reduction benefiting Aix and Marseilles, see Duchesne, *Fastes* 1.98-99, who notes the result: "Quand les querelles des cités furent devenues des querelles d'évêques, on vit souvent les évêques d'Arles en froid avec leurs collègues d'Aix et de Marseille."

67. "mirati admodum sumus dum . . . relatio tua . . . legeretur, quod, dum assertioni et desideriis tuis cupis esse consultum, praetermissa veri fide, relationem tuam sub honestatis specie colorasti, asserens in aliena provincia ab alio non debere fieri sacerdotes, cum utique debueris, non quid tibi rectum videatur, sed quid habuerit antiqua consuetudo, suggerere." See Duchesne, *Fastes* 1.98, and Langgärtner, *Gallienpolitik* p.49.

Hilarius even argued that the status of his see had been sanctioned by an earlier bishop of Rome, to which Zosimus responded, "That which you deceitfully claim was obtained from the apostolic see has been made void."[68]

Hilarius, of course, was on firm legal ground in making these objections, and Zosimus once again fell back on the Trophimus legend, and threateningly concluded:

> We constrain you by this authority, so that you should recognize the limitation of the just prescription which has been issued on account of your presumption, which you seem to have exhibited contrary to established practice. . . . If you attempt to do anything contrary to these things which we have decreed according to the judgment of God, dearest brother, you must believe not only that those whom you favor will be unable to obtain the episcopate, but also that you yourself, separated from catholic communion, will lament too late your illicit presumptions.[69]

That Hilarius may indeed have reached some kind of accord with Patroclus is seen by the latter's ordination a few years later of a new bishop for Lodève, a see in Hilarius' province.[70]

Simplicius of Vienne also complained about the change, encouraged to do so by Proculus himself. In a letter addressed to the bishops of Viennensis and Narbonensis Secunda, Zosimus noted: "[Proculus] has recruited Simplicius of Vienne as an ally, who demands with a not dissimilar impudence that he too be permitted the right of creating bishops in the province of Viennensis."[71] Zosimus totally ignored the metropolitan status assigned to Simplicius at Turin, despite a later forged letter to the contrary, there is no evidence that Simplicius ever accepted Zosimus' ruling.[72]

---

68. "vacuato eo quod obtinuisse a sede apostolica subreptitie comprobaris" (*Epist.* "Mirati admodum": *M.G.H. Epist.* 3.9-10); see Pietri, *Roma* 2.999-1000 n.5. Narbonensis Prima had become an independent province in the late fourth century (see chapter 1 above, n.8), at which time the bishop of Narbonne may have sought some ecclesiastical recognition of his metropolitan status. Langgärtner, *Gallienpolitik* p.25, however, supposes that before 417 there had been "no legitimate metropolitan in Narbonensis."

69. "hac te auctoritate constringimus, ut praesumptioni tuae, quam extulisse contra veterem consuetudinem videbaris, modum noveris iustae praescriptionis indictum. . . . si quid contra haec, frater carissime, quae a nobis sunt sub dei iudicia statuta, tentaveris, non solum quos faciendos credideris episcopatum obtinere non posse, sed etiam ipse catholica communione discretus, sero de illicitis praesumptionibus ingemiscas."

70. See chapter 4 below and Batiffol, "Les églises" p.164; Ganshof, "L'élection" pp.485-486; and McShane, *Romanitas* p.277.

71. "socium sibi Simplicium Viennensis civitatis adscivit: qui non dissimili impudentia postularet, ut sibi quoque in Viennensium provincia creandorum sacerdotum permitteretur arbitrium" ("Multa contra veterem": *M.G.H. Epist.* 3.11 [29 September]).

72. See the letter, supposedly by Zosimus, "Revelatum est nobis" (*P.L.* 20.704); and Griffe, *Gaule* 2.148, who admits the forgery but still accepts the contents as genuine. The letter affirms

Yet another round of letters sent to Gaul by Zosimus in March 418 demonstrates further his lack of success in enforcing his rulings. Once again, his primary target was Proculus of Marseilles. In a letter addressed "to the clergy, senatorial order, and plebs residing at Marseilles," Zosimus, referring to the disturbances (*turbatio*) Proculus supposedly had been causing in Marseilles, admitted the ineffectiveness of his Gallic decrees: "I do not marvel that Proculus persists still in his accustomed effrontery, and absolutely shamelessly commits damnable deeds daily, nor does he ever desist, so that having been warned and forbidden many times he does not cease."[73] He then repeated a sentence of deposition against Proculus and placed the church of Marseilles in the hands of Patroclus, but his admission that he was doing so *iterum*, "again," indicates how ineffectual his reiterated decree would have been.[74]

In another letter of the same date to Patroclus himself, Zosimus rebuked the bishop of Arles for not being able to bring Proculus to heel ("Cum et in": *M.G.H. Epist.* 3.12):

Given that you not only learned in our presence but also yourself have been advised in repeated letters from us that with your metropolitan authority, supported by the rigor and censure which you wield for the sake of the confirmation of the statutes . . . you ought to resist Proculus' adventures and endeavors, with which until now he thinks he can disturb anything . . . I marvel at what, after all this, is permitted to Proculus. He either is free to do that to which he was accustomed, or commits even worse acts.[75]

Zosimus also reported a subsequent *rumor* which had reached him (ibid.), "that Proculus, so to speak, is mocking the customary practices and is demonstrating his usual character, that he has associated with

---

the Council of Turin and returns to Vienne its metropolitan status. Zosimus is unlikely to have done either. Batiffol, "Les églises" p.163, without basis asserts that Hilarius and Simplicius were summoned to Rome. McShane, *Romanitas* p.277 supposes that Simplicius "reçut le coup avec résignation." See also Langgärtner, *Gallienpolitik* p.50

73. "non miror Proculum in consueta adhuc fronte durare, et oblito penitus pudore cotidie digna damnatione committere, nec aliquando desistere, ut totiens commonitus prohibitusque non cesset" (*Epist.*"Non miror": *M.G.H. Epist.* 3.13 [5 March]).

74. "cum ipse iam non sit episcopus." The initial sentence is not extant, unless it was implied in the "damnation" of Proculus at the council of the previous September. Some, such as McShane, *Romanitas* p.277, presume Proculus actually was deposed. For the ineffectiveness of the decree, see Palanque, *Marseilles* p.20. Langgärtner, *Gallienpolitik* p.52, supposes that the result is unknown.

75. "cum et in praesenti cognoveris, et frequentibus a nobis litteris ipse sis monitus, ut auctoritate metropolitani . . . Proculi ausibus conatibusque illis, quibus adhuc se putat aliqua posse turbare . . . occurreres, renitens rigore censuraque, quam pro regularum confirmatione susceperas . . . miror quid post ista Proculo liceat, aut vacet illa quae consueverat, aut peiora committere."

himself certain men suited for creating disturbances, and that he has carried out ordinations after we had forbidden him to do so."[76] Zosimus concluded by ordering the invalidation of these ordinations, but once again one can imagine how successful the order was.

Such strong support for Patroclus by the bishop of Rome may have served to confirm Proculus' conversion from one who favored foreign ties to a more "isolationist" viewpoint: if the bishop of Rome was going to attack him so fiercely, then Proculus, and many other Gauls, could not but have felt alienated from him. The apparent decline of the influence of the bishop of Milan, with whom Proculus had worked so closely in the past, also would have forced Proculus and his partisans back upon their own local resources.

If anything, Zosimus' attempts to regulate the church of Gaul served only to unify Gallic resistance to him. As of 417, Proculus of Marseilles became the focal point of Gallic opposition to Roman, and Arlesian, aspirations, and the *de facto* leader of an influential cabal including at least Hilarius of Narbonne and Simplicius of Vienne. Given that Patroclus had the support not only of Zosimus, but also of the patrician Constantius, old adherents of the anti-Felician school of thought regarding foreign ties, such as Proculus and Simplicius, would no longer have any basis for such a viewpoint. For them, there would be no more support forthcoming from outside Gaul. Another result of this affair, therefore, was to encourage Gallic bishops (other than Patroclus and his partisans) to restrict their ties and interests to within Gaul even more than they had in the past.

BONIFACE, PATROCLUS, AND MAXIMUS OF VALENCE

In early 418 Zosimus of Rome died after only about a year in office, and the ensuing dissension over the election of a new bishop rent the church of Rome.[77] The leading contenders were Boniface and Eulalius, and the controversy became so intense that the imperial government finally stepped in; eventually even transmarine bishops were invited to help consider the case.[78] The ultimate victor was Boniface, and in a letter of 7 April to the proconsul of Africa, the emperor Honorius noted (*Epist. imp.* 35: *C.S.E.L.* 35.81-82),

---

76. "Proculum quasi consuetis ludere, et uti moribus suis, iunxisse sibi quosdam idoneos turbationibus homines, et post illa quae illi interdiximus ordinasse."

77. See Cristo, "Schism" and Pietri, "Le schisme de 419," *Roma* 1.452-460; 2.948-950.

78. See *Epist. imp.* 26-28, invitations to the Africans to come to Spoleto; *Epist. imp.* 25 was a special invitation to Paulinus of Nola.

When indeed a controversy was occurring concerning the confirmation of the bishop of the eternal city, and those bishops, who were gathered together, thought that they were too few for coming to a decision, it was thought proper that more bishops should come from the African and Gallic provinces....[79]

Honorius then informed him that the matter already had been decided and that it was not necessary for any more bishops to come to Rome. Similar letters may have been sent to the imperial authorities in Gaul as well.

It is likely that Patroclus of Arles was one of the foreign bishops who became involved in the dispute. His penchant for such activities already has been seen in his involvement in the election of Zosimus, and he may have viewed the controversy in Italy as another opportunity to fish in troubled waters. This time he probably was not so successful. His patron Constantius initially had backed the nomination of Eulalius, and Patroclus hardly could have avoided doing the same. But Eulalius had lost, and the victor Boniface would have felt antipathy toward both Constantius and Patroclus.[80] It remains to be seen how well Patroclus would be able to maintain his extraordinary authority in Gaul now that he no longer had, it seems, the support of the bishop of Rome.

In 419 Boniface became involved in Gallic ecclesiastical politics when he was appealed to by the enemies of bishop Maximus of Valence.[81] In a letter addressed to fourteen named bishops as well as to "the other bishops resident throughout Gaul and the Seven Provinces," Boniface began, "Clerics from the city of Valence have approached us putting forth in a letter the crimes which they assert Maximus, with the entire province as a witness, has committed."[82] Boniface went on to note that this was a problem which previously had been considered "by my predecessors," and that Maximus had refused to attend a council assembled to consider the case. There were two charges against him. The first was that he previously had been involved in Manicheism, and the second was that he was one "whom they accuse also of having come to be subjected, in his rage and mad

79. "cum enim de confirmando episcopo urbis aeternae controversia tractaretur, atque hi, qui in unum positi erant, episcopi de tanto negotio paucos se aestimarent ad sententiam proferendam, placuerat . . . ut ex Africanis et Gallicanis provinciis plures episcopi commearent. . . ."

80. For Constantius', and Galla Placidia's, support for Eulalius, see Cristo, "Schism" pp.164-166; Oost, *Placidia* p.158; and Wermelinger, *Pelagius* p.242.

81. For Maximus, see Duchesne, *Fastes* 1.109-110; Griffe, *Gaule* 1.180-181; Langgärtner, *Gallienpolitik* pp.53-54; and Pietri, *Roma* 2.1005.

82. "Valentinae nos clerici civitatis adierunt, proponentes per libellum crimina, quae Maximum teste tota provincia asserunt commisisse" ("Valentinae nos": *P.L.* 20.756 [13 June]).

rashness, to an inquiry before the tribunals of secular judges, which is most shameful even in a common person, and with evidence displayed in public they assert that he was condemned as a homicide."[83]

Some of the opposition to Maximus may have been because he was guilty at least of association with the usurper Jovinus; it was to Valence that Jovinus fled just before he was captured.[84] If so, Maximus, like Proculus of Marseilles, was strong enough to resist any attempts to unseat him after Jovinus' fall. This may have been, in part, because, unlike some of the bishops patronized by the usurpers, Maximus was a native of his episcopal see.[85] Maximus also may once have been a secular official, perhaps even a provincial governor. This would explain the accusation of homicide against him, which would have resulted from his having passed the death sentence.[86]

The charge of Manicheism, moreover, perhaps concealed an accusation of Priscillianism, just as it had in the 380s.[87] If so, Maximus at one time may have been associated with the anti-Felician party of Martin and Ambrose, which had opposed imperial intervention in the controversy. A similar confusion of Priscillianism with Manicheism also just might explain an otherwise mysterious reference in Ado of Vienne's ninth-century account of Simplicius of Vienne, another suggested anti-Felician: "at that time the insane heresy of the Manichees arises."[88] The anti-Felician Proculus' connections to so-called Priscillianism at this time likewise are suggested, at least, by the favor he showed to Tuentius, who had been accused of Priscillianism in the past. Proculus, of course, also had been a protégé of the tyrants. In one way or another, then, several bishops with anti-Rome, anti-imperial sentiments also were associated with reports or accusations of Priscillianism-cum-Manicheism.

Prosopographical considerations provide another indication that Maximus may have been associated with Proculus. Boniface's letter was addressed to the authors of the earlier letter to him, beginning with the names of Patroclus [of Arles], Remigius [of Aix], a Maximus, and Hilarius [of Narbonne].[89] Notably absent, however, are the names,

83. "quem furore suo et insana temeritate ad saecularium quoque iudicum tribunalia subditum quaestioni, quod in vili quoque persona turpissimum est, obiicerent pervenisse et homicidii damnatum asserunt gestis prolatis in medium...."
84. *Chron. gall.* 452 no.71 s.a.411, "Valentia nobilissima Galliarum civitas a Gothis effringitur, ad quam se fugiens Iovinus contulerat."
85. He was charged with acting "in propriae civitatis infamiam."
86. For the deposition of Chelidonius of Besançon on a similar charge in the 440s, see chapter 7 below.
87. For the "inquiries" into Gallic Manicheism, see Kidd, *Church* p.387, see also Aug. *De mor. man.* 2: *P.L.* 42.1373-1378. For the confusion, see chapter 1 above.
88. "tunc temporis insana Manichaeorum haeresis oritur" (Duchesne, *Fastes* 1.182).
89. Is this Maximus of Valence? Boniface stated that he had learned of the affair "ex vestra-

for example, of Proculus of Marseilles and Simplicius of Vienne. Given that Patroclus and Remigius were two of Proculus' most implacable enemies, Proculus' refusal to associate with them in this matter is hardly surprising. Simplicius, too, must have had little stomach for participating. According to the terms of the Council of Turin, Valence belonged under his own metropolitan jurisdiction. His failure to participate in the proceedings against Maximus of Valence, therefore, can only be an indication of his displeasure at the interference of other bishops.

There is no evidence that Boniface was any more successful in controlling Maximus than his predecessors had been. The most he could do was to refer the case back to the provincials (*Epist.* "Valentinae nos": *P.L.* 20.756):

> We decree that your hearing should be within the province and that a synod should be assembled before the first day of November, so that if he wishes to attend, he might respond to the accusations in person, if he has the confidence to do so; if, however, he declines to attend, let him gain no delay of the sentence because of his absence.[90]

Just what did Boniface mean here by "the province?" He apparently was not addressing this request to all the bishops in his list of addressees, for they represented several provinces. Nor was he referring to all of Gaul loosely as a single province, for later in his letter he could say, "We are directing letters throughout all the provinces [of Gaul], lest [Maximus] have for himself an excuse of ignorance, so that he will be compelled to come to the provincial [synod]."[91] Boniface was well aware that there were several provinces in Gaul. His reference, therefore, must have been to the province of a single individual. This could only have been Patroclus, whose place at the head of the list confirms the extraordinary status Boniface continued to grant him.[92] Boniface was commanding Patroclus to convene a synod in order to review the

---

rum quoque chartarum instructione" (Sirmond's reading of "vestrarum" is to be preferred to the "nostrarum" of *P.L.*), and Maximus hardly would have informed on himself. Therefore, the Maximus in the list of addressees either must be someone else, or Boniface simply inserted his name gratuitously. If this Hilarius is Hilarius of Narbonne, then his capitulation to Patroclus would be confirmed.

90. "decrevimus vestrum debere intra provinciam esse iudicium et congregari synodum ante diem Kalendarum Novembrium, ut si adesse voluerit, praesens se confidit ad obiecta respondeat, si vero adesse neglexerit, dilectionem sententiae de absentia non lucretur. . . ."

91. "nos autem per omnes provincias litteras dirigimus, ne excusationem sibi ignorationis obtendat, ut ad provinciam venire cogatur."

92. Patroclus clearly was not senior by tenure status: Remigius greatly outranked him there. Langgärtner, *Gallienpolitik* p.57, explains Patroclus' presence at the head of the list as a result of his "grosses Ansehen in Südgallien."

case of Maximus.[93] As of 419, Boniface still recognized Patroclus as having extraordinary authority in southern Gaul, authority which extended into the area of Viennensis which, according to the Council of Turin, should have been overseen by Simplicius of Vienne.

There is no evidence that this council ever met, or that the Gauls obeyed Boniface's final demand: "Furthermore, whatever Your Charity thinks must be decreed about this matter, when it has been reported to us, necessarily must be confirmed, as is fitting, by our authority."[94] Very probably, Maximus continued to serve as bishop of Valence and all the fuss over his status came to nought. In the long run, however, this incident did give the bishops of Rome one more precedent to cite for their own status as a court of appeal for disaffected Gauls. In this context, it is interesting to note one of Boniface's reasons for finding against Maximus: "Because he declined to present himself here to be heard, lest he perhaps be convicted by the accusations of his clergy."[95] Once again, Gallic clerics undertaking the journey to Rome were able to obtain a favorable decision, even against their own bishop. This consequence, along with the pope's willingness to give heed to the complaints of lesser clergy, could not but encourage additional appeals to Rome in the future.

THE AUTHORITY OF PATROCLUS OF ARLES

If the Maximus affair suggests that the bishop of Rome still recognized Patroclus as having exceptional authority in Gaul, another incident gives further insight into Patroclus' continued attempts to appropriate extraordinary powers. A letter in the recently discovered correspondence of Augustine, written after 418 to Augustine by the Balearic priest Consentius, describes an accusation of Priscillianism in Spain.[96] Consentius had instructed the cleric Fronto to spy out the situation, but Fronto made the mistake of accusing a relative of Count Asterius of heresy.[97] Finding himself opposed by "the force of a great

93. Langgärtner, *Gallienpolitik* pp.53-54 suggests that Patroclus had ordained Maximus against the will of the people and that the letter was aimed against him. He presumes that Patroclus was not rebuked by name because Constantius was still alive. A more reasonable conclusion, however, might be that it was Patroclus who had helped to instigate the recent attacks on Maximus.

94. "quidquid autem vestra caritas de hac causa duxerit decernendum, cum ad nos relatum fuerit, nostra, ut condecet, necesse est auctoritate firmetur."

95. "quia audiendus hic praesentare se noluit, ne convictus forsitan ab accusantibus se clericis."

96. *Epist.* 11*, J. Divjak ed., *C.S.E.L.* 88 (Vienna, 1981) pp.51-70.

97. Asterius: *PLRE II* p.171 (c. 420/422).

faction," Fronto then fled precipitously to Gaul.[98] There, as he reported back to Consentius, he found a new ally (Aug. *Epist.* 11*.23.1-3):

... I quickly sought the assistance of the blessed Patroclus, bishop of Arles, whose most renowned persecution of this heresy used to be praised. With no difficulty I obtained this from him, that all of those, both the guilty and the judges, who had perverted the weight of justice in their unfair proceedings, would gather at a council. Whether or not it has met in the town of Béziers, as was announced, I do not know.[99]

Consentius, however, supposed that it would be difficult to summon such a council, and suggested an alternative (Aug. *Epist.* 11*.24.2-3):

The Spanish bishops by no means will attend the council which your brother Patroclus, aroused not by the virtue of his power but by his piety, announced. But this same brother of yours and the other Gallic bishops perhaps also will take pains to refer this matter to the ears of the renowned prince.[100]

Consentius then concluded by asking Augustine to send a response not to himself, but to Patroclus, "through whom the aforementioned diversity of provinces, persons, and teachings might suggest that a different sentence ought to be promulgated."[101]

Consentius' fears seem to have been justified, and there is no evidence that this council ever met. Nevertheless, this incident does show that Patroclus intended not only to exercise the authority over the entire Tres Provinciae granted to him by Zosimus, but even, given the opportunity, to extend it into Spain. His choice of Béziers, only a few miles from Narbonne, would have been a demonstration of his authority over Hilarius of Narbonne, with or without the latter's cooperation.[102]

As a result of the refusal of the Spaniards to attend, the most such a council could have done would have been to refer the matter to the *inclitus princeps.* Now, if this letter was written in 419, as Divjak sug-

---

98. "adversum tantae vim factionis" (Aug. *Epist.* 11*.5.1).

99. "ut ... ad sancti ac beatissimi Patrocli Arelatensis episcopi, cuius clarissima in insectatione huius haereseos constantia laudabatur, auxilium convolarem. a quo quidem non difficulter obtinui, ut cuncti tam rei quam iudices qui iniquo examine pondus iustitiae perverterunt ad concilium convenirent quod utrumne in oppido Biterrensi sicut indictum est, adhuc agitandum sit ignoramus...."

100. "Hispanos episcopos ad concilium, quod ... frater vester Patroclus non potestatis sed pietatis virtute commotus indixit, nequaqaum esse venturos. sed idem ... frater vester et ceteri episcopi Gallicani ... fortasse haec etiam ad aures incliti principis referentes elaborabunt...."

101. "per quam et provinciarum et personarum et dogmatum diversitas declarata diversam doceat proferri debere sententiam" (*Epist.* 11*.26.1-2).

102. Consentius himself may have had family ties to Narbonne: note the grammarian Consentius of Narbonne and his son, also Consentius, who served as a *tribunus et notarius* under Valentinian III and *cura palatii* under Avitus (*P.L.R.E. II* pp.308-310).

gests, the "prince" would have been Honorius. The only basis for this date, however, is Consentius' statement in another letter that it was written a year after he received Zosimus' account of the investigation into Pelagianism of 418.[103] If Consentius had not received his copy immediately, the prince in question may rather have been Patroclus' patron Constantius. If so, the stress upon an appeal to the emperor is more understandable: Patroclus had no known influence with Honorius, but he was a close ally of Constantius. In this case, the incident would have occurred in 421, during the months when Constantius was emperor. At that time, Patroclus could indeed have hoped to summon the Spanish bishops to a council, and Constantius' subsequent death would explain why the council never met.

Consentius seems to have sought a tie to Patroclus in their mutual opposition to "Priscillianism." Along with his reference to Patroclus' previous "persecution" of Priscillianism, Consentius also noted that Patroclus had asked him to write "against the Priscillianists, by whom even the Gauls used to be devastated (*vastabantur*)." Even Consentius, therefore, apparently did recognize that Priscillianism no longer was a problem in Gaul.[104] Just what, one might ask, had been Patroclus' concern with Priscillianism? It may be no coincidence that, as just seen, several of Patroclus' opponents in Gaul were in some manner connected with Priscillianism-cum-Manicheism. Consentius' reference may be to these very insinuations. If so, it would be one more example of the role played by such charges in the rhetoric of Gallic ecclesiastical politics at this time.

Consentius also tried to demonstrate his orthodoxy and good will to both Patroclus and Augustine by inserting himself into a further controversy. In another letter to Augustine, Consentius included a copy of a letter he had sent to Patroclus containing "those matters which I dare to write against the propositions of Pelagius and which I wished to forward, in an imperfect state."[105] Consentius, therefore, already had established consensus with Patroclus on the one ground which united all Gallic ecclesiastics, their condemnation of Pelagianism. Augustine, of course, shared this sentiment. To ingratiate himself still further with Augustine, Consentius also attempted to draw analogies between Priscillianism and Donatism.[106] It would appear that

---

103. Aug. *Epist.* 12*.16.

104. Aug. *Epist.* 11*.1.1. This passage has been used to suggest that at this time Priscillianism was "flourishing in . . . Provence," see Birley, "Magnus Maximus" p.41. Consentius' verb tense, however, does not support this contention.

105. "ea quae adversus quaestiones Pelagii scribere audeo vel imperfecta transmittere voluissem" (Aug. *Epist.* 12*.15.3).

106. Aug. *Epist.* 11*.26-27.

Consentius was pulling out all the stops in his quest for help from influential western ecclesiastics.

Patroclus, of course, would have been happy to use this incident as a pretext for extending his authority. In doing so, he may even have been patterning his activities on those of the bishops of Rome, who likewise gave a ready ear to appeals. As of c.420, Rome did not offer the only court of appeal. Consentius, for one, believed that he would find a more receptive audience in Gaul and Africa.[107] Nor is there any indication that Consentius ever made, or intended to make, any similar appeal to Boniface of Rome.

THE SITUATION CIRCA 420

Zosimus had attempted to establish Arles as the metropolitan see of the entire Tres Provinciae. In doing so, however, he aroused much Gallic opposition against both himself and Patroclus. The preceding discussion suggests that the ties among Proculus, Simplicius, and Maximus, and very possibly others as well, were not merely fleeting or coincidental. Earlier in the century, all seem to have had anti-Felician points of view, and to have welcomed foreign contacts. After the Felician controversy died down c.400, however, many such as they threw in their lot with the local usurpers: Proculus certainly did, and Maximus may have. The fall of the usurpers then saw the rise of the see of Arles with the support of the bishop of Rome. At the same time, some ecclesiastical supporters of the usurpers lost their sees.

Because of these developments, individuals with an anti-Felician outlook, such as Proculus, were forced to adopt an altered viewpoint. The old anti-Felician party now became an anti-Rome, anti-Arles party. Presumably, many of the old Felician school of thought joined in as well. The difference between Felicians and anti-Felicians now would have been passé. Metropolitans such as Proculus, Simplicius, and Hilarius had to join forces in their attempts to protect their own metropolitan privileges. However loose the connections among these individuals might have been, they foreshadow the composition of the group which was to continue to oppose the interests of Arles for the next three decades and more.

Zosimus' activities also established another pattern which was to hold true for the rest of the fifth century regarding the relations between the Roman and Gallic churches. On the one hand, powerful and independently minded Gallic bishops like Proculus and Maximus could flout the wishes of the bishop of Rome at will, provided that

---

107. For Africans in Gaul at this time, see Aug. *Epist.* 7*.1, 15*.2, 16*.2.

they had sufficiently strong Gallic support. If summoned to a council, they simply refused to attend. And on the other, the bishop of Rome would not be able to assert his authority in Gaul unless he had his own powerful support there. Zosimus, realizing this, had attempted to enlist Patroclus of Arles, who already had strong secular backing, as his agent in Gaul.[108] Unless Patroclus himself were able to enforce Zosimus' rulings, they would have little chance of success.

In the future, the same patterns were to hold true, even if the alliances were to shift. The bishops of Rome learned not to intervene in Gaul unless they had the support of some party there. By being responsive to appeals, they increasingly strengthened their position as a court of appeal for disaffected Gauls, who could hope to receive a favorable reception in Rome. Thus, even rulings such as these of Zosimus, which were observed primarily in their breach, served their purpose over the long term in establishing precedents for the jurisdiction of the bishop of Rome in Gaul.

108. In March, 418, for example, Zosimus ordered Patroclus (*Epist.* "Cum et in": *M.G.H. Epist.* 3.12), "sciant, quibus hanc epistolam volumus in notitiam pervenire."

CHAPTER 4

THE LÉRINS FACTION, PART I

ORIGIN AND PRACTICES

THE FALL OF PATROCLUS

During the 420s nearly all the earlier important participants in both the secular and ecclesiastical spheres in Gaul were to die, including such as Constantius, Patroclus of Arles, Proculus of Marseilles, Hilarius of Narbonne, and Simplicius of Vienne. At the same time, a new coalition of prominent ecclesiastics associated with the monastery of Lérins acquired increasing influence.

Constantius, after having been made augustus in 421, died later in the year. As long as he was alive, Boniface of Rome may have had to give tacit recognition to Patroclus' preeminence in Gaul. Once Patroclus had lost his imperial patron, however, Boniface apparently decided the time was right to attempt to restrict his authority. On 9 February 422 he decreed the removal of at least some of Patroclus' extraordinary metropolitan jurisdiction.[1] In a letter addressed to bishop Hilarius of Narbonne, Boniface reported (*Epist.* "Difficile quidem": *P.L.* 20.772–773),

The clergy, the senate, and the plebs of the church of Lodève have sent their pleas and tears to us, with great grief, as much as can be understood, saying that our fellow bishop Patroclus has ordained in the place of the deceased bishop some unknown individual, having bypassed the metropolitan and against the statutes of the fathers.[2]

---

1. See Duchesne, *Fastes* 1.110-111; Franses, *Leo* pp.20-21; Kidd, *Church* p.355; and Langgärtner, *Gallienpolitik* pp.53-54.
2. "Lutubensis ecclesiae cleri ordo, vel plebis, preces suas et lacrimas ad nos, quantum datur intelligi, magno cum dolore miserunt, dicentes coepiscopum nostrum Patroclum ... in locum decedentis episcopi nescioquem in alia provincia, praetermisso metropolitano, contra patrum regulas ordinasse...."

Boniface then decreed that "in every province it is fitting to have individual metropolitans, nor should two [provinces] be subjected to anyone."[3] He ordered Hilarius,

Whence, if this situation does indeed exist and if the borders of your province do contain the aforementioned church, having been addressed by our authority, care for the wishes and desires of the suppliants, which you in fact ought to have done of your own will; hasten to the same place in which such an ordination is said to have been celebrated, fortified by your metropolitan status and supported by our instructions . . . See to it that when all this has been done your report will make clear to the apostolic see whatever you, to whom clearly the control of the entire province has been entrusted, decide. Let no one, therefore, as a rash fool exceed his boundaries. . . .[4]

The complaint evidently had not come from Hilarius, the supposedly aggrieved party, but rather from the citizens of Lodève. Does this imply that Hilarius was continuing to recognize Patroclus' extraordinary metropolitan authority? Other activities of Patroclus in Narbonensis Prima would suggest that this was the case. Twenty-eight years later, in 450, the bishop Constantius of Uzès attested that he, and perhaps one or more of his predecessors, had been ordained by the bishops of Arles.[5] Now, Constantius himself had been ordained c.429, and because Patroclus was bishop until 426, at least one of Constantius' predecessors could have been ordained by Patroclus, who may, in fact, have been responsible for raising the *castrum* to the status of an episcopal see in the first place.[6] If this were so, Patroclus would have been doing in Narbonensis Prima no more than Proculus of Marseilles currently was doing in Narbonensis Secunda. Nor does Hilarius of Narbonne seem to have raised any objections to this action either.

Even if Patroclus was not mentioned by name, Boniface's ruling would have been a direct attack on the extended metropolitan authority which even Boniface had conceded to Patroclus in 419. Significantly, Boniface made no reference to Zosimus' decree granting this extraordinary authority.[7] Surely he was not unaware of it; he may

---

3. "per unamquamque provinciam ius metropolitanos singulos habere debere, nec cuiquam duas esse subiectas."

4. "unde . . . si ita res sunt et ecclesiam supradictam provinciae tuae limes includit, nostra auctoritate commonitus, quod quidem facere sponte deberes, desideriis supplicantium et voluntate respecta, ad eundem locum in quo ordinatio talis celebrata dicitur, metropolitani iure munitus, et praeceptionibus nostris fretus, accede . . . ita ut peractis omnibus, apostolicae sedi quidquid statueris te referente clarescat, cui totius provinciae ordinationem liquet esse mandatam. nemo ergo eorum terminos audax temerator excedat. . . ."

5. "ab huius ecclesiae sacerdote tam decessores nostros quam nos ipsos . . . consecratos" (*Epist*. "Memores quantum": *M.G.H. Epist*. 3.17-20); see chapter 8 below.

6. For Constantius' date of ordination, see appendix "Episcopal Hierarchy."

7. See Bardy et. al., *Eglise* p.255.

have found it more convenient simply to ignore it. He thereby would have avoided discussing the status of northern Viennensis, Narbonensis Secunda, and Alpes Maritimae. His failure to mention these provinces has led some to suggest that he continued to recognize Patroclus' metropolitan status in these provinces, even if he no longer did so in Narbonensis Prima.[8] This interpretation, however, would be contrary to Boniface's explicit statement that no metropolitan was to oversee more than one province. Even if Boniface was reluctant to say specifically that Patroclus was to be limited to Viennensis, a ruling he may have felt that he had no way of enforcing, it is clear that he was determined to weaken the authority of the bishop of Arles as much as he could.

It also might be asked whether Boniface's order ever was obeyed. Did Hilarius ever investigate the ordination at Lodève? Did he ever forward the demanded explanation? If so, no evidence of either survives. What can be said, however, is that once again the bishop of Rome had used the requests for aid from a disgruntled Gallic party to attempt to exercise authority in Gaul. One might wonder how many truly believed the opening statement of Boniface's letter: "With difficulty do we grant faith to complaints whose assault afflicts the bishops of the Lord."[9]

Little else is known of Gallic affairs at this time until after the death of Honorius in 423, and the proclamation in Rome of the *primicerius notariorum* Johannes.[10] This disruption apparently led to unrest at Arles, for according to Prosper, "Exsuperantius of Poitiers, the praetorian prefect of Gaul, is killed at Arles during a military revolt, and this was not avenged by Johannes."[11] Either Johannes approved of this action, or, more likely, he simply had little authority in Gaul.

Another indication of Johannes' lack of influence in Gaul might be the ease with which imperial authority was restored, and the lack of evidence for purges such as those following the revolts of a decade earlier. Indeed, a special effort of the old dynasty to consolidate its support in Gaul is suggested by a *novel* of Johannes' successor Valentinian III, dated 9 July 425 and addressed to the Gallic prefect Amatius, which restored to the church the privileges "which the tyrant had

---

8. See Duchesne, *Fastes* 1.87, and McShane, *Romanitas* p.277. Langgärtner, *Gallienpolitik* pp.58, 61, however, suggests that Boniface recognized Patroclus only in southern Viennensis.

9. "difficile quidem fidem querimoniis commodamus, quarum sacerdotes domini pulsat intentio."

10. For Johannes, see Oost, *Placidia* p.186; *P.L.R.E. II* pp.594-595; Seeck, *Untergang* pp.90-96; and Stein, *Geschichte* 1.428.

11. "Exuperantius Pictavus praefectus praetorio Galliarum in civitate Arelatense militum seditione occisus est, idque apud Iohannem inultum fuit" (*Chron.* 1285 s.a.424). See also *Chron. gall.* 452 no.97, "in Galliis Exuperantis praefectus a militibus interficitur."

begrudged [it]."[12] The same constitution went on to introduce, or re-introduce, anti-Pelagian legislation into Gaul:

We command that those various bishops who follow the nefarious error of the teaching of Pelagius and Caelestius are to be assembled by Patroclus, bishop by sacrosanct law. We are confident they will be corrected. If they have not corrected their errors and returned themselves to the catholic faith within twenty days of the time of the synod, which period we grant for the purpose of deliberation, they are to be expelled from the Gallic regions and in their place a more faithful priesthood is to be installed. . . . [13]

The extensive powers granted to the bishop of Arles gave him the rights 1) to convene church councils, 2) to depose offending bishops, and 3) to ordain successors in their place. They indicate that even if Patroclus had lost the backing of the bishop of Rome, he still had influential allies in the secular sphere.[14] Some of his support probably came from Valentinian's mother Galla Placidia, the wife of his old patron Constantius, who once again was in a position of power.[15] When she returned to Rome she presumably would have fallen back upon old friends and old alliances, and Patroclus of Arles apparently was one of the beneficiaries. There is no evidence, moreover, that Pelagianism was as rampant in Gaul at this time as this law would imply.[16] Either the government in Rome was overreacting to a per-ceived problem, or this was simply a pretext for the granting of addi-tional powers to Patroclus. In the parallel laws of this time applying to other areas, the only other ecclesiastical enforcer named was the bishop of Rome, in the law against the Manichees addressed to the *praefectus urbi Romae*.[17] In this context, at least, Patroclus and Boni-

---

12. "quae . . . tyrannus inviderat" (*Sirm.* 6). Matthews, *Aristocracies* pp.379-308 suggests that Johannes had subjected Gallic clerics to secular jurisdiction. Amatius (*P.L.R.E. II* p.68) seems not to have been a Gaul: the name does not otherwise occur there. He probably was an Italian supporter of the new government. Perhaps the new regime was unsure of its position in Gaul, or had not yet had an opportunity to consolidate its authority there.

13. "diversos vero episcopos nefarium Pelagiani et Caelestiani dogmatis errorem sequentes per Patroclum sacrosanctae legis antistitem praecipimus conveniri: quos quia confidimus emen-dari, nisi intra viginti dies ex conventionis tempore, intra quos deliberandi tribuimus facultatem, errata correxerint seseque catholicae fidei reddiderint, Gallicanis regionibus expelli atque in eorum loco sacerdotium fidelius subrogari. . . ."

14. Langgärtner, *Gallienpolitik* p.61, who asserts that there was "keinen Wechsel der staat-lichen Haltung gegenüber den Massnahmen des apostolischen Stuhles," cannot make this ex-traordinary grant consistent with his view that the ecclesiastical authority of Arles was limited to southern Viennensis.

15. See Oost, *Placidia* pp.150, 208, 211.

16. For the status of the Pelagian controversy in Gaul in the late 420s, see chapter 6 below.

17. *C. Th.* 16.5.62 (17 July 425), also against "heretics and schismatics" in general. Other versions of the law, addressed to the *comes rei privatae* (*C. Th.* 16.5.64: 6 August 425) and to the *proconsul Africae* (*C. Th.* 16.5.63: 4 August 425), likewise cited "Manichees, heretics, and schis-matics," but named no ecclesiastical enforcers.

face had been given similar powers. Furthermore, just as "Manicheism" apparently continued to serve as a convenient catchall accusation in Rome, "Pelagianism" now seems to have fulfilled the same function in Gaul.[18]

Patroclus' regained ascendancy, however, was not to last. In 425 Valentinian, with the apparent support of Galla Placidia, also appointed a new *patricius et magister utriusque militiae*, Fl. Constantius Felix.[19] In the next year, Felix had dealings of his own with Patroclus, as reported by Prosper Tiro (*Chron.* 1292 s.a.426),

The bishop Patroclus of Arles, mangled by many wounds, was killed by a certain tribune Barnabus: this crime was attributed to a secret order of the master of soldiers Felix, through whose initiative it also was believed that the deacon Titus, a blessed man, was killed while distributing money to the poor at Rome.[20]

One can only speculate as to what chain of circumstances could have led one protégé of Galla Placidia to plot the murder of another. Patroclus did have a history of becoming involved in intrigues at the very highest levels of Italian ecclesiastical politics. Felix' own involvement in the same sphere is attested not only by his murder of the Roman deacon, but also by his and his wife's building of a church in Rome, and by his own murder in 430, when another deacon was killed along with him.[21] Italian church politics, therefore, may have been one arena in which these two came into conflict, especially because Felix himself is not known to have had any particular dealings with Gaul.

What may have induced Patroclus to put himself at risk is a desire to have his extraordinary metropolitan status recognized by the new bishop of Rome, Celestine, who had succeeded Boniface in 422. He also may have become involved with Felix' enemy Fl. Aetius.[22] At that very time, Aetius was just beginning to make his mark in Roman politics. As master of soldiers in Gaul, he drove the Goths away from Arles c.425/426, at which time he certainly would have met the bishop of the city. Whatever Patroclus' plans were, he was murdered for his

18. For other accusations of "Manicheism" in Rome, see chapter 7 below.

19. Felix: *P.L.R.E. II* pp.461-462. For Felix and Placidia, see Oost, *Placidia* pp.210-211.

20. "Patroclus Arelatensis episcopus a tribuno quodam Barnabo multis vulneribus laniatus occiditur: quod facinus ad occultam iussionem Felicis magistri militum referebatur cuius impulsu creditum est etiam Titus diaconus vir sanctus Romae pecunias pauperibus distribuens interemptus." See *apparatus criticus* in *M.G.H. A.A.* 9.471 for readings. The two murders apparently, although not necessarily, were two separate incidents.

21. *I.L.S.* no.1293, "Fl. Felix v.c. magister utriusque militiae, patricius et cons. ord. et Padusia eius inl. femina, voti compotes de proprio fecerunt." Murder: see n.27 below.

22. Aetius: *P.L.R.E. II* pp.21-29. For the enmity between Aetius and Felix, see Prosp. *Chron.* 1303 s.a.430.

efforts, and once again a change in the Gallic secular power structure resulted in the replacement of the bishop of Arles.

News of Patroclus' death was met with rejoicing by his Gallic rivals, as noted in a rebuking letter of 26 July 428 from Celestine to the bishops of Viennensis and Narbonensis (*Epist.* "Cuperemus quidem": *P.L.* 50.435–436):

As to the bishop of Marseilles, who is reported—terrible to say—to have rejoiced so much at the death of his brother that he rushed to meet one who arrived spattered with his blood in order to share it with him, we also delegate the investigation of him to your [episcopal] college. . . .[23]

This gloating Massiliote bishop must have been Patroclus' old enemy, the aged Proculus, and his glee indicates how hard the feelings were between them.[24] One notes, moreover, Proculus' alleged meeting with one of those implicated in the murder. If this were so, all the more reason for Patroclus to have allied himself with Aetius. If Proculus were aligned with the party of Felix, the bishop of Arles could have hoped for little support from that quarter.

Proculus and his party then may have been behind another attempt to weaken further the status of Arles. In his letter of 428, Celestine renewed the earlier decree of Boniface, and once again limited the authority of the bishop of Arles to his own province.[25] Thus, any efforts by Patroclus before his death to regain papal recognition of his extraordinary metropolitan status were unsuccessful. It also would have become increasingly clear to the bishops of Arles that they could no longer expect support from Rome in their quest for extraordinary authority.

AETIUS AND THE GALLIC ARISTOCRACY

In 430, Fl. Felix met his own end at the hands of the individual who was to be the master of the secular, and in some ways even the ecclesiastical, affairs of Gaul for the next quarter century, Fl. Aetius.[26] According to Prosper, "Aetius murders Felix, along with his wife Padusia and the deacon Grunitus, when he apprehends them plotting

23. "Massiliensis vero ecclesiae sacerdotem, qui dicitur, quod dictu nefas est, in necem fratris sui taliter gratulatus, ut huic, qui eius sanguine cruentus advenerat, portionem cum eodem habiturus occurreret, et vestro eum audiendum collegio delegamus."

24. Proculus is first attested at Aquileia in 381; Griffe, *Gaule* 1.339, has him alive only as late as 418, but there is no evidence that he did not survive longer, see Duchesne, *Fastes* 1.274. Langgärtner, *Gallienpolitik* p.60, presumes this reference is to Proculus' successor, whom he leaves unnamed.

25. See chapter 5 below, n.34.

26. For Aetius and Gaul, see Moss, "Policies"; Stroheker, *Adel* pp.50-51; Twyman, "Aetius"; and Zecchini, *Aezio* passim.

against him."[27] Aetius, however, did not benefit immediately from Felix' death, and for the next several years was engaged in a another struggle for influence, this time primarily with the count of Africa, Boniface.[28]

The canvassing by these two for allies seems to have extended even to Gaul, for Sidonius recalled how an unnamed Cadurcan chose to follow Boniface and his son Sebastian, whereas the Ligurian Quintianus opted for Aetius.[29] Because both were "the greatest comrades" of Sidonius' father and his friends, the perceived need to choose sides might have been distressing indeed.

In 432, Aetius was defeated, and Boniface killed, near Rimini. Aetius then was forced into retirement, and after "a certain enemy" attempted to kill him, he fled to his friends among the Huns.[30] With their support, he returned to power and became first *magister militum* in 433 and then *patricius* in 435.[31] For the rest of his life, Aetius spent much of his time campaigning in Gaul, perhaps because he considered it essential for the defense of the empire, perhaps because that was where he had the strongest support, or perhaps both.[32] Any aristocratic Gauls associated with him now would have been in an advantageous position.

The extant evidence indicates that on both the secular and ecclesiastical levels some Gauls got along with the patrician very well.[33] In general, the Gallic sources portray him in a favorable light, including *The Gallic Chronicle of 452*, Constantius of Lyons' *Vita s. Germani Autissiodorensis*, and Sidonius Apollinaris, not to mention the Spanish bishop Hydatius.[34] One Gaul who cooperated with Aetius was Epar-

27. "Aetius Felicem cum uxore Padusia et Grunito diacono, cum eos insidiari sibi praesensisset, interimit" (*Chron.* 1303 s.a.430). Hydatius (*Chron.* 94) notes "Felix qui dicebatur patricius Ravenna tumulto occiditur militari."

28. For this conflict, see Bury, *L.R.E.* pp.240-249; Oost, *Placidia* pp.232-233; Seeck, *Untergang* pp.113-117; and Stein, *Geschichte* pp.478-479.

29. *Carm.* 9.277-295. The Cadurcan ultimately surfaced in Athens, his change of home perhaps, in part, a result of the fortunes of his party in the west. On him, see Mathisen, "Aquitania" p.164 n.18. In 413, Boniface had driven the Visigoths from Marseilles and acquired supporters there (Olymp. fr.21).

30. Prosp. *Chron.* 1310 s.a.432.

31. *P.L.R.E.* II p.24.

32. For Aetius and the Gallic aristocracy, see Matthews, *Aristocracies* pp.338-339; Moss, "Policies" pp.716-718; Oost, *Placidia* pp.235-238; and Twyman, "Aetius" pp.485-487, 494-500.

33. Ecclesiastics: chapter 7, nn.62-65 below. There is no evidence, however, that "a group of Gallic landowners" supported Aetius in the senate at Rome, as suggested by Moss, "Policy" p.716.

34. *Chron. gall.* 452 nos.100, 102, 106, 109, 111-112, 115, 118, 123, 127, 139; Sid. Apoll. *Carm.* 5.120, 275, 306, 7.230-359, *Epist.* 7.12.3; *VGermani* 28. See also the later *VOrientii* and *VAniani*. The only Gallic writer, and he an expatriate, to portray Aetius negatively was Prosper Tiro in his *Chronicle* (s.a.430, 432, 439, 440, 454); see Täckholm, "Aetius" p.260; as well as Seeck, *Untergang* p.114; and Stein, *Geschichte* 1.477-478.

chius Avitus, who fought with him in 435 against the Burgundians, became *magister militum per Gallias* in 438 and *praefectus praetorio Galliarum* in 439, and helped Aetius obtain the help of the Visigoths against Attila in 451.[35] In this last instance, assistance also was rendered by another Gallic aristocrat, the praetorian prefect of Gaul, Tonantius Ferreolus.[36] Aetius also sent the Gaul Constantius to serve as the *notarius* of Attila, and, presumably, to spy upon him as well.[37]

Some landowners, however, would have had no love for Aetius, for in 442 "The Alans, to whom lands in the further part of Gaul were granted by the patrician Aetius to be divided with the inhabitants, overcame armed resistance and having expelled the owners seize possession of the land by force."[38] Other evidence concerns Aetius' role in Gallic ecclesiastical politics. It will be seen below that he was every bit as involved in this arena as had been Constantine III and Constantius before him.

THE CIRCLE OF LÉRINS: ECCLESIASTICAL, FAMILIAL, LITERARY, SECULAR[39]

After the assassination of Patroclus in 426, the see of Arles fell into the control of a group of aristocratic, influential, and often interrelated monks, many of whom were not even from Provence but rather had their origins further north, primarily in eastern Lugdunensis.[40] One of these was Honoratus, whose life was described in a eulogy, the *Sermo de vita s. Honorati*, delivered circa 430 by his relative and successor as bishop of Arles, Hilary.[41]

Honoratus, a member of a consular family, left the north early in the century and traveled in the east, where his brother Venantius died in Greece, and to Italy (*VHonorati* 12-14). He then returned to Gaul and settled c.400/410 with a certain Caprasius on the barren island of Lerinum (Lérins, St. Honorat), off the Gallic coast between Antibes

---

35. Sid. Apoll. *Carm.* 7.230ff; *P.L.R.E. II* pp.196-198.
36. Sid. Apoll. *Epist.* 7.12; *P.L.R.E. II* pp.465-466.
37. Priscus fr.8; *P.L.R.E. II* p.319.
38. "Alani, quibus terrae Galliae ulterioris cum incolis dividendae a patricio Aetio traditae fuerant, resistentes armis subigunt et expulsis dominis terrae possessionem vi adipiscuntur...." (*Chron. gall. 452* no.127 s.a.442).
39. For Lérins, see Bardy et. al., *Eglise* p.403; Jalland, *Leo* p.113ff; Koch, *Faustus* pp.5-6; Pricoco, *L'isola*; Prinz, *Mönchtum* pp.1-48; Stroheker, *Adel* p.72; and Travers-Smith, *Gaul* pp.259-272.
40. On the homeland of these monks, see Mathisen, "Hilarius" passim; Prinz, *Mönchtum* pp.47-49.
41. For Honoratus, see Griffe, *Gaule* 2.241ff; Heinzelmann, "Prosopographie" p.626; Mathisen, "Addenda" p.376; Prinz, *Mönchtum* pp.47-49; and Stroheker, *Adel* p.196.

and Fréjus, "enchanted by the nearness and embraced by the affection of bishop Leontius [of Fréjus]."[42] He apparently, therefore, had the cooperation of the bishop who had jurisdiction over the island. Leontius, or someone, then ordained him as a presbyter, but Hilary also stated that (ibid.16),

he appeared there as a presbyter most worthy not only of double but even of multiple honor, in whose presence episcopal office acknowledged no difference in rank, no nominal privilege. No bishop ever usurped so much to himself that he considered himself a colleague of that presbyter.[43]

From the beginning, then, it seems that Honoratus did not fully recognize the status and authority of several local bishops, and Hilary's rosy picture of cooperation among them cannot conceal this reality.

Hilary also rhetorically asked, "What land, moreover, what nation does not have its citizens in that monastery?" and asserted that Honoratus assembled a "congregation gathered from different parts of the land," where "all thought that in it their homeland and family and all like things had been returned to them."[44] These other monks included Honoratus' family and friends, and other northerners.[45] One such was Salvian, a native of perhaps Trier or Cologne, who later became a presbyter at Marseilles.[46] Even after his departure, Salvian wrote back to his ex-brethren asking them to accept into the monastery a young relative of his who had fled from Cologne, indicating that he remained on good terms with them.[47]

In the early to mid 420s Honoratus induced his younger relative Hilary, who seems to have come from near Dijon, to join him at

---

42. "Leonti episcopi [sc. Foroiuliensis] oblectatus vicinia et caritate constrictus" (ibid.15): see Pricoco, L'isola pp.35-40 and Prinz, Mönchtum pp.47-50. On Lerinum and its neighbor Lero see Pliny H.N. 3.79; Ptol. Geog. 2.9/21; and Strabo 4.1; see also Pricoco, L'isola p.25. A late and derivative vita (A.A.S.S. June I pp.75-78) describes Caprasius as "spectabilis genere" and a philosopher: see Heinzelmann, "Prosopographie" p.574.

43. "apparuit illic presbyter non duplici tantum sed et multiplici honore dignissimus, coram quo nullam sacerdotii distantiam, nullum nominis privilegium episcopatus agnosceret. nemo umquam episcoporum sibi tantum usurpavit, ut se presbyteri illius collegam conputaret." For Honoratus' office, see also Paul. Nol. Epist. 51.1, "conpresbyter meus Honoratus."

44. "quae adhuc terra, quae natio in monasterio illius cives suos non habet.... congregatio ... ex diversa terrarum parte collecta ... omnes ... in illo sibi patriam ac propinquos et omnia simul reddita conputantes" (VHonorati 17-19). Cassian of Marseilles described Honoratus as (Coll. 11 praef.1) "ingenti fratrum coenobio praesidens," and Ennodius (VAntonii: M.G.H. A.A. 7.185-190) described the monastery as "illam dominici gregis legionem ... variatam gentibus." Hilary also noted, however (VHonorati 33), that some monks later decided to return home.

45. For the identity of the monks, see Pricoco, L'isola pp.40-59: "Gli asceti di Lerino da Onorato a Fausto. Dati prosopografici" and Prinz, Mönchtum pp.47-54.

46. Salvian: Chadwick, Poetry pp.160-163; Griffe, Gaule 2.40ff; Heinzelmann, "Prosopographie" p.688; Mathisen, "Addenda" pp.383-384; Pricoco, L'isola pp.53-54; and Prinz, Mönchtum pp.53-54. Travers-Smith, Gaul p.336 suggests he moved c.429/430.

47. Salv. Epist. 1.

Lérins.[48] Hilary may have been a relative, even the son, of the Hilarius who was prefect of Gaul in 396 and prefect of Rome in 408.[49] Shortly thereafter, c.425/426, he was joined by the brothers Vincentius and Lupus of Toul, the former being an ex-secular official, and the latter the husband of Hilary's sister Pimeniola.[50] At about the same time Maximus, a native of Riez, entered the monastery as Honoratus' successor.[51] His biographer Faustus noted that "for a long time he served as a soldier for Christ in secular garb," and that he became a monk "after secular service."[52] Maximus' secular office, however, is unknown.[53] At about the same time would have appeared Maximus' protégé the Briton, or perhaps Breton, Faustus, who was to succeed his mentor both as abbot at Lérins and as bishop of Riez.[54] Later in the century, monastic recruits included a certain Antiolus, probably another northerner, who was described by Sidonius as "a cellmate of the Lupuses and Maximuses," and the monk Antonius of Valeria in Pannonia, the nephew of a bishop Constantius.[55]

48. Hilary: Cristiani, *Lérins* pp.99ff; Griffe, *Gaule* 2.244-250; Heinzelmann, "Prosopographie" p.625; Kidd, *Church* pp.355-359; and Prinz, *Mönchtum* p.50. Origin: Mathisen, "Hilarius" pp.167-168. Pricoco, *L'isola* pp.38-39, 49-50, suggests he was from Belgica, whereas Duval, *Gaule* p.725, repeats the older error that he was from Provence. He was forty-eight at the time of his death in 449 (*VHilarii* 18[24]); he therefore was born c.401/402.

49. See Heinzelmann, "Prosopographie" p.624, and Mathisen, "Petronius" pp.106-112.

50. Vincentius: Vinc. *Comm.* 1, "cum aliquandiu variis ac tristibus saecularis militiae turbinibus volveremur" and Greg. Tur. *Glor. conf.* 66; see Griffe, *Gaule* 3.375ff; Heinzelmann, "Prosopographie" p.715; Pricoco, *L'isola* p.52-53; and Prinz, *Mönchtum* p.52. Lupus: *VLupi* passim; see Griffe, *Gaule* 2.301-304; Heinzelmann, "Prosopographie" p.641; Pricoco, *L'isola* pp.51-52 (see n.102 for the validity of the *vita*); and Prinz, *Mönchtum* p.51. The date is based upon *VLupi* 1-4: Lupus spent one year at Lérins, and became bishop two years before going to Britain in 429.

51. Maximus: Griffe, *Gaule* 2.260-262; Heinzelmann, "Prosopographie" p.651; and Pricoco, *L'isola* p.48.

52. "diu ille sub habitu saeculari, Christi militem gessit" (*VMaximi*: *P.L.S.* 3.633).

53. Faustus' allusions to Maximus as a *dux* do not necessarily mean that he was a high-ranking military officer: such terminology was common in the ecclesiastical writings of this period. Maximus' involvement with *leges* (ibid.), however, could suggest that, like Germanus of Auxerre, he had been an *advocatus*. The late sixth-century *Vita Maximi* by the patrician Dynamius of Marseilles (*P.L.* 80.31-40) adds little of substance except that Maximus was a native of the *vicus Decomecus* (Château-Redon near Digne: Prinz, *Mönchtum* p.55). See also Greg. Tur. *Glor. conf.* 82.

54. For Faustus' origin, see Sid. Apoll. *Epist.* 9.9.6 ("Britannis tuis") and Alc. Avit. *Epist.* 4 ("ortu Britannum"). Prinz, *Mönchtum* pp.54, 65, suggests that Faustus left Britain when the island was evacuated by Rome. For a Breton origin, see Griffe, *Gaule*, 2.262; the common objection that the term "Britannus" could not refer to an Armorican this early is belied, for example, by Sidonius (*Epist.* 1.7.5, 3.9.2, 9.9.6) and *Corp. chr. lat.* 148.148, where an "episcopus Britannorum" attended a council in Lugdunensis III in 461. See also N. Chadwick, "Contacts" pp.254-263 and *Poetry* pp.192-207; Engelbrecht, *C.S.E.L.* 21.vi-xi; Griffe, *Gaule* 2.145ff, 2.262-265, 3.340ff; Heinzelmann, "Prosopographie" p.607; Koch, *Faustus* passim; Morris, *Arthur* pp.338-343; and Weigel, *Faustus* passim.

55. Antiolus: "Luporum concellita Maximorumque" (Sid. Apoll. *Epist.* 8.14.2): he was a good friend of Principius of Soissons and Remigius of Rheims, hence his probable northern origin. See Pricoco, *L'isola* pp.56-57; he is omitted from Heinzelmann, "Prosopographie." An-

Nor was Honoratus' the only monastery to be founded in the area. By about 410 a Eucherius, who may have been another northerner, had established a monastery of his own on the neighboring island of Lero (St. Marguerite) with his wife Galla and two sons Salonius and Veranus.[56] By c.420, he and his family had moved to Lérins.[57] In 431 he encouraged his relative Valerianus, probably the son of the praetorian prefect of Gaul Priscus Valerianus, to take up the monastic life, and he too seems to have become a monk at Lérins.[58]

In his *De laude heremi*, moreover, Eucherius discussed the personnel at Lérins after the departure of Honoratus in 426/427: "It now holds his successor, the notable Maximus by name. . . . It had Lupus of the worshipful name, it had his brother Vincentius, it now possesses Caprasius, venerable in age, it now has those blessed elders. . . ."[59] There is no indication who the "blessed elders" are; perhaps they are to be identified with at least some of the *patres* mentioned by Cassian and by the *Gallic Chronicle*.[60]

The close ties among these monks and their associates soon became a commonplace for contemporary and later writers. Cassian of Marseilles, for example, linked Honoratus, Leontius of Fréjus, Eucherius, and another likely monk of Lérins, Helladius.[61] The *Gallic Chronicle*

---

tonius: Ennod. *VAntonii* (*M.G.H. A.A.* 7.185–190). Only his last two years were spent at Lérins; previously he had lived in the mountains near Como in Italy; see Heinzelmann, "Prosopographie" p.555. For the tradition that St. Patrick of Ireland stayed at Lérins, see note 125 below.

56. Lero: Paul. Nol. *Epist.* 51.2. Eucherius: de Montauzan, "Saint Eucher"; Gouilloud, *St. Eucher*; Mellier, *Vita*; and Prinz, *Mönchtum* pp.52-53. Eucherius' ties to Lugdunensis are suggested by his relative Priscus Valerianus of Lyons (see Mathisen, "Petronius" pp.110-112), although a late *vita* of his supposed daughter Consortia (*A.A.S.S.* June V pp.214-217) places the family in the valley of the Durance (but in the early sixth century).

57. See Cristiani, *Lérins* pp.193-275; Griffe, *Gaule* 2.286-289, 3.376 (c.420); Heinzelmann, "Prosopographie" p.598 (c.410), 709; Prinz, *Mönchtum* pp.47, 52 (after 426); and Travers-Smith, *Gaul* p.322 (c.409/410).

58. Valerianus' father and father-in-law were both of illustrious rank (Euch. *Epist. ad Valer.* p.712); for the identification, see Mathisen, "Petronius" p.111. Eucherius stated that he wrote his letter in the 185th year after the millenium (A.D.247), that is, in 431 (*P.L.* 50.722). Valerianus later wrote an extant letter to his brethren of Lérins (*P.L.* 755-758, see also *Corp. chr. lat.* 148.132), on which see Bardy, "Ecoles" p.17 and Prinz, *Mönchtum* pp.57-60. Pricoco, *L'isola* pp.58-60 and Weiss, "Valérien" pp.144-145, however, question whether the author of the letter ever was a monk at Lérins.

59. "haec nunc successorem eius [sc. Honorati] tenet, Maximum nomine, clarum . . . haec habuit reverendi nominis Lupum . . . haec habuit germanum eius Vincentium . . . haec nunc possidet venerabilem gravitate Caprasium . . . haec nunc habet sanctos senes illos. . . ." (*De laud. herem.* 42).

60. In the mid 420s, Cassian dedicated various parts of his *Collationes* to Castor, Honoratus, Eucherius, Iovinianus, Minervius, Leontius, and Theodorus. Note also *Chron. gall. 452* no.86 (s.a.419): "Honoratus, Minervius, Castor, Iovianus singulorum monasteriorum patres in Galliis florent." Like Eucherius, some may have relocated to Lérins.

61. Cass. *Coll. praef.*

of 452 discussed Hilary, Honoratus, and Eucherius, as well as Cassian and Germanus of Auxerre.[62] Faustus, after becoming bishop of Riez, recalled the ties between Honoratus and Caprasius.[63] The author of the late fifth-century *Vita Hilarii*, himself named Honoratus and a protégé, as well as a probable relative, of Hilary, told of the latter's friendship with Caprasius, the presbyter and future abbot Faustus, and the monks and *sacerdotes* Theodorus [later of Fréjus] and Maximus [later of Riez], the last two of whom he had come and live with him at Arles c.430.[64]

Sidonius Apollinaris noted the ties among Faustus, then bishop of Riez, and Caprasius, Honoratus, Maximus, Eucherius and Hilary; among Antiolus, Lupus, and Maximus, and between Lupus and Germanus of Auxerre.[65] Constantius of Lyons told of Germanus' friendship with Hilary, Lupus and Eucherius.[66] In 568 Nicetius of Trier could recall the association among Hilary, Germanus, and Lupus.[67] Even the twelfth-century *Chronicle* of Sigisbert noted under the year 435, "Germanus Antisiodorensis, Lupus Trecassinus, Eucherius Lugdunensis, Hilarius Arelatensis episcopi in Galliis clarent."[68]

The late *Vita Domitiani*, moreover, provides a virtual gazetteer of the Lérins circle.[69] Supposedly born at Rome "at the time of the emperor Constantius," Domitianus then

traveled all the way to Marseilles, whence, having remained for a while with "Silvanus" [i.e. Salvianus], he continued on to the island of Lérins, where, having remained for one year, he related everything which had happened to him to the father Vincentius, a most learned and erudite presbyter, and to the brothers....[70]

Then, after spending some time with Hilary of Arles, and having been ordained a presbyter, "hearing of the sanctity of the blessed Eu-

---

62. *Chron. gall. 452* nos. 86, 104, 114, 134. For Germanus' ties to the circle, see n.111 below.

63. *Sermo in depositione s. Honorati* (*P.L.S.* 3.691).

64. Honoratus: Gennad. *Vir. ill.* 100, Hilary: *VHilarii* 9(12).

65. *Carm.* 16.104-115; *Epist.* 8.14.2, 8.15.1.

66. *VGerm.* 12-19, 23; see note 111 below.

67. *M.G.H. Epist.* 3.121.

68. *M.G.H. S.S.* 6.308. The source of this reference is unclear: no known earlier source mentioned these four all together; the *Gallic Chronicle* does mention Hilary, Germanus, and Eucherius, but not Lupus.

69. *A.A.S.S.* July I pp.44-50, see Heinzelmann, "Prosopographie" p.592, where the *vita* is dated "kaum vor dem 9. Jh."

70. "Marsiliam usque pervenit, ubi cum Silvano [sic] eruditissimo presbytero aliquamdiu commoratus, Lirinensem usque peragravit insulam, in qua uno anno conversatus, cuncta, quae ei acciderant, patri Vincentio doctissimo ac disertissimo presbytero narravit, et fratribus...." (*VDomitiani* 3). The Constantius generally is assumed to have been Constantius II (A.D.337-361), but it would be more consistent with the rest of the *vita* if he were Constantius III (A.D.421).

cherius, bishop of Lyons, a famous city of Gaul, he entered Lyons with the greatest haste, desiring to see him."[71] Eucherius then established him in a monastery in the territory of Lyons.[72] In spite of, or perhaps because of, its late date, this *vita* exemplifies the great influence that this tightly knit monastic circle had upon the later Gallic imagination.

Now, some of these aristocratic monks, like Honoratus, Faustus, Vincentius, and Salvian, also obtained clerical office.[73] Most, however, remained laymen, and, as seen already in the case of Honoratus, were under the direct authority not of the neighboring bishop of Fréjus but of the abbot, who was chosen by the monks themselves.[74]

One can only speculate about why so many aristocrats from influential families decided to retreat into an isolated southern monastery. Certainly, true religious motivations and convictions were a primary consideration. Much attention, for example, has been given to their pursuit of isolation and the ascetic ideal.[75] Paulinus of Nola wrote to Eucherius about escape "from the confusion of this world."[76] Hilary of Arles told how Honoratus settled on an "island, uninhabited on account of its excess of squalor, and unvisited for fear of venemous animals."[77] Vincentius wrote, "Avoiding the turmoil and crowds of cities, I inhabit a little dwelling on a remote farmstead and within it the retreat of a monastery."[78] Faustus preached, "We will imitate God, moreover, by abandoning the world, by not avenging injuries, by forsaking our own desires ... by refusing honors."[79]

The disillusionment of the Lerinenses with the secular world was summed up by Eucherius in 431 in his *Letter on the Contempt of the World and Secular Philosophy* (*P.L.* 50.717):

71. "audiens beati Eucherii sanctitatem, episcopi Lugdunensis inclytae urbis Galliarum summa cum festinatione, illum videre desiderans, Lugdunum ingreditur. . . ." (ibid.4).

72. Domitianus also is described by Ado (*Mart.* [July 1]: *P.L.*123.295) as one "qui primum illic [in territorio Lugdunensi] eremiticam vitam exercuit."

73. Faustus: *VHilarii* 9[12]; Vincentius and Salvian: Gennad. *Vir. ill.* 65, 68. They need not, however, have obtained their offices at Lérins.

74. "omnis laica multitudo ad curam abbatis pertineat. . . . laica vero omnis congregatio ad solam ac liberam abbatis proprii quem sibi elegerit ordinationem dispositionemque pertineat" (*Corp. chr. lat.* 148.134), see also chapter 8 below, and Jones, *L.R.E.* p.933, and Prinz, *Mönchtum* p.57.

75. See Fontaine, "L'ascétisme" pp.87-115; Heinzelmann, *Bischofsherrschaft* pp.73-98,185-211; and Pricoco, *L'isola* pp.25-59, 131-186.

76. "ab istius mundi strepitu" (*Epist.* 51.2).

77. "vacantem itaque insulam ob nimietatem squaloris et inaccessam venenatorum animalium metu" (*VHonorati* 15).

78. "urbium frequentiam turbasque vitantes remotioris villulae et in ea secretum monasterii incolamus habitaculum. . . ." (*Comm.* 1).

79. "imitabimur autem deum neglegendo saeculum, iniurias non persequendo, voluntates proprias respuendo ... honores ... declinando" (*Serm.* 2, *De nativitate*: *C.S.E.L.* 21.229).

There now is a certain tale among us of recent and renowned kingdoms: all those things which were great here now are non-existent. Nothing, I think, or rather I certainly know, from those powers, honors, kingdoms did they take with them, unless, if there was any in them, the substance of faith and piety.[80]

Such thoughts seem to express the attitude of Eucherius and his circle not only about secular ideals in general, but also about the suppression of the earlier Gallic revolts in particular.

Such sentiments, however, do not completely explain the phenomenon. The desire for solitude and withdrawal from secular life could have been fulfilled equally well closer to home. In search of a further explanation, some have seen the monasteries as aristocratic refuges from the barbarian invasions in the north.[81] Others have noted Hilary's remark about Honoratus, "To what extent did he not alleviate barbarism," and suggested that the monasteries were a response to a socio-cultural crisis caused by the barbarian inroads.[82] These reasons also are not totally satisfactory. Even if trouble in the far north, as around Trier and Cologne, could explain the departures of such as Salvian, the area of eastern Lugdunensis remained relatively untouched by the barbarian occupation.

It may be that some of the monks' disenchantment with the secular world also was influenced by more immediate, personal considerations. Circa 428, Eucherius, after asking in his *De laude heremi*, "Who indeed can fittingly enumerate the benefits of the monastery?", responded, "There the human ordinances of accusations and crimes do not transmit their force and assert avenging laws concerning capital crimes."[83] A strange point to make if some did not have exactly such thoughts in mind. Added to this is Faustus' claim that Maximus escaped to Lérins c.427 "from the dangers of an enemy"; an idle reader might assume the enemy was Satan, but perhaps someone more corporeal was meant.[84]

The large influx of new monks such as Hilary, Lupus, Vincentius, Faustus, and Maximus in the mid-420s occurred at the same time as

---

80. "recentium inclytorumque regnorum apud nos iam quaedam fabula est, omnia illa, quae hic erant magna, modo iam nulla sunt. nihil, ut puto, immo, ut certo scio, ex illis opibus, honoribus, regnis, secum abstulerunt, nisi (si qua in his fuit) fidei pietatisque substantiam."

81. See Prinz, "Lerinum als 'Flüctlingskloster' der nordgallischen Aristokratie," *Mönchtum* pp.147-158.

82. "quam ille barbariem non mitigavit?" (*VHonorati* 17). See Pricoco, *L'isola* pp.61-63.

83. "quis enim enumerare beneficia eremi digne queat . . . non illic humana criminum facinorumque praescripta vim suam resonant nec se ultricia capitalium delictorum iura exserunt. . . ." (*De laud. herem.* 31, 35). Faustus, in a more religious context, also mentions "capitalibus criminibus" and "capitala crimina" (*Serm.* 24 *Ad monachos II*: *C.S.E.L.* 21.319-320).

84. "ab inimici periculis" (*P.L.S.* 3.634).

great secular turmoil. There was the usurpation of Johannes at Rome, the murder of a prefect at Arles, the Valentinian restoration, the Visigothic attack on Arles, and the murder of Patroclus. Memories of the imperial purges after the last series of revolts would have been very fresh in everyone's mind. What better place to seek security, therefore, than in an isolated southern monastery?[85] These aristocrats could not have anticipated that the imperial restoration in Gaul would be accomplished as smoothly as it seems to have been. When this did turn out to be the case, some of the new arrivals may have felt secure enough to leave: Lupus remained only one year, and Hilary went to Arles soon thereafter.[86]

Perhaps a sense of danger shared and avoided, therefore, also helped to foster a strong sense of solidarity among these monks of Lérins. Additional factors would have been their similar aristocratic status, place of origin, monastic experience, and blood ties.[87] One significant way in which this sense of solidarity manifested itself was in their joint pursuit of literary interests.[88] The monks' love of literature is seen in the great number of extant works which they wrote. No fewer than six contemporaries of Lérins, for example, wrote extant letters (Hilary [1], Eucherius [6], Salvian [10], Lupus [1], Valerianus [1], and Faustus [11]).[89] Furthermore, Hilary noted that Honoratus too was an epistolographer, saying, "He carried out his duties of letter-writing."[90] None of his letters survive, although he is known to have corresponded with the expatriate Gaul Meropius Pontius Paulinus, who became bishop of Nola in the early fifth century: on one occasion Honoratus sent the three monks Gelasius, Augendus, and Tigridius to visit him.[91]

Of course, in a group many of whose members ultimately were to be dispersed throughout Gaul, letter-writing would have been one of the most appropriate ways for them to stay in touch.[92] Eucherius

85. On similar possible ulterior motives for the earlier withdrawal of Paulinus of Nola, see Matthews, *Aristocracies* p.152 and Moricca, "Morte violenta."

86. Vincentius and Salvian may have left at about this time as well.

87. See Heinzelmann, *Bischofsherrschaft* p.81; Langgärtner, *Gallienpolitik* p.65; Mathisen, "Hilarius" passim and "Epistolography" pp.104-106; and Pricoco, *L'isola* pp.59-61, who sees this as a "processo per il le ultime famiglie senatoriali si trasformarono in famiglie sacerdotali."

88. Most if not all the monks had received the standard classical education. Some scholars, such as Bardy, "Ecoles" pp.101-103 and Hagendahl, *Tertullian* p.95, suppose that pagan literature had no place at Lérins, but others believe the monks did not totally abandon their classical heritage, see Courcelle, "Culture" and Glorie, "Culture." Faustus of Riez, for example, was not averse to citing classical authors such as Vergil and Juvenal (*C.S.E.L.* 31.468).

89. For these works, see Mathisen, "Epistolography" pp.104-107.

90. "litterarum officia perlata sunt" (*VHonorati* 22).

91. Paul. Nol. *Epist.* 51: *C.S.E.L.* 29.424.

92. See Matthews, *Aristocracies* pp.152-153, for "how important it was considered that such friendships among social equals should be fostered by the frequent exchange of letters."

would not have been the only one of them to write, as he did to Hilary c.428, "You demand that I respond more copiously to your most lengthy and most learned letters."[93] Circa 450, Valerianus of Cimiez could write to the monks, "Nor, indeed, do I travel a road unknown to spiritual men if I express my solicitude for your edification in writings of epistolary eloquence."[94] Epistolography even was seen as a literary genre especially appropriate for clerics. Sidonius later could assert, "I have transferred every kind of care to the cultivation of letter-writing, so that I would not be guilty of writing poetry."[95]

The Lerinenses also wrote other works. Hilary wrote poetry, a *Sermo de vita s. Genesii*, and the *Sermo de vita s. Honorati*.[96] Eucherius wrote an epitome of Cassian's *Institutiones*, a *Passio acaunensium martyrum*, and educational texts for his sons, as well as other works "necessary for both ecclesiastical and monastic studies."[97] Vincentius wrote a *Commonitorium* and some *Excerpta* from Augustine.[98] Salvian wrote the extant *De gubernatione dei* (or *De praesenti iudicio*), the *Ad ecclesiam* (or *Adversus avaritiam*), several letters, as well as a lost *Commentary on Ecclesiastes*, a *De virginitate bono*, a verse *Hexaemeron*, homilies and *sacramentarii*.[99] Faustus' extant works include a *De gratia*, a *De spiritu sancto*, a *De ratione fidei*, an *Adversus Arrianos et Macedonianos*, and several letters.[100] Eucherius, Valerianus, and Faustus also published sermons.[101]

A good indication of the combined familial-cultural atmosphere provided by the monastery is seen in the education of the boys Salonius and Veranus not only by their father Eucherius but also by Hilary, Salvian, Honoratus, and Vincentius.[102] Even after they were separated

93. "quia me respondere copiosius spatiosissimis ac facundissimis litteris tuis saepe postulas" (*De laud. herem.* 3).

94. "nec sane incognitam spiritalibus viam teneo, si aedificationis vestrae sollicitudinem sermonibus eloqui epistolaris expromo" (*P.L.* 52.755).

95. "ad epistularum / transtuli cultum genus omne curae / ne reus cantu . . . / sim" (*Epist.* 9.16.3 *carm.* 49-52).

96. Gennad. *Vir. ill.* 70. Poetry: *Anth. lat.* 1.2.37 no.487, cf. *VHilarii* 11(14). See *Clavis* nos.500-509.

97. "tam ecclesiasticis quam monasticis studiis necessaria" (Gennad. *Vir. ill.* 64). See *Clavis* nos.488-498, 2326. An *Epistula de situ Hierusolimae ad Faustum presbyterum* (*Corp. chr. lat.* 175; *C.S.E.L.* 39.125-134) attributed to Eucherius, even if it is spurious, still attests recollections of the literary circle of Lérins.

98. Gennad. *Vir. ill.* 65; see *Clavis* nos.510-511.

99. Gennad. *Vir. ill.* 68; see *Clavis* nos.485-487.

100. Gennad. *Vir. ill.* 86; see *Clavis* nos.961-977.

101. See *Clavis* nos.966-975a, 1002, 1004; *Corp. chr. lat.* 101 (3 vols.); and *P.L.S.* 3.545ff. See also Bergmann, *Predigtliteratur* pp.1-17; Buytaert, *L'héritage*; Koch, *Faustus* pp.33-39; Leroy, *L'oeuvre*; and Pricoco, *L'isola* pp.55-56 n.123.

102. Euch. *Instruc. ad Salonium praef.* Eucherius also dedicated his *Formulae spiritalis intelligentiae* to his other son Veranus (*C.S.E.L.* 31.3-6). See Mathisen, "Epistolography" pp.105-106. It is difficult to accept the view of Bardy, "Ecoles" p.103, that this is just an isolated example and that the monks otherwise lived isolated lives in their "cells."

from each other, Salvian's and Hilary's ties to the family of Eucherius continued. They corresponded with Eucherius, he sent them review copies of his *Instructiones ad Salonium*, and Salvian corresponded with Salonius and dedicated to him the *De gubernatione dei*.[103] Eucherius, on the other hand, addressed his *De laude heremi* to Hilary.[104] Eucherius' sons, moreover, went on to exercise their literary talents in their own right.[105]

MONKS AS BISHOPS

The phenomenon of monks becoming bishops was particularly common in Gaul. The monk-cum-bishop Martin of Tours saw many of his disciples do so.[106] Nearly a century later, Sidonius Apollinaris could cite the three obvious choices for bishop as a cleric, a monk, and a layman.[107] The bishops of Rome repeatedly, and futilely, attempted to restrict the widespread practice of electing monks, just as they likewise tried to prevent the ordination of *saeculares* "per saltum."[108] In 418, the bishop of Rome, Boniface, wrote to the bishop of Salona (*Epist*. "Exigit dilectio": *P.L.* 20.669ff),

You indicate that [not only] some from the local crowd of monks, but also laymen are hastening to the episcopate. This in particular, however, is known to have been forbidden, both by my predecessors and recently by me, in letters sent to Gaul and Spain, in which areas this presumption is common....[109]

These letters to Gaul and Spain do not survive, but a well-known Gallic example of the practice, perhaps one of the cases of which Boniface spoke, occurred on 7 July 418, in the same year as Boniface's

103. See Salv. *Epist*. 2, 8 (to Eucherius), 9 (to Salonius), and *De gub. praef.*; Hilary (to Eucherius) in *C.S.E.L.* 31.197-198.

104. *C.S.E.L.* 31.177-194; see Opelt, "De laude eremi."

105. *P.L.* 54.887, see also Besson, "Un évêque"; *Clavis* no.499; Curti, *Salonii Commentarii*, *Salonii De evangelio*, and *Due Commentarii*; Pricoco, *L'isola* p.48; and Schanz, *Geschichte* p.529. For suggestions of later dates for some of these works, see Flint, "True Author" and Weiss, "Essai."

106. Sulp. Sev. *VMart*. 10.

107. *Epist*. 7.9.9-14.

108. Note Innoc. *Epist*. "Etsi tibi" (forbidding ordination of *curiales*) and Zos. *Epist*. "Quid de Proculi." See also Duchesne, *Fastes* 1.112-113; Griffe, *Gaule* 1.366-381; Hefele-Leclercq, *Conciles* 2.430-431; Parisot, "Ordinationes"; and Prinz, *Mönchtum* pp.59-62.

109. "significas nonnullos ex monachorum populari coetu ... sed et laicos ad sacerdotium festinare. hoc autem specialiter et sub praedecessoribus nostris, et nuper a nobis interdictum constat, litteris ad Gallias Hispaniasque transmissis, in quibus regionibus familiaris est ista praesumptio...." There was no known imperial ruling on this matter. *C. Th*. 16.2.32 [26 July 398] did allow bishops to ordain monks as priests, and *C. Th*. 16.2.33 [27 July 398] suggested that parish clergy should be local people. For other laws, see Joannou, *Legislation* passim. For similar letters to Gaul and Spain, see Jaffé, no.338 p.50.

letter, when the *dux* Germanus was forcibly consecrated bishop of
Auxerre.[110] Now, Germanus was a good friend of both Eucherius and
Hilary, and like them, a native of eastern Lugdunensis.[111] Even
though he is not known to have been a monk at Lérins, like his brethren to the south he did found his own monastery outside Auxerre.[112]

It was in a similar acquisition of episcopal office that the group
solidarity and shared interests of the monks of Lérins also manifested
themselves. As early as 428, Eucherius could claim that Lérins "both
nourished the most outstanding monks and sent forth the most
sought-after bishops."[113] By the mid-420s this group of expatriate
northerners and allied southerners had gained sufficient influence and
prestige so as to be able to obtain, on a fairly regular basis (at least
until c.540), not only the see of Arles, the most prestigious and powerful one in Gaul, but also several other ones as well. They often did
so, as will be seen, with the support of the secular authorities in Gaul,
and therefore continued the pattern, which had been established under Constantine III and Constantius, of outsiders becoming the bishops of Arles with or without the support of the locals.

The successor of the murdered Patroclus of Arles in 426 was a
shadowy figure named Helladius, or perhaps Euladius, whose tenure
in office seems to have been less than a year and whose very existence
was questioned until recently.[114] Helladius appears first in the mid-

110. *VGermani* 2, see Duchesne, *Fastes* 2.439-445; *P.L.R.E. II* pp.504-505. He usually is assumed to have been *dux tractus Armoricani et Nervicani*. Wood, "End" pp.9-12, however, denies
Germanus' *ducatus* altogether, insisting that it is merely "allegorical." According to a late version
of his *vita* (*A.A.S.S.* July VII p.202), Germanus was ordained with the permission of the Gallic
prefect "Julius," who has been identified with the contemporary prefect Agricola (*P.L.R.E. II*
p.642).

111. Hilary: *VGermani* 23-24, *VHilarii* 16(21). Eucherius: *VGermani* 23, where Germanus
visits Lyons c.435, and "diversae infirmitates passim benedictione sanantur, praedicationibus
civitas recreatur." He could not have carried out such ministries without the blessing of the
bishop, presumably Eucherius (Borius, *Germain* p.96, suggests that Eucherius' predecessor Senator was still in office, but see appendix "Episcopal Hierarchy" below). Germanus also had other
ties to the area around Lyons. Both he and Eucherius had a special devotion to the martyrs of
the Theban Legion at Acaunum (see Borius, *Germain* pp.28-29). Just west of Lyons, Germanus
later was said to have established the proper date for the festival of St. Julianus at Brioude
(Greg. Tur. *Virt. Iul.* 39). Furthermore, the request for the composition of Germanus' life
came not from the bishop of Auxerre, but from the bishop of Lyons, Patiens, in the 470s, and
the *vita* was written by a Lyonese author, Constantius (Const. *Epist. ad Pat.*: *Sources chrétiennes*
121.112; see Bardy, "Copies" pp.38-39). See also Prinz, *Mönchtum* p.63 and Mathisen, "Hilarius"
pp.161-168.

112. *VGermani* 6. Koch, *Faustus* p.6, and Langgärtner, *Gallienpolitik* p.57 n.16, do suppose
that Germanus was an alumnus of Lérins.

113. "et praestantissimos alat monachos et ambiendos proferat sacerdotes" (*De laud herem.*
42). See also Sid. Apoll. *Carm.* 16.109-110, which has Faustus of Riez "relating to the brothers
how many 'mountains' [i.e. bishops] that flat island sent into the sky."

114. Helladius, even though he appears in the episcopal *fasti* of Arles, was omitted by Duchesne (*Fastes* 1.256). His existence was proven, however, by O. Chadwick, "Euladius" pp.200-
205; see also Griffe, *Gaule* 2.239-241.

420s as an *anachoreta* (monk) as one of dedicatees, along with Leontius of Fréjus and Castor of Apt, of the first ten books of the *Collationes* of Cassian of Marseilles. Shortly thereafter, in the prologue to books 11-17 of the same work, he appears again, this time as a bishop, along with Leontius and two new entries, the *fratres* Honoratus and Eucherius.[115] His only other appearance, as bishop of Arles, is in a letter from Prosper of Aquitaine to Augustine written at about the same time.[116]

Helladius thus was a monk who then became bishop of Arles. One notes, moreover, that his affiliations in the dedications all are with the monastery of Lérins, for Leontius was the neighboring bishop, and Honoratus and Eucherius, of course, were two of its most distinguished alumni. Helladius himself, therefore, perhaps was another monk of Lérins, and as such possibly a northerner, a suggestion which draws support from the evidence of nomenclature. The name Helladius at this time was common in eastern Lugdunensis at Auxerre, where Germanus had just become bishop. In the mid-fourth century a Helladius had been bishop of Auxerre, in the mid-fifth Germanus himself was succeeded by another, an ex-monk of his monastery, and in the late sixth a third Helladius was a presbyter there.[117] It remains unclear, however, whether Helladius, like his predecessors, was the nominee of a high-ranking secular potentate.

Helladius' successor was Honoratus, the founder and first abbot of the monastery of Lérins. He, it would appear, was not a unanimous choice. Immediately after his election in late 426 or early 427, according to his successor and biographer Hilary (*VHonorati* 28),

> his first concern was for concord, and a particular task was to intertwine with a reciprocal affection the faction-ridden fraternity, for special interests were still seething over the episcopal election.... Like an upright Israelite charioteer he rightly knew that it is difficult to exercise any rule over the discordant ... immediately, therefore, discord was excluded....[118]

Given that Hilary was a friendly source, and writing but a few years after these events occurred, one must suppose that Honoratus was indeed faced with serious opposition both before and immediately after his election. Just who these opponents were is not clear. Perhaps

---

115. For the date of Helladius' episcopate, see appendix "Episcopal Hierarchy" below.

116. Aug. *Epist.* 225.9: see chapter 6 below, n.57.

117. Duchesne, *Fastes* 2.444; *Corp. chr. lat.* 148A.271 ("Illadius"). For others, see Mathisen, *Ecclesiastical Aristocracy* pp.439-442.

118. "prima cura ei concordia fuit, et praecipuus labor fraternitatem calentibus adhuc de adsumendo episcopo studiis dissidentem, mutuo amore connectere tamquam probatus Israelis agitator probe noverat non facile quicquam discordantibus imperari ... confestim itaque exclusa discordia...." For the dates, see appendix "Episcopal Hierarchy" below.

the locals, and the party of Patroclus, had their own candidate or candidates.

Although Hilary did not specifically discuss the circumstances of Honoratus' election, he did give a brief but revealing account of his "qualifications" for the job when he rhetorically asked the Arlesians (*VHonorati* 25),

But how did it come about, I ask you, that one so unknown could be summoned from so far? Who fixed in your hearts that favor for one who was absent, not even seen before? Who indeed aroused that desire, so that having orphaned those to whom he had been granted by the lord in the monastery he should be produced for you? It was He, of course, who dispenses all things. . . .[119]

Honoratus, therefore, at least according to Hilary, had been a virtual unknown in Arles before his election. How, then, had he been able to become bishop of such a prestigious see? Hilary's own attribution of the choice to divine intervention, commendable for its piety, may conceal support Honoratus received from influential *saeculares*. For two years later Honoratus died "with powerful men, the prefect and men of praetorian rank, flocking to him," and surrounded by "packed crowds of high-ranking men."[120]

Even though Hilary judiciously refrained from discussing any role played by such potentates in Honoratus' election, it is difficult to see how an unknown outsider could have been elected bishop of Arles without their support. Such men certainly were involved in the election of Honoratus' successor Hilary, as reported by Hilary's biographer Honoratus of Marseilles. After the death of Honoratus, perhaps on 16 January 429, Hilary made the *de rigueur* flight from the city, hoping, perhaps, to be able to fulfil the *topos* of being *raptus ad episcopatum*.[121] Then, according to the younger Honoratus, "That divine power suddenly enflamed the spirit of the illustrious Cassius, who then commanded the soldiers, to seek out an unknown, located afar, hastening, in fact, to isolation. . . . He led a picked number of citizens along with a goodly band of soldiers. . . ."[122]

---

119. "sed unde illud, quaeso, quod tam e longinquo tam ignotus expetitur? quis illam absentis nec prius visi gratiam vestris pectoribus affixit? quis illud desiderium suscitavit, ut orbatis his quibus a domino apud eremum indultus erat, vobis nasceretur? ille utique qui cuncta dispensat. . . ."

120. "confluentibus autem ad se potestatibus praefecto et praefectoriis viris" (*VHonorati* 32); "crebra sublimium virorum agmina" (*VHilarii* 6[9]). In contemporary sources these claims cannot be rejected as mere *topoi*. There is little evidence for who these individuals may have been. Aetius may have been there, as well as Agricola the prefect of 418. The name of the current prefect is unknown; it is unlikely that Amatius, the prefect of 425, still was in office.

121. See Hodgkin, *Italy* 2.428, for "the harmless comedy of the *nolo episcopari*, which was so commonly played in those days." For the date, see appendix "Episcopal Hierarchy" below.

122. "sed illa divinitatis potentia, quae . . . illustris Cassii, qui tunc praeerat militibus, ani-

The similarity between Honoratus' and Hilary's status before their elections, with both being referred to as virtually unknown in the city, is striking. The source of Hilary's support, however, is more clear. He not only was, presumably, the choice of his predecessor and an alumnus of a respected monastery, he also had the backing of an army general, influential citizens, and a troop of soldiers at least.[123] After Hilary had been run to earth "by those packed crowds and guards of civilians and soldiers," the will of the Lord supposedly was made clear when a dove landed on his head and refused to be shooed away.[124] Hilary then duly was ordained bishop, and he, like Germanus, founded a new monastery, the so-called Hilarianum, outside Arles.[125]

A combination of the accounts of Honoratus' and Hilary's elections shows that between them they had the support of secular officials, both civil and military, at the very highest levels in Gaul. If they had such powerful assistance, it becomes easier to explain how these outsiders could be chosen as bishops of the city. Some of the secular adherents of this group, moreover, also may have been northerners. It has been suggested that after the imperial withdrawal from Trier and the north in or soon after 395, many displaced officials and aristocrats settled in the south, especially at Arles.[126] If so, northern ecclesiastics such as Honoratus, Hilary, and others would have had a natural, and influential, secular constituency in the south upon whose support they could draw.

Nor was the see of Arles the only one which partisans of the circle of Lérins were able to occupy. By the year 434 at least eight others of the group also had found sees of their own. The case of Germanus already has been discussed. Others of this group who became bishops were actual ex-monks of Lérins. Lupus, a native of Toul with prop-

---

mum repente succendit, ut ignotum, ut longe positum, ut denique ad eremum properantem ardenter expeteret. . . . electum civium numerum cum non parva manu dirigit militantum. . . ." (*VHilarii* 6[9]).

123. For the otherwise unknown Cassius, see *P.L.R.E. II* p.269, which suggests he was "probably successor of Fl. Aetius 7 as MVM *per Gallias*." Aetius was promoted in 429 (Prosp. *Chron.* s.a.429), which is consistent with Hilary's being ordained in January of that year. See also Mathisen, "Addenda" p.369. The subsequent passage makes it clear that the *militantes* were in fact soldiers, and not civil servants.

124. "ab illis civium militumque frequentibus turbis atque custodiis" (*VHilarii* 6[9]).

125. See *VHilarii* 8(11) and *VCaesarii* 1.12, as well as Benoit, "L'Hilarianum"; Pricoco, *L'isola* p.50; and Prinz, *Mönchtum* p.62. St. Patrick also is said to have been an alumnus variously of Lérins, of Hilary's monastery at Arles, or of Germanus' monastery at Auxerre (see Pricoco, *L'isola* pp.57-58, and Prinz, *Mönchtum* pp.62-63), another indication of the perceived relationship between these two bishops.

126. See Prinz, *Mönchtum* p.48; note the *rationalis* Geminus of Cologne (*P.L.R.E. I* p.389); the *vir praesidalis* Paulus of Rheims (*P.L.R.E. II* p.851); and the Briton Tolosanus, the son of a proconsul (*P.L.R.E. I* p.921).

erty at Mâcon, after but one year of service at the monastery became
bishop of Troyes, also in Lugdunensis Prima, in 427 and served until
c.475.[127] Lupus was both a neighbor and a particularly close associate
of Germanus.[128] He also seems to have faced the same kind of dissension in his clergy as Honoratus did, for his biographer noted, "He
controlled his own clergy with the reins of a vigorous justice."[129] Later
in the century, the aforementioned Antiolus also became a bishop,
presumably in the north where he was a close associate of Principius
of Soissons and Remigius of Rheims.[130]

Eucherius, one of the earliest settlers on the islands, became bishop
of Lyons, the metropolitan city of Lugdunensis Prima, c.427/433.[131] If
he, as suggested above, was a native of that area, he would have been
able to return home to a very powerful position. Like his confrères,
he either founded, or supported, his own local monastery, on the Insula barbara.[132] His two sons Salonius and Veranus later were able to
obtain sees of their own, at Geneva, in the north, and Vence, near
Cimiez, respectively, creating an even more influential ecclesiastical
dynasty.[133] His relative Valerianus became bishop of Cimiez at about
the same time as Eucherius.[134]

The circumstances of two immediately subsequent episcopal elections involving Lerinenses are discussed in the *Sermon on St. Maximus,
Bishop, and Abbot of Lérins* delivered at Riez by Maximus' protégé
Faustus.[135] In 426/427, Maximus, an ex-secular official, had become
Honoratus' successor as abbot at Lérins, apparently at the same time
that he entered the monastery.[136] Faustus then noted that "different
regions sought him [as bishop], but most especially the city closest to
the monastery, which, as you know, lies between here and the island."[137] This was the strategic see of Fréjus, which had Lérins itself

127. See note 50 above.
128. *VGermani* 12-19, *VLupi* 4ff.
129. "clerum quoque suum . . . habenis iustitiae strenuae gubernabat" (*VLupi* 3).
130. Sid. Apoll. *Epist*. 8.14.2. Sidonius calls him a "spectabile caput," i.e. abbot, at Lérins: if
this is true, he could not have become abbot until after the early 450s when Faustus, who had
succeeded Honoratus' successor Maximus, became bishop of Riez.
131. For the date, see appendix "Episcopal Hierarchy."
132. Note a spurious letter supposedly written by Eucherius to these monks (*P.L.* 50.1213;
Clavis no.496).
133. Duchesne, *Fastes* 1.227, 294. For possible ties of the Eucherii in the south in the area of
Vence, see above, note 56. Koch, *Faustus* p.6, wrongly has Salonius as the successor of Eucherius
at Lyons, Veranus as bishop of Geneva, and Constantius of Lyons as a priest at Vienne.
134. For the date, see appendix "Episcopal Hierarchy" below.
135. *Sermo* 34, *De s. Maximo, et episcopo et abbati Lirinensi* (*P.L.S.* 3.633-640).
136. Faustus gives no suggestion that any time passed between the time when Maximus
entered the monastery ("Lirinensis sedem . . . petit") and when he became abbot ("et . . . ibidem
Christi gregem pavit") (*P.L.S.* 3.634). For the date, see appendix "Episcopal Hierarchy" below.
137. "ambiebant illum diversae patriae, sed vel maxime proxima eremi civitas . . . quae inter
locum hunc et insulam (ut nostis) interiacet" (*P.L.S.* 3.636).

under its jurisdiction.[138] According to Faustus, Maximus then fled and hid. Now, if this were only the playing out of the customary "nolo episcopari," something then may have gone awry, for not Maximus but his fellow monk of Lérins Theodorus was named bishop. If Maximus had indeed desired the see, this incident could have been a factor in the bad blood which seems to have existed later between him, as well as his protégé Faustus, and Theodorus.[139] It may be, however, that this evasion was intentional, for "not long afterward [in 433/434], as you remember, when this church [of Riez] had been deprived of a shepherd for its people, a suppliant homeland entrusted to its sons a pious legation, and demanded back its pledge and deposit for more just needs."[140] Once again, Maximus fled, but this time he was apprehended and consecrated bishop of Riez, "no less carried off than elected, and even though he was unwilling."[141] One might suspect that Maximus would not have been disappointed to acquire his home see. He too, then, seems to have founded his own monastery at Riez.[142]

During the years c.426-434, therefore, many monks of Lérins became bishops, usually, with the exception of the bishops of Arles, in their homelands, whether in the north or south.[143] Faustus' justification for Maximus' withdrawal to the monastery and subsequent return home as bishop might also be applied to bishops such as Lupus and others who did the same (P.L.S. 3.635, 640):

He was enriched there so that he might bear interest here, there he was illuminated so that he might shine here . . . he was absent a short while from his homeland so that he might bring overseas wealth and riches back to his homeland. . . . Lucky is the land which bore such a one, and gained a patron in place of a pupil.[144]

Faustus' implied reference was to the spiritual riches and patronage that such a bishop would bring back to his homeland as a result of his

---

138. In point of fact, Antibes is more nearly between Riez and Lérins geographically, but Faustus surely is referring to where these places lay on the Roman road (to get to Antibes, one had to go through Fréjus); and, in any event, Antibes already had a bishop, Armentarius, at this time.

139. See chapter 8 below.

140. "non post longum tempus, ut meministis, sancto orbata pastore populi praesenti ecclesia, piam supplex filiis mandat legationem, reposcit patria iustioribus desideriis pignus ac depositum" (P.L.S. 3.637). For the date, see appendix "Episcopal Hierarchy" below.

141. "non minus raptus quam electus, et quamvis invitus" (Dyn. VMaximi 6).

142. Faust. Epist. 6, 9, 12; see Pricoco, L'isola p.56.

143. These are only the known Lerinenses who became bishops during this period: other bishops who regularly supported this faction also were ordained c.427-433 (see chapter 5 and appendix "Episcopal Hierarchy" below): one can only speculate as to whether they too may have been monks at Lérins.

144. "illic ditatus, ut hic foenararet, illic illuminatus, ut hic refulgeret . . . absentat paulisper a patriae, ut novas opes ac divitias transmarinas reportet ad patriam . . . felix terra quae talem genuit, ac de alumno patronum . . . remisit."

monastic experiences. The citizens involved, however, also might have had more substantial benefits in mind: those which could accrue from having as bishop an influential aristocrat who had equally influential friends and contacts throughout Gaul in both the secular and ecclesiastical worlds.

CHAPTER 5

THE LÉRINS FACTION, PART II

CONSOLIDATION OF INFLUENCE

In the first quarter of the fifth century the monks of Lérins came to form a closely-knit ecclesio-aristocratic group. They had been able to expand their influence by the holding of important episcopal sees in the north and the south, and especially that of Arles. Another of the reasons for their success was the assistance which they received from high-ranking secular officials. As the following discussion will show, they adopted several methods of consolidating their influence: through their participation in an expanded literary circle, through the acquisition of still more episcopal partisans, and by the convening of regular church councils.

THE LITERARY FRIENDS OF LÉRINS

One manifestation of the ties the Lérins circle had in the secular world is the even wider literary circle in which the monks and bishops took part.[1] Hilary's local circle at Arles comprised the most eminent *litterati* of the city. The *Vita Hilarii* notes that the participants included "the superior authors of that time, who most deservedly shone through their writings, Silvius, Eusebius, Domnulus."[2] Silvius would have been the *palatinus* Polemius Silvius, about whom the *Gallic Chronicle of 452* noted: "Silvius, very mentally disturbed, writes a few things on religion after his official service in the palace had been fulfilled."[3] In 449 Silvius dedicated his extant *Laterculus* to Eucherius,

---

1. See Mathisen, "Epistolography" pp.104-107.
2. "eiusdem praelati auctores temporis, qui suis scriptis meritissime claruerunt, Silvius, Eusebius, Domnulus" (*VHilarii* 11[14]).
3. "Silvius turbatae admodum mentis post militiae in palatio exactae munera aliqua de religione conscribit" (no.121, s.a.438: *M.G.H. A.A.* 9.660). See Heinzelmann, "Prosopographie" p.695 and *P.L.R.E. II* pp.1012-1013. Silvius' religious works do not survive, perhaps because they

attesting further his ties to the literary circle of Lérins.[4] Eusebius was a rhetorician who was one of the instructors of Sidonius.[5] Domnulus apparently was the Domnulus who was a friend of Sidonius Apollinaris and served as *quaestor sacri palatii*, perhaps under Majorian, before becoming a monk himself outside Lyons.[6] Domnulus also has been identified with the Rusticius Helpidius Domnulus who wrote the extant poems *Carmen de Christi Iesu beneficiis* and *Historiarum testamenti veteris et novi*, and who transcribed a manuscript at Ravenna.[7]

Another member of the Arlesian circle was "Livius, a famous poet and author of that time."[8] He probably is to be identified with the *vir inlustris* Livius who in the early 460s was a member of the literary circle of Narbonne and also a friend of Sidonius.[9] His rank would indicate that he too, like Domnulus and Silvius, probably had held a high secular office.[10] Another rhetor who belonged to this circle was "the blessed Aedesius, a man most skilled in rhetorical eloquence and metrical art," who praised Hilary in an extant poem.[11]

An especially noteworthy member of Hilary's literary circle was "Auxiliaris, the source of Roman eloquence," who served as praetorian prefect of Gaul during the mid-430s and later as prefect of Rome.[12] While in Gaul, Auxiliaris assisted Hilary's friend Germanus of Auxerre, who had traveled to Arles seeking tax relief for his city.[13] According to the *Vita Germani* (ch.23),

---

were considered unorthodox in Gaul. The adjective *turbatus* sometimes was applied to individuals with heretical views; Augustine, for example, described the Gaul Leporius as *exturbatus* (*Epist.* 219.1, see chapter 6 below).

4. *M.G.H. A.A.* 9.518-523.

5. Sid. Apoll. *Epist.* 4.1.3. The two entries for "Eusebius" in Heinzelmann, "Prosopographie" p.602 and *P.L.R.E. II* p.430 (nos.12,13) surely refer to the same man.

6. Sid. Apoll. *Epist.* 4.25, 9.13.4, 9.15.1 *Carm.* 38, *Carm.* 14 *ep.* 2; see Heinzelmann, "Prosopographie" p.593; Mathisen, "Resistance" pp.612-618; and *P.L.R.E. II* pp.374-375, 537.

7. See Mathisen, "Resistance" pp.612-613.

8. "Livius, temporis illius poeta et auctor insignis" (*VHilarii* 11[14]).

9. Sid. Apoll. *Carm.* 23.445; see Heinzelmann, "Prosopographie" p.639 and *P.L.R.E. II* p.685.

10. He may have been related to the Livia who was the mother of the *vir inlustris* Pontius Leontius of Bordeaux, a relative of Paulinus of Nola who was described by Sidonius as "facile primus Aquitanorum" (*Epist.* 8.12.5).

11. "sanctus Aedesius, rhetoricae facundiae et metricae artis peritissimus vir" (*VHilarii* 12[15], 18[23]). See Heinzelmann, "Prosopographie" p.594 and *P.L.R.E. II* p.386; both call him "Edesius."

12. "Auxiliaris, auctor Romanae facundiae" (*VHilarii* 11[14]). See *C.I.L.* 12.5494; *Nov. Val.* 8; see also Heinzelmann, "Prosopographie" p.566; *P.L.R.E. II* p.206; and chapter 7 below.

13. The only certain date for Auxiliaris in Gaul is 435/436, the date of a milestone from between Arles and Marseilles (*C.I.L.* 12.5494 = *I.L.S.* no. 806). The visit may have been connected to the regular 15-year tax revision of 432 (the last had been in 417, see Seeck, *Regesten* p.334). A similar date of 433 might be suggested by the *Chron. gall. 452.* no. 114 which notes

At that time the city [of Arles] was rendered illustrious by the bishop Hilary, a man made precious by his manifold virtues; he was indeed a torrent of celestial eloquence, burning with faith, and a tireless worker of the divine precept. He exalted the venerable saint [sc. Germanus] with affection as a father, with reverence as an apostle.[14]

The *vita* then immediately continued (ch.24), "Indeed, Auxiliaris, who at that time was ruling the praetorian prefecture throughout the Gauls, received the bishop with a double joy....."[15] The high opinion of Hilary expressed by Germanus' biographer probably reflects not only Hilary's close ties to Germanus but also the great esteem in which Hilary continued to be held later in the century.[16] As for Auxiliaris, he did grant the requested tax alleviation, after Germanus supposedly had cured his wife. The cooperation of Auxiliaris, the highest imperial official in Gaul, with Hilary and his circle, therefore, extended beyond his polite participation in a local literary circle.

Yet another powerful *saecularis* with literary inclinations who may have been affiliated to the monastic circle of Lérins is the patrician, and *magister utriusque militiae* in 443, Merobaudes, a Spaniard whom the chronicler Hydatius praised as "comparable to the ancients in the excellence of his eloquence and especially in his poetic endeavors."[17] He apparently was the Merobaudes who granted land to the monastery of Mantaniacum (Mantenay-sur-Seine) near the see of Lupus of Troyes.[18] Directly or indirectly, he had several other connections to Gaul. He wrote at least two panegyrics in honor of Aetius, and his father-in-law Astyrius entered the consulate in 449 at Arles. Furthermore, Sidonius attests that Merobaudes was one of the "greatest comrades" of his own father and of the father of his friend Rusticus of Lyons.[19] The details of his ties to Lupus, and thence to the Lerinenses, however, remain unclear.

---

under that year "Germanus episcopus Altisiodori virtutibus et vitae districtione clarescit"; this reference, however, also may be a rather late allusion to Germanus' voyage to Britain in 429 (see n.49 below).

14. "inlustrabatur eo tempore civitas Hilario sacerdote multimoda virtute pretioso, erat enim fide igneus torrens caelestis eloquii et praeceptionis divinae operarius indefessus. qui venerabilem sanctum affectu ut patrem, reverentia ut apostolum sublimabat."

15. "Auxiliaris etiam regebat tum per Gallias apicem praefecturae, qui praesentiam sacerdotis duplicata gratulatione suscepit ..."

16. Borius, *Germain* p.96, however, dismisses these lines as "très conventionelles," and Thompson, *Germanus* p.58 sees in them a "distinct lack of warmth and fervour."

17. "eloquentiae merito vel maxime in poematis studio veteribus comparandus" (Hyd. *Chron*. 128). See *Clavis* nos.1433-1436.

18. See Clover, *Merobaudes* pp.7-8; Mathisen, "Patricians" pp.47-48; *P.L.R.E. II* pp.756-758 and Prinz, *Mönchtum* pp.70-71

19. Sid. Apoll. *Carm*. 9.277-278, 296-301.

Another individual with close literary ties to the Lerinenses was Cassian of Marseilles, who dedicated sections of his *Collationes* to Helladius and Honoratus of Arles, Eucherius of Lyons, and Theodorus of Fréjus.[20] Yet another Massiliote product of this literary circle perhaps is the so-called *Gallic Chronicle of 452*, which continued the *Chronicle* of Jerome from 379 to 452.[21] It long has been accepted that the anonymous author of the chronicle was writing in southern Gaul, possibly Marseilles, because of the detailed references to persons and events there.[22] It would appear, moreover, that his ties to the literary circle of Lérins were more than merely geographical. For one thing, he not only mentioned but usually praised individuals connected with it, such as Honoratus (no.86), Germanus (no.114), and Hilary and Eucherius (no.134), as well as Cassian of Marseilles (no.104) and Hilary's friend Polemius Silvius (no.121: not quite so laudatory). Moreover, he showed a detailed knowledge of, and willingness to report, events involving Lugdunensis (nos.9, 117, 119, 127, 133), the homeland of many of the Lerinenses, and Britain (nos. 6-7, 62, 126), which may have been the *patria* of Faustus of Riez. His ties to the Lérins faction are perhaps also suggested by the sides he took in contemporary controversies. He was very critical, for example, of Patroclus of Arles, the predecessor of the Lerinenses, whom he accused of simony (no.74). He also, as will be seen below, supported the Lerinenses in the controversy over predestination.[23] The extension of this circle to the north, finally, is seen in the dedication by an Agroecius, presumably the later bishop of Sens, of his *De orthographia* to Eucherius of Lyons.[24]

THE ACTIVITIES OF THE LÉRINS FACTION:

HONORATUS OF ARLES

The monastic and episcopal circle of Lérins, therefore, was extremely influential. It included a number of aristocrats who were

20. *C.S.E.L.* 13.3, 311-312, 503-504. Cassian's other extant works include the *De institutis coenobiorum* and the *De incarnatione* (*C.S.E.L.* 17). Lost works include a *De habitu monachi*, *De canonico orationum modo*, and *De origine* (Gennad. *Vir. ill.* 62).

21. *M.G.H. A.A.* 9.646-662. The reliability of the chronicle has been challenged by Miller, "Last Entry" pp.315-318, but convincingly reaffirmed by Muhlberger, "Gallic Chronicle" pp.23-33; see also Casey, "Magnus Maximus" p.78 n.17.

22. See Mommsen, *M.G.H. A.A.* 9.617-618; Demougeot, "Constantin" p.92; and Duchesne, *Fastes* 1.97 n.1 (from Provence). Note also that the four monks whom the chronicle (s.a. 419) singles out for special mention are all included among the dedicatees of Cassian of Marseilles' *Collationes*. It also spoke favorably of Proculus of Marseilles (s.a. 408). Both its author and Salvian of Marseilles even discussed some of the same events: the fall of Carthage, the Bacaudae, and the general decline of Roman authority.

23. See chapter 6 below, n.26.

24. H. Keil, *Gram. lat.* 7.113-125. See Heinzelmann, "Prosopographie" p.548 and *P.L.R.E. II* p.39.

among the leading literary luminaries of their day. It also had close ties to the secular authorities, some of whom, at least, were willing to use their influence on behalf of partisans of the faction. Several Lerinenses became bishops of some of the most important sees in Gaul. They maintained their contacts not only by correspondence, but also by visits, on which occasions they even preached in each other's churches.[25]

It is no surprise, then, that the monks of Lérins made such attractive episcopal candidates. Their religious credentials would have been acceptable, whatever their actual clerical backgrounds. Their reputation for holiness came to be established through the many accounts written, often by their confrères, of their lives.[26] Furthermore, in this age when a bishop's ability to get things done in the secular world was every bit as important as his divine contacts, the monks' secular connections and aristocratic status would have been most attractive. Finally, their group solidarity would have meant that any candidate from Lérins could count on the active support of his brethren.[27]

A primary means by which the Lerinenses, led by the bishops of Arles, extended their influence was by supporting their own partisans in vacant (or otherwise) episcopal sees, especially metropolitan ones. Some of these would have been fellow monks of Lérins, such as Lupus, Valerianus, Eucherius, Theodorus, and Maximus. Others would have been some of the bishops who in 450 asserted, "It is known that our predecessors, just as we ourselves, were consecrated in episcopal office by the bishop of [Arles]."[28] Included among these were such as Nectarius of Avignon, Julius of Apt, Claudius of Castellane, Asclepius of Cavaillon, and Auspicius of Vaison. All of them are known by their episcopal status to have been ordained between 425 and 434, and all, as will be seen, religiously supported the bishops of Arles in subsequent years.[29]

It might be asked, moreover, whether it is mere coincidence that,

---

25. See *VGermani* 23 (Germanus at Lyons); Faustus, *De natali sancti Felicis* (*C.S.E.L.* 21.259-262) (Faustus at Arles); and Faustus, *Sermo de sancta Blandina lugdunensi* (*P.L.* 50.859-861) (Faustus at Lyons).

26. Such as Hilary's life of Honoratus, Faustus' of Maximus, and Honoratus of Marseilles' of Hilary, not to mention Eucherius' *De laude heremi* and Constantius of Lyons' life of Germanus.

27. Even if on occasion faction partisans had to be left unsatisfied: Hilary reports how Honoratus, on his deathbed, had whispered to him (*VHonorati* 33), "excusa ... sancto illi fieri non potuisse quod voluit," "Excuse me to that blessed [brother] for not having been able to do what he wished."

28. "ab huius ecclesiae [sc. Arelatensis] sacerdote tam decessores nostros, quam nos ipsos, constat in summum sacerdotium ... consecratos" (*Epist.* "Memores quantum": *M.G.H. Epist.* 3.18-20).

29. See appendix "Episcopal Hierarchy" below.

at the very time that the Lérins faction was installing its members in so many Gallic sees, the bishop of Rome, Celestine, chose to issue a decree attempting to regulate episcopal ordinations and practices in Gaul.[30] In his letter "Cuperemus quidem" addressed to the bishops of Viennensis and Narbonensis (*P.L.* 50.430-436: 26 July 428) he declared, for example, that laymen were not to be ordained as bishops (ch.3):

> We have learned that certain individuals, who had been trained in no ecclesiastical orders, have been ordained bishops, through the usurpation of one who recognizes that he has done this.... But now it is not merely laymen who are ordained, whom no rank permits to become [bishops]: even those whose crimes are known far and wide throughout all the provinces are ordained....[31]

Outsiders, moreover, were not to be ordained bishops (ch.4-5):

> Nor should foreigners and outsiders, and those who were unknown beforehand, be proposed to the exclusion of those who are deserving in the judgment of their fellow citizens.... Let no one be given as bishop to the unwilling: the agreement and desire of the clergy, plebs, and [local senatorial] order is required ... Let each cleric enjoy the fruits of his service in the church in which he passed his life in all the ranks.... [32]

Nor were priests and bishops to dress in the garb of monks (ch. 1).

Later in the letter, Celestine reiterated and refined his prohibition of "illegal" ordinations: "Let no layman, no one who has been married twice, no one who is or was married to a widow, be ordained ... and if such illicit ordinations have been done, let them be revoked...."[33] Finally, Celestine also pointedly reaffirmed Boniface's decree of 422 that metropolitans were to limit themselves to a single province: "Let each province be content with its own metropolitan, as contained in the decrees of our predecessor given to the bishop of Narbonne, nor should the opportunity of usurpation be conceded to one bishop to

---

30. See Franses, *Leo* p.21; Pricoco, *L'isola* p.66; and Prinz, *Mönchtum* p.48, who sees the decree as a response to the ordination of dispossessed northern aristocrats.

31. "ordinatos vero quosdam ... episcopos qui nullis ecclesiasticis ordinibus ... fuerint instituti ... huius ursupatione, qui se hoc recognoscit fecisse, didicimus.... sed iam non satis est laicos ordinare, quos nullus fieri ordo permittit: sed etiam ii quorum crimina longe lateque per omnes paene sunt nota provincias, ordinantur...."

32. "nec ... peregrini et extranei, et qui ante ignorati sint, ad exclusionem eorum, qui bene de suorum civium merentur testimonio, praeponantur ... nullus invitis detur episcopus: cleri, plebis et ordinis consensus ac desiderium requiratur ... habeat unusquisque clericorum suae fructum militiae in ecclesia, in qua suam per omnia officia transegit aetatem...." The letter "Exigit dilectio" (*P.L.* 20.75), supposedly written by the bishop of Rome Anastasius c.398/401 "Ad omnes Germaniae ac Burgundiae episcopos," commands, "transmarinos homines ... in clericatus honore nolite suscipere." It has been condemned, however, as a forgery (ibid.).

33. "nullus ex laicis, nullus digamus, nullus qui sit viduae maritus, aut fuerit, ordinetur ... et si quae factae sunt ordinationes illicitae removeantur...." (ch.6).

the injury of another...."[34] Celestine's decree, like Boniface's, specifically mentioned only Narbonensis Prima. Even if their intention was to limit the authority of the bishop of Arles, both refrained from specifying him by name. Celestine identified a particular transgressor only as "the one who recognizes that he has done this."[35] His identity might be suggested by the one case which Celestine did mention in particular, that of the foreigner Daniel.[36]

Celestine claimed to have received letters from the east accusing this Daniel of all sorts of crimes: "Many shameful acts have been reported by many individuals ... he has been burdened by such great testimony, afflicted by so much accusation of crimes, to the extent that he is said to be polluted by unchaste relations with the sacred virgins...."[37] As a result, he said, "a letter was sent to the bishop of Arles ordering that he be brought before episcopal judgment." In the meantime, however, "[Daniel] crept into the episcopal dignity at the time when he was called to having his case heard in the letters sent by us.... It would be more suitable that the one who ordained him should lose his rank by ordaining such a one than that the one ordained should obtain it...."[38]

The bishop of Arles, however, clearly failed to react, either to Celestine's letter or to Daniel's ordination. As a result, Celestine then took matters into his own hands and decreed, "Daniel, as I have said, who believed that he could evade prosecution through his pontifical rank, and achieved such a status by hiding from his accusers, should know that he has been in the meantime removed from your [episcopal] assembly...."[39] One might suggest, moreover, that it was the

---

34. "unaquaeque provincia suo metropolitano contenta sit, ut decessoris nostri data ad Narbonensem episcopum continent constituta, nec usurpationis locus alicui sacerdoti in alterius concedatur iniuriam...." (ch.4).

35. "qui se hoc recognoscit fecisse" (ch.3). Langgärtner, *Gallienpolitik* p.58 wrongly asserts that Celestine explicitly named the bishops of Vienne and Marseilles.

36. See Batiffol, "Eglises" p.166 and Langgärtner, *Gallienpolitik* pp.57-58.

37. "multa a multis obiecta flagitia ... tantis gravatus testimoniis, tanta facinorum accusatione pulsatus, sacrarum ut dicitur virginum pollutus incestu...." (ch.3).

38. "in pontificii dignitatem hoc tempore, quo ad causam dicendam missis a nobis litteris vocabatur, obrepsit ... facilius est, ut hanc dignitatem tali dando ipse amiserit ordinator, quam eam obtineat ordinatus...." (ch.3). Langgärtner, *Gallienpolitik* pp.57-58, suggests that Daniel had been ordained by the bishop of Vienne. He supposes that the bishop of Arles would not have been put in charge of the investigation if he had done the ordination, but he fails to note that the letter to the bishop of Arles was sent before the ordination occurred.

39. "Daniel, ut diximus, qui accusationem pontificali honore subterfugere se posse credidit, et ad fastigium tantum accusatores suos latendo pervenit, a sanctitatis vestrae coetu interim se noverit segregatum" (ch.6). Celestine's language is vague, perhaps purposely so. Is he removing Daniel from office, excommunicating him, or merely forbidding him from attending church councils? For varying meanings of the word "coetus," see *Corp. chr. lat.* 148.4, 9, 204, 206 and Hil. *Epist.* "Qualiter contra sedis."

bishop of Arles, Honoratus himself, with whom Celestine was piqued, even if he was reluctant to chastise him by name. Not only had Honoratus clearly failed to fulfil Celestine's demands, but Celestine's letter also condemned one of the standard practices of Lérins: the ordination of laymen, foreign or Gallic, both monks of Lérins and others. Celestine's reiteration of Boniface's prohibition against metropolitans holding authority in more than one province only serves to suggest that Boniface had been ignored, and that Honoratus was continuing the policy of his predecessor Patroclus in claiming extraordinary metropolitan jurisdiction. Daniel, meanwhile, presumably continued to hold his office.

One further indication of Honoratus' activities may survive in the tradition that the first bishop of Tarentaise, a certain Jacobus, was a disciple of Honoratus at Lérins, and later, after Honoratus had become bishop of Arles, was ordained by him as bishop for the Ceutrones.[40] If this story were true, it would be consistent with the very accusation Celestine was making about interference in another province. The ordination also would have given the Lérins faction control of another important see. Even though the bishop of Tarentaise is not known to have exercised the role of metropolitan actively as of this time, by the sixth century the city was the official metropolitan see of Alpes Graiae.[41] He may have had some local predominance in the fifth century too. The interest of the Lerinenses in this province is seen again in Eucherius of Lyons' composition of his *Passio acaunensium martyrum* at the request of bishop Salvius of Octodorum.[42] Attempts of the group to extend its presence into Alpes Graiae also would have served to counter the influence of the bishop of Vienne, who seems to have claimed rights there as well.[43]

It also may have been at this time, if not before, that the bishops of Arles raised Toulon, previously a dependency of Marseilles, to the status of an episcopal see. Its first attested bishop, Augustalis (ordained c.440), was closely associated with the circle of Lérins, supported the metropolitan pretensions of Ravennius of Arles in 449, and even died

---

40. See *A.A.S.S.* January II p.268, also Duchesne, *Fastes* 1.243-244, and Prinz, *Mönchtum* p.60.

41. See Griffe, *Gaule* 1.336 n.10. In the *Notitia galliarum* (*M.G.H. A.A.* 9.598-600), Alpes Graiae et Poeninae are not given a metropolis, even though the province is known to have had a *praeses* (ibid.554). Mommsen calls this an "administrative oddity" (ibid.557-558); Harries, "*Notitia*" p.32, calls the lack of a metropolis a "mistake." In either case, there would have been a tradition of local administation which could have been appropriated by a provincial bishop in a *de facto* metropolitan capacity.

42. *P.L.* 50.827-832. See Curti, "'Passio'" pp.297-327 and Pricoco, *L'isola* pp.204-244.

43. See Leo, *Epist.* "Lectis dilectionis" of 450 which recognized the authority of the bishop of Vienne over Tarentaise, and chapter 8 below.

at Arles.[44] It may be significant that the extant episcopal *fasti* of Toulon begin with an Honoratus, perhaps a doublet of the bishop of Arles who created the see.[45]

HILARY OF ARLES AND THE ROLE OF CHURCH COUNCILS

One now might turn to the more well-attested activities of Honoratus' successor, Hilary.[46] One of Hilary's earliest undertakings, it seems, involved the mission of his partisans Germanus of Auxerre and Lupus of Troyes to Britain to combat Pelagianism in 429. According to Germanus' biographer Constantius of Lyons, this came about when "an embassy sent to the Gallic bishops from Britain announced that the Pelagian perversity was widely taking hold of the population in that area ... for which reason a large synod was summoned, and by the judgment of all Germanus and Lupus were approached...."[47] This account indicates that the Gauls sent their delegation on their own authority. Their legal justification could have been supplied by Valentinian's law of 425 granting the bishop of Arles imperial authority to try Pelagians.[48] The Gauls therefore could claim that they had adequate legal precedent for their unilateral action.

The only other independent evidence for this mission comes from Prosper. In his chronicle, he gave a rather different account (*Chron.* 1301 s.a.429: *M.G.H. A.A.* 9.472):

The Pelagian Agricola, son of the Pelagian bishop Severianus, corrupts the churches of Britain with the insinuation of his teaching. But at the insinua-

44. See Duchesne, *Fastes* 1.100, 257 n.3, 277-278. See also chapter 8 and appendix "Episcopal Hierarchy" below.

45. Ibid. 1.277 n.8. The first bishop of the newly created see may even have been the aforementioned Daniel; perhaps Honoratus' name was substituted for his in the *fasti* after his disgrace.

46. Hilary conventionally has been portrayed as being solely responsible for the activities of his faction; see Heinzelmann, *Bischofsherrschaft* pp.78-84; Kidd, *Church* p.356; Langgärtner, *Gallienpolitik* pp.61-91; Morrison, *Tradition* p.92ff; and Stein, *Geschichte* pp.328-329. For Hilary as responsible for making his partisans bishops, see Duchesne, *Fastes* 1.114 ("il s'occupait aussi de recruter l'épiscopat") and Prinz, *Mönchtum* pp.59-63. Jalland, *Leo* 124, however, sees the trend to such bishops as a result of "laxity in the standard of Christian life" and the need for men "of undoubted integrity."

47. "ex Britaniis directa legatio Gallicanis episcopis nuntiavit Pelagianam perversitatem in locis suis late populos occupasse ... ob quam causam synodus numerosa collecta est, omniumque iudicio ... ambiuntur Germanus ac Lupus...." (*VGermani* 12). It is suggested by Hefele-Leclercq, *Conciles* 2.216-217, that the council met at Troyes; a more likely, as well as more accessible, meeting place might have been further south, perhaps at Lyons. This synod is erroneously dated in *Corp. chr. lat.* 148.106 to 446.

48. *Sirm.* 6, see chapter 4 above, n.13. The law had assumed that such Pelagians would actually be present at Arles, an impossibility in this case.

tion of the deacon Palladius, Pope Celestine sends bishop Germanus of Auxerre as his representative, and with the heretics having been confounded he returns the Britons to the catholic faith.[49]

Prosper characteristically ignored the Gallic council and claimed that the bishop of Rome was the initiator of this mission to Britain, whereas Constantius did not mention him at all.[50] As noted above, the Gauls did have some legal justification for taking independent action; moreover, Prosper's pro-Roman bias is notorious. It may be that Prosper's assertion exaggerates Celestine's role, and that any papal authorization was *ex post facto* in nature. The Gauls perhaps did send a deacon Palladius to inform Celestine of the results of the mission.[51] A case even has been made for Palladius being a deacon of Auxerre. If so, he may have accompanied Germanus in 429 and thus had first-hand knowledge of the situation in Britain.[52] Once again, then, the varying accounts of the same incident indicate how factional affiliations could influence the portrayal of events.

The Council of Riez [53]

More specific evidence for Hilary's attempts to solidify his and his partisans' authority in the south comes from a series of three church councils held in mid-November in the years 439, 441, and 442. The meeting of these councils perhaps was facilitated by the treaties made by Aetius with the Franks, Burgundians, and Visigoths during the period 432-439, and the return of some degree of peace to the Gallic

---

49. "Agricola Pelagianus, Severiani episcopi Pelagiani filius, ecclesias Brittaniae dogmatis sui insinuatione corrumpit. sed ad insinuationem Palladii diaconi papa Caelestinus Germanum Autisidorensem episcopum vice sua mittit et deturbatis hereticis Britannos ad catholicam fidem dirigit" The accounts in the *VLupi* 4 and Bede, *Hist. eccl.* 1.17-20 merely repeat that of the *VGermani.* See also Prosp. *Contr. coll.* 21(41) (*P.L.* 51.271), which omitted Germanus' role altogether: "nec vero segniore cura ab hoc eodem morbo Britannias [Caelestinus] liberavit, quando quosdam inimicos gratiae . . . exclusit."

50. Prosper also neglected to mention the British embassy and the presence of Lupus, nor was there any mention of any role of Palladius beyond that of a mere messenger. Prosper's account usually is accepted at face value; see de Plinval, *Pélage* p.349 and Wood, "End" p.10, who asserts that Prosper "was rather better placed to understand events," without explaining how Prosper would have understood Gallic events better than the Gauls themselves.

51. Wood, "End" p.10, suggests that Palladius was "responsible for obtaining papal approval of the mission." This same Palladius was sent as a bishop to Ireland in 431 (Prosp. *Chron.* 1307), see also Prosp. *Contr. coll.* 21(41) (*P.L.* 51.271), "ordinato Scotis episcopo, dum Romanam insulam studet servare catholicam, [Caelestinus] fecit etiam barbaram Christianam."

52. See Grosjean, *Analecta bollandiana* 63(1945) p.73ff and Borius, *Germain* p.81, who suggest that Palladius was a deacon of Rome. For Palladius and Patrick of Ireland as the same person, see Grosjean, "Palladius" pp.317-326. For the Palladii of Bourges and eastern Lugdunensis, see Mathisen, *Ecclesiastical Aristocracy* pp.316-319.

53. For the text, see *Corp. chr. lat.* 148.61-75. See also Griffe, *Gaule* 2.155-158; Hefele-Leclercq, *Conciles* 2.423-430; and Langgärtner, *Gallienpolitik* pp.63-64.

scene.[54] The councils drew bishops not only from Hilary's province of Viennensis, but from three or more others as well.

The first council adjourned on 29 November 439. Its very location is instructive. Even though it met at Riez in Narbonensis Secunda, outside Hilary's own province, Hilary nonetheless presided: his signature comes first and he referred to his fellow bishops as those "who subscribed along with me."[55] Hilary, therefore, clearly was exercising his ecclesiastical authority in another province, and by doing so was making a direct attack upon the authority of the bishops of both Aix, the *de iure* metropolitan see, and Marseilles, apparently still the *de facto* one. The bishop of Riez, of course, was Hilary's partisan Maximus, the ex-abbot of Lérins. The council may have been held there because it concerned Alpes Maritimae, which still was looked upon as an ecclesiastical appendage of Narbonensis Secunda.

The prologue of the extant conciliar canons states the pretext for the synod (*Corp. chr. lat.* 148.63):

Because a remedy is sought for a transgression which has occurred in the church of Embrun, where, without the presence of three [bishops], without letters to the fellow provincials, and without the authority of the metropolitan, it is clear that an illegal fiction of an ordination was arrogated by two rashly assembled bishops.[56]

Now, Embrun was itself the metropolitan see of the province. The charge that there was no metropolitan at the ordination, therefore, is meaningful only if the bishops at the council refused to accept this, and instead recognized someone else, presumably Hilary, as the rightful metropolitan.

The events which had provoked the council then were elaborately detailed as follows (can.1: *Corp. chr. lat.* 148.64-65):

It seemed that before everything else counsel had to be taken quickly about the church of Embrun, because having been in need of a bishop for twenty months it more gravely grew sick to the point that the clergy, innocent and properly mindful of discipline, troubled by the insolence and manifold troublesomeness of certain laymen, recently suffered, to their peril in a most savage assault, dangerous threats and opprobrium and a most harsh attack, nor could the summoning of good men, mindful of discipline, be postponed, lest the wishes of obstinate and restless individuals seem to be flattered, whose conspiracies and machinations in the past, to the extent which they

54. *P.L.R.E. II* pp.24-25.
55. "qui mecum subscripserunt" (*Corp. chr. lat.* 148.71-72).
56. "cum ... transgressionis apud Ebrodunensem ecclesiam habitae remedium quaereretur, qua ... absque trium praesentia, absque comprovincialium litteris, sine metropolitani auctoritate, irritam ordinationis speciem a duobus temere convenientibus praesumptam esse clarebat. ..."

can be apprehended, must be punished by ecclesiastical reproach, and anticipated in the future.[57]

The bishops also claimed not so much that Embrun lacked a bishop, but that it lacked a "legitimate" one. A certain Armentarius had in fact been ordained. The assembled bishops asserted that he then had attempted to resign the office, "because he had sent letters to the clergy, in which he recognized that he had not obtained the episcopate. He renounced his claim, petitioning that his name be erased [from the *fasti*]."[58] Later, however, supported by "the great insolence of his supporters," he supposedly had reasserted his claim to the office.[59]

The council responded to these perceived irregularities by declaring Armentarius deposed. It also claimed to be inclined to mercy because Armentarius was only a "youngster" and "because in some degree he has ceased from juvenile frivolity."[60] It therefore made use of a ruling of the Council of Nicaea designed to apply to schismatics and allowed him to preside over a single *parochia* not as a full bishop but as a *chorepiscopus*.[61] As such, he was forbidden to ordain "even the lowest ranking cleric," or to obtain another see in Alpes Maritimae. The council further decreed, "Let not any place be chosen for him which is ennobled by its status of *civitas* or the rank of its local senate ... nor should he ever at all obtain control over two churches."[62] Such restrictions would effectively restrict any ambitions he may have had. He was allowed to take precedence over his own priests, but was compelled to yield to all other bishops, no matter how junior. The bishops

57. "Ebrodunensi ecclesiae ante omnia mature visum est consulendum quia, quattuor de biennio mensibus sacerdote legitimo destituta, hoc gravius aegrotaverat, quod clerus innocens ac disciplinae, ut probatum est, memor, quorumdam laicorum insolentia ac varia perturbatione vexatus, etiam in sacerdotibus ac ministris minas ac iurgia et vim acerbissimam periculose nuper caede pertulerat, nec poterat differri bonorum ac disciplinae memorum expectatio, ne viderentur contumacium et inquietorum vota palpari, quorum conspirationes machinationesque et in praeteritum, quantum deprehendi possint, animadversione ecclesiastica puniendae, et in futurum anticipandae erant."

58. "quod epistulas ad clerum ipsum emiserat, quibus episcopatum quem se non indeptum agnoscebat, appetere renuntiaverat, eradi nomen suum petens" (can.2).

59. "multa assentatorum insolentia" (can.2).

60. "quod iuvenilibus titillationibus aliqua in parte cessissit" (can.2).

61. Can.3. Attributed to Leo of Rome is an undated letter "Cum in dei" (*P.L.* 20.661, 54.1256) addressed to the bishops of Gaul and Germany and entitled "De privilegio chorepiscoporum sive presbyterorum." Given that these are the very matters discussed at Riez, one might wonder whether there is some connection: did Armentarius perhaps appeal to Rome? On *chorepiscopi*, see Gillmann, "Institut" p.40ff; Gottlob, *Chorepiskopat*; Jalland, *Leo* p.111; and McShane, *Romanitas* pp.248-249.

62. "ne quisquam ei locus decernatur quem curiae et civitatis species aut ordo nobilitat ... nec omnino unquam duarum ecclesiarum gubernationem obtineat" (can.3). Nor was he permitted to substitute for an absent bishop in any *civitas*.

had no objections to Armentarius being a bishop, they were concerned only about where he was a bishop. The controversy was really over ecclesiastical authority, with Hilary and his party asserting their own preeminence in Alpes Maritimae.

The efforts to render Armentarius impotent apparently were successful, for he never is heard from again.[63] As an additional punishment, some of the clerics he had ordained, those who supposedly had been excommunicated by someone unnamed, also were declared deposed. The "upright" clerics, however, were either to be retained at Embrun or sent with Armentarius to his new see, at the discretion of the new bishop of Embrun. This measure would allow Armentarius' successor to expel any potential troublemakers.

The two bishops who ordained him also were disciplined (can.1):

Therefore, it is pleasing that those who usurped such improper and destabilizing powers be received in communion and fellowship to this extent, as they understand according to the most recent and salubrious decree of the Synod of Turin, that they otherwise attend no ordinations and no ordinary councils, for it is expected that nothing useful would be suggested by them.[64]

Typically, the bishops derived their authority from their own earlier council at Turin, rather than from any ruling of the bishop of Rome, or anyone else.[65] This punishment would have served to warn other bishops of what could happen to them if they presumed to oppose Hilary and his partisans.

The council then attempted to place stricter controls upon the elections of new bishops, decreeing that in order to act "against scandals of this nature," after a bishop died only the neighboring bishop could attend the funeral, "who, moreover, should take the most strict care of this same church, lest he allow before the ordination [of the new bishop] anything to be done by the subversion of clerics discordant in their new status."[66] To prevent any future "scandals," the election was to be overseen by the metropolitan. His summons was required before

63. Griffe, *Gaule* 2.157 n.43, and Langgärtner, *Gallienpolitik* pp.63-64 n.4, suggest that this Armentarius is Armentarius of Antibes, but this is impossible, for the latter was in office by c.425 (see appendix "Episcopal Hierarchy" below).

64. "itaque eos qui tam incondita ac tam instabilia usurpaverant placuit ... ita in communionem dilectionemque recipi, ut scirent secundam recentem ac saluberrimam Taurinatis synodi definitionem ... nullis se de cetero ordinationibus, nullis ordinariis interfuturos esse conciliis, quia nihil salubre ab illis statuendum expectaretur. . . ." The "ordinary" councils seem to have been provincial ones. For the distinction, see Griffe, *Gaule* 1.341.

65. See *Conc. Taur.* 3, where a transgressor is "in conciliis minime retenturum" (*Corp. chr. lat.* 148.56).

66. "qui tamen statim ecclesiae ipsius curam districtissime gereret, ne quid ante ordinationem discordantium in novitatibus clericorum subversioni liceret" (can.5).

anyone else could attend, "lest he be misled by the populace and appear to have wished to allow a forcible consecration."[67]

It is clear that this metropolitan was to be Hilary himself. This
requirement would give Hilary, and his partisans, virtual control over
the naming of bishops in southern Gaul, and the opportunity to solidify their control over the ecclesiastical hierarchy even further. It was
all too common at this time to have bishops chosen by mob action at
the local level; Germanus of Auxerre, of course, had been, and even
Hilary's own ordination was essentially of this sort. But for Hilary and
his confrères to retain their influence, they needed to have as much
control as possible over episcopal elections. On-the-spot ordinations at
the local level were no longer desirable, and due process now became
the watchword.[68]

The case of the new bishop of Embrun, a certain Ingenuus, shows
this policy in action. He was ordained by Hilary himself, presumably
immediately after the council.[69] He was a good choice, for he faith-
fully supported Hilary and his policies as long as the latter was alive.
He dutifully attended Hilary's councils, and his signature only in the
position determined by his tenure in office indicates that he acquiesced
to the exalted status of the bishop of Arles, even if it meant restrictions
upon the exercise of his own authority.[70] The suggestion that Ingenuus was "trop négligent ou trop indifférent" to assert his status fails
to recognize that Ingenuus would have been Hilary's partisan from
the very beginning.[71] Such deference presumably would have been the
quid pro quo for his election in the first place. After Hilary's death,

---

67. "ne a plebe decipiatur et vim pati voluisse videatur" (can.6). This requirement is very
similar to one in *De sept. ord. eccl.* 6 (*P.L.* 30.156), where, to avoid "scandals," "nuper episcopalis
electio ad metropolitanum remissa est." It conventionally has been assumed that this is a reference to Zosimus' grant of extraordinary metropolitan authority to the bishop of Arles (see Beck,
Pastoral Care pp.15-16). A problem with this interpretation, however, is that the *De sept. ord.
eccl.* seems to presume the existence not of one but of several metropolitans. It may be rather
that these very canons of the Council of Riez served as the model instead.

68. Nevertheless, forcible ordinations seem to have continued in Gaul, and eventually, the
imperial government itself entered the controversy. A law issued by Majorian on 28 May 460
entitled "Ne quis invitus clericus ordinetur" (*Nov. Maj.* 11) asserted that "indeed, the persuasion
of some bishops imposes [the priesthood] upon those who are resisting, with the result that the
offense of an interceding violence provides unready minds to the disgust of holy religion." The
law concluded, "si quis sane invitus episcopus fuerit ordinatus, hanc consecrationem nulla violari
accusatione permittimus." Reluctant bishops, apparently, were the exception and were compelled
to serve. The source of this activity is suggested by where the law was issued, Arles, and the
source of the complaint perhaps by the individual who was to adjudicate such cases, the bishop
of Rome.

69. The Gallic letter of 449/450, *Epist.* "Memores quantum," notes that the subscribers,
among whom was Ingenuus (Leo, *Epist.* "Lectis dilectionis"), had been ordained by the bishop
of Arles.

70. See Duchesne, *Fastes* 1.113 for Embrun as "un simple évêché" under Hilary.

71. Griffe, *Gaule* 2.166.

Ingenuus showed himself neither negligent nor indifferent in the pursuit of his rights.[72] Ingenuus, and other metropolitans, recognized that their collegiate interests could be pursued more effectively under a single, strong leader.

The Council of Riez was attended by thirteen other bishops besides Hilary. Because the council supported his expanded authority, one must assume that most, if not all, of them were his supporters. From Viennensis came Audentius of Die, Auspicius of Vaison, Nectarius of Avignon, a presbyter Vincentius representing Constantianus of Carpentras, Asclepius of Cavaillon, and an Arcadius, perhaps of Orange.[73] From Alpes Maritimae came Severianus of Thorâme, Severus of Vence, Claudius of Castellane, and Valerianus of Cimiez. Narbonensis Secunda was represented by Theodorus of Fréjus, Maximus of Riez, and Julius of Apt. Three of these, it will be noted, Valerianus, Theodorus, and Maximus, are known alumni of Lérins. As seen above, moreover, Asclepius, Nectarius, Julius, Claudius, and Auspicius all were ordained by the bishop of Arles. All these sees were to send representatives to at least one of Hilary's two other attested councils.

The final canon of the Council of Riez called for concord among bishops at future councils: "Certainly, in the midst of their worries of whatever sort, having put aside their personal and local concerns . . . let them search out a remedy for the church alone, having removed all animosity and any itch for revenge. . . ."[74] It also decreed that regular councils were to be convened "twice a year if the times are peaceful."[75] "Peace" of whatever sort, however, never prevailed sufficiently for such semi-annual councils to be held, and it was not until 441 that the next one met.[76] Political unrest of several kinds may have caused the delay. In 439 had come the showdown between Aetius and the Visigoths, in which the Roman army of Huns under Litorius had been defeated outside Toulouse. The Goths, too exhausted to continue, then did return to their federate status through the intercession of the Arvernian senator Eparchius Avitus.[77]

72. See chapter 9 below.

73. For these bishops, see appendix "Episcopal Hierarchy."

74. "certe inter quaslibet anxietates neglectis propriis ac domesticis necessitatibus . . . solum ecclesiae remedium, remota ultionis prurigine atque omni animositate quaesissent. . . ." (can.7).

75. "si quies temporum erit bis in anno" (ibid.). A variant Spanish version of the canons specifies that the first council was to be three weeks after Easter and the second on the Ides of October (13 October) (Corp. chr. lat. 148.73). Boniface of Rome in his letter "Valentinae nos" had specified 31 October as a meeting date (chapter 3 above). The semi-annual ideal was repeated by Avitus of Vienne in his invitation of 517 to the Council of Epao: "conventus ergo, quos bis per annum a sacerdotibus fieri cura seniorum decreverat . . . assiduitate vel singulos post biennia faceremus. . . ." (Corp. chr. lat. 148A.22).

76. There is no evidence for an intervening council whose acta are lost.

77. Sid. Apoll. Carm. 7.246-315.

The year 440 also had been a busy one for Aetius in other regards. According to the *Gallic Chronicle*, "The deserted fields of the city of Valence, having been surveyed, are granted to the Alans under the command of Sambida."[78] Prosper reported that in the same year a new bishop of Rome was elected, the deacon Leo, "who was being detained in Gaul while he patched up the friendship between Aetius and Albinus."[79] It usually is assumed that this Albinus was Fl. Albinus, prefect of Rome in 426 and of Italy in 443-449, and it has been suggested that he was prefect of Gaul in 440, although this would be inconsistent with the contemporary imperial policy of using only Gauls in high Gallic office.[80] Nor is there any indication of the nature of the quarrel which Leo was to patch up. It may have been serious enough, and, in spite of Prosper's claim, unresolved enough, that Aetius had to give it his personal attention, for the *Gallic Chronicle* also notes for the year 440 that "after the revolts in Gaul had been put down, Aetius returned to Italy."[81] If Leo and Aetius met at Arles, Hilary, if not directly involved in the negotiations, at least would have had the opportunity to meet Leo. The two therefore could have made some assessment of each other. One only can wonder if this visit had any effect upon Leo's later Gallic policy.

The Council of Orange [82]

Barbarian settlements on the one hand, therefore, and high-level factional disputes on the other may have prevented the convening of a Gallic council in 440. In the next year, however, the Council of Orange, with Hilary once again presiding, did assemble on 8 November. Perhaps because it was more centrally located in southern Gaul than the Council of Riez, it attracted a greater attendance. With the exception of Cavaillon, the same sees were represented here as at Riez, Justus having replaced Arcadius (it seems) at Orange. A new attendee from the south was Augustalis, the recently ordained bishop of Toulon.

More significantly, the council also was attended by Claudius of

---

78. "deserta Valentinae urbis rura Alanis, quibus Sambida praeerat, partienda traduntur" (*Chron. gall. 452* no.124).

79. "quem tunc inter Aetius et Albinum amicitias redintegrantem Galliae detinebant": Prosp. *Chron.* 1341. Leo returned to Rome and was consecrated on 29 September (Jalland, *Leo* p.38; Jaffé no.390). Nor was this Leo's first experience with Gaul: Leo earlier had solicited Cassian of Marseilles to write the *De incarnatione* (chapter 6 below, n.36).

80. *P.L.R.E. II* p.53. See Jalland, *Leo* p.38; Moss, "Policies"; and Twyman, "Aetius."

81. "pacatis motibus Galliarum Aetius ad Italiam regreditur" (no.123). Prosper, being friendly to Leo, may have exaggerated just how successful Leo actually was.

82. For the text, see *Corp. chr. lat.* 148.76-93. See also Griffe, *Gaule* 2.157-158; Hefele-Leclercq, *Conciles* 2.430-454; and Langgärtner, *Gallienpolitik* p.64.

Vienne and two of his suffragans, Ceretius of Grenoble and Salonius of Geneva.[83] Now, Salonius, being the son of Eucherius of Lyons, already had close ties to the Lérins circle. Claudius, too, seems to have had connections, for he was the dedicatee of a lost *Commentary on Ecclesiastes* by Salvian of Marseilles.[84] Perhaps because of such ties to Hilary's circle, Claudius now was induced to grant the luster of his presence to the council. Moreover, because this is Claudius' first attested appearance anywhere, he may have been elected but recently, perhaps even with Hilary's support. With the addition of Claudius and his suffragans, attendance from Viennensis was complete save for the bishops of Valence and the minor sees of Trois-Châteaux and Aps/Viviers.[85]

The province of Narbonensis Secunda was represented by the same three bishops who had attended Riez, so Hilary's faction had made no gains there. The delegation from Alpes Maritimae, moreover, was represented only by Ingenuus of Embrun; Severianus of Thorâme, Severus of Vence, and Valerianus of Cimiez all were absent. The first two of these may have been the consecrators of Armentarius of Embrun and if so forbidden to attend; Valerianus may have been absent for other reasons. Or, given that all three were from the same area, there simply may have been travel difficulties.[86]

The council would have gained additional prestige from the presence of Eucherius of Lyons, who was accompanied by his other son Veranus, then a deacon, and who also noted in his subscription, "I foresee the assent of my blessed fellow provincial bishops to these matters."[87] Eucherius, of course, not only was a close associate of Hilary, but also was metropolitan bishop of Lugdunensis Prima, the homeland of many of the monks of Lérins. His statement could be seen as a subtle reminder of his own metropolitan status, even though

83. Claudius' other suffragan in Viennensis, the bishop of Valence, may still have been preoccupied by the settlement of the Alans and thus unable to attend. The bishop of Tarentaise also was absent.

84. Gennad. *Vir. ill.* 68; the work was written when Claudius was already bishop. See also Ado, *Chron.* 6 (*P.L.* 123.104) (as a presbyter "Claudianus," but clearly not Mamertus Claudianus). Vienne had its own monastery at Grigny on the Rhône, which Sidonius (*Epist.* 7.17.3) seemed to associate with Lérins ("secundum statuta Lirinensium patrum vel Grinincensium"). Avitus of Vienne also spent time there (*Epist.* 74, see also *VAbbAcaun.* 9); see Griffe, *Gaule* 3.234, 323.

85. The absence of Aps may indicate that it was at roughly this time that the city was destroyed, and the episcopal see moved to Viviers: the last bishop of Aps, Auxonius, is last attested in 431 and the first of Viviers, Eulalius, is first seen in 451: see Duchesne, *Fastes* 1.237. Trois-Châteaux: chapter 7 below. Valence: note 83 above.

86. Or some names may have dropped out of the list: whereas sixteen bishops are named, one list cites the total as seventeen (XVII) and another as twenty-two (XXII, an easy corruption of XVII) (*Corp. chr. lat.* 148.87-90).

87. "sanctorum sacerdotum comprovincialium meorum super his expectaturus adsensum" (*Corp. chr. lat.* 148.87-89). See Langgärtner, *Gallienpolitik* p.65.

in the subscriptions his name appears only in the position determined by his tenure in office. Eucherius' attendance at the council, moreover, need not mean that he was relinquishing his metropolitan rights, any more than the attendance of Agrestius of Lugo in Galicia, who probably was a refugee from the Suevic takeover, means that Hilary was claiming metropolitan rights in Spain.[88]

The attendance at this council suggests that Hilary had been able to unify his party in south central Gaul even further. In order to do so, however, he was compelled to acknowledge the metropolitan status of Claudius of Vienne. Claudius' name appears second in the list of subscribers, immediately after that of Hilary. The only way Claudius could have acquired such status so soon would be by having recognized metropolitan rights.[89] This consideration in and of itself should put to rest any suggestions that Hilary wished to extend his metropolitan authority over all Gaul.[90]

Most of the canons of the Council of Orange were uncontroversial, in contrast to those of Riez, and dealt with general matters of church discipline which few would question. A few, however, deserve amplification. The twentieth, for example, reiterated the decree of Riez that ordination by only two bishops was forbidden: does this imply that it was still going on, or only that confirmation by such as Claudius and Eucherius was deemed useful?[91] The twenty-third once again drew its authority from the Synod of Turin ("Taurinatis synodi sequendam esse sententiam"), indicating the continued Gallic reliance upon Turin for precedents. The bishops, although continuing to recognize the

88. Agrestius has been identified as the Agrestius who wrote a poem "Inter Christicolas," also known as the *De fide*, attesting to his orthodoxy (see Smolak, *Agrestius*). In the context of the Council of Orange, such a declaration would be justified, if written by a foreign bishop wishing to participate in Gallic ecclesiastical life. Recent legislation (*Nov. Theo.* 3: 31 January 438) again had condemned Priscillianists and Manichees; any foreigner might be potentially suspect. The poem is addressed to an "illustrious Avitus." If the author of the poem is in fact Agrestius of Luco, this would have to be Eparchius Avitus, praetorian prefect of Gaul in 439, who was responsible for the enforcement of this, and other, laws against heresy. Agrestius' attendance at the Council of Orange indicates that Avitus validated his orthodoxy.

89. Claudius would have been ordained only very recently, as successor to the ephemeral Paschasius. Both are poorly known; on Claudius, even *Gallia christiana* 16.12-13 has only four lines, and Ado thought he was bishop in the time of Constantine. The metropolitans Eucherius, and Ingenuus, may only have been accorded their tenure status because they were from outside the province.

90. As by Langgärtner, *Gallienpolitik* pp.64-65. He dismisses Agrestius' presence as "zufälligen" ("accidental"). Duchesne, *Fastes* 1.113, suggests that Claudius "avait, ce semble, admis qu'Arles était la véritable métropole de la Viennoise," whereas Langgärtner, *Gallienpolitik* p.64, assumes that his presence signifies a renewed division of the province, although he also suggests (p.65) that Claudius recognized Hilary's "Obermetropolitanrechte." Franses, *Leo* p.22, calls it only a "peace."

91. Such ordination by only two bishops seems to have been a common practice in the north. In the two detailed accounts of episcopal ordinations discussed by Sidonius c.470, at Chalon-sur-Saône (*Epist.* 4.25) and Bourges (ibid.7.9), only two bishops presided.

value of holding semi-annual synods, realized "that this is difficult for us because of the nature of the times."[92] They therefore proclaimed, "We desire that no council be adjourned without the scheduling of another council," and they planned the next one for 18 October 442, also at Orange, "so that there will be no opportunity for excuse or need for an invitation."[93]

One remaining problem was bishops who had not attended. As to them, the council decreed, "We leave those others, who were absent, to the solicitude of our blessed brother Hilary, to be informed of these matters through copies forwarded to them."[94] The bishops made clear that the canons were to apply equally to those "who shirk attending the synod either in person or through written consent or through representatives sent in their place."[95] Mere failure to attend, they contended, did not absolve a bishop from responsibility for adherence.

Church councils were expected to reach unanimous decisions.[96] They therefore provided an important means by which Hilary's faction could achieve consensus and reassert its corporate authority. It could do so, however, only if bishops actually attended. Hilary, therefore, as the presiding bishop and faction leader also was given the role of "enforcer." Nor was that all, for the discussion of shirking bishops seems to have resulted in the final canon (no. 30):

After all these matters the question of the weaknesses of human frailty arises, so that if any bishop falls ill through any infirmity of weakness or dullness of the senses, or loses the function of speech, let him not permit those things which are done only through bishops to be done by presbyters in his presence, but let him call forth a bishop upon whom he can impose that which must be done in church.[97]

It is unclear, however, whether the infirm bishop was to summon a neighboring bishop or actually to name a successor.

92. "quod nobis pro temporum qualitate difficile est" (can.28[29]: *Corp. chr. lat.* 148.85).

93. "optamus ut nullus conventus sine alterius conventus denuntiatione solvatur . . . ut tam excusationis libertas quam invitationis necessitas non sit" (can.28[29]). For such invitations, see *Corp. chr. lat.* 148.132. The council was to meet "in Arausico territorio" at a place called in the manuscripts "Iustinianum," "Iustianum," and "Lucianum" (*Corp. chr. lat.* 148.86). The Council of Orange of 440 had been held "in ecclesia Iustinianensi," so perhaps the same place was meant.

94. "reliquos qui defuerunt, beatissimi fratris nostri Hilarii sollicitudini relinquimus, datis ad ipsos horum exemplaribus commonendus" (can 28[29]).

95. "qui synodo aut per se aut per consensus suos vel ad vicem sui per legatos destinandos adesse detrectant. . . ." (can.28[29]).

96. See, for example, *Epist. imp.* 40 (*C.S.E.L.* 35.91) ("concordantibus universis sacerdotibus et unanimiter deo servientibus"), and *Corp. chr. lat.* 148.56 (Turin), 70 (Riez), 85-86 (Orange), 150-151 (Vannes), 213 (Agde). See also Oehler, "Consensus omnium."

97. "post omnia occurrit de imbecillitatibus fragilitatis humanae, ut si quis episcopus per infirmitatem debilitatemve aliquam aut hebetudinem sensus inciderit, aut officium oris amiserit, ea quae nonnisi per episcopos geruntur, non sub praesentia sua presbyteros agere permittat, sed episcopum evocet cui quod in ecclesia agendum fuerit imponat."

The Council of Vaison [98]

Something, apparently, went awry with the plan to hold the next council at Orange on 18 October 442, for it did not convene until 13 November and at the more inaccessible neighboring city of Vaison.[99] The presiding officer, moreover, was Auspicius, bishop of the host city, and his name headed the list of subscribers, with Hilary's coming only second.[100] Perhaps this was a conciliatory move intended to mollify any bishops who had balked at the extraordinary status Hilary had assumed. The opening canon also was meant to promote harmony (*Corp. chr. lat.* 148.96):

> As a result of the discussion, therefore, it was our opinion that bishops attending from the Gallic provinces need not be examined, but that it should suffice if no one refused to take communion with anyone; because among those who are neighbors and are nearly all known to each other, an upright man does not need pointing out so much as a depraved one needs to be noted and denounced.[101]

This canon provides an important statement of how the bishops established unity and consensus among themselves. Bishops were not to examine each other too closely; differences which did not result in excommunication were to be played down in the desire to achieve harmony. This clause may have allowed the return of the excluded Alpine bishops. The bishops punished at the Council of Riez were specifically not forbidden communion, and Severianus of Thorâme and Severus of Vence do indeed reappear at Vaison. It also could have been a conciliatory move toward other Gallic bishops who still were not attending the councils. There is no evidence that any Gallic bishops recently had excommunicated each other, so unless any of the Felician excommunications were still in effect, this canon may have been a call for bishops estranged from one another for other reasons to be reconciled.[102]

If this was the case, the move may have had its desired effect. The

---

98. For the text, see *Corp. chr. lat.* 148.94-104; see also Griffe, *Gaule* 2.158; Hefele-Leclercq, *Conciles* 2.454-460; and Langgärtner, *Gallienpolitik* pp.65-66.

99. Orange was located on the major north-south Roman road, Vaison not on any important road; see Cunze, *Geographie*; Desjardins, *Géographie*; and Sitwell, *Roman Roads*.

100. Moreover, the incipit states that the synod was held "in civitate Vasensi apud Auspicium episcopum" (*Corp. chr. lat.* 148.96).

101. "placuit ergo tractatu habito episcopos de Gallicanis provinciis venientes intra Gallias non discutiendos, sed solum sufficere si nullus communionem alicuius interdixerit; quia inter circumhabitantes ac sibi pene invicem notos, non tam testimonio indiget probus quam denotatione et denuntiationibus depravatus."

102. Duchesne, *Fastes* 1.124, suggests that none of the other bishops in Gaul ever broke communion with Arles.

attendance at this council was even more complete than at the previous ones, with twenty-two cities represented, compared with seventeen at Orange and fifteen at Riez. From Viennensis came all the bishops who had attended either of the first two, with the addition of the archdeacon Galatheus representing Chariatto of Valence, who perhaps still was occupied with the Alans. Claudius of Vienne, moreover, retained his metropolitan status, again subscribing immediately after Hilary.[103] The contingent from Narbonensis Secunda was augmented by the aged Armentarius of Antibes, apparently a new recruit to Hilary's party, for he had been in office since c.420/425.[104] Alpine representatives also included Valerianus of Cimiez, and another newcomer, Superventor, the son of bishop Claudius of Castellane, but of an unknown see.

Also attending was Constantius of Uzès, who, even though technically a suffragan of Rusticus of Narbonne, had been ordained by either Honoratus or Hilary.[105] He not only seems to have abandoned his *de iure* metropolitan, but he also was to go on to become one of Hilary's strongest supporters.[106] Missing this time, however, was Eucherius of Lyons.[107]

Several other canons also were intended to restrict dissension, and to ensure that the Gallic bishops maintained solidarity. Canon 5, for example, asserted that "if anyone does not agree with the sentence of his bishop, let him have recourse to a synod."[108] The sixth stated,

If there is an enemy of any bishop, do not expect him to speak to you: do not wish to be friends with him. . . . When anyone is at fault, when he desires to restore himself to the good graces of all of you, let him hasten quickly to be reconciled to the one in charge [sc. the bishop], so that through him he might return to safety. . . . Moreover, let a cleric therefore realize that there is reason

---

103. In the ninth century, Ado of Vienne referred to (*P.L.* 123.92), "Nectarius Viennensis episcopus . . . qui in Vasensi illa synodo venerabili primus interfuit." Ado may have confused Nectarius of Vienne with Nectarius of Avignon, who did attend. See Hefele-Leclercq, *Conciles* 2.296 and Langgärtner, *Gallienpolitik* pp.65-66.

104. Had Armentarius been sympathetic to Hilary in 439, he surely would have been represented at the nearby Council of Riez. Could he perhaps have been a relative of the Armentarius who was deposed? For his date of ordination, see appendix "Episcopal Hierarchy" below.

105. For Uzès and Arles, see chapter 4 above, n.5. Griffe, *Gaule* 2.158, suggests that the see of Uzès was organized only c.440, but Constantius clearly had been in office roughly ten years longer.

106. Griffe, *Gaule* 2.158, suggests that Constantius was Rusticus' "representative" at Vaison, but given Rusticus' total lack of cooperation with Hilary (see chapter 6 below), and Constantius' later extraordinary support for Hilary, this scarcely seems likely.

107. Perhaps his presence was not considered crucial; perhaps he felt one appearance was sufficient to make his point; perhaps he had other business; or perhaps he was even upset over not having been allowed clear metropolitan status the year before.

108. "si quis episcopi sui sententiae non adquiescit recurrat ad synodum."

for an accusation if anyone is discovered in this evil as a comforter of the wicked and a subverter of discipline.[109]

The seventh and eighth canons reiterated the first, asserting that bishops were to refrain from frivolous accusations. Investigations were only to be *de crimine*, and bishops, or clerics of one bishop, accused by another bishop were to remain in the communion of all except the accuser until the accusation was proven. All these canons demonstrate the desire of these Gallic bishops to solve their problems themselves; nowhere is there any hint of any higher court of appeal.

It was very rare during late antiquity, however, that a problem could be solved simply by passing a law against it, and there is no indication that the case was any different in Gaul. Perhaps the most that can be said for canons such as these is that they demonstrate the extent to which dissension existed. If it were to be restrained, other, more substantial, measures would have to be taken. One such would be the corporate pressure allied bishops could bring to bear in the context of these church councils. Another would be the influence of powerful, and sympathetic, *saeculares*.

The role of the bishop of Arles in the summoning of church councils also is seen in the canons of the so-called "Second Council of Arles," the first known Gallic attempt to codify past conciliar canons.[110] The collection includes canons of the Councils of Arles (314), Nicaea (325), Valence (374), Riez (439), Orange (441), and Vaison (442). It presumably, therefore, was assembled at some time after 442, although exactly when and by whom is uncertain.[111] Although most of the canons merely repeat canons of these earlier Gallic councils, some do introduce measures new to Gaul. They are even more specific on the right of the bishop of Arles to summon councils (can.18):

A synod must be assembled at the instigation of the bishop of Arles, at which city we read that a council and assembly was held from all parts of the world at the time of the blessed Marinus [A.D. 314]. If anyone invited is absent by reason of illness, let him send someone in his place.[112]

109. "si inimicus est alicui [sc. episcopo] pro actibus suis vos nolite expectare ut ipse vobis dicat: cum illo nolite amici esse. . . . ut unusquisque qui in culpa est, dum cupit omnium vestrum sibi gratiam reparare, festinet citius reconciliari ei qui omnibus praeest, ut per hoc redeat ad salutem. . . . sciat itaque deinceps clerus ad reatum . . . si quis in hoc vitio malorum confortator et disciplinae subversor agnoscitur."

110. *Corp. chr. lat.* 148. 111-130.

111. See *Corp. chr. lat.* 148.111; Duchesne, *Fastes* 1.143 and Langgärtner, *Gallienpolitik* p.66. For suggested dates, see Beck, *Pastoral Care* p.17 (452); Hefele-Leclercq, *Conciles* 2.460-476 (443/452); Munier, *Corp. chr. lat.* 148.111 (442/506); and Turner, "Arles" pp.236-247 (c.450).

112. "ad Arelatensis episcopi arbitrium synodus congreganda, ad quam urbem ex omnibus mundi partibus sub sancti Marini tempore [sc. anno 314] legimus celebratum fuisse concilium atque conventum, si quis commonitus infirmitatis causa defuerit, personam vice sua dirigat."

The author apparently cited the earliest precedent for the authority of Arles that he could find. The collection also reemphasized the importance of attending councils: absenteeism and early departure were punishable by excommunication (can.19).

Along with friendly encouragement, at either the individual or the conciliar level, there also may have been other ways in which Hilary consolidated his support. A later bishop of Rome, Hilarus, for example, in December of 462 referred to "parishes of the church of Arles transferred to others by [Leontius of Arles'] predecessor Hilary."[113] Hilary, therefore, had been alienating some of the parishes of his church.[114] The beneficiaries presumably would have been one or more bishops of the immediately adjacent sees, which included Marseilles, Nîmes, Avignon, Cavaillon, and perhaps Uzès. Now, it is unlikely that Hilary would have ceded any of his parishes to Venerius of Marseilles, or to the bishop of Nîmes, a suffragan of Rusticus of Narbonne.[115] He may, however, have assigned them to Nectarius of Avignon or Constantius of Uzès, who, coincidentally or otherwise, were to appear as two of his very strongest supporters in the years to come. Perhaps he returned parishes, even on the far side of the Rhône, which had been appropriated by Patroclus in the past. Hilary's alienation of these parishes would illustrate, again, the spirit of cooperation which united his party, and give the lie to the view that he was a power-hungry expansionist.

As of the mid-440s, then, Hilary and his faction had met with widespread success. Many of their partisans had been installed in episcopal sees. They had influential friends in the highest Gallic secular offices. Their members made up the premier literary circle of Gaul. Under Hilary's leadership, they exercised their collegiate authority in regular church councils. Their influence extended not only over Viennensis, Narbonensis Secunda, and Alpes Maritimae, but also into Narbonensis Prima in the west, and north into the Lugdunenses. All of which could lead these episcopal allies to assert in 450 that the prestige

---

The emphasis on the authority of Arles would be consistent with a date of soon after 442 for the compilation, although the restrictions placed upon metropolitans (cans.54, 56) might indicate a later date.

113. "parochias Arelatensis ecclesiae a praedecessore suo Hilario in alios ... translatas" (*Epist.* "Quamquam notitiam": *M.G.H. Epist.* 3.27).

114. The alienation of church lands was not an uncommon practice. Sidonius (*Epist.* 4.25.2) tells how a candidate for bishop of Chalon hoped to gain support: "tacita pactione promiserat ecclesiastica plorosibus suis praedae praedia fore."

115. On the enmity of the bishops of Narbonne and Marseilles toward the bishop of Arles, see chapter 6 below. For Hilary's supposed unwillingness to alienate any parishes, see Thiel, *Epistolae* p.146 n.15.

of the bishop of Arles had become so great, "that he not only oversees under his authority these [three] provinces, but he also holds nearly all the Gauls under every ecclesiastical rule."[116]

The nominal leaders of the Lérins faction effectively exercised the authority which had been granted by Zosimus to Patroclus of Arles, however much Boniface and his immediate successors may have attempted to restrict it. Hilary's authority, however, came from a very different source from that of Patroclus. Patroclus had had very close ties not only to the imperial administration of both Gaul and Rome, but also to the bishop of Rome himself. There is no evidence, however, that the Lérins bishops of Arles had, or sought, any secular or ecclesiastical support from Rome. From 420 until 450, no Roman pontiff appears in any way to have viewed the bishop of Arles as his "representative" in Gaul; nor did the Gauls make any overtures to him. They preferred to acquire their authority from their unity and councils, not from the bishop of Rome or the imperial government.[117] In so doing, they pursued an "isolationist" policy similar to that of the Felicians in the late fourth century and the adherents of the usurpers in the early fifth. The ability of the Lerinenses to extend their ecclesiastical authority in Gaul without the help of the Roman see would only have weakened the pope's influence there.

---

116. "ut non tantum has [tres] provincias potestate gubernaret, verumtamen omnes Gallias ... sub omni ecclesiastica regula contineret" (*Epist.* "Memores quantum": *M.G.H. Epist.* 3.17-20).

117. It may be significant that Patroclus is not known to have sponsored, or attended, a single Gallic council.

CHAPTER 6

THE LÉRINS FACTION,
PART III

CONTROVERSY AND OPPOSITION
IN GAUL

The preceding discussion has indicated that during the period c.425-442 the party of Lérins was remarkably successful in establishing itself in southern Gaul. This does not mean, however, that there was no opposition to the rising influence of Lérins. No, the policies of Hilary and his allies were to bring them into conflict with other powerful parties, first in Gaul and then in Rome.

THE OPPOSITION IN GAUL:
THE EVIDENCE OF HILARY'S COUNCILS

One indication of who opposed Hilary comes from studying those who regularly absented themselves from his councils. Now, one or two such absences might have been justified by illness, travel difficulties, or other business. Persistent and regular absence, however, especially by influential clerics, might have been deliberate, and can suggest failure to cooperate, passive resistance, or even out and out opposition to the pretensions of Hilary and his partisans.

It already has been noted that at the Council of Riez in 439 the bishop of Vienne and his suffragans in Viennensis (Grenoble, Valence, and Geneva) were conspicuously absent. It is unclear, however, who the bishop of Vienne at this time was.[1] If the absence of all these bishops can be taken to indicate opposition, then Claudius probably had not yet become bishop of Vienne, for he did attend the Councils of Orange and Vaison. The bishop in 439 therefore probably was either the aged, influential Simplicius or his successor, the ephemeral

1. For the bishops of Vienne during this period, see Duchesne, *Fastes* 1.147-205.

Paschasius.[2] The latter may be the more likely of the two. Perhaps Simplicius had died recently, and the presence of a new and untried bishop at Vienne encouraged Hilary to act. This would explain why he allowed the situation at Embrun to fester for nearly two years before he finally took action. The new bishop Paschasius would have been very junior and hardly in a position to challenge Hilary openly, even if he resisted him passively.

Other bishops were absent from all three councils. With the exception only of Constantius of Uzès in 442, Rusticus of Narbonne and all his suffragans of Narbonensis Prima also failed to attend any of these councils.[3] From Narbonensis Secunda, only the Lerinenses Theodorus of Fréjus and Maximus of Riez attended, along with Julius of Apt and, in 442 only, Armentarius of Antibes. Although Julius' affiliations are unknown, his predecessor Castor, another well-known monk, was associated with Honoratus of Lérins under the year 419 in the *Gallic Chronicle of 452* (no.86). Castor also not only was the dedicatee of Cassian's *Institutes* and of the epitome of the same work by Eucherius of Lyons, he also was included with several Lerinenses among the dedicatees of Cassian's *Collationes*.[4] One could suggest, at least, that Julius inherited his predecessor's affiliations.

The other bishops concerned with the province, however, including the two presumptive metropolitans from Marseilles and Aix, were pointedly absent from all three of these councils.[5] The former was Venerius, who by 431 had succeeded the elderly Proculus. According to the canons of Turin, the metropolitan status of Marseilles then should have passed to Aix, but later events will show that Venerius nonetheless had metropolitan aspirations of his own. Furthermore, the bishop of Aix, whose name is unknown, presumably also would have wished to exercise the metropolitan rights which were *de iure* his, but which now had been appropriated by Arles. As a result, he would have been all the more isolated because of the traditional antipathy of his see toward Marseilles.

The bishop of Aix seems to have responded to the pretensions of the bishop of Arles in the same way as did a successor of his in the

---

2. See chapter 5 above, n.89.

3. Duchesne wrongly asserts (*Fastes* 1.127) that Rusticus is seen "assister volontiers aux conciles arlésiens et prendre part à toutes les affaires ecclésiastiques du midi de la Gaule." This statement is applicable only to the special circumstances of the years 449-450 (chapter 8 below).

4. *P.L.* 49.55, q.v. 53-54 for a supposed letter from Castor to Cassian. For the epitome of this letter published in *P.L.* 50.867-894, see Diekamp, "Titelfälschung" pp.341-355.

5. Duchesne (*Fastes* 1.113) refers to "l'abstention platonique d'Aix et de Marseille," and (1.124, cf. 1.99, 298) to their "opposition tacite." See also Griffe, "Primatie" p.72; Langgärtner, *Gallienpolitik* p.66; Palanque, "Evêchés" pp.122-125 and "Premiers" p.381; and Weiss, "Valérien" pp.121-122.

early sixth century, when Symmachus, bishop of Rome, wrote to Caesarius of Arles, yet another alumnus of Lérins (*Epist.* "Quantum in
omnibus": *M.G.H. Epist.* 3.42),

Indeed, see to it that the bishop of the city of Aix is advised by the decisions
of Your Sanctity, so that when he is summoned to a synod by the metropolitan bishop of the church of Arles, or when holy religion demands his presence as necessary for some reason of ordination, he does not at all decline
to come.[6]

The bishops of Aix, therefore, had a long history of passive resistance
to the bishop of Arles. The bishop of Marseilles well may have done
the same. Both can be expected to have opposed Hilary's attempts to
extend his own metropolitan authority into Narbonensis Secunda, just
as Proculus had resisted Patroclus. One means by which they did so
was by refusing to attend any of Hilary's councils.

The Monastic Circle of Marseilles

Nor are any ties among this opposition to Hilary merely to be inferred from a shared resistance to Arles. It is known, for example, that
Rusticus of Narbonne and Venerius of Marseilles were close to each
other. In the early 420s they had been fellow monks and co-presbyters
under Proculus at Marseilles, presumably in the monastery of St.
Victor.[7] They continued to maintain the ties formed there after both
became bishops, for in 445 Venerius contributed at least 100 solidi for
Rusticus' restoration of the cathedral of Narbonne (*C.I.L.* 12.5336): no
such contributions were forthcoming from any of the Lerinenses.
Indeed, the dedicatory inscription even emphasized the ties between
the two bishops: "The bishop Rusticus, son of the bishop Bonosus,
nephew of the bishop Arator through his sister, comrade and fellow-
presbyter of Venerius in the monastery at Marseilles...."[8]

The parallels between the practices of the alumni of Lérins and St.
Victor are clear, even though those of the latter are less well documented. Like their brethren from Lérins, Rusticus and Venerius had

6. "Aquensis etiam civitatis episcopum sanctitatis vestrae moneri praecipite constitutis,
ut dum a metropolitano antistite ecclesiae Arelatensis ad synodale concilium fuerit evocatus,
vel aliqua ordinationis causa eum sibi postulet religio divina necessarium, minime venire
frustretur...."

7. Rusticus seems to have adopted the monastic life c.414; Jerome (*Epist.* 125.17) wrote to
him "vive in monasterio, ut clericus esse merearis...et te vel populus vel pontifex civitatis in
clerum adlegerit," apparently suggesting the role of the monastic life as a steppingstone to
greater things.

8. "Rusticus ep[iscopu]s Bonosi filius / ep[iscop]i Aratoris de sorore nepus / ep[iscop]i Veneri
soci[us] in monasterio / conpr[es]b[yteri] eccle[siae] Massiliens[is] ..." On this inscription, see
Marrou, "Dossier" passim. For a contemporary cultural bond between Narbonne and Marseilles,
see Ward-Perkins, "Sculpture" pp.85-86.

a shared monastic experience in their background, and both had been raised to the rank of presbyter by Proculus. Furthermore, the monks of St. Victor likewise participated actively in literary activities. Massiliote ecclesiastical authors included the presbyters Cassian, Salvian (after he left Lérins), Musaeus, Vincentius, and Gennadius, as well as the Massiliote bishop Honoratus.[9] Moreover, there can be little doubt but that Rusticus gained the see of Narbonne with the aid of his powerful patron Proculus, just as Honoratus and Hilary aided their partisans at the same time. Likewise, Venerius would have succeeded Proculus in just the way that Hilary had succeeded his fellow monk Honoratus. Later in the century, another cleric of Marseilles, Eutropius, was able to become bishop of Orange.[10] One can only guess at how many other monks of St. Victor also became bishops.[11]

Rusticus and The Church of Narbonne

One of the most powerful Gallic bishops of this period was Rusticus of Narbonne, who was ordained on 9 October 427 as the successor to Hilarius.[12] Rusticus, with the assistance of his clergy, was an indefatigable church builder, not only in Narbonne, but also in the far corners of his diocese.[13] His building activities would have been one of the means he used to assert, and magnify, his local influence and status. The dedicatory inscription cited above shows that, like some of the Lerinenses, Rusticus too was a member of an ecclesiastical dynasty: his father and uncle also had been bishops.

An indication of Rusticus' independent-mindedness is seen in his practice of dating events by the years of his own episcopate; only on occasion did he also include the more standard consular years.[14] One possible reason for Rusticus' show of autonomy may have been the exposed position of his see, bordering on the eastern edge of the Visigothic kingdom. Although the sees of Narbonne, Béziers, Lodève, Nîmes, and, in theory, Uzès in the eastern half of his province appear to have remained under his jurisdiction, the west, including Toulouse, was controlled by the Goths. This consideration perhaps forced Rusticus all the more to focus his attention upon the east when it came to involvements in Gallic ecclesiastical affairs.

9. Gennad. *Vir. ill.* 62, 68, 80, 81, 100, and 101 respectively. Other Massiliote writers included the rhetor Victorinus (ibid.61) and Paulinus of Pella.

10. See chapter 9 below, n.40.

11. For the importance of the monastery of St. Victor as a source of bishops, see Palanque, *Marseilles* p.24 and Prinz, *Mönchtum* p. 61.

12. Duchesne, *Fastes* 1.303, cf. 1.127-128; see also Griffe, *Gaule* 2.265-268 and Heinzelmann, *Bischofsherrschaft* p.109.

13. See Chalon, "Inscriptions" p.224ff and Marrou, "Dossier" pp.339-346.

14. See Chalon, "Inscriptions" passim and Marrou, "Dossier" passim.

Like his brethren associated with Lérins, Rusticus had influential
allies not only in the church, but also in the secular world. Another
contributor, of at least 1200 solidi, to the restoration of the cathedral
of Narbonne was the praetorian prefect of Gaul c.441-443 Marcellus,
who may have had family ties in the city.[15] If Marcellus were indeed
a partisan of Rusticus, a curious passage from the *Vita Hilarii* might
belong in this context, especially if Rusticus and Hilary were actively
opposed to one another. Hilary's biographer said of him (*VHilarii*
10[13]):

And how much strictness he had in the cause of justice he made clear most
openly, to the extent that he did not even spare the dignity of the prefecture ... for after [Hilary] had often secretly warned the prefect of that time
that he should restrain himself from unjust judgments, and [the prefect] with
his accustomed error was borne forward headlong, it happened that while
the sacred rites were being celebrated in the Basilica Constantia ... suddenly
the prefect entered with his retinue. When Hilary saw him waiting there, he
ceased preaching ... and [the prefect], smitten with a fitting confusion,
departed....[16]

Now, other evidence has shown that Hilary usually was on good terms
with the high secular authorities of Gaul. This section seems to indicate, however, that one prefect in particular did suffer Hilary's ire.
Although the *vita* does not state that Marcellus was the prefect concerned here, he is an attractive candidate. During Marcellus' tenure in
the early 440s Hilary's influence was at its height, and if he were going
to embarrass a hostile prefect, this was the time to do it. If Marcellus
were a partisan of Rusticus, all the more reason for him to have opposed Hilary, especially if he were one of the individuals whom Hilary
later was accused of wrongly excommunicating.[17]

Like other powerful Gallic bishops, Rusticus seems to have been

15. On Marcellus' connections, see Mathisen, "Resistance," pp.598-603. *P.L.R.E. II* p.712 cites
the figure as 1200 solidi; Marrou, "Dossier" p.340 and Chalon, "Inscriptions" p.228 give for
Marcellus a total of 2100 solidi. The inscription itself (*C.I.L.* 12.5336) reads, "Marcellus
Gall[iarum] pr[a]ef[ectus] d[e]i cultor prece exegit ep[iscopu]m hoc on[u]s suscip[ere] inpendia
necessar[ia] repromittens quae per bienn[ium] administ[rationis] suae pr[a]ebu[it] artifi[ci]b[us]
merced[em] sol[idos] DC ad oper[a] et ceter[a] sol[idos] ID." *C.I.L.* suggests the "ID" represents
"mille quingentos," or 1500 solidi, but *P.L.R.E.* presumably supposes it merely means "IDEM,"
i.e. an additional 600.

16. "quantum igitur districtionis habuerit in causa iustitiae apertissime declaravit, ita ut ne
dignitati quidem pepercerit praefecturae. nam cum saepius praefectum temporis illius secrete
monuisset ut ab iniustis iudiciis se temperaret et consuetudinario lapso ille ferretur in praeceps,
accidit ut dum in basilica Constantia sacra solemnia celebrantur ... subito cum suo ingrederetur
officio praefectura, quam dum ibidem cerneret immorantem a praedicatione cessavit ... at ubi
ille digna confusione perfusus egressus est...." Note also Gennad. *Vir. ill.* 70, "absque personarum acceptione omnibus castigatum opus praedicationis ingessit" ("[Hilary] entered the task of
preaching censuring everyone, without any allowance for individuals").

17. See chapter 7 below, n.56.

concerned with finding episcopal sees for his ecclesiastical supporters and protégés. His deacon, archdeacon, and presbyter Hermes, who also aided in the reconstruction of the cathedral, obtained the neighboring see of Béziers.[18] Individuals with the same names as other Narbonese clerics who contributed to Rusticus' building projects also later appear in the south as bishops, and likewise may have benefited from Rusticus' support.[19] Rusticus, then, apparently was the leader of another highly organized ecclesiastical faction in southern Gaul which operated in much the same way as the party of Lérins, even if in a rather more restricted venue.

The circle of Lérins, therefore, did not have a monopoly when it came to the placing of its alumni in episcopal sees; others, such as the monastery of Marseilles, and the party of Rusticus, did the same. Given the small number of available sees, there well may have been competition over them in the years after 425, and it should be no surprise if controversies and even animosities were the result. Rusticus, for example, hardly could have been pleased with the *de facto* control of the see of Uzès by the bishops of Arles.

THE CHURCH OF MARSEILLES: AUGUSTINE, PELAGIANISM, AND PREDESTINATION

At Marseilles, the powerful bishop Proculus had organized an influential monastery which predated even that of Lérins and which housed Cassian and Salvian, both of whom had close ties to Lérins. Shortly after 400, Proculus even had attempted to gain the services of Honoratus himself after the latter left home, as noted by Hilary: "This very one [sc. Honoratus], whose memory we today cherish, the church of Marseilles then nearly snatched from this city, with the bishop of that city [sc. Proculus] encouraging him and rejoicing in such a colleague."[20] Shortly thereafter, Salvian transferred from Lérins to the monastery of St. Victor, nor did his relations with his

---

18. See Marrou, "Dossier" p. 332 and chapter 9 below.

19. Contributors: a presbyter Ursus in 445 (*C.I.L.* 12.5336), and a presbyter Projectus and a deacon Avitianus in 456 (Espérandieu, no.604). Bishops of these names, from unknown southern sees, later appear in Gallic ecclesiastical proceedings—Ursus in 451 (*Corp. chr. lat.* 148.109; identified by Marrou, "Dossier" p.339), and Projectus, Ursus, and Avitianus in 464 (*M.G.H. Epist.* 3.30-32). Marrou ("Dossier" p.340) also identifies another contributor, Oresius, with a bishop of "Tarragona." Oresius of Tarraconensis, however, seems to have been a layman (Sid. Apoll. *Epist.* 9.12; *P.L.R.E. II* p.810).

20. "hunc ipsum [sc. Honoratum] iam tunc cuius hodie memoria pascimur, urbi huic Massiliensis ecclesia paene praeripuit, hortante illius urbis antistite, et tali eo gaudente collegio" (*VHonorati* 13). See Duchesne, *Fastes* 1.107.

past brethren seem to suffer.[21] In the early part of the century, there-fore, even if the bishops of Arles and Marseilles did not get along, relations between the monastic circles of Marseilles and Lérins appear to have been cordial.

A theological controversy which arose at Marseilles in the mid 420s also seems to have involved some of the Lerinenses.[22] Much of the rhetoric in this dispute concerned Pelagianism, although this phase of the Pelagian controversy in Gaul was not over Pelagianism *per se* at all, but over Augustine's theory of predestination.[23] Nevertheless, because Pelagianism had been such a *cause celèbre*, those on both sides of this, and other, theological controversies tended to use it as a straw man.

Now, in nearly every regard, Augustine was greatly respected in Gaul, and every fifth-century Gallic theologian cited him, at least on occasion, as an authority.[24] His anti-Pelagian stand was consistent with the prevalent condemnation of the belief in Gaul: The *Gallic Chronicle of 452*, for example, could state under the year 400, "The insane Pelagius attempts to befoul the churches with his execrable teaching."[25]

The sticking point, however, was Augustine's concept of predesti-nation, and the same *Gallic Chronicle* also noted under the year 418, "The heresy of the predestinarians, which is said to have received its impetus from Augustine, once arisen creeps along."[26] The pro-predestinarian letter written by Augustine at roughly the same time to the ex-Gallic prefect Dardanus, by then comfortably ensconsced in

21. See chapter 4 above, n.47.

22. For the "écoles théologiques" at Marseilles and Lérins c.425-430, see Bardy, "Ecoles" pp.101-102.

23. On the decline of Pelagianism in Gaul, see Kidd, *Church* p.383. On the Gallic opposition to Augustine, see Bardy et. al., *Eglise* pp.399-404; von Harnack, *Lehrbuch* pp.240-257; Kidd, *Church* p.360 (the "excesses . . . of Augustine"); and Turner, "Arles and Rome" p.244.

24. Note the *Excerpta* from Augustine of Vincentius of Lérins (J. Madoz ed. [Madrid, 1940]) on the trinity and the incarnation; Cass. *De incarn.* 7.27 (a backhanded reference to "Augustinus Hipponae Regiensis oppidi magnus sacerdos"); and the two citations by Faustus of Riez (*C.S.E.L.* 21.468); see Bardy et al., *Eglise* p.402. Note also the sermon, ascribed to Faustus, *In depositione s. Augustini* (*C.S.E.L.* 21.330-334), on which see Engelbrecht, *Studien* pp.27, 90ff; Bergmann, *Predigtliteratur* pp.248-255; and Morin, "Critique" p.59, the latter two of whom deny Faustus' authorship, and suggest Caesarius of Arles. For Mamertus Claudianus' use of Augus-tine, see chapter 10 below.

25. "Pelagius vesanus doctrina execrabili ecclesias conmaculare conatur" (no. 44).

26. "praedestinatorum haeresis quae ab Augustino accepisse initium dicitur his temporibus serpere exorsa" (no. 81). Note, e.g., Morris, *Arthur*, p.72, who, apparently unaware of the entry for the year 400, assumes that the *Chronicle of 452* must be pro-Pelagian, viz. because it is anti-predestinarian. 418 was the date of Augustine's letter (*Epist.* 194) on predestination and grace to the priest Sixtus, (Wermelinger, *Pelagius* p.248 presumes not only that this is Sixtus, the later bishop of Rome, but also that he was in Gaul at the time of the letter). One might at least note contemporary Gallic pagan opposition to Augustine, as discussed by Cameron, "Rutilius" and Dufourcq, "Rutilius."

his refuge at Theopolis, might even indicate Augustine's recognition of the Gallic opposition to his position.[27] Predestination was seen as smacking of fatalism, Priscillianism, or Manichean dualism.[28]

The schizophrenic Gallic attitude toward Augustine is seen in the controversy which arose over certain of his teachings in the neighborhood of Marseilles in the mid-420s in conjunction with the publication of his *De correptione et gratia* (*P.L.* 44). In 426, Cassian of Marseilles published the second installment of his *Collationes*, and book thirteen contained a discussion of the need for human effort along with grace, and an attack upon both Pelagianism and unconditional predestination.[29] As was the custom of the times, however, Cassian genteelly refrained from attacking his distinguished opponent by name.[30]

Circa 426 two of Augustine's supporters, the laymen Hilarius and Prosper, wrote extant letters to him from Marseilles decrying the situation in Gaul.[31] Hilarius reported, "These are the charges being aired about in Marseilles and even in other places in Gaul: that your idea

27. *Epist.* 187 (*C.S.E.L.* 57.81-108); see Wermelinger, *Pelagius* p.245.

28. Fatalism and Priscillianism: Vincentius *Comm.* 26ff; see Bardy et al., *Eglise* pp.402-403. Fatalism and Manicheism: Prosp. *Epist. ad Rufin.* 3 ("dicentes ... ut scilicet tantae pietatis viro paganorum et Manichaeorum ascribatur impietas"); see Wermelinger, *Pelagius* p.245.

29. This section was published while Helladius was bishop of Arles, on whom see chapter 4 above. For Cassian's arguments, see von Harnack, *Lehrbuch* pp.243-244. Cassian had been ordained a deacon by John Chrysostom in Constantinople (Cass. *De incarn.* 7.31; Gennad. *Vir. ill.* 62), and, apparently before 410, had carried a letter from Chrysostom to Innocent of Rome, where he may have met Leo. He subsequently was ordained a presbyter, either by Innocent or, more likely, by Proculus of Marseilles after his arrival in Gaul by c.410. See Cass. *De incarn. praef.*, *Coll.* 24.1; Pallad. *Dial.* 3; and Soz. *H.E.* 8.26; see also Bardy et al., *Eglise* pp.398-399; Chadwick, *Cassian* pp.32-33; and Gibson, *Cassian* pp.183-188 (who suggests Cassian was a native of Provence).

30. Other opponents of predestination ostentatiously disassociated Augustine from the heresy. The so-called *Praedestinatus*, for example, in its list of heresies concluded (ch.90), "nonagesima haeresis, quam ... de nomine Augustini episcopi esse mentitam, praedestinatorum nomen accepit." This work has been attributed with some cause to the mid-fifth-century Italian writer Arnobius Junior, see Altaner, *Patrology* p.546; *Clavis* no.243; McClure, "Handbooks" pp.192-193; and Morin, "Examen" pp.419-432. This same Arnobius, in his commentary *In psalmum centesimum octavum* (*P.L.* 53.495), also discussed the heresy "quae dicit deum alios praedestinasse ad benedictionem, alios ad maledictionem," although elsewhere he dutifully noted, "quis enim nesciat Augustinum orthodoxum semper fuisse doctorem."

31. For Hilarius and Prosper, see von Harnack, *Lehrbuch* p.242ff. For Prosper's works, see *Clavis* nos.516-535. For his anti-Pelagianism, see Koch, *Faustus* pp.40-44; Turner, "Arles and Rome" p.244; and Wermelinger, *Pelagius* p.244ff; for his Augustinianism, see Griffe, *Gaule* 2.173-174; and Lorenz, "Augustinismus" pp.217-252. Wermelinger, *Pelagius* (pp.245-246, 276-278, 334) supposes Hilarius was the now-dead Hilarius of Narbonne. Hilarius seems to have been a transient in Marseilles, and he was about to leave when he wrote his letter; perhaps he was the same Hilarius who wrote to Augustine c.415 about Pelagians in Sicily (Aug. *Epist.* 156-157, see Wermelinger, *Pelagius* pp.75-77, 177-179, 291-292). There is no evidence to support the contention of von Harnack, *Lehrbuch* p.245, that Prosper was "in den berühmten Klöstern der Provence heimisch." Prosper's letter is sometimes dated wrongly to 429 because the bishop of Arles, Helladius, mentioned in it has been confused with Hilary of Arles; see Chadwick, "Euladius" passim; Jalland, *Leo* p.122 n.36; and Kidd, *Church* p.356.

that certain individuals are designated as the elect according to a fixed purpose is an innovation and is useless for preaching."[32] Prosper's letter gave a similar account: "Many of the servants of Christ who live in Marseilles think that, in the writings which Your Sanctity composed against the Pelagian heretics, whatever you said in them about the choice of the elect according to the fixed purpose of God is contrary to the opinion of the fathers and to ecclesiastical feeling."[33]

In another letter of about the same time to a certain Rufinus, who seems to have been an anti-Augustinian himself, Prosper ironically attempted to refute the Gallic attack on Augustine (*P.L.* 51.79):

If these things are true, why are they [sc. the anti-Augustinians] so negligent, or rather should I say impious, that ... they do not oppose such insane preaching, or do not at least challenge the one from whom such teaching emanates with writings of some sort? Indeed, they would act in the interest of humankind, to their own great credit, if they were to recall Augustine from error.... If we are rebuked justly, why are we not convincingly exposed? If we do not deserve to be exposed, why are we gnawed at by secret disparagement?[34]

Of course, the fact that Augustine's opponents were indeed attacking him openly and in writing would have had no effect on Prosper's rhetoric. Prosper then went on to write his 1000-line *De ingratis carmen* (*Poem on the Opponents of Grace*) and the *Epigrammata in obtrectatorem Augustini* (*Epigrams against the Detractor of Augustine*).[35]

Meanwhile, Gallic theological discussions were complicated even further in 429 when Cassian of Marseilles was requested by the deacon, later bishop, Leo of Rome to compose a tract condemning

32. "haec sunt itaque quae Massiliae vel etiam aliquibus locis in Gallia ventilantur: novum et inutile esse praedicationi, quod quidam secundum propositum eligendi dicantur...." (*apud* Aug. *Epist.* 226).

33. "multi ergo servorum Christi qui in Massiliensi urbe consistunt in sanctitatis tuae scriptis, quae adversus Pelagianos haereticos condidisti, contrarium putant patrum opinioni et ecclesiastico sensui, quidquid in eis de vocatione electorum secundum dei propositum disputasti...." (*apud* Aug. *Epist.* 225). See Pelland, *Prosperi* pp.37-44 (dated wrongly to late 428/early 429).

34. "quae si vera sunt, cur ipsi tam negligentes, ne dicam tam impii, sunt, ut ... tam insanis praedicationibus non resistant, nec saltem aliquibus scriptis eum, a quo talis emanat doctrina, conveniant? magna enim gloria sua humano generi consuluerint, si Augustinum ab errore revocaverint.... si recte reprehendimur, cur non constanter arguimur? si arguendi non sumus, cur occulta obtrectatione mordemur?" For discussion, and date of c.426/427, see Pelland, *Prosperi* pp.23-36.

35. *De ingratis*: *P.L.* 51.91-148; Huegelmeyer, *Carmen*; and Pelland, *Prosperi* pp.45-53. The title comes from Augustine's *Contra Iulianum Pelagianum* 4.3.15 (*P.L.* 44.744), "O ingrati gratiae dei. O inimici gratiae Christi ..." *Epigrammata*: *P.L.* 51.149-152. The *obtrectator* wrote under a pseudonym: "nec te mutato defendi nomine credas / si pastorem ovium laedere vis, lupus es...." (*P.L.* 51.150). Vincentius of Lérins did write a pseudonymous *Commonitorium* (see n.86 below) some years later, and the reference to the *obtrectator* as a "lupus" may even be a reference to Vincentius' brother Lupus of Troyes, who was at Lérins at this time.

the Christological views of bishop Nestorius of Constantinople, who wished to separate the human from the divine nature of Christ.[36] In the resultant work, the *De incarnatione Christi*, Cassian made a connection between Nestorianism and Pelagianism: "Therefore, you say that Christ was born only as a mere man. Certainly, that heresy of the Pelagian impiety, as I clearly showed in the first book, also preached this, that Christ was born only as a mere man.... Therefore, you see that you vomit the Pelagian poison, that you hiss with the Pelagian spirit." [37]

As an example of the relation between Nestorianism and Pelagianism, Cassian recalled the case of the Gallic monk Leporius, apparently another displaced northern aristocrat.[38] He, and others, had been expelled from Marseilles and elsewhere for deviant beliefs.[39] Cassian refered to "Leporius ... who as one of the primary or greatest assertors of the aforementioned heresy [sc. Nestorianism] in Gaul, a descendent of the teaching, or rather the depravity, of Pelagius, was warned by me, but corrected by God...." [40] Cassian's bishop Proculus also became involved in the controversy and, in conjunction with an otherwise unknown bishop Cillenius, sent Leporius to Augustine, who later wrote back to them (*Epist.* 219.1: *C.S.E.L.* 57.428),

When our son Leporius, who deservedly and suitably had been rebuked for the presumption of his error by Your Sanctity, arrived in our presence, after

36. Gennadius *Vir. ill.* 62.

37. "dicis ergo Christum hominem tantummodo solitarium natum esse. hoc utique et illa, quam in primo libro evidenter ostendimus, Pelagianae impietatis haeresis praedicavit, Christum hominem tantummodo solitarium natum esse.... ergo vides Pelagianum te virus vomere, Pelagiano te spiritu sibilare...." (*De incarn.* 5.2, cf. 1.3). For the work, see *C.S.E.L.* 17.235-391. Modern views on Cassian's reasoning differ: compare Chadwick (*Cassian* p.147) ("the similarity ... was not in the least justified by the facts") with Gibson (*Cassian* p.190) (the association shows "the writer's keen penetration"). Nestorius had received Pelagians in Constantinople (*De incarn.* 1.3; see Chadwick, *Cassian* pp.141-147), and had written to Celestine of Rome on behalf of some exiled Pelagian bishops (*De incarn.* 1.3). Marius Mercator also made such a connection (Chadwick, ibid. pp.141-147), and Prosper claimed that Celestine had freed the east from the "double plague" of Nestorianism and Pelagianism (*Contr. coll.* 21[41]); he also wrote an *Epitaphium Nestorianae et Pelagianae haereseon* (*P.L.* 51.153-154). See also Bardy, "Controverses" pp.25-26; Disdier, "Pélagianisme" pp.314-333; von Harnack, *Lehrbuch* pp.186-187; Pietri, *Roma* 2.954; Plagnieux, "Grief" pp.391-402; and Spiegl, "Pelagianismus" pp.1-14.

38. Rank: *Conc. Carth. a. 525* (*Corp. chr. lat.* 149.280): "presbyterum Leporium quamvis saeculi natalibus clarum et apud suos honestissimo loco natum." Northern origin: *De incarn.* 1.2 ("Beligarum urbe"); Trier is suggested by Duval, *Gaule* pp.678-679.

39. For suggested dates and discussion, see Chadwick, *Cassian* pp.137-138 (c.418); Griffe, *Gaule* 3.356-358 (c.418); Hefele-Leclercq, *Conciles* 2.215-216 (c.426); Morel, "Leporius" pp.31-52; and Palanque, *Marseilles* p.25 (427).

40. "Leporius ... qui ex Pelagii, ut supra diximus, institutione, vel potius pravitate, descendens apud Gallias assertor praedictae haereseos, ut inter primos aut inter maximos, fuit a nobis admonitus, a deo emendatus...." (*De incarn.* 1.4). For Nestorius, Leporius and Pelagianism, see also *De incarn.* 7.21. For Leporius as a Pelagian, see Gibson, *Cassian* p.190; this is denied, however, by Bardy, "Controverses" p.26.

he had become deranged, we received the confused one so that he might be soundly corrected and healed. For just as you obeyed the precept of the apostle, that you should rebuke those who are disturbed, thus we likewise obey the precept that the weak should be consoled and that we should support the feeble.[41]

Ultimately, Leporius wrote a letter of retraction addressed "to nearly all the cities of Gaul."[42] He also chose to remain in Africa, where he had been made a presbyter by Augustine. He may have found the surroundings there more congenial, and have suspected that, in spite of his recantation, he would not have found a welcome reception back in Gaul.[43]

The role of Proculus of Marseilles deserves some amplification. Once again, he was intimately involved in a Gallic ecclesiastical controversy. In this case, not only does he appear to have been anti-Pelagian, but he also seems to have enjoyed cordial relations with Augustine and the African bishops.[44] If such relations continued into the 420s, then Proculus, like Hilarius and Prosper, may not have opposed predestination. If so, Proculus necessarily would have been opposed theologically by other Gauls, such as his own presbyter Cassian, who were decidedly anti-predestinarian. Cassian's curious failure to mention either Proculus or Augustine in his account of the Leporius affair, even though he hardly could have been unaware of their involvement, certainly seems to suggest he was at odds with them both about something. The end result could have been the very dissension discussed by Prosper.

A problem with Cassian's account of the Leporius affair is that whereas he stressed Leporius' Pelagian tendencies, the letter of Augustine and the African bishops confirming Leporius' recantation made no mention of them at all. They discussed only Leporius' Christological errors: "He is a man preoccupied in some sort of error about the only begotten son of God . . . denying that He was made man, and not realizing that he is introducing a fourth person into the trinity. . . . [He] rashly presumed that it was possible to separate the son of man

41. "filium nostrum Leporium apud vestram sanctitatem pro sui erroris praesumptione merito idoneeque correptum, cum ad nos, posteaquam exinde exturbatus est, advenisset, salubriter perturbatum corrigendum sanandumque suscepimus. nam sicut vos oboedistis apostolo, ut corriperetis inquietos, ita et nos, ut consolaremur pusillanimes et susciperemus infirmos." Proculus' role in these proceedings could suggest that the Ursus whom Proculus also condemned before 417 (chapter 3 above, n.54) was one of the others expelled with Leporius.

42. Partially extant in Cass. De incarn. 1.5.

43. Cassian noted (De incarn. 1.4) that Leporius, "tunc monachus, modo presbyter," wrote his recantation "in Africa, ubi tunc erat atque nunc est." A presbyter Leporius, very likely the Gaul, is attested with Augustine at Hippo (see Aug. Epist. 213.1 and Serm. 356.10).

44. The Massiliote connections to Africa also may be reflected in the many African references in the Gallic Chronicle of 452 (e.g. nos.56, 59, 75, 96, 98, 108-109, 129).

from the son of God."[45] Moreover, even in the response of Leporius to the Gallic bishops cited by Cassian, this was the only topic addressed: "We believe that God and man were united."[46] This failure to mention Pelagianism has led one Cassian scholar to assert that Cassian "did not understand the opinion which he was condemning."[47] Such a conclusion, however, also incorporates the *a priori* assumption that the Leporius affair "can hardly be earlier than 418, when Pelagius was condemned."[48]

This condemnation of 418, however, was that of the Roman state and church, which would have been of little moment in Gaul, where anti-Pelagians were being placed in high ecclesiastical office perhaps as early as c.410. If the Leporius incident occurred before 418, it may be that he and his partisans were accused of Pelagianism and expelled from Gaul as early as the reigns of Constantine III and Jovinus, possibly c.410/413.[49] Leporius could have come south as a result of either the barbarian invasions or the Gallic revolts. Augustine's very failure to mention the accusation of Pelagianism in his letter suggests that Pelagianism had not yet become one of his concerns when he received Leporius in Africa.

A dating of the Leporius affair to the early or middle part of the second decade of the fifth century would obviate the otherwise unresolvable conflict between the testimony of Cassian and that of Augustine. Augustine would have been responding to what he saw as the only deviant aspect of Leporius' beliefs. Cassian, however, writing in the late 420s, would have placed much more emphasis on any whiff of Pelagianism. Its continued topicality, and the universal Gallic condemnation of it, could have led to the stress upon that particular charge in Cassian's tract, regardless of its validity. Priscillianism in the past, and now predestination, had been purposefully, even if misleadingly, equated with the universally condemned Manicheism. Now, any teaching, such as Leporius' "Nestorianism," which anyone happened to oppose similarly could be likened to Pelagianism. Eventually, Leporius was thought to have been tainted with Pelagianism alone.

45. "praeoccupatus esset homo in aliquo delicto ... de unigenito filio dei ... negans deum hominem factum ... nec videns quartam se subintroducere in trinitate personam.... incaute praesumpsit filium hominis a filio dei posse separari" (Aug. *Epist.* 219.1-3: *C.S.E.L.* 57.428-431).

46. "putemus deum hominemque commixtum" (*De incarn.* 1.5).

47. Chadwick, *Cassian* p.138. He also, however, (pp.137-138) has Leporius as the "chief champion of ... Pelagius in Gaul."

48. Chadwick, *Cassian* p.137.

49. In an apparent reference to Leporius (*De incarn.* 1.2), Cassian noted, "nuper quoque, id est in diebus nostris, emersisse haeresim venenosam, et maxime Beligarum urbe conspeximus, certi erroris incerti nominis. ..." (*P.L.* 50.18-19). His need to qualify "nuper", viz. "that is, in my own time," would imply that the incident had not occurred *too* recently.

At the end of the century Gennadius of Marseilles, repeating the assessment of Cassian, noted, "He began to follow the teaching of the Pelagians, but he was rebuked by the Gallic authorities."[50] Like Cassian, he made no mention of Augustine's or Proculus' roles at all.

Nor was Cassian the only Gallic theologian of the time to attempt to tar his opponents with the Pelagian brush. Prosper did the same in his aforementioned letter to Augustine on the Gallic opposition to predestination. Even though Prosper admitted that the Gallic antipredestinarians accepted grace and original sin, the two main Augustinian tenets denied by the Pelagians, he nonetheless referred to their "spirit of Pelagianism," claimed that "some actually fail to avoid Pelagian errors," and described some of their teachings as the "remnants of the Pelagian depravity."[51] Prosper also made clear, however, that their primary complaint concerned predestination, which they thought smacked of Manicheism. The Gauls also accused Augustine of having a flawed conception of grace: "They say that [Augustine] has eliminated free will and that in the guise of grace he preaches fatal necessity [i.e. predestination]."[52]

Given the *a priori* absurdity of Prosper's charge, that the Gallic anti-Pelagians were themselves guilty of Pelagianism, one well might conclude that these accusations were more rhetorical than real.[53] Not only would they draw attention away from the true point of contention, predestination, but they also would be effective for another reason: Pelagianism had been intertwined with the recent political unrest in Gaul, and continued to be a concern of the Italian government, as attested by the imperial edict of 425. To be accused of it could put anyone on the defensive. Prosper would have been aware that if Gallic condemnations of Pelagianism served as a ritual method of expressing consensus, accusations of it could be used as a means of exclusion. Finally, it even has been suggested that Prosper himself may have been a disenchanted Pelagian: if so, all the more reason to deflect the charge from himself, just as Augustine had to atone for his earlier ties to Manicheism.[54]

Nonetheless, Prosper's accusation of Pelagianism has gained suffi-

---

50. "Pelagianum dogma coeperat sequi, sed a Gallicanis doctoribus admonitus" (*Vir. ill.* 59).

51. *apud* Aug. *Epist.* 225.2-4. For the falsity of this accusation, see Lumpe, "Ennodius" p.31. Compare Cassian's description (*De incarn.* 1.4) of Leporius as "ex Pelagii ... pravitate descendens."

52. "dicentes eum liberum arbitrium penitus submovere et sub gratiae nomine necessitatem praedicare fatalem...." (Prosp. *Epist. ad Rufin.* 3: *P.L.* 51.79); see note 28 above.

53. Even a staunch defender of Prosper (Pelland, *Prosperi* p.48 n.1) must ask "utrum Prosper adversariorum errores exaggeraverit..."

54. For the suggestion that Prosper was the author of the Pelagian-tinged *Carmen de providentia divina* (*P.L.* 51.617-638), see Myers, "Pelagus" p.31.

cient credence so that the anti-predestinarian party in Gaul has been saddled with the misleading misnomer "semi-Pelagian."[55] And this in spite of the fact that all known influential Gallic theologians, including the so-called semi-Pelagians, condemned Pelagianism every bit as heartily as Augustine himself.[56]

A rather more correct depiction of the sentiments of the Gallic anti-predestinarians is given by Prosper himself in the same letter to Augustine, when he reported about the short-lived bishop Helladius of Arles (*apud* Aug. *Epist.* 225.9):

Your Beatitude should know that he is an admirer and follower of your teaching in all other things, and with regard to that which he calls into question [i.e. predestination], he already wished to convey his own thoughts to Your Sanctity through correspondence, but because it is unclear whether he is going to do this or to what purpose he is going to do it . . .[57]

If Helladius ever did write the letter in question, no record of it survives. It perhaps is more prudent to conclude either that he chose not to, or that he died before he could. Helladius, like other influential Gallic ecclesiastics of his time, would have remained staunchly anti-Pelagian at the same time that he continued to oppose Augustinian ideas on predestination. His role here could suggest that the Lérins circle already was a center of anti-predestinarian sentiment.[58]

In 430, Prosper's patron Augustine died. Shortly thereafter, Prosper, now seeing himself as the defender of Augustine in the struggle against the anti-predestinarians, returned to the attack in his *Pro Augustino responsiones ad excerpta Genuensium*.[59] This work was addressed to Camillus and Theodorus, two otherwise unknown Genoese presbyters who had suggested that nine excerpts from Augustine's defenses of predestination, the *De dono perseverantiae* and the *De praedestinatione sanctorum*, were "either unusual or not absolutely clear."[60]

---

55. See Altaner, *Patrology* pp.538-539; Cappuyns, "Capitula" pp.156-170; Chadwick, *Poetry* pp.170-239; Duckett, *Writers* p.201; Gibson, *Cassian* passim; von Harnack, *Lehrbuch* p.240; Jalland, *Leo* pp.122 n.36; Koch, *Faustus* pp.39-207; Prinz, *Mönchtum* pp.53-56, 65; Travers-Smith, *Gaul* pp.272-322; and Weigel, *Faustus* p.49ff. For the incorrectness of this appellation, see Chadwick p.180, who calls it a "malicious term."

56. For the "semi-Pelagians" as actually non-Pelagians, see Bardy et al., *Eglise* p.403.

57. "sciat beatitudo tua admiratorem sectatoremque in aliis omnibus tuae esse doctrinae et de hoc, quod [sc. praedestinationem] in querelam trahit, iam pridem apud sanctitatem tuam sensum suum per litteras velle conferre, sed quia, utrum hoc facturus aut quo fine sit facturus, incertum est . . ."

58. See Bardy et. al., *Eglise* pp.400-404. For Helladius' suggested ties to Lérins, see chapter 4 above, n.114.

59. *P.L.* 51.187-202. See Pelland, *Prosperi* pp.54-65.

60. "vel insolita aut minus clara" (*P.L.* 51.187). Augustine's works: *P.L.* 44.959-992 and 45.993-1034 respectively. See Wermelinger, *Pelagius* p.246.

Prosper suspected that his Gallic opponents had been the source of their doubts, and he replied, "I marvel that Your Sanctity cannot tell the objections of calumniators [sc. the Gauls] from the person of the defender of grace [sc. Augustine], and that you prefer the words of detractors to him who responded to his detractors."[61] His arguments, however, stemmed mostly from the assertion of Augustine's authority, and were not fully convincing.[62]

Meanwhile, the opponents of predestination in Gaul, unimpressed by Augustine's, and much less by Prosper's, arguments, had entered the pamphlet war themselves. By 431, it seems, Prosper felt called upon to respond to them in the tracts *Pro Augustino responsiones ad capitula objectionum Gallorum calumniantium* and *Pro Augustino responsiones ad capitula objectionum vincentianarum.*[63] Neither of these anti-Augustinian works survives; the author of the first is unknown, but the author of the second will have been the Vincentius who was an influential monk of Lérins, and the brother of Lupus of Troyes.[64] Prosper's responses, however, give a good idea of what the objections were. Augustine was accused of fatalism; of denying that all share the chance for salvation; and even of asserting that predestination compelled some to sin, and that those predestined to salvation had no need to lead a Christian life, to be baptized, or to have free will. These works of Prosper, too, apparently had no effect.

Then, when it appeared to Prosper that he was unable to sway his Gallic opponents with his rhetoric, he and Hilarius exercised the increasingly popular last resort of so many disgruntled Gallic ecclesiastics. They went to Rome and appealed to its bishop.[65] As a result, Celestine shortly afterward, probably in 431, addressed the letter "Apostolici verba" (*P.L.* 50.528-537) to the bishops Venerius [of Mar-

61. "stupeo sanctitatem vestram objectionem calumniantium a persona defensoris gratiae non potuisse discernere, et verba obtrectantium ei ipsi qui obtrectatoribus suis respondet aptasse" (*P.L.* 51.199). These two individuals are otherwise unknown, but their names were common in Gaul: a Camillus was a *vir inlustris* of Arles in 461 (Sid. Apoll. *Epist.* 1.11.10: *P.L.R.E. II* p.255), and one Theodorus was the aforementioned bishop of Fréjus, and another was a noble relative of Eparchius Avitus c.425 (Sid. Apoll. *Carm.* 7.215-220: *P.L.R.E. II* pp.1087-1088). These two doubters of predestination, therefore, may have had their own connections in Gaul.

62. See Pelland, *Prosperi* p.64, "nullam lucem dubio Genuensium attulerit."

63. *P.L.* 51.155-174 and 51.177-186 respectively. The term "calumniantes" suggests the identity of these Gauls with the "calumniators" who had influenced the Genoese priests. For discussion and dates, see Pelland, *Prosperi* pp.66-99. Von Harnack, *Lehrbuch* p.245 identifies the Gauls as from "der Kreis Cassians."

64. For these two, see chapter 4 above, n.50. For this Vincentius as he of Lérins, see Schanz, *Geschichte* p.522, although some refuse to accept Vincentius of Lérins as the author, and attribute this work to the presbyter Vincentius, perhaps of Marseilles, said by Gennadius (*Vir. ill.* 81) only to have written a commentary on the *Psalms*: see Pelland, *Prosperi* pp.66-69.

65. For Prosper and Celestine, see Wermelinger, *Pelagius* pp.244-249.

seilles], Marinus, Leontius [?of Trois-Châteaux], Auxonius [?of Aps/ Viviers], Arcadius [?of Orange], and Fillucius.[66]

Now, the name of Venerius at the head of the list requires an explanation. Given his brief tenure in office as of 431, it is very unlikely that he was the most senior bishop. Could it be, then, that Celestine was continuing to accord to Venerius the same irregular metropolitan status of Proculus? Or was Venerius, as bishop of the city where the problems were occurring, merely the one who was most involved in the controversy; or, perhaps, the one whom Celestine thought would be the most able, or inclined, to support him in the matter? And why is it that neither the bishop of Arles nor any of his known supporters (with the possible exception of Arcadius) are mentioned? [67]

Celestine (ch.1) wrote to the Gallic bishops that he became involved because

our sons Prosper and Hilarius, in our presence, have charged that so much is permitted to certain presbyters there [sc. in Gaul] that, raising undisciplined inquiries in public, they stubbornly preach things contrary to the truth. . . . [Hilary and Prosper] had recourse to an appeal to the apostolic see, complaining to us about these problems which dissension incites. Let these men know, if they indeed are considered presbyters, that they are subject to your authority. . . .[68]

Prosper and Hilarius had claimed, it seems, that Gallic bishops, perhaps the very ones addressed, were not taking sufficient steps to repress these individuals, for Celestine also noted (ch.1),

What hope is there [in Gaul], when, with the teachers silent, those speak out who (if this is true) were not their pupils? . . . In such cases taciturnity draws suspicion. . . . If this is indeed the case, let novelty cease to afflict antiquity, let unrest cease to upset the peace of the churches . . . for what do you do in church, if they hold the right of preaching? [69]

---

66. Griffe, *Gaule* 3.367 presumes Leontius was bishop of Fréjus and responsible for Lérins; for Trois-Châteaux, see chapter 7 below, n.94. But this Leontius was ranked third of the six bishops, and Leontius of Fréjus was ordained c.432, perhaps after this letter was written; it also is unlikely that four of the six bishops addressed all would have been ordained in the year or less preceding Celestine's letter. Kidd, *Church* p.356 wrongly has the letter addressed to Venerius alone. See also Bardy et al., *Eglise* pp.399-400. The date is inferred from the consideration that at the time the letter was sent, Augustine was dead, but Celestine was still alive.

67. A bishop Arcadius of an unknown see did attend the Council of Riez (*Corp. chr. lat.* 148.71-72).

68. "filii nostri praesentes Prosper et Hilarius . . . tantum nescio quibus presbyteris illic licere qui dissensioni ecclesiarum studeant, sunt apud nos prosecuti, ut indisciplinatas quaestiones vocantes in medium, pertinaciter eos dicant praedicare adversantia veritati. . . . recurrerunt ad apostolicam praedicti sedem, haec ipsa nobis quae tentat perturbatio conquerentes . . . sciant se, si tamen censentur presbyteri, dignitate vobis esse subjectos. . . ."

69. "quid illic spei est, ubi, magistris tacentibus, ii loquuntur qui, si ita est, eorum discipuli non fuerunt? . . . in talibus causis non caret suspicione taciturnitas . . . desinat, si ita res sunt,

In this context, Celestine also was able to introduce one of his favorite complaints, suggesting (ch.1), "Unless, perhaps, there is this problem, which is allowed by no authority, nor even by any reason, that some of the brothers, perhaps recently admitted into our order from the ranks of the laity, do not know what they ought to vindicate to themselves. . . ."[70] The layman Hilarius had suggested the same thing about the identity of these individuals in his letter to Augustine when he reported that "some of them are such individuals that laymen must exhibit the greatest respect for them by ecclesiastical custom."[71] Both accounts, therefore, would suggest that influential laymen who had entered the clergy were involved, the very type of persons who were associated with the Lérins party.

This much of the discussion indicates that Celestine was operating solely on the reports of Prosper and Hilarius, and even though he did exhibit some caution as to the validity of their claims, he nonetheless did not hesitate to act upon them. Once again, the willingness of disaffected Gauls to undertake the journey to Rome resulted in quick action and a favorable response by the bishop of the city.

Who, then, were these rambunctious presbyters and what were their improper teachings?[72] Celestine gave a hint when he lamented (ch.1-2),

Nor, moreover, can we marvel if those who struggled to vilify the memory even of brothers who have died, now dare such things toward the living. We always have held Augustine, a man of blessed memory . . . in our communion, nor has even the rumor of perverse suspicion tainted him. . . . For what reason is he opposed by such men, whom we see evilly increasing?[73]

Prosper and Hilarius, therefore, were merely continuing their opposition to the anti-Augustinian, anti-predestinarian, party in Gaul, and

---

incessere novitas vetustatem, desinat ecclesiarum quietem inquietudo turbare . . . nam quid in ecclesiis vos agitis, si illi summam teneant praedicandi?"

70. "nisi forte illud obsistat, quod non auctoritate, non adhuc ratione colligitur, ut aliqui e fratrum numero, nuper de laicorum consortio in collegium nostrum fortassis admissi, nesciant quid sibi debeant vindicare. . . ." Celestine also opposed the practice in Italy, for in 429 he wrote to the bishops of Apulia and Calabria (*Epist.* "Nulli sacerdotum": *P.L.* 50.436), "commonemus, ne quis laicum ad ordinem clericatus admittat."

71. "sunt ex parte tales personae, ut his consuetudine ecclesiastica laicos summam reverentiam necesse sit exhibere" (*apud* Aug. *Epist.* 226.9).

72. Given that Venerius is addressed first, the names of Cassian and Salvian of Marseilles, not to mention Vincentius of Lérins, have been proposed; see Gibson, *Cassian* p.192 and Griffe, *Gaule* 1.183, 2.173. All had close ties to Lérins. Marrou, "Dossier" p.338, identifies them as "les Marseillais, avec leur théorie sur les 'futurs conditionnels'."

73. "nec tamen mirari possumus si haec erga viventes hi nunc tentare audent, qui nituntur etiam quiescentium fratrum memoriam dissipare. Augustinum sanctae recordationis virum . . . in nostra communione semper habuimus, nec umquam hunc sinistrae suspicionis saltem rumor aspersit. . . . unde resistatur talibus, quos male crescere videmus?"

now had enlisted the bishop of Rome in their cause.[74] Their portrayal
of the views of their Gallic opponents is suggested by the documents
which Celestine appended to his letter (ch.12ff): a condemnation of
Pelagianism and an attack "against the enemies of the grace of God,"
along with a defense of the Augustinian version of free will, "through
which, with the aid and support of God, free will is not eliminated,
but rather set free."[75]

Celestine, therefore, had been led to believe that the Gauls were
infected with Pelagianism and on this basis were questioning the Augustinian interpretation of free will. Only by assuming this can one
understand Celestine's otherwise incomprehensible attack on Pelagianism, when Prosper's opponents were in fact the Gallic anti-Pelagians. Prosper realized that Pelagianism still was a valid issue in Italy,
and that he could be assured of support against anyone who was accused of it.[76] Prosper and Hilarius apparently had found a sure way
to obtain Italian support for their attack on the Gallic view of grace,
by accusing their Gallic opponents of being pro-Pelagian rather than
anti-predestinarian. Celestine's letter is searched in vain for any reference to the real reason why the Gauls opposed Augustine.

It may be, moreover, that it is in the context of this controversy that
one is to place the troublesome little tract entitled *On the Seven Offices
of the Church*.[77] Although the piece has been transmitted among the
works of Jerome, it now generally is believed to have been addressed
to a bishop in early fifth-century Gaul.[78] The content of the work is
very consistent with contemporary Gallic ecclesiastical concerns. It especially emphasized the rights of presbyters. It complained that these
rights were observed in Rome, the east, Italy, Crete, Cyprus, Africa,
Illyricum, Spain, and Britain, but only partly in Gaul, and it called
the failure to do so an "illicita praesumptio" on the part of a bishop.[79]
It also stressed one such privilege in particular: "Therefore, no bishop,
inflated with the jealousy of a diabolical ambition, becomes aroused
in church if the presbyters occasionally exhort the people, if they
sometimes preach in church. . . ."[80] This, of course, is exactly the sort
of activity about which Celestine had been complaining.

74. See also Prosp. *Contr. coll.* 21(41), where Celestine responded against those "qui sanctae
memoriae Augustini scripta reprehendunt."

75. "quo utique auxilio et munere dei non aufertur liberum arbitrium, sed liberatur."

76. For Pelagianism in Italy at this time, see Kidd, *Church* p.115ff.

77. Text of the *De septem ordinibus ecclesiae*: *P.L.* 30.148-162; see also Kalff, *De septem ordinibus ecclesiae* and Morin, "Portion" pp.310-318.

78. See *Clavis* no.764; Duval, *Gaule* pp.775-777; Griffe, *Gaule* 2.322; and Morin, "Portion"
passim.

79. *De sept. ord. eccl.* 6.

80. "nemo hinc episcoporum invidia diabolicae tentationis inflatus irascitur in templa si
presbyteri interdum exhortentur plebem, si in ecclesiis praedicent. . . ." (ibid.). See Griffe, *Gaule*

In some manuscripts the treatise is addressed to a bishop Rusticus, and at one point it was suggested that it had been dedicated to Rusticus of Narbonne by Faustus, then a presbyter of Lérins.[81] Even though the Faustian authorship was subsequently rejected, it still may be that Rusticus of Narbonne was the recipient.[82] For one thing, Rusticus was a metropolitan, and it has been suggested elsewhere that the recipient was one.[83] Furthermore, the attention to the rights of presbyters seems to reflect Massiliote practices, and the tone of the letter indicates that it was written by a priest who was an intimate of a recently ordained bishop.[84] Is it possible, therefore, that the newly elected Rusticus requested Venerius, his old comrade in Proculus' monastery at Marseilles, to compose for him a discussion of the seven ranks of the ecclesiastical hierarchy? If Venerius were the one who had stressed the rights of presbyters, all the more reason for Celestine to single him out for special attention.

Shortly after the succession of Sixtus as bishop of Rome on 31 July 432, Prosper returned to the fray with his *De gratia et libero arbitrio contra collatorem*.[85] The *collator*, of course, was Cassian, who some six years earlier had attacked Augustine's ideas on grace in his *Collationes*. Just as Cassian courteously avoided mentioning Augustine by name, Prosper did not name Cassian, although his title would have left no doubt as to whom he was attacking.

None of these defenses of predestination, however, had any effect upon the Gallic theologians, and the definitive Gallic response to Celestine and Prosper came in 434, when Vincentius of Lérins wrote his *Commonitorium*, a tract ostensibly issued as a general handbook on how to distinguish heresy from orthodoxy.[86] Vincentius, stating that

---

2.316-317, who relates this expanded power of priests to the foundation of new parishes in the countryside.

81. Morin, "Hiérarchie" pp.97-104, who, however, assumes that "Rustique avait été moine à Lérins"; see also Bergmann, *Predigtliteratur* pp.117-125 and Koch, *Faustus* p.32.

82. Morin, "Le destinataire" pp.229-244, where he suggests Patroclus of Arles as the author.

83. See Griffe, "L'apocryphe" pp.215-224 and *Gaule* 2.313-322; and Pietri, *Roma* 2.1000.

84. For example, "te non pudeat paulisper minorem esse dum discis: quia seposito ... privilegio dignitatis, habes de nobis amplius quod quaeras" (*De sept. ord. eccl. praef.*).

85. *P.L.* 51.215-276; he mentioned Sixtus (21[44]: p.273), and noted that it was twenty-one years since Augustine had first attacked the Pelagians (1.2: p.216) circa 412/413. See Bardy et al., *Eglise* p.402 and von Harnack, *Lehrbuch* pp.245-247.

86. Discussion: Bardy et al., *Eglise* pp.400-402 and Heurtley, *Commonitory* passim. Text: Moxon, *Commonitorium* and *P.L.* 50.637-686. Vincentius wrote in some kind of monastery: "remotioris villulae et in ea secretum monasterii incolamus habitaculum" (*Comm.* 1). This, however, may not have been at Lérins. Circa 428, Eucherius had indicated he was no longer there (*De laud. herem.* 42): "haec *habuit* ... Vincentium." Griffe, *Gaule* 3.376 suggests he may have moved back to Troyes with his brother Lupus. He also may have been back at Lérins by 434, or even at Marseilles; for similarities between Vincentius and Cassian, see Pastorini, "Concetto" pp.37-46.

"the fraudulence of new heretics demands great care and attention," soon narrowed his discussion down to a discussion of *novitas*.[87] It becomes clear, however, that Vincentius' real purpose was to respond to Celestine's letter of a few years before, and to defend the Gallic anti-predestinarian position even though, as usual, Augustine was not mentioned by name.[88] He made it clear, for example, that he was particularly concerned with recent heresies, saying, "But all heresies are not attacked in this way all the time but only new, recent ones when they first arise."[89] Which is exactly what the Gauls were doing.[90] Moreover, Vincentius' discussion of the question, "Here, perhaps, someone might ask whether heretics too use the testimony of divine scripture. They clearly do, and effectively indeed, . . ." might well have been a reference to the rhetorical abilities of Augustine.[91]

It becomes most clear in his concluding remarks that Vincentius was responding to the charges that the Gauls were wrongly attacking Augustine. In his final argument against *novitas*, he brazenly turned Celestine's own arguments against him, noting, "Although all these arguments together abundantly suffice for overthrowing and extinguishing these novelties, nevertheless . . . we have added at the end the twofold authority of the apostolic see."[92] He then included a lengthy discussion of Celestine's own letter:

In the letter which he sent to the Gallic bishops, rebuking them for their connivance because, forsaking the ancient faith by their silence, they allowed profane novelties [sc. attacks upon Augustine] to arise . . . someone here per-

87. "novorum haereticorum fraudulentia multum curae et attentionis indicat" (*Comm.* 1, see also *Comm.* 24).
88. See Bardy et al., *Eglise* pp.401-402; von Harnack, *Lehrbuch* p.243; Heurtley, *Commonitory* p.127; Morrison, *Tradition* p.3; Pelland, *Prosperi* p.66; Turner, "Arles and Rome" p.244; and Wermelinger, *Pelagius* p.246. Griffe, on the other hand, *Gaule* 3.379, denies this was Vincentius' intent, but his sole argument is that Vincentius never named Augustine. This, however, was merely standard practice. Elsewhere ("Pro Vincentio" pp.26-32), even Griffe recognizes Vincentius' "réserves les plus expresses . . . de la grâce et de la prédestination." See also Madoz, "¿Contra quién" pp.5-34 and "El concepto" pp.59-89; as well as d'Alès, "La fortune" pp.334-356.
89. "sed neque semper neque omnes haereses hoc modo impugnandae sunt, sed novitiae recentesque tantummodo cum primum scilicet exoriuntur" (*Comm.* 28).
90. Griffe, *Gaule* 3.379, and Pricoco, *L'isola* p.266 n.121, suppose that Nestorianism was Vincentius' "recent" heresy, even though it never had been of great moment in Gaul (even Cassian had linked it to Pelagianism), and would have been even less so after the Council of Ephesus in 431.
91. "hic fortasse aliquis interroget an et haeretici divinae scripturae testimoniis utantur. utuntur plane, et vehementer quidem, . . ." (*Comm.* 25).
92. "quae omnia licet cumulata abundeque sufficerent ad profanas quasque novitates obruendas et exstinguendas, tamen . . . ad extremum adjecimus geminam apostolicae sedis auctoritatem" (ibid.32). This would have been a calculated reply to Prosper, who had used the same letter of Celestine as evidence for "quantum sibi [sc. Coelestino] praesumptionis istius novitas displiceret" (*Contr. coll.* 21[41]: *P.L.* 51.271).

haps might wonder who these individuals might be, whom he forbids to have free speech according to their will: the proclaimers of tradition or inventors of novelty? Let him speak himself, let him destroy the doubts of our readers himself. He said, "Let novelty cease to assault tradition."[93]

It was the "inventors of novelty," therefore, whoever they might be, who should be condemned.

Vincentius concluded by arguing that because Pelagius, Caelestius, and Nestorius all had been condemned, therefore "it is immediately necessary for all catholics who desire to show themselves to be legitimate sons of the mother church to detest, dread, pursue, and persecute the profane novelties of the profane...."[94] Vincentius clearly had in mind some other recent "novelties," not those he had just used as examples. Predestination, too, was *novitas*, and as such was condemned rightly. By using Celestine's own arguments for tradition on his and the Gauls' behalf, he rejected Celestine-cum-Prosper's claims that the Gallic anti-predestinarian presbyters were guilty of any wrong doing. So much, therefore, for predestination, at least as far as the Gauls were concerned. Once again the Gauls showed that, however much they might respect authorities such as Augustine and the bishop of Rome, they reserved the final judgment for themselves. And once again the Gallic local party of Lérins triumphed over those, such as Prosper, who sought foreign support.

For the rest of the century, the Gallic theological establishment continued to reject predestination, and to define ever more carefully its own conception of the interaction among grace, effort, and free will.[95] In the 490s, for example, Gennadius of Marseilles repeated the orthodox Gallic opinion that Cassian was right and Prosper wrong: "I also read [Prosper's] book attacking works under the name of Cassian which the church of God judges to be useful, [but which] he denigrated as harmful."[96] All of which is not to say, however, that there did not continue to be predestinarians in Gaul, or that everyone agreed with the views expressed by Vincentius. Gennadius even reported that the

93. "in epistola quam Gallorum sacerdotibus misit, arguens eorum conniventiam quod antiquam fidem silentio destituentes, profanas novitates exsurgere paterentur ... hic aliquis fortasse addubitet quinam sint illi quos habere prohibeat liberum pro voluntate sermonem, vetustatis praedicatores, an novitatis adinventores. ipse dicat, dubitationem legentium ipse dissolvat. sequitur enim: "desinat ... incessere novitas vetustatem" (ibid.).

94. "necesse est profecto omnibus deinceps catholicis, qui sese ecclesiae matris legitimos filios probare student ut ... profanas vero profanorum novitates detestentur, horrescant, insectentur, persequantur" (*Comm.* 33).

95. Circa 450, for example, Valerianus of Cimiez quoted *James II* 26, "fides sine operibus mortua est" (*Epist. ad. mon.* : *P.L.* 52.758). See also chapter 10 below.

96. "legi et librum adversus opuscula sub persona Cassiani, quae ecclesia dei salutaria probat, ille infamat nociva" (*Vir. ill.* 85).

reason Vincentius' second book survived only in outline form was because the complete version had been stolen.[97]

The preceding analysis also can offer some additional insight into the factional affiliations of these Gallic ecclesiastics. On the one hand, the activities of Helladius, Cassian, and Vincentius, as well as the lack of Lerinenses among the addressees of Celestine's letter, indicate that the circle of Lérins was very much involved in the Gallic opposition to Augustine's and Prosper's views on predestination. On the other, however, it also may be that the bishops of Marseilles, perhaps Narbonne, and elsewhere, were not so strongly opposed to Augustinian views. Proculus of Marseilles earlier had sent Leporius to Augustine for correction. His protégé Venerius had been the first addressee of Celestine's letter. Presumably it is no accident that Venerius and others were asked for help whereas the Lerinenses were not.

It even may be that the addressees of Celestine's letter were suggested to him by Prosper, who perhaps was attempting to profit from Gallic dissension by singling out for special attention from Rome those not known as rabid anti-predestinarians. If this were the case, the letter of Celestine can suggest who some of the opponents of Lérins were. The fact that most of them cannot be identified with known individuals, moreover, indicates only that many of the adherents of this group were not very well placed.

Vincentius' treatise is the last extant evidence for the controversy over predestination for nearly forty years. Prosper apparently gave up his efforts to influence the Gauls, admitted defeat, and moved to Rome for good.[98] His interest in the Pelagian and predestinarian controversies seems to have waned. There is no further mention of them even in his chronicle. It may be that Celestine and others finally realized what Prosper had been up to, and that the Gallic controversy did not involve Pelagianism at all. Furthermore, if Celestine's successor Sixtus once had Pelagian inclinations himself, he may not have been very receptive to accusations of it.[99]

It has been suggested that Prosper revived his activities on behalf of predestination under Leo of Rome, but little evidence of this survives, and Leo himself may not have strongly endorsed it.[100] Like the

---

97. "a quibusdam furatam" (*Vir. ill.* 65).

98. For discussion of the common belief that Prosper settled in Rome c.433/434, see Markus, "Prosper" pp.31-43.

99. For Sixtus as favorable to the Pelagians, see Bardy et al., *Eglise* p.258; Kidd, *Church* pp.100, 114; Pietri, *Roma* 1.452, 2.1185; and Wermelinger, *Pelagius* pp.248-249 (who even suggests that Sixtus had Gallic ties). For support, see Aug. *Epist.* 191 and 194 (to a priest Sixtus), and Prosp. *Contr. coll.* 21(44): *P.L.* 51.273.

100. Prosper: Pelland, *Prosperi* pp.112-116. Photius (*Bibliotheca* 54: *P.G.* 103.97) noted that "certain ones spoke freely in Rome about heresy, but a certain Prosper, a man truly of God,

Gauls, Leo does seem to have opposed recurrences of "Pelagianism."[101] It is noteworthy that in the later quarrel between Hilary of Arles and Leo of Rome, neither questioned the orthodoxy of the other, implying that neither's was in question.[102] Prosper's accusations of Gallic Pelagianism, therefore, apparently made little lasting impact in Rome.

In Gaul, the antipathy of Hilary and his party toward Pelagianism continued. Circa the early 440s, perhaps in 444, Germanus of Auxerre went to Britain a second time to combat Pelagianism, this time accompanied by a bishop Severus, apparently of Trier.[103] This Severus was himself a pupil of Germanus' comrade in 429, Lupus, who probably recommended him. Another pupil of Lupus was Albinus, bishop of Châlons. These examples indicate how the extent of the influence of the Lérins party was widening all the time.[104]

Now, Germanus and Severus presumably did not undertake such a mission simply on their own authority, and probably were, as before, acting in concert with Hilary and his partisans. Indeed, it would appear that Germanus had some sort of imperial authority, for according to his biographer, the result of the voyage was that "those responsible for this depravity, expelled from the island, are consigned to be carried off to the Mediterranean regions so that they might enjoy both imperial absolution and correction."[105] Germanus' quasi-official capacity perhaps was based again upon the imperial decree of 425, which assigned to the bishop of Arles the responsibility for combating Gallic Pelagianism, and decreed that offending bishops were to be expelled from Gaul. Hilary even may have visited Germanus at Auxerre for the purpose of arranging this mission.[106] Furthermore, one at

confounded them in inscrutable publications against them while Leo guided the Roman see." This heresy probably is Eutychianism, although some suggest Pelagianism: see McShane, *Romanitas* p.370 and Pelland, *Prosperi* p.144, who sees this as a reference to the *De vocatione omnium gentium* (*P.L.* 51.647-722), a work defending Augustine which has been attributed to Prosper (*Clavis* no.528). For Leo's possible association of predestination with Priscillianism, which he vehemently opposed (chapter 7 below), see Bardy et al., *Eglise* p.43.

101. In Aquileia: see Leo, *Epist.* "Relatione sancti" (*P.L.* 54.593-594); see also Kidd, *Church* pp.388-389 and Pietri, *Roma* 2.943. Note also the alleged Pelagian anathematizations, "qui scripta sunt in urbe Roma de exemplaribus papae sancti Leonis" (Turner, "Arles and Rome" p.242).

102. See chapter 7 below.

103. See Duchesne, *Fastes*, 3.36; for the date, see Mathisen, "Last Year."

104. *VLupi* 11: Severus is called the apostle of Germania Prima. Lupus also was acquainted with Polichronius of Verdun (ibid.). Albinus' own *vita* goes so far as to claim that he had accompanied Germanus and Lupus on their first voyage to Britain in 429 (*A.A.S.S.* September III pp.85-89, see also *VLupi* 11).

105. "pravitatis auctores, expulsi insula, sacerdotibus addicuntur ad mediterranea deferendi ut et regio absolutione et illi emendatione fruerentur" (*VGermani* 27).

106. See Mathisen, "Hilarius" and "Last Year."

least might mention persistant suggestions that at this time Aetius himself may have been interested in intervening in Britain.[107] If such were the case, this visit of Germanus to the island could have been consistent with the plans of the patrician.

Hilary and his partisans were not without opposition as they attempted to expand their ecclesiastical influence in Gaul. Other southern metropolitans, such as Venerius of Marseilles, and especially Rusticus of Narbonne, belonged to a faction organized similarly to that of Lérins, and competed for the right to install their own candidates in episcopal sees. Furthermore, the objections of the Lerinenses to Augustinian predestination seem to have provoked further resistance, apparently centered at Marseilles. Such purely local opposition, however, seems to have caused little difficulty for the partisans of Lérins. Some of their theological rivals, for example, simply left Gaul altogether. But there also were others, outside Gaul, who would have been taken aback to see Hilary and his associates gaining not only extraordinary ecclesiastical authority but also secular influence as well, and who were concerned by the ever closer ties between the Lerinenses and the secular hierarchy in Gaul. Dealing with them would be another problem altogether.

107. See Johnstone, "Vortigern" pp.16-21, and Moss, "Policies" p.721; as well as the reference of Gildas, *De excidio* (ch.20) to a letter containing "Agitio ter consuli gemites Britannorum."

CHAPTER 7

HILARY AND LEO

At the same time that Hilary was expanding his influence in Gaul, the new bishop Leo of Rome was doing the same on an even greater scale.[1] Powerful *saeculares* assisted him in this, and he eventually was able to bring the full weight of the imperial government to bear against any opposition. Ultimately, he could not avoid coming into conflict with the powerful isolationist bishops of Gaul.

LEO AND THE PRIMACY OF ROME

In Africa, Leo renewed papal attempts to establish his authority over the independently minded bishops.[2] Here, he had only marginal success. In Illyricum, however, he was able to build upon the work of his predecessors and consolidate his authority. In 444 he wrote to the metropolitan bishops there reiterating his contention that the primacy of Peter gave him the care of all the churches, and appointing Anastasius of Thessalonica as his representative.[3] Anastasius was assigned the right to consecrate metropolitan bishops and to convene synods in which episcopal quarrels were to be settled; Leo reserved to himself the right to decide matters which the Illyrians could not.

This settlement, however, seems not to have met with total acceptance. In 446, Leo wrote again to the Illyrian metropolitans to remind them of Anastasius' privileges and to complain of "illegal" ordinations by the metropolitan of Achaea.[4] In another letter he rebuked Anastasius for exceeding his authority, and introduced many ecclesiastical regulations.[5] Anastasius must have responded satisfactorily, for in 449

1. For Leo, see Gore, *Leo the Great*; Hunt, *St. Leo*; Jalland, *Leo and Church* pp.301-313; Rahner, "Leo der Grosse"; and Sieben, "Leo der Grosse."
2. Papal problems in Africa: Bardy et al., *Eglise* p.263; Jalland, *Church* pp.280-291; and Kidd, *Church* pp.392-394. Leo and Africa: Lepelley, "Saint Léon" pp. 189-204.
3. See Leo, *Epist.* "Omnis admonitio" (*P.L.* 54.614, Jaffé, p.59 no.403) and "Omnium quidem litteras" (*P.L.* 54.616, Jaffé p.60 no.404).
4. *Epist.* "Grato animo epistulas": *P.L.* 54.663 (Jaffé p.60 no.409).
5. *Epist.* "Quanta fraternitati": *P.L.* 54.666 (Jaffé p.61 no.411).

Leo wrote to him again to thank him for not attending the Council of Ephesus, which Leo had boycotted.[6]

The example of Illyricum demonstrates what could happen when an influential metropolitan did concur with Leo's concept of how the church hierarchy should be organized. Of course, Anastasius may have had his own motives for doing so, such as a preference for the distant authority of Rome rather than the close supervision of Constantinople. However that may be, the prestige and authority of Leo would have been increased as a result.

In Rome itself, Leo continued the papal policy of persecuting schismatic and heretical sects. Under Celestine, the last Novatianist churches had been closed, and in 425 the Manichees and others had been expelled from Rome.[7] In 443, Leo attacked the so-called New Manichees in Rome.[8] In early 444 he united a coalition of ecclesiastics and influential laymen at a council whose pretext was an investigation into heretical activities: "Therefore, when there had been seated in my presence the bishops and presbyters, and in the same assembly Christian and noble men had been gathered, we ordered the elect of their men and women to be brought forth."[9] They were duly condemned; some recanted, some were exiled, and some fled.[10]

Subsequently, in 445, Leo was able to impetrate from Valentinian III a rescript which first asked, "Indeed, what deeds, and how obscene to speak and hear, have been discovered in the hearings of the blessed pope Leo, in the presence of the fullest senate, by the very confession of the accused?" and then went on to condemn the Manichees throughout the empire, and expel them from all the cities.[11] Leo, therefore, had been able to gain the support of the imperial administration, including the senate, at the very highest levels.

There remains, however, a problem with this account. Deeper in-

---

6. *Epist.* "Quantum relatione": *P.L.* 54.839 (Jaffé p.63 no.440).

7. Novatianists: Soc. *H.E.* 7.11. Note also *C. Th.* 16.5.65 (30 May 428) which includes the Novatianists in a blanket condemnation of twenty-three heresies; curiously, the Pelagians are omitted. Manichees: *C. Th.* 16.5.62 (17 July 425). See Pietri, *Roma* 1.446-448.

8. Prosp. *Chron.* 1350 s.a. 443, "plurimos Manichaeos intra urbem latere diligentiae papae Leonis innotuit." See Kidd, *Church* pp.386-388; Lauras, "Saint Léon" pp.203-209; and McShane, *Romanitas* pp.375-376.

9. "residentibus itaque mecum episcopis ac presbyteris ac in eumdem consessum Christianis viris ac nobilibus congregatis, electos et electas eorum [sc. Manichaeorum] iussimus praesentari" (*Serm.* 16.4: *P.L.* 54.178). For the role of laymen, see McShane, *Romanitas* pp.375-376.

10. Leo, *Epist.* "In consortium vos" (*P.L.* 54.620-621: Jaffé p.60 no.405: 30 January 444), "plurimos impietatis Manichaeae sequaces et doctores in urbe investigatio nostra reperit... quos potuimus emendare, correximus... aliquanti... per publicos judices perpetuo sunt exsilio relegati... aliquantos... cognovimus aufugisse." See Hefele-Leclercq, *Conciles* 2.476-477.

11. "quae enim et quam dictu audituque obscena in iudicio beatissimi papae Leonis coram senatu amplissimo manifestissima ipsorum confessione patefacta sunt?" (*Nov. Val.* 18: 19 June). See Ensslin, "Novellen XVII und XVIII" pp.367-374.

vestigation suggests that at least some of these individuals may not have been Manichees at all, but Priscillianists. In the 440s there had been another resurgence of Priscillianism, or at least of accusations of it, in Spain. The opposition to it had been led by bishop Turribius of Asturias in Galicia.[12] In an undated letter of this period to the bishops Hydatius (the chronographer) and Ceponius, Turribius complained about the revival of the *vetus error*, "which, indeed, has grown more freely during the misfortunes of our time as a result of the cessation of synodal councils and decrees."[13] He especially condemned the use of apocryphal scriptures, "through which the Manichees and Priscillianists attempt to justify their entire heresy."[14]

Hydatius, too, under the year 445 referred to Turribius' problems: "In the city of Asturias in Galicia certain Manichees, who had been hiding for several years, were discovered in episcopal investigations which were forwarded to Antoninus, bishop of Merida, by the bishops Hydatius and Turribius, who had tried them."[15] Then, under the same year, Hydatius also stated that "reports about the Manichees were distributed throughout the provinces by the bishop then presiding at Rome."[16] Now, these "reports" presumably refer to Leo's investigations of 444 and the imperial edict of 445, but Hydatius' uncertainty about who the bishop of Rome was at this time also suggests that as of 445 there was not yet any direct contact between Leo and the Galician bishops.

The report of the investigations into the "Manichees" in Rome may have given the Spaniards an idea about how they could proceed against their own Priscillianists: by stressing a connection between the two heresies. The association of Priscillianists with Manichees, of course, was nothing new.[17] Turribius may have decided to play upon it when he wrote to Leo and requested his support.[18] In Leo's reply to him in 447, Leo made the same connection. He began by noting, on the basis of Turribius' letter, that "the most fetid dregs of the Priscil-

---

12. See Thompson, *Romans* pp.194-199, who notes possible references to Priscillianist activities in 433 and 441. For Spanish Priscillianism c.420, see chapter 3 above. See also Hefele-Leclercq, *Conciles* 2.480-487.

13. "quod quidem per mala temporis nostri, synodorum conventibus decretisque cessantibus, liberius crevit" (*Epist.* "Molesta semper": *P.L.* 54.693-695). For the date, see note 22 below.

14. "ex quibus Manichaei et Priscillianistae ... omnem haeresim suam confirmare nituntur" (ibid.). Note that the singular, *haeresim*, is used, indicating that the two were viewed as a single heresy.

15. "in Asturicensi urbe Gallaeciae quidam ante aliquot annos latentes Manichaei gestis episcopalibus deteguntur, quae ab Hydatio et Thoribio episcopis, qui eos audierant, ad Antoninum Emeritensem episcopum directa" (*Chron.* 130).

16. "per episcopum Romae tunc praesidentem gesta de Manichaeis per provincias diriguntur" (ibid.133).

17. See chapters 1, 3 above.

18. For Leo and Spanish Priscillianism, see Kidd, *Church* pp.372-374.

lianists have boiled up among you."[19] He also discussed the problems of maintaining ecclesiastical unity in Spain: "Wherefore, moreover, a hostile invasion besets many provinces, and the storms of warfare preclude the carrying out of the laws. Wherefore, travel is difficult and the councils of the bishops have begun to be rare; hidden treachery has found an opportunity as a result of the general disorder. . . ."[20]

Leo then went on to associate the Priscillianists firmly with the Manichees: "The Priscillianists do this, so do the Manichees, whose spirits are so tied to theirs that they are different only in name; they are found to be united, however, in their sacrileges. . . ."[21] Leo concluded by ordering a council of all the Spanish bishops to be assembled, but if this was impossible, at least a synod of the Galicians.[22]

Leo's equation of Priscillianism with Manicheism should come as no surprise: Manicheism was topical in Rome, Priscillianism was not; Manicheism had been specifically condemned in an imperial rescript of two years before, Priscillianism had not. Indeed, Turribius, in his lost letter to Leo, may have stressed the connection for these very reasons, just as Prosper had accused the Gallic anti-predestinarians of Pelagianism the year after a similar imperial decree.

Meanwhile, back in Spain, accusations of Manicheism continued. According to Hydatius, "The bishop Antoninus apprehends at Merida a certain Manichee, Pascentius of Rome, who had fled from Asturias, and having examined him orders him expelled from Lusitania."[23] Is it possible that this Pascentius was one of those expelled from Rome circa 444/445?[24] If so, why would he have fled to Spain, at a time when those who could were leaving, if not because he was a Spaniard?[25] If he was, an accusation of Manicheism against him probably conceals his actual Priscillianist sentiments. Leo's response to Turribius suggests that in Rome it would have been difficult to tell the two

19. "Priscillianistarum foetidissimam apud vos recaluisse sentinam" ("Quam laudabiliter": *P.L.* 54.678-679); Turribius' own letter is not extant.

20. "ex quo autem multas provincias hostilis occupavit irruptio, et executionem legum tempestates interclusere bellorum. ex quo inter sacerdotes dei difficiles commeatus et rari coeperunt esse conventus, invenit ob publicam perturbationem secreta perfidia libertatem. . . ." (ibid. p.680).

21. "faciunt hoc Priscillianistae, faciunt Manichei, quorum cum istis tam foederata sunt corda, ut solis nominibus discreti, sacrilegiis autem suis inveniantur uniti . . ." (ibid. p.689).

22. Leo mentioned by name only Hydatius and Ceponius as ones who should attend. This would suggest that Leo had seen their names in the aforementioned letter Turribius wrote to them, which indicates that Turribius' letter was written before Leo's. The consideration that Turribius' letter contains no mention of Leo or of the synod he ordered to be assembled leads to the same conclusion.

23. "Pascentium quendam urbis Romae, qui de Asturica diffugerat, Manichaeum Antoninus episcopus Emerita comprehendit auditumque etiam de provincia Lusitania facit expelli" (*Chron.* 138, s.a.448).

24. See n.10 above.

25. For examples of such flight, see Mathisen, "Aquitania" p.159.

heresies apart, even if anyone had wished to do so. It may be, then, that the "New Manichees" of Rome were in fact Priscillianists, from Spain and perhaps elsewhere, who had sought refuge there.

Once again, the accusation of an old, well-known, and universally condemned heresy apparently was used to facilitate attacks on a more obscure, and in Spain perhaps a more popular, one. Leo's involvement in this entire affair also allowed him to establish his authority over the church of Spain. In this instance, both the fragmentation caused by the barbarian incursions and the inability of the Spanish bishops to settle their theological disputes among themselves had given the bishop of Rome an opportunity to intervene.[26]

LEO AND GAUL

This leaves to be considered the relations between the see of Rome and Gaul. Sixtus of Rome (432-440) appears to have ignored Gaul altogether; there is no surviving record of any Gallic contacts by him.[27] Leo, however, hardly could have been happy with the situation there. But how was he to assert his authority in an area where the leading ecclesiastics, Hilary and his partisans, had not sought out any rapprochement; where the authority of the imperial government was relatively weak; and where what imperial officials there were usually were aligned on the side of the Gauls? In Spain, theological disagreements and the difficulties of holding church councils had resulted in a lack of ecclesiastical unity which eventually worked to Leo's advantage. No such conditions existed, however, in Gaul.

Leo's opportunity, as always, came from dissaffected Gallic bishops. Hilary's enemies, apparently feeling themselves unable to offer appropriate resistance by themselves, took the step taken by so many other disgruntled Gallic ecclesiastics in the past, and appealed for help to the bishop of Rome. The resultant quarrel between Hilary and Leo probably was unavoidable.[28] Hilary was attempting to secure Gallic ecclesiastical leadership for himself and his colleagues at the same time that Leo himself was seeking extraordinary precedence for him-

---

26. See Thompson, *Romans* p.197: the bishop of Rome was "to be feared abjectly [in Spain] . . . his authority was undisputed." Ideas vary on the significance of the barbarian invasions for the expansion of the authority of the see of Rome: Kidd, *Church* p.394 suggests that they slowed the development of Roman control, whereas Bardy et al., *Eglise* p.263 suggest that they helped it.

27. See Bardy et al., *Eglise* pp.258-259.

28. See Kidd, *Church* 357. The quarrel customarily is portrayed as involving Hilary and Leo alone, see Duchesne, *Fastes* 1.114-119; Franses, *Leo* passim; Griffe, *Gaule* 2.153-163, 200-212; Kidd, *Church* pp.356-360; Langgärtner, *Gallienpolitik* p.76; Prinz, *Mönchtum* p.51; and Stein, *Geschichte* 1.488. Heinzelmann, *Bischofsherrschaft* pp.80-83 views it as a result of the Gallic aversion to rule from Italy.

self and the see of Rome. Ultimately, this controversy was to involve not only religious personnel, but also the imperial administration at the very highest levels. One of the most noteworthy aspects of the conflict, moreover, is the tremendously tendentious accounts of it which are found in the Roman sources on the one hand, and the Gallic ones on the other.[29]

Leo, it will be recalled, as a deacon already had had some relations with Gaul: in 429 he had encouraged Cassian of Marseilles to compose the *De incarnatione*, and in 440 he had been in Arles trying to patch up the quarrel between Aetius and Albinus. After becoming bishop in 440, however, he seems to have maintained a low profile with regard to Gaul, and no official contact is known certainly to have occurred before 445.[30]

Not until some time in early 445, it seems, in his letter "Divinae cultum" addressed "To all my beloved brothers situated throughout the province of Viennensis," did Leo begin his offensive against Hilary, whom he singled out as the sole object of his grievance.[31] Leo laid out his general complaints as follows ("Divinae cultum" ch.2):

But Hilary, intending to disturb the condition of the churches and the concord of the bishops, has strayed from this path [sc. of obedience to Rome] which always was well followed and salubriously guarded by our ancestors; thus, [he has been] wishing to subjugate you to his own power, and he does not allow himself to be subjected to the blessed apostle Peter, appropriating for himself ordinations in all the churches throughout Gaul, and transferring to himself the authority owed to the metropolitan bishops; also by diminish-

29. Nearly all writers follow the version of Leo, see Duchesne, *Fastes* 1.114-119; Hefele-Leclercq, *Conciles* 2.477-478; Hunt, *Leo* p.39; and Jalland, *Leo* pp.113-124, although even he (p.119) notes that Leo's version was "perhaps somewhat exaggerated," and (p.122) that "Leo derived most of his information ... from the appellants." The *Vita Hilarii*, which gives Hilary's side of the story, usually is given short shrift. Wood, "End" p.15 n.113, calls it "propagandist," but accepts Leo's account at face value. Prinz, *Mönchtum* p.50, calls it unreliable because it tried to "hush up" the conflict with Leo. Thompson, *Germanus* p.58, does caution that "the *Vita S. Hilarii* itself gives us a clear indication that the story was more complex than historians usually allow."

30. Palanque, "Marseilles" p.24, mentions (without documentation) a late tradition that c.440 Leo consecrated two basilicas at Marseilles.

31. Thompson, *Germanus* p.58, objects that "the date of the pope's [letter] is unknown and it is mere guesswork to say that it can hardly be much earlier than Valentinian's *Novel 17* [of 8 July 445]. The date when the entire affair began is therefore altogether unknown." Even though Leo's letter is undated, it is unlikely that it was issued long before Valentinian's edict. For one thing, Valentinian referred to the events in it as a "recens ... exemplum." Moreover, in Leo's parallel offensive against the Manichees, only a year or so intervened between Leo's hearing and the issuance of *Nov. Val.* 13. If the Gallic case was handled similarly, Leo's winter hearing perhaps is to be dated to either 443/444 or 444/445, with the latter date being the more likely. "Divinae cultum" then would have been issued soon afterward. For the conventional date of circa June, 445, see Jaffé, p.60 no.407 and Seeck, *Regesten* p.374.

ing the reverence for the most blessed Peter with his rather arrogant
words....[32]

Leo was accusing Hilary, therefore, not only of lack of respect for
himself, but also of carrying out improper ordinations by supplanting
the authority of other metropolitans.

Later in the letter, Leo became a bit more specific on this latter
accusation when he asked, "What does Hilary seek in the province of
another, what does he usurp, and this being that which none of his
predecessors before Patroclus had? Is it also that very thing which
seemed to have been granted by the apostolic see to Patroclus temporarily, and afterward was removed by wiser judgement?"[33] Leo realized that one of Hilary's justifications for his pretensions was the
grant of extraordinary status to the bishop of Arles by Leo's own predecessor Zosimus. He dismissed it by simply asserting that it had been
withdrawn.

THE CHELIDONIUS AFFAIR

So much, then, for the general tenor of Leo's complaints. He was
more specifically concerned with two charges in particular against
Hilary, which had been laid before him by disgruntled Gallic bishops.
The first was that of bishop Chelidonius, who, having been deposed
as bishop of Besançon, the metropolitan see of Maxima Sequanorum,
had traveled to Rome and appealed his case to Leo.[34] With regard to
the circumstances of Chelidonius' expulsion, however, Leo merely
noted ("Divinae cultum" ch.3),

The arrangement of matters contained in the enclosed documents explains
what was decided in the case of bishop Chelidonius, which was considered

32. "sed hunc tramitem semper inter maiores nostros et bene tentum et salubriter custoditum Hilarius, ecclesiarum statum et concordiam sacerdotum novis praesumptionibus turbaturus,
excessit; ita suae vos cupiens subdere potestati, ut se beato apostolo Petro non patiatur esse
subiectum, ordinationes sibi omnium per Gallias ecclesiarum vindicans, et debitam metropoli-
tanis sacerdotibus in suam transferens dignitatem; ipsius quoque beatissimi Petri reverentiam
verbis arrogantioribus minuendo ..."

33. "quid sibi Hilarius quaerit in aliena provincia, et id quod nullus decessorum ipsius ante
Patroclum habuit, quid usurpat? cum et ipsum, quod Patroclo a sede apostolica temporaliter
videbatur esse concessum, postmodum sit sententia meliore sublatum?" ("Divinae cultum" ch.4).

34. See Bardy et al., *Eglise* pp.261-262; Franses, *Leo* pp.27-33; Griffe, *Gaule* 2.159, 200-201;
Jalland, *Leo* pp.114-118; Kidd, *Church* pp.356-357; Langgärtner, *Gallienpolitik* pp.67-68; Mathisen, "Hilarius"; and Prinz, *Stadtherrschaft* pp.13-15. Chelidonius' deposition is conventionally
dated to 444, although recently a date in the mid 430s has been suggested (see Thompson,
Germanus pp.55-70 and Wood, "End" p.15). This earlier date, however, would require an inor-
dinately long delay between Chelidonius' appeal (before 438) and Valentinian's response (445).
Moreover, Leo gives no indication that Chelidonius had appealed to his predecessor Sixtus,
rather than to himself, as this analysis would require.

in our presence. . . . Through the clear testimony of witnesses, he demonstrated that he was unjustly deposed from his episcopal office . . . because [of the accusation that] as the husband of a widow he could not hold a priesthood. . . .[35]

All that comes out of Leo's testimony, therefore, is that Chelidonius had been convicted of having an uncanonical marriage and accordingly deposed. No other charges were mentioned or even suggested.

It is useful to compare this account with the Gallic version contained in the rather later *Vita Hilarii*, composed near the end of the century by Hilary's pupil and likely relative, the bishop of Marseilles, Honoratus.[36] According to him, Hilary's presence in the north at the time of the controversy was purely adventitious. He was there to visit an old friend: "Who will expand upon how much advantage his presence brought to the Gallic cities by repeatedly seeking out Saint Germanus, with whom he oversaw the supervision and activity of bishops and clergy, as well as their advancements and departures?"[37] Hilary did not become involved, Honoratus went on, until he was already there (ibid.):

When his arrival became known, the enflamed desires of nobles and commoners flocked to them both [sc. Hilary and Germanus], claiming that Chelidonius had married a widow, which the authority of the apostolic see and the statutes of the canons prohibit, and saying at the same time that while he was serving in the secular administration he had sentenced several to capital punishment. Aroused by the novelty of such a charge, they order witnesses to be summoned. The most upright bishops gather from other places, the affair is investigated with all intelligence and prudence, the accusation is confirmed by testimony, a true and simple rule is brought forth, that he whom the rules of scripture remove ought to remove himself of his own will. But [Chelidonius] believed that he should go to Rome, and there he claims that he had been condemned by an unjust strictness.[38]

35. "Quae igitur apud nos in causa Chelidonii episcopi gesta confecta sint, . . . inditus chartis rerum ordo demonstrat. . . . se iniuste sacerdotio fuisse deiectum, manifesta testium responsione . . . monstraverat . . . quod tamquam viduae maritus sacerdotium tenere non posset. . . ."

36. For the text, see Cavallin, *Vitae*. For the author and date, see Gennad.*Vir. ill.* 100: "sanctorum quoque patrum vitas . . . [Honoratus Massiliensis] coaptat ipse legendas, praecipue nutritoris sui Hilarii Arelatensis episcopi." Honoratus was bishop in the mid-490s (see Duchesne, *Fastes* 1.274-275); Wood, "End" p.15, exaggerates the work's lateness. Honoratus probably was related to Hilary through the latter's relative Honoratus of Arles. Honoratus wrote under the pseudonym "Reverentius" (see Thompson, *Germanus* p.57).

37. "quis . . . explicabit, quantum eius praesentia profectum contulerit civitatibus Gallicanis sanctum Germanum saepius expetendo, cum quo sacerdotum ministrorumque curam et vitam, nec non profectus excessusque tractabat?" (*VHilarii* 16[21]). On Germanus and Hilary, see Franses, *Leo* pp.38-39 and Mathisen, "Hilarius."

38. "ubi eius adventus innotuit, flammata ad utrosque nobilium et mediocrium studia convolarunt, astruentes Chelidonium internuptam suo adhibuisse consortio—quod apostolicae sedis auctoritas et canonum prohibent statuta—simul ingerentes saeculi administratione perfunctum

The mere mention of Germanus at all in the *vita* of another saint suggests that he played in important part in the proceedings.[39] As the senior bishop there, he may even have presided.[40]

Several significant discrepancies between the two accounts are immediately apparent. For one thing, Leo attempted to lay the entire blame for the deposition on Hilary's shoulders, and made no mention at all of Germanus' presence or of the church council. This council is confirmed, however, by the early sixth-century *vita* of Romanus of St. Claude, which reports that Romanus encountered Hilary at Besançon "when the clerics had been summoned for the case [of Chelidonius]."[41] Moreover, Leo implied that Hilary had been out to depose Chelidonius all along, whereas Honoratus claimed that his presence was purely fortuitous. Finally, Honoratus noted that there were two charges against Chelidonius, whereas Leo mentioned only the accusation that he had married a widow, ignoring the perhaps more heinous one about Chelidonius' imposition of the death sentence.

Now, the marital charge would have been especially timely. Leo himself, on 8 October 443, had expressly forbidden the ordination of those married to widows, and had ordered, "If any brother contrives to go against these measures, let him know he must be removed from

---

capitali aliquos condemnasse sententia. tantae rei novitate permoti testes imperant praeparari. conveniunt ex aliis locis probatissimi sacerdotes; res omni ratione prudentiaque discutitur; accusatio testimoniis confirmatur; adhibetur vera simplexque definitio, ut quem scripturarum regulae removebant, voluntate propria se removere deberet. ille urbem credidit expetendam, ibique se iniusto rigore astruit condemnatum."

39. Some have attempted to play down Germanus' role. Thompson, *Germanus* p.57 n.13, suggests that after the word *imperant*, "the rest of the story is about Hilary alone with no further reference to Germanus"; and Wood, "End" p.15, asserts that after the initial accusations, the *Vita Hilarii* "forgets about Germanus." In fact, however, there is no further reference to Hilary either; the rest of the story either is in the passive voice or has both (or others) as the subject. Furthermore, the *vita* also is very clear that Hilary and Germanus consulted *saepius*, and that this was not merely an isolated incident. Nor need it be significant that there is "no hint as to ... how long it took them to obtain" the evidence against Chelidonius (Thompson, p.58): this presumably already had been done, and all that remained to do was to assemble an *ad hoc* synod. The *Vita Romani* (note 41 below), ignored by the critics, also suggests that the process took very little time.

40. Hefele-Leclercq, *Conciles*, 2.477-478 n.4, raise the possibility that Eucherius may have presided, and wrongly make Hilary as the "plus ancien"; Germanus had been in office since 418, Hilary only since 429.

41. "missis in causa clericis" (*VRomani* 18). For the text and reliability of the *vita*, see F. Martine, *Vie des pères du Jura*, Sources chrétiennes no.142 (Paris, 1968). It is customary to assert, as Duchesne, *Fastes* 1.114; Hefele-Leclercq, *Conciles* 2.477; Jalland, *Leo* p.114; and McShane, *Romanitas* p.278, that Hilary called the council on his own authority: there is no evidence for this. Langgärtner, *Gallienpolitik* p.57, even asserts that Hilary himself deposed Chelidonius. Some, such as Franses, *Leo* pp.27-33, simply deny the evidence of the *Vita Romani*. Leo's own failure to mention Germanus (or anyone else) does not mean that Germanus did not take part, as suggested by Franses, *Leo* p.36ff; Thompson, *Germanus* p.59; and Wood, "End" p.15, but only that Leo was prosecuting Hilary, no one else.

his office."[42] The Gauls themselves, moreover, had forbidden husbands of widows to advance beyond the subdiaconate as early as the Council of Valence in 374, and had reiterated the restriction as recently as 441.[43] Chelidonius seems simply to have denied this charge. The second charge, however, might have been more difficult to disavow: presumably records of Chelidonius' official activities would have been on file in Rome. Leo just ignored this accusation.[44]

There can, of course, be little doubt that both Leo and Honoratus presented their cases in the most favorable light. One might rightly doubt that Hilary's presence in the north at the time was strictly fortuitous: even if he had not come to depose Chelidonius, he may have been there with regard to Germanus' second mission to Britain.[45] One also might wonder what kind of a hearing Chelidonius really received. This area was the homeland of the Lérins faction, and its adherents, such as Hilary and Germanus, would have had a great deal of influence there. Of course, Chelidonius must have been influential in his own right, for in order to have passed the death sentence in secular life he would have to have been at least a provincial governor. He even may have been *praeses Maximae Sequanorum*, and if so, like many of the day, he may have been serving near his homeland.[46] Then, also like many others, he probably went directly to episcopal office. If such were the case, the entire affair would have been one more example of an originally local conflict among powerful aristocrats over ecclesiastical office and authority which eventually drew other, more distant, potentates into it.[47]

There are some interesting similarities, moreover, between this case and that of Armentarius of Embrun, who had been deposed by Hilary's faction in 439. First and foremost, both were bishops of metropolitan sees.[48] This consideration brings to mind Leo's charge that Hilary was appropriating the rights of other metropolitans. The cases of Armentarius and Chelidonius show one means by which Hilary

---

42. "si quis fratrum contra haec constituta venire tentaverit . . . a suo se noverit officia submovendum" (*Epist.* "Ut nobis gratulationem": *P.L.* 54.644) addressed "to the bishops of Campania, Picenum, Tuscia, and all the provinces." A similar restriction had been specified by Innocent in 404 (*Epist.* "Etsi tibi" 4, to Victricius of Rouen).

43. Can.1 (*Corp. chr. lat.* 148.38), repeated at Orange in 441 (can.24[25]: ibid. p.84) and in the canons of the "Second Council of Arles" (can.45: ibid. p.123).

44. Many others have done likewise, see Langgärtner, *Gallienpolitik* pp.67-68.

45. See Mathisen, "Last Year" pp.158-159. For the assumption that Hilary was in the north only for Chelidonius, see Hefele-Leclercq, *Conciles* 2.477.

46. See Mathisen, "Hilarius" p.164 and "Addenda" p.369.

47. See Mathisen, "Hilarius" passim.

48. Duchesne, *Fastes* 1.115, notes that "il est douteux que Besançon fut alors considérée comme une métropole ecclésiastique," which, however, means denying the evidence of both the *Notitia Galliarum* and the *VRomani* 18, which specifically calls Besançon a metropolitan see at the time: see Hefele-Leclercq, *Conciles*, 2.477 n.3.

was able to do so: by replacing opponents with his own partisans. It has been seen that Ingenuus, the new bishop of Embrun, loyally supported Hilary. In the case of Besançon, however, neither Leo nor the *Vita Hilarii* mention the ordination of any successor to Chelidonius. But the episcopal *fasti* of the city do: after the name of Chelidonius they note, "The false bishop Inportunus is received but [then is] dishonorably expelled."[49]

There is no other extant reference to this Inportunus, and, indeed, this may be only a pseudonym. Whoever he was, he presumably was the successor to Chelidonius selected by Hilary and his party, which would have given the faction metropolitan authority in yet another Gallic province. The Chelidonius case, however, also had a significant difference from that of Armentarius. The latter had been appeased with a chorepiscopate and, it seems, had caused no further trouble. Chelidonius, however, was not to be put off so easily. He apparently was an older, more influential individual than the younger Armentarius, and could be neither satisfied nor overawed. Therefore, like others before him, he took his case to Rome.

Leo's second specific accusation against Hilary was similar, involving a bishop Projectus of an unknown see ("Divinae cultum" ch.4):

> With his [sc. Chelidonius'] business finished, the complaint of our brother and fellow bishop Projectus was taken up, whose tearful and grief-stricken account of the ordination of a bishop in his place was directed to us. A letter also was included from the citizens of his city, and was strengthened by the numerous signatures of individuals, full of the most serious complaints against Hilary, [saying] that the bishop Projectus was not free to become ill, that his episcopate had been transferred to another without his approval, and so to speak changed into an ownerless possession by the invader Hilary, a legacy of one who was still living....[50]

Nothing further is known about the background of this case, except that Projectus' see was not in Viennensis, as indicated by Leo's query, "What does Hilary seek for himself in the province of another?"[51]

---

49. "Inportunus pseudo-episcopus receptus sed turpiter eiectus" (Duchesne, *Fastes* 3.198, 212). Jalland, *Leo* p.116 n.16, wrongly has Inportunus as the bishop who replaced a Projectus (n.50 below). Langgärtner, *Gallienpolitik* p.67 n.17, denies Inportunus existed at all.

50. "huic negotio sic finito, fratris et coepiscopi nostri Proiecti querela successit: cuius ad nos litterae lacrymabiles et dolendae, de superordinato sibi episcopo, sunt directae. epistola quoque ingesta est civium ipsius, et numerosa singulorum subscriptione firmata, invidiosissimis contra Hilarium plena querimoniis: quod Proiecto episcopo suo aegrotare liberum non fuisset, eiusque sacerdotium in alium praeter suam notitiam esse translatam, et tamquam in vacuam possessionem ab Hilario pervasore haeredem viventis inductum...." See Franses, *Leo* pp.33-34 and Langgärtner, *Gallienpolitik* pp.67-68. McShane (*Romanitas* p.331) asserts that Projectus went to Rome himself, but this passage indicates that only his complaints did.

51. "quid sibi Hilarius quaerit in aliena provincia?" ("Divinae cultum" ch.4). For Narbonensis Prima as the province, see Hunt, *Leo* p.41 n.13 and Jalland, *Leo* p.116 n.15. Franses, *Leo*

Now, if this case were consistent with what is otherwise known about Hilary's policies, Projectus too may have been a metropolitan bishop. Furthermore, the evidence of nomenclature could suggest that he was a southerner, for Projecti appear at Arles and Narbonne during this period, and one of these may have been the Projectus who was the bishop of an unknown southern see c.464.[52] Indeed, Sidonius knew a southern Projectus whose grandfather had been a bishop, perhaps the very one under consideration here, if the usual pattern of nomenclature held.[53] Finally, the failure of this Projectus to appear at any of the Gallic councils of 439-442 also suggests that he was one of Hilary's opponents.

It also can be presumed that Hilary and his party had some canonical justification for Projectus' replacement, and believed that they had observed all the legal niceties. Such may have been provided by the final canon of the Council of Orange in 441, which stated that infirm bishops were to be replaced, at least temporarily.[54] Leo, of course, even though he did draw attention to Projectus' illness, gave no hint that the replacement might have been justified, or authorized by a Gallic council, and he asserted that the entire affair was carried out "by the invader Hilary."

With all these considerations in mind, one might tentatively suggest that Projectus, a southern bishop opposed to Hilary, was the as-yet-unnamed bishop of Aix. By replacing him Hilary would have gained another metropolitan bishop among his supporters and removed a troublesome thorn in his side as well. After all, the only other certain examples of episcopal replacements by Hilary's party also involved metropolitans, those of Embrun and Besançon. If this analysis is correct, it would mean that as of c.445, the Lérins party had been very successful in consolidating its ecclesiastical authority. Over the years no fewer than six metropolitans would have been recruited or appointed: Hilary of Arles and Claudius of Vienne in Viennensis, Ingenuus of Embrun in Alpes Maritimae, Projectus' unknown replacement at Aix in Narbonensis Secunda, Eucherius of Lyons in

---

p.43, suggests Narbonensis Secunda, and Langgärtner, *Gallienpolitik* p.73, opts for Alpes Maritimae.

52. Arles: *C.I.L.* 12.958, 965. Narbonne: Espérandieu, *Inscriptions* no.604, a presbyter in 456. Bishop: *P.L.* 58.28, see chapter 6 above, n.19. If Projectus of 445 were from Narbonne, he also may have been a protégé of Hilary's rival Rusticus of Narbonne, and therefore all the more worthy of replacement.

53. *Epist.* 2.4.1.

54. See chapter 5 above, n.97. Most simply assume Hilary's action was unjustified; see Jalland, *Leo* pp.116,118. Franses, *Leo* pp.42-43, suggests his authority came from the metropolitan authority of Arles which was not recognized by Leo.

Lugdunensis Prima, and Inportunus of Besançon in Maxima Sequanorum. The bishop of Sens, metropolitan see of Lugdunensis Quarta, also may have been involved. Not only was this the province of Germanus of Auxerre, but the city also was the see of Eucherius' literary confrère Agroecius, although it is unclear whether he was in office this early.[55]

Such a faction would have been very potent. Small wonder that it gave Leo pause, and caused him to seek to lessen its influence. If he could not do so, his own authority in Gaul would be negligible. It also would have been clear that he would have to act quickly, for his potential Gallic support would have been eroding rapidly. As of 445, the only strong opponents of the Lerinenses in southern Gaul would have been Venerius of Marseilles and Rusticus of Narbonne. How long would they, and whatever partisans they had, be able to hold out?

Yet another of Leo's causes for concern, finally, might be behind a further command which he issued to Hilary ("Divinae cultum" ch.8):

Let communion be easily denied to no Christian, nor let that which a somewhat unwilling and grieving spirit of the judge ought to inflict in the avenging of a great guilt be done arbitrarily by an indignant bishop. Indeed, we have learned that certain individuals have been excluded from communion because of trivial deeds and words.... But what wonder that [Hilary] acts in such a manner toward laymen when he is in the habit of rejoicing over the damnation of bishops?[56]

This accusation may even be a reference to Hilary's aforementioned exclusion of the prefect from church.[57] It would have given Leo yet more ammunition to use against Hilary, and might indicate that Leo was aware of Hilary's involvement not only with ecclesiastics, but with powerful laymen as well.

HILARY'S SUPPORT IN 445

Several sources suggest just how strong Hilary's secular support in the early 440s was. The early sixth-century *vita* of the abbot Romanus

---

55. Agroecius is attested only c.470, already an old man (Sid. Apoll. *Epist.* 7.5). For the date, see Duchesne, *Fastes* 2.415. Jacobus of Tarentaise also may have been involved and one also might wonder whether the Lerinenses had anything to do with the expulsion c. 430 of Brictius from Tours, another metropolitan see (chapter 1 above, n.91).

56. "nulli Christianorum facile communio denegetur, nec ad indignantis fiat hoc arbitrium sacerdotis, quod in magni reatus ultionem invitus et dolens quodammodo debet inferre animus iudicantis. cognovimus enim pro commissis et levibus verbis quosdam a gratia communionis exclusos.... sed quid mirum eum in laicos talem existere, qui soleat de sacerdotum damnatione gaudere?"

57. See chapter 6 above, n.16.

of St. Claude, for example, gave the following account of the Chelidonius affair (*VRomani* 18-19):

For when the fame of the aforementioned [monks of St. Claude] became
known, Saint Hilary, bishop of Arles, when clerics had been summoned for
the case [of Chelidonius], had the blessed Romanus meet him not far from
the city of Besançon, and praising his motivation and life in a most worthy
proclamation and having imposed on him the office of presbyter, he permitted him to return honorably to his monastery. In fact, the aforementioned
Hilary, supported by the patrician and the prefect, seizing for himself an
unjustified monarchy throughout the Gauls, for no clear reason deposed the
venerable Chelidonius, patriarch of the aforementioned metropolis, from his
episcopal see. . . . There is extant, moreover, a letter of the aforementioned
and venerable father [sc. Leo] to the bishops of Gaul. . . .[58]

This account clearly was influenced by the very unfavorable depiction
of Hilary in Leo's letter to the Gauls, which the sixth-century author
adopted. The other elements, however, those presumably dependent
upon local tradition, not only contradict Leo but also contribute otherwise unattested material.

It is clear, for example, that Romanus was yet another of Hilary's
partisans. On the one hand, he was ordained a presbyter by him. And
on the other, the *vita* also states that he had spent time in the monastery of the Insula barbara near Lyons, under the jurisdiction of
Eucherius, and had borrowed there a "*Book of the Life of the Blessed
Fathers* and the exceptional *Institutes of the Abbots*," perhaps Eucherius' epitome of Cassian's *Institutes*.[59] This suggests yet another, albeit
tenuous, connection between Romanus and the Lerinenses.

Romanus also had connections of some sort near Besançon, for the
martyrology of the ninth-century bishop Ado of Vienne noted that,
even though Romanus' monastery was in the territory of Lyons, "his
body was buried within the boundary of Besançon."[60] Romanus therefore would have been a valuable local ally for Hilary and his party at

58. "audita namque memoratorum fama, sanctus Hilarius Arelatensis episcopus, missis in
causa clericis, beatissimum Romanum haud longe sibi a Vesontionensi urbe fecit occurrere, cuius
incitamentum vitamque dignissima praedicatione sustollens, inposito honore presbyterii, ad
monasterium honorifice repedare permisit. siquidem antedictus Hilarius venerabilem Caelidonium supradictae metropolis patriarcham, patricio praefectorioque fultus favore indebitam sibi
per Gallias vindicans monarchiam, a sede episcopali memoratum Caelidonium nulla exsistente
ratione deiecerat. . . . exstat denique exinde antedicti ac venerabilis papae ad Galliae episcopos
. . . epistula. . . ." For the *vita*, see note 41 above.

59. "librum vitae sanctorum patrum eximiasque institutiones abbatum" (*VRomani* 11). The
abbot of the monastery was a certain Sabinus, on whom see Martine, *Pères* pp.250-251 n.3.

60. "corpus eius situm est in finibus Vesontionum" (*P.L.* 123.234); Ado also affirmed that
Romanus' monastery lay "in territorio Lugdunensi locis Iurensibus," and that his brother Lupicinus likewise was buried "in finibus Vesontionum, apud Laoconense monasterium" (*P.L.*
123.241).

the time of Chelidonius' deposition, and the alliance may have been pointedly ratified by his ordination as presbyter near Besançon. The ordination also shows that Hilary was exercising episcopal rights in another province, and indicates that here, as in the south, a metropolitan bishop, either Eucherius of Lyons or Inportunus of Besançon, was yielding precedence to him.[61]

Most significant of all is the explicit statement that Hilary was supported in his activities "by the favor of the patrician and the prefect." Now the patrician would have been Flavius Aetius himself, the current "patrician and master of soldiers."[62] Aetius is known to have been closely involved with other ecclesiastics in Gaul as well. In 431, the Spanish bishop Hydatius "undertook an embassy to the *dux* Aetius, who was campaigning in Gaul."[63] In 439, Aetius used the bishop Orientius of Auch as an ambassador to the Goths.[64] Later, in 451, when Anianus of Orléans went to inform Aetius about the approach of the Huns, he encountered there "many bishops . . . who because of their own needs already had been waiting there for many days."[65]

The identity of the prefect, unfortunately, is unknown: Marcellus of Narbonne would have been out of office by then, and the next known prefect, the father of Sidonius Apollinaris, is not attested until 449.[66] Whoever he was, it is clear that as of 445 Hilary had support at the very highest levels of the Gallic secular administration.

Leo himself, moreover, rhetorically attested the extent of Hilary's secular support when he asserted ("Divinae cultum" ch.6):

A military band, as we have learned, follows this bishop around the provinces, and he is assisted by the supporting presumption of an armed guard in his tumultous invasions of churches which have lost their own bishops. Those to be ordained are dragged before this tribunal, unknown in those cities which they are to oversee. Even when a known and approved individual is sought peacefully, one who is brought forth as an unknown is of necessity imposed by force.[67]

---

61. See also Prinz, *Mönchtum* pp.23,26.

62. See Heinzelmann, *Bischofsherrschaft* p.83. Langgärtner, *Gallienpolitik* pp.74-77, sees a connection between Hilary's presence at Besançon and Aetius' settlement of the Burgundians in Sapaudia in 443.

63. "ad Aetium ducem, qui expeditionem agebat in Gallis, suscipit legationem" (*Chron.*96).

64. *VOrientii* 3, cf. Salv. *De gub.* 7.9.

65. "multorum episcoporum qui pro necessitatibus eorum illuc iam multis diebus resedebant" (*VAniani* 7).

66. For the assumption that the prefect was Marcellus, see Hefele-Leclercq, *Conciles* 2.478 n.3. This, however, is impossible, for *C.I.L.* 12.5336 states that Marcellus was prefect for only two years, c.441-443. For Sidonius' father, perhaps named Alcimus, see Mathisen, "Epistolography" p.100.

67. "militaris manus, ut didicimus, per provincias sequitur sacerdotem et armati praesidii praesumptione suffulto ad invadendas per tumultum famulatur ecclesias, quae proprios amise-

Now, if Hilary actually did have military support in his activities, it could have occurred only with the connivance of Aetius, the master of soldiers.[68] Of course, precedents for such collusion already had been set. Earlier bishops of Arles had cooperated with secular officials at the highest levels, including Heros with Constantine III and Patroclus with Constantius. Later, the master of soldiers Cassius had used soldiers in Hilary's election. So Leo's accusation, however extravagantly it may have been expressed, probably was grounded in fact at least in so far as it implies influential secular support for Hilary. This is one thing upon which all the otherwise disparate sources do agree.

Here, then, the pattern established by Constantine III and Constantius had been repeated on a much wider scale. With the support of the secular authorities of Gaul, Hilary and his monkish, aristocratic, and largely northern associates had been able to introduce themselves into the most influential southern, as well as northern, sees, and into many others as well. As outsiders, they would initially have been very beholden to their secular supporters. But as the years went by, their personal authority would have grown as well.

It is difficult, however, to find much evidence for Leo's accusation of the forceful imposition of unknowns.[69] Most of the Lerinenses who became bishops, including Lupus of Troyes, Maximus of Riez, Antiolus, and probably Eucherius of Lyons and his son Salonius of Geneva, not to mention Germanus of Auxerre, did so in or near their homelands.[70] In fact, the only certainly attested non-native bishops, and the ones whom Leo probably had in mind, were the bishops of Arles themselves, such as Honoratus, Hilary, and probably Helladius.

Elsewhere in his discussion, moreover, Leo revealed perhaps more accurately the means that Hilary's faction used to put its supporters in episcopal sees. In his decision about metropolitan bishops, Leo decreed,

---

rint sacerdotes. trahuntur ordinandi ante hoc officium, his quibus praeficiendi sunt civitatibus ignotus adducitur, imponatur." This charge recalls that of Zosimus, that Proculus of Marseilles had "associated with himself certain men suited for creating disturbances" (chapter 3 above, n.76).

68. For Hilary's "militaris manus," see Heinzelmann, *Bischofsherrschaft* p.82 and Prinz, *Klerus* p.43. Private persons could and did raise personal armies at this time (see Diesner, "Buccellariertum"), but for a fifth-century Gallic bishop to have done so is absolutely unprecedented.

69. Small matter that the bishops of Rome were themselves guilty of the same practice. When Peter Chrysologus, archdeacon of Cornelia, was imposed upon the church of Ravenna by Pope Sixtus (432–440), "Some said, 'He is not from our flock, but he has suddenly invaded our cathedral like a bandit'" (Agnell. *Lib. pont. eccl. rav.* 49).

70. Eucherius' relative Valerianus of Cimiez and other son Veranus of Vence may have had family ties of their own in the south: see chapter 4 above, n.56. The origin of Theodorus of Fréjus is unknown.

Let each be contented with his own borders and boundaries, and let him know that he is not permitted to be able to transfer his due privilege to another. Because if anyone, neglecting the apostolic sanctions and attributing more to personal favor, wishes to be a deserter of his rank, let not the one to whom he yielded but the one who outranks the other bishops within the province in episcopal tenure assume for himself the right to ordain bishops.[71]

Hilary's extended metropolitan rights, therefore, even according to Leo, had not been seized from unwilling metropolitans, but had been ceded willingly to him by the metropolitans concerned, for the sake of *gratia personalis*. Now, this is only the conclusion which already has been reached above, where it has been suggested that Ingenuus of Embrun, Claudius of Vienne, Inportunus of Besançon, Eucherius of Lyons, and others had, to some degree or other, allowed Hilary to assume extraordinary precedence.

Hilary, then, was hardly acting on his own. He was supported by a powerful faction, which included high secular officials and several metropolitan bishops, not to mention lesser lights such as local bishops and influential lay aristocrats both at Lérins and elsewhere. How, then, was Leo to try to extend his own influence into Gaul?

LEO'S OFFENSIVE AGAINST HILARY

Leo used several justifications for his intervention. One was the standard claim that the see of Rome had received its authority from St. Peter. Leo realistically recognized, however, that this claim might not carry much weight, as when he asserted, "Whoever believes that the leadership ought to be denied to [Peter] in no way is able to diminish his authority."[72] Another justification was the authority which the bishop of Rome could summon from the imperial administration. A third was the customary use of appeals to *vetustas* and *antiquitas*, and to the *statutes* or *canones patrum* or *apostolicae*, and the assertion that he was "not instituting novelties, but renewing traditions."[73]

One of Leo's most effective weapons, however, had been provided by the Gauls themselves: the repeated appeals to Rome by dissatisfied

---

71. "suis limitibus, suis terminis sit unusquisque contentus, et privilegium sibi debitum in alium transferre se posse, noverit non licere. quod si quis negligens apostolicas sanctiones, plus gratiae tribuens personali, sui honoris desertor esse voluerit, privilegium suum in alium transferre posse se credens, non is cui cesserit, sed is qui intra provinciam antiquitate episcopali caeteros praevenit sacerdotes, ordinandi sibi vindicet potestatem" (*Epist.* "Divinae cultum" ch.6). For such voluntary yielding of metropolitan rights to Hilary, see Duchesne, *Fastes* 1.117, and Jalland, *Leo* p.120 n.22.

72. "cui [sc. Petro] quisquis principatum aestimat denegandum, illius quidem nullo modo potest minuere dignitatem" (*Epist.* "Divinae cultum" ch.2).

73. "non nova instituentes, sed vetera renovantes" ("Divinae cultum" ch.2).

ecclesiastics in the past. The papal chancery would have provided him with many examples of them.[74] Regardless of the outcome of such appeals, they had set precedents through which the bishop of Rome was able to portray himself as the arbiter of the affairs of other churches. In the quarrel with Hilary, Leo took full advantage of them. He reminded the Gallic bishops ("Divinae cultum" ch.2),

Along with us, therefore, let Your Fraternity recall that the apostolic see has been consulted in innumerable cases on account of the reverence felt for it by the bishops even of your provinces and that judgments either have been reversed or upheld through the appeal of diverse cases, to the extent that the ancient custom demands ... with letters traveling back and forth.[75]

Leo was well aware that it was the Gauls themselves who had given to him and his predecessors additional precedents for their involvement in Gaul. It was the appeals of Chelidonius and Projectus which gave Leo his real opening, and once again the willingness of disgruntled Gauls to seek redress at Rome gave a bishop of Rome the chance to assert himself in Gaul.

In several regards, however, Leo seems to have underestimated Hilary, for the Gallic bishop appears to have been not only more determined but also better-supported than Leo had anticipated. For one thing, Leo presumably had expected to have a free hand at least in Rome, his own see, when he conducted his inquiries into the Gallic complaints. After all, when Zosimus had favored Patroclus, for example, only one side had been represented in Rome. Hilary, however, when he learned of Leo's intentions, immediately traveled to Rome, braving the rigors of a winter journey, and arrived to oppose Leo on his own ground.

Not unexpectedly, there are very contradictory accounts of their confrontation.[76] According to Leo ("Divinae cultum" ch.3),

That which Hilary said while he was heard with the same aforementioned bishop [sc. Chelidonius] present, the sequence of events embedded in the documents demonstrates. When afterward Hilary did not have anything sensible to respond in the synod of the sanctified bishops, the hidden thoughts of his heart transferred themselves to those things which no layman should speak and no bishop should hear. We were unwilling to exacerbate these wounds which he inflicted through the insolent words of his spirit, and the

74. For these records, see Jalland, *Leo* p.117; McShane, *Romanitas* pp.328-332; and Silva-Tarouca, "Nuovi Studi" pp.349-425.

75. "nobiscum itaque vestra fraternitas recognoscat apostolicam sedem, pro sui reverentia a vestrae etiam provinciae sacerdotibus, innumeris relationibus esse consultam, et per diversarum, quemadmodum vetus consuetudo poscebat, appellationem causarum, aut retractata, aut confirmata fuisse iudicia: adeo ... commeantibus hinc inde litteris. ..."

76. For the proceedings, see Franses, *Leo* pp.37-41 and Jalland, *Leo* pp.114-122.

very one whom we had received as a brother we struggled more to soothe than to sadden with our interlocutions, even though he implicated himself with his responses.[77]

Leo, therefore, portrayed himself as being conciliatory, and Hilary as responsible for the final break. In doing so, however, he also indicated that Hilary was not about to be overawed and went so far as to beard the lion in his own den. Leo's decision, presumably, would have been foreordained, and Hilary verbalized exactly what he thought about it.[78]

Leo's version of what happened next, moreover, is equally interesting, for he referred to Hilary as one ("Divinae cultum" ch.7)

who, knowledgeable of his own worth, when he was sought at the hearing decided to absent himself in shameful flight, not sharing in apostolic communion, whose participant he did not deserve to be: we believe this was an act of God, who drew him to our deliberations with us totally unsuspecting, and who brought it about in the midst of our examinations that he should secretly abscond, lest he be a participant in our communion.[79]

The unexpected nature of Hilary's arrival—Leo could attribute it only to divine intervention—would indicate that Hilary had not even been invited to the hearing of his own case.[80] Leo also apparently felt the need to explain why Hilary, after going to the trouble of coming to Italy, did not remain until the end of the proceedings. He could attribute that as well only to divine action. In doing so, he also revealed that it was not he who refused communion to Hilary, but Hilary who excommunicated him.[81]

Leo was not very specific, however, about what caused Hilary's precipitate departure, and for further enlightenment one must turn to

77. "quae Hilarius dixerit, dum cum eodem praesente supradicto episcopo audiretur, inditus chartis rerum ordo demonstrat. ubi postquam Hilarius rationabile, quod in sanctorum concilio sacerdotum posset respondere, non habuit, ad ea se occulta cordis ipsius transtulerunt, quae nullus laicorum dicere, nullus sacerdotum posset audire.... nolebamus etenim ea illi exacerbare vulnera, quae suae animae insolentibus subinde sermonibus infligebat, et quem susceperamus ut fratrem, delinire magis ipsum, quamvis ipse se suis responsionibus innodaret, quam contristare nostris interlocutionibus, nitebamur."

78. Duchesne, *Fastes* 1.115, faults Hilary for not bringing as witnesses those who had testified against Chelidonius at Besançon: it might be asked whether that would have been either possible or worthwhile.

79. "qui meriti sui conscius, cum quaereretur ad causam, turpi fuga se credidit subtrahendum, exsors apostolicae communionis, cuius particeps esse non meruit: Deo, ut credimus, hoc agente, qui illum, inopinantibus nobis, et ad iudicia nostra pertraxit, et inter examinationes habitas, ne communionis nostrae consors fieret, ut abscederet latenter, effecit."

80. McShane, *Romanitas* p.331, nevertheless supposes that "Hilaire avait été sommé devenir à Rome."

81. It is unclear, however, whether Hilary broke with Leo because of Leo's treatment of him, or because Leo was in communion with Chelidonius.

the Gallic version of this encounter preserved in Honoratus' *Vita Hilarii*, which offers a very different account (*VHilarii* 17[22]):

[Hilary] presents himself immediately to the blessed pope Leo, granting compliance with reverence, and requesting humbly that Leo order the organization of the churches in the accustomed manner, asserting that some in Gaul [e.g. Chelidonius] had received a public sentence deservedly, and were present at the sacred altars [i.e. accepted into communion] in Rome. He demands and enjoins that if Leo receives advice freely he should order emendation privately; and he says that he had come from duty, not to argue a case, and that he was advising him of what had been done for the purpose of a protest, not of an accusation. He went on to say, moreover, that if Leo wished anything else, he would not be troublesome. And because I do not dare to air in this narrative judgments of such great men already called to supernal grace, let it suffice to have touched upon it briefly [and to say] that he alone restrained such great men; that he feared those threatening not at all; that he instructed those who were inquisitive; that he overcame the quarrelsome; that he did not yield to the powerful; [and] that, placed in danger of his life, he did not at all acquiesce to be joined in communion with the one whom he had damned [sc. Chelidonius?] along with such great men, because, having been placed under guard, in the raging fury of winter, he decided that he had to forsake those whom he could not influence by reason.[82]

This version helps to clarify the sequence of events after Hilary's arrival in Rome. First of all, Hilary's "organization of the churches in the accustomed manner" may have referred to the understanding that Patroclus had had with Zosimus. Hilary may have offered to grant tacit recognition to Leo's authority in Gaul in exchange for Leo's stamp of approval upon Hilary's own jurisdiction. Honoratus seems to indicate, moreover, that Hilary intended this to be agreed upon at some private, personal level, not in an open council. Hilary and Leo, however, had no known history of cooperation and no grounds upon

---

82. "beato Leoni papae ilico se praesentat, cum reverentia impendens obsequium, et cum humilitate deposcens ut ecclesiarum statum more solito ordinaret: astruens aliquos apud Gallias publicam merito excepisse sententiam, et in urbe sacris altaribus interesse. rogat atque constringit ut si suggestionem suam libenter excepit, secrete iubeat emendare, et se ad officia, non ad causam venisse; protestandi ordine, non accusandi, quae sunt acta suggerere. porro autem si aliud velit, se non futurum esse molestum. et quia tantorum virorum praesertim iam ad supernam gratiam vocatorum, nec in narratione audeo iudicia ventilare, hoc breviter tetigisse sufficiet, quod solus tantos sustinuit, quod nequaquam minantes expavit, quod inquirentes edocuit, quod altercantes vicit, quod potentibus non cessit, quod in discrimine vitae positus communioni eius, quem cum tantis viris damnaverat, coniungi nullatenus acquievit, quod custodibus appositis, hiemis rigore saeviente, quos ratione non flexerat, credidit relinquendos." Thompson, *Germanus* p.58, asserts that the *Vita Hilarii* "suppresses all mention of the pope's other two accusations and also of the fact that the pope championed Celidonius." The *aliqui* mentioned here, however, could cover both (or even others), as also would Hilary's refusal to share communion with Chelidonius: shared communion was the Gallic test of acceptability (chapter 5 above, n.101).

which to build any, and in this Hilary was rebuffed. Leo could not accept Hilary's fundamental refusal to acquiesce to Leo's absolute, unquestioned authority in Gaul.[83]

As a result, Hilary delivered the diatribe mentioned by both Honoratus and Leo. Only Honoratus, however, indicated the nature of the "unspeakable things" which Hilary uttered. Hilary made it very clear that, unlike disaffected Gauls in the past, he had not come to Rome to have Leo adjudicate his case. He was willing to treat with Leo as an equal, but not to submit to his judgment. Furthermore, Leo's protest in his reply to the Gauls that he was "not instituting novelties" suggests that Hilary accused him of doing just that, a suggestion corroborated by Leo's subsequent reassurance to the Gauls that "we do not in fact claim for ourselves the right to ordain in your provinces, as Hilary, as he is accustomed, might possibly lie in order to deceive the spirits of Your Sanctity."[84] Leo presumably would not have felt the need to make such a disclaimer unless others besides Hilary felt that he was doing just that.

Honoratus' account also offers a more believable explanation for Hilary's rapid departure. The repeated references to the *potentes* arrayed against him suggest that it was not only ecclesiastics who were behind Leo, but powerful *saeculares* as well. It already has been seen that Leo's support in his campaign against the "New Manichees" in 443-445 included "noble Christians," the senate as a body, and imperial administrators. Such men, with or without Leo's blessing, apparently went so far as first to threaten Hilary and then to place him under house arrest. Hilary's response was to excommunicate Leo and withdraw hastily to Gaul.[85] Leo, meanwhile, was left to decide what to do with this intractable Gaul now that he, Leo, seemed to have the upper hand.

LEO'S SETTLEMENT OF 445[86]

After Hilary had left Rome, Leo was free to decree his own settlement of the situation in Gaul. In the case of Chelidonius, Leo, as was

---

83. It has been suggested that Hilary argued that according to the Council of Sardica, any review of the Gallic appeals should have taken place in Gaul; see Hess, *Sardica*; Holmes, *Church* p.369; Jalland, *Leo* pp.114-115; and Kidd, *Church* p.357.

84. "non enim nobis ordinationes vestrarum provinciarum defendimus, quod potest forsitan ad depravandos vestrae sanctitatis animos Hilarius pro suo more mentiri. . . ." ("Divinae cultum" ch.9).

85. Some, like Travers-Smith, *Gaul* p.270, suppose that Hilary actually was imprisoned. Heinzelmann, *Bischofsherrschaft* p.79, concludes he just had "too many enemies."

86. See, Duchesne, *Fastes* 1.117-119; Franses, *Leo* pp.35-36; Griffe, *Gaule* 2.159-160, 202-206; Jalland, *Leo* pp.117-130; Kidd, *Church* p.359ff; Langgärtner, *Gallienpolitik* pp.68-91; McShane,

the papal custom when appellants came to Rome, ordered his restoration ("Divinae cultum" ch.3):

Bishop Chelidonius has been absolved because he demonstrated that he was expelled from his see unjustly, with the clear testimony of witnesses and with himself [sc. Chelidonius] present, so that Hilary, sitting among us, had nothing to offer in opposition ... but he would have remained subject to the sentence which had been passed, if the truth of the charges had been proven. Our fellow bishop Chelidonius has been returned, therefore, to his church, and to that dignity which he ought not to have lost, as the series of actions, and the decision passed by us after a thorough examination, attests.[87]

The *fasti* of Besançon suggest that he did indeed reoccupy the see after the "dishonorable" expulsion of his successor Inportunus.[88] Likewise, in the case of Projectus, Leo stated, "We also decree ... not only that one improperly ordained should be deposed but also that bishop Projectus ought to remain in his office."[89] There is no indication, however, of whether this command ever went into effect. Leo also attempted to invalidate other Gallic ordinations on the basis of supposed technical violations, such as the failure to carry out the ceremony on a Saturday night or a Sunday (ch.6).

Nor did Leo stop there. Hilary's open opposition to him in Rome itself would have made him all the more determined to bring this troublesome Gaul to heel. Leo therefore took several measures intended to dismantle Hilary's Gallic support. As already noted, Leo proposed that Hilary alone was responsible for any crimes committed in Gaul; he alone, therefore, should bear the brunt of any retributions. Leo would have known that he could hardly hope to depose Hilary altogether; the lesson of Proculus of Marseilles would have been well learned. He could, however, take advantage of the existing factional conflicts in Gaul, and try to isolate Hilary and induce at least some of his followers to abandon him.

Romanitas pp.278-280; and Täckholm, "Aetius" p.26off. Hunt, *Leo* p.42, notes that "several of Leo's remarks are extremely bitter"; and Travers-Smith, *Gaul* p.270, calls Leo's response an example of the "unscrupulous tyranny" of Rome.

87. "absolutus est Celidonius episcopus, quoniam se iniuste sacerdotio fuisse deiectum, manifesta testium responsione, ipso etiam praesente, monstraverat; ita ut, quod Hilarius nobiscum residens posset opponere, non haberet ... mansisset namque in illum prolata sententia, si obiectorum veritas exstitisset. redditus itaque est ecclesiae suae, et huic, quam amittere non debuit, dignitati coepiscopus noster Celidonius, sicut gestorum series, et post decursam cognitionem sententia, quae a nobis est prolata, testatur."

88. Duchesne, *Fastes* 3.198, 212.

89. "nos tamen ... et male ordinatum submoveri, et episcopum Projectum in suo sacerdotio permanere debere decrevimus...." (ibid. ch.5). See Griffe, *Gaule* 2.202-203 and Langgärtner, *Gallienpolitik* pp.70-73.

Leo therefore decreed that Hilary was to be punished as follows ("Divinae cultum" ch.7):

Let each province be content with its own councils, nor any longer is Hilary to dare to convene synodal gatherings, and to stir them up by inserting himself into judgments of the bishops of the Lord. Let him know that he not only is stripped of any extra-provincial authority, but that he also is deprived of power in the province of Viennensis, which he wrongly usurped.... Let him not, therefore, attend any ordination, let him not perform an ordination . . .[90]

Nor, said Leo, was one metropolitan any longer to yield his status to anyone else. Leo realized that Hilary's strength lay in the organization of his faction, which was manifested in the control of ordinations, in the convening of church councils, and in the extraordinary status ceded to the bishop of Arles.

Leo's claim that Hilary had "wrongly usurped" metropolitan authority even in Viennensis would be yet another Roman attack upon the settlements of the Council of Turin.[91] If this authority were to be denied, and if Hilary no longer was to convene councils and ordain bishops, who, then, was to exercise these responsibilities? Here, Leo seems not to have had any canonical solution. Rather than identifying a legitimate metropolitan see, such as the logical Vienne, Leo temporized, and simply decreed ("Divinae cultum" ch.9),

And because age always must be honored, we desire, if it is pleasing to you, our brother and fellow bishop Leontius, an upright priest, to be endowed with this rank: so that without his consent no council will be convened by Your Sanctity in another province and so that he might be honored by all of you, to the extent that his age and uprightness demand, with the dignity of his metropolitan status preserved....[92]

There is no indication as to who this Leontius is; he must have been quite senior and, because he was to assume Hilary's metropolitan

90. "suis unaquaeque provincia sit contenta conciliis, nec ultra Hilarius audeat conventus indicere synodales, et sacerdotum domini iudicia se interserendo turbare, qui non tantum noverit se ab alieno iure depulsum, sed etiam Viennensis provinciae, quam male usurpaverat, potestate privatum.... non ergo intersit ulli ordinationi, non ordinet...."

91. Leo would not seem to be referring to any usurpation only in northern Viennensis, for, as seen above, Claudius of Vienne retained his metropolitan status there.

92. "et quoniam honoranda est semper antiquitas, fratrem et coepiscopum nostrum Leontium probabilem sacerdotem, hac, si vobis placet, dignitate volumus decorari: ut praeter eius consensum alterius provinciae non indicatur a vestra sanctitate concilium, et a vobis omnibus, quemadmodum vetustas eius et probitas exigit, honoretur, metropolitani[s] privilegii sui dignitate servata...." For Gallic primates, see Duchesne, *Fastes* 1.117. In Boniface of Rome's letter "Si inter episcopos," traditionally addressed to the Gallic bishops (*P.L.* 20.789: Jaffé p.53 no.354), questions of canon law which cannot be solved by the metropolitan are to be referred to the primate.

status, he presumably held a see in Viennensis.[93] If so, there would be only two possibilities, Trois-Châteaux and Aps/Viviers, for the bishops of all the other sees of Viennensis at this time are known. Because two bishops of Aps c.430/450 may be known, neither of them named Leontius, the most likely possibility would appear to be Trois-Châteaux.[94]

Now, this Leontius also may be the bishop Leontius of an unknown see who was addressed in Celestine's letter "Apostolici verba" in 431.[95] It already has been suggested that this letter included among its addressees some enemies of Lérins. The later Leontius' own enmity to Hilary and his party is sufficiently attested by his failure to appear, or be represented, at any of Hilary's attested councils, or in any of the other activities, such as the literary circle, in which the Lerinenses engaged. This Leontius, then, apparently was a long-time holdout against Hilary, and by 445 he could have been the most senior opponent as well. It is interesting to see that Leo yielded to him the very power he had just forbidden to anyone: that of convening extra-provincial councils.

Nor did Leo stop here in his attempts to lessen Hilary's influence. He also would have been aware of the extent of Hilary's secular support. This too would have to be neutralized if Hilary truly were to be restrained. Leo, therefore, pursued his Gallic offensive by impetrating from the emperor Valentinian III a rescript entitled "On the ordination of bishops," which not only confirmed Leo's judgments against Hilary but also promulgated the primacy of the see of Rome.[96] Valen-

93. Jalland, *Leo* p.123 n.38, asserts that this is Leontius of Fréjus, forgetting that this Leontius had been dead for over ten years. Ewig, *Trier* p.39ff, makes the equally impossible suggestion (questioned by Boshof, "Trierer" pp.105-106) that it was Leontius of Trier. That Leontius' see was in Viennensis also is suggested by the address of Leo's letter, to the bishops of that province only.

94. Duchesne, *Fastes* 1.237, has the last attested bishop of Aps as an Auxonius, at some time after 396, perhaps the Auxonius named in the letter of Celestine of 431 (chapter 6 above, n.66). The first bishop of Viviers, which replaced Aps after the latter was destroyed, may have been an Eulalius (ibid., n.2), who may be the Eulalius who signed the Gallic letter to Leo in 451 (appendix "The Names in Ravennius' Letter to Leo" below.) Trois-Châteaux: Duchesne, *Fastes* 1.264. Florentius (A.D.517) is preceded in the episcopal *fasti* only by a Paulus, whom Duchesne identifies as the Paulus who attended the Council of Valence in 374. This Paulus seems to have been another northerner, a native of Rheims: see *Analecta bollandiana* 11 (1892) pp.374-383. His appellation "Remus" is sometimes misread as "Romus"; *lectio difficilior* clearly applies here. For this Paulus as a fifth-century bishop, see chapters 9-10 below.

95. He is less likely to be the Leontius who was addressed in the letter of Boniface in 419, "Valentinae nos." The Leontii of 419 and 431, moreover, apparently are not the same man because he of 419 ranked before Marinus and he of 431 ranked after him.

96. "De episcoporum ordinatione" (*Nov. Val.* 17: 8 July 445). Oost, *Placidia* p.207, sees the decree as part of the policy of Placidia and Valentinian to "ally the state with the church." For the view that the rescript was "full of false statements, both in fact and law" see Travers-Smith, *Gaul* p.271. See also Ensslin, "Novellen XVII und XVIII" pp.374-378; Kidd, *Church* pp.358-359; Langgärtner, *Gallienpolitik* pp.74-77; and Morrison, *Tradition* pp.50-55.

tinian's own assertion, however, that Leo's "sentence alone would be valid throughout Gaul even without imperial sanction" only suggests that the opposite was the case, and helps to explain why Leo felt that imperial intervention was necessary if he was to exercise any authority there.[97]

The content of the novel makes it clear that it was based solely upon Leo's version of events, viz. (*Nov. Val.* 17):

Hilary of Arles, as we have learned from a reliable report of the venerable man Leo, pope of Rome, with a contumacious audacity has attempted to undertake certain illicit acts, and as a result an abominable tumult has afflicted the transalpine churches, as a recent incident in particular attests. For Hilary ... armed only with the temerity of a usurper, has appropriated for himself undeserved ordinations of bishops: some he has wrongfully removed, others he has indecently ordained with the citizens unwilling and protesting. When they were not accepted easily by those who did not choose them, he recruited for himself an armed band. . . .[98]

The state made no effort at all to carry out an impartial investigation; it merely acted as an enforcement arm for the church in Rome, much as, of course, the secular authorities in Gaul seem to have supported the activities of Hilary and his partisans.

The imperial decision might have been written by Leo himself.[99] Valentinian, like Leo, realized the impossibility of actually deposing Hilary. He therefore saved face by asserting that only the imperial *humanitas* allowed Hilary to remain bishop. State authority then was placed behind the bishop of Rome, for it also was decreed that (*Nov. Val.* 17),

It is not permitted either to the bishops of Gaul or to those of the other provinces to undertake anything contrary to the ancient customs without the authority of the venerable pope of the eternal city; but whatever the authority of the apostolic see has ordained, or shall have ordained, will be taken as law by all of them. Thus, any bishop who fails to come when summoned to the judgment of the bishop of Rome shall be compelled to appear by the governor of his respective province. . . .[100]

97. See Jalland, *Leo* pp.124-126, who suggests that the decree was a result of the "not entirely unanimous" reception of Leo's judgment.

98. "Hilarius Arelatensis, sicut venerabilis viri Leonis Romani papae fideli relatione conperimus, contumaci ausu inlicita quaedam praesumenda temptavit ideo transalpinas ecclesias abominabilis tumultus invasit: quod recens maxime testatur exemplum. Hilarius enim ... indebitas sibi ordinationes episcoporum sola temeritate usurpantis invasit. nam alios inconpetenter removit, indecenter alios invitis et repugnantibus civibus ordinavit. qui quoniam non facile ab his, qui non elegerant, recipiebantur, manum sibi contrahebat armatam. . . ."

99. Suggested by Jalland, *Leo* p.126.

100. "ne quid tam episcopis gallicanis, quam aliarum provinciarum, contra consuetudinem veterem liceat, sine viri venerabilis papae urbis aeternae auctoritate temptare: sed hoc illis om-

Leo, then, used the case of Hilary as a pretext for a grant of sweeping authority.

What is particularly significant about this edict is the individual to whom it is addressed. Not to the praetorian prefect of Gaul, as one might expect, but to the general "Aetius, the illustrious patrician, count, and master of both services."[101] Now, it already has been seen that Aetius, on occasion, had supported Hilary and his partisans.[102] Valentinian, therefore, if not Leo as well, apparently felt that it was necessary to command Aetius directly to obey, suggesting, at least, that he might have been inclined to do otherwise.[103] If Leo's earlier arbitration between Aetius and Albinus had been on the side of the latter, Leo would have had all the more reason to worry about the patrician's response. Moreover, any enemies of Aetius in Rome, and he certainly had many, also would have favored any attempt to weaken his position, or at least embarrass him, in Gaul.[104] Leo, therefore, by taking advantage of Hilary's enemies in Gaul, and perhaps Aetius' in Rome, was very successful in being able to bring imperial authority to bear against Hilary and his partisans.

HILARY'S DIPLOMATIC OFFENSIVE

Once he realized how great the opposition against him was, Hilary had no option but to adopt a new strategy: "Having returned to Arles, although broken by bodily weakness, nevertheless he was blessed by perfection and most ready to do his duty, and he turned himself totally then to placating the spirit of the blessed Leo with an improved hu-

---

nibusque pro lege sit, quidquid sanxit vel sanxerit apostolicae sedis auctoritas. ita ut quisquis episcoporum ad iudicium Romani antistitis evocatus venire neglexerit, per moderatorem eiusdem provinciae adesse cogatur. . . ."

101. Heinzelmann, *Bischofsherrschaft* p.80, presumes, without manuscript or other support, that the decree also would have been addressed to all "episcopi Gallicani" and "moderatores provinciae." Of the forty-six extant *Novella Valentiniani*, twenty-eight are addressed to the appropriate praetorian prefect, and only one other one to a *magister militum*, *Nov. Val.* 6.1 to Sigisvult, which predictably concerned military matters. The other extant post-revolt imperial constitutions addressed to Gaul all had single addressees: in 416 to the patrician Constantius (*C. Th.* 15.14.14); in 418 to the prefect Agricola (Haenel, *Corp. leg.* p.238 no.1171; *M.G.H. Epist.* 3.13-15); in 425 to the prefect Amatius (*Sirm.* 6); and in 451, again to Aetius (as patrician only) (*Nov. Val.* 33).

102. See Heinzelmann, *Bischofsherrschaft* p.282ff; Langgärtner, *Gallienpolitik* pp.74-77; Prinz, *Mönchtum* p.43; and note 68 above.

103. Prinz, *Stadtherrschaft* p.15, presumes the edict was addressed to Aetius because he was on Leo's side; Ensslin, "Novellen XVII und XVIII" p.378, because Aetius was "der damalige leitende Staatsmann" in the west; and Duchesne, *Fastes* 1.118, because Aetius was "représentant de l'empire dans les Gaules." None notes any irregularity.

104. On Aetius' Roman enemies, see Täckholm, p.260 (for Leo as Aetius' enemy) and Twyman, "Aetius" passim.

mility."[105] He first sent his presbyter and eventual successor, Ravennius, to Rome, but Ravennius seems to have accomplished little.
Hilary then dispatched a delegation of two bishops, Nectarius of Avignon and Constantius of Uzès, the former being a long-time supporter
and the latter a more recent recruit from the province of Narbonensis
Prima. On this occasion Hilary also attempted to make use of his own
contacts in Rome, and in particular his old friend the ex-prefect of
Gaul Auxiliaris.

Now, Auxiliaris was a Roman aristocrat of some standing, for he
also appears as the subject of two rescripts of Valentinian dated 440
and 441 concerning a quarrel with a certain *vir inlustris* Apollodorus
over a house which Auxiliaris claimed.[106] In the first rescript, dated 9
June, Valentinian referred to Auxiliaris' "great record of virtues demonstrated by his long service in our administration."[107] Auxiliaris,
therefore, had served in several imperial offices. He claimed that on
the occasion of a recent absence, probably his Gallic prefecture, his
house had been appropriated. The first rescript ordered its restoration
and commanded, "We forbid anyone from pursuing further lawsuits
and cases over this matter."[108] Nevertheless, a second rescript obtained
by Apollodorus and dated 27 January 441 reversed the decision.[109]
Auxiliaris, then, was involved in high-level Roman politics, in this
instance in a losing cause.

Hilary's biographer apparently thought that this was a very touchy
situation, for he noted, "And because I am unable in any way to piece
together what sort of things [Hilary] said in this instance, I decided to
insert what the opinion of Auxiliaris, a prefect of that time, was."[110]

---

105. "in civitatem regressus, licet corporali infirmitate fractus, tamen perfectione sanctus et
pietate promptissimus, totum se ad placandum tunc animum sancti Leonis inclinata humilitate
convertit...." (*VHilarii* 17[22]). See Thompson, *Germanus* pp.58-60 and Duchesne, *Fastes* 1.118.
McShane, *Romanitas* p.280, wrongly supposes that the negotiations occurred "quelques années
plus tard."

106. Nothing is known about this Apollodorus beyond his involvement in this affair.
P.L.R.E. II p.119 suggests he may have been the son of Petronius Apollodorus, attested as a
Roman senator in 370 (*P.L.R.E. I* p.84).

107. "magna adsertio virtutum multis perennitati nostrae administrationibus conprobata"
(*Nov. Val.* 8.1).

108. "quem ulterius prosequi lites causasque non patimur earum rerum" (ibid.).

109. *Nov. Val.* 8.2.

110. "et quia quanta in hac causa dictaverit, huic operi nulla possum ratione connectere,
Auxiliaris tunc praefecti quae fuerit sententia credidi inserendam...." (*VHilarii* 17[22]). On this
basis, *P.L.R.E. II* (p.206) assumes that Auxiliaris was prefect of Rome in 445. Jalland, *Leo* p.127,
has Auxiliaris as Gallic prefect, on a "visit" to Rome. Langgärtner, *Gallienpolitik* p.78, wrongly
suggests that Auxiliaris was prefect of Italy (it was Fl. Albinus: *P.L.R.E. II* p.1248). *P.L.R.E.* has
separate entries for the Gallic prefect Auxiliaris whom Hilary knew and who owned the house
in Rome, and for the Roman prefect Auxiliaris whom Hilary also knew. Undoubtedly, both are
the same man; see Heinzelmann, "Prosopographie" p.566.

Honoratus then appended excerpts from a letter which Auxiliaris had sent back to Hilary (*VHilarii* 17[22]):

I received the bishops Nectarius and Constantius, arriving on behalf of Your Beatitude, with appropriate admiration. I spoke with them often about the virtue and constancy of spirit, and the contempt of human affairs with which you, in the midst of our frailties, always are blessed. For what good fortune can there be in this corporeal life, which, although it is miserable, is nonetheless not perpetual? I also spoke with the saintly father Leo. At this point, I believe, you give a little mental shudder: but because you are firm in your purpose and always even tempered, and because you are torn by no poisonous anxiety just as you are carried away by no joyful pleasures, I cannot recall the least deed of Your Beatitude which was contaminated with the contagion of arrogance. But men have little concern, if I may speak frankly, with how we perceive ourselves. The ears of the Romans are influenced above all by a certain submissiveness, to which if Your Sanctity from time to time lowers itself, you will gain more and lose nothing. Grant me this, and blot out this insignificant gloom with the tranquility of a small reconsideration.[111]

Hilary, then, did have support in Rome at least from Auxiliaris. The latter's reply, however, makes it clear that in this instance there was little he could do unless Hilary were willing to back down to some degree. Indeed, Auxiliaris' loss in the aforementioned case over the house might suggest that his own support in Rome had waned, or was outweighed by that of others. Ultimately, the efforts of Nectarius and Constantius to achieve a reconciliation also met with failure, probably because Hilary declined to follow Auxiliaris' advice and simply refused to be sufficiently "submissive."[112] If there had been a reconciliation, Honoratus surely would have mentioned it, but this is all that he has to say about the matter.

It is possible, however, that Hilary made yet another attempt to

---

111. "sanctos Nectarium et Constantium sacerdotes de beatitudinis tuae parte venientes digna admiratione suscepi. cum his saepius sum locutus de virtute animi atque constantia, contemptuque rerum humanarum, quo inter fragilitates nostras semper beatus es. nam quid potest in hac corporea vita esse secundum, quae cum sit misera, tamen non potest esse perpetua? locutus sum etiam cum sancto papa Leone. hoc loco, credo, aliquantum animo perhorrescis; sed cum propositi tui tenax sis, et semper aequalis, nulloque commotionis felle rapiaris, sicut nullis extolleris illecebris gaudiorum, ego nec minimum quidem factum beatitudinis tuae arrogantiae memini contagione fuscari. sed impatienter ferunt homines, si sic loquamur, quomodo nobis conscii sumus. aures praeterea Romanorum quadam teneritudine plus trahuntur; in quam si se sanctitas tua subinde demittat, plurimum, tu, nihil perditurus, acquiris. da mihi hoc, et exiguas nubes parvae mutationis serenitate compesce." Honoratus clearly had Auxiliaris' letter in mind when he wrote elsewhere of Hilary (*VHilarii* 10[13]), "reliquit exemplum, qualiter constantiae virtute mundanae contemni debeant potestates."

112. There is extant a very servile poem supposedly written from Hilary to Leo saying, for example, "tu capitis primique caput, tu fontis origo / primus apex rerum, primus sator, omnia condens" ("Metrum in Genesim": *P.L.* 50.1287-1292). It is not accepted as genuine. Note also the suggestion of Thompson, *Germanus* p.58, that "there may well have been other goings to and fro of which we hear nothing."

influence the Roman imperial administration at the very highest levels, although any details of this offensive do not survive. At just about this time, it seems, Germanus of Auxerre was able to stop an attack of the Alans upon the rebelling Armoricans on condition that he seek pardon "from the emperor as well as from Aetius."[113] The Alan king, Goar, may have realized that Germanus, a partisan of Aetius, would have no problem at that source, hence his additional condition that Germanus undertake the long and arduous trip to the Italian court. Would he be willing to do so? It may be that another consideration helped him to decide to go. Given the temporal context of his trip, perhaps in early 446, one cannot help but wonder if Germanus also may have hoped to regain some imperial favor there for himself and his partisans in Gaul.[114]

When Germanus reached Ravenna he began to move in the highest circles of the Roman aristocracy. It was reported, for example, that he cured the son of a certain Volusianus, the *cancellarius* of the patrician and master of soldiers Sigisvult.[115] Although this Volusianus is otherwise unknown, his name would indicate that he was related, for example, to Rufius Antonius Agrypnius Volusianus, praetorian prefect of Italy in 428-429 and the son of Ceionius Rufius Albinus.[116] The latter was a friend of the Gaul Rutilius Namatianus, and may have had other Gallic ties as well; he also presumably would have been related in some degree to the Fl. Albinus who arguably was the Albinus who quarreled with Aetius in 440.[117] If Germanus were in fact attempting to end the hostilities between Italian officialdom and his own party in Gaul, he would have been moving in the right circles to do so.

Germanus interacted with other court officials as well. He was said to have cured a servant of the *praepositus sacri cubiculi* Acolus, who had Germanus' body embalmed after his death.[118] He also reportedly got along very well with Valentinian and his mother Galla Placidia.[119]

---

113. "ab imperatore vel ab Aetio" (*VGermani* 28). See Mathisen, "Last Year." Thompson, *Germanus* pp.73-75, has shown that Constantius' "vel" is to be translated "and," and not the more conventional "or." Germanus' previous service as *dux* in this area, and his recent journey to Britain, would have made him a logical patron for the Armoricans.

114. For the date, see Mathisen, "Last Year" passim. Thompson, *Germanus* p.59, wonders why "Germanus is not associated ... with ... Hilary's subsequent negotiations with Leo." This analysis would suggest that he was. Elsewhere (p.60), Thompson suggests that Germanus may have "consulted with" Hilary at Arles on this journey, but Germanus' path took him over the Alps (*VGermani* 31), upon the *Via Cottia*, not through Arles.

115. *VGermani* 38.

116. See *P.L.R.E. II* pp.1183-1184.

117. Rutil. Namat. *De red. suo* 1.167-178.

118. *VGermani* 39, 44.

119. *VGermani* 35, 43. Oost, *Placidia* pp.254-256, however, has suggested that Valentinian was not in Ravenna at the time. This is possible, for the most contemporary laws have him at Rome on 10 December 445 (*Nov. Val.* 19) and on 21 October 446 (ibid. 21). For contra, see Thompson, *Germanus* pp.68-69.

Germanus ultimately was unsuccessful, however, in achieving his stated purpose, prevented from successfully ending the revolt, says Constantius, by a "perfidious" renewal of hostilities by the Armorican leader Tibatto.[120] He apparently was equally unsuccessful in any unstated mission as well. In any event, Germanus died on 31 July of the same year in Ravenna. He was the first of Hilary's powerful faction to die, although many others, including Hilary himself, were soon to follow.[121]

Any attempts at a reconciliation between the parties of Hilary and Leo, therefore, seem to have ended in failure. Both bishops remained equally recalcitrant. Hilary was willing to make amends but not, apparently, to make any substantive concessions or submission. Leo, realizing that he now was in a position of strength, made no known effort at all to reach an agreement. Nor is there any indication that Leo's decrees concerning the Gallic church ever went into widespread effect.[122] Even though there is no evidence for any councils being called or ordinations being made by Hilary during his few remaining years, his successor Ravennius felt no qualms about doing both in the years 449-450, in spite of Leo's prohibition.[123]

The only other thing that can be inferred for the period 445-449 in this context is that the bishop of Vienne was not at all happy with Leo's decision to grant metropolitan status in Viennensis to the aged Leontius. As a result, he mounted a campaign of his own, and Leo's letter "Lectis dilectionis," dated 5 May 450, recalled that "this [metropolitan] power, having been removed from Hilary, we believed should be entrusted to the bishop of Vienne."[124] At some time between 445 and 450, therefore, Leo did in fact restore metropolitan authority in Viennensis to the bishop of Vienne.[125] One might won-

120. The only other reference to Tibatto occurs in the *Gallic Chronicle of year 452* under the year 437 (no. 119, *M.G.H. A.A.* 9.660), where he reportedly was captured by the imperial government. This has led to the suggestion (Thompson, *Germanus* pp.55-70 and Wood, "End" passim) that Germanus' intervention also must date to the late 430s.

121. For the date, see Ado, *Mart.* (31 July: *P.L.* 123.312), also cited under 1 October (ibid.371-373), the day he was entombed in Auxerre.

122. Scholars in the past have assumed *a priori* that Leo's rulings were put into effect, but none has offered any evidence for this. See Bardy et al., *Eglise* p.262; Duchesne, *Fastes* 1.118; Kidd, *Church* p.359; and Jalland, *Leo* pp.127-129, who suggests not only that Hilary "accepted the Roman verdict," but also that he "retained a sort of informal primacy [in] southern Gaul," and (p.130) that the bishops of southern Gaul still considered him their "legitimate metropolitan." As noted above, it does appear that Chelidonius was able to reoccupy his see, perhaps because Germanus of Auxerre, his most powerful local opponent, now was dead.

123. See chapter 8 below.

124. "quam potestatem [sc. metropolitanam] Hilario episcopo ablatam, Viennensi episcopo credidimus deputandum." Is it only coincidence that the letter is dated one year to the day after Hilary's death?

125. Here one must consider the problematical letter "Quali pertinacia" (*P.L.* 54.1237), supposedly written on 6 January (or 11) 450 to the bishop of Vienne, presumably Nicetas (see chapter

der, indeed, why Leo had not done so in the first place. It may be that the grant to Leontius was only a temporizing move, made in the hope that Hilary might yet be induced to capitulate: such a strategy was utilized by Hilarus of Rome in 462 in Narbonensis Prima.[126] The ultimate grant to Vienne probably came when the superannuated Leontius died soon after 445, and may be the final sign of Leo's disgust with Hilary's continuing intransigence.

It is clear that Hilary went to his death (5 May 449) unrepentant, and still reviling Leo as he had done in Rome four years earlier.[127] In the death-bed speech reported by Honoratus, Hilary stated (*VHilarii* 20[26]):

Although I have quarreled with the princes of this world ... I believe that I will be absolved and set free in the judgment of my Lord which will come with His blessing. In order to attain these rewards, you must undertake your struggles with a diligent course, and he, who has condemned himself through his own spite, who sniffs out conflicts from afar ... as if all ought to be under his authority, made crafty by his long experience, tricky through subtlety, and skilled in the art and practice of deception, he who ... is fattened by the condemnation of the upright, [and] considers the salvation of another to be his own punishment ... he, an enemy of human salvation, must be guarded against, he must be assailed and resisted at every opportunity.... If human frailty does not deceive me, a great storm threatens this city, a serious, not a minor, affliction overhangs us.[128]

A generous, or uninformed, reader might conclude that Hilary was speaking of Satan, but one more knowledgeable of his past might conclude that he had someone more concrete in mind as well.[129]

After his death, as in life, Hilary was to remain a controversial

---

8 below). The letter states that "quia principis apostolorum ... moderationem ... Arelatensis episcopus [Hilarius] non exspectavit, a privilegio suae civitatis submotus humili loco discat ... sitque redintegratum Viennensi archiepiscopo privilegium." The letter usually is condemned as a later Viennese forgery, although Jalland, *Leo* pp.167-168, remains unsure and Babut, *Turin* p.265ff, argues that it is genuine. Even if the letter is genuine, it still has serious difficulties: Leo had removed Hilary's metropolitan rank in 445, not in 450, and the bishop of Vienne already had regained it as of 450 (see preceding note).

126. See chapter 9 below, n.30.

127. Date: Ado, *Chron* (5 May: *P.L.* 123.260).

128. "cum istius mundi principibus ... confliximus ... absolutum me et liberatum ad domini mei intuitum credo eodem propitiante venturum. ad ea praemia obtinenda perseveranti cursu vobis sunt peragenda certamina, ille utique, qui se livore proprio perdidit, qui procul odoratur bellum ... quasi cuncti esse debeant in sua potestate, diutina antiquitate callidus, subtilitate dolosus, decipiendi assiduitate atque arte peritus, qui ... perditione perfectorum saginatur, poenam propriam, salutem reputat alienam.... hic salutis humanae inimicus cavendus est; huic omnimodis oppugnandum est et resistendum... si me humana non fallit illusio, grandis tempestas huic imminet civitati; non mediocris, sed satis gravis incumbit afflictio."

129. Langgärtner, *Gallienpolitik* pp.78-79, doubts that Hilary was unrepentant.

figure. Even his biographer referred to him in his final eulogy as "factious and long-suffering."[130] His extant epitaph recalled his influence and his ambition, calling him "gem of bishops, and master of the people and the world."[131] It was his great accomplishment to organize a unified and powerful ecclesio-political faction which had great influence in both southern and central Gaul. Ultimately, however, his faction became so strong that it attracted the opposition of even stronger factions to the south. However well Hilary might have been able to hold his partisans together even right up to his death, after he died his party was to be rent by dissension, and another opportunity for ecclesiastical unity in Gaul was to be lost.

130. "turbulentus et patiens" (VHilarii 23[30]).
131. "gemma sacerdotum plebisque orbisque magister" (Anth. lat. 2.1.325 no.688).

CHAPTER 8

RAVENNIUS, RUSTICUS
AND MAMERTUS

THE FRAGMENTATION OF
THE LÉRINS FACTION

On 5 May 449 Hilary of Arles died, perhaps in part because of the rigors of his winter journey to Rome in 444/445.[1] Shortly thereafter he was followed in death by several of the other leading Gallic prelates of the time, including Eucherius of Lyons and Nicetas of Vienne. As a result, the years c.449-452 saw new faces in some of the most important Gallic sees.

After Hilary's death, a group of twelve southern bishops, mainly if not exclusively from Viennensis and Narbonensis, gathered to choose and consecrate Hilary's successor. The ceremony also seems to have been the occasion of an impromptu church council, for the bishops took the opportunity to co-author a letter to Leo of Rome informing him of the result of the election.[2]

The new bishop of Arles was the presbyter Ravennius who had been Hilary's first ambassador to Rome in early 446. He therefore presumably was a protégé of Hilary, even though there is no evidence that he ever had been a monk at Lérins. His consecrators included not only Nicetas of Vienne, but also Rusticus of Narbonne, the most influential opponent of Hilary. Presumably, Ravennius was an individual acceptable to them both and one who they felt would not attempt to revive Hilary's pretensions to hegemony in the south. Indeed, the presence of Rusticus and at least one of his suffragans (who, being from Narbonensis Prima, technically should not have been taking part at

---

1. See Duchesne, *Fastes* 1.119, 256, and Griffe, *Gaule* 2.249-250; as well as the *VHilarii* 21-23(27-30).

2. What is known of this lost letter comes from Leo, *Epist.* "Justa et rationabilis": *M.G.H. Epist.* 3.15-16. See Duchesne, *Fastes* 1.120; Jalland, *Leo* pp.128-129; and Langgärtner, *Gallienpolitik* pp.81-82.

all) could be seen not only as a show of solidarity among the prelates of southern Gaul, but also as an attempt of Rusticus, à la Hilary, to extend his own influence beyond his own province.[3]

After being informed of the ordination of the new bishop, Leo of Rome expressed his satisfaction in a letter dated 22 August 449. He praised the choice and approved its orderly nature: "You have unanimously ordained a man indeed acceptable to us, the brother Ravennius, in accordance with the wishes of the clergy, the nobility and the plebs. . . . We believe that his election was peaceful and harmonious . . . nor was there a lack of eagerness by the citizenry."[4] The Gallic stress upon the lack of discord in the election perhaps was intended to forestall any complaints to the contrary. Leo, meanwhile, conventionally described Hilary as "of blessed memory," and gave no indication of the past bad feeling between them.

At the same time, Leo also wrote a separate letter to Ravennius himself, recalling their previous acquaintance and implicitly advising him to be more circumspect than his predecessor: "You are not unaware of what I feel about the sincerity of your spirit as a result of our previous meeting. . . . May patience restrain rashness, and with pride avoided, which is next to killing it off, may humility be loved."[5] Leo also attempted to establish the proper relationship between himself and the bishop of Arles with his concluding advice, "You should make us aware more often of the pattern of your activities."[6]

Despite his approval, Leo would have been placed in a rather awkward position by Rusticus of Narbonne's uncanonical participation in the election. It ran directly counter to Leo's ruling of 445, issued specifically to the Gauls, that new bishops were to be chosen and consecrated only by the metropolitan and bishops of the province in question, and that outside interference was absolutely forbidden. It may have been Leo's own realization of this problem which led him to the unusual hierarchical organization he adopted in addressing his reply.

---

3. It usually is assumed that all of the consecrators but Rusticus were from southern Viennensis, see Duchesne, *Fastes* 1.120, and Ganshof, "Note" p.489. Duchesne even insists that the Florus who was bishop of Lodève at this time cannot be the one who appears here (*Fastes* 1.313-314 n.7). Rusticus, however, well may have brought one or more of his own suffragans along; and it hitherto has escaped notice that wherever Florus appears, he always accompanies Rusticus, a strange trait for a suffragan of Arles.

4. "virum etiam nobis probatum, fratrem Ravennium, secundum desideria cleri, honoratorum et plebis, unanimiter consecrastis. . . . electionem pacificam atque concordem . . . nec studia civium defuerunt . . . credimus fuisse" (*Epist.* "Justa et rationabilis": *M.G.H. Epist.* 3.15-16).

5. "non ignoras, quid de sinceritate animi tui secundum praecedentem notitiam senserimus. . . . patientia contineat libertatem, et declinata superbia, cui proximum est ut decidat, ametur humilitas. . . ." ("Provectionem dilectionis": *M.G.H. Epist.* 3.16-17). For Leo's satisfaction with Ravennius, see Griffe, *Gaule* 2.194, and Jalland, *Leo* pp.129, 136.

6. "saepius nos de processu actuum tuorum facias certiores" (ibid.).

Rather than appearing at the head of the list, as would be dictated by standard ecclesiastical protocol, the names of the metropolitans Rusticus of Narbonne and Nicetas of Vienne occur third and fifth respectively.[7] Rusticus' position is consistent with his date of ordination in 427, and Leo seems to have resolved his dilemma by treating Rusticus, in this instance, as just an ordinary provincial bishop.[8] In spite of its irregularities, Leo did recognize the election, accepting the *fait accompli*.

Then, only four days after writing this letter, on 26 August 449, Leo exhibited his favor for Ravennius by delegating to him the responsibility for tracking down a certain Petronianus, who Ravennius had reported was making his way around southern Gaul passing himself off as a deacon of the church of Rome.[9] Later events will suggest that this was an early indication that Leo was willing to reach the rapprochement with Ravennius which he had denied to Hilary. But if the bishops of Narbonne, Vienne and, perhaps, Rome thought that in Ravennius they had a tractable and impotent colleague, they soon were disabused of the notion, for two incidents soon were to show that Ravennius had ambitions and pretensions of his own.

Even before the end of 449, it seems, the bishop of Vaison, Auspicius, a long-time partisan of Hilary, died.[10] According to Leo's settlements, a successor should have been ordained by the bishop of Vienne, but characteristically, the will of the bishop of Rome was ignored and the new bishop, Fonteius, was consecrated by Ravennius.[11] The understandably unhappy Nicetas of Vienne responded by dispatching a delegation to Leo in Rome with a petition "complaining that the bishop of Arles had usurped for himself the ordination of a bishop of Vaison."[12] Nicetas would have been angry at what he saw as abroga-

---

7. See Duchesne, *Fastes* 1.120 n.1.

8. See appendix, "Episcopal Hierarchy" (refuting the suggestion of Langgärtner, *Gallienpolitik* p.79, that this Rusticus may not have been the bishop of Narbonne). Nicetas, however, was not yet in office in 442, when his predecessor Claudius attended the Council of Vaison, yet he precedes several bishops ordained by 430. Nicetas' name is too high to be a result of his tenure status, but too low for his metropolitan status. Either Leo made a mistake, or perhaps this is not Nicetas of Vienne at all. Langgärtner (ibid.) also presumes that Ravennius was "merely" a suffragan of Vienne, but had this been so, Leo surely would have listed Nicetas first.

9. Leo, *Epist.* "Circumspectum te": *M.G.H. Epist.* 3.16. See Jalland, *Leo* pp.129-130, 136, and Babut, *Turin* p.196, who (n.1) dates this letter later in the year.

10. For the date, see Jalland, *Leo* p.130 (early 450) and Langgärtner, *Gallienpolitik* pp.80-81.

11. See Duchesne, *Fastes* 1.121, 262; Griffe, *Gaule* 2.160 and Jalland, *Leo* pp.130-134. Fonteius perhaps is to be identified with the presbyter "Fontedius" of Vaison who attended the Councils of Orange and Vaison in 441-442, or the deacon Fontedius of Avignon, also at Vaison in 442 (*Corp. chr. lat.* 148.87, 102).

12. "conquerens Arelatensem episcopum ordinationem sibi Vasensis antistitis usurpasse" (Leo, *Epist.* "Lectis dilectionis": *M.G.H. Epist.* 3.20-21). See Langgärtner, *Gallienpolitik* p.80.

tions not only of Leo's settlement, but also of any understanding he may have had with Ravennius when the latter was ordained.[13]

Ravennius' second move was even more audacious. After having exercised *de facto* metropolitan rights in Viennensis by his ordination at Vaison, he then gained the support of nineteen bishops of southern Gaul, all of whom had been ordained by the bishop of Arles. In early 450, if not late 449, they subscribed to a letter to Leo, "Memores quantum," requesting him to recognize Ravennius as holding all the previous rights of Arles.[14] At the same time, they disparagingly referred to "the city of Vienne, which now impudently and remarkably demands for itself an undeserved primacy."[15]

Significantly, these bishops were from not only Viennensis (Constantianus of Carpentras, Audentius of Die, Nectarius of Avignon, Asclepius of Cavaillon, Justus of Orange, and Fonteius of Vaison), but also Narbonensis Secunda (Armentarius of Antibes, Theodorus of Fréjus), Alpes Maritimae (Severianus of Thorâme, Ingenuus of Embrun), and even Narbonensis Prima (Constantius of Uzès). The sees of the five other bishops who subscribed are not known for certain.[16] These nineteen bishops include some of the most dependable and persistent supporters of Hilary, and thus there can be little doubt that this move was an attempt to revive Hilary's coalition and policies in southern Gaul.

In the interests of continued collegiality it would seem that once again Ingenuus of Embrun had yielded his metropolitan status to the bishop of Arles, for his name appears only fourteenth in the list. This, and the presence of the names of bishops from outside Viennensis,

13. For Nicetas as bishop see Jalland, *Leo* p.130. His successor Mamertus was not ordained until 451 at the earliest, for in the spring of that year, still a layman, he was visited by his friend Anianus, bishop of Orléans (*VAniani* 5).

14. See Leo, *Epist.* 65-67 = *Epist. arel.* 12-14: M.G.H. *Epist.* 3.17-22. Leo's reply was written 5 May 450, but not until after he had detained Ravennius' representatives in Rome: "diu filios nostros Petronium presbyterum et Regulum diaconum in urbe tenuimus" (Leo, *Epist.* "Diu filios": M.G.H. *Epist.* 3.22). Leo explained that he had wished the Gauls to be present at the *tractatus* ("deliberation") which considered the events in the east. Silva-Tarouca, "Nuovi Studi" pp.393-394, assumes that this had occurred in October of 449, and that the Gallic meeting had occurred in the fall of 449 (ibid. p.394, n.1), but this may be too early. The meeting probably was of an *ad hoc* nature early in 450; see Griffe, *Gaule* 2.160, 171, 195 and Hefele-Leclercq, *Conciles* 2.626-627. Gundlach, M.G.H. *Epist.* 3.17-18, and Langgärtner, *Gallienpolitik* p.80, suggest April but do not take into account the Gauls' delay in Rome. See also Duchesne, *Fastes* 1.120-121; Jalland, *Leo* pp.130-134 and McShane, *Romanitas* p.280.

15. "Viennensis civitas, quae sibi nunc impudenter ac notabiliter primatus exposcit indebitos" (*Epist.* "Memores quantum" ch.2).

16. Also subscribing were a Venantius, a Superventor, a Palladius, an Ursus, a Stephanus, and a Maximus, apparently not Maximus of Riez; see appendix "Episcopal Hierarchy" below. For the provenance of these bishops, see also Duchesne, *Fastes* 1.121-122 (who calls the nineteen bishops "suffragans" of Arles); Griffe, *Gaule* 2.160; and Jalland, *Leo* p.131 n.67.

could be taken as an indication that the bishops were requesting that the bishop of Arles be granted metropolitan status not over the province of Viennensis alone, but over the entire Tres Provinciae of Viennensis, Narbonensis Prima, and Narbonensis Secunda. Such a conclusion also is suggested by the bishops' reference to Zosimus' decree of 417 ("Memores quantum": *M.G.H. Epist.* 3.18-20):

Whence it happened that the bishop of the church of Arles recovered the [right of] ordination not only of the province of Viennensis, but even of the Three Provinces, out of respect for Saint Trophimus. Indeed, this honor and dignity was added to him, so that he not only governed these provinces by his own authority, but he also gathered to himself all the Gauls, with authority to act in place of the apostolic see having been granted.[17]

Such a request would explain the absence of the names of the other bishops with metropolitan pretensions in the south—those of Vienne, Aix, Marseilles, and Narbonne.[18]

The bishops began by using flattery in an attempt to conciliate Leo, saying, "Mindful of how much reverence and honor always has been due, and always ought to be due, to the most blessed apostolic see, which Our Lord Jesus Christ desires you to oversee on account of your merits of sanctity . . . "[19] They then went on to draw an elaborate analogy, which began, "Thus, just as the blessed church of Rome has the rule over all the churches of the whole world through the blessed Peter, prince of the apostles . . . "[20] Now, this clause has been cited as proof that the Gauls recognized Leo's absolute authority.[21] The rest of the analogy, however, indicates that the Gauls had a wholly different purpose in mind: "Likewise also within Gaul the church of Arles,

---

17. "unde factum est, ut non solum provinciae Viennensis ordinationem, sed etiam trium provinciarum contemplatione sancti Trophimi. . . . Arelatensis ecclesiae sacerdos . . . revocarit. cui id etiam honoris dignitasque collatum est, ut non tantum has provincias potestate propria gubernaret, verum etiam omnes Gallias, sibi apostolicae sedis vice mandata . . . contineret." For Sirmond's "contemplatione" Gundlach reads "contemplationem"; it is unclear, however, what a "contemplation of the Three Provinces" would be, and this reading also would leave "s. Trophimi" without a context. Alpes Maritimae here still apparently was not viewed as an independent ecclesiastical province; if it had been, Ravennius would have had to ask for authority over "Quattuor Provinciae." Ingenuus' continued cession of his metropolitan powers would be yet another violation of Leo's decree of 445.

18. See Duchesne, *Fastes* 1.121, 124, 126. Hefele-Leclercq, *Conciles* 2.426 n.1, inexplicably assert that the bishop of Aix subscribed to the request.

19. "memores quantum honoris et reverentiae beatissimae sedi apostolicae, cui vos dominus noster Iesus Christus pro meritis sanctitatis voluit praesidere, semper debitum fuerit, semperque debeatur . . . " (*Epist.* "Memores quantum": *M.G.H. Epist.* 3.18-20). See Duchesne, *Fastes* 1.120-123.

20. "ut sicut per beatissimum Petrum apostolorum principem sacrosancta ecclesia romana teneret supra omnes totius mundi ecclesias principatum . . . "

21. See Jalland, *Church* p.304.

which deserved to have as its bishop St. Trophimus, sent by the apostles, claims the right of ordaining a bishop."[22] If the primacy of Rome over the world was valid, the Gauls sophistically argued, then the primacy of Arles over Gaul was equally valid: to deny one would be to deny the other.[23] In spite of their role here as suppliants, the Gallic bishops also attempted to keep their distance from Rome.

Along with the legendary evangelization of Gaul by Trophimus, the Gauls also cited the preference shown by past bishops of Rome for the bishop of Arles as a justification for their request.[24] Great stress also was laid upon the purely secular status of Arles ("Memores quantum": *M.G.H. Epist.* 3.18-20):

The city was specially honored to such an extent by Constantine of most glorious memory that it received its name Constantina from his. Valentinian and Honorius, most faithful emperors of most clement memory, adorned it with special privileges. In this city ... one accepts and grants the consulate. The sublime office of prefect always inhabits it, as do the remaining officials....[25]

Presumably, such an argument would have been used only if the Gauls believed that Leo would have been responsive to it. Given Leo's own very recent reliance upon the secular arm, he hardly could not have been.

The Gauls also cited Leo's own recent response to Ravennius: "Now, moreover, having looked over the letters of Your Beatitude, we clearly recognize the great love with which you embrace him."[26] They also made in this context their only reference to Leo's quarrel with Hilary:

Nor indeed is it fair that that matter, wherein another man offended Your Piety, should diminish the status of him whom, as we can attest, you greatly

22. "ita etiam intra Gallias Arelatensis ecclesia quae sanctum Trophimum ab apostolis missum sacerdotem habere meruisset, ordinandi pontificium vindicaret."

23. See Jalland, *Leo* p.132 n.74. The claim here that Trophimus was sent by both Peter *and* Paul (see Jalland, *Leo* p.169) could be meant to weaken the primacy of Peter alone, and contrasts with the Gauls' earlier statement that Trophimus had been sent "a beatissimo Petro apostolo."

24. It probably is a mistake to suggest, as Langgärtner, *Gallienpolitik* p.82, that the bishops knowingly used false evidence.

25. "haec in tantum a gloriosissimae memoriae Constantino peculiariter honorata est, ut ab eius vocabulo ... Constantina nomen acceperit. hanc clementissimae recordationis Valentinianus et Honorius fidelissimi principes specialibus privilegiis ... decorarunt. in hac urbe ... consulatum suscepit et dedit. hanc sublimissima praefectura, hanc reliquae potestates ... semper inhabitant" See Duchesne, *Fastes* 1.122-128; Griffe, *Gaule* 2.161; Jalland, *Leo* p.132; and Langgärtner, *Gallienpolitik* pp.82-83. This argument may have been stressed because Asterius had assumed the office of consul at Arles on 1 January 449, on which see Sid. Apoll. *Epist.* 8.6.5-6 and Griffe, *Gaule* 2.249 n.37. The secular authorities may even have overseen the election to ensure that it was peaceful.

26. "perceptis nunc tamen beatitudinis vestrae litteris, quanta eum caritate complectamini, evidenter agnovimus" (*Epist.* "Memores quantum").

esteem. We perceive that it is certainly clear that the favor of divine grace accompanies the church of Arles, which happens to possess such a bishop, through whom it might rejoice that its privileges of ancient rank, which it was grieving as temporarily lost, have been perpetually restored by more recent decrees of the apostolic see.[27]

The Gauls, therefore, argued that Leo's decree removing Hilary's status was but a temporary thing, made for personal reasons.[28]

The Gauls elaborated their argument that precedent and tradition were on their side by using Leo's own statements in his "Divinae cultum" against him. The Gallic bishops claimed that they wished "non aliqua nova institui, sed prisca ... et antiqua reparari," an obvious echo, and contradiction, of Leo's own protestation in 445 that he was "non nova instituentes, sed vetera renovantes" ("Divinae cultum" ch. 2). To counter Leo's claim of 445 that he was acting according to *antiquitas*, *primitia*, and *traditio*, the Gallic bishops in 449/450 responded by saying not once but nine times that their own claims were based upon *antiquitas*, *primitia*, and *traditio*. The bishops then concluded with their actual request:

We beseech the crown of Your Sanctimoniousness that, as we have shown above, whatever the church of Arles either received from antiquity or afterwards gained by the authority of the apostolic see, the authority of Your Beatitude shall order that the bishop of this same church shall recover all of it, under his own authority, to remain perpetually....[29]

The bishops stressed that they were not asking Leo for anything new, only for the recovery of what rightly belonged to the church of Arles.

This letter, demanding the return of all the rights that Arles had ever possessed, might suggest that the faction organized by Hilary still was strong in the south, and that it would continue to give organizational unity to the church in southern Gaul. The very end of the letter, however, hints at another problem that this party of bishops would have had to face, for it states that the bishops would have brought their petition to Rome in person, "if infirmity had not prevented some

---

27. "nec enim iustum est, ut honorem eius, quem, ut probavimus, inpense diligitis, illa res minuat, quod pietatem vestram alter offendit. et sane manifestum [est] ecclesiae Arelatensi divinae gratiae favorem adesse perspicimus, cui talem habere contigit sacerdotem per quem privilegia dignitatis antiquae, quae dolebat sibi pro tempore diminuta, gauderet in perpetuum recentioribus apostolicae sedis auctoritatibus reformata" (ibid.).

28. Langgärtner, *Gallienpolitik* pp.81-82 presumes that Leo's decree of 445 also was to apply to Hilary's successors, arguing that Nicetas' complaints about Fonteius would have been "senseless" otherwise. Nicetas, however, had claims of antiquity of his own, and his metropolitan status was not based simply upon Leo's recent decree.

29. "obsecramus coronam sanctimoniae vestrae ... ut quicquid Arelatensis ecclesiae, sicut superius indicavimus, vel ab antiquitate suscepit, vel postea auctoritate sedis apostolicae vindicavit, id omne ad suum pontificium revocare eiusdem ecclesiae sacerdotem beatitudinis vestrae auctoritas in perpetuum mansura praecipiat..." (*Epist.* "Memores quantum").

and the penury of the present year others."[30] Many of the Lerinenses by now were quite elderly: of the nineteen who subscribed, eleven had been ordained c.430 or before, and only two, Fonteius of Vaison (who predictably supported the pretensions of his patron Ravennius) and Palladius, had been ordained within the previous ten years.[31] In the succeeding years, many of these individuals were going to die, and they were not going to be replaced, apparently, by men with similar sentiments.

The arrival in Rome of Ravennius' representatives, the presbyter Petronius and the deacon Regulus, had been preceded by the arrival of the delegation of the bishop of Vienne, as Leo noted in his response: "But the bishop of Vienne, having sent letters and legates, anticipated the petition of Your Fraternity with his own request."[32] This was a situation which the bishops of Rome must have yearned for: to be appealed to, not by some petty local cleric, but by two of the most powerful metropolitans in Gaul. Leo now had the chance to have a papal decision in Gaul actually be observed, but only if he could induce these two bishops to enforce it. The case, therefore, had to be handled very delicately.

The presence of both delegations in Rome, both asking for his patronage, also would have placed Leo in a quandary.[33] For one thing, the bishops of Rome in the past regularly had favored the party which brought its appeal to Rome. What was Leo to do now that two suppliant groups had come? If his response were to be consistent with his past rulings, he would have to condemn Ravennius for his illegal ordination and deny out of hand the request for his restoration of the metropolitan rights of Arles.

The situation, however, was not so straightforward. For one thing, Leo already had shown Ravennius some favor. Moreover, Leo himself was involved in a theological dispute with the east. In 449 the Council of Ephesus, the so-called *Latrocinium*, had favored the monophysites. Leo then found himself in dire need of support for his own position, which was set forth in his *Epistula ad Flavianum* (13 June 449).[34] For

---

30. "nisi alios infirmitas alios anni praesentis peniuria . . . revocasset" (*Epist.* "Memores quantum"). Such a statement also would have been strictly *pro forma*: under no circumstances would a horde of Gallic bishops have descended upon Rome during this period.

31. For the ordination dates of these bishops, see appendix "Episcopal Hierarchy" below.

32. "sed petitionem fraternitatis vestrae Viennensis episcopus, missis litteris et legatis, sua suggestione praevenerat" (*Epist.* "Lectis dilectionis": *M.G.H. Epist.* 3.20-21). Some, such as Jalland, *Leo* pp.130-131, wrongly assert that the Arles delegation arrived first; for the correct translation, see Duchesne, *Fastes* 1.121. Langgärtner, *Gallienpolitik* p.83, mistakenly has the delegations arriving at the same time.

33. See Jalland, *Leo* p.134, for Leo's "embarrassment."

34. Leo, *Epist.* 28 = the *Epistola dogmatica*, the so-called *Tome*, written against the presbyter Eutyches. For Prosper of Aquitaine as the author, see Gennad. *Vir. ill.* 85 and Ado of Vienne,

Leo, this controversy would have been vastly more important than metropolitan bickering in Gaul. Therefore, in deciding between Arles and Vienne, Leo also might have wished to find a solution which would alienate as little potential support in Gaul as possible.[35]

LEO'S NEW GALLIC SETTLEMENT

After a long delay, Leo eventually attempted to satisfy both sides at once, even though this meant repudiating his decree of 445.[36] In his response to the supporters of Ravennius ("Lectis dilectionis": *M.G.H. Epist*. 3.20-21), he declared that he simply could not choose between the two cities:

having indeed considered the allegations of each party of clerics who were present, we thus discovered that the cities of Vienne and Arles both have always been famous within the province, so that through the alternating result of certain considerations at one time one excelled in ecclesiastical privilege and at another time the other [did]. . . .[37]

Leo solved his dilemma by dismembering the province, giving to the bishop of Vienne metropolitan rights over Valence, Geneva, and Grenoble in Viennensis as well over Tarentaise in Alpes Graiae, and granting the rest to Arles.[38]

Given his recent decrees, Leo hardly could ignore the claims of Vienne altogether.[39] But he also would have recognized that Ravennius was continuing to ignore his rulings and was exercising metropolitan status within the province. It was clear Ravennius meant to do so with or without Leo's blessing.[40] Ravennius would prefer, of

---

Chron. (*P.L*. 123.104). See also Di Capua, *Ritmo Prosaico* pp.202-203; Gaidioz, "Prosper"; Mc-Shane, *Romanitas* pp.370-374; and Silva-Tarouca, "Nuovi Studi" pp.571-572. For the Council of Ephesus of 449, see Hefele-Leclercq, *Conciles* 2.555-622.

35. See Duchesne, *Fastes* 1.120; Langgärtner, *Gallienpolitik* p.86-90; and Jalland, *Leo*, pp.134-137, who presumes that Leo meant to "safeguard the churches of Gaul against false teaching." It is doubtful, however, that there was a real concern that monophysitism might spread to Gaul. On Leo's need for the "unanimous backing of the church of Gaul" see Kidd, *Church* p.359.

36. For the delay, see note 14 above.

37. "consideratis enim allegationibus utriusque partis praesentium clericorum, ita semper intra provinciam vestram et Viennensem et Arelatensem civitatem claras fuisse reperimus, ut quarumdam causarum alterna ratione, nunc illa in ecclesiasticis privilegiis, nunc ista praecelleret. . . ." Duchesne, *Fastes* 1.123, suggests that Leo had studied up on the past administration of Gaul. Leo also carefully acted as if he were taking into account only ecclesiastical status.

38. After listing the cities to be under Vienne, Leo added encouragingly, "ut cum eis ipsa Vienna sit quinta." Jalland, *Leo* 135 n.82, mistakenly places Tarentaise in the province of Viennensis.

39. Leo's continued recognition of the rights of Vienne may indicate that Vienne continued to be the civil metropolitan city even while Arles was the seat of the prefect.

40. For the Gallic failure to abide by Leo's decree of 445, see Griffe, *Gaule* 2.159-163.

course, to have it, but he also had enough support in Gaul that he did not require it. Leo, therefore, accepted his inability to introduce innovations into Gallic ecclesiastical administration, and tacitly fell back upon the decision reached by the Council of Turin.[41]

Leo's repetition of Turin, however, was by now somewhat anachronistic. How, for example, did he justify placing Tarentaise, a city in another province and perhaps a metropolitan see itself, under the jurisdiction of Vienne?[42] Perhaps Tarentaise had not had a bishop at the time of Turin, in which case its supervision by Vienne could have been understandable, assuming that this even had been done then.[43] By the early fifth century, however, the Alpine provinces had fallen under the influence of the bishops of Arles, and a reversion to the earlier division may have been difficult to implement.[44] What is certain is that the bishop of Tarentaise took part in none of the known activities of the bishop of Vienne and his other suffragans at this time. This must mean either that Tarentaise still had no bishop, an unlikely case, or that its bishop was employing the same passive resistance against Vienne that some of the southern bishops had used against Arles.

At the same time, Leo tactfully ignored some of the specific points raised by the two delegations. On the one hand, he made no mention at all of the case of Fonteius, whose ordination therefore was tacitly accepted; and on the other, the question of the bishop of Arles' authority over the Tres Provinciae was left hanging.[45] Leo's order that Ravennius was to have authority over "the remaining cities of this same province" would seem to suggest that he meant Ravennius to administer cities only in Viennensis.[46] Nevertheless, Leo's failure to be more specific has led some to suppose that he did in fact restore the metropolitan authority of the bishop of Arles over most of the Three Provinces.[47] This, however, is unlikely. In the context of c.450, Ravennius would have had no reasonable expectation of being able to

---

41. See Griffe, *Gaule* 1.340; Jalland, *Leo* p.136 n.82; and Langgärtner, *Gallienpolitik* p.85. Others miss this precedent: see Duchesne, *Fastes* 1.122-124, and Klingshirn, "Charity" pp.193-194. McShane, *Romanitas* p.281, anachronistically suggests that "Vienne gouvernera les régions occupées par les barbares, Arles les régions contrôlées par les Romains." Jalland (*Leo* p.140) nevertheless claims that Leo "refused to act on expediency."

42. For the Alpine provinces, see chapter 1 above.

43. As assumed by Langgärtner, *Gallienpolitik* p.85.

44. See chapter 5 above.

45. See Jalland, *Leo* p.136.

46. "reliquae vero civitates eiusdem provinciae" (*Epist.* "Lectis dilectionis"). See Babut, *Turin* p.209; Griffe, *Gaule* 2.162-163 n.49; Gundlach, "Der Streit" p.332 n.2 (which assumes that Narbonensis Secunda and the Alpes still did not have their own metropolitans); Jalland, *Leo* pp.134-136; and Langgärtner, *Gallienpolitik* pp.83-85.

47. See Duchesne, *Fastes* 1.124; Hefele-Leclercq, *Conciles*, 2.426 n.1; Kidd, *Church* p.359; Klingshirn, "Charity" p.194; and McShane, *Romanitas* p.280. Duchesne also suggests (p.125) that

establish his authority over Rusticus of Narbonne, however much he might have wished to do so. Moreover, Leo already had shown himself to be adamantly against such extended metropolitan jurisdiction.

Leo's lack of precision on what cities were to be under Ravennius probably was a result of other considerations. For one thing, an enumeration of all nine of them would have angered the bishop of Vienne even more over Leo's *volte-face*. Moreover, there remained the anomalous position of Venerius of Marseilles, who continued to claim the same extraordinary status which had been granted to his predecessor Proculus. To have named Marseilles specifically as a suffragan of Arles would have gained for Leo yet another powerful adversary in Gaul. So from Leo's point of view, it was both prudent and politic to be vague about exactly what cities Ravennius was to oversee. He apparently left it to Ravennius to make of it what he could.

Ravennius seems to have been satisfied with Leo's decision. Official recognition by the Roman see of his metropolitan status, and the abrogation of Leo's settlement of 445, would have seemed to him at least a step in the right direction. It would appear that Nicetas of Vienne concurred as well, if it was he to whom Leo's successor Hilarus was referring in 464 when he said of Nicetas' successor Mamertus, "Instructed at least by the example of his predecessor, let him emulate his temperance."[48] As for Leo, he may have felt that he was the real winner, for he now truly could portray himself as the overseer of the ecclesiastical affairs of Gaul. Such an opportunity never would have occurred during the era of Hilary.[49]

On the same day, 5 May 450, that he wrote his letter renewing the metropolitan privileges of Arles, Leo wrote a second letter, addressed only to Ravennius, in which he requested the latter's support in his doctrinal quarrel with the east.[50] After apologizing for delaying the return of Ravennius' representatives, Leo continued (*Epist.* "Diu filios": *M.G.H. Epist.* 3.22),

In fact, we desired them to be present at our deliberation and to understand everything which we wish through you to come to the notice of all our brothers and fellow bishops.... You have a good opportunity to render the

---

Arles now became "un grand centre d'information et de communications." The territory of Vienne, of course, would have been exempted even in this interpretation.

48. "decessoris sui saltem instructus exemplo, illius imitaretur temperantiam" (*Epist.* "Sollicitis admodum": *M.G.H. Epist.* 3.30-32). See chapter 9 below, n.32.

49. The lack of effect of this decree, however, is suggested by the notation appended to some of the manuscripts, "hoc praeceptum domini Leonis confirmatum est a sede apostolica praesidenti Symmacho papa, Probo v.c. consule" (A.D.502) (*M.G.H. Epist.* 3.21).

50. Dated wrongly to 451 in *Corp. chr. lat.* 148.107.

beginning of your episcopate agreeable to all the churches and to our God, if you fulfil these matters, dearest brother, thus, as we plan and command.[51]

Given the contents of Leo's other letter, the *quid pro quo* in this one is self-evident. After the show of strength Ravennius had just made, Leo expected that he would be the bishop best able to marshall Gallic support for Leo's theological offensive in the east.

Leo's reliance upon Ravennius, moreover, went even further than this, as seen in his conclusion of the second letter (*Epist.* "Diu filios"): "As to those matters which should not be committed to writing, when you are informed by the report of the aforementioned brothers of ours, you will fulfil them, supported by the aid of the Lord, efficiently, as I have said, and laudably."[52] These secret, verbal instructions already show Ravennius in the special role of trusted confidante and ally of Leo, at least in the opinion of the latter.[53]

There remain Leo's relations with the bishop of Vienne. It appears that Leo also sent a copy of the *Epistula ad Flavianum* back with the representatives of the bishop of Vienne, with instructions to circulate it on their way back, for Eusebius, the bishop of Milan, obtained a copy of the *Epistula* from Ceretius of Grenoble, "according to [Leo's] instructions."[54] Now, there were not many occasions when a bishop of Grenoble would have been passing through Milan on his way north from Rome in the early 450s. One such opportunity would have occurred if Ceretius had been the leader of the Viennese delegation to Rome in late 449, for he surely would have stopped at Milan on his way back home.[55] The representatives from Arles would not have stopped there themselves; they would have returned by the coast road or by

---

51. "voluimus enim eos nostro interesse tractatui, et universa cognoscere, quae per te cupimus ad omnium fratrum et consacerdotum nostrorum notitiam pervenire. . . . habes probabilem facultatem, qua cunctis ecclesiis et deo nostro episcopatus tui possis commendare primordia, si haec ita, ut credimus atque mandamus, impleveris, frater carissime."

52. "quae autem committenda litteris non fuerunt, cum praedictorum filiorum nostrorum insinuatione didiceris, domini fretus auxilio efficaciter, ut diximus, ac laudabiliter exequeris."

53. It was not uncommon for letter writers to send verbal as well as written messages, see Sid. Apoll. *Epist.* 4.12.4. It has been suggested, as by Jalland, *Leo* p.137 n.86, that the secret instructions included a request for support for Leo's attack on Eutychianism, but this is what Leo had asked in the extant letter. Leo may have asked the Gauls to write directly to the eastern emperor Theodosius II, for in their response they did mention that they had considered doing so (see n.64); see Griffe, *Gaule* 2.171-172.

54. "ex vestra [sc. Leonis] admonitione" (*P.L.* 54.945-950).

55. The best route from Italy to Gaul, the *Via Cottia*, led through the Alps directly from Milan to Grenoble and Vienne. See Sitwell, *Roads* p.73: the Alpine road was "much more popular" for all land travel between Gaul and Italy than the more difficult *Via Iulia Augusta* on the coast. At the Council of Milan in August/September 451, the letter brought by Ceretius had to be "requisita," "hunted for" (*P.L.* 54.946), implying that it had been delivered some time in the past, and the return of the delegation to Vienne circa May of 450 would be the only known

sea.[56] Leo also may have included a request for support addressed to the bishop of Vienne similar to that which he had sent to Ravennius.

THE GALLIC RESPONSE TO LEO

What is most immediately striking about the Gallic response to Leo's request for support is its dilatoriness. Leo's letter was written on 5 May 450, but the Gauls did not finally deliver their response until January of 452. This delay certainly was annoying to Leo.[57] In the ultimate letter of support, signed by forty-four bishops and delivered by Ingenuus of Embrun, the Gauls began by apologizing for their tardiness. They would have replied "immediately," they said (*Epist.* "Perlata ad nos" 1: *Corp. chr. lat.* 148.107),

if the distances which separate us from each other or the intemperateness of the weather, which was worse than usual in our area, had not caused difficulty for us whereby we were unable to unite together quickly. May Your Apostolacy, therefore, grant pardon to our tardiness, which came about not from sloth or dissimulation, but from definite necessity.[58]

The need for a Gallic apology is seen in Leo's response of 27 January 452, which disapprovingly began, "We indeed would have wished to receive the letters of Your Fraternity at the time when you had promised them...."[59] It went on to say, "But, although many obstacles caused your unexpected delay, we gratefully received the letters, however late and long awaited...."[60]

Given the issue made of the Gallic delay, one might wonder at its

---

opportunity. Later legends also connected Ceretius with Milan: he supposedly had been educated by Ambrose (*A.A.S.S.* June I p.697). For the view that Ravennius distributed the only Gallic copy of the letter, see Bardy, "La répercussion" p.774, and Silva-Tarouca, "Nuovi Studi" pp.395-396.

56. For the sea route, see Rutilius Namatianus' *De reditu suo* passim.

57. The delay is so unusual that some have failed to notice it (see *Corp. chr. lat.* 148.107). Silva-Tarouca, "Nuovi Studi" p.394, dates the Gallic meeting to the summer of 451; Jalland, *Leo* p.137 n.90, to the fall; and Griffe, *Gaule* 2.171, to the end of the year, the usual time for holding Gallic councils. See also Duchesne, *Fastes* 1.125-126, and Bardy et al., *Eglise* p.267.

58. "nisi nobis difficultatem, qua in unum cleriter non potuimus convenire, vel spatia quibus a nobis dispalati sumus, longa terrarum vel aurarum, quae in regionibus nostris praeter consuetudinem fuit, intemperies attulisset. det ergo apostolatus vester nostrae veniam tarditati, quae non de otio aut dissimulatione, sed de certa necessitate descendit...." Bardy, "Répercussions" pp.29-39, recognizes that the Gallic excuses are not sufficiently convincing to warrant such a delay, but his only alternative is that the Gauls "n'aient pas mesuré la gravité des événéments..."

59. "optassemus quidem fraternitatis vestrae litteras eo tempore quo promiseratis accipere ..." (*Epist.* "Optassemus quidem": *A.C.O.* 2.4.53-55).

60. "sed cum multa obstacula inopinatam vobis intulerint tarditatem, quamlibet seras et diu expectatas epistolas ... gratanter accepimus...."

cause. The Gallic excuse about the difficulties caused by distance and weather do not ring true; councils had been held many times in the past without being delayed by such problems. Perhaps the Gauls' mention of "certain necessity" and Leo's of "many obstacles" might have other explanations. Some have attributed the delay to the invasion of Gaul by the Huns, but they were in Gaul only from April through June of 451 (and even then only in northern Gaul). This explanation could not account for the entire delay, from May, 450 until January, 452.[61] Moreover, if the Huns had been the cause of the delay, it is remarkable that the Gauls neglected to mention such an eminently reasonable excuse. Nor is there any evidence at all, or any reason to suspect, that the delay was caused by Gallic disagreements with Leo's theological position: even in the era of Hilary there had been no such differences between Gaul and Italy. It may be better to look elsewhere for the causes of the Gallic tardiness.

For one thing, the Gallic protest that their tardiness was not the result of *dissimulatio* could be taken as an indication of their fear that the opposite would be thought.[62] Furthermore, Leo's complaint that the Gallic response had not arrived "at the time when you had promised" implies that Ravennius had committed himself to obtaining Gallic adhesion at some earlier time, probably in time for it to be used in the deliberations at Chalcedon.[63] Nevertheless, he was unable to do so. Just what might have been the cause of Ravennius' inability to obtain Gallic support for Leo?

It would appear that the Gauls did hold a meeting of some sort in late 450, for Ravennius later reported to Leo, "We would have wished to send letters to the emperor on this matter but after the arrival of the news from the east we deemed this to be less necessary."[64] The "news" presumably was of the death of Theodosius II on 28 July 450. Either Ravennius was lying, or the Gallic bishops actually did meet in late 450. If they did, and did not at the same time forward their adherence to Leo, it can only be because they could not agree to do so.

61. See Duchesne, *Fastes* 1.126 n.2, and Jalland, *Leo* p.137 n.87. For Attila's dates, see Demougeot, "Attila" p.29. Others, such as Griffe, *Gaule* 2.171, accept the Gallic excuses.
62. For a similar use of *dissimulatio*, see the letter of Hilarus of Rome "Etsi meminerimus," in which he accuses the bishop of Arles of doing just that (chapter 9 below, n.120).
63. On 20 July 451 Leo wrote another letter to Ravennius, ostensibly on the date of Easter for 452 (Leo *Epist.* "Ad praecipuum": *P.L.* 54.945). The bearer of this letter may have carried another verbal message to Ravennius: to forward his support while there still was time for it to be used at Chalcedon, which convened on 8 October 451 (Seeck, *Regesten* p.391).
64. "optassemus etiam ad . . . principem super eadem causa litteras dare . . . nisi ad nos de orientalibus partibus nuntio perlato, fieri hoc minime necessarium putassemus" (*Epist.* "Perlata ad nos" 4: *Corp. chr. lat.* 148.108). The news of the election of Marcian, then unrecognized in the west, also may have made such a letter "less necessary."

It was not until either the very end of 451, or early January of 452, that Ravennius and forty-three other bishops, whose sees, unfortunately, are not given, forwarded their letter of support to Leo.[65] The list of subscribers was headed by Ravennius of Arles, Rusticus of Narbonne, and Venerius of Marseilles, demonstrating Ravennius' success at securing the adhesion of the other two most important prelates of Provence. Rusticus, the metropolitan of Narbonensis Prima, had been one of Ravennius' consecrators, so his signature is not unexpected. That of Venerius, however, in the third position, is significant, for it would imply that Ravennius, and Rusticus, recognized Venerius' anomalous claim to extraordinary status, even though he was not a bishop of a regular metropolitan see.[66]

Ravennius' ability to conciliate Venerius is surprising, for the latter had held aloof from Ravennius' ordination, and, predictably, had not subscribed to the letter to Leo requesting the revival of Ravennius' metropolitan authority. Ravennius' recognition, in the letter to Leo, of the metropolitan status of both Rusticus and Venerius must mean that as of 451 he had dropped any lingering claims to authority over the entire Tres Provinciae. Whether he recognized the rights of the bishop of Vienne in northern Viennensis or not, it does appear that he did yield authority in Narbonensis Prima to Rusticus and in Marseilles, and perhaps even in other places such as Nice, to Venerius. Venerius' status in Narbonensis Secunda, however, may have been left unclear.

This was an offer Venerius could not refuse; he would have snatched at any opportunity to have his ever-more-irregular metropolitan status recognized by his peers. As for Rusticus, he may have had other reasons for coming to terms with Ravennius. As the ambitious doyen of the southern Gallic metropolitans, and one who to some degree had been responsible for Ravennius' very election, he may have seen himself as the logical successor to the aspirations of Hilary. In the matter of the letter to Leo, he would wish to portray himself as a leader, not as an isolated malcontent.

Perhaps, therefore, it was the continuing controversy over the allocation of metropolitan authority in southern Gaul which led to the

---

65. *Epist.* "Perlata ad nos" (*Corp. chr. lat.* 148.107-110). Leo's response (*Epist.* "Optassemus quidem"), dated 27 January, indicated that he sent back the Gallic representative as soon as possible: "nam fratrem Ingenuum noluimus hac expectatione tardari, cum ob hoc ipsum properantius remeare deberet...." It seems unlikely, therefore, that Ingenuus could have left Gaul before early January. The Gallic letter is dated to 451 by Munier, *Corp. chr. lat.* 148.107-110 and Duchesne, *Fastes* 1.369; and to late 451 by Jalland, *Leo* p.137. Southern bishops seem to have subscribed in person, whereas more distant ones apparently forwarded their subscriptions by messenger, see appendix "The Names in Ravennius' Letter to Leo" below.

66. Venerius' name precedes those of several bishops who had been in office longer than he. See Palanque, "Evêchés" pp.124-125.

delay in the Gallic letter to Leo. Only Ravennius' restriction of his own status had induced Rusticus and Venerius, not to mention their partisans, to subscribe. On the other hand, however, the metropolitan authority of the bishop of Aix in Narbonensis Secunda seems not to have been recognized, at least in this letter, for the fourth signer was Constantianus of Carpentras, a non-metropolitan. Apparently, then, the bishop of Aix was continuing his boycott of church councils.

Leo himself concurred with this arrangement, for he addressed his reply to Ravennius, Rusticus, and Venerius first, granting them alone extraordinary metropolitan status. Little matter if, according to his own decrees, Venerius did not warrant it. A coalition of these three sees was a far cry from the dissension among them during the tenure of Hilary, and at least in this regard Ravennius finally had been successful in welding together an acceptable response to Leo.[67]

THE GALLIC OPPOSITION TO RAVENNIUS

The names of other influential Gallic bishops, however, were conspicuously absent from the Ravennius-sponsored letter. The bishop of Vienne and his suffragans, as well as Theodorus of Fréjus, do not appear. Nor do powerful northerners such as Euphronius of Autun, Patiens of Lyons, and Lupus of Troyes. Just what might have been the reasons for their abstention?

In 450 or 451, the bishop of Vienne would have been reminded of his loss of southern Viennensis when Audentius of Die died and was succeeded by a possible protégé of Ravennius: the new bishop Petronius perhaps is to be identified with the presbyter Petronius who delivered to Rome Ravennius' request for the reestablishment of his metropolitan privileges.[68] By the end of 451, moreover, Nicetas of Vienne had been succeeded by Mamertus, who appears to have been every bit as opposed to Ravennius as his predecessor had become.[69]

Perhaps as a result of his pique over Ravennius' revived status, Mamertus and his suffragans refrained from subscribing to the letter of support organized by Ravennius.[70] So as not to be totally mute on the matter, however, they also took the step of co-authoring an extant

---

67. For the assumption that Ravennius was successful in reestablishing the authority of Arles, see Bardy et al., *Eglise* pp.262, and Jalland, *Leo* p.138, who also sees him now as "a natural intermediary between the Roman see" and Gaul.

68. Date: see appendix "Episcopal Hierarchy" below. For the presbyter, see Leo *Epist.* "Lectis dilectionis" (*M.G.H. Epist.* 3.20-21) and "Diu filios" (*M.G.H. Epist.* 3.22).

69. As of early 451, Mamertus was not yet bishop (*VAniani* 5).

70. For their absence, see Bardy, "La répercussion" p.774 n.11; Hunt, *Leo* p.137; and Jalland, *Leo* p.137.

letter of their own to Leo on the same subject.[71] As it survives, the letter has only three signatures: Ceretius of Grenoble, Salonius of Geneva, and Veranus, Salonius' brother and the newly elected bishop of Vence in Alpes Maritimae.[72] These three signatures, however, are preceded, like the subscriptions to Ravennius' letter, by an elaborate anonymous subscription identified only by the formula *et alia manu*.[73] Now, just as the anonymous subscription in the Arles letter has been attributed, without doubt correctly, to the metropolitan Ravennius, the subscription on this letter equally certainly should be attributed to the metropolitan bishop of Vienne, Mamertus.[74] The suffragans of Vienne, therefore, not only obtained their own copy of Leo's *Epistula*, they also forwarded their own response.

This undated letter probably also was written c.451/452, at about the same time as the letter sponsored by Ravennius.[75] Although it too speaks favorably of Leo's *Tome*, it also is equivocal and temporizing. The bishops stalled by asking for a revised copy ("Recensita epistola": *P.L.* 54.889):

We request Your Sanctity to glance over the work and if anything is lacking through an error of the copyist, deign to emend it, or if you have accumulated by some additional study of yours a page which is salutary for those who shall read it, with solicitous piety may you command it to be added to your letter.[76]

To ask for a fair copy might seem a bit strange, given that Ceretius already had brought one directly from Rome. The request that Leo

71. "Recensita epistola" (*P.L.* 54.887-890). This letter conventionally is dated only to c.442/461, see Pricoco, *L'isola* p.47 n.78, and Silva-Tarouca, "Nuovi Studi" pp.395-396.

72. The appearance of Veranus, who was ordained after Mamertus, shows that Mamertus by this time had become bishop of Vienne (see appendix "Episcopal Hierarchy" below). As usual, Mamertus' supposed suffragan of Tarentaise is absent, as is the bishop of Valence.

73. For this formula, see Di Capua, *Ritmo Prosaico* pp.199-204, 234-235; and Silva-Tarouca, "Et alia manu," in "Nuovi Studi" pp.361-374. The subscription reads "Memorem coronam vestram humilitatis nostrae Christus dominus longaeva aetate conservet, domine sancte, beatissime pater et apostolica sede dignissime papa," and clearly was written by an individual of rank and importance, whose name has not survived. The anonymous Arles subscription reads "Ora pro me domine merito beatissime et apostolico honore venerande papa" (*Corp. chr. lat.* 148.108).

74. In the Arles letter, Ravennius' name does appear at the head of the salutations, but has dropped out of the subscriptions. For the restoration of his name, see *Corp. chr. lat.* 148.108 n.2 and Jalland, *Leo* p.137 n. 89. The same thing happened at the Council of Valence in 374 (*Corp. chr. lat.* 148.40, see also *Corp. chr. lat.* 149.277, 278, 281). In such circumstances, it may have been felt that the presiding bishop's status made his actual name superfluous.

75. For dates, see Silva-Tarouca, "Nuovi Studi" pp.395-396 (before the summer of 451); Griffe, *Gaule* 2.172 n.6 (late 451); and Jalland, *Leo* p.137 n.91 (early 452 at the latest). See also note 108 below for a date circa December 451/January 452.

76. "deprecamur ut opus ... sanctitas vestra percurrere et si quid librarii errore defuerit, emendare dignetur, vel si salutarem lecturis omnibus paginam aliquo studii vestri accumulastis augmento, idipsum addi libello huic sollicita pietate iubeatis. . . ."

review the text may in fact have been an excuse for withholding a definitive response.[77]

The opening of their letter, moreover, seems to imply that Mamertus and his colleagues were aware that their reply would not come up to Leo's expectations: "Having read the letter of Your Beatitude, we thought it fitting that we should render proper thanks at least with the offered duty of a letter...."[78] The word *saltem* seems curiously restrained. Surely, if these bishops had been giving Leo what he wanted, they would not have phrased their response so modestly.

The purpose of the letter may have been twofold: both to emphasize Mamertus' own independence of action vis-à-vis Ravennius in Viennensis, as well as, perhaps, to embarrass Ravennius in the eyes of Leo.[79] Mamertus' reply also may have been intended to display his dissatisfaction with Leo's handling of the situation in Viennensis. At the close of the letter, Mamertus even presumed to instruct Leo, "We wish those whom we sent to return soon, if you think it proper," an allusion, perhaps, to the long delay experienced by the previous Viennese embassy to Rome.

The presence of Veranus of Vence among the signers also is interesting. His see was in Alpes Maritimae, and he should have signed Ravennius' letter, along with his fellow provincials Ingenuus of Embrun (his metropolitan) and Valerianus of Cimiez.[80] At this time, however, Veranus would not have held the office of bishop for more than several months. It may be that his ties to the north, where his brother Salonius was bishop of Geneva and where his father Eucherius of Lyons had just died, allied him more closely to the party of Mamertus than to that of Ravennius.[81]

THE BISHOPS OF NORTHERN GAUL

It would be a mistake, however, to see in Mamertus and his partisans an anti-Lérins faction. What they represent seems rather to be a

77. Jalland, however, *Leo* p.138, concludes that "the writers spare no pains to testify of their devotion" to Leo. See also Bardy, "La répercussion" p.774.

78. "recensita epistola beatitudinis vestrae ... dignum esse censuimus, ut ... debitas gratias saltem oblato litterarum officio redderemus...."

79. Most commentators exaggerate Ravennius' authority. See Griffe, *Gaule* 2.172 n.6; Silva-Tarouca, "Nuovi Studi" pp.395-397; and Jalland, *Leo* p.138, who asserts that Ravennius had regained his "preeminent position" immediately after discussing the Viennese letter but also admits (p.143 n.117) that Rusticus of Narbonne acted independently at this time.

80. Jalland, *Leo* pp.137-138, inexplicably asserts that this Viennese letter was written by the bishops of Alpes Maritimae, although only one of the signers, Veranus, and he the most junior, was from that province.

81. The presence of Veranus, a bishop from Alpes Maritimae, in this group can be explained only by his relationship to Salonius, and confirms the common assumption that this Veranus was

splinter group of the old Lerinenses. After all, Salonius and Veranus were the sons of Eucherius, one of the monastery's founders, and Mamertus has been identified as a relative of his predecessor Claudius, who had his own ties to Lérins.[82] What this may be is the beginning of geographically based fragmentation of the old party of Lérins, with a northern group breaking away as local interests, in this case Mamertus' desire to protect his metropolitan status, took predominance over the veneer of factional unity which had prevailed under Hilary.

Farther north, at Lyons, the bishop Eucherius died in late 451 or early 452, and was succeeded by a hitherto unattested Patiens.[83] Now, neither Eucherius nor Patiens appear among the subscribers to Ravennius' letter to Leo. Nor do the names of two other famous northern bishops, Euphronius of Autun, and the ex-monk of Lérins Lupus of Troyes.[84] One might wonder why their names are absent. The presence in Ravennius' list of such bishops as, it seems, Helladius of Auxerre and Eparchius of Clermont would suggest that mere distance from Arles probably was not the primary reason why the names of these three preëminent prelates do not appear.[85]

Nor would it appear that these abstentions were the result of any contemporary turmoil and dislocation.[86] Indeed, as of the 450s there is increasing evidence rather for a strong sense of solidarity among some of the influential northern Gallic bishops. The *Vita Aniani* (ch.5), for example, singles out Mamertus of Vienne as a special friend of Anianus of Orléans in the year 451. Shortly thereafter, Lupus of Troyes and Euphronius of Autun co-authored an extant letter on ecclesiastical discipline addressed to Thalassius of Angers, in western Lugdunensis.[87]

Salonius' brother (as assumed by Duchesne, *Fastes* 1.294, although still questioned by Pricoco, *L'isola* p.47 n.78).

82. The relationship is suggested by the name of Mamertus' brother, the presbyter Mamertus Claudianus; see Heinzelmann, *Bischofsherrschaft* p.226.

83. See appendix "Episcopal Hierarchy" below.

84. For Lupus, see chapter 4 above, n.50. The *Gallic Chronicle of 511* (no. 616, M.G.H. A.A 11.663) wrongly notes, between Attila's invasions of Gaul in 451 and Italy in 452, that "Euphronius episcopus Augustiduno sepelitur": he clearly was alive some twenty years later. Perhaps one should read instead a word like "ordinatur" or "claret." This is his first attestation.

85. Eparchius: Duchesne, *Fastes* 2.34 and n.120 below. Helladius: ibid. 2.444 and chapter 4 above, n.117. The signers' sees, unfortunately, are not given. Note also a Victurus, perhaps Victurius of Le Mans, and a Eustachius, who may be Eustochius of Tours. See appendix "The names in Ravennius' Letter to Leo" below.

86. Duchesne, *Fastes* 1.126, attributes the absences to the Huns, but they were a factor for only a few months. Similarly, any delay caused by Eucherius' death also could not have lasted long.

87. "Commonitorium quod": *Corp. chr. lat.* 148.140-141. Euphronius, although not known to have visited Lérins, did follow that pattern: as a presbyter, he founded a monastery of Sym-

Further insight into the tightly knit organization of the bishops of Lugdunensis can be gleaned from a collection of documents assembled by this same Thalassius (*Corp. chr. lat.* 148.135-158). It includes the canons of three church councils, which met at Angers in 453, at Tours in 461, and at Vannes at some time later.[88] These councils show that the ecclesiastical situation in Lugdunensis was much the same as that in southern Gaul. Northern bishops, too, used councils not only to consolidate their episcopal authority but also to mitigate dissension within their own ranks, as at the Council of Tours (canon 9: *Corp. chr. lat.* 148.146):

> If any bishop attempts to exert his own authority against the rights of his brother, so that he seizes the churches of another by transgressing the boundaries established by the fathers, or presumes to promote clerics ordained by others, let him have no doubt that he shall be excluded from communion.[89]

Clearly, the churches of the north had an organization of their own. Northern bishops attended northern councils just as southern bishops attended southern ones. The Council of Tours, for example, drew bishops from as far away as Châlons-sur-Marne. There would be no reason to expect, moreover, that the interests of the northerners would always be the same as those of their southern brethren. This may explain why Lupus, Patiens, Euphronius, and others, in spite of any past ties to the circle of Lérins, refrained from aligning themselves with the bishop of Arles in the theological discussions of 450-451. This is not to say, however, that these northern bishops, like Mamertus and his partisans, could not also have forwarded their own letter of support to Leo. The survival of the Mamertus letter is purely fortuitous; others, such as one sponsored by Patiens and Euphronius, well could have perished.[90]

---

phorianus at Autun. His ties with the west also are demonstrated by his offering at the tomb of Martin of Tours (Greg. Tur. *H.F.* 2.15, 10.31).

88. The Council of Vannes is undated; Hefele-Leclercq, *Conciles* 2.1382, suggest before 470; *Corp. chr. lat.* 148.50 more conservatively suggests only 461/491. The dates of the other documents in Thalassius' corpus (453-461) would suggest a date in the 460s. See also Silva-Tarouca, "Nuovi Studi" pp.9-10.

89. "si quis episcopus in ius fratris sui suam conatus fuerit inserere potestatem, ut aut dioceses alienas, transgrediendo terminos a patribus constitutos, pervadat, aut clericos aliis ordinatos promovere praesumat ... communione se alienum efficiendum non dubitet."

90. If Helladius of Auxerre did in fact subscribe to the Arlesian letter, it would mean that some northerners continued to affiliate themselves with the southern ecclesiastical establishment.

THE CONTROVERSY OVER LÉRINS

Other evidence for dissension among the ranks of the old Lérins faction, as well as for additional opposition to Ravennius, involves Theodorus of Fréjus, an ex-monk of Lérins and a veteran partisan of Hilary. His name too is missing from the list of subscribers to Ravennius' letter. Given the time and effort expended by Ravennius to achieve as much unanimity as he could, Theodorus' absence may be the result of something more than old age, distance, or bad weather. The reasons for Theodorus' resentment against his erstwhile partisans might be found in the record of a council which assembled at Arles in the early 450s.[91]

The first evidence of the controversy, variously described as a *scandalum*, an *atrocitas*, and a *querela*, occurs in an extant "generalized copy of a letter sent to the bishops who were summoned to an investigation of the island of Lérins."[92] The council was to settle a dispute "between the blessed bishop Theodorus, and the blessed Valerianus and the blessed Maximus, both bishops, and the abbot Faustus and likewise the other brothers of the island of Lérins."[93] Some readers of this passage have assumed that the quarrel aligned Theodorus, Valerianus and Maximus against Faustus and his brethren.[94] Both grammar and phrasing, however, as well as historical probability, argue against this. Grammatically, *atque* expresses closer connection than *et*, and therefore Valerianus and Maximus more likely were associated with Faustus than with Theodorus.[95] Furthermore, if Theodorus, Valerianus, and Maximus all were grouped together, there would have been no need to describe Theodorus as *episcopum* on the one hand and Valerianus and Maximus together as *item episcopos* on the other: all could have been described equally as *episcopos*.[96]

There also are other reasons for supposing that Theodorus was the odd man out. It is very unlikely that Faustus, otherwise the protégé

91. The *acta* of this council (*Corp. chr. lat.* 148.131-134) survive only among the documents cited at the Council of Carthage in 525 as evidence for monastic privileges (*Corp. chr. lat.* 149.282). Perhaps the Eugenius who subscribed to Ravennius' letter to Leo was the African bishop Eugenius, who was in exile in Albi in Gaul at roughly this time (Greg. Tur. *H.F.* 2.3), and took the record back with him.

92. "exemplar epistulae generalis quae ad episcopos invitandos in causa insulae Lerinensis missa est" (*Corp. chr. lat.* 148.132).

93. "inter sanctum episcopum Theodorum et sanctum Valerianum vel sanctum Maximum item episcopos atque abbatem Faustum necnon et reliquos fratres insulae Lerinensis" (*Corp. chr. lat.* 148.132). See Duchesne, *Fastes* 1.126-127 and Griffe, *Gaule* 2.145-146.

94. See Weiss, "Valérien" pp.144-145.

95. See C.E. Bennett, *New Latin Grammar* (Boston, 1918) pp. 223-224.

96. For a parallel situation, note the Council of Turin, where four named bishops are grouped as "episcopos" (*Corp. chr. lat.* 148.56).

of Maximus and his successor as both abbot of Lérins and bishop of
Riez, would have been opposed by him in this isolated instance. Maximus' opposition to Theodorus here also would be consistent with any
antipathy between them which had arisen over the contest for the see
of Fréjus just after 430.[97] One must accept that in this controversy it
was Theodorus who was opposed by all the others.[98]

Specifically, the quarrel was over who was to have jurisdiction over
the personnel of the monastery. It had escalated to the point where
Faustus was publicly vilifying Theodorus, who had responded by excommunicating him. For Gallic clerics, who only rarely took such a
step, this would have been a very serious matter. Faustus' particular
complaint seems to have been that Theodorus, in whose diocese the
monastery lay, was attempting to assume control over the lay congregation, *omnis laica multitudo*, of the monastery. This control traditionally had been in the hands of the abbot.[99]

The council, scheduled for 30 December, assembled in the *secretar-
ium* of the basilica at Arles and was attended by thirteen bishops.[100]
Included among them were not only Rusticus of Narbonne, but also
at least two of his suffragans, Florus of Lodève and Constantius of
Uzès. Indeed, Ravennius had issued Rusticus a personal invitation to
attend: "To the blessed Rusticus: We first of all pray that Your Beatitude in particular will attend, because a more serious illness necessarily demands the most skilled physicians."[101] A similar special invitation was issued "to those who are on the island": "truly, it is fitting
that Your Beatitude in particular attend, you whom that very island,
nurturing as if in a mother's bosom, has promoted to that grace which
now, at the instigation of the Lord, is within you."[102]

Now, Rusticus had pointedly ignored the church councils spon-

97. See chapter 4 above, n.139.
98. See Koch, *Faustus* pp.11-12 and Mathisen, "Petronius" pp.110-111.
99. See chapter 4 above, n.74.
100. "tertio Kalendas Ianuarias audientiae dies est constitutus" (*Corp. chr. lat.* 148.132). Like
the Council of Vaison (chapter 5 above, n.98), this council need not necessarily have met on its
scheduled date. Suggestions for the council's date include 449 (Babut, *Turin* p.304 n.1), 451
(Hefele-Leclercq, *Conciles* 2.579; Koch, *Faustus* p.12); circa 452 (Griffe, *Gaule* 2.145; Duval,
Gaule p.342; Palanque "Evêchés" p.125 and "Diocèse de Aix" p.17); 455 (Bardy et al., *Eglise*
p.404; Duchesne, *Fastes* 1.265, 296; Jones, *L.R.E.* p.933; *P.L.R.E. II* s.v. "Salonius"); and 449/461
(Munier, *Corp. chr. lat.* 148.131).
101. "Ad sanctum Rusticum: ac praecipue beatitudo vestra ut adsit primum deprecamur,
quia gravior infirmitas necessarie medicos peritissimos inquirit" (*Corp. chr. lat.* 148.132).
102. "Ad eos qui in insula sunt: beatitudinem vero vestram praecipue adesse convenit, quos
insula ipsa velut sinu quodam genitricis fovens, ad eam gratiam quae nunc in vobis est, domino
instigante produxit" (*Corp. chr. lat.* 148.132). There is no indication that any monks actually
attended; only bishops were named as present. Griffe, *Gaule* 2.146, suggests that this invitation
was directed at bishops who once had been monks at Lérins, even though the verb "sunt" is in
the present tense.

sored by the bishop of Arles during the era of Hilary. His attendance here with his suffragans may reflect the spirit of cooperation which seems to have existed between Rusticus and Ravennius ever since the latter's ordination. It also may be another sign of Rusticus' desire to extend his own influence. Other attendees included: from Viennensis, Nectarius of Avignon, Asclepius of Cavaillon, Justus of Orange, and Salonius of Geneva; from Alpes Maritimae, its metropolitan Ingenuus of Embrun; and from Narbonensis Secunda, Maximus of Riez. Still others, from unknown sees, included Venantius, Zoticus, and Chrysanthius.[103]

Technically, this council should not even have had jurisdiction in the case: both Fréjus and Lérins lay outside of Ravennius' province and under the jurisdiction of the metropolitan of Narbonensis Secunda. Both Venerius of Marseilles and the unnamed bishop of Aix had claims to this position; not surprisingly, neither seems to have attended.[104] With the exception of Maximus of Riez, none of the other bishops of the province seem to have come either.[105] This attempt by the bishops of Arles and Narbonne jointly to adjudicate a dispute in Narbonensis Secunda is yet another indication of the continuing extent to which the *de iure* metropolitans of the lesser provinces of southern Gaul, Alpes Maritimae and Narbonensis Secunda, still were unable to assert their independent status and fell victim to the pretensions of their more influential colleagues. Even the *de iure* metropolitan Ingenuus of Embrun, who did attend, was kept in a subordinate position.

The decision of the council gives an additional reason why Theodorus chose to be absent, for Faustus' position was sustained. Theodorus was ordered to restore him to communion and to maintain the arrangement which had been initiated between Theodorus' predecessor Leontius and the monastery's founder Honoratus. The bishop of Fréjus would continue to have his canonical right of ordaining "clerics and ministers at the altar." As to the administration of the monastery, the bishops decreed (*Corp. chr. lat.* 148.134),

Truly, let the entire lay multitude belong in the care of the abbot, nor let the bishop appropriate anything from it for himself or presume to any cleric from

103. Chrysanthius may be the Chrysaphius who helped to consecrate Ravennius and subscribed to Ravennius' letter to Leo; his appearance with Rusticus in both places, but nowhere else, could suggest that he, like Florus (see note 3 above) and Constantius, was another suffragan of Rusticus.

104. The bishop of Aix at this time probably was Victurus (see chapter 9 below, n.37). For the pointed absence of the bishop of Marseilles, see Duchesne, *Fastes* 1.126-127, who observes that Rusticus attended "malgré ses attaches marseillaises."

105. For Maximus as Maximus of Riez, see appendix "Episcopal Hierarchy" below.

it except at the request of the abbot.... Truly, the entire lay congregation belongs in the sole and free care and disposition of the abbot alone.[106]

Finally, in an attempt to terminate the bad blood between Theodorus and Faustus, the council also stated, "Nor should anyone continually repeat verbally or keep in mind those things which [Theodorus] charged brother Faustus had done to him."[107]

Such a clear-cut rejection of his prerogatives would have alienated Theodorus from the party of Ravennius. Theodorus may have been all the more upset because in 449 he had supported the restoration of the rights of Arles, whereas Maximus had not. If their doing so were related to their quarrel, one can understand all the better Theodorus' pique during the Lérins affair, when Ravennius sided with Maximus and against him. All this may have led to Theodorus' failure to subscribe to Ravennius' letter to Leo. If this were the case, it could suggest a date for the hitherto undated council on Lérins. One then could presume that Theodorus' estrangement from Ravennius antedated the sending of the letter to Leo, and that the Lérins council therefore had met by early 452. Because Ravennius was elected in 449, the possibilities then would be limited to the years 449, 450, and 451.

The year 449 can be ruled out because of Theodorus' support for Ravennius in early 450, and 451 would appear to be the more likely of the remaining two possibilities in part because of several coincidences. First of all, with but two exceptions, Zoticus and Salonius, the individuals who attended the council on Lérins also subscribed to the letter to Leo which was delivered in January 452.[108] The appearance at Arles of Rusticus and his suffragans on both occasions is particularly noteworthy. These considerations could suggest that the council and the signing of the letter occurred at the same time, when the same individuals were in town. Also noteworthy is the convening of both councils in December (or perhaps January) at a time when church councils customarily were held in October/November. It is unlikely

106. "monasterii vero omnis laica multitudo ad curam abbatis pertineat, neque ex ea sibi episcopus quidquam vindicet aut aliquem ex illa clericum nisi abbate petente praesumat.... laica vero omnis congregatio ad solam ac liberam abbatis proprii ... ordinationem dispositionemque pertineat."

107. "nec quisquam deinceps ex his quae sibi fratrem Faustum arguebat fecisse aut verbis repeteret aut animo retineret...." (*Corp. chr. lat.* 148.133).

108. Salonius may have failed to subscribe to Ravennius' letter to Leo because he already had signed the one sponsored by Mamertus (see n.72 above). This seems not to have prevented him from taking part in the council on Lérins, in which his prior residence at the monastery would have given him a personal interest. Salonius also was a relative of Valerianus of Cimiez, one of those directly concerned. Perhaps he even was representing Valerianus, who did not attend the council. Zoticus is otherwise unknown.

that these sets of such similar circumstances would have occurred at two different times but a few years apart.

Support for the simultaneity of these two meetings also comes from Ravennius' invitation. For one thing, Ravennius' request that the bishops should "tire themselves out without interruption" over the Lérins case suggests not only that they already were in Arles on other business, but also that the other business had been completed. And finally, in 451, 30 December, the scheduled date for the council, did in fact fall on a Sunday.[109] It may be, therefore, that the council on Lérins met on 30 December 451, shortly after the bishops had completed the business of subscribing to the letter to Leo. Some of the bishops, such as Valerianus, who had attended the first meeting perhaps decided not to stay—after all, it was the Christmas season. This would explain why not all the signers of the Leo letter attended the Lérins council.

This reconstruction also can explain the unusual presence of Rusticus and his suffragans at the council on Lérins. With such an important prelate present in the city for the letter to Leo, Ravennius would have been hard-pressed to snub him when it came to issuing invitations to the council on Lérins, especially given that Rusticus had but recently played a role in Ravennius' own election as bishop. Furthermore, the council could have been viewed as a potential infringement on any authority which Ravennius' new ally Venerius of Marseilles, who perhaps already had returned home, might still claim in Narbonensis Secunda. Venerius' partisan Rusticus therefore could have attended *vice Venerii*. This would allow Ravennius to argue that Venerius' interests had in fact been represented. Of course, another possible explanation of Venerius' absence is that he simply refused to attend, in which case his rapprochement with Ravennius would have been short-lived indeed.

It would appear, moreover, that Theodorus chose a method similar to that of Mamertus for showing his displeasure with Ravennius. Soon after the council, in early 452, he, too, took it upon himself to send a letter of his own to Leo, which Leo answered on 10 June 452.[110] This letter was written on the pretext of obtaining answers to some questions of Theodorus about penitence, but one might wonder whether Theodorus also was wishing in this way to show that there was "noth-

---

109. See Bickerman, *Chronology* p.60, for the calculation. For the years 449 through 456, 451 was the only year when 30 December fell on a Sunday. Of course, not all church councils actually met on Sunday, but the scheduled date for the Gallic council of 442 also was on a Sunday (*Corp. chr. lat.* 148.86).

110. *Epist.* "Sollicitudinis quidem" (*P.L.* 54.1011-1014).

ing personal" in his failure to support Leo in Ravennius' letter of a few months before.[111] Leo's response also is noteworthy. After a perfunctory rebuke of Theodorus for not having consulted his metropolitan first—did he mean the bishop of Aix, Marseilles, or Arles?—Leo went on to answer Theodorus' questions anyway.[112]

CHURCH AND STATE IN THE 450S

If the evidence for Gallic ecclesiastical affairs in the 450s is sparse, that for the interaction between Gallic ecclesiastics and secular officialdom is virtually nonexistent. There are, however, indications that ecclesiastical and secular authorities continued to work together. In 451, as noted above, many bishops, presumably in the south, were attendant upon Aetius with various requests.[113] In northern Gaul, too, cordial relations existed between church and state officials, at least near Autun, for Hydatius reported, "At the time of the following Easter [in 451], certain things which were seen in the sky in the territory of Gaul are clearly described in a letter about them of Euphronius, bishop of Autun, sent to Count Agrippinus."[114]

Several conciliar canons from western Lugdunensis at this time also suggest that clerics could not resist becoming involved in secular affairs. The Council of Angers of 453 had to decree, "Clerics, too, who having abandoned their ecclesiastical office betake themselves to the laity and secular office are justifiably excluded from church."[115] This requirement was reiterated at the Council of Tours just eight years

111. Griffe, *Gaule* 2.178, sees the letter as intended simply "pour s'éclairer sur des points de discipline."

112. This example of continued local Gallic episcopal independence generally is overlooked: Jalland, *Leo* pp.140-143, for example, weakly suggests that Theodorus had written to Leo directly because he did not know who his metropolitan was. Griffe, *Gaule* 2.178, assumes the bishop of Aix was meant.

113. *VAniani* 7, see chapter 7 above, n.65, and Bardy et al., *Eglise* p.392. Heinzelmann, "Prosopographie" p.546, supposes that these meetings occurred in Arles. Note also a late tradition that "Arvatius," bishop of Tongres, went to Rome in a fruitless search for aid against the Huns (Greg. Tur. *H.F.* 2.5); he actually was Servatius, a fourth-century bishop (Duchesne, *Fastes* 3.188-189).

114. "in diebus insequentis paschae visa quaedam in caelo regionibus Galliarum epistola de his Eufroni Augustodunensis episcopi ad Agrippinum comitem facta evidenter ostendit" (*Chron.* 151). The Spaniards seem to have been in regular contact with Gaul: under the year 450 Hydatius noted, "de Gallis epistolae deferuntur Flaviani episcopi ad Leonem episcopum missae.... et Leonis ad eundem responsa, quae cum aliorum episcoporum et gestis et scriptis per ecclesias diriguntur" (ibid. 145). For other communications, see Mathisen, "Third Regnal Year" pp.332-334 and "Resistance" pp.618-620. For Agrippinus as the *comes Augustodunensis*, see Mathisen, "Resistance" pp.614-615.

115. "clerici quoque qui relicto clero se ad saecularem militiam et ad laicos contulerint, non iniuste ab ecclesia . . . amoventur" (can.7: *Corp. chr. lat.* 148.138).

later: "If any cleric . . . wishes to live the life of a layman, or to return to secular service, let him suffer the punishment of excommunication."[116] One can only wonder what kind of secular service these individuals were engaging in at a time when the Roman administration supposedly had vanished. The Council of Angers further ordered, "Moreover, if any are discovered to have been involved in the betrayal or the capture of cities, let them not only be excluded from communion, but they also ought not to be admitted as participants in any gatherings. . . ."[117]

Even more lamentable is the total lack of information on the position of the Gallic prelates during the reign of the Arvernian emperor Eparchius Avitus from June of 455 until October of 456.[118] Did many of the isolationist Gallic bishops side with the Gallic emperor? Any who had been unhappy with Leo of Rome's use of state authority on his own behalf ten years earlier could not but have been pleased to see the tables turned. What advantage, if any, they took of the situation is unknown. Nor is there any evidence that Avitus used his influence on behalf of one Gallic ecclesiastical faction or another: he may have been too concerned about his own status to become very involved in theirs.

Perhaps the most that can be said is that after Avitus' fall, Gallic aristocrats increasingly took refuge in the church. Avitus himself was forcibly consecrated bishop of Piacenza at the end of October, 456.[119] Circa 469 his son-in-law Sidonius Apollinaris not only became bishop of Avitus' birthplace Clermont, but also encouraged other powerful aristocrats to do likewise. Furthermore, the Eparchius whom Sidonius succeeded surely was another relative of the emperor, perhaps a brother, who already had entered the religious life. He may be the Eparchius who subscribed to Ravennius' letter to Leo of 451/452.[120]

Further insight into secular-ecclesiastical relations at this time may be gleaned from a curious tale involving the aforementioned Count Agrippinus and the abbot Lupicinus of St. Claude, just northeast of

116. "si quis vero clericus . . . laicam voluerit vitam, vel se militiae tradiderit, excommunicationis poena feriatur" (can.5: *Corp. chr. lat.* 148.145).

117. "tum si qui tradendis vel capiendis civitatibus fuerint interfuisse detecti, non solum a communione habeantur alieni, sed nec conviviorum quidem admittantur esse participes. . . ." (can.4: *Corp. chr. lat.* 148.138).

118. For Avitus' reign, see Mathisen, "Avitus" and "Third Regnal Year."

119. Eusebius of Milan presided over Avitus' own rather irregular ordination (*M.G.H. A.A.* 9.304). Eusebius had his own ties to Gaul, for Ceretius of Grenoble had left him a copy of Leo's letter to Flavianus. Perhaps he had ideas about reviving his predecessors' status in Gaul. For Avitus' fall, see Mathisen, "Third Regnal Year," and for Gaul afterward, see Mathisen, "Resistance" and "Sidonius."

120. *Corp. chr. lat.* 148.107-110; Duchesne, *Fastes* 2.34.

Lyons.[121] Agrippinus, it seems, had been a supporter of Avitus, whereas a rival of his, the general Aegidius, became an early protégé of the new emperor Majorian (457-461). Aegidius proceeded to accuse Agrippinus of various kinds of treachery, "[saying] that he, jealous of Roman authority, undoubtedly favored the barbarians and was attempting with clandestine plotting to detach provinces from Roman rule."[122] Agrippinus, accompanied by Lupicinus, then was taken under guard to Rome, where he was sentenced to death by the emperor and imprisoned to await execution. In the meantime, however, he was able to escape, and to take refuge in the church of St. Peter. Subsequently, with Lupicinus' help, he was pardoned, and he returned to Gaul "exalted with honors."[123] At the same time he probably also became the client of Ricimer. Although the details of this story might be questioned, it appears as if the ecclesiastical *topos* of appeals to Rome by disaffected clerics has here been applied by a hagiographer to a secular incident.[124]

Finally, there is the equally peculiar report that an archdeacon of Lyons requested the eastern emperor Leo to remit the taxes on the city, an incident which, if genuine, perhaps occurred c.457/458 as part of the revolt of Lyons against Ricimer and Majorian.[125] Now, if an archdeacon of Lyons were in Constantinople, it could only have been with the permission of his bishop, Patiens, and there is a known context in which this might have occurred. In the year 458, according to the *Chronicle* of Count Marcellinus, "the emperor Leo sent individual letters speaking out on behalf of the *Tome* of Chalcedon to individual orthodox bishops throughout the entire world, so that all might demonstrate in their own responses what they felt about this same *Tome*. He received the unanimous letters of all these bishops. . . ."[126] There is no record of any other possible Gallic response to this request, but if Patiens did send his archdeacon to Constantinople on this pretext, he also may have included a request for a remission of taxes.[127]

---

121. *VLupicini* 11-14; see Mathisen, "Resistance" pp.614-618.

122. "eo quod Romanis fascibus livens, barbaris procul dubio favens, subreptione clandestina provincias a publica niteretur ditione deiscere" (*VLupicini* 11).

123. "sublimatus honoribus" (*VLupicini* 14).

124. Agrippinus probably never went to Rome at all: see Mathisen, "Resistance" pp.614-618. The same source discussed Chelidonius' appeal to Leo.

125. Greg. Tur. *Glor. conf.* 62. For the revolt, see Mathisen, "Resistance" pp.604-614.

126. "Leo imperator pro tomo Chalcedonense per universum orbem singulis orthodoxorum episcopis singulas consonantesque misit epistulas, quo sibi quid de eodem tomo sentirent cuncti suis rescriptionibus indicarent. horum omnium episcoporum ita conspirantes suscepit epistulas. . . ." (*M.G.H. A.A.* 11.87).

127. Such a remission was in fact granted by Majorian in 459, see Mathisen, "Resistance" ibid.

BISHOP LEO AND GAUL AFTER
THE FALL OF AVITUS

For the years between 453 and 461 direct evidence about the ecclesiastical affairs of Gaul is limited to two letters of Leo.[128] They may indicate a shift in Leo's policy in Gaul as a result of Ravennius' failure not only to gain sufficiently timely support for Leo's *Epistula ad Flavianum*, but also to gain support for another of Leo's pet projects: a uniform date for Easter.[129] In the mid-440s, Leo had given his support to the Alexandrian method of determining the date for the festival, and in 451 he had written the letter "Ad praecipuum" to Ravennius announcing 23 March as the date of Easter for 452.[130] He had concluded his letter, "We wished notice of it also to be brought to all through Your Worship, dearest brother."[131]

Here, too, however, Ravennius again may have failed to deliver.[132] On 28 July 454, Leo sent another letter, "Cum in omnibus," announcing 24 April as the date of Easter for 455.[133] This letter not only asserted that Leo's date had the support of the emperor Marcian, it also wished to forestall the *praesumptio* of those who might prefer a different date. Both points might suggest that Leo felt that some Gauls needed further convincing. That Ravennius might have been one of them is suggested by the address of the letter. Whereas Leo's similar letter of 451 had been addressed to Ravennius alone, the second letter was addressed "to all the most beloved catholic bishops located throughout Gaul and Spain." Might this change suggest that Leo no longer considered Ravennius to be his spokesman in Gaul? Such a loss of favor already may have been hinted at in Leo's letter of 452,

128. See Jalland, *Leo* p.139. Leo may have been preoccupied by concerns closer to home: Attila's invasion of Italy in 452, the sack of Rome by the Vandals in 455, Avitus' assumption of power in 455-456, and the civil wars of 456-459. A final example of Leo's attitude to Gaul during this period is known only from a letter of his successor Hilarus and will be discussed in chapter 9 below.

129. It generally is assumed that Leo remained favorably disposed toward Ravennius, see McShane, *Romanitas* p.281.

130. *P.L.* 54.945. See also *M.G.H. A.A.* 9.755; Jaffé p.59 no.401 and p.61 no.414; and Mommsen, "Ostertafel" pp.589-601. For a possible involvement of Prosper of Aquitaine, see Bede, *De temporum ratione* 43 (*Corp.chr.lat.* 123B.417). For Leo's conflict with the bishop of Alexandria in 455, see Prosp. *Chron.* 1376. According to Leo, the problem had arisen because of a typographical error; see *P.L.* 54.1055, 1058, 1085 (Jaffé p.70 nos.496-498).

131. "cuius notitiam per dilectionem quoque tuam, frater carissime, omnibus voluimus declarari." For this letter as an indication that Ravennius still enjoyed Leo's favor, see Jalland, *Leo* p.138.

132. See Prinz, *Mönchtum* p.65, who suggests that Ravennius refused to cooperate.

133. *P.L.* 54.1101-1102. A similar letter to Britain also survives (Jaffé p.71 no.513: *Mon. hist. Brit.* 1.830).

"Impletis per," forwarding to Gaul the results of the Council of Chalcedon.[134] Whereas the addressees in the letter "Optassemus quidem" of 27 January 452 had begun with the names Ravennius, Rusticus, and Venerius, this shortly subsequent letter had the order changed, viz. Rusticus, Ravennius, and Venerius.[135]

In and of themselves, such variations might appear inconsequential, but Leo's other post-452 letter bears out the suggestion that he now was showing greater favor to Rusticus, whose influence and ambitions have been attested several times above. Leo's final extant letter to Gaul, probably dating to c.456/458, was addressed to Rusticus himself.[136]

In it Leo answered for Rusticus several questions of a theological nature, much as he had done for Theodorus of Fréjus in 452.[137] The contents also suggest, moreover, that Rusticus himself had fallen victim to dissension within his own city, for Leo noted:

We have read, then, what you stated in your entire letter and we have reviewed what took place at the investigation conducted by the bishops and leading men. We thus found out that the priests Sabinianus and Leo lacked confidence in what you were doing and that they had no just complaint left, because of their own accord they withdrew from the discussion that had been started. I leave to your determination what procedure and what measure of justice you should hold to in their regard.[138]

Rusticus, therefore, had been troubled by two rebellious presbyters, and to deal with them had summoned a council attended both by bishops and by high-ranking laymen.[139] The result of the council seems to have been that the two priests were overawed and withdrew.

The probable context for such resistance to a powerful bishop within his own church is the troubled time during and after Avitus' abortive snatch at imperial power in 455-456, for Narbonne seems to have been a stronghold of his support.[140] Furthermore, the subsequent

---

134. *A.C.O.* 2.4.155-156.

135. See Bardy, "Répercussions" p.31 n.21, who can respond only, "on ne saurait d'ailleurs pas répondre à cette question." Jalland, *Leo* p.39 n.102, attributes the discrepancy to Rusticus' being "senior by consecration," but whereas this certainly was true, it hardly explains the change, for in that case Rusticus should have preceded Ravennius in the earlier instances.

136. "Epistolas fraternitatis": *P.L.* 54.1199-1205. Leo's letter has been dated as early as c.450 (Griffe, "Pratique" p.250), but Leo's reference to persecution "by fire and sword" may be a reference to the Vandal sack of Rome in 455, and Jaffé's date of 458-459 (*Regesta* no.544 p.74, cf. *P.L.* 54.1198) has been used by Griffe himself, *Gaule* 2.178, 196 n.62, and Jalland, *Leo* p.143.

137. See Jalland, *Leo* pp.143-151.

138. "unde totius sermonis tui allegatione comperta [vel concepta] et gestis, quae in episcoporum honoratorumque examine confecta sunt, recensitis, Sabiniano et Leoni presbyteris actionis tuae intelleximus fiduciam defuisse: nec eis iustam superesse querimoniam, qui se ab inchoatis disceptationibus sponte subtraxerint. circa quos quam formam, quamve mensuram debeas tenere iustitiae, tuo relinquo moderamini. . . ."

139. Jalland, *Leo* p.143, suggests that the controversy concerned adultery.

140. See Mathisen, "Resistance" pp.598-607 and "Third Regnal Year."

"Marcellan conspiracy to seize the diadem" also seems to have been centered at Narbonne.[141] If Rusticus had supported Avitus, and been involved in the conspiracy, the failure of both may have emboldened his local opponents to resist him more openly.[142] The role of the *honorati* in the deliberations also could suggest that Leo's and Sabinianus' offenses were not entirely ecclesiastical, and had some connection with the political troubles of the times.[143] In the end, Rusticus was able to mobilize the local secular and ecclesiastical aristocracies on his behalf, and the resistance was crushed.

As portrayed by Leo, the dissension at Narbonne was so serious that Rusticus even expressed a desire to be relieved of his episcopal duties, to which Leo replied (*Epist.* "Epistolas fraternitatis"),

I am amazed that Your Worship is so overcome with tribulation from scandals, no matter from what occasion they may arise, that you say you desire rather to be freed from the labors of your bishopric and prefer to live in silence and leisure rather than continue handling those problems which were entrusted to you.[144]

Leo advised Rusticus that it is necessary to persevere, "when the ravages of persecution are inflicted by differences of character, by the perversity of the disobedient, and by the barbs of slanderous tongues."[145]

One might wonder, however, whether the strong-willed and ambitious Rusticus truly was nearly hounded from office. Might he rather have been deliberately misleading in the reasons he gave Leo for why he wished to resign, because he feared Leo would be less sympathetic to the real reasons? Perhaps the now elderly Rusticus, who had been in office since 427, intended to name his own successor while he was still alive. Leo, too, may have been dissimulating, pretending that Rusticus wished to retire because of the troubles of the times, and advising against it on these grounds, rather than simply forbidding him to do so, a demand which he had no means of enforcing.

The questions in the rest of Rusticus' letter dealt primarily with

---

141. Sid. Apoll. *Epist.* 1.11.6; see Mathisen, "Resistance" ibid.

142. Rusticus also suffered the presence of another presumptuous priest. In 450, the presbyter Othia dedicated a basilica between Narbonne and Béziers "anno xxxiii presbyteratus" (*C.I.L.* 12.4311). This method of dating is clearly modeled on Rusticus' own, but for a priest to do so is even more unprecedented. See Marrou, "Dossier" pp.346-348, for Othia's "autonomie."

143. Could this be the troublemaker Sabinianus alluded to by Sidonius (*Epist.* 3.6.3): "quamdiu nos Sabini familia rexerit, Sabiniani familiam non timendam"?

144. "miror autem dilectionem tuam in tantum scandalorum quacumque occasione nascentium adversitate turbari, ut vacationem ab episcopatus laboribus praeoptare te dicas, et malle in silentio atque otio vitam degere, quam in his quae tibi commissa sunt permanere. . . ." Note Rusticus' conventional assertion of the senatorial ideal: a desire to enjoy *otium*. See Griffe, *Gaule* 2.196.

145. "cum persecutionum saevitiam suppleant et dissimilitudines morum, et contumaciae inobedientium, et malignarum tela linguarum. . . ."

ecclesiastical practice, such as marriage and baptism. But the first one, with Leo's response, is potentially interesting:

> Concerning the priests, or deacons, who falsely claim to be bishops . . . there is no basis for considering those to be bishops who have been neither elected by the clergy, nor sought by the people, nor consecrated by the provincial bishops with the metropolitan presiding . . . Such an ordination must be considered void, which was neither based upon precedent nor supported by authority.[146]

Although Rusticus seems to have worded his query in general terms, he may have had some specific cases in mind. What he wanted, apparently, was prior approval for the deposition of bishops who, perhaps, had been consecrated without his approval.[147] He might have learned from the example of Hilary that it was prudent at least to have consulted the bishop of Rome ahead of time, even if he intended to proceed under any circumstances. If this were his purpose, he did obtain that much of what he wanted from Rome.

All in all, the fragmentary extant evidence would seem to indicate that, after a momentary revival in the early 450s, the policy of the bishop of Rome of favoring the bishop of Arles over his brethren again had gone into abeyance, and that Leo was treating with the Gallic bishops, whether Rusticus, Theodorus, or whomever, individually. Not since the time of Patroclus and Zosimus had there been a close working relationship between the sees of Arles and Rome. In Gaul, meanwhile, the church became increasingly factionally fragmented. The old Lérins faction broke into several splinters. In the south, it was rent by the quarrel between Faustus and Theodorus. To the north, old affiliates of Lérins began to go their own ways as well.

Ravennius did make a short-lived attempt to reassert the preëminence of the bishop of Arles, but after initially coming to terms with the bishops of Vienne and Narbonne, he was not able to maintain a leading role. By reasserting his metropolitan status in Viennensis, he gained the hostility of the bishop of Vienne, and after his unsatisfactory handling of the *Tome* and the dating of Easter he apparently lost the patronage of Leo. One of Ravennius' few successes was in inducing the bishop of Marseilles to abandon his customary policy of opposition to the bishop of Arles, although even this may not have lasted long. One price paid for it, however, was the recognition of some sort

146. "de presbytero, vel diacono, qui se episcopos esse mentiti sunt . . . nulla ratio sinit, ut inter episcopos habeantur, qui nec a clericis sunt electi, nec a plebibus expetiti, nec a provincialibus episcopis cum metropolitani iudicio consecrati. . . . vana habenda est ordinatio, quae nec loco fundata est, nec auctoritate munita."

147. Some of their sees may have been in the Visigothic kingdom, effectively outside Rusticus' direct control.

of continuing extraordinary status for Marseilles, which could only complicate southern Gallic ecclesiastical politics still further.

Additional evidence for the loss of ecclesiastical unity in southern Gaul, as well as for the loss of prestige and authority by the bishop of Arles, is seen in the apparent hiatus in the holding of southern Gallic councils. Between 439 and 451 no fewer than ten councils had been sponsored by the bishop of Arles.[148] This string of regular councils seems to have been brought to an end by that on Lérins. The next known Gallic council would not be assembled until 463. This interruption in church synods also suggests that consensus among the bishops of southern Gaul no longer could be reached in the decade and more after 451.

Such dissension within the ranks of the Gallic ecclesiastical establishment worked to the advantage of Leo, who expanded his supervisory role in Gaul at the request of the quarreling Gauls themselves, something he never had been able to do during the tenure of Hilary. After 450 the Gallic bishops, rather than settling any questions or quarrels among themselves, as they had done for the previous quarter century, began to turn to Leo as the deciding authority in matters of church doctrine and administration. As long as the Gauls could not resolve their own differences, the authority of the bishop of Rome in Gaul would continue to grow.

148. Including the council scheduled for 440 which was not held.

CHAPTER 9

LEONTIUS, MAMERTUS
AND INGENUUS

THE GROWTH OF
GERMANIC INTERFERENCE

In 460 or 461 the lackluster Ravennius of Arles died, and was succeeded by a certain Leontius.[1] Leontius' background is unknown; he might be the Leontius, a deacon of Arles, who attended the council of Vaison in 442.[2] Meanwhile, Leo of Rome died on 10 November 461, and was succeeded on 12 November by his archdeacon Hilarus.[3] Although little Gallic evidence for this period survives, Hilarus' own extant correspondence illustrates three cases in which he attempted to establish his authority in Gaul.[4]

HERMES OF NARBONNE

On 3 November 462, Hilarus wrote to Leontius rebuking him for not having consulted him, "Because, with a most shameful usurpation, a certain Hermes has presumed to the episcopate of the city of Narbonne with an execrable rashness. . . ."[5] Hilarus had only learned of the incident, he said, "from the deacon John, who was recom-

---

1. See Duchesne, *Fastes* 1.128,257. Kidd, *Church* p.359, dates the transfer too early, to 455, as does Langgärtner, *Gallienpolitik* p.92, who professes that Ravennius' successor is unknown. For the inaccuracy of the suggestion that he was succeeded by an Augustalis (actually of Toulon), see Duchesne, *Fastes* 1.257 n.3, and Thiel, *Epistolae* p.137 n.1.

2. *Corp. chr. lat.* 148.102. Perhaps he was related to Leontius of Fréjus (chapter 4 above, n.42).

3. Jaffé, *Regesta* p.75. Duchesne, *Fastes* 1.128, concludes that Ravennius died before Leo.

4. Thiel's 1867 edition is more complete and often preferable to that of Gundlach in *M.G.H. Epist.* 3.

5. "quod iniquissima usurpatione quidam Hermes episcopatum civitatis Narbonensis execrabili temeritate praesumpserit. . . ." (Hil. *Epist.* "Miramur fraternitatem": *M.G.H. Epist.* 3.22-23). See Demandt, "Magister militum" cols.690-691; Duchesne, *Fastes* 1.128-130; Griffe, *Gaule* 2.183-185; and Langgärtner, *Gallienpolitik* pp.93-95.

mended to us by our son, the magnificent man Fridericus, in his letter. . . ."[6] Now, this Fridericus, the so-called *filius* of Hilarus of Rome, can be none other than the Arian brother of the Visigothic king Theoderic II.[7]

The Hermes in question had had a long career as a cleric of Rusticus of Narbonne, and is attested as a deacon in 445, an archdeacon in the late 450s, and finally a presbyter soon after.[8] Circa 460, he was made bishop of the nearby city of Béziers, located just northeast of Narbonne.[9] The ties between the aristocratic circles, at least, of Béziers and Narbonne seem to have been quite close. Sidonius Apollinaris noted in the early 460s that littérateurs from both cities socialized with each other.[10] Furthermore, Hermes' predecessor seems to have been a Dynamius, probably the same bishop Dynamius who in 445 was one of the many to contribute to Rusticus' church-building activities in Narbonne.[11] Rusticus, therefore, probably had some influence in Béziers, a conclusion also suggested by the propinquity of the two cities, and Hermes presumably became bishop of the city with Rusticus' support and blessing.[12] Then, after Rusticus' death in 461, Hermes abandoned his post at Béziers and was made bishop of Narbonne.[13]

Hilarus' immediate response to Fridericus' report was to dash off the aforementioned letter to Leontius of Arles, berating him for having allowed this to occur and for having done nothing about it "because you either do not wish to or are unable to."[14] He demanded, "Making no excuses, send to us an account, signed by your own hand, not only of Your Worship but also of our brothers, either through the bearer of my letter or through one whom you yourself choose. . . ."[15]

6. "a diacono Iohanne, qui a magnifico viro filio nostro Friderico litteris suis nobis insinuatus est. . . ." (ibid.).

7. Fridericus: *P.L.R.E. II* p.484. Wenzlowsky, *Päpstbriefe* 6.38 n.1, suggests that the appellation "our son" indicates that Fridericus was Catholic; for denial, see Langgärtner, *Gallienpolitik* pp.94, 98-99 n.29.

8. Deacon: Marrou, "Dossier" pp.332,339; in the mid to late 450s he traveled to Rome as an archdeacon (Leo *Epist.* "Epistolas fraternitatis": *P.L.* 54.1199); and as a presbyter he dedicated an altar in the chapel of St. Lupus in Narbonne (*C.I.L.* 12.5338).

9. Duchesne, *Fastes* 1.128-129, 309.

10. *Epist.* 8.4.2: "nunc Narbonensibus cantitanda, nunc Biterrensibus."

11. Duchesne, *Fastes* 1.309 n.3; *C.I.L.* 12.5336. Marrou, "Dossier" p.340, suggests the Dynamius of 445 was the presumably long-dead Dynamius of Angoulême (chapter 3 above, n.22).

12. For other bishops supported by Rusticus, see chapter 6 above, nn.18-19.

13. Leo of Rome died just after having learned of Hermes' ordination (Hil. *Epist.* "Quamquam notitiam": *M.G.H. Epist.* 3.25-28). Rusticus' death, therefore, probably occurred circa mid-461.

14. "si ipse aut non vis aut non potes" (Hil. *Epist.* "Miramur fraternitatem": *M.G.H. Epist.* 3.22-23).

15. "seposita excusatione, ad nos tam tuae dilectionis quam fratrum nostrorum aut per portitorem litterarum, aut per quem ipse elegeritis, subscriptam manuum vestrarum relationem transmittatis. . . ." (ibid.). Wallace-Hadrill, "Gothia" p.230, asserts that Hilarus wrote to Leontius

Long before Leontius could have replied to this letter, however, Hilarus had an opportunity to take the matter even further into his own hands when there arrived in Rome two Gallic bishops, Faustus and Auxanius. Faustus, ex-abbot of Lérins, had succeeded his mentor Maximus as bishop of Riez, perhaps c.455.[16] Like other Lerinenses who became bishops, he continued his monastic practices in his new office. Sidonius later said to him, "You have transferred [the island prayers] from the exercise ground of the monastic congregation and from the senate of Lérins into your city. Nothing of the abbot has been lost in the bishop. . . ."[17] Faustus also maintained his ties with his island confrères by regular visits.[18] Auxanius' see is uncertain; he may have been bishop of Apt.[19]

The two Gauls then attended a church council held at Rome on 19 November 462, barely two weeks after Hilarus had sent his initial letter about Hermes to Leontius.[20] Here Hilarus took it upon himself to introduce several measures involving the Gallic church, not the least of which concerned the case of Hermes of Narbonne. Hilarus presumably would have welcomed the Gauls at his synod, for it would have imparted an appearance of Gallic participation to the proceedings.

On 3 December Hilarus then wrote another letter, addressed to the bishops of Viennensis, Lugdunensis, Narbonensis Prima and Secunda, and Alpes "Poeninae."[21] This letter indicates that Hilarus had acted

---

"ordering him to remove his suffragan of Narbonne"; this is doubly wrong: Hilarus issued no such order, and Hermes was not Leontius' suffragan.

16. This is Faustus' first attestation as bishop; see Duchesne, *Fastes* 1.284. Some suggest, without grounds, that he was bishop as early as c.452; see Bergmann, *Predigtliteratur* p.119, and Koch, *Faustus* pp.13-14. For the date, see appendix "Episcopal Hierarchy" below.

17. "quas de palaestra congregationis heremitidis et de senatu Lirinensium cellulanorum in urbem quoque . . . transtulisti, nil ab abbate mutatus per sacerdotem. . . ." (*Epist.* 9.3.4).

18. Sid. Apoll. *Carm.* 16.104-106, "Lirinus . . . qua . . . saepe . . . venis"; see also *Epist.* 9.9.13.

19. An Auxanius appears at this time in some unreliable *fasti* of Apt, see Duchesne, *Fastes* 1.282 n.5 and chapter 10 below, n.74. For Auxanius as bishop of either Apt or Aix, see Thiel, *Epistolae* p.143, and for him as bishop of Aix, see Griffe, *Gaule* 2.174 n.11; Koch, *Faustus* p.13; Langgärtner, *Gallienpolitik* p.94; and Palanque, "Evêchés" pp.124, 125, 129. Aix, however, is impossible, because Basilius was bishop of Aix c.470, at the Council of Arles, which Auxanius also attended. Palanque, "Evêchés" pp.123-128, however, argues that the Auxanius of 462/464 is not the Auxanius of c.470. Even if this were the case, the Auxanius of 462/464 still could not have been bishop of Aix, for at the council of 463, metropolitan bishops were named first (see nn.37-38 below), but Auxanius' name appears far down the list.

20. Council: Hilarus *Epist.* "Etsi meminerimus" (*M.G.H. Epist.* 3.29-30) and *Epist.* "Quamquam notitiam" (ibid.3.25-28). In the latter, some mss. read "praesidentibus" for "praesentibus" (the reading preferred by Gundlach and Thiel), and this has led some erroneously to suppose that Faustus and Auxanius presided at the council; the occurrence of the word "praeside" in the previous line probably caused the error. Hefele-Leclercq, *Conciles* 2.900, groundlessly assert that there was "un grand nombre" of Gallic bishops at the council.

21. "Quamquam notitiam": *M.G.H. Epist.* 3.25-28. Hilarus' geography is faulty: the province of Alpes Poeninae no longer existed.

rashly in his initial response. What had happened, Hilarus now confessed, was that "previously, therefore, the rulers of the aforementioned cities [viz. Narbonne and Béziers] reported even then their problems to my predecessor [Leo] of hallowed memory no less than to me, by daring to pursue with illicit petitions that which scarcely may be granted leniency by the lone plea of necessity."[22] Both petitions, it seems, favored Hermes' transferal. Hilarus went on to give Hermes' side of the story: the trouble had arisen "because our brother, now, and fellow bishop Hermes believed that he had been received by the Narbonese church legally because, he says, he was wrongly expelled by the inhabitants of Béziers, by whom he had been ordained."[23] It is striking how Hermes, in the eyes of Hilarus, had gone from "quidam" to "coepiscopus noster." Regardless of the circumstances of his "expulsion" from Béziers, Hermes, the ranking member of the party of Rusticus, presumably would have been happy to obtain in exchange the much more prestigious see of Narbonne.

There remain to be considered the particular roles of Faustus and Auxanius. Hilarus' reference in the same letter to the "opinion which we brought forth after the testimony of both delegations which had been sent here" sometimes has been taken to mean that Faustus and Auxanius were official Gallic delegates in the Hermes case, sent in response to Hilarus' order.[24] This reference, however, probably is to the aforementioned delegations from Béziers and Narbonne. It surely would have been very irregular for Faustus and Auxanius to be participating in the decision, as Hilarus stresses they did, if they were the appellants. Furthermore, there would not have been time for an official delegation to be assembled and sent: Hilarus did not write to Leontius until 3 November and Faustus and Auxanius already had arrived by the date of the council, 19 November. Finally, Hilarus elsewhere referred to "all those matters which were considered by us with our brothers and fellow bishops Faustus and Auxanius."[25] The two, therefore, participated in other matters besides the Hermes case, and

22. "olim igitur urbium praesides praedictarum sanctae memoriae decessori meo non minus quam nobis, etiamtunc attulerunt dolores, illicitis petitionibus audendo prosequi, quod vix apud patientiam nostram solum necessitatum potuit deploratione leniri...." (ibid.). For "praesides," Gundlach reads "praesidum desideria." The Ballerini (*P.L.* 54.1231-1232) date the appeals to 460, with Rusticus still alive; this would imply that Leo then did nothing for a year or more.

23. "cum ideo se frater iam et coepiscopus noster Hermes a Narbonensi ecclesia credidit iure suscipi, quia indigne a Biterrensibus, quibus ordinatus est, dicebat excludi...." (Hil. *Epist.* "Quamquam notitiam": *M.G.H. Epist.* 3.25-28).

24. "sententia, quam sub adsertione utriusque legationis inde directae ... protulimus" (ibid.). Gundlach's reading "adsertione" is to be preferred to Thiel's "adversione." See Duchesne, *Fastes* 1.130; Koch, *Faustus* p.13; Langgärtner, *Gallienpolitik* pp.94, 102; and Thiel, *Epistolae* p.143 n.8.

25. "omnia quae a nobis sunt per fratres et coepiscopos nostros Faustum et Auxanium definita" (*Epist.* "Etsi meminerimus": *M.G.H. Epist.* 3.29-30).

Hilarus gives no indication that they had any personal or particular concern in it.

The Barbarian Factor

Those who wrote Leo to obtain *ex post facto* approval for Hermes' irregular move may have been anticipating appeals to Rome by his enemies, who perhaps included Rusticus' nemeses Leo and Sabinianus, as well as the deacon John. This is exactly what happened in 462, when John, with the support of the Visigoth Fridericus, complained to Hilarus. Such unprecedented Germanic interference would have followed immediately upon the cession of the city to the Visigoths in this very year.[26] The Gothic presence gave the losers in the Narbonese disputes an added opportunity: now they could appeal not only to Rome, but also to the barbarians. For fifty years the Germans had limited their involvement to secular affairs; they now were to become interested in the ecclesiastical sphere as well.[27]

Nor would Fridericus have been loathe to lend his support, for Hermes, it seems, was involved with the established Gallo-Roman, and anti-German, aristocracy of Narbonne.[28] In his description of the literary circle of Narbonne, Sidonius included Hermes along with such as Magnus (who had been Avitus' master of offices and Majorian's Gallic prefect) and Avitus' *cura palatii* Consentius.[29] Hermes hardly could escape being labeled as a Roman sympathizer. He also might have inherited the same independence of action which had characterized his predecessor Rusticus. All this could have made him *persona non grata* with the Visigoths.

In this instance, however, neither Fridericus nor Hilarus could take any effective action. Fridericus soon was dead, and Hilarus, lacking influential Gallo-Roman support, could do nothing more than accept the *fait accompli*. There is no evidence that Leontius of Arles either disapproved of Hermes' election, much less desired to take action against him, or ever forwarded the *relatio* requested by Hilarus in his first letter on the matter.

Hilarus did attempt to save face by declaring Hermes relieved of his position as metropolitan of Narbonensis Prima. In doing so he

26. Hydatius, *Chron.* 217; see Mathisen, "Resistance" pp.614-618.

27. At the same time, they were becoming more acceptable in Gallo-Roman aristocratic circles, see Sid. Apoll. *Epist.* 1.2, 4.17.

28. In the recent past, Narbonne had fiercely resisted the Visigoths, see Sid. Apoll. *Carm.* 7.475-480; 22 *epist.* 1; 23.59-79.

29. Sid. Apoll. *Carm.* 23.436-487. For the Narbonese faction in imperial politics, see Mathisen, "Resistance" pp.598-604, and for these individuals, see also the appropriate entries in *P.L.R.E. II*.

adopted the same method as Leo had in 445 in his quarrel with Hilary of Arles (*Epist.* "Quamquam notitiam"):

From him who now is allowed to preside over the church of Narbonne we remove, because of these perverse deeds, the right of ordaining bishops, which we decree now belongs to our brother and fellow bishop Constantius, overseer of the church of Uzès, because he is said to be primate because of his tenure in office. . . .[30]

Hilarus also decreed that after Hermes' death, metropolitan status would return to his successor.

This Constantius had been an old partisan of Hilary of Arles, in whose favor he had abandoned his legitimate metropolitan Rusticus. Constantius even had traveled to Rome on Hilary's behalf in 446. None of these actions would have endeared him to the party of Rusticus and Hermes, and the antipathy they may have felt toward Constantius could have made Hilarus' decree doubly galling. As in the case of Hilary of Arles, however, there is no indication that Hilarus' decision ever went into effect. Constantius, as the elderly bishop of an outlying and very minor see, and no longer backed by the powerful Lérins faction of Hilary's day, very probably would have had little opportunity to exercise the metropolitan status so magnanimously granted him by Hilarus.

As for Hermes, his influence probably was more effectively curtailed by the Visigothic expansion. Now that nearly the entire province, including his own see, was under Gothic control, he no longer could hope to play the important role in Gallic ecclesiastical politics that his predecessor Rusticus had. The bishop of Narbonne took no known part in Gallic ecclesiastical activities for the next forty years.[31]

MAMERTUS OF VIENNE

Barbarian interference occurred again in a case involving ecclesiastical jurisdiction in Viennensis. In a letter dated 10 October 463 and addressed, again, to Leontius of Arles, Hilarus complained about the ordination by Mamertus of Vienne of a new bishop, Marcellus, for the

---

30. "ei qui nunc ecclesiae Narbonensi praesidere permittitur, ordinandorum episcoporum, ob haec quae prave facta sunt, sustulimus potestatem, quam ita ad fratrem et coepiscopum nostrum Constantium Uceticae ecclesiae antistitem, quia aevo honoris primas esse dicitur, pertinere censuimus. . . ." Constantius had been in office since c.430 (see below, appendix "Episcopal Hierarchy"), and undoubtedly was the provincial primate: see Thiel, *Epistolae* pp.143-144 n.10. Duchesne, *Fastes* 1.130, suggests that Hilarus chose Constantius because Uzès was still in Roman hands.

31. See Duchesne, *Fastes* 1.303-304. For Narbonne under the Goths, see Greg. Tur. *Glor. mart.* 92.

city of Die. According to Leo's division of 450, Die was supposed to be overseen by the bishop of Arles. Nevertheless, the source of the complaint was not Leontius, who presumably would have been the aggrieved party. It came instead from a rather unexpected quarter:

Indeed, it has been pointed out by the report of my son, the illustrious master of soldiers Gundioc, how the aforementioned bishop [sc. Mamertus], against the will of the inhabitants of Die, who do not in fact, as I read in our chancery, belong to his allocation of churches, which the authority of the apostolic see granted to him, occupying the city, so it is said, in a hostile manner, presumed to ordain the bishop.[32]

Hilarus went on to request Leontius to investigate the matter at a church council and to learn there from Mamertus himself exactly why this irregularity had occurred. Leontius then was to inform Hilarus of his findings, "so that I may ordain what must be done to repress illicit endeavors."[33]

In this instance, a synod actually did convene, probably in November 463, to discuss the Mamertus affair. It was attended by twenty-one bishops from the provinces of Viennensis, Narbonensis Secunda, and Alpes Maritimae.[34] Significantly, some names are noticeably lacking. Neither Mamertus and his suffragans, nor Marcellus the newly consecrated bishop of Die, attended. The name of Leontius of Arles, whom Hilarus painstakingly attempted to depict as the aggrieved party, is absent as well.[35] Therefore, both parties whom Hilarus had specifically instructed to attend the council chose not to do so.

The names of those who did attend are equally interesting. The

32. "quantum enim filii nostri, viri illustris, magistri militum Gunduici sermone est indicatum, praedictus episcopus invitis Deensibus, et qui ad ecclesiarum eius numerum, quas ei apostolicae sedis deputavit auctoritas, sicut in scriniis nostris legimus, minime pertinebat, hostili more, ut dicitur, occupans civitatem, episcopum consecrare praesumpsit. . . ." (Hil. *Epist.* "Qualiter contra sedis": *M.G.H. Epist.* 3.28-29). Hilarus uses against Mamertus the same rhetoric Leo used against Hilary in 445; see Heinzelmann, *Bishchofsherrschaft* p.226: Hilarus presumably had found that letter in the chancery as well. See also Demandt, "Magister militum" col.694; Duchesne, *Fastes* 1.129-131; Griffe, *Gaule* 2.163, 270; and Langgärtner, *Gallienpolitik* pp.98-101. Thiel, *Epistolae* p.147 n.3, interprets the appellation *filius noster* to mean that Gundioc was a Catholic at the time.

33. "ut quod . . . faciendum est ad comprimendos conatos illicitos ordinemus."

34. The attendees are inferred from the addressees of Hilarus' letter "Sollicitis admodum" (*M.G.H. Epist.* 3.30-32) sent back to them, with the addition of Antonius, who delivered the letter to Rome.

35. It always has been assumed that the bishop Leontius, whose name appears last, is Leontius of Arles; see Duchesne, *Fastes* 1.130; Hefele-Leclercq, *Conciles* 2.902; Langgärtner, *Gallienpolitik* p.99; and Griffe, *Gaule* 2.167. This is impossible for two reasons: 1) protocol would not have allowed Leontius of Arles' name to be placed last, especially when the names of other metropolitans head the list, and 2) the list of bishops attending the Council of Arles of c.470 (chapter 10 below) has two Leontii: one who heads the list, certainly Leontius of Arles, and another of an unknown see who appears further down, in the same position as that held by the Leontius of 463, who therefore cannot be Leontius of Arles.

first four in the list are Victurus, Ingenuus, Hydatius, and Eustasius. Of these, Ingenuus and Eustasius are identifiable as the bishops of Embrun and Marseilles respectively. Hydatius probably is the Hydatius who subscribed to Ravennius' letter to Leo of 451/452, and his see is uncertain. This leaves Victurus, who heads the list. In an attempt to identify him, one first might note that Eustasius of Marseilles clearly has been accorded some kind of exceptional status in the list, because if his hierarchical rank had been determined solely by his tenure in office, Fonteius of Vaison should have ranked ahead of him.[36] Eustasius, therefore, seems here still to have been granted the irregular metropolitan status which had been held by his predecessors Proculus and Venerius.

Now, if Eustasius was accorded metropolitan status, the three bishops who precede him of necessity must have had it as well. Once it is agreed that the first four names are those of metropolitans, it then might be suggested that the bishop of Aix was none other than the Victurus whose name came first.[37] If the ordering of the names of the metropolitans were determined by their tenures in office, moreover, Victurus then would have been ordained before Ingenuus, who had been consecrated in 439.[38]

Hydatius' own claims to metropolitan status could have been justified if he were the bishop of Tarentaise in Alpes Graiae. If so, he may have been taking the opportunity to emphasize his independence of Vienne, to which his city had been apportioned by Leo. It is noteworthy that even in those instances where the suffragans of Vienne displayed obvious solidarity with their metropolitan, as in their letter to Leo of c.452, the bishop of Tarentaise never appears. He may have been holding aloof from his would-be metropolitan, much as the bishop of Aix had refused to cooperate with the bishop of Arles. If this were so, Hydatius' signature to Ravennius' letter to Leo in 451/452 also now can be seen as a declaration of his independence.

Perhaps the most noteworthy thing about the council is that it met at all. After all, the sees of the two individuals most concerned, Mamertus and Marcellus, both were in Viennensis. None of the metropolitans who attended, however, claimed any jurisdiction there. In-

---

36. When Fonteius signed the letter to Leo of 451/452, Eustasius' predecessor Venerius still was alive.

37. Given that his name was first, one also could suggest that the council was held at Aix. Langgärtner, *Gallienpolitik* p.101, identifies Victurus as Victurius of Le Mans, but this would be impossible if Victurus were a metropolitan. The Victurus who signed Ravennius' letter to Leo in 451/452 may be this one, or Victurius of Le Mans, who attended the councils of Angers (453) and Tours (461) (Duchesne, *Fastes* 2.336-337).

38. What is known of the other bishops is consistent with this hypothesis: Ingenuus first appears in 439, Hydatius in 451/452, and Eustasius not until later.

genuus of Embrun, accompanied by at least two of his suffragans (Veranus of Vence and Memorialis of Digne), had authority only in Alpes Maritimae. Victurus, if he was in fact bishop of Aix, was metropolitan only in Narbonensis Secunda, whence came also Faustus of Riez and perhaps Auxanius. From Viennensis came Eustasius of Marseilles, Fonteius of Vaison, Eutropius of Orange, and Paulus of Trois-Châteaux.[39] Of these, Eustasius did have some pretensions to metropolitan power, but not in Viennensis.

Supposedly, the Viennese bishops were suffragans of Leontius of Arles: what were they doing at a council from which their own metropolitan was pointedly absent? Do they represent an anti-Leontian faction within Leontius' own province? Eutropius, at least, was a protégé of Eustasius. After "serving for a time in secular office," he had been forcibly ordained a deacon: "He did not escape the notice of that noteworthy man, the blessed Eustasius, bishop of Marseilles . . . he is seized by order of the bishop."[40]

In the Roman opinion, at least, these bishops should have had no jurisdiction in the affair. After all, Leo already had decreed that bishops, and especially metropolitans, of one province were absolutely forbidden to interfere in the ecclesiastical affairs of another. Nevertheless, once it became clear that Leontius was not going to summon the council that Hilarus had demanded, these neighboring metropolitans may have seized the opportunity to exhibit their own authority and independence by doing so themselves, without either Leontius or Mamertus. They may, however, have had little else upon which to agree. The bishops of Marseilles, Embrun, and Aix all would have had concerns of their own. Eustasius may have seen this council, in the absence of Leontius, as an opportunity to reestablish the status of his own see in the south. The only claim of his see to metropolitan authority, however, had been in the province of Narbonensis Secunda, and this may have brought him into conflict with the bishop of Aix. Moreover, as will be seen, Eustasius and Ingenuus seem to have been in the midst of a quarrel of their own over the see of Nice.

Given their lack of authority to act, as well as the possible disharmony among them, the bishops must have been aware that there was little they could accomplish without the cooperation of Leontius or

39. The Viventius named in the sixth position cannot be Viventius of Grenoble (Duchesne, *Fastes* 1.231): he precedes Veranus, who c.451/452 subscribed to the letter to Leo while Ceretius of Grenoble was still alive. Viventius of Grenoble must be a second Viventius, who subscribed after this Viventius at the Council of Arles of c.470. For Paulus, see chapters 7 above (n.94) and 10 below.

40. "aliquandiu saeculo serviens . . . sanctum Eustasium Massiliensium episcopum virum eximium non latuit . . . rapitur iussu pontificis" (*VEutropii* p.54). See Palanque, *Marseilles* p.21. For forcible ordinations into lesser orders, see chapter 5 above, n.68.

Mamertus. The most they could do was to refer the case back to Hilarus, whose own desire to show authority in Gaul apparently led him to recognize the validity of this irregular council. On 24 February 464 he replied: "Therefore, as both the account of Your Worship and the recommendation of our brother and fellow bishop Antonius has disclosed, let it be clear that the aforementioned bishop [sc. Mamertus], by desiring [to have] more, desires to lose his privileges, which had been enclosed within fixed boundaries...."[41] Hilarus went on to say that Marcellus also deserved to be removed as bishop of Die.

In an effort to compel Mamertus to comply, Hilarus cited the example of Hilary of Arles, and asked: "Does not the bishop Mamertus remember that the status of the church of Vienne was raised once because of the transgression of the bishop of Arles?"[42] He also subsequently threatened twice that further such infractions by Mamertus would result in his metropolitan privileges being returned to Arles. Hilarus, like Leo, saw grants of metropolitan status as one of his few negotiating tools. Hilarus concluded by demanding from Mamertus a statement "in which he will testify that the will of the apostolic see always must be obeyed."[43]

Hilarus also, however, realized the impossibility of taking any concrete action, and ultimately could do no more than recognize the status quo: "Wherefore, dearest brothers, it is fitting to tolerate the presumption of the aforementioned individual, which led to the disgrace of our brother and fellow bishop Leontius, as being now immune, for the time being, from a worthy retribution...."[44] In the end, the ordination stood and both Mamertus and Marcellus went unpunished.[45]

Once again, the bishop of Rome was unable to exercise any effective

---

41. "sicut ergo et vestrae dilectionis relatio et fratris et coepiscopi nostri Antonii insinuatio reseravit, claret praedictum privilegia certis conclusa terminis velle perdere plus volendo...." (Hil. Epist. "Sollicitis admodum": M.G.H. Epist. 3.30-32). The bishop Antonius, of an unknown see, carried the council's report to Rome. His verbal account was referred to by Hilarus as an *insinuatio*, the same word Hilarus used for the reports of Fridericus (Epist. "Miramur fraternitatem": M.G.H. Epist. 3.22-23) and Gundioc (Epist. "Qualiter contra sedis": M.G.H. Epist. 3.28-29).

42. "non dignitatem Viennensis ecclesiae Mamertus episcopus meminit Arelatensis antistitis quondam transgressione crevisse?" (Epist. "Sollicitis admodum").

43. "qua definitionem sedis apostolicae ... semper conservandam ... testetur" (ibid.).

44. "unde, fratres carissimi, praesumptionem praedicti, quae in fratris et coepiscopi nostri Leontii processit iniuriam, ita convenit tolerari, dignae nunc interim ultionis immunem...." (ibid.). See also Epist. "Etsi meminerimus": "de cuius facto vindictae congruae sententiam differentes."

45. The conventional view is that Hilarus was in full control. Griffe, Gaule 2.270, concludes that Hilarus allowed the ordination to stand because Marcellus was "un homme méritant." Duchesne, Fastes 1.130-131, suggests that Hilarus was inclined to leniency by "renseignements favorables" given by the courier Antonius. For the lack of effect, see Thiel, Epistolae p.150 n.12, who also supposes that Die remained under Vienne.

authority in Gaul. As in the past, he had seized an opportunity to
intervene there without first ascertaining how much real support he
had. In this instance he had been motivated by the report of another
barbarian. Die, like Narbonne, had but recently fallen to the Germans.[46] Unlike the Visigoth Fridericus at Narbonne, however, the
new ruler of Die, the Burgundian Gundioc, was not only a barbarian
king, but also a legitimate Roman official, a master of soldiers.[47] His
ambiguous position could have made the local networks of loyalty and
authority even more confused at Die than they had been at Narbonne.[48] After their candidate lost to Marcellus, disaffected locals at
Die may have found in this situation an additional opportunity for an
appeal, and Gundioc, like Fridericus, was happy to lend his support.[49]
The existence of such an anti-Marcellan faction is attested in the *Vita
Marcelli* itself, which recalled the strife over Marcellus' election:
"Therefore, as customarily occurs in the election of a bishop, when
one man is sought, part of the people turns to another. . . ."[50]

The newly elected bishop Marcellus, of course, surely would have
had his own supporters in the city, and all the more so because he was
the brother of his predecessor Petronius.[51] This Petronius, moreover,
himself may have had Arlesian connections: in 441 a deacon Petronius
accompanied Hilary to the Council of Orange, and in 442 a presbyter
Petronius, presumably the same man, went with him to Vaison.[52] If
so, Marcellus too may have had similar ties to Arles which caused
Leontius to be content with his ordination.[53] Even if Hilarus viewed
the ordination as an injury to Leontius, the latter apparently did not,

46. See Duchesne, *Fastes* 1.129.

47. Gundioc: *P.L.R.E. II* pp.523-524. Gundioc also was an ally of the Visigoths (*Auct. Prosp.
Haun.* s.a.457: *M.G.H. A.A.* 9.305).

48. Some Gallo-Roman senators, at least, had cooperated with Gundioc's Burgundians and
divided their land with them (Mar. Avit. *Chron.* s.a.456: *M.G.H. A.A.* 11.232; see Goffart, *Barbarians* p.107).

49. Duchesne, *Fastes* 1.129, sees Gundioc, and Fridericus, as portraying themselves as "les
champions de la discipline canonique" in an attempt to rid themselves of patriotic pro-Roman
bishops. Heinzelmann, *Bischofsherrschaft* p.226, suggests that Gundioc's appeal was motivated by
a concern over Mamertus' supposed use of soldiers.

50. Ch.3: "igitur, ut adsolet in electione pontificis, dum unus petitur, pars populi vertitur in
alterum. . . ." (Dolbeau, "Marcel" p.115; Kirner, *Due vite* p.304). Dolbeau (p.112) suggests that
the author of the *vita* may have had access to Hilarus' letter. A canon of the "Second Council of
Arles" recognized that the *topos* of unanimity might not always be fulfilled: "quod si inter partes
aliqua fuerit nata dubitatio, maiori numero metropolitanus in electione consentiat" (can.5: *Corp.
chr. lat.* 148.115).

51. *VMarcelli* 2: Dolbeau, "Marcel" p.114. Marcellus was said to have been a native of
Avignon.

52. *Corp. chr. lat.* 148.87, 102.

53. Marcellus later went into exile at Arles (Dolbeau, "Marcel" p.118). Duchesne, *Fastes*
1.129, attributes Leontius' acquiescence to his patriotic desire to forestall barbarian inroads;
Griffe, *Gaule* 2.163, to "les circonstances politiques."

and did nothing. Indeed, this lack of response may be behind Hilarus' references to Leontius' "moderation."[54] As for Gundioc, after reporting to Hilarus, he was unwilling, or unable, to take any further action.

In an effort to find some Gallic support, Hilarus did appoint a Gallic mediator: "Whence, holding to the authority of our moderation, we have sent letters to our brother and fellow bishop Veranus to the effect that he should meet with the aforementioned individual [sc. Mamertus] so that he might be informed as to what you have decided about him."[55] Veranus of Vence would have been a reasonable choice for Hilarus to use as his go-between for several reasons. First of all, Veranus had known ties to Rome. In the early 450s, as will be seen, he had been responsible for writing a letter to Leo on behalf of the authority of Ingenuus of Embrun. Veranus also was familiar with the case, having been one of the attendees at the Gallic council on the matter in 463. Finally, Veranus would have been perceived as having some influence with Mamertus, for c.452 he, along with Mamertus, Ceretius, and his brother Salonius, had subscribed to the separate letter to Leo.[56] Whether Veranus ever had any such meeting with Mamertus is unknown. If he did, one might suspect that it would have had as little effect as the other measures taken to control Mamertus.

Realizing how little support he had in Gaul, Hilarus ultimately could only proclaim, "It has been decreed also by the law of the Christian princes that whatever the bishop of the apostolic see has promulgated in his examination for the elimination of disputes is to be accepted reverently...."[57] This secular authority, however, would have been a good deal weaker in Gaul in 463 than it had been in 445, when Leo had relied upon it himself.

CHURCH AND STATE IN THE 460S

Any authority of the imperial government in Gaul in the early 460s would have been minimal, even though the political relations between Gaul and Italy remained a very real concern. After the fall of Majorian, the Gallic generalissimo Aegidius had rebelled openly against

54. *Epist.* "Sollicitis admodum": "cum ... Leontii moderatio formam continentiae praebere debuerit ambienti [sc. Mamerto]."

55. "unde moderationis nostrae nomen tenentes, ad Veranum fratrem et coepiscopum nostrum scripta direximus, ut praedictum ex nostra delegatione conveniat, quatenus quid de eo retuleritis agnoscat...." (*Epist.* "Sollicitis admodum": *M.G.H. Epist.* 3.32).

56. For Veranus' "crédit particulier auprès de Mamert," see Duchesne, *Fastes* 1.131. Letter: chapter 8 above, n.71.

57. "Christianorum quoque principum lege decretum est, ut quidquid ... in auferendis confusionibus apostolicae sedis antistes suo pronuntiasset examine, veneranter accipi...." (*Epist.* "Sollicitis admodum": *M.G.H. Epist.* 3.30-32).

Ricimer and the Italian government, and even gone so far as to enter
into negotiations with the Vandals.[58] Ricimer's only powerful Gallo-
Roman ally seems to have been Aegidius' rival Agrippinus, who in
462 had surrendered Narbonne to the Visigoths on the patrician's behalf.[59] Ricimer had another Gallic ally in the Visigothic king Theoderic, who was induced, in part by the cession of Narbonne, to send
his brother Fridericus into the field against Aegidius. Fridericus, however, was killed in 464 in fighting around Orléans, and Aegidius died
not long after, some said by poison.[60]

Both Agrippinus and Aegidius had influential Gallic ecclesiastical
contacts and supporters. Aegidius, for example, received very favorable notices in several west-central Gallic ecclesiastical sources. Circa
480, Paulinus of Périgueux described him as "a man illustrious in
bravery, but more distinguished because of his gentle nature, and great
in faith, in which he stood out more conspicuously."[61] According to
Gregory of Tours, he won a victory "by invoking the blessed man
[Martin]."[62] Both were describing Aegidius' defeat of the Visigoths
outside the walls of Arles in 458.[63] Hydatius described him as "a man
both commendable by reputation and pleasing to the Lord through
his good works."[64]

Agrippinus, on the other hand, cooperated with Anianus of Orléans, corresponded with Euphronius of Autun, and was described in
the life of Lupicinus, abbot of St. Claude, as "endowed with a singular
wisdom."[65] Lupicinus even was said to have traveled to Rome c.458
on Agrippinus' behalf.[66] This last source also described Agrippinus'
enemy Aegidius as *callidus* ("tricky") and *malitiosus* ("malicious").

Agrippinus' attested ties, therefore, seem to be concentrated in the
eastern part of Lugdunensis (writers from no other area have anything
good to say about him), and his confidante Euphronius of Autun was
part of the "northern" party of Gallic bishops. On the other hand,

58. Priscus, fr.30; Hyd. *Chron.* 224 s.a.464. See Bury, *L.R.E.* p.333 and Stein, *Geschichte*
1.563-565.
59. For Aegidius and Agrippinus, see chapter 8 above.
60. Death of Fridericus: *Chron. gall.511* no.638 (*M.G.H. A.A.* 9.664); Hyd. *Chron.* 218
(ibid.11.33) and Mar. Avit. *Chron.* s.a.463 (ibid.11.232). Death of Aegidius: Hyd. *Chron.* 228
(ibid.11.33) and Greg. Tur. *H.F.* 2.18.
61. "inlustrem virtute virum, sed moribus almis / plus clarum magnumque fide, qua celsior
extat" (*VMartini* 6.111-112).
62. "per invocationem beati viri [sc. Martini]" (*Virt. Mart.* 1.2).
63. See Mathisen, "Resistance" pp.618-620.
64. "virum et fama commendatum et Deo bonis operibus complacentem" (*Chron.* 218
s.a.463). Was Hydatius so well informed on the affairs of Aegidius because the latter's envoys to
the Vandals passed that way?
65. *VAniani* 3; Hyd. *Chron.* 151 s.a.452; "sagacitate praeditus singulari" (*VLupicini* 11).
66. See chapter 8 above, n.121.

Aegidius' defense of Arles, and Agrippinus' cession of Narbonne, would suggest that Aegidius was popular in the south, as well as in western Lugdunensis and Belgica.[67]

It remains unclear just how close the ties were between Gallic ecclesiastics and secular potentates at this time, and to what extent there were parallel secular and ecclesiastical factions.[68] It does appear that the control which secular officialdom had exerted over the ecclesiastical hierarchy in southern Gaul before the 450s had disappeared by the 460s. Some Gallic ecclesiastics may have been not at all unhappy to see imperial authority in Gaul decline as powerful laymen such as Aegidius, Agrippinus, and others attempted to carve out their own spheres of influence. As long as these potentates were contending among themselves, they would be less likely to become deeply involved in the affairs of the church.

This decline of imperial authority in Gaul may have been one reason why Hilarus was willing to associate himself with "his sons" the Germanic warlords. Even though his granting of credence to the "insinuatio" of Fridericus and the "relatio certa" of Gundioc hardly can have been received well in Gaul, Hilarus may have seen in such unlikely alliances a way to gain secular support. Fridericus and Gundioc themselves also may have been seeking pretexts for inserting themselves into Gallo-Roman factionalism, on one side or the other. In so doing they could not only broaden their own base of support within Gaul but also fragment the Gallic aristocracy even further as they advanced toward the Mediterranean.

INGENUUS OF EMBRUN

A third incident from the 460s concerned the exercise of metropolitan authority by the bishops of the minor metropolitan sees of Provence.[69] In Narbonensis Secunda, the bishop of Aix was supposed to have become metropolitan after the death of Proculus of Marseilles. Nevertheless, as has been seen, it appears that Proculus' successor Venerius did not easily relinquish his claims, and as late as the 450s he was accorded extraordinary status not only by the bishops of southern Gaul, including Ravennius of Arles, but also by the bishop of Rome.

---

67. For the opposite conclusion, that Agrippinus represented a southern party and Aegidius a northern one, see Nesselhauf, *Verwaltung* p.34ff.

68. One such possible connection is suggested by the fact that Leontius' letter to Rome was delivered not by a cleric but by the otherwise unknown *vir spectabilis* Pappolus (Hil. *Epist.* "Dilectioni meae").

69. See Griffe, *Gaule* 2.137-146; Thiel, *Epistolae* pp.152-153 n.3; and Weiss, "Valérien" pp.112-138.

Even in the 460s Eustasius of Marseilles seems to have retained some kind of supernormal status as well. Such status could have been partially at the expense of the bishop of Aix, whose dissatisfaction with his own standing apparently was reflected in his abstention from participation in extant Gallic ecclesiastical activities before 463.[70]

As for Alpes Maritimae, it often has been assumed that it remained a dependency of Narbonensis Secunda for much of the fifth century, even though bishops of the province had taken it upon themselves to consecrate a new bishop of Embrun as early as 437.[71] It also has been presumed that during the tenure of Hilary of Arles, at least up until 445, the bishops of both Aix and Embrun lacked metropolitan status, or that Embrun did not obtain it until 465.[72] Evidence to the contrary, however, comes from Leo's letter of 445: "Let individual metropolitans maintain for themselves ordination in their own provinces, with this right restored to them through us. . . . Let each one know that it is not permitted him to be able to transfer to another the privilege due to himself."[73] Some metropolitans of southern Gaul, therefore, had been yielding their rights of ordination freely to Hilary. If they were not *de iure* metropolitans, they would have had no rights of ordination either to yield or be restored. One such metropolitan who yielded his metropolitan rights was Ingenuus of Embrun; one who did not concede so willingly was the bishop of Aix.[74] As of early in the fifth century, therefore, the bishops of both Aix and Embrun had at least *de iure* metropolitan status; what varied was the extent to which they were able to exercise it.

Certainly, by the time of Hilarus the ecclesiastical independence of both the Alpine provinces and Narbonensis Secunda was recognized. Hilarus' letter "Quamquam notitiam" of 462 was addressed "to the bishops of Viennensis, Lugdunensis, Narbonensis Prima and Secunda, and Alpes Poeninae"; and "Etsi meminerimus" of 464 was sent to "the

70. See Babut, *Turin* p.135 and Palanque, "Evêchés" pp.122-125; denied by Griffe, "Primatie" p.67.

71. *Corp. chr. lat.* 148.64-70 and chapter 5 above, n.56; see Griffe, *Gaule* 2.165-166. Langgärtner, *Gallienpolitik* p.101, has it as a dependency of Arles. For independence, see Thiel, *Epistolae* pp.152-153 n.3.

72. See Duchesne, *Fastes* 1.124, 297-298; Griffe, *Gaule* 2.165-166; Kidd, *Church* p.358; and Palanque, "Evêchés" p.125.

73. "ordinationem sibi . . . singuli metropolitani suarum provinciarum . . . restituto sibi per nos iure defendant. . . . unusquisque . . . privilegium sibi debitum in alium transferre se posse, noverit non licere" ("Divinae cultum" ch.6: *P.L.* 54.628-636). This passage belies the assertion of Griffe, "Primatie" p.68, that this letter "ne fait aucune allusion aux divers metropolitains de la région du sud-est." In at least two other places as well ("Divinae cultum" ch.5, 9) Leo also mentioned the existence of other metropolitans.

74. See Duchesne, *Fastes* 1.113; Griffe, *Gaule* 2.165 n.55; and chapters 6-7 above.

bishops of Viennensis, Lugdunensis, Narbonensis Prima and Secunda, and Alpes." If Narbonensis Secunda and one, or as it seems both, of the Alpine provinces were recognized as separate, the bishops of their metropolitan sees, Aix, Embrun, and presumably Tarentaise, *a priori* would have been recognized by Rome as metropolitan bishops. Such recognition may have encouraged them to take part in, and even organize, the council on Mamertus.

THE CONTROVERSY OVER NICE

On 19 November 465, Ingenuus of Embrun and Saturninus of Avignon were in Rome, and once again Gauls were allowed to participate, and speak freely, in a church council presided over by Hilarus.[75] The reasons for Saturninus' visit are unclear: he may have been there in support of Ingenuus, or he may have had some unknown mission of his own.[76] The purpose of Ingenuus' visit was to persuade Hilarus to support him in a quarrel concerning his authority as metropolitan of Alpes Maritimae. Part of the price for such support may have been Ingenuus' extant public acknowledgement of papal authority. After Maximus of Turin had spoken, Ingenuus continued (Thiel, *Epistolae* p.164),

I have the same opinion about all these matters, by which I constrain myself so that I never will attempt any of those things which are forbidden, because I am mindful of my status and position. Concerning the other matters, I certainly think that whoever appears as a transgressor of the statutes should know that he is entangled in the noose of the ecclesiastical rules and shall incur the condemnation of the apostolic see.[77]

Ingenuus' strong support of papal authority may help to explain Hilarus' equally cooperative response.

The undated letter, "Movemur ratione," which Hilarus sent back to Gaul began by saying,

Our brother and fellow bishop Ingenuus of Embrun, therefore, always supported by his rank of metropolitan of the province of the Maritime Alps,

---

75. Mansi 7.960-968; *P.L.* 58.12-17, 67.315-320, 130.923-926; Thiel, *Epistolae* pp.159-165. See Di Capua, *Ritmo Prosaico* pp.87-91. Ingenuus subscribed in the third position, after Hilarus and Maximus of Turin, and Saturninus in the fifth position, after the unnamed bishop of Milan.

76. Saturninus' see, of course, was in Viennensis. He also could have been in Rome representing Leontius' interests.

77. "mihi quoque eadem de omnibus partibus sententia est, qua me ipse constringo, ne quid a me unquam de his quae sunt interdicta tentetur, quia novi statum et professionem meam. de ceteris etiam censeo, ut quisquis statutorum transgressor exstiterit, sciat se ecclesiasticae regulae laqueis innodari et reatum apostolicae sedis incurrere."

recounts that, as the appended documents demonstrate, we had established certain matters detrimental to him at the instigation of our brother and fellow bishop Auxanius, which are contrary to all the evidence in the case.[78]

The injurious declaration which Auxanius had obtained would have been granted in conjunction with Auxanius' own visit to Rome in 462, when he and Faustus of Riez had attended the council which met on 19 November. Presumably, this would have been the real reason why Auxanius went to Rome, not the Hermes case.

Hilarus' letter then continued (ibid.):

Indeed, if you review the referral to our judgment which our brother and fellow bishop Veranus, together with the other bishops of the province, sent to my predecessor of blessed memory, and the clear response which was then forthcoming, it is clear that nothing further ought to be in contention, and that it is not right for anything detrimental to the synodal regulations to be established. . . .[79]

The ruling obtained by Auxanius, therefore, contradicted an even earlier ruling obtained from Hilarus' predecessor Leo after a letter had been sent to him by Veranus and "the other bishops of the province [sc. Alpes Maritimae]."[80]

This decision, favorable to Ingenuus, very probably was obtained from Leo in early 452, when Ingenuus himself was in Rome as the bearer of the Gallic letter to Leo.[81] Ingenuus may have seen in the arduous journey to Rome an opportunity to pursue his own provincial interests as well. The letter of support from his suffragans would have

78. "frater igitur et coepiscopus noster Ingenuus Ebredunensis, Alpium Maritimarum provinciae metropolitani semper honore subnixus in praeiudicium suum, sicut annexa declarant, quaedam nos, petente fratre et coepiscopo nostro Auxanio, statuisse commemorat, quae universis in hac eadem causa defensionibus contrairent. . . ." (Hilarus *Epist.* "Movemur ratione" [Thiel, *Epistolae* pp.152-155]), see Babut, *Turin* pp.287-289, and Weiss, "Valérien" pp.126-127. The letter must have been written after the council, probably in late 465 or early 466; see Duchesne, *Fastes* 1.297, and Weiss, "Valérien" p.136 n.7. Latouche, "Nice" pp.321-358, wrongly suggests 463/465, and Griffe, *Gaule* 2.122, after first opting for the impossible date of 464, later favored 465 or later (ibid.168 n.58).

79. "siquidem relationibus in nostro iudicio recensitis, quas frater et coepiscopus noster Veranus ad sanctae memoriae decessorem meum cum ceteris provinciae sacerdotibus misit, et apostolicae sedis, quae tunc directa fuerat, responsione patefacta manifestum est, nihil postea debuisse tentari, nec ad iniuriam synodalium regularum quidquam per obreptionem, quae proxime facta est, oportere constitui. . . ."

80. Duchesne (*Fastes* 1.297 n.1) suggests that the bishops may have been "de la province ecclésiastique d'Arles," but does not explain why Veranus, a bishop of Alpes Maritimae, would have been representing bishops of Viennensis on behalf of another Alpine bishop, Ingenuus. He does state elsewhere (ibid.1.126) that Ingenuus acted "soutenu par les évêques des Alpes Maritimes."

81. See Leo, *Epist.* "Perlata ad nos" (chapter 8 above, n.58); Duchesne, *Fastes* 1.126, cf. 2.296, and Jalland, *Leo* p.138. This decision is dated to c.455/461 by Weiss, "Valérien" pp.134-135. Griffe, *Gaule* 2.166, and Palanque, "Evêchés" p.126, date it only to c.451/461. Dates after 452 would mean that Ingenuus made a third otherwise unknown trip to Rome.

followed the precedent set in 449/450 when the supporters of Ravennius had written to Leo on behalf of Ravennius' metropolitan pretensions. Just as Ravennius may have considered it improper for himself
to have been the author of a letter on his own behalf, Ingenuus too
may have decided that a letter from his suffragans would give added
weight to his plea, especially if Leo was concerned with just how
much Gallic support an appellant had. There is no need to assume
that Ingenuus was "trop négligent ou trop indifférent" and that Veranus therefore had to take matters into his own hands.[82] The principal
role of Veranus in the writing of this letter, moreover, is consistent
with the part he played at the same time in the forwarding of Mamertus' letter to Leo: both letters would have been contrary to the
interests of the bishop of Arles.

It was not until the very end of Hilarus' letter that he specifically
discussed what the quarrel was about ("Movemur ratione": Thiel,
Epistolae pp.152-155):

> Let our brother and fellow bishop Ingenuus, therefore, have the pontificate
> of his own province, concerning the illicit relinquishing of which he recently
> was reproached by the apostolic see, and having taken into custody every-
> thing which the authority of my predecessor of blessed memory defined, as
> we said, about the churches of the city of Cimiez and the *castellum* of Nice,
> let him harm nothing of the right of these churches because a bishop recently
> was consecrated in one of the aforementioned churches by the aforemen-
> tioned brother [sc. Ingenuus] in order to prevent, as he asserted, the greed of
> another's ambition.[83]

A persistent misconception has to do with the "illicit relinquishing
(*cessio*)" of his metropolitan status, for which Ingenuus recently had
been rebuked. It has been asserted, for example, that "sans doute" this

---

82. Griffe, *Gaule* 2.166. One also cannot agree with Palanque ("Evêchés" p.126 n.85), see
also the Ballerini, *P.L.* 54.1232, that the sending of the letter by Veranus and the others "proves"
that Ingenuus was not involved: was Ravennius, therefore, also "not involved" in the letter
of 449?

83. "habeat itaque pontificium frater et coepiscopus noster Ingenuus provinciae suae, de
cuius dudum ab apostolica sede est illicita cessione culpatus: et custoditis omnibus, quae super
ecclesiis Cemelensis civitatis, vel castelli Nicensis, sicut diximus, sanctae memoriae decessoris
mei definivit auctoritas, nihil ecclesiarum iuri noceat, quod in altera memoratarum a praedicto
fratre, ad excludendam cupiditatem, quemadmodum perhibuit, ambitionis alienae, proxime est
episcopus consecratus...." The "aforementioned" consecrator must have been Ingenuus, Auxanius, or even Veranus, the only bishops mentioned in the letter by name. The view of Duchesne,
Fastes 1.297; Griffe, *Gaule* 2.168; and Thiel, *Epistolae* p.155 n.12 that Ingenuus is to be identified
with the *praedictus* probably is correct, for two reasons: 1) the name of Auxanius had occurred
so far back in the text, even before that of Veranus, that, for the sake of clarity, any reference
back to him would have to be more specific, and 2) the phrase "quemadmodum perhibuit"
demonstrates that it was this same "aforementioned brother" who was justifying himself to
Hilarus, and it was Ingenuus not Auxanius who was in Rome in 465. For the view that Auxanius
had consecrated the new bishop, see Babut, *Turin* p.292; Palanque "Evêchés" p.126 and *Aix* p.17;
and Weiss, "Valérien" p.136 n.76.

rebuke occurred after 451.[84] It more likely occurred, however, in 445, when Leo decreed that "if anyone wishes to desert his rank," the one who should obtain it was "not he to whom he yielded (*cesserit*)."[85]

An even more pervasive controversy has existed over what the quarrel was about. Some believe that it involved Ingenuus' loss of his very metropolitan status, but the conflict actually seems to have concerned only the status of the churches of Cimiez and Nice.[86] Hilarus even specified with the words "sicut diximus" that his decision, like the earlier one of Leo's, concerned these two churches.

The problem was that Nice, called variously a *portus* or a *castellum*, during the fourth century had been an ecclesiastical dependency of Marseilles, even though it was located in the territory of the *civitas Cemelensis*, which was in the province of Alpes Maritimae and which apparently did not then have a bishop of its own.[87] Cimiez seems not to have acquired its first bishop until the early fifth century, and this resulted in the anomaly of two bishops within a single *civitas*, each dependent upon a different metropolitan. Now, over Cimiez there was no contention, for it clearly belonged under the jurisdiction of the metropolitan of Alpes Maritimae. It was Nice which caused the problem: the bishop of Marseilles could claim it on the basis of antiquity, the bishop of Embrun could claim that it was in his province, and even the bishop of Aix may have had a claim, for according to the Council of Turin, he was to inherit the metropolitan rights of the bishop of Marseilles.[88] The short history of the separate existence of these two sees, therefore, became closely intertwined with the factional disputes of the mid-fifth century.

The first attested bishop of Cimiez was Valerianus, elected c.429, a partisan of Hilary and the monks of Lérins. The installation of a bishop at Cimiez may have been viewed by the Lérins faction as a means of striking at the authority of the bishop of Marseilles, who

84. Griffe, *Gaule* 2.166. Weiss, "Valérien" p.129, suggests 450, when Ingenuus and the others requested the restoration of Ravennius' extended metropolitan rights.

85. "si quis ... sui honoris desertor esse voluerit ... non is cui cesserit" (*Epist.* "Divinae cultum" 6: *P.L.* 54.628-636); see chapter 7 above. This obvious parallel was noted long ago by the Ballerini (*P.L.* 54.1232); see also Langgärtner, *Gallienpolitik* p.73 (cf. pp.101-102), who translates "dudum" as "längst."

86. Metropolitan status: Griffe, *Gaule* 2.167-168. Nice and Cimiez: Babut, *Turin* p.287; Duchesne, *Fastes* 1.297; Latouche, "Nice" p.339; Palanque, "Evêchés" pp.125-127; Thiel, *Epistolae* pp.152, 154 n.5; and Weiss, "Valérien" p.128. The appropriation of Nice by another metropolitan was itself a sufficient infringement of Ingenuus' metropolitan rights to allow Hilarus to state (*Epist.* "Movemur ratione": Thiel, *Epistolae* p.154), "nec in alterius provincia sacerdotis alterum ius habere permittimus."

87. See Duchesne, *Fastes* 1.296-298; Griffe, "Primatie" pp.72-74; Latouche, "Nice" pp.331-358; Palanque, "Prémiers" p.382; and Weiss, "Valérien" pp.109-146.

88. For a potential claim by the bishop of Aix, see also Palanque, "Prémier" p.382, who argues for propinquity. Jalland, *Leo* p.138 n.96, suggests the bishop of Arles.

would have ordained the current bishop of Nice, who now could be seen as superfluous. Such a move might have been encouraged by the death of the old and powerful Proculus of Marseilles and the succession of the untried Venerius.

Then, in early 452, after the death of Hilary, Ingenuus, armed with the letter written by Veranus and his other suffragans, traveled to Rome and obtained the ruling from Leo decreeing 1) that Ingenuus was to have authority over both Nice and Cimiez, and 2) that the two sees ultimately were to be united.[89] A potential objection to this analysis, however, might be that as recently as 449 Ingenuus had not openly insisted upon the recognition of his metropolitan status.[90] Not only had he subscribed to the letter requesting the restoration of Ravennius' metropolitan rights, his name also appeared in it only in the position accorded by his tenure in office. How can one explain such an apparently rapid about face, with Ingenuus suddenly asserting his metropolitan status in 452? The key, it seems, lies in the timing and circumstances of Ingenuus' visit to Rome.

Ravennius, under pressure to secure Gallic adhesion to Leo's theological position, had been compelled to recognize the metropolitan status not only of Rusticus of Narbonne but even of Venerius of Marseilles. It may be that Ingenuus, like many other old Lerinenses, became disenchanted with Ravennius' leadership. On the one hand, this was how he was repaid for subordinating himself in 449. And on the other, in the quarrel over Nice, Ingenuus' most bitter opponent would have been Ravennius' new ally Venerius of Marseilles. Ingenuus, perhaps, viewed himself as the odd man out, and the one most likely to suffer if these two powerful churchmen became allies. Already, Ravennius had recognized Venerius' metropolitan status, but not Ingenuus'. Ingenuus, therefore, could hardly expect support from Ravennius in the controversy over Nice.

Like so many disgruntled Gallic ecclesiastics, Ingenuus then determined to take his case to Rome. When the opportunity came in early 452 to deliver the Gallic letter to Leo, he seized it. As a result of Ingenuus' appeal, Leo declared that the sees of Nice and Cimiez were to be consolidated under Ingenuus' authority. At some time during the 450s the two sees then presumably were united under a single bishop. This bishop just may have been Valerianus of Cimiez, for a monastic martyrology noted under 24 July that a bishop "Valerius",

---

89. "sed statutae correctionis forma permaneat, ut ad unius antistitis regimen praedicta loca revertantur, quae in duos dividi non decuit sacerdotes" (Hil. *Epist.* "Movemur ratione": Thiel, *Epistolae* p.155). See Duchesne, *Fastes* 1.126.

90. See the Ballerini, *P.L.* 54.1232.

an ex-monk of Lérins, died, not at Cimiez, but at Nice.[91] This controversy, therefore, marks one more facet of the fragmentation of the old Lérins faction in the 450s.

Nor did the matter end there. Several years later, in 462, Auxanius and Faustus of Riez went to Rome where Auxanius took advantage of the good nature, inexperience, ignorance, and possibly ambition of the newly elected bishop Hilarus to have the see of Nice placed under the metropolitan authority of someone other than the bishop of Embrun.[92] Shortly afterward, this metropolitan moved to consecrate a new bishop of Nice, and Ingenuus could prevent it only by making a preemptive ordination of his own.[93]

The question remains of just who Ingenuus' opponent was. Hilarus warned him that "the fruit of our ministry should not be sought in an expansion of one's control," and repeated Ingenuus' assertion that the ordination at Nice had occurred "in order to prevent the greed of another's ambition."[94] Just who was this ambitious outsider on whose behalf Auxanius had acted? If the controversy was over whether Ingenuus were to have metropolitan status at all, likely candidates would be the bishop of Arles, or perhaps Aix.[95] But once one accepts that the only point of contention was jurisdiction over the see of Nice, the most likely suggestion is that the bishop of Marseilles was seeking to restore his previous authority over the *castellum*.[96]

In 462 the bishop of Marseilles would have been Eustasius, who was bishop as of 461 and probably earlier.[97] It already has been seen that Eustasius was accorded some kind of extraordinary status by Hi-

91. See *P.L.* 52.762 and Vincent Barralis, *Chronologia sanctorum* (Lyons, 1613) 1.203: "de sancto Valerio episcopo Niciensi et monacho Lerinensi." Weiss, "Valérien," argues that Valerianus (of Cimiez) and "Valerius" (of Nice) were two different contemporaries.

92. This is the only specific concern Hilarus attributes to either of them. Langgärtner, *Gallienpolitik* p.102, however, supposes that Faustus and Auxanius were in Rome for the Hermes case, and that Auxanius merely took the opportunity to bring up Nice as well.

93. Hilarus had to remind Ingenuus not to depose either of the two bishops. In 465, Ingenuus presumably wished to reunite the two sees immediately; he argued not only that he had performed the ordination under duress, but also "that it also is rumored that the very one who earned [the post] did not wish any gain" ("Movemur ratione": Thiel, *Epistolae* pp.152-155). It rightly is assumed that it was at Nice, not Cimiez, where the new bishop was installed, for Cimiez would indisputably have been under Ingenuus' authority; see Babut, *Turin* p.292; Duchesne, *Fastes* 1.297; Griffe, "Primatie" p.73 n.19; Palanque, "Evêchés" p.126; Thiel, *Epistolae* p.155 n.12; and Weiss, "Valérien" p.136 n.76.

94. "expectatio fructus nostri ministerii non in latitudine regionum . . . ponitur," "ad excludendam cupiditatem . . . ambitionis alienae" ("Movemur ratione": Thiel, *Epistolae* pp.152-155).

95. For Arles as the beneficiary, see Babut, *Turin* p.299 and Jalland, *Leo* p.138. For Aix, see Griffe, *Gaule* 2.166-167; Langgärtner, *Gallienpolitik* p.101; Palanque, "Prémiers" p.382; and Weiss, "Valérien" p.136. Thiel, *Epistolae* p.155 n.12, suggests that Auxanius himself was the "alienus."

96. Suggested by Duchesne, *Fastes* 1.297-298.

97. Duchesne, *Fastes* 1.274, cites the year 463 as Eustasius' earliest attestation, neglecting Gennad. *Vir. ill.* 80, which has "Eustachius" of Marseilles in office by 461 at the very latest.

larus in 464. One way in which he could have obtained, or strengthened, it would have been by Auxanius' mission to Rome in 462, through which Eustasius' authority over Nice, at least, had been reestablished. There is no way to tell, however, how much, if any, of Narbonensis Secunda he controlled. Nice may have been all he had.

Even though Eustasius is very poorly known, he probably had the same powerful local support and independence of spirit which characterized other, better known, Gallic prelates of the time. Sidonius, for example, does mention his cooperation with the *comes civitatis Massiliensis*, and Gennadius attests his involvement in the Massiliote literary circle.[98] As has been seen, his ties extended even to Orange, where his protégé Eutropius became bishop at just this time. On the local level, at least, he would have been a force to be reckoned with.

A final consideration in the controversy over Nice is those to whom Hilarus' letter of settlement was addressed: the three bishops Leontius, Veranus, and Victurus. Although Hilarus made clear to them how he would like to have the case settled, he also disavowed any responsibility for making, or enforcing, the final decision, asserting, "Lest I be influenced by enmity or preference, which is not proper in the judgment of disputes, I delegate to Your Charity the jurisdiction in the appended complaint."[99] Hilarus, it seems, had learned it was necessary to find strong Gallic support if his decisions were to have any effect. It was best to deal with potential supporters circumspectly, and to conciliate rather than try to intimidate them. This was a far cry from his treatment of Leontius four years earlier.

Why, one now might ask, were these three bishops singled out? For one thing, as the designated adjudicators, they could not have been directly involved. Leontius, of course, was the bishop of Arles and in some sense Hilarus' Gallic "representative." Moreover, the bishops of Arles in the past had had presumptions of extraordinary metropolitan authority extending into Alpes Maritimae. Leontius also was Eustasius' *de iure* metropolitan. Leontius' presence, then, is not surprising.[100]

Veranus, bishop of Vence, would have been the senior Alpine bishop back in Gaul. Ingenuus would still have been at Rome when the letter was written, and it would have been rather comical to address it to him. Ingenuus also was one of the parties to the dispute. Furthermore, as seen above, Veranus had a special standing with the

98. Sid. Apoll. *Epist.* 7.2.5; Gennad. *Vir. ill.* 80.

99. "ne odio vel gratia moveamur, quae in causarum disceptationibus esse non debet, ita vestrae caritati cognitionem annexae querimoniae delegamus" ("Movemur ratione": Thiel, *Epistolae* pp.152-155).

100. Duchesne, *Fastes* 1.297 n.3, rightly notes that Leontius could not have been both judge and a party to the quarrel. Curiously, this letter was omitted, like Leo's "Divinae cultum," from the *Epistulae arelatenses*: was it considered somehow contrary to the interests of the see of Arles?

bishop of Rome: he had authored the letter of the Alpine bishops to
Leo in 452, in which he had shown a particular interest in the controversy over Nice, and he had been a special delegate of Hilarus himself
in 463. So Veranus' inclusion is understandable as well.

But what of Victurus? What status did he have to warrant his
involvement? Once one accepts that the controversy did not concern
an attempt by the bishop of Aix to appropriate metropolitan status in
Alpes Maritimae, the reasonable conclusion, as already suggested
above, is that Victurus was the bishop of Aix.[101] As metropolitan of
the neighboring province of Narbonensis Secunda, he would have
been a logical, or even necessary, person for Hilarus to include. Hilarus' letter therefore would have been addressed to the highest-ranking
representatives in Gaul of the three provinces which conceivably could
have been involved in the controversy.[102]

Veranus could be expected to support the position of Ingenuus because he had done so in the past. Leontius would not have been unhappy to see his suffragan Eustasius' metropolitan pretensions sup-
pressed. And Victurus might have been influenced by the past rivalry
between Aix and Marseilles to support any move that would weaken
the status of the latter see. Hilarus may have reasoned that if his
settlement was in the best interests of those he named to confirm and
enforce it, they would be more likely to do so.[103] As for the influential
Eustasius, one can note only that his name is conspicuously absent
from Hilarus' letter. This, too, could suggest that he might not have
been inclined to support the decision.

ARLES AND ROME

One now can attempt to define the terms of the relationship between the bishops of Arles and Rome in the 460s. From the very
beginning of his tenure in office, Hilarus seems to have regarded
Leontius as his Gallic representative. Hilarus may have had no alternative but to try to revive the occasionally implemented alliance be-

101. If so, then Auxanius, again, could not have been bishop of Aix (as shown in note 19
above), and was not a metropolitan.

102. Most writers have simply avoided the difficult question of the identity of Victurus:
Griffe, *Gaule* 2.166 n.56, fails to mention him at all in this context, whereas Palanque, "Prémiers" p.381, seems at least to be aware of the possibility that Victurus could be bishop of Aix,
but he elsewhere had committed himself to Auxanius as bishop of Aix, and can only suggest
that Victurus was "le doyen de l'épiscopat de ces provinces" ("Evêchés" p.127).

103. The two sees were eventually combined, although the first evidence for this does not
appear until 549 (Duchesne, *Fastes* 1.295-299); soon afterward, Cimiez was destroyed by the
Lombards.

tween Rome and Arles.[104] Any idea that Leo may have had of favoring Rusticus of Narbonne over the discredited Ravennius of Arles would have been passé by the time of Hilarus. Not only were all of them dead, but the church of Narbonne now was embroiled in controversy of its own, and the city was in the hands of the Visigoths.

In his initial letter of 25 January 462, Hilarus notified Leontius of his election and asked that it be announced "at the order of Your Fraternity to all the brothers and bishops throughout the entire province."[105] Leontius, on the other hand, had anticipated Hilarus. Even before Hilarus' letter arrived, Leontius had sent one of his own to the new bishop. Although this letter is lost, Hilarus' reply, written around the end of April, gives an idea of what it contained.[106] Hilarus responded to him, "I recognize that you are intent upon this concern, that you wish me to be devoted to the preservation of the regulations of the paternal canons."[107] He also promised that he would make no changes without informing Leontius first. Just what were these regulations which Leontius wished Hilarus to preserve? Was Leontius merely speaking in general terms, or did he have something more specific in mind? If the latter, the only regulations he could have meant would have involved the status of the see of Arles in southern Gaul.

The affair of Hermes of Narbonne, at first appearance, might suggest that Leontius had been successful in obtaining recognition of his extended rights.[108] After all, Hilarus was of the opinion that the offense had occurred "in a province which belongs to your monarchy."[109] Either his geography was very faulty, or he did indeed believe

104. Jalland, *Leo* p.140, asserts that Leontius "succeeded in obtaining most of the privileges refused to his predecessor."

105. "dispositione tuae fraternitatis omnibus per universam provinciam fratribus et consacerdotibus" (*Epist.* "Quantum reverentiae").

106. "Quantum reverentiae": *M.G.H. Epist.* 3.23. See Di Capua, *Ritmo Prosaico* pp.83-84. An extant letter "Quod Leonem" (*P.L.* 58.22-23) purporting to be the letter Leontius wrote generally is believed to be a forgery, see Di Capua, *Ritmo Prosaico* pp.70-73, and Rahner, *Vignier* pp.129-142. In his response, Hilarus expressed surprise that his letter of 25 January had not yet been received. Now, a representative travel time between Rome and Arles was five weeks (see Haenel, *Corp. leg.* p.238 no.1171). Leontius' letter thus may have been sent circa mid-March (Gundlach's date of early February [*M.G.H. Epist.* 3.24] probably is too early), and would have arrived around the end of April; Hilarus' second letter then would have been sent. Hilarus perhaps suspected that Leontius had feigned ignorance of his first letter in order to write his own as if he had not read it.

107. "ei sollicitudini intentum te esse cognosco, ut custodiendis paternorum canonum regulis studere me cupias" (*Epist.* "Dilectioni meae").

108. Langgärtner, *Gallienpolitik* p.93, supposes that Hilarus granted to Leontius an "Obermetropolitangewalt über ganz Gallien."

109. "in provincia quae ad monarchiam tuam pertinet" ("Miramur fraternitatem": *M.G.H. Epist.* 3.22-23). The only other use of this word applied to the bishop of Arles occurs in the

that Leontius had some kind of supervisory authority in Narbonensis Prima. But of what kind? Was Leontius in fact trying to revive the defunct pretensions of the bishops of Arles to metropolitan authority over the entire Tres Provinciae? If so, he would have been faced with an apparently insurmountable task. There is no evidence that he had nearly the support that Hilary, or even Ravennius, had enjoyed. Furthermore, even the minor metropolitans of southern Gaul, those of Embrun, Aix, and even Marseilles and perhaps Tarentaise, were asserting their own independence at this very time. Unless Leontius were being very unrealistic, it might be prudent to look elsewhere for the source of his supposed authority in Narbonensis Prima.

In doing so, one must bear in mind that it was not Leontius himself who had claimed, at least in any extant document, such power. It was rather Hilarus who had attributed it to him. It may be that Hilarus was presuming that his relationship with Leontius was similar to that which Leo had established with Anastasius of Thessalonica in the 440s. Anastasius had been named Leo's representative in the Illyrian prefecture, and was assigned the right to consecrate metropolitans and to convene inter-provincial councils for the settling of episcopal quarrels: the bishop of Rome, however, retained the final word.[110] This is just the model Hilarus appears to have followed in his treatment of the bishop of Arles. Leontius had jurisdiction in the Hermes affair because Narbonne was a metropolitan see and Leontius should have presided at the ordination.[111] In the case of Mamertus, on the other hand, the bishop of Vienne, according to Hilarus, had performed an illegal ordination in another's province, and it was up to Leontius to summon a council to deal with it.

An arrangement in Gaul patterned on that in Illyricum also would have given Hilarus the right to structure the operations of the Gallic church as he saw fit. His measures, however, contained little which had not already been ordained by the Gauls themselves. This is seen in Hilarus' repeated desire that the Gauls hold yearly councils. He promulgated this rule first at the Council of Rome attended by Faustus and Auxanius on 12 November 462, and stated in his letter of 3 December 462, "In each year, therefore, let it be understood that an

---

VRomani 18, accusing Hilary of Arles of "indebitam sibi per Gallias vindicans monarchiam." See also Greg. Tur. VPat. 1.2.

110. See chapter 7 above, n.3.

111. Hitherto, the similarity has been unrecognized. Duchesne, Fastes 1.131, notes only that "Hilaire attachait une certaine importance aux pouvoirs supérieurs de l'évêque d'Arles," and refers to "la 'monarchie' d'Arles." Hefele-Leclercq, Conciles 2.427 n.2, likewise speak of the privileges accorded Leontius' "monarchie."

episcopal council is to be assembled from all possible provinces, in a manner so that it might take place at a convenient place and time under the supervision of our brother and fellow bishop Leontius. . . ."[112] He even called the refusal to attend a *superba rebellio*.[113] He referred to this policy again in his letter of 10 October 463, in which he ordered Leontius to convene a council, "which must be assembled yearly under your presidency according to my decrees."[114] In 464 he ordered, "that yearly synodal councils should be held whose highest place should be that of our brother and fellow bishop Leontius, bishop of the church of Arles."[115]

The Gauls, however, already had recognized the usefulness of having not annual but semi-annual councils, and at Orange in 441 had decided that each council should conclude by scheduling the next one in advance.[116] This policy, however, was never implemented. If the Gauls could not abide by their own regulations, they could hardly adhere to Hilarus', whose repeated requests merely underline the Gallic failure to obey them. Nor is there any evidence that they abided by Hilarus' other standard demand either: "In the discussion of more weighty matters, and those which cannot be resolved there, let the opinion of the apostolic see be consulted."[117] What followed, in fact, was a thirty-year hiatus in papal correspondence with Gaul.

Hilarus also instructed metropolitans to give *litterae formatae* to clerics traveling outside their province.[118] This measure, too, however,

---

112. "per annos itaque singulos, ex provinciis quibus potuerit, congregari, habeatur episcopale concilium; ita ut opportunis locis atque temporibus secundum dispositionem fratris et coepiscopi nostri Leontii . . . celebretur" ("Quamquam notitiam": *M.G.H. Epist.* 3.25-28). The addressees included the bishops of Viennensis, Lugdunensis, Narbonensis I and II, and Alpes Maritimae (cf. the addressees of "Etsi meminerimus"). Conspicuously absent were the Visigothic provinces of Novempopulana and Aquitania I and II, which here no longer are included, even in theory, in the regular ecclesiastical structure of Gaul. Hilarus therefore recognized that the Germanic presence might prevent some from attending, see Thiel, *Epistolae* p.144 n.11.

113. He may have had this in mind when he said of Mamertus (*Epist.* "Sollicitis admodum"), "cui umquam profuit mens rebellis? aut quem superbiae non inclinavit elatio?"

114. "qui secundum statuta nostra annis singulis te sibi praesidente est congregandus" ("Qualiter contra sedis": *M.G.H. Epist.* 3.28-29).

115. "ut . . . synodalia quotannis concilia quorum maxime in fratre et coepiscopo nostro Leontio Arelatensis ecclesiae sacerdote summa placuit esse celebrentur" (*Epist.* "Etsi meminerimus").

116. *Corp. chr. lat.* 148.85; see chapter 5 above, and Thiel, *Epistolae* p.145 n.13.

117. "in dirimendis sane gravioribus causis, et quae illic non potuerint terminari, apostolicae sedis sententia consulatur" (*Epist.* "Quamquam notitiam"). For the same terms expressed to the Illyrian bishops, see Leo's letter "Omnium quidem litteras" (*P.L.* 54.616; Jaffé pp.59-60 no.404). These *causae graviores* would be equivalent to the *magnae causae* of Zosimus (*Epist.* "Placuit apostolicae") and the *maiores causae* of Innocent (*Epist.* "Etsi tibi").

118. *Epist.* "Quamquam notitiam". This was a variant of Zosimus' decree in which even bishops traveling to Rome had to obtain such letters from the bishop of Arles: *Epist.* "Placuit

already had been introduced by the Gauls themselves, at Angers in 453 and Tours in 461.[119] Hilarus merely added the requirement that disputes were to be settled by the bishop of Arles.

Leontius, however, had equally firm ideas about the tenor of the relationship between Arles and Rome. He pointedly ignored, as far as is known, every single one of Hilarus' directives. He neither investigated nor reported on the Hermes case. He refused to convene a council to consider Mamertus, even though the neighboring bishops did. He paid no attention at all to the order that he convene yearly councils. Even Hilarus indicated how little affect his demands had had when he irritably began his letter to the Gallic bishops of 24 February 464, "Even if I were aware that Your Fraternity was mindful of those matters which had been decreed by me, and that you did not ignore anything which I have written. . . ."[120] The Gallic bishops, of course, were doing just that. Nor was his plea in the same letter, "Nevertheless, with repeated letters I now also decree that these same matters must be observed," likely to induce the Gauls to follow the Roman line.[121] All it does is to underline how ineffectual Hilarus had been in implementing his Gallic policy.[122]

Hilarus' main problem was that he had absolutely no way of enforcing his will. Imperial power was eroding rapidly, and Ricimer and his puppet Severus had little if any authority in Gaul. Any hopes that Hilarus may have had of taking advantage of Germanic cooperation had not been fulfilled. All he could rely upon was Gallic good will, and the Gauls usually had agendas of their own.

Hilarus' lack of success in gaining Leontius' cooperation may have resulted, at least in part, from a grudge which Leontius bore against him. In 462, Leontius had gone so far as to request Hilarus' assistance, as Hilarus reported back to the Gallic bishops on 7 December: "Moreover, a letter of this same brother [sc. Leontius] has been delivered to us in which he asserts that parishes of the church of Arles were transferred to others by his predecessor Hilary, which is not permitted,

---

apostolicae"; see Thiel, *Epistolae* p.145 n.12. Langgärtner, *Gallienpolitik* pp.95-96, sees Hilarus' decree as weakening that of Zosimus, but they actually were two different things.

119. *Corp. chr. lat.* 148.137, 147.

120. "etsi meminerimus fraternitatem vestram ea quae a nobis sunt statuta retinere, nec aliquid ex his dissimulare quae scripsimus. . . ." ("Etsi meminerimus": *M.G.H. Epist.* 3.29-30).

121. "tamen repetitis litteris eadem nunc quoque observanda decernimus. . . ."

122. For the orthodox view that Hilarus did "regulate the affairs" of the church of Gaul, see Jalland, *Church* p.314. Hodgkin, *Italy* 3.147-148, states that Hilarus was successful in his "attempts to assert the Papal supremacy over the churches of Gaul and Spain in a more despotic style. . . ."

asking that they be restored to their original status by our authority. . . ."[123] Hilarus' response was that the matter should be considered at one of the regular yearly Gallic councils. Leontius may have viewed this as a self-seeking way to maneuver him into complying with the order to hold yearly councils.[124] Leontius' pique only would have been increased by the consideration that if he had been able to settle the matter in Gaul, he never would have resorted to asking for help from the bishop of Rome. Leontius, therefore, had lessened his own prestige by referring the case to Hilarus, and had gained nothing by doing so.

In the rest of Gaul, too, the bishop of Rome seemed ever more distant and insubstantial. No correspondence between him and any Gaul at all survives for the years 465-494. The influential bishop Patiens of Lyons could chauvinistically compare the patron saints of his own city with those of Rome: "We hold and exalt especially enclosed in the bosum of this city twin palms, rivals of the triumph of the apostolic city, and having also ourselves our own Peter and Paul, we match this pair of patrons against [those of] that sublime see. . . ."[125] In 472, Sidonius Apollinaris even described Lupus of Troyes as residing "in an apostolic see."[126]

As of the 460s, then, any real authority of the bishop of Rome in Gaul seems to have been minimal. Disaffected Gauls did continue to appeal to Rome, at least in the first half of the decade, but Hilarus had no effective means of implementing any decisions. He encouraged such appeals, however, by consistently rendering favorable decisions to appellants who actually journeyed to Rome, even, as in 462 and 465, when the ruling directly contradicted an earlier one. As in the days of Leo, however, Gaul does not seem to have been a primary concern of the bishops of Rome. In the cases of Hermes and Ingenuus, Hilarus did not even take the trouble to seek out any precedents or past correspondence. Gaul seems to have been placed in the same category as

123. "praeterea eiusdem fratris libellus oblatus est nobis, quo perhibet paroecias Arelatensis ecclesiae a praedecessore suo Hilario in alios, quod non licuit, fuisse translatas, petens illas pristino iuri nostra auctoritate restitui. . . ." (*Epist.* "Quamquam notitiam"). Duchesne, *Fastes* 1.98-101, and Griffe, *Gaule* 2.122-124, 186, suggest that the parishes were in the hands of the bishop of Marseilles. If so, they may have been Citharista and Gargaria, over which Patroclus and Proculus argued in 417 (chapter 3 above, n.40). It is unlikely, however, that Hilary would have transferred any of his parishes to the bishop of Marseilles (see chapter 5 above, n.115).

124. Langgärtner, *Gallienpolitik* p.97, suggests not only that the council met, but also that Leontius regained his parishes at it; there is no evidence for either.

125. "intra gremium civitatis huius peculiariter conclusum tenemus et geminas palmas triumphi aemulas apostolici urbi attollimus, atque habentes et nos Petrum Paulumque nostrum, cum sublimi illa sede binos suffragatores certamus. . . ." (*De sanctis martyribus Epipodio et Alexandro: Corp. chr. lat.* 101A.639-640). See Van Dam, *Leadership* p.171.

126. "in apostolica sede" (*Epist.* 6.1.3).

the prefecture of Illyricum, regardless of whether the policy used there worked in Gaul or not. In the pontiffs' relations with Gaul, it was enough to have been consulted. It may have been less important whether this or that judgment went into effect, than that it had been sought, rendered, and was available as yet one more precedent establishing Rome as a final court of appeal.

CHAPTER 10

FAUSTUS, INTELLECTUAL CONTROVERSY, AND THE END OF ROMAN GAUL[1]

As of circa 470, Gaul was in intellectual ferment. Several theological debates occupied Gallic intellectuals in both the north and south. One, over the nature of the soul, seems to have been conducted by pamphlet, by correspondence, and in small groups. Another, involving a revival of the discussion of some of the views of Pelagius and Augustine, was to result in the convening of at least two church councils. One person who had a key role in both these controversies was the old alumnus and abbot of Lérins, Faustus, bishop of Riez.

FAUSTUS, MAMERTUS CLAUDIANUS, AND THE NATURE OF THE SOUL[2]

The most controversial aspect of the debate over the soul concerned whether it was corporeal or incorporeal, and it pitted against each other the the two foremost Christian philosophers in Gaul, Faustus and the priest Mamertus Claudianus of Vienne. The controversy flared up when an unnamed bishop wrote to Faustus asking him three theological questions. The last of them was "In human affairs, which things must be considered corporeal and which incorporeal?"[3] He was especially concerned about the nature of the soul. He apparently leaned toward the incorporealist viewpoint, for Faustus wrote back to him, "But you also deny that the soul is corporeal, because in the

---

1. The two numbers for the letters of Faustus refer to those in the editions of Krusch (*M.G.H. A.A.* 8) and Engelbrecht (*C.S.E.L.* 21) respectively.

2. For Faustus and Claudianus, see Mathisen, "Addenda" pp.372-373, 378. For the controversy, see Arnold, *Caesarius* p.325; de la Broise, *Mamerti* pp.29-32; von Harnack, *Lehrbuch* p.253; Koch, *Faustus* pp.15-17; and Loyen, "Etudes sur Sidoine" p.87.

3. "quae in rebus humanis corporea quaeve incorporea sentienda sint" (Faust. *Epist.* 20/3, also *C.S.E.L.* 11.3-17).

opinion of some it is not localized nor is it defined by quality or quantity."[4] Faustus, however, argued that the soul was contained in the body, and therefore was corporeal. He concluded that God alone was incorporeal. As support, he cited the authority of *eruditissimi* such as his old mentor, Cassian of Marseilles, who had opined, "It is clearly understood that nothing is incorporeal except God alone."[5] Faustus' letter then circulated, sometimes anonymously, in Gallic intellectual circles.[6]

Circa 469/470, the Viennese priest Mamertus Claudianus, the brother of bishop Mamertus of Vienne, denounced Faustus' views on the soul in his *De statu animae*.[7] Claudianus based his rebuttal upon his interpretation of *Genesis* 1.26-27: "And God said, 'Let us make man in our own image and likeness,' and He made man in His own image and likeness."[8] Claudianus argued, "If the human soul is the image of God, it of course is the image of incorporeality; if it is the image of incorporeality, it itself at least is incorporeal."[9] He also concluded, "God is incorporeal, the human soul, moreover, is the image of God, because man was made in the likeness and image of God. Now, the body cannot be the image of incorporeality, therefore because the human soul is the image of God, the human soul is incorporeal."[10]

Like Faustus, Claudianus argued from authority, stating, "Aurelius Augustine, in the acuity of his intelligence and the multitude of his topics and the mass of his work ... spoke thus in his *On the Origin of*

4. "sed inter haec ideo tu animam negas esse corpoream, quia iuxta aliquorum opinionem nec localis sit nec qualitate aut quantitate subsistat. . . ." (ibid.).

5. "pro manifesto colligitur nihil esse incorporeum nisi solum deum. . . ." (*Coll.* 7.13). See Koch, *Faustus* pp.15-16. Faustus also cited Jerome.

6. Gennadius (*Vir. ill.* 86) thought that this was the only matter the letter discussed, "legi eius . . . libellum . . . adversus eos qui dicunt esse in creaturis aliquid incorporeum, . . ." unaware that what he called the "Contra Arianos ac Macedonianos" was another part of the same letter.

7. Sidonius Apollinaris was still a layman when Claudianus began his edition (*C.S.E.L.* 11.18: "Praefectorio patricio . . . Sollio Sidonio"), but in the epilogue Claudianus addressed Sidonius as "venerande vir," implying that by then Sidonius had become a bishop (see Jerg, *Vir venerabilis* passim). Sidonius was prefect in 468, and a bishop by c.470. Not long after its publication, Sidonius certainly was a bishop (Sid. Apoll. *Epist.* 4.2: "Claudianus Sidonio papae salutem"). Weigel, *Faustus* p.87, dates Faustus' letter to the unnamed bishop (whom he groundlessly identifies [p.84 n.30] as the monk Marinus) to 467/468, and Claudianus' dedicatory letter to Sidonius to 468/469. For the date of the *De statu animae*, Chadwick (*Poetry* p.207) suggests c.470 and Griffe (*Gaule* 3.382 n.81) 469-470.

8. "et dixit deus, 'faciamus hominem ad imaginem et similitudinem nostram.' et fecit hominem ad imaginem et similitudinem suam" (*De statu animae* 1.5). Faustus later interpreted this passage less literally (n.40 below).

9. "si imago dei est humana anima, incorporei videlicet imago est, si incorporei imago est, incorporea utique ipsa est" (ibid.).

10. "deus incorporeus est, imago autem dei humanus animus, quoniam ad similitudinem et imaginem dei factus est homo. enimvero imago incorporei corpus esse non potest, igitur quia imago dei est humanus animus, incorporeus est animus humanus" (ibid. 3.16.1).

the Soul [dedicated] to Jerome: 'the soul is incorporeal'."[11] It already
has been seen, however, that many Gauls did not accept all of Augustine's teachings.[12] Claudianus emphasized most of all the support of
Eucherius of Lyons, whom he described as "most subtle in intelligence ... by far the greatest of the great bishops of his age," and
whom he quoted as saying, "There are two things incorporeal, that is,
the soul and God."[13] By aligning Eucherius on the side of the incor-
porealists, Claudianus had adlected to his own party one of the most
respected theologians of Lérins. He then could say that his opponents
were so wrong "that they prefer to choose outsiders along with falsehood and to condemn Eucherius along with the truth. ... I, truly,
would choose to be rejected, along with Eucherius, by them, than to
be condemned, along with them, by the truth."[14] Such an argument
would have been especially germane if, as suggested by Claudianus,
Faustus himself had been a pupil of Eucherius.[15]

Claudianus, who hardly could have been unaware that Faustus was
the author of the tract he was attacking, used the cloak of its anonym-
ity to score rhetorical points at the expense of its supposedly unknown
author: "I enquire as to the author; his name is produced in neither
the spoken nor written word. ... If you know you dispute well, why
do you conceal your name? If you fear to be known, why do you
produce such work, dare I say, why do you write such things at all?"[16]
Claudianus also felt free to make blanket denunciations of his detractors (*De statu animae* 1.1):

There is added to this also the hostility of their ever-souring spite, the fault
and punishment of an envious spirit. For if anything truthful, of general
usefulness, is produced by those whom they assault with an unjust hatred,
they immediately advertise the opposite, even if they feel the same way, and

11. "Aurelius Augustinus et acumine ingenii et rerum multitudine et operis mole ... libro
ad Hieronymum de origine animae sic pronuntiat: incorpoream esse animam. ..." (*De statu
animae* 2.9). Claudianus also drew support from Ambrose, Jerome, and Hilary of Poitiers, not to
mention Chrysippus, Zeno, and Varro.

12. See chapter 6 above; see also n.59 below.

13. "ingenii subtilissimus ... magnorum saeculi sui pontificum longe maximus ... duo illa
incorporea, id est anima et deus" (*De statu animae* 2.9).

14. "ut extraneos mallent cum falsitate prae[e]ligere et Eucherium cum veritate damnare ...
ego vero prae[e]legerim ab istis cum Eucherio reici, quam cum istis a veritate damnari" (ibid.).

15. *De statu animae* 2.9, "cedo mihi nunc illos [sc. such as Faustus], qui aeque talibus instituti
ab hisce doctrinis degeneraverunt pessum facientes salubria sua et alienis semet noxiis obnox-
iantes iniusto amantium sui odio eo usque prolapsi"; see de la Broise, *Mamerti* p.31.

16. "percontor de nomine: nec responso nec scripto proditur. ... si bene conscius disputas,
cur nomen occultas? si agnosci metuis, cur opus prodis, ne dicam, cur ista conscribis?" (*De statu
animae* 1.2). Krusch (*M.G.H. A.A.* 8.lx) believes that Claudianus really did not know the name
of the author; Engelbrecht (*C.S.E.L.* 21.xix-xx) more reasonably concludes that "aperte se nomen
scriptoris ignorare profitetur"; see also Weigel, *Faustus* p.85. Claudianus quoted at least sixteen
times from Faustus' letter (listed in *C.S.E.L.* 11 and 21 passim).

thus they fear not at all to have made a mockery of the truth because of their inexhaustible and confirmed hatred for those whom it has been ordained that they hate. Therefore, they hate the one closest to them, and they also hate God. . . . [but] this is much the greatest and by far the more dangerous fault, that they stupidly conceive, they vainly put forth, they proudly advertise opinions inimical to catholic well-being; they write with temerity and they support themselves by making accusations. . . .[17]

At the conclusion of his three volumes, Claudianus conventionally denied any personal animus, but at the same time took one last opportunity to attack his rival: "Now, whoever you are against whose writings the injury caused by your writings compelled me to speak out, I beg and beseech you not to be angry with me, for I neither rendered invective nor repaid opprobrium. I have done no more than repay to you, in a like manner, truth alone for falsehood."[18]

Both Faustus' and Claudianus' works found ready audiences. They even circulated together, presumably to facilitate discussion and appreciation of the complex arguments which both Faustus and Claudianus so clearly relished.[19] The circulation of Faustus' tract is attested by Claudianus himself, as when he derogatorily noted in his own work, "Recently I fell in with several individuals here in town who were studiously rereading a certain little tract [Faustus' letter] and, by human nature, seduced by the recognition of a new work, they hastened to grasp it with an eager spirit."[20] Claudianus, on the other hand, indicated the number and prestige of his own supporters when he said in his dedicatory letter to Sidonius Apollinaris, "You have demanded from me an edition of the books *On the Nature of the Soul* which I have composed. . . . Many of the very greatest men have themselves,

---

17. "accedit ad hoc etiam acescentis semper livoris intentio, invidentis animi crimen et poena. nam si quid ab his, quos iniquo lacessunt odio, ad utilitatem publicam veri prodatur, diversum protinus adstruunt, etsi idem sentiant, ac sic inexhausto firmatoque odio cum his, quos sibi odisse institutum est, nequaquam metuunt veritatis fecisse iacturam. oderunt igitur proximum, oderunt et deum . . . illud multo maximum longeque periculosius crimen est, quod catholicae sanitati opiniones inimicas stulte concipiunt, vane proferunt, superbe adstruunt, cum temeritate scribunt, cum intentione defendunt. . . ." These sentiments belie Sidonius' eulogistic assessment of Claudianus' tolerance (*Epist.* 4.11.3).

18. "te nunc, quisque ille es adversus cuius scripta nosmet iniuria scriptorum tuorum dicere conpulit, oro quaesoque non obirascaris mihi, neque enim convicium rettuli neque rependi maledictum. solam tibi pro falsitate veritatem haud pari vicissitudine reponderavi. . . ." (*De statu animae* 3.18). Weigel (*Faustus* pp.85-86) misconstrues Claudianus' disclaimer as genuine, and concludes that he "ingratiatingly apologises."

19. Engelbrecht notes (*C.S.E.L.* 21.xx) that all the manuscripts of Claudianus which he saw included the third section of Faustus' letter. In these cases, however, Faustus was never named; in some mss. Faustus' letter even was referred to as an "ignoti heretici tractatus" (*C.S.E.L.* 11.8 n).

20. "nuper etenim offendi in quosdam, qui chartulam quandam oppido studiose lectitabant, et quia mortalium generi mos est, novi operis agnitione pellecti ad id percipiendum sedulo animo intenderant. . . ." (*De statu animae* 1.1).

along with you, given me the very same task."[21] One of these "great men" presumably would have been Claudianus' own brother Mamertus. Given the very close ties between the two, Mamertus would have been hard pressed to disavow, even had he been so inclined, a share in the polemics which his brother leveled against Faustus.[22] The dissemination of Claudianus' work is seen in Sidonius' lending of his own copy to his friend Nymphidius, to whom he described Claudianus as "the most learned Christian philosopher."[23]

As for Faustus, he continued to proselytize on behalf of his own position. On one occasion, Paulinus of Bordeaux, probably the son of Pontius Leontius, wrote to him asking, "either whether the soul, enclosed in a corporeal bond, is contained in some sort of custody or is held by a closed prison, or whether it is tossed about uncertainly among the winds. . . . I would like to know whether the soul itself is better described as corporeal or incorporeal."[24] Faustus, not surprisingly, responded, "That which coincides with God, this alone is incorporeal. . . . [But] the soul is enclosed in a localized space. . . . What is that which, removed from its supernal home, submits to a place, if not corporeal?"[25]

Sidonius himself, whether his personal theological sentiments inclined him thus or not, was deeply implicated in the publication of Claudianus' work.[26] After all, he had encouraged Claudianus to publish it, even though this may have been merely his exercise of the accepted literary convention of the day. Furthermore, not only had Claudianus made him the dedicatee, he also had attempted to recruit him as an incorporealist by making use of another such convention (C.S.E.L. 11.20):

21. "editionem libellorum mihi quos de animae statu condidi. . . . imperasti . . . multi hoc idem mihi et idem ipsi tecum magni admodum viri negotium dedere. . . ." (De statu animae praef.: C.S.E.L. 11.18).

22. Ties: Sid. Apoll. Epist. 4.11.5-6.

23. Epist. 5.2.1. Nymphidius: Sid. Apoll. Carm. 15.200; P.L.R.E. II p.789. Wood, "End" p.22, supposes that another opponent of Faustus would have been Constantius of Lyons: "Constantius and Faustus had no direct contact (their theology differed too much)." The two, however, certainly associated on the occasion of the dedication of Patiens' basilica (Sid. Apoll. Epist. 2.10, 9.3.5), and there is no clear evidence either for what Constantius' theology was, or that differences of this nature prevented personal associations.

24. "aut utrum anima vinculo seclusa corporeo custodia aliqua mancipetur an carcere clausa teneatur aut utrum inter auras incerta iactetur. . . . aut ipsa anima corporea an incorporea melius vocetur, edocear" (apud Faust. Epist. 14/4). For Paulinus and Pontius Leontius, see P.L.R.E. II pp.847, 674-675. Paulinus had been discussing the matter with the hermit Marinus.

25. "quod soli deo conpetit, hoc tantum incorporeum esse cognosce. . . . anima . . . localibus spatiis continetur. . . . quid est enim nisi corporeum, quod de supernis sedibus proturbatum loco cessit?" (Epist. 15/5.25-27).

26. Some would assert that Sidonius had no aptitude for such topics: for his supposed "theological ignorance," see Stevens, Sidonius p.135.

You should only take care to remember, not without care for yourself, that it is fitting for me to produce what you order me to publish. . . . Accordingly, protect and defend your counsel, because if I run any risk by being the author of this work, you do so also by being the editor.[27]

As a result, Sidonius may have antagonized his other good friend, Faustus.[28]

It may have been Sidonius' fear of alienating Faustus all the more which caused him to neglect to acknowledge Claudianus' dedication.[29] This breach of contemporary literary protocol ultimately resulted in a peevish letter from Claudianus, who complained, "I do not think this can be perpetrated against the laws of friendship with impunity. Even now I sorrowfully remain silent because you have not acknowledged with any reply those books which you did not disdain to have ennobled by your name."[30] Sidonius' response was conventionally deprecating: he had delayed because he was reluctant to submit his meager writing to Claudianus' judgment. He then went on to deliver the expected and customary fulsome praise of Claudianus' work.[31]

Sidonius' association with the incorporealist party does seem to have turned Faustus against him. Circa 470, for example, the priest and monk Riochatus, who was delivering copies of one of Faustus' theological tracts to the Bretons of Lugdunensis III, stopped at Clermont.[32] He did not, however, bring with him a letter from Faustus to

27. "tu modo faxis uti memineris non absque cura tui prodi oportere, quod publicari iubes. . . . proinde consilium tuum adserito et defensitato: quoniam si in his secus aliquid, ego conscriptionis periclitabor, sed tu editionis. . . ."

28. For Sidonius' ties to Faustus, see Sid. Apoll. Carm. 16, Epist. 2.10.3; 9.3; 9.9, and nn.67-69 below; for those to Claudianus, see Sid. Apoll. Epist. 4.2-3,11; Mamert. Claud. Epist. 1 and De statu animae praef. (C.S.E.L. 11. 198-199, 18-20).

29. Sidonius' problems as a new bishop (Sid. Apoll. Epist. 3.2) also could have kept him from his epistolary duties.

30. "non arbitror amicitiae legibus impune committi. illud etiamnum dolenter faxo tacitum, quod libellos illos, quos tuo nomine nobilitari non abnuis, nullo umquam inpertivisti rescripto" (Sid. Apoll. Epist. 4.2.2). Krusch (M.G.H. A.A. 8.lx) concludes that Sidonius did not know whom Claudianus was attacking when Sidonius alluded to "eum, quem contra loquitur" (Epist. 4.3.6). One might wonder, however, whether Sidonius truly was so unaware of the intellectual activities of his times, and Engelbrecht (C.S.E.L. 21.xx) probably is correct when he suggests that Sidonius did know the identity of Claudianus' opponent; see also Weigel, Faustus p.86, for the delay being a result of Sidonius' embarrassment.

31. Epist. 4.3. For the suggestion that Sidonius included Claudianus' letter in his own corpus (Epist. 4.2) in order to show Faustus that he had praised Claudianus only under duress, see Engelbrecht, C.S.E.L. 21.xx, and Weigel, Faustus p.87 n.3.

32. The trip occurred "donec gentium concitatarum procella defremeret" (Sid. Apoll. Epist. 9.9.6), probably sometime in 469 or shortly afterward, when the Bretons of Riothamus were engaged by Anthemius to oppose the Visigoths (Chron. gall. 511, no. 649 s.a.471: M.G.H. A.A. 9.664, Greg. Tur.H.F. 2.18, Jord. Get. 237-238, and Sid. Apoll. Epist. 3.9). Loyen, Lettres 3.218, associates the disturbances with Anthemius' invasion of Gaul in 471; but this directly affected only southern Gaul. Chadwick (Poetry p.196) inexplicably dates this letter to after 478.

Sidonius, even though Sidonius and his confrères usually seized upon every possible opportunity to maintain their epistolary ties.[33] Riochatus even had been expressly instructed by Faustus not to show Sidonius the tract he was carrying.[34] Furthermore, in Sidonius' rhetorical imaginings as to why Faustus had slighted him—envy, sycophancy, junior status, lack of learning—his last possibility rings most true: "Or for some reason have we become estranged, so that it was thought I would be derogatory toward these books which you have authored?"[35]

If Faustus saw Sidonius as a partisan of Claudianus, it probably would be safe to assume that this is exactly what Faustus did think, and that momentarily, at least, Faustus and Sidonius were alienated from each other.[36] Ultimately, however, any bad feeling wore off, and epistolary intercourse between them resumed. Sidonius later wrote to Faustus, "You complained that for a long time we had maintained our mutual silence."[37]

FAUSTUS AND THE CHURCH OF MARSEILLES

It would appear, moreover, that Faustus' position on the soul prevailed in Gaul.[38] Claudianus seems to have suffered obloquy after his death, which occurred soon afterward, as noted by Sidonius in a letter to Claudianus' nephew Petreius: "For also because of the fact that there is scant faith kept even among the living, you should not think it strange if you should find that there are very few indeed who love the dead."[39] In his *De gratia* of shortly after 470, Faustus seems to have taken the opportunity to have the last word when he, perhaps in response to Claudianus' interpretation of *Genesis* 1.26-27, asserted, "The likeness is possessed not in physical appearance but in moral

---

33. Sid. Apoll. *Epist.* 9.9.2, 6. Faustus also failed to answer one of Sidonius' letters at this time, perhaps not simply because Faustus had been out of town, as Sidonius later purported to be willing to believe (*Epist.* 9.9.1).

34. Sid. Apoll. *Epist.* 9.9.3, 6-7.

35. "an aliquo casu dissidebamus, ut putaremur his quos edidissetis libellis derogaturi?" (Sid. Apoll. *Epist.* 9.9.5).

36. See Pricoco, "Studi" pp.133-140, and de la Broise, *Mamerti* pp.43-44 n.3.

37. "longum tacere ... nos in commune dequestus es" (*Epist.* 9.9.1, see also *Epist.* 9.3).

38. One cannot agree with Griffe (*Gaule* 3.381) that Faustus' views on the soul did not have much success in Gaul; see Momigliano, "Cassiodorus" p.210: "[Claudianus'] follower was in Italy rather than in France."

39. "namque et ex hoc, quod vix reservatur imaginaria fides vel superstitibus, non praeter aequum opinabere, si perpaucos esse conicias, qui mortuos ament" (Sid. Apoll. *Epist.* 4.11.7). Loyen, *Lettres* 2.252, dates this letter to 471/477. For the more commonly held view that Claudianus died c.473/474, see Altaner, *Patrology* p.567; Chadwick, *Poetry* p.207; Engelbrecht, "Sprache" p.426; and Schanz, *Geschichte* p.547.

virtues.... Those who think that justice and the other virtues of the soul have substance are in error."[40]

Later Gallic writers also supported the corporealist position. This last statement of Faustus may have influenced the assessment of Gennadius of Marseilles in his *Liber sive definitio ecclesiasticorum dogmatum* (55[88]): "In response to the new little legislators, who claim that the soul is created so much in the image of God that, because God rightly is believed to be incorporeal, the soul too is incorporeal, we freely confess that the eternal image finds its likeness in moral virtues."[41] Elsewhere, Gennadius backhandedly complimented Claudianus as a "man ingenious in speech and precise in argumentation."[42]

Gennadius' support of corporeality also is suggested by his entry on Julianus Pomerius, an African rhetor relocated to Arles, in which he reported without comment that Pomerius had written a *De natura animae et qualitate eius* (now lost), about "whether the soul should be considered corporeal or incorporeal," composed in the late fifth century "with fitting language and sentiment" (that is, presumably Gennadius agreed with him).[43] Gennadius did not say which side Pomerius supported, but the seventh-century Spanish writer Isidore of Seville did. In his own *De viris inlustribus* Isidore not only repeated Gennadius' account, but also editorialized, "Agreeing with the errors of Tertullian, he asserted that the soul is corporeal, attempting to prove this with certain false arguments."[44] Pomerius, therefore, favored Faustus' view that the soul was corporeal, and because Pomerius was one of the leaders of the intellectual circle of Arles before and after A.D.500, and was the mentor of Caesarius of Arles, his views on the soul too presumably would have been acceptable in those circles.[45]

Gennadius also noted that Pomerius had composed this work "at

40. "similitudo non in vultibus, sed in virtutibus possidetur.... errant ergo qui iustitiam reliquasque virtutes animae putant esse substantiam" (*De gratia* 2.9).

41. "propter novellos legislatores, qui ideo animam tantum ad imaginem dei creatam dicunt ut quia deus incorporeus recte creditur etiam incorporea anima esse credatur, libere confitemur imaginem in aeternitate similitudinem in moribus inveniri." Text: Turner, "Liber," cf. *P.L.* 42.1222, 58.1000; see also *Clavis* no.958. For the same sentiments, see the pseudo-Eucherian *Commentarii in Genesim* (*P.L.* 50.900), "sed in interiore homine est conditoris sui imago, imago in immortalitate, similitudo in moribus...." For similar terminology, see Faust. *De gratia* 1.8, "audi legislatorem de voluntatis arbitrio disputantem," and *De sept. ord. eccl. praef.*, "si modo ad injuriam non revoces novelli exhortatoris."

42. "vir ad loquendum artifex et disputandum subtilis" (*Vir. ill.* 84). Gennadius' is alluding to Claudianus' own statement (*De statu animae epil.*) that he had written "subtilissima disputatione." For Gennadius' opposition to Claudianus, see Morin, "Liber dogmatum" p.488.

43. "utrum anima corporea an incorporea debeat credi ... sermone ingenioque apto" (*Vir. ill.* 99). Gennadius describes Julianus Pomerius as an African.

44. "Tertulliani erroribus consentiens, animam corpoream esse dixit, quibusdam hoc fallacibus argumentis astruere contendens" (*Vir. ill.* 12).

45. Pomerius also was a friend of the bishop Aeonius and the aristocrat Firminus of Arles, see *VCaesarii* 1.8-9 and Ruric. *Epist.* 1.17, 2.10.

the request of the bishop Julianus and the presbyter Verus."[46] Julianus perhaps is Julianus, bishop of Avignon in the 470s, who therefore would have been another of Faustus' partisans in this controversy.[47] Verus, on the other hand, may be the Verus who succeeded Eutropius as bishop of Orange. He wrote his predecessor's extant *vita*, and may have shared his Massiliote ties.[48] If Verus, assuming his priesthood also was at Orange, made his request with the assent of his bishop, then Eutropius too will have supported Faustus in the controversy over the soul.

Any Massiliotes who supported Faustus, however, may have done so against the wishes of their bishop. Graecus, bishop of Marseilles in the 470s, did not always see eye-to-eye with the bishop of Riez. He probably is to be identified with the deacon Graecus who, perhaps before 451, wrote a work which Faustus accused of being tainted with Nestorianism.[49] Faustus was especially severe in his assessment of Graecus' work (*Epist.* 17/7):

In this little writing, which you thought it proper to send me, there appears no eloquence, no wisdom, no understanding, no organization at all of ordered or refined speech, but rather this writing, heaped together most confusingly from the point of view of ease of memory, attests the rashness of an incautious spirit.[50]

Now, at a time when Gallic *litterati* were generally restrained in their criticisms of each other, Faustus was uncharacteristically, and insultingly, harsh.

Graecus' resentment may have festered over the years, and after becoming bishop of Marseilles he may have been reluctant to support Faustus' position in other debates. Perhaps it was one of these controversies to which Sidonius was referring when he consoled Graecus in the early 470s because "recently you have suffered much grief on account of certain brothers."[51] The clergy of Marseilles, of course,

---

46. "interrogantibus Juliano episcopo et Vero presbytero" (*Vir. ill.* 99.).

47. Julianus: Duchesne, *Fastes* 1.267. Sid. Apoll. *Epist.* 9.5 is to a bishop Julianus, presumably this one.

48. Verus: Duchesne, *Fastes* 1.266; for the *vita*, see the *Bulletin du Comité Historique des Monuments Ecrits de l'Histoire de France* 1(1849) pp.52-64. Eutropius: chapters 6 (n.10), 9 (n.40) above. Heinzelmann, "Prosopographie" pp.636, 664, dates the life to c.500.

49. For the date, see de la Broise, *Mamerti* p.33 n.1; Engelbrecht, *C.S.E.L.* 21.xxi-xxii; and Griffe, *Gaule* 3.373 n.60. For the view that this dispute concerned monophysitism rather than Nestorianism, see Duckett, *Writers* pp.199, 251 n.31. See also Bergmann, *Predigtliteratur* pp.250-252.

50. "in hac autem scripturula, quam ad me dirigere dignatus es, non eloquentia, non scientia, non ratio, non aedificatio aliqua ordinati aut conpuncti sermonis adparet, sed testimonia confusissime pro memoriae facilitate congesta temeritatem incauti cordis adcusant."

51. "nuper quorumpiam fratrum necessitate multos pertuleritis angores...." (*Epist.* 9.4.2). This letter is dated to 473 by Loyen, *Lettres* 3.218.

had a long history of opposition to their bishop, and Faustus himself had been involved with the malcontents in the past.[52] If Graecus opposed Faustus, for example, on the nature of the soul, and Gennadius and others with Massiliote ties, such as Eutropius, favored him, dissension certainly could have arisen.[53] Furthermore, Sidonius' own close friendship with Graecus in the early 470s may have added to the strain in Sidonius' relations with Faustus.[54]

The controversy over the nature of the soul, then, provides some helpful insight into the intellectual affiliations of Gallic ecclesiastics c.470. The corporealist party of Faustus, which included Gennadius and Julianus Pomerius, not to mention, perhaps, Julianus of Avignon and Eutropius of Orange, seems to have overwhelmed its opponents, who included Mamertus Claudianus and others, such as his brother Mamertus, perhaps Graecus of Marseilles, and maybe even Sidonius. In doing so, the Gauls also dismissed another of the teachings of Augustine. Indeed, one of Mamertus Claudianus' mistakes may have been in aligning himself too closely with the African doctor.[55] This taking of sides, coincidentally or otherwise, repeats the conventional factional division of earlier in the century, with the Lerinenses, such as Faustus, opposed, *inter alios*, to the bishops of Vienne and Marseilles.[56] One also notes the great number of controversies in which Faustus seems to have been centrally involved. His activities apparently encouraged partisanship, and it might be asked whether his opponents, and supporters, were more concerned with his views or simply with him.

THE LUCIDUS AFFAIR AND
THE COUNCILS OF ARLES AND LYONS

In the years after 470, Gallic opposition to Augustinian predestination was in no way mitigated. At Marseilles, the center of such sentiments in the 420s, the priest Gennadius said of Augustine circa 490 (*Vir. ill.* 39),

---

52. See chapter 6 above. For Faustus' ties to John Cassian of Marseilles, see Chadwick, *Cassian* pp.149-152. There is no evidence that Paulinus of Pella, who lived in Marseilles in the late 450s (see Mathisen, "Aquitania" pp.162-165), took any part in these controversies. He seems to have been something of an outsider.

53. Eutropius also had been close to an unnamed Massiliote abbot, whom the Bollandists (*A.A.S.S.* May VI p.694) suggest may have been Cassian.

54. Sidonius included in his published corpus of letters no fewer than five to Graecus (*Epist.* 6.8, 7.2, 7, 10[11], 9.4), more than to any other individual, and only two (ibid.9.3,9) to Faustus.

55. For Claudianus as an Augustinian, see Altaner, *Patrology* p.567; Fortin, *Christianisme* pp.75-128; and Schmid, "Claudianus" col.175-178. Sidonius even could go so far as to compare the two (*Epist.* 4.3.7).

56. For Faustus' continued ties to Lérins, see Sid. *Carm.* 16.104-106 and chapter 9 above, n.18.

Whence, that which the Holy Spirit said through Solomon, 'In verbosity you shall not escape sin,' also happened to one who said a great deal. . . . Nevertheless error was incurred, as I said, by the excessive speaking of that man, was enlarged by the attack of his enemies, and not yet has escaped the accusation of heresy.[57]

Gennadius also is thought to have been the author of a rather earlier short *Adversus omnes haereseos*, which more specifically condemned predestination: "The predestinarians are those who say that God did not create all men so that all might be saved, but so that the earth might be adorned with a multitude of inhabitants."[58]

The leader of the Gallic anti-predestinarians was Faustus of Riez. Like most Gallic theologians, he did not condemn Augustine *in toto*, but only certain of his premises. In his letter to the deacon Graecus he had noted, "Even if some part of the works of the blessed bishop Augustine is thought to be suspect by the most learned men, you should know that there is nothing reprehensible in those sections which you thought should be condemned."[59] Graecus, apparently, had been overly enthusiastic in his denunciations of Augustine and had to be restrained. Only specialists, Faustus went on to say, were qualified to evaluate and criticize Augustine.

Faustus' opposition to Augustine is seen more clearly, however, in his role in the most important theological controversy of this period, which concerned certain teachings of Pelagius and, in particular, Augustine regarding grace, labor, free will, and, especially, predestination. It began perhaps just before 470, when the theological views of the priest Lucidus, whose city is unknown, were challenged by Faustus.[60] Briefly put, Lucidus was accused of denying the role of human labor and of favoring Augustinian predestination.[61] The resultant discussions ultimately culminated in one council held at Arles, which brought together some thirty bishops from throughout Gaul, and another held at Lyons.

---

57. "unde et multa loquenti accidit, quod dixit per Salomonem spiritus sanctus, 'in multiloquio non effugies peccatum' . . . error tamen illius sermone multo, ut dixi, contractus, lucta hostium exaggeratus, necdum haeresis questionem absolvit." For Gennadius' similar condemnation of Augustine's supporter Prosper, see chapter 6 above, n.96.

58. "praedestinatiani sunt qui dicunt quod deus non omnes homines ad hoc creavit ut omnes salventur, sed ut multitudine hominum ornetur mundus" (*P.L.* 81.644). This section is appended to Ps.-Jerome, *Indiculus de haeresibus* (*P.L.* 81.636-644), with the note "haec vero quae sequuntur a sancto Gennadio Massiliensi presbytero sunt posita." See Morin, "Trois" pp.451-454.

59. "in scriptis sancti pontificis Augustini etiamsi quid apud doctissimos viros putatur esse suspectum, ex his quae damnanda iudicasti nihil noveris reprehensum" (*Epist.* 17/7). For the "quid" as a reference to predestination, see Bergmann, *Predigtliteratur* p.251. See also Koch, *Faustus* pp.39-128.

60. See Engelbrecht, *C.S.E.L.* 21.xiii-xv; Griffe, *Gaule* 3.370-373; Koch, *Faustus* p.18; and Lumpe, "Ennodius" p.31ff.

61. Faust. *Epist.* 18-19/1-2.

The Letter to Lucidus

Faustus attempted to prevail upon Lucidus to recant first through personal confrontation, and then by correspondence: "How can I speak with Your Singlemindedness about this matter, at your wish, in correspondence, when in much sweet and humble discussion I was not able to draw you to the road of truth?"[62] This letter contained a list of anathemas, condemning both predestination and Pelagianism, to which Lucidus was requested to subscribe. Faustus concluded by saying:

> I am keeping with me a copy of this letter to be presented, if such should be necessary, in the council of the holy bishops. If Your Fraternity thinks it should be acknowledged, you should either return it quickly signed by your own hand, or respond in a subsequent answer that you reject it altogether.[63]

This letter survives in two versions, one of which is subscribed to only by Faustus himself, and the other of which has not only his name but also those of ten other bishops:[64]

Auxanius
Faustus
Paulus
Eutropius
Pragmatius
Patiens
Euphronius
Megethius
Claudius
Leocadius
Julianus

In the past, some have questioned the authenticity of these signatures, suggesting, for example, that the entire list was concocted by Faustus or that the additional names were a later interpolation.[65] The first

---

62. "quid possum de hoc sensu, sicut vis, cum unanimitate tua per litteras loqui, cum te praesens multa et blanda et humili conlocutione numquam potuerim ad viam veritatis adtrahere" (Faust. *Epist.* 18/1).

63. "huius autem epistulae exemplar mecum retineo in conventu sanctorum antistitum, si ita necesse fuerit, proferendum. quam si suscipiendam putaverit fraternitas tua, aut subscriptam manu propria mox remittat aut sequentibus scriptis omnino se improbasse respondeat" (ibid.).

64. Faust. *Epist.* 18/1: see the manuscript traditions in *C.S.E.L.* 21.164-165 and *M.G.H. A.A.* 8.290.

65. See Weigel, *Faustus* pp.94-100. For the suggestion that Faustus sent one copy to Lucidus with his own signature, and then obtained those of the others at the Council of Arles, see Engelbrecht, *C.S.E.L.* 21.xiv, although he cannot explain why "non omnes, at complures" (actually only one-third) of the bishops there subscribed.

suggestion, however, can be dismissed out of hand: all of the bishops
involved also seem to have attended the Council of Arles, and Faustus
would have fooled no one. This suggestion may have arisen because
the name of Lucidus follows those of the bishops; perhaps he actually
was compelled to subscribe at Arles. The possibility that the list is an
interpolation, on the other hand, can be considered best by determining whether or not it is internally consistent. If it is, the chances that
the names in it were assembled haphazardly by a later copyist would
be vanishingly small. Any analysis of this letter which accepts the list
as genuine, moreover, also must explain the anomalous ordering of
the names. They clearly are not in the normal hierarchical order. The
names of Patiens of Lyons, the metropolitan of Lugdunensis Prima,
and of the aged Euphronius of Autun, for example, appear only sixth
and seventh. A study of this list might begin by investigating the
personal preferences and affiliations of the individuals involved.

Faustus and the North. One person involved in the controversy from
the very beginning was Faustus, whose ties were very strong in Lyons
and the north. Faustus' friendship with Sidonius Apollinaris, a native
of Lyons, already has been mentioned.[66] Sidonius' otherwise unknown
brother was a student of Faustus, and Sidonius visited Faustus at Riez;
Sidonius also heard Faustus preach many times.[67] Along with two
letters, Sidonius dedicated a lengthy poem to Faustus, the only one of
his *carmina* addressed to a cleric.[68]

Faustus himself visited Lyons at least once, when the bishop Patiens
was dedicating a new church of St. Justus. Sidonius said of the occasion, "Then, especially, when at the week-long celebration of the dedication of the church at Lyons you were beseeched by the request of
your sacrosanct colleagues to deliver an oration...."[69] Furthermore,
Faustus not only seems to have been a pupil of Eucherius of Lyons,
but even went so far as to refer to Lyons as "Lugdunus nostra."[70]

Faustus also had broader ties throughout Lugdunensis. He himself
was of either British or, perhaps, Breton, origin.[71] He sent the afore-

66. See n.28 above, and Chadwick, *Poetry* pp.193-198; Griffe, *Gaule* 2.263-264; and Krusch,
*M.G.H. A.A.*8.lvii.

67. Sid. Apoll. *Carm.* 16.78-126, *Epist.* 9.3.5.

68. *Epist.* 9.3, 9.9, *Carm.* 16.

69. "tunc praecipue, cum in Lugdunensis ecclesiae dedicatae festis hebdomadalibus collega-
rum sacrosanctorum rogatu exorareris, ut perorares...." (Sid. Apoll. *Epist.* 9.3.5, see also 2.10.2).
Chadwick (*Poetry* pp.193-195) supposes that on this occasion Sidonius composed his *Carmen* 16
for Faustus, but the poem is too juvenile to have been written this late (see Stevens, *Sidonius*
p.132ff), and the preaching mentioned in *Carm.* 16.124-126 occurred at Riez, not at Lyons.

70. See Faustus' sermon *De sancta Blandina lugdunensis* (*P.L.* 50.859-861) for his presence in
and references to Lyons. See also Griffe, *Gaule* 2.263, 323-324, 328, 334, 3.219-221, who suggests
that Faustus may have had family ties there. Eucherius: see note 15 above.

71. See chapter 4 above, n.54.

mentioned Riochatus to the Bretons of Lugdunensis III with copies of theological tracts, perhaps the *De spiritu sancto* or the *De gratia*, in the early 470s.[72] He also interceded with Ruricius, bishop of Limoges, on behalf of a presbyter who was trying to free his wife and daughter from captivity in Lugdunensis.[73] Finally, Faustus served first as a monk and then as abbot at the monastery of Lérins, most of whose monks were from the north, and particularly from Lugdunensis Prima.

Faustus and Auxanius. The Auxanius whose name heads the list of the signers of the Lucidus letter apparently is to be identified with the bishop Auxanius who was present with Faustus in Rome in 462, and who seems to have been acting on behalf of the bishop of Marseilles. Presumably, therefore, Faustus and Auxanius were acquainted. Unfortunately, Auxanius' see is unknown. There is, however, an admittedly unreliable tradition which claims that the successor of Julius of Apt was an Auxanius.[74] This assertion might be considered in the light of a letter written by Sidonius c.470, in which he mentioned why Faustus had not replied to his immediately previous letter: "When it arrived at Riez, you, who then were at Apt, were aptly absent."[75] Not much, but enough to suggest that Faustus was a friend of the bishop of Apt, who just may have been Auxanius.[76]

It is possible that Auxanius, like Faustus, also had ties in the north. In 468, for example, another Auxanius, the son of a praetorian prefect, accompanied Sidonius as a member of an Arvernian delegation to Rome, and shortly thereafter an Auxanius, probably the same man, became abbot of the monastery of St. Abraham outside Clermont.[77] Later, in the 540s, an Auxanius and his lover Papianilla, the granddaughter of the Arvernian emperor Eparchius Avitus, were murdered by her husband Parthenius.[78]

Eutropius, Patiens, and Leocadius. Three more of the subscribers to

---

72. Sid. Apoll. *Epist.* 9.9.6-16. De la Broise (*Mamerti* p.43 n.3); Engelbrecht (*C.S.E.L.* 21.xv-xvi); and Krusch (*M.G.H. A.A.* 8.lvii) conjecture that the work sent was the *De gratia*, but others suggest the *De spiritu sancto*: see Bergmann, *Predigtliteratur* pp.35-55; Loyen, "Etudes" pp.83-90; and Pricoco, "Studi" pp.71-151. Loyen's date of 471 for Sidonius' letter (*Lettres* 3.218) would be consistent with the work being the *De gratia*.

73. Faust. *Epist.* 4/11.

74. Duchesne, *Fastes* 1.282 n.5, citing Polycarp. Auxanius could not have been bishop of Aix, see chapter 9 above, n.19.

75. "cum Reios advenerant, qui tunc Aptae fuistis, aptissime defuistis" (*Epist.* 9.9.1). For the date, see note 32 above.

76. If so, Auxanius' actions in 462 would indicate, again, not only that the bishop of Marseilles, Eustasius, claimed metropolitan status in Narbonensis II, but also that Auxanius supported him.

77. Sid. Apoll. *Epist.* 1.7.6-7, 7.17.4; see *P.L.R.E. II* pp.203-204

78. Greg. Tur. *H.F.* 3.36. In 545 another Auxanius was bishop of Arles, see *Epist. arel.* 41-42: *M.G.H. Epist.* 3.60-63.

the letter to Lucidus are associated in a passage from the *Vita Eutropii*, composed by Verus of Orange, the successor of the Eutropius who was one of the signers.[79] After reporting how Eutropius provided for his people during a famine, Verus went on to say, describing Eutropius' approaching death, "Not long afterward, having summoned his people and having notified Patiens and Leocadius, after revealing that he now was passing to the Lord the blessed man began to await the final day."[80] It seems likely that the Patiens and Leocadius who were the associates of Eutropius are the bishops of these names who, with Eutropius, subscribed to the letter to Lucidus. This tie between the bishops of Orange and Lyons apparently continued even after Eutropius', and Patiens', deaths, for it was Patiens' own successor Stephanus who requested Verus to compose the *vita*.

Patiens, of course, was bishop of Lyons, and Eutropius' ties to him may be clarified to a slight degree, for in a letter to Patiens, Sidonius gave his own description of the famine mentioned in the *Vita Eutropii*.[81] In Sidonius' version, however, it was Patiens who provided relief not only for the cities of Arles, Riez, Avignon, Viviers, Valence, Trois-Châteaux, and Clermont, but also for Orange itself. After making allowances for the circumstances under which both accounts were written, the one in honor of Eutropius and the other to Patiens, one might suggest that Patiens and Eutropius were cooperating with each other, a not unlikely possibility under the circumstances, and all the more probable given the other evidence for the ties between the two men. Such cooperation, moreover, would have occurred at about the same time as the Lucidus affair.[82]

Little more can be said about Leocadius; not even his see is known. Like Auxanius, he may have had northern connections. The grandmother of the Arvernian Gregory of Tours was a Leucadia, and one of her ancestors may have been the senator Leocadius of Bourges, who also may be the *praeses* Leocadius on whose behalf Martin of Tours interceded with Magnus Maximus c.383/388.[83] In 431, moreover, a *sacrata puella* Leucadia was buried at Lyons, and in the early sixth

---

79. For the *vita*, see above, note 48.

80. "cum ante multum tempus, vocatis suis, admonitis sanctus vir Patiente et Leucadio, ut ad dominum iam pergeret, prodidisset, expectare coepit diem ultimum. . . ." (*VEutropi* pp. 62-63). Heinzelmann, "Prosopographie" pp.636, 664, assumes that the word *suis* refers to Patiens and Leocadius, and he makes them Eutropius' relatives. If so, the locution would be very awkward, with two verbs in the same construction. It might be more prudent to assume that there are two ablatives absolute in sequence here.

81. *Epist.* 6.12.8.

82. Loyen (*Lettres* 3.188, 214) dates Sidonius' letter, and the famine, to the winter of 471-472. For a third version, see Greg. Tur. *H.F.* 2.24, who attributed the relief to Patiens and Ecdicius, the son of the emperor Avitus and Sidonius' brother-in-law.

83. Greg. Tur. *Vit. pat.* 6.1; Sulp. Sev. *Dial.* 3.11.8: see *P.L.R.E. I* p.504.

century, a presbyter "Lovocatus" (?Leocadius) was involved in a doctrinal dispute in Lugdunensis III.[84]

A more tenuous link may connect Eutropius and Julianus. Both, as
was seen above, seem to have supported Faustus in the controversy
over the soul. This could suggest, at least, that they may have favored
him here as well.

Euphronius, Patiens, and Iohannes. It already has been suggested that
the failure of both Patiens and Euphronius to subscribe to the Gallic
letter to Leo in 451/452 reflected their increasing pursuit of their own
interests in the north.[85] The two appear together in an account given
by Sidonius of the election c.470 of a new bishop of Chalon-sur-
Saône.[86] After the death of the bishop Paulus, a "pontifical council"
under the direction of Patiens and Euphronius, and attended by the
other bishops of the province, was assembled for the purpose of choosing a successor. Sidonius stressed both the contention over the selection of the new bishop and the arbitrary nature of Patiens' and Euphronius' final choice: the archdeacon Iohannes.[87]

Iohannes, then, presumably was a partisan of Patiens and Euphronius, and he customarily is identified as the bishop Iohannes who
attended the Council of Arles c.470, whose very junior position (he
subscribed twenty-eighth of thirty) would indicate that he indeed had
been elected only recently.[88] His predecessor Paulus, however, probably is not to be identified as the Paulus who subscribed to the letter
to Lucidus, for that Paulus appears again at the Council of Arles, in
the same position as he did in the letter to Lucidus, and at the council
of 463. This Paulus perhaps was the Paulus attested in the fifth century as bishop of Trois-Châteaux, who was himself a northerner, a
refugee from Rheims, and perhaps an ex-provincial governor.[89]

Pragmatius. The see of the Pragmatius who subscribed to the letter
to Lucidus is unknown. Nevertheless, he too may have had ties not
only in the north, but also to several of the other bishops who signed.
He probably is to be identified with the bishop Pragmatius of an unknown see who was requested by Sidonius to settle a lawsuit between

84. *C.I.L.* 13.2354; Jülicher, "Bischofsschreiben" pp.664-671. Jülicher emends the name
"Lovocatus" to "Leocadius." No Leucadii at all are known from southern Gaul.

85. See chapter 8 above.

86. *Epist.* 4.25.1-5.

87. For other influential Iohannes in Lugdunensis Prima, see Mathisen, "Hilarius," pp.
167-168.

88. See Duchesne, *Fastes* 1.132, and Weigel, *Faustus* p.107.

89. See Duchesne, *Fastes* 1.264, and chapters 4 (n.126) and 7 (n.94) above. His *vita* (*Analecta
bollandiana* 11[1892] pp.374-383) describes him as an "incola civitatis Remensis," and he perhaps
is to be identified with the *vir praesidalis* Paulus whose son Aelianus was buried at Lyons
(*P.L.R.E. II* p.851; see *C.I.L.* 13.1796).

the "venerabilis matrona" Eutropia and her daughter-in-law's father, the presbyter Agrippinus, one of Pragmatius' clerics.[90] Sidonius' involvement would suggest that Pragmatius' see was close to Clermont, as would other evidence for the provenance of the Agrippini: in 452 the aforementioned Count Agrippinus had been the recipient of a letter from Euphronius of Autun.[91]

Sidonius also referred to a *vir inlustris* Pragmatius, the son-in-law of the ex-praetorian prefect Priscus Valerianus of Lyons. This Pragmatius therefore would have been an *adfinis* of Eucherius of Lyons.[92] If the bishop Pragmatius were related to, or even identical with, this aristocrat, his affiliation to the northern party of Gallic bishops would be even more strongly suggested. Finally, Euphronius of Autun himself ultimately was succeeded by a Pragmatius.[93] All these considerations suggest that the bishop Pragmatius of c.470, if not from the north himself, had close ties there, and that his sympathies in the Lucidus controversy would have lain with the northern party of Faustus.

Sidonius and the Literary Circle. Another factor which connects most of the signers of the Lucidus letter is their appearances in the correspondence of Sidonius Apollinaris. Sidonius' connections to Faustus already have been discussed; others who received letters from him include Euphronius of Autun, Eutropius of Orange, Pragmatius, Patiens of Lyons, Megethius of Besançon and Julianus of Avignon (see Table 1).[94] Sidonius' letters to these individuals are concerned primarily with the pursuit of their mutual literary interests, the most personal form of interaction among Gallo-Roman aristocrats of the time, and one of the identifying marks of an aristocratic circle.[95]

Euphronius, for example, requested Sidonius to publish some of his works; Eutropius was asked by Sidonius for copies of his *exhortationes*; Patiens prevailed upon Sidonius to compose verses for the apse of his new church of St. Justus; Sidonius copied extracts from a work of Faustus; and Megethius received a copy of Sidonius' otherwise unknown *contestatiunculae*.[96] Circa 469, moreover, Sidonius canvassed

---

90. *Epist.* 6.2; see Mathisen, "Addenda" p.372, and chapters 8-9 above.

91. Hydatius *Chron.* 151, see chapter 8 above. The count even could have been the presbyter to whom Sidonius referred, if he, like many others of this period, finished his career in the church.

92. *Epist.* 5.10.1-2. For Valerianus' relationship to Eucherius, see Mathisen, "Petronius" pp.106-112, and chapter 4 above.

93. Duchesne, *Fastes* 1.278: he first appears in 517.

94. Sid. Apoll. *Epist.* 7.8, 9.2; 6.6; 6.2; 6.12; 7.3; 9.5.

95. See Chadwick, *Poetry* pp.197-198 and Mathisen, "Epistolography" pp.95-109.

96. *Epist.* 9.2; 6.6.2; 2.10.4; 9.9.8; 7.3.

TABLE I. *Addressees of Lucidus' Letter of Retraction to the Bishops Who Attended the Council of Arles*

Name	See	Province	Reference	Correspondence with Sidonius
1. Euphronius (#)	Autun	Lugdunensis I	D2.188	*Ep.*7.8; 9.2
2. Leontius (*)	Arles	Viennensis	D1.257	*Ep.*6.3
3. Fonteius	Vaison	Viennensis	D1.262	*Ep.*6.7; 7.4
4. Viventius		?Lugdunensis III	D2.344–380	
5. Mamertus (*)	Vienne	Viennensis	D1.205	*Ep.*7.1
6. Patiens (*)(#)	Lyons	Lugdunensis I	D2.163	*Ep.*6.12
7. Veranus	Vence	Alpes Maritimae	D1.294, 370n.5	
8. Auxanius (#)	?Apt	?Narbonensis II		
9. Faustus (#)	Riez	Narbonensis II	D1.284	*C.*16; *Ep.*9.3,9
10. Paulus (#)	Trois-Châteaux	Viennensis	D1.264.	
11. Megethius (*)(#)	Besançon	Maxima Sequan.	D3.201	*Ep.*7.3
12. Graecus (*?)	Marseilles	Viennensis	D1.274	*Ep.*6.8; 7.2,7,10; 9.4
13. Eutropius (#)	Orange	Viennensis	D1.265-6	*Ep.*6.6
14. Leontius				
15. Claudius (#)				
16. Marcellus	Die	Viennensis	D1.234	
17. Crocus	Nîmes	Narbonensis I	D1.312n	
18. Basilius (*)	Aix	Narbonensis II	D1.280	*Ep.*7.6
19. Claudius				
20. Ursicinus	?Paris	?Lugdunensis IV	D2.470	
21. Praetextatus				
22. Pragmatius (#)				*Ep.*6.2
23. Theoplastus	Geneva	Viennensis	D1.227–8	*Ep.*6.5
24. Leocadius (#)				
25. Viventius	Grenoble	Viennensis	D1.231	
26. Julianus (#)	Avignon	Viennensis	D1.267	*Ep.*9.5
27. Amicalis				
28. Iohannes	Chalon	Lugdunensis I	D2.192–3	
29. Opilio				
30. Licinius				

* Metropolitan status of some kind.   # Signed original letter to Lucidus
D = Duchesne, *Fastes.*

Euphronius of Autun, as well as Agroecius of Sens, in the matter of the election of a bishop for Bourges.[97] It appears that, at least through their mutual ties to Sidonius, these individuals shared not only close ecclesiastical ties, but also similar cultural and intellectual interests.

By one means or another, then, nearly all the signatories of the Lucidus letter but Claudius have been shown to have had varied interrelationships with several of their fellows. It is extremely unlikely,

97. *Epist.* 7.5; 7.8.

therefore, that the list of signers of the letter to Lucidus resulted from interpolations. They form, rather, an aristocratic, as well as an ecclesiastical, circle unified by ties of friendship, proximity, and mutual interests, and there can be little doubt but that the list of subscriptions appended to the letter must be accepted as genuine.

The Circumstances of the Lucidus Letter

The letter to Lucidus itself now can be considered. It already has been noted that the names in the subscriptions do not appear in their normal hierarchical order. There are several possible explanations for this. The list may have been corrupted, or the bishops, for some unfathomable reason, may have chosen to sign helter-skelter. But a more likely explanation, perhaps, is that not all the bishops subscribed at the same time. As in the case of the Ravennius-sponsored letter to Leo, a later group of signatures may have been appended to an earlier one.[98]

It may be that after Lucidus initially refused to concede, Faustus, Auxanius, and other sympathetic southern bishops assembled first, and subscribed to Faustus' letter condemning Lucidus. Then, probably soon afterward, an opportunity arose for them to present their case before some of their partisans in the north. Just such an opportunity may have occurred at the aforementioned dedication of Patiens' new church of St. Justus at Lyons. Faustus is known to have been present, and such celebrations often gave the opportunity for an impromptu church synod.[99] Moreover, the strong representation of bishops from the area of Lugdunensis Prima among the final six signers, viz. Patiens of Lyons, Euphronius of Autun, and Megethius of nearby Besançon, also is consistent with a meeting at Lyons. If this interpretation is correct, the gathering could not have taken place after c.469/470, for if it had, surely Sidonius, who was present, and a bishop himself since c.470, would have subscribed as well.[100]

Patiens' own interest in such theological matters, at least, is attested

---

98. See appendix "The Names in Ravennius' Letter to Leo."

99. Such a meeting would be consistent with the date of c.470 for the dedication suggested by Griffe, *Gaule* 2.288, 324, and Loyen, *Lettres* 3.247. Justus' festivals fell in October (the 14th and 21st) (Duchesne, *Fastes* 2.162), the customary time for Gallic church councils. Sidonius (*Epist.* 5.17.4) confirms that the celebration was in the fall. Weigel, *Faustus* p.80, ludicrously believes that the consecration was of Patiens himself. Other such impromptu councils could be occasioned by the dedication of a new church (*Corp. chr. lat.* 148A.42-46, 53-79), by the election of a new bishop (ibid.148.151, see also Hefele-Leclercq, *Conciles* 2.906-907), or by the celebration of a church festival (ibid.148.143). Such incidents illustrate again the irregular and *ad hoc* nature of many Gallic councils.

100. For Sidonius' election c.469/470, see Stevens, *Sidonius* p.207. Sidonius' accounts (*Epist.* 2.10.2, 9.3.5) give no indication whatsoever that he was a bishop.

elsewhere.[101] A Paris manuscript, for example, contains a section entitled "A notation excerpted from the *Book of Ecclesiastical Dogmas*, which saint Patiens brought forth."[102] Now, the contents of this notation are identical to chapter 21 of the *Liber sive definitio ecclesiasticorum dogmatum* now attributed to Gennadius of Marseilles, which deals with free will.[103] If Patiens supported the views of the antipredestinarian, and pro-Faustian, Gennadius on this question, he presumably would have favored Faustus' interpretation of grace in the Lucidus controversy. It also can be no accident that in a letter written to Patiens at the same time, Sidonius praised him for his opposition to heretics, and then qualified his statement by saying, perhaps referring to this very meeting, "even if, nonetheless, some of these activities must be shared, perhaps, with the rest of your colleagues."[104] The only heretics Sidonius named, however, were "Photinians," who were hardly a Gallic concern; perhaps Sidonius had some other group in mind, such as the Arian Burgundians, whom it would have been impolitic to mention by name.[105]

If the letter to Lucidus were signed in this manner, the anomalous ordering of the names could be explained. Presuming that the like-named bishops who attended the Council of Arles are the same as those who subscribed to the letter to Lucidus, the list of those who signed the letter breaks up into two halves whose members subscribed in the same relative order as they did at the Council of Arles (see Table 1). Auxanius, Faustus, Paulus, Eutropius, and Pragmatius, the first five to sign the Lucidus letter, appear at Arles in the eighth, ninth, tenth, thirteenth, and twenty-second positions. On the other

101. Other evidence for theological discussions in the north occurred c.470, when Sidonius recommended Lupus of Troyes and Auspicius of Toul to Arbogast, the count of Trier, as the most learned expositors of church doctrine in northern Gaul (*Epist.* 4.17.3). Sidonius said only that Arbogast had asked him to be an interpreter "de paginis . . . spiritalibus" (*Epist.* 4.17.3). Anderson (*Sidonius* 2.129) translates this merely as "Holy Writ," but Arbogast may have had something more specific in mind, perhaps Faustus' *De spiritu sancto*.

102. "adnotatio excerpta de Libro ecclesiasticorum dogmatum, quem sanctus Patiens protulit" (*Corp. chr. lat.* 148.161). It is unclear whether Patiens wrote the book himself, in which case "protulit" should be translated "published," or whether he took an excerpt from someone else's work with this title.

103. *P.L.* 42.985-986, 58.1000. See McClure, "Handbooks" p.189, Morin, "Liber dogmatum" passim, and Turner, "*Liber.*" Similar sentiments were expressed by Faustus (*De gratia* 1.9).

104. "et horum aliqua tamen cum reliquis forsitan communicanda collegis" (*Epist.*21.12.5).

105. The fourth-century Photinians were, in fact, loosely related to the Arians, (see the Council of Aquileia of 381 [*P.L.* 16.944]; Alc. Avit. *Contra arrianos* 7 [*M.G.H. A.A.* 6.2.4]; and Paul. Nol. *Epist.*21.4ff). The reference to Photinians in canon 16 of the "Second Council of Arles" (*Corp. chr. lat.* 148.114-125) merely repeats one of the canons of the Council of Nicaea. There is, moreover, a verbal similarity between "Photiniani" and "Pelagiani," even to the number of syllables, and Pelagianism, as will be seen, was a point of contention in the Lucidus controversy. For a date of 471-472 for the letter, see Loyen, *Lettres* 2.214.

hand, Patiens, Euphronius, Megethius, Claudius, Leocadius, and Julianus, the remaining six to sign the Lucidus letter, appear in the sixth,
first, eleventh, fifteenth or nineteenth (there were two Claudii at
Arles), twenty-fourth, and twenty-sixth positions at Arles. Only Euphronius is out of place, but this can be explained: at a purely provincial council, as when Patiens' church was dedicated, the metropolitan,
Patiens, would sign first. But at a multi-provincial council, as at Arles,
sometimes extraordinary precedence could be assigned simply on the
basis of tenure in office, and Euphronius seems to have been allowed
the honor of signing first because he was the most senior by consecration of all the bishops present.[106]

The first group of five bishops, therefore, seems to have subscribed
to the letter to Lucidus first, in their normal hierarchical order, and
later the second group did so as well. This conclusion is consistent
with the previous suggestion that all the bishops of the first group
probably were southern bishops, an inference which again indicates
that Paulus was the bishop of Trois-Châteaux. Pragmatius, whose see
is unknown, also may have had a see in the area.

Not all the southern bishops, however, signed then, for Julianus,
the bishop of Avignon, appears in the second group. He, then, would
have subscribed at Lyons.[107] His willingness to make the trip, perhaps
with Faustus, confirms his commitment to the policies of the northern
group: it already has been suggested that he supported Faustus in the
controversy over the soul. Finally, one can only note at this point the
absence of the bishop of Vienne and his suffragans from the subscriptions to the letter to Lucidus, and wonder whether this was by accident or design. The memory of Faustus' quarrel with Claudianus may
have been too fresh.

It may be significant, moreover, that the sees of the southern bishops who subscribed, Faustus of Riez, Auxanius (of Apt?), Eutropius
of Orange, Julianus of Avignon, and Paulus of Trois-Châteaux, are
nearly contiguous, with Apt in the center. The proximity of these sees
could suggest that the Lucidus controversy arose in this area, and even
that Lucidus was a presbyter of one of these five bishops. Now, in
spite of Faustus' deep concern in the case, he seems not to have been
Lucidus' bishop: his use of correspondence to contact Lucidus seems

106. See also n.115 below. Even in the letter to Lucidus, Euphronius' subscription was the
most elaborate of all those who signed (*C.S.E.L.* 21.164, *M.G.H. A.A.* 8.290), and perhaps was
intended to demonstrate his senior status.

107. Eutropius, too, whose predecessor coincidentally also was named Justus, may have made
the journey, for in a letter to him (*Epist.* 6.6.1), Sidonius indicated that they had met only once,
apparently c.470, and the dedication of Patiens' basilica would have been as good an occasion
as any.

too awkward for that.[108] It may be, rather, that the prestigious and influential Faustus was asked for help by his neighbor Auxanius. If Auxanius were the bishop most concerned in the case, it could explain why his name appears first in the list, just before that of Faustus, even though Faustus had preceded him in 463. The two then may have prevailed upon other local bishops for support.

THE COUNCIL OF ARLES

The affair of the Lucidus letter indicates that, as in the 450s and 460s, influential northern bishops maintained corporate interests in church dogma and practices. In this instance, one group of them was assisted by several southerners, at least two of whom, Faustus and Paulus, were expatriate northerners. But in spite of their best efforts, Lucidus still refused to yield, and Faustus' threat was carried out. A full-scale church council was convened under Leontius at Arles, perhaps c.470, or very shortly thereafter.[109] The only document surviving from the council is the resultant letter of retraction which Lucidus addressed to the thirty bishops who attended.[110] A discussion of the council, therefore, might begin with an analysis of the list of addressees (Table 1), and what their viewpoints are likely to have been.[111]

Because the letter of retraction lists only the attendees' names, not all of their sees are known. Those which are known serve to set this

108. Faustus also referred to his dealings "with an absent one" (*Epist.* 18/1). Duchesne, *Fastes* 1.132; Krusch (*M.G.H.A.A.* 8.lvi) and Koch, *Faustus* p.18, do suppose that Lucidus was a presbyter at Riez.

109. Faust. *Epist.* 19/2, see *Corp. chr. lat.* 148.159-160 for a summary of the sources for the council. This date was suggested above as a *terminus ante quem* for the letter to Lucidus; it is presumed that the council occurred shortly thereafter. Suggested dates for this council, and the subsequent one at Lyons, none based upon very firm evidence, vary between 470 and 475. Chadwick, *Poetry* p.199, and Schanz, *Geschichte* p.542, support 475. Duchesne, *Fastes* 1.132, offers 474-475, and Duckett, *Writers* p.201, who wrongly believes there was only a single council at Lyons, prefers 474. Altaner, *Patrology* p.566; Rusch, *Latin Fathers* p.171; and Weigel, *Faustus* pp.80, 93-109, opt for 473-474; and Lumpe, "Ennodius" suggests 473/475. Koch, *Faustus* p.18, and Engelbrecht, *C.S.E.L.* 21.xv, prefer 473; and Krusch, *M.G.H. A.A.* 8.lvi, merely some date before 475. Griffe, *Gaule* 2.289, 3.371-373, however, favors 470-471; and Munier, *Corp. chr. lat.* 148.159, suggests c.470. Engelbrecht and Griffe depend upon their estimated dates for the exile of bishop Crocus of Nîmes, neither one realizing that even after his exile he still could have attended.

110. The only mention of a council at Arles appears in the prologue to Faustus' subsequent *De gratia*: Lucidus' statement does not specify where the council took place. It is assumed that Faustus and Lucidus were referring to the same council.

111. For the list, see Faust. *Epist.* 19/2: *Corp. chr. lat.* 148.159, *C.S.E.L.* 21.165, *M.G.H. A.A.* 8.290. The ordering of names is that preserved in the ninth-century *Codex sangellensis* 190. The same order (mistakenly copied by rows rather than columns) is given by Hincmar in the *Liber de praedestinatione dei et libero arbitrio* 1. The list also is preserved in the ninth-century *Codex parisinus* 2166, with great confusion in the middle and with three names (Crocus, Claudius, and Ursicinus) omitted.

meeting apart from every other fifth-century Gallic council. Not only did some bishops come from Septem Provinciae (Viennensis, Narbonensis I and II, and Alpes Maritimae), but others also came from the more northern provinces of Gallia (Lugdunensis I, perhaps III and IV, and Maxima Sequanorum). In only one other instance, the Council of Orange of 441, did even one northern bishop, Eucherius of Lyons, attend a southern council in the fifth century.[112] The Council of Arles also marked the first time that the influential bishops of Arles, Marseilles, Aix, Vienne, and Lyons all sat down together at the same council.[113] As many as six, or even more, bishops with metropolitan status of some kind attended.[114]

Perhaps because of continuing controversies over precedence, the seating arrangements at Arles seem to have been unusually democratic. The list of bishops was headed by the name of Euphronius of Autun, apparently in his capacity as both eldest and senior bishop by consecration.[115] Leontius did, however, as host and metropolitan bishop of Arles, reserve for himself the second position. The remainder subscribed in strict order of tenure status, even the metropolitans.[116]

The "northern" party of Faustus was especially well represented. All eleven bishops who signed the letter to Lucidus made the journey to Arles, as did Iohannes of Chalon, the newly elected protégé of Patiens and Euphronius. Furthermore, the Ursicinus who attended perhaps is to be identified with the Ursicinus who was bishop of Paris in Lugdunensis Quarta. At least one bishop from Lugdunensis Tertia (the first Viventius) also may have attended.[117]

Of the remaining sixteen bishops, all ten who can be identified

112. In 451/452 it appears that some northerners did sign Ravennius' letter to Leo, but they do not seem to have gone actually to Arles, see appendix "The Names in Ravennius' Letter to Leo."

113. The absence of the bishop of Narbonne presumably was a result of the notorious Visigothic interference in church affairs at this time, not of a boycott.

114. The metropolitans of the Alpine provinces, whose identities are not known, perhaps would have been present as well. It is unclear whether Graecus retained any vestigial metropolitan status.

115. In a letter to Leontius, Sidonius (*Epist.* 6.3.1) listed the factors which established episcopal status: "chronological age, tenure in office, status of see."

116. An observation which demonstrates that the order of names given in the *Codex sangallensis* is indeed correct. An exception appears to be Graecus of Marseilles, who at Arles subscribed four places ahead of Marcellus of Die. Marcellus had been ordained by 463, at which time Graecus' predecessor Eustasius was still in office. Graecus also seems to have been junior to Basilius of Aix (Sid. Apoll. *Epist.* 7.6.10).

117. The first Viventius in the Arles list perhaps is to be identified with the Viventius of Lugdunensis Tertia who attended the Council of Angers in 453 (*Corp. chr. lat.* 148.137; Duchesne, *Fastes* 2.244, 274-380); his tenure status would be consistent with his having been in office by 453. It is unclear whether this is the same Viventius who also was in office by the early 450s and who attended the council of 463 (chapter 9 above).

came from Vienne and points south.[118] Most of these were from Viennensis, including Leontius (Arles), Fonteius (Vaison), Viventius (Grenoble), Mamertus (Vienne), Graecus (Marseilles), Marcellus (Die),
and Theoplastus (Geneva). From Narbonensis Prima came Crocus
(Nîmes), from Narbonensis Secunda, Basilius (Aix), and from Alpes
Maritimae, Veranus (Vence).

This leaves six bishops unaccounted for: the second Leontius, one
of the Claudii (the other having signed the letter to Lucidus), Praetextatus, Amicalis, Opilio, and Licinius. This latter Leontius may be
the Leontius who was a subdeacon at Riez in 442, when he attended
the Council of Vaison.[119] Similarly, at the same council a deacon Claudius of Grenoble was in attendance, and he eventually may have obtained his own see as a partisan of his possible relative Mamertus of
Vienne.[120] The name Praetextatus occurs twice in southern episcopal
contexts: one was bishop of Apt c.515/545 and another was bishop of
Cavaillon c.550.[121] Regarding the rest, little can be said at all. Opilio's
name suggests that he may have had Italian ties.[122]

Factional Considerations

It already has been shown that a group of influential northern bishops supported Faustus in his campaign against Lucidus. Some southern bishops, however, in the past had not cooperated effectively either
among themselves or with Faustus. Eight of the bishops at Arles (Fonteius, the first Viventius, Veranus, Auxanius, Faustus, Paulus, Eutropius, and the second Leontius) had attended the council of 463 on the
Mamertus affair.[123] That council, however, had been boycotted by
Leontius of Arles, not to mention Mamertus of Vienne, and appar-

118. The name of Sidonius is notably absent from the list. Is this because he was prevented
from attending because of Visigothic hostilities (no bishops from Aquitania I-II or Novempopulana attended), because he was not yet bishop (in which case the council would have been
earlier than is thought), or because he preferred not to put himself once again into the middle
of a theological controversy?

119. *Corp. chr. lat.* 148.102.

120. For Claudii in this area during the fifth century, see Heinzelmann, *Bischofsherrschaft*
pp.220-232. Only three sees in Viennensis did not have known representatives at Arles, Toulon,
Carpentras and Cavaillon. Leontius or Claudius may have held any of these sees. Other sees not
known to have been represented at Arles whose bishops had participated in earlier Gallic councils include Embrun, Thorâme, Castellane, and Cimiez, all in Alpes Maritimae, and Antibes in
Narbonensis II.

121. Duchesne, *Fastes* 1.282, 271. Other sixth-century Gallic Praetextati include a grandson
and a great-granddaughter of Remigius of Rheims (*P.L.* 65.973-974) and a bishop of Rouen who
died in 586 (Duchesne, *Fastes* 2.207).

122. For the Italian Opiliones, see Sundwall, *Abhandlungen* pp.142-144. Neither of the
names Opilio or Amicalis occur elsewhere in the surviving sources for fifth- and sixth-century
Gaul.

123. Because they subscribed in the same relative positions at both these councils, they presumably are the same individuals. See chapter 9 above.

ently had met against their wishes. Furthermore, Faustus had quarreled in the past with Theodorus of Fréjus, Graecus of Marseilles, and
perhaps others. Nor would Mamertus of Vienne have been pleased by
Faustus' recent attacks on his brother Claudianus.[124] Marcellus of Die,
moreover, of necessity would have supported his patron Mamertus. It
remains to be seen, therefore, whether all these bishops would be able
to find some common ground at Arles.[125]

The Points under Consideration

This council also is set apart from earlier Gallic councils for another
reason. It is the first fifth-century Gallic council known to have discussed serious matters of church doctrine. Earlier synods had concentrated upon matters of authority, organization, and discipline. This
council, however, went beyond the mere condemnation of Lucidus,
although this remained one of its intents. As Faustus wrote to Leontius afterward, "For the sake of pastoral care, blessed pope Leontius,
you have convened a council of the highest-ranking clerics in order to
condemn the error of predestination."[126] The primary function of the
council, therefore, was to place on record the half-century-old Gallic
opposition to Augustinian predestination.[127] Faustus and his party, it
seems, had been able to induce the Gallic ecclesiastical establishment
to meet in order to come to a corporate decision on what they all
should believe. It is no surprise, therefore, that the debate aroused
great interest throughout southern and central Gaul.

It is possible to gain some insight into the questions discussed at
Arles by identifying the important points under consideration at each
stage of the controversy. The original letter to Lucidus began by sum-
marizing what proper belief, according to Faustus, ought to be (Faust.
Epist. 18/1):

Briefly, therefore, I might explain, as much as I am able to speak with one
who is absent, what you ought to believe with the catholic church, that is,
that you always link the deeds of the baptized servant with the grace of God,
and that you condemn, along with the teaching of Pelagius, also the one who
preached predestination to the exclusion of human labor.[128]

---

124. von Harnack, *Lehrbuch* p.253 n.2, suggests that Mamertus Claudianus also would
have opposed Faustus on the question of predestination (as a "Metaphysiker Gegner des
Semipelagianismus").

125. See Duchesne, *Fastes* 1.132, for the assumption that "les vieilles rancunes étaient ob-
liées." See also Weigel, *Faustus* p.106.

126. "pro sollicitudine pastorali, beate papa Leonti, in condemnando praedestinationis errore
concilium summorum antistitum congregastis" (*De gratia prol.: C.S.E.L.* 21.3).

127. See Duchesne, *Fastes* 1.132-133, who sees the council as a response to the need for Gallic
unity in the face of the barbarians, and the whole Lucidus controversy as just a pretext.

128. "breviter ergo dicam, quantum cum absente loqui possum, quid sentire cum catholica

Lucidus was ordered, therefore, to condemn the two individuals who had taught that either grace or labor was preeminent. One of these, Pelagius, was cited by name, but the other, Augustine, was prudently left anonymous. All of the teachings of Pelagius, of course, had been officially declared heretical, so no restraint was needed in his case. Augustine, however, continued to be respected. Even if some of his teachings were condemned, his name never was mentioned. The letter continued by listing six specific anathemas, and several assertions, to which Lucidus refused to subscribe.

Subsequently, at the Council of Arles, Lucidus was compelled to subscribe to a list of anathemas and assertions which were drawn up "according to the recent statutes of the council."[129] These canons were unequivocal in their opposition to Augustinian predestination. Lucidus' reply to the assembled bishops began with a list of nine condemnations, five of which paralleled either the assertions or the anathemas of the letter to Lucidus. The condemnations were followed by seven assertions of belief, some of which likewise reflected the condemnations and statements in the letter to Lucidus. If anything, the council was even harder on Augustine than Faustus had been.

The most obvious divergence between Faustus' letter to Lucidus and Lucidus' reply to the Council of Arles, however, is in their treatment of Pelagius, and in the emphasis they placed upon grace.[130] The letter to Lucidus clearly condemned Pelagius twice by name, and anathematized three of his teachings in particular: 1) the rejection of original sin; 2) that one could gain salvation by deeds alone; and its corollary 3) that it was possible to gain salvation without grace. Lucidus' response to the Council of Arles, on the other hand, nowhere condemned Pelagius by name, and was much more perfunctory in its condemnations of his teachings. Its list of anathemas stated only that it was improper to assert that "labor must not be linked to grace," and the statements of belief said only that "the striving of man and the undertaking of grace always" are to be linked.[131] Nowhere, moreover, did it specify exactly what the role of grace was, and how significant it was in comparison to labor. All it did, in essence, was to recognize that grace existed.

It would appear, then, that the Council of Arles was unanimous in its condemnation of certain of the teachings of Augustine, especially

---

ecclesia debeas, id est, ut cum gratia domini operationem baptizati famuli semper adiungas et eum, qui praedestinationem excluso labore hominis adserit, cum Pelagii dogmate detesteris."

129. "iuxta praedicandi recentia statuta concilii" (Faust. *Epist.* 19/2).

130. Faust. *Epist.*18/1.

131. Faust. *Epist.*19/2.

those relating to predestination. With regard to the condemnation of particular Pelagian teachings, however, and to defining the specific role of grace, feelings were mixed. Faustus and the other signers of the letter to Lucidus, of course, already had condemned Pelagius categorically and by name. It therefore must have been those outside Faustus' circle, primarily southerners, who were responsible for any Gallic equivocation at Arles.

This created a problem. Church councils were expected to reach consensus, and their canons to have unanimous approval.[132] In order to reach this unanimity, concessions, even if only in wording, often had to be made. The northerners, therefore, may have had to soften their condemnations of Pelagius. There still remains the question of why the southerners would have opposed such condemnations at all. One possibility, of course, is that they harbored Pelagian-appearing sentiments themselves. If they did, Faustus and his partisans, ardent anti-Pelagians all, were surprisingly mild in their treatment of them. Furthermore, given that Pelagianism had been officially condemned now for over fifty years, one would think that any sympathizers would have been all the more eager to escape suspicion by condemning Pelagius at least by name.

Some southerners are more likely to have argued, rather, that the bishops were there only to consider Lucidus, and predestination: even Faustus admitted that this was the reason Leontius had summoned the council. It may have been unclear to some why Faustus and his partisans wished to discuss Pelagianism at all; for them Pelagius and Pelagian beliefs simply may not have been an issue. Others may have felt that Faustus, whose career did extend back to a time when Pelagianism was a controversial issue, was simply unreasonably apprehensive about it. They may have feared that to raise the issue would have been to create problems where none really existed. Finally, given Faustus' reputation, there may even have been some who perversely welcomed an opportunity to hinder the implementation of the full theological agenda of the froward bishop of Riez.

Faustus and the 'De gratia'

Faustus and his party, however, may have argued that a natural result of an official condemnation of predestination was the need to define a Gallic position on related matters, and especially on the role of grace. They may have warned that a strict Augustinian, unsympathetic to their views, could see in their denial of predestination a concomitant denial of grace, and make unwarranted accusations of

132. See Oehler, "Consensus omnium" pp.119-120 and chapter 5 above.

Pelagianism against them. Faustus, at least, would recall how Prosper had done so in the past. Whether for this particular reason or not, the southerners too were willing to compromise. Even though they balked at undertaking a detailed discussion of the role of grace at the council, they did authorize Leontius to commission Faustus to compose a position paper explaining the Gallic viewpoint. As Faustus later wrote to Leontius, "The one undertakes the task for defending grace competently and soundly who offers the obedience of an attendant labor...."[133] The resultant work was the *De gratia.*[134]

Presumably, it would have been understood that Faustus' statement would reflect the conclusions of the council, that is, would show how the Gallic view permitted the existence of grace while at the same time denying predestination. If Faustus did no more than this, one would expect the contents of the *De gratia* closely to reflect the list of condemnations and assertions included in Lucidus' letter of retraction. In one regard, this was the case. In the heading to his prologue, for example, Faustus condemned only the predestinarians: "On the one hand, they defend fate like the pagans, and on the other they deny free will like the Manichees...."[135] Here again Faustus had recourse to the conventional accusation of Manicheism. In several places Faustus referred to an assertor of such beliefs as a "haereticus."[136] A generous reader might translate this as "a heretic," but it would not be difficult also to take it to mean "the heretic," that is, Augustine himself.[137]

Elsewhere, however, the *De gratia* included material which was not directly drawn from the Council of Arles. Once again, as in the original letter to Lucidus, Faustus condemned Pelagius openly and by name. In his summary at the very beginning of the work, he emphasized the point by asserting (*De gratia* 1.1),

We intend to consider ... the grace of God and the insufficiency of free will. In the first place, we believe that the blasphemies of Pelagius must be con-

---

133. "studium asserendae gratiae conpetenter et salubriter suscipit qui oboedientiam famuli laboris adiungit...." (*De gratia prol.*).

134. *C.S.E.L.* 21.1-98, with the letter to Leontius on pp.3-4. It presumably was written immediately after the councils of Arles and Lyons (note 109 above). For discussion of the content, see Tibiletti, "Libero arbitrio" pp.259-285, and Chadwick, *Poetry* pp.180-181.

135. "hinc fatum cum gentilibus asserunt, inde liberum arbitrium cum Manichaeis negant ..." See also *De gratia* 1.5, "dum Pelagii impietatem nescis refugere, ad Manichaeorum dogma pestiferum, qui liberum arbitrium totum denegant, te intellege declinare."

136. *De gratia* 1.7, 1.12.

137. Elsewhere (1.10), Faustus referred to a "liberi interemptor arbitrii" who "omnia ex praedestinatione statuta et definita esse pronuntiat," a clear reference to Augustine. In a rare instance where Faustus did name Augustine, it was to point out his sophistry (*De gratia* 1.5): "the priest Augustine insinuates that not everything which is left unmentioned is denied."

demned, because, among the other abominations of his teachings, he attempted to assert with damnable elation that human labor can be sufficient without grace. . . . We will take care to make clear his nefarious meanings, so that any concerned person shall recognize that it is one thing to join the responsibility of labor to salutary grace, and another to support with a rashness of spirit labor alone without the aid of grace.[138]

He even went so far as to associate Pelagius with Augustine (*De gratia* 1.1),

This one [Pelagius], therefore, when forgetful of divine fear he extolled human weakness too highly, lost the sanity of his judgment, and thus fell into another error, when he preached that the freedom of will was complete and unweakened, the same error as those [e.g. Augustine] who assert that [freedom of will] was totally destroyed. Here, therefore, both errors contradict themselves, for, with the path and rule of truth abandoned, one [Augustine] stresses only grace and the other [Pelagius] only labor, disparate by the kind of beliefs, but similar in impiety through their equally divergent approach, they hiss with the spirit of a single serpent, of whom one, that is the supporter of grace alone, with a distinguished facade hides his venom under the guise of piety, whereas the other, that is the assertor of labor, openly displays his conspicuous arrogance in his shameless elation.[139]

Faustus not only accused Augustine and Pelagius of being equally wrong, but found in this wrongness an antithetical link between them. This connection may have been intended, rhetorically, to forestall any accusations of a relationship between anti-predestinarianism and Pelagianism. In this way, the Gallic position, which saw the need for both grace and human labor, could be demarcated as a mean between two equally heretical extremes.

Faustus, by reintroducing a condemnation of Pelagianism, was well aware that he might be exceeding the scope of the task which had been assigned to him. He therefore, in his cover letter to Leontius, offered the following justification for his additions (*De gratia prol.*):

138. "de gratia dei et tenuitate liberi arbitrii . . . tractaturi; primo loco Pelagii blasphemias . . . praestringendas esse credidimus, pro eo quod inter reliquas dogmatis sui abominationes etiam laborem hominis valere posse sine gratia elatione damnabili adfirmare conatus est. . . . nefarios sensus suos . . . proferre curabimus, ut sollicitus quisque cognoscat multo aliud esse salutari gratiae officium laboris adiungere, aliud vero nudum absque patrocinio gratiae laborem temeritate una cordis asserere."

139. "hic ergo dum altius humanam fragilitatem immemor divini timoris extollit, iudicii sui perdidit sanitatem [et] ita ex parte alia cecidit, dum arbitrii libertatem integram praedicat et inlaesam, sicut illi, qui eam ex toto asserunt fuisse evacuatam. hoc itaque loco gemini inter se conluctantur errores, quorum unus solam gratiam, alter solum laborem relicto tramite atque mensura veritatis insinuat. sectarum genere dispares, sed inpietate consimiles diverso quidem studio, sed spiritu unius serpentis insibilant. quorum unus, id est solius gratiae praedicator prima quidem fronte venenum suum sub specie pietatis occultat, alter, id est laboris assertor protinus extantem tumorem inproba elatione manifestat."

Indeed, because Pelagius insolently exalted labor by itself, and, like a mad-man, stupidly believed that human infirmity can be sufficient in and of itself without grace ... we deemed it necessary to blunt and refute his blasphemies in a short discussion, lest, perhaps, one who denies the role of labor, while we assert that God's pity must be assisted by faith and good works, lacking discretion overemphasize the teachings of Pelagius, and falling to the right, having deviated from the true path, believe that we have slipped to the left, and lest when we speak of labor as the servant of grace we seem to place an obstacle before the feet of the ignorant.... We therefore have produced an expanded work on prescience and predestination, so that those matters which seemed obscure will be made more clear for the slow-witted.[140]

Faustus here showed his conviction that the Council of Arles' con-demnation of predestination had been too narrow, and that some of his fellow bishops, perhaps, could not foresee the need to condemn Pelagianism as well in order to forestall future accusations against themselves of that very heresy.[141]

THE COUNCIL OF LYONS

Faustus, therefore, believed that in order to define the Gallic posi-tion on grace adequately, Pelagian views of it also had to be con-demned. On what grounds was he to do so? His use of *iudicavimus* rather than *iudicavi* at least suggests that he was relying on some cor-porate authority. His concluding remark to Leontius confirms this suspicion: "Indeed, when new errors were detected after the signing ceremony of the Council of Arles, the Synod of Lyons demanded that a few matters be added to this work."[142]

---

140. "verum quia Pelagius nudum laborem inportunius exaltat et humanam demens infir-mitatem sine gratia sibi posse sufficere stulte credidit ... blasphemias eius brevi sermone prae-stringere et confutare necessarium iudicavimus, ne forte is, qui donum laboris ... excludit, asse-rentibus nobis, quod dei misericordia fide et operibus promerenda est, catholicam vocem ad Pelagii sensum discretionis nescius adplicaret et omissa via regia in dexteram cadens in sinistram declinare nos crederet, et dum de labore servo gratiae loquimur, offendiculum ante pedes caeci opposuisse videremur.... latius utcumque sermonem de praescientia et praedestinatione pro-duximus, ut quae putabantur obscura absolutiora tardioribus redderentur."

141. Faustus, of course, was right, and this is exactly what modern theologians have done. For Faustus as a "Semi-Pelagian," see Altaner, *Patrology* p.566; Engelbrecht, *C.S.E.L.* 21.xviii; Loyen, *L'esprit* p.158; Schanz, *Geschichte* p.542; and Schmid, "Claudianus" col.172. The mis-taken belief that Faustus was tinged with Pelagianism arose, in part, from the *Vita Fulgentii* (*A.A.S.S.* January I p.43), which says of Faustus: "contra gratiam subdolo sermone composuit favens occulte Pelagianis, sed catholicus tamen volens videri." For the more correct view of Faustus as an anti-Pelagian, see Ado of Vienne, *Chron.* s.a.492 (*P.L.* 123.107), "Pelagianum dogma destruere conatus in errorem labitur": Ado felt that Faustus' mistake was in believing that free will was a gift of nature rather than of Christ. For "Semi-Pelagianism," see chapter 6 above, n.55.

142. "in quo quidem opusculo post Arelatensis concilii subscriptionem novis erroribus de-prehensis adici aliqua synodus Lugdunensis exegit" (*De gratia prol.*).

This second council, at Lyons, very possibly came about as a result of the dissatisfaction of Faustus and his partisans with the Council of Arles. Shortly thereafter, at the same place where the letter to Lucidus itself probably had been signed, specific anti-Pelagian resolutions were introduced to be incorporated by Faustus into the *De gratia*.[143] Unfortunately, there is no list of attendees. Patiens, of course, and presumably Faustus, would have been there, and probably other northern signers of the letter to Lucidus as well.[144]

Traces of attempts to forestall any possible opposition to this *fait accompli* may be found in Faustus' cover letter to Leontius, where he wrote, "But, truly, you have entrusted to infirm shoulders the labor and responsibility for expressing those matters which you presented most learnedly in the public gathering . . . You have burdened me with the judgment of your affection, yourself with the danger of the choice."[145] Faustus seems shrewdly to have intended both to conciliate Leontius and to implicate him as responsible for the work. In doing so, Faustus would have done to Leontius exactly what Mamertus Claudianus had done to Sidonius only shortly before.

The summoning of this second council shows again how strongly Faustus and his partisans felt about their opposition to both predestination and Pelagianism. They used condemnations of them both to mark out the limits of their own intermediate position on grace. One should not suppose, however, that either predestinarianism or Pelagianism was rampant in Gaul. Nor should one suppose that the unfortunate Lucidus was himself guilty of all the beliefs he was compelled to anathemetize.[146] Denunciations of heretical beliefs served rather as a ritual, rhetorical, and intellectual means by which not only Faustus and his party, but also those whose beliefs were challenged, could reaffirm their own orthodoxy.[147] Only after this had been done could Faustus describe in detail the interaction between grace and free will.

The express condemnations of Pelagianism clearly were more of an issue with Faustus and his confrères than with the southerners. Although there is no record of it, some northerners even may have

143. For this timing, see Koch, *Faustus* p.19. If the council of Arles had met in the fall, the northern bishops would have been able to assemble at Lyons on their way home. There is no reason to believe (as does Weigel, *Faustus* p.108, cf. 79-80) that a year separated the two councils. For a possible reference to the council, see Sid. Apoll. *Epist.* 6.12.5 (n.104 above).

144. Because Faustus felt it necessary to inform Leontius that the Council of Lyons had occurred, one might conclude that Leontius, at least, had not attended it.

145. "quod vero ad ordinanda ea, quae conlatione publica doctissime protulistis, operam infirmis humeris curamque mandastis . . . me iudicio caritatis, vos periculo electionis onerastis" (*De grat. prol.*).

146. Nor, presumably, did he disagree with all the tenets which he was forced to espouse.

147. One might compare Lucidus' statement to that of Agrestius (chapter 5 above, n.88). Once delivered, both presumably were accepted into the ecclesiastical fold.

suspected that some of their southern brethren continued to harbor Pelagian-appearing beliefs. It may be in this context that one is to interpret Faustus' otherwise curious charge that Graecus, later bishop of Marseilles, was guilty of Nestorianism. Only the uninformed reader would have been unaware that Faustus' mentor Cassian had equated Nestorianism with Pelagianism.[148] If this were the case, it is then even more remarkable that these usually contentious Gallic bishops were able not only to sit down together at Arles but even to hammer out a document upon which all could agree. They apparently were willing to put aside their differences over this or that theological point in an effort to reach a broader consensus.

Even if the additions of Faustus and his partisans at the Council of Lyons came as something of a surprise to the southern bishops, there was no significant opposition to Faustus' definition.[149] Even Faustus discussed Pelagianism in only two of the thirty chapters of his *De gratia*. For him too, apparently, it was of secondary importance, and was included only for the sake of completeness. The primary concern of the bishops before and after Arles was to condemn Augustinian predestination. Gennadius of Marseilles, Faustus' ally in the controversy over the soul, later wrote, "[Faustus] also wrote an excellent work on the grace of God, by which we are saved, and the free will of the human spirit, in which work he instructs that the grace of God always encourages, leads, and assists our will."[150] Gennadius appreciated Faustus' point: grace was paramount, but human labor also was important.

The theological views of Faustus and his supporters, therefore, now became dogmatic throughout Gaul. Perhaps this should be no surprise. It already has been seen that, however contentious the Gauls could be over other matters, they had few differences on matters of orthodoxy. If anything, their ability to reach consensus here only re-affirms how small their theological differences must have been. The views of Faustus' party had been largely accepted anyway. Only, perhaps, matters of wording, emphasis, and presentation remained to be worked out at Arles.

This controversy resulted in a lengthy exposition of what the "official" Gallic positions on predestination, grace, free will, and human labor were to be. Only a single possible example of any contemporary opposition to Faustus' anti-predestinarian views survives. An apocry-

---

148. See chapter 6 above, n.37.

149. See Weigel, *Faustus* p.106 and von Harnack, *Lehrbuch* p.250.

150. "edidit quoque opus egregium de gratia dei, qua salvamur, et libero humanae mentis arbitrio, in quo opere docet gratiam dei semper et invitare et praecedere et adiuvare voluntatem nostram" (*Vir. ill.* 86). See Koch, *Faustus* pp.48–51.

phal document apparently composed in southern Gaul shortly after the publication of the *De Gratia*, the so-called *Decretum Gelasianum de recipiendis et non recipiendis libris*, supposedly written in Rome c.495, condemned in two neighboring entries "opuscula Cassiani presbyteri Galliarum apocrypha" and "opuscula Fausti Regiensis Galliarum apocrypha."[151] This attempt to anathematize the works of both assian and his protégé Faustus does not appear at that time to have met with any favor.

The overall success of Faustus in promulgating his views is seen in the high respect in which he was held in sixth-century Gaul, even by those who opposed him on individual points. Avitus of Vienne, in a letter to the Burgundian king Gundobad denouncing Faustus' views on repentance, adopted the subterfuge that the Faustus he was attacking was not Faustus of Riez, but rather the African Faustus the Manichee.[152]

Even in northern Italy, the deacon Ennodius of Milan, later bishop of Pavia, himself born in Arles c.470, wrote to his friend Constantius in 503 on the subject of predestination, and the need for human labor (*Epist*. 2.19.16),

I see where the poisons of the Libyan plague extend. The sandy snake not only holds these pernicious beliefs which he discloses: the matters which he confesses must be understood in the consideration of his hidden crimes. He even wishes to go so far [as to say] that no one perishes by his own sin or negligence. . . .[153]

It was not until the 520s that Faustus' teachings on grace were seriously questioned in the west.[154] Yet, even when they were condemned in Gaul in 529 at the Council of Orange, Caesarius of Arles

151. See von Dobschütz, *Decretum,* and Thiel, Epistolae pp.454-471 (who, like others of his age, accepts its Gelasian origin). The list of the approved writers concludes with Augustine, Prosper, and Leo, and that of the condemned writers with Cassian and Faustus (pp.9,13), suggesting what the true focus of the author may have been. Engelbrecht (*C.S.E.L.* 21.xvi), however, suggests that the anathematization of Faustus was an interpolation. For the origin of the document in southern Gaul c.500, see *Clavis* no.1676; von Harnack, *Lehrbuch* p.251; Rusch, *Latin Fathers* p.171; and E. Schwartz, *Zeitschrift der Savigny-Stiftung, Kanonistische Abteilung* 56(1936) p.63 n.2.

152. *Epist*. 4. See Duckett, *Writers* p.199; Engelbrecht, *C.S.E.L.* 21.xvii,183; Krusch *M.G.H. A.A.* 8.lx; and Weigel, *Faustus* pp.7,90-91.

153. "video quo se toxica Libycae pestis extendant. arenosus coluber non haec sola habet perniciosa quae reserat: ad aestimationem occultorum facinorum ferenda sunt, quae fatetur. vult enim ad illud pertingere, neminem suo vitio aut neglegentia perire. . . ." Lumpe, "Ennodius" pp.31-33, correctly identifies Augustine as the "Libycae pestis," and suggests that Ennodius had ties of his own to Lérins, as reflected in his *Vita Antonii lerinensis* (*M.G.A. A.A.* 7.185-190). Vogel, *M.G.H. A.A.* 7.356, curiously sees this as an attack on Pelagianism, although he does correctly identify the "doctorem Libycum" of Ennod. *Epist*. 1.4.6 as Augustine.

154. See von Dobschütz, *Decretum* p.317; Duckett, *Writers* p.201; Engelbrecht, *C.S.E.L.* 21. xvi-xvii; Griffe, *Gaule* 3.373; von Harnack, *Lehrbuch* pp.251-253; and Krusch, *M.G.H. A.A.* 8.lix.

and the Gallic bishops still refrained from mentioning Faustus by name.[155]

Meanwhile, the continuing Gallic concern with establishing theological orthodoxy during this period probably also was behind the work known as the *Statuta ecclesiae antiqua*, which has been attributed to Gennadius of Marseilles, or to Caesarius of Arles.[156] It included a detailed description of the theological beliefs all bishops were expected to hold before they could be consecrated, and it rejected Arian, Nestorian, and monophysite beliefs, even though these heresies were not mentioned by name. It also appears to deny predestination, for it stated, "[the candidate] must be asked whether the devil became evil not through his creation but through his own will."[157]

THE EPISCOPAL EMBASSY TO EURIC[158]

At the Council of Arles, Gallic bishops from the most important sees in central and southern Gaul were able to meet, and, however great their differences had been in the past, to reach consensus. The point finally had been reached when, at least momentarily, the Gallic episcopal factions, whether political or theological, had been able to achieve reconciliation. Another manifestation of this new-found spirit of cooperation, moreover, may be seen in a rather different incident which occurred shortly thereafter, in a secular context.

By the mid-470s, Roman imperial authority in Gaul was restricted primarily to Provence. In central Gaul, only the Auvergne continued to resist the Visigoths. The attempted offensives of Anthemius in 469 on the Loire and in 471 in the south had failed dismally, and as a result the Visigothic kingdom had expanded still farther. In 475, the

155. A posthumous chapter in Gennadius' *De viris inlustribus* (no.87) was added on Caesarius, stating "de gratia quoque et libero arbitrio edidit testimonia . . . ubi docet hominem nihil de proprio agere boni posse, nisi eum divina gratia praevenerit." This section apparently was added to compensate for Gennadius' own pro-Faustian, anti-Augustinian stand in *Vir. ill.* 86, the preceding chapter. It even gave an incorrect date for Caesarius, "floruit hic eo tempore quo et Faustus," indicating whom the anonymous interpolator had in mind. For this second Council of Orange, see Altaner, *Patrology* p.569; Chadwick, *Poetry* p.185; Duckett, *Writers* p.201; Engelbrecht, *C.S.E.L.* 21.xviii; Griffe, *Gaule* 3.373; von Harnack, *Lehrbuch* pp.253-257; Koch, *Faustus* pp.50-55; Krusch, *M.G.H. A.A.* 8.lix; Weigel, *Faustus* p.137; and Woods, *Canons*. Some, such as Rusch, *Latin Fathers* p.179, mistakenly assert that Faustus was condemned by name, and Tibiletti, "Libero arbitrio" p.284 n.142, thinks it "strange" that Faustus' name was not mentioned.

156. *Corp. chr. lat.* 148.162-168; Morin, "Hiérarchie" p.99 and "Liber dogmatum" p.447, places the work in Arles c.500; see also Palanque, *Marseilles* p.27 and Turner, "Arles and Rome" p.247.

157. "quaerendum . . . si diabolus non per conditionem sed per arbitrium factus sit malus" (*Stat. eccl. ant.* 1: *Corp. chr. lat.* 148.165). This statement also would reject Manichean dualism.

158. See Koch, *Faustus* pp.19-20; Stevens, *Sidonius* pp.157-160, 207-211; and Weigel, *Faustus* pp.111-116.

new emperor Julius Nepos attempted to negotiate a settlement with
the Visigothic king Euric which apparently was intended to consolidate the Roman holdings in Provence and improve the security of
Italy.[159] Significantly, the new emperor used not imperial officials as
his negotiators, but Roman bishops. In the spring of 475 he sent to
Euric Epiphanius of Pavia, who returned "with the bond of peace
having been undertaken."[160] Epiphanius, it seems, had ties of his own
in Gaul. On his return from Toulouse, for example, he stopped off to
visit Lérins.[161] Subsequently, he was involved in the ransoming of
Gallic captives, and in the early 490s he served as Gelasius of Rome's
emissary to the Gallic bishops in the case of Acacius.[162]

Nepos then sent to Toulouse a delegation of four bishops from
southern Gaul, Leontius of Arles, Faustus of Riez, Graecus of Marseilles, and Basilius of Aix, to work out the actual terms of the
treaty.[163] One individual who was very concerned in the progress of
these negotiations was Sidonius Apollinaris, now the bishop of Clermont and one of the leaders of the Arvernian resistance against the
Goths. Apparently, however, as at Die in the 460s, there were divided
loyalties even in Sidonius' own city. At one point, Sidonius even had
had to call upon his friend Constantius of Lyons to encourage the
citizenry when their will to resist began to flag: "When you found the
city emptied no less by civic dissension than by barbaric invasion,
preaching peace to all, and love to them, you returned them to their
homeland."[164]

Upon learning of the negotiations, Sidonius wrote to Basilius of Aix
about his views on the matter.[165] For Sidonius, the most important
issue was Visigothic interference in episcopal elections. He cited
eleven sees in Aquitania I and II, Novempopulana, and Narbonensis
I where ordinations of new bishops had been prevented or living bishops had been exiled. He declared to Basilius (*Epist.* 7.6.6, 10),

I fear not so much that [Euric] will threaten Roman walls as Christian practices. . . . Carry things out to the extent that this might be the principal agree-

159. See Stevens, *Sidonius* pp.158, 209-210, who suggests that the Goths had occupied Provence in 473-474, but that a threatened imperial invasion induced Euric to come to terms.

160. "inito etiam pactionis vinculo": Ennod. *VEpiphanii* 91.

161. Ennod. *VEpiphanii* 93-94.

162. Gelas. *Epist.* "Inter inguentium" (25 January 494): *P.L.* 59.138. The captives were described as "gentis suae": does this mean simply Roman, or that they were related to Epiphanius?

163. Ennodius, the source for Epiphanius' mission, does not mention the Gauls, and Sidonius (*Epist.* 7.6-7), the source for the Gallic embassy, does not mention Epiphanius. The reconstruction of Stevens, *Sidonius* pp.207-211, seems the most reasonable.

164. "cum inveneris civitatem non minus civica simultate quam barbarica incursione vacu-
atam, pacem omnibus suadens caritatem illis, illos patriae reddidisti" (*Epist.* 3.2.2).

165. For whatever reasons, he did not write to any of the other three, for he noted to Basilius
(*Epist.* 7.6.2), "I carry my pleas to you, with no offense intended toward the others. . . ."

ment of the treaty, that, with episcopal ordinations permitted, we might hold
the peoples of Gaul, whom the boundary of the Gothic kingdom encloses, by
faith even if we do not hold them by treaty.[166]

In a later letter, written to Graecus of Marseilles after the negotiations
had begun, Sidonius also gave his impression of the four bishops' authority: "Through you delegations come and go; to you, first of all, in
the absence of the emperor, peace is not only reported when it has
been negotiated, it is even entrusted to be negotiated."[167] A great deal
of authority, it would seem, had been granted to these bishops in the
secular arena, to go along with that which they already had assumed
in the ecclesiastical sphere.

Imagine Sidonius' shock, then, when he learned that the episcopal
embassy proposed to cede the Auvergne to the Goths. In the bitter
reproaches he addressed to Graecus of Marseilles for what he considered Graecus' shameful betrayal of the Arvernians, Sidonius gave his
opinion of the caliber of episcopal cooperation in contemporary Gaul
(Epist. 7.7.4):

You consult in common too little, and, when you come into a council, you
are less concerned with remedying public dangers than with pursuing
your own private interests; by doing this without fail every time and for a
long time you begin to be not the first but the last among your fellow
provincials.[168]

Sidonius' words, spoken in disappointment and despair, are probably some of his most heartfelt. It made no difference if the settlement
made by Graecus and his colleagues was in the strategic best interest
of the empire at the time, and perhaps had been mandated by the
imperial government and not by the bishops at all.[169] Sidonius' observations would in no way lose their force, for he himself was responding from the point of view of his own narrow regional perspective.
The fragmented political condition of Gaul in the 470s only exacer-

166. "non tam Romanis moenibus quam legibus Christianis insidiaturum pavesco. . . . agite,
quatenus haec sit amicitiae concordia principalis, ut episcopali ordinatione permissa populos
Galliarum, quos limes Gothicae sortis incluserit, teneamus ex fide, etsi non tenemus ex foedere."

167. "per vos legationes meant; vobis primum pax quamquam principe absente non solum
tractata reseratur, verum etiam tractanda committitur" (Epist. 7.7.4). The peace which had "been
negotiated" presumably is that of Epiphanius, and this statement could suggest that the Gauls
had supervised even that earlier embassy.

168. "parum in commune consulitis; et cum in concilium convenitis, non tam curae est
publicis mederi periculis quam privatis suadere fortunis; quod utique saepe diuque facientes
iam non primi comprovincialium coepistis esse, sed ultimi." Anderson, Sidonius 2.329 n.4, suggests that the word concilium refers to the concilium septem provinciarum; there is no indication,
however, either that this council met at this time, or that bishops attended.

169. See Hodgkin, Italy 2.504 and Stevens, Sidonius pp.207-211.

bated the current tendencies of aristocrats to be concerned primarily with their own local well being.

The presence of Faustus in this embassy, along with at least one of his earlier adversaries, is striking. This incident demonstrates once again the mutability of personal and factional alignments at this time. The mere fact that Faustus and Graecus once had held opposing views in matters of religious dogma would not at all preclude their acting in concert, and even having the same views, in matters of politics. Perhaps Faustus, too, whatever his sentimental ties to the north, concurred in the final settlement. After all, his own see was in the protected area in the south. If so, it may have led to a second break in the epistolary ties between him and Sidonius in 475/476, after the latter's exile by Euric, for Sidonius wrote to him, "But I think that it would be safest to renounce our rather frequent correspondence and, with the sedulity of our interchange of speech put aside for a time, assume rather concern for silence." [170]

This treaty marks the last gasp of the Roman imperial presence in Gaul. Within ten years, the few remaining Roman enclaves would be annexed by the barbarian kingdoms. [171] The Visigothic expansion also served to dissolve the short-lived spirit of Gallic episcopal unity. By 475 Crocus of Nîmes, not to mention Simplicius of Bourges, also had been exiled, and they and Sidonius were joined c.477 by both Marcellus of Die and Faustus himself. [172] Under such circumstances, there would be no more opportunities for bishops from throughout Gaul to meet as they had at Arles. The cessation of communications between Faustus and Sidonius only reflected the breakdown of ties among bishops throughout Gaul.

The early 470s represented a very brief period during which the central and southern Gallic bishops were able to cooperate and manage their ecclesiastical affairs by themselves. At the very time when all Gaul was about to fall to the barbarians, it seems that the Gallic bishops finally learned how to settle their own differences. The bishop of Rome no longer was consulted by anyone, nor did he try to intervene in Gaul. [173] The imperial government had lost nearly all its authority, and the barbarian kings had yet to consolidate theirs. The Gallic epis-

170. "reor ac saluberrimum ... stilo frequentiori renuntiare dilataque tantisper mutui sedulitate sermonis curam potius assumere conticescendi" (*Epist.* 9.3.1). For the date of the letter, see Loyen, *Lettres* 3.218.

171. Syagrius, of course, held out in the north until c.486. See Levison, "Chlodowech" pp.42-67; Schmidt, "Ende" pp.611-618; and Seeck, *Untergang* vol.5 passim.

172. See Mathisen, "Aquitania" p.168.

173. Hanson, "Church" p.3, notes that Sidonius never even mentions the bishop of Rome, and applies "popely" titles to Gallic bishops.

copal establishment even served as a stand-in for the imperial government, providing a kind of a "caretaker" government. Even though
this period was only transitional, it nonetheless represented the cul-
mination of Gallic episcopal practices and interactions which had begun early in the century. The Gallic bishops had been able to achieve
their influence and unity, however, only in default of any strong, centralized secular authority. What was to follow was to be the beginning
of a new tradition in which Gallic bishops became the "clients" of the
local king, and in which any concept of a "Gallic" ecclesiastical establishment was to be lost. But that is another story.

EPILOGUE

By the 480s, Gaul had been partitioned among the Franks in the north, the Visigoths in the southwest, and the Burgundians in the Rhône valley, not to mention smaller enclaves of Alemanni, Alans, Armoricans, and others. By circa 500, the Gallic church was operating in a new and in many ways more repressive atmosphere. The continuing powerful local influence of the Gallic bishops during the sixth century is well known. What has been insufficiently appreciated, however, is the loss of corporate freedom which the Gallic episcopal establishment suffered. Building upon the precedents set by Fridericus, Gundioc, and Euric, the Germans took control of significant elements of the operation of the Gallic church. Episcopal appointments now required at least the consent of the king, and many were preordained by him.

There also were new restrictions on the assembly of church councils. The days when bishops could meet in private on their own authority were gone: now the summoning authority of the king was required, and church councils were limited to the residents of a particular kingdom. The new spirit of servility which was imposed on Gallic bishops wishing to assemble is seen, for example, in the preamble to the Council of Agde, held in 506 (*Corp. chr. lat.* 148.192):

When in the name of the Lord, with the permission of Our Lord the Most Glorious, Magnificent and Pious King [Alaric] ... the blessed synod had gathered, and there with our knees bent to the ground we prayed for his kingdom and for his long life, so that the Lord might expand the realm of him who had permitted to us the opportunity to meet....[1]

Similarly, the canons of the Council of Orléans, held in 511, were addressed as follows: "All the bishops, whom you commanded to come to the council, to Their Lord Clovis, Son of the Catholic

---

1. "cum in nomine domini ex permissu domini nostri gloriosissimi magnificentissimi piissimique regis ... sancta synodus convenisset, ibique flexis in terram genibus, pro regno eius, pro longaevitate ... deprecaremur, ut qui nobis congregationis permiserat potestatem, regnum eius dominus ... extenderet...."

Church, Most Glorious King, ..." and began, "When, under the authority of God, at the command of the Most Glorious King Clovis, the council of the bishops had gathered ..."[2]

The period of roughly a century during which influential Gallic ecclesiastics were free to interact throughout Gaul was over. Which is not to say, of course, that the Gallic church did not remain as faction-ridden in the sixth century as it had been in the fifth. Sixth-century factionalism, however, was no longer on the grand scale that it had been before, when Hilary and his partisans could presume to extend their influence over much of southern and central Gaul; and when Gallic bishops from Arles to Autun could assemble freely to discuss theological issues; and when the will of the bishop of Rome could be blithely ignored. No, the Gallic dissension of the sixth century was to be on a more strictly local scale. A bishop's primary concern became the welfare of his own city vis-à-vis the local king.

One beneficiary from all this, as usual, was to be the bishop of Rome, who, faced with an even less organized Gallic ecclesiastical establishment than before, could use the precedents of the fifth century to consolidate his authority in Gaul. This became apparent, for example, in the 490s, when there was a revival of the quarrel between the bishops of Arles and Vienne over the extent of their metropolitan jurisdiction in Viennensis. Avitus of Vienne attempted to argue that the dividing line should be the border between the Burgundian and Visigothic kingdoms, and this led to a series of renewed appeals to the bishop of Rome.[3] Later in the sixth century, bishops of Rome effectively played the Gallic bishops against one another by the granting of this or that privilege, and by instituting a true "papal vicariate" in Gaul.[4]

THE LEGACY OF LÉRINS

In the early part of the fifth century a large contingent of monks, mostly laymen, and many of them from the area of Lugdunensis

---

2. "domno suo catholicae ecclesiae filio Chlothovecho gloriosissimo regi omnes sacerdotes, quos ad concilium venire iussistis ... cum auctore deo ex evocatione gloriosissimi regis Clothovechi ... fuisset concilium summorum antestitum congregatum ... " (*Corp. chr. lat.* 148A.4). After the occupation of Provence by the Ostrogoths, the bishops there seem to have had a bit more freedom, perhaps because of the distance separating them from the Italian court, see *Corp. chr. lat.* 148A.43, 48, 55 and passim.

3. See Symm. *Epist.* "Movit equidem": *M.G.H. Epist.* 3.34 (21 October 499); Symm. *Epist.* "Dilectionis tuae": ibid.3.34-35 (29 September 500); Symm. *Epist.*"Non debuit": Thiel, *Epistolae* no.4 pp.656-657 (13 October 501); and Symm. *Epist.* "Sedis apostolicae": ibid. no.14 pp.722-723 (6 November 513).

4. See Kellett, *Gregory.*

Prima, established themselves at Lérins. By the later 420s they began to appropriate for themselves episcopal sees, and in particular the see of Arles. Under the leadership of Hilary of Arles, and with the help of powerful secular allies, they were able to exercise their influence throughout central and southern Gaul. After the death of Hilary in 449, however, dissension broke out within the group, and it seems to have lost its former unity.

Nevertheless, even after the disappearance of Roman imperial authority from Gaul and the fragmentation of Gaul into several Germanic kingdoms, the Lerinenses were able to appropriate important sees in the south, including that at Arles. A certain Honoratus, for example, a relative of Hilary of Arles, was bishop of Marseilles in the 490s.[5] The Lérins faction, therefore, finally may have been able to gain control of Marseilles, although it is unknown whether this Honoratus actually was a monk at Lérins. Better evidence comes from the *vita* of another native of Lugdunensis Prima, Caesarius, who came from Chalon. After spending two years in the monastery of Silvester of Chalon, then "the blessed novice [Caesarius] sought the monastery of Lérins," where he was received by the abbot Porcarius.[6]

Subsequently, because of bad health, Caesarius moved to Arles, where the bishop Aeonius reportedly exclaimed to him, "My son, you are my fellow townsman and relative, for I not only remember your parents well, I also embrace our blood tie with parental memory."[7] Caesarius presumably would have been aware of this relationship. Aeonius himself, therefore, also was a native of Lugdunensis Prima; there is no evidence, however, as to whether he ever had been a monk at Lérins. Then, in 502 (*VCaesarii* 1.13), "The blessed Aeonius addressed his clergy and citizenry, and requested the masters of affairs [the Visigoths] that they choose as his successor no one other than the blessed Caesarius...."[8] When Aeonius died later that year, Caesarius duly was ordained. Once again, then, a monk of Lérins from Lugdunensis Prima not only had become bishop of Arles, but also had done so with the aid of the secular authorities, in this instance the Visi-

5. Duchesne, *Fastes* 1.274-275. Gennadius, *Vir. ill.* 100 contains an interesting report that his orthodoxy was challenged, but affirmed by Gelasius of Rome: "sanctus quoque papa Gelasius, Romanae urbis pontifex, per scripturam agnoscens eius fidei integritatem, rescripto probatam iudicavit." Perhaps the Gauls' previous reluctance to challenge each others' orthodoxy was lessening.

6. "Lerinense monasterium tiro sanctus expetiit" (*VCaesarii* 1.5).

7. "meus es, fili, concives pariter et propinquus, nam et parentes tuos reminiscor optime et per consanguinitatem parentali recordatione complector" (ibid. 1.10).

8. "Aeonius sanctus clerum vel cives adloquitur et ipsos dominos rerum per internuntios rogat ut ... nullum sibi alterum quam sanctum Caesarium eligerent fieri successorem...."

goths.[9] Like his predecessors from Lérins, Caesarius retained his monastic ties: Venantius Fortunatus said that he "remained a pontifical monk."[10]

Northerners continued to maintain their curious hold on the see of Arles later in the century. Aurelianus, for example, bishop from at least 546 to 550, died in Lyons and was buried there; presumably, he had close ties in the area.[11] Virgilius, bishop c.591-601, previously had been an abbot at Autun, and according to Gregory of Tours was made bishop of Arles at the request of Syagrius, bishop of Autun.[12]

Other evidence as well attests the continuing tradition of a strong connection between central Gaul and Lérins. The *Vita Iohannis Reomaensis* tells how Johannes, a native of Langres, adopted the religious life at about the age of twenty.[13] Then, accompanied by two comrades (ibid. 4), "seeking the religious lifestyle, he arrived at the monastery of Lérins, where then the monastic rule of the venerable Honoratus guided many, and taught them to hold to the norm of discipline."[14] After a year and a half at the monastery, however, bishop Gregorius of Langres wrote to the abbot of Lérins requesting that Johannes be allowed to return, which he then did. It would appear, therefore, that in the early sixth century, a stop at Lérins, even if only for a year or two, was still common, just as it had been for Lupus of Troyes and Hilary of Arles back in the 420s.

The *Vita Leobini* provides additional evidence for the continuing importance of Lérins as a waystation in one's monastic career at this time.[15] Leobinus, a native of Poitiers, first spent eight years in a monastery at home, and then entered the monastery of Avitus at Miciacum. Even this did not satisfy his yen for travel, so (*VLeobini* 4[11]), "wishing to go to Lérins, he met a certain brother who said that he scarcely would be able to bear the unpleasantness of the weather there.

---

9. The episcopal *fasti* of Arles list between Aeonius and Caesarius a Johannes, whose existence is rejected by Duchesne (*Fastes* 1.250,257 n.8) on the grounds that "il est sûr que Césaire succédé immédiatement à Aeonius" (presumably because Johannes does not appear in the *Vita Caesarii*). One might wonder, however, whether the *fasti* can be rejected so easily, especially because the Johannes also were an influential family of Lugdunensis Prima (see Mathisen, "Hilarius" p.168, and note Johannes Reomaensis below).

10. Ven. Fort. *Carm.* 5.2.68-70, "regula Caesarii praesulis alma pii / qui fuit antistes Arelas de sorte Lerini / et mansit monachus pontificale decus."

11. Duchesne, *Fastes* 1.258. His career before becoming bishop, however, is unknown.,

12. *H.F.* 9.23. Prinz, *Mönchtum* p.60 n.83, argues that Virgilius also was a monk, and perhaps even the abbot, at Lérins. This, however, is by no means certain.

13. *VIohannis* 1-4: M.G.H. *Scr. rer. merov.* 3.502-517, written in 659.

14. "religiosorum mores perquirens, ad Lirinense monasterium pervenit, ubi tunc venerabilis Honorati religionis forma plures instruebat et regularis disciplinae normam tenere eos commonebat. . . ."

15. M.G.H. *A.A.* 4.2.73-82, sometimes attributed to Venantius Fortunatus (ibid., p. xxviii).

Hearing this, he held back from the journey which he had begun." [16]

After subsequent stops at monasteries at Javols, Lyons, Orléans, Miciacum, and Chartres, Leobinus and a comrade Albinus finally did get to Arles. After being asked by Caesarius why they had come, Albinus responded (*VLeobini* 13[41]), "truly, the blessed Leobinus, having left behind the brothers whose charge he had, was hastening to Lérins, where, having left behind the brothers of his own monastery, he would be subordinate to all the brothers there at Lérins." [17] In this instance, however, Caesarius advised Leobinus to return home and attend to his responsibilities there. Even if Leobinus did not actually enter the monastery at Lérins, his example confirms the continuing attractiveness of the monastery to the monks of Lugdunensis.

Even during the sixth century, therefore, the monastery of Lérins continued to attract monks from the north. Some became bishops in the south, others eventually returned home. [18] Despite the political fragmentation of Gaul, Lérins maintained its tradition, established in the fifth century, of serving as a center, perhaps now the only center, of Gallic ecclesiastical unity.

16. "volens Lirinum pervenire, quendam fratrem Lirinensem repperit dicentem se non posse illic temperiei incommoditatem vix ferre. quo dicto ab itinere quod coeperat revocatur."

17. "beatum vero Leobinum derelictis fratribus quibus praepositus fuerat Lirino properaturum, ubi fratribus eiusdem monasterii derelictis Lirino foret subiciendus ... ibi omnibus fratribus."

18. For the monk Siffredus of Lérins later becoming bishop of Carpentras, see Prinz, *Mönchtum* p.60; see also Duchesne, *Fastes* 1.272.

EPISCOPAL HIERARCHY AND TENURE IN OFFICE

ESTABLISHING DATES FOR SOME GALLIC BISHOPS[1]

One problem with dealing with fifth-century Gallic bishops in detail is that for most of them, their dates of ordination are not known. This means that it is not clear when their activities as bishops began. Most bishops appear for the first time at a church council, but there is no indication given of how long they had been in office before that council. It would be very useful if some method could be established for calculating with some accuracy the tenures in office, and thus the ordination dates, of these Gallic bishops. In order to do so, one might begin by establishing as many absolute dates of ordination for as many bishops as possible.

THE BISHOPS OF ARLES

Much of the episcopal chronology of the 420s and later depends upon the dates of the death of Honoratus of Arles and the ordination of his successor Hilary immediately afterward. Two pieces of evidence help to establish these dates with some degree of certainty. According to the *VHilarii* 6(9), Honoratus died "emenso biennio," that is, after about two years in office. Additional evidence for the date of Honoratus' death comes from Hilary's *Sermo de vita Honorati* 29, which states that Honoratus died shortly after Epiphany (6 January). This date for Honoratus' death is confirmed by the martyrologies, which place his death on 16 January.[2]

Honoratus' year of ordination, however, is not given. It depends

---

1. Presented under the title "Episcopal Hierarchy and Episcopal Careers in Fifth-Century Gaul," Medieval Studies Congress, Western Michigan University, May, 1982.

2. See Ado, *Mart.* s.d. Jan.16 (*P.L.* 123.216).

upon how long his predecessor, the ephemeral Helladius, was in office. Helladius would have been ordained at some time in 426, in succession to the murdered Patroclus. It appears, moreover, that he did not survive long. For one thing, as seen above, his very existence was long in doubt. And for another, his appearances in the prologues of Cassian's *Collationes* also do not suggest a long tenure in office. In the prologue to books 1-10 he is addressed as a monk. In the prologue to books 11-17, he has become a bishop, and in the prologue to books 18-24, Honoratus now is the bishop. Unless Cassian dragged out the composition of his work over several years, Helladius could not have been in office for more than several months. If such were the case, and if Helladius therefore died late in 426, or even very early in 427, Honoratus then would have died in 429. In the less likely case that Helladius lasted until late 427 or early 428, Honoratus would have died in 430.[3]

In support of a date of 429, a further argument can be made from a careful reading of Hilary's account of Honoratus' death (*VHonorati* 29):

He gave his last sermon in church on the day of Epiphany. . . . his illness, prolonged for a long time, . . . growing worse, on the eighth or ninth [or eleventh] day after the aforementioned solemnity prostrated him by weakening him little by little. Scarcely on the fourth day, moreover, he denied his presence to us at the sacrament of communion. . . .[4]

There are several uncertainties in this passage. For one thing, one reading has Honoratus falling sick on the thirteenth or fourteenth of January, and another on the sixteenth, the day he died. Furthermore, it is unclear what the "fourth day" on which he absented himself from communion is related to. The fourth day after Epiphany? The fourth day before he fell sick?[5] Or the fourth day before he died?

One also might ask why such emphasis was placed upon Honoratus missing communion. If this was a daily occurrence, it seems that his missing it would have no special significance. Perhaps, therefore, Hilary meant a Sunday communion service. If this were the case, one now can look for appropriate Sundays in the years under consideration. On these grounds, it does not appear that the "fourth day" re-

3. For 429, see Duchesne, *Fastes* 1.112,256, and Griffe, *Gaule* 3.190; for 430, see Chadwick, "Euladius" pp.200-205, and McShane, *Romanitas* p.277.

4. "ultimum . . . epiphaniorum die in ecclesia sermonem habuit. . . . diu dilata infirmitas . . . ingravescens, octavo eum vel nono [*vel* undecimo] die a solemnitate praedicta, paulatim extenuando confecit. vix quatriduo tamen nobis suam in officiis charitati deditis praesentiam denegavit. . . ."

5. It could not be the fourth day after he fell sick, because that would have been after he was already dead.

ferred to the fourth day after Epiphany, for that day was a Sunday only in 427, and then not again until 438. What about, then, the fourth day before Honoratus fell ill? If this was on the eighth or ninth day after Epiphany, the only years fitting this qualification would be 426, 431, and 432, all of them impossible. If it was on the eleventh day after Epiphany, however, the communion would have fallen on a Sunday in 429.[6] There remains the fourth day before he died. Here too, one discovers, that in 429, the fourth day before 16 January, 13 January, also was a Sunday. A tenuous chain of reasoning, perhaps, but at least consistent with the other evidence for a date of 429.

On the basis of these analyses, therefore, it would indeed appear that Honoratus' death, and Hilary's election, occurred in early 429. Honoratus would have been elected in 426 or very early 427, with the former date being *a priori* more likely. Helladius, then, would have served for just a few months in the middle to latter part of 426.

THE DATES OF ORDINATION OF OTHER GALLIC BISHOPS

These dates now can be used to date the abbacy and episcopate of Maximus of Riez. Faustus said of him, "He oversaw the flock of Christ there [at Lérins] for seven full years."[7] Maximus succeeded Honoratus as abbot at Lérins, and therefore became bishop of Riez in 433 or 434. Because Maximus' election was "not long after" that of Theodorus of Fréjus, the latter's election would have occurred in the early 430s.[8]

A few other dates of episcopal ordinations are independently known. The *VLupi* 4 notes that Lupus of Troyes was ordained two years before his voyage to Britain with Germanus of Auxerre, viz. in 427. Inscriptions of Narbonne indicate that Rusticus was ordained on 9 October 427.[9] Another secure date is that of 439 for the ordination of Ingenuus of Embrun, immediately after the deposition of Armentarius at the Council of Riez.[10]

Other absolute dates of ordination are known less exactly, but still closely enough to be useful in establishing an absolute chronology. Castor of Apt, for example, was alive when Cassian of Marseilles dedi-

---

6. If one accepts this reading, Honoratus also would have missed communion on the fourth day before he fell ill.

7. "nam plenis septum annis ibidem Christi gregem pavit" (*P.L.S.* 3.634).

8. "non post longum tempus" (ibid.637).

9. Duchesne, *Fastes* 1.303 and Marrou, "Dossier."

10. See chapter 5 above, n.69.

cated books 1-10 of his *Collationes* to him, but by the time Cassian published books 11-17, in 426, Castor had been succeeded by Julius.[11] Julius, therefore, probably became bishop in 425 or 426. Furthermore, if the "Constantius" who was an addressee of Boniface of Rome's letter "Valentinae nos" in 419 is to be identified with Constantianus of Carpentras, he thus would have been in office by 419. The bishop Arcadius addressed in Celestine's letter "Apostolici verba" in 431 may be the Arcadius who attended the Council of Riez, who therefore also would have been in office by 431. Absolute dates such as these now can be used to approximate the dates of ordination and tenures in office of other fifth-century Gallic bishops.

GALLIC EPISCOPAL LISTS AND TENURE IN OFFICE

Many fifth-century documents pertaining to Gaul contain lists of bishops. An analysis of these lists shows that, with few exceptions, a strict hierarchy was maintained in the ordering of the names, that is, the same order is preserved when the same names occur in different lists. By juxtaposing these lists in chronological order, and aligning the recurrences of the same individuals' names, it is possible to establish a relative hierarchy among the bishops whose names appear. Then, by adding the dates for those bishops whose dates of ordination are known, it is possible to estimate with a surprising degree of accuracy ordination dates for the other bishops who appear in the lists.

This method works best, of course, when a large number of bishops reappear in lists over a relatively short period of time. This is just the situation in Gaul c.439-470, for which period there are extant no fewer than nine lists of names, from 1) the Council of Riez (439), 2) the Council of Orange (441), 3) the Council of Vaison (442), 4) the consecrators of Ravennius (449), 5) the letter to Leo on behalf of Arles (449/450), 6) the Gallic letter to Leo (451/452), 7) the council on Lérins (?451), 8) the council on Mamertus (463), and 9) the Council of Arles (c.470). The names of the bishops which appear in these documents may be arranged as in the accompanying Table 2, in the same order as they appear in their respective documents.

The table demonstrates that there is a very high degree of consistency from one list to the next as to the relative hierarchy of the names of the bishops who appear. Some anomalies, of course, can be found. Metropolitans, for example, often signed first. Occasionally the host bishop, such as Auspicius of Vaison in 442, could be allowed to sign

---

11. Books 11-17 were published when Helladius was bishop of Arles, see chapter 4 above.

TABLE 2. *Orders of Appearance of Gallic Bishops on Different Occasions (c.439–470)*

Attended Council of Riez (439)	Attended Council of Orange (441)	Attended Council of Vaison (442)	Consecrators of Ravennius of Arles (449)	Arles Privilege Supporters (449/450)	Signed Letter to Leo (451/452)	Attended Council of Arles (?451)	Attended Council on Mamertus (463)	Attended Council of Arles (c.470)
Hilarius (Arles)	Hilarius (Arles)	Auspicius (Vaison)			Ravennius (Arles)	Ravennius (Arles)	Victurus (Aix?)	Euphronius (Autun)
	Claudius (Vienne)	Hilarius (Arles)			Rusticus (Narbonne)	Rusticus (Narbonne)	Ingenuus (Embrun)	Leontius (Arles)
		Claudius (Vienne)			Venerius (Marseilles)		Hydatius	
							Eustasius (Marseilles)	

-------- METROPOLITANS AND BISHOPS OF EXTRAORDINARY STATUS ABOVE --------

283

TABLE 2. Continued

Attended Council of Riez (439)	Attended Council of Orange (441)	Attended Council of Vaison (442)	Consecrators of Ravennius of Arles (449)	Arles Privilege Supporters (449/450)	Signed Letter to Leo (451/452)	Attended Council of Arles (?451)	Attended Council on Mamertus (463)	Attended Council of Arles (c.470)
	Constantianus (Carpentras)	Constantianus (Carpentras)	Constantianus (Carpentras)	Constantianus (Carpentras)	Constantianus (Carpentras)	Constantianus (Carpentras)		
					Maximus			
419 · · · · · · Severianus (Thorâme)		Severianus (Thorâme)		Severianus (Thorâme)				
		Armentarius (Antibes)		Armentarius (Antibes)	Armentarius (Antibes)			
Audentius (Die)	Audentius (Die)	Audentius (Die)	Audentius (Die)	Audentius (Die)				
	Agrestius (Galicia)							
c.425 · · Julius (Apt)	Julius (Apt)	Julius (Apt)						
			Rusticus (Narbonne)					
427 · · · · · · Arcadius (Orange?)								
431? · · · · · · Auspicius (Vaison)	Auspicius (Vaison)		Auspicius (Vaison)					
Severus (Vence)		Severus (Vence)						

284

Claudius
(Castellane)

Eucherius
(Lyons)

Nicetas
(Vienne)

Florus
  (Lodève)
Sabinus
Valerianus
  (Cimiez)

Nectarius
  (Avignon)

Florus
  (Lodève)
Constantius
  (Uzès)

Asclepius
  (Cavaillon)

Valerianus
  (Cimiez)

Valerianus
  (Cimiez)
Ursus
Stephanus

Nectarius
  (Avignon)

Constantius
  (Uzès)
Maximus
Asclepius
  (Cavaillon)

Constantius
  (Uzès)

Nectarius
  (Avignon)

Nicetas
(Vienne)

Nectarius
  (Avignon)
Florus
  (Lodève)

Asclepius
  (Cavaillon)

Valerianus
(Cimiez)

Asclepius
  (Cavaillon)
Ceretius
  (Grenoble)
Salonius
  (Geneva)
Augustalis
  (Toulon)
Theodorus
  (Fréjus)

Theodorus
(Fréjus)

Nectarius
(Avignon)

Nectarius
  (Avignon)

Ceretius
(Grenoble)

Asclepius
(Cavaillon)

Asclepius
  (Cavaillon)

Theodorus
(Fréjus)

Theodorus
(Fréjus)

TABLE 2. *Continued*

	Attended Council of Riez (439)	Attended Council of Orange (441)	Attended Council of Vaison (442)	Consecrators of Ravennius of Arles (449)	Arles Privilege Supporters (449/450)	Signed Letter to Leo (451/452)	Attended Council of Arles (?451)	Attended Council on Mamertus (463)	Attended Council of Arles (c.470)
433···	Maximus (Riez)	Maximus (Riez)	Maximus (Riez)			Maximus (Riez)	Maximus (Riez)		
						Ursus			
						Ingenuus (Embrun)			
	Justus (Orange)	Justus (Orange)	Justus (Orange)	Justus (Orange)	Justus (Orange)	Justus (Orange)	Justus (Orange)		
							Salonius (Geneva)		
439········		Ingenuus (Embrun)	Ingenuus (Embrun)		Ingenuus (Embrun)		Ingenuus (Embrun)		
		Augustalis (Toulon)		Augustalis (Toulon)	Augustalis (Toulon)				
		Salonius (Geneva)							
						Valerius			
441········			Superventor (Alpes)		Superventor (Alpes)	Superventor (Alpes)			
442········				Antonius					
				Venantius	Venantius		Venantius		
							Zoticus		

286

449 · · · · · · · · · Chrysaphius

449 · · · · · · · · · Chrysaphius · · · · · · · · · Fonteius (Vaison)

Eulalius (?Viviers)
· · ·
Chrysaphius

Chrysaphius
Petronius (Die)
· · ·
Fonteius (Vaison)

Fonteius (Vaison)

Viventius

Fonteius (Vaison)
Viventius
Eulalius (?Viviers)

Hydatius
· · ·

Palladius
· · ·

450 · · · · · · · · · Palladius

Venantius

c.451 · · · · · · · · · Mamertus (Vienne)

c.451 · · · · · · · · · Patiens (Lyons)

Veranus (Vence)
Faustus (Riez)
Auxanius

Veranus (Vence)
Auxanius
Faustus (Riez)

TABLE 2. *Continued*

Attended Council of Riez (439)	Attended Council of Orange (441)	Attended Council of Vaison (442)	Consecrators of Ravennius of Arles (449)	Arles Privilege Supporters (449/450)	Signed Letter to Leo (451/452)	Attended Council of Arles (?451)	Attended Council on Mamertus (463)	Attended Council of Arles (c.470)
							Proculus	
							Ausonius	
							Paulus	Paulus
							(Trois-Châteaux)	
							Memorialis	
							Caelestius	
							Projectus	
								Megethius (Besançon)
								Graccus (Marseilles)
							Eutropius (Orange)	Eutropius (Orange)
							Avitianus	
							Ursus	
							Leontius	Leontius
463 · · · · · · · · ·								Claudius
463 · · · · · · · · ·								Marcellus (Die)
								Crocus (Nîmes)

Basilius
(Aix)
Claudius
Ursicinus
(Paris?)
Praetextatus
Pragmatius
Theoplastus
(Geneva)
Leocadius
Viventius
(Grenoble)
Julianus
(Avignon)
Amicalis
Johannes
(Chalon)
Opilio
Licinius

c.470···

first. Other minor variations, such as in the relative positions of Constantius of Uzès and Florus of Lodève, may have been caused by their having been ordained in the same year, by their not knowing their correct place in line, or even by copyists' errors. Such variations, however, do not alter the basic structure of the table.

When known dates are inserted, such as those for the ordinations of Julius of Apt, Rusticus of Narbonne, Maximus of Riez, and Ingenuus of Embrun, the dates of the other bishops in the lists usually can be established within the span of a few years. Valerianus of Cimiez, for example, must have been ordained between 427, or even 431, and 434. The dates for the other bishops may be estimated in a like manner.

Patiens of Lyons

This method can help to clear up some uncertainty in the sources about the date of ordination of Patiens of Lyons. Patiens' predecessor Eucherius usually is thought to have died in 449, the date given by the *Chron. gall. 452* no. 134 (*M.G.H. A.A.* 9.662): "Eucherius Lugdunensis episcopus et Hilarius Arelatensis egregiam vitam morte consummant."[12] But there is something wrong here. At the Council of Arles of c.470 (*Corp. chr. lat.* 148.159), Patiens' name followed that of Mamertus of Vienne, who did not become bishop of Vienne until after early 451 (*VAniani* 5, and chapters 8-9 above). Moreover, Gennadius (*Vir. ill.* 64), claims that Eucherius died "sub Valentiniano et Marciano principibus," i.e. between 450 and 455. The date in the *Gallic Chronicle*, then, would appear to be wrong, and Eucherius' death may have been attracted to that of his more famous colleague Hilary of Arles because of the close association between them. A *terminus ante quem* for Patiens' election also is found at the same Council of Arles, for his name appears immediately before that of Veranus of Vence, who not only subscribed to Mamertus' letter to Leo (circa 451/452), but also attended the council on Lérins (as suggested above, in December 451).[13] Patiens, therefore, probably became bishop in late 451 or early 452.[14]

Faustus of Riez

The date of ordination of Faustus of Riez remains problematical. He last appears as abbot of Lérins at the council on Lérins of December, c.451. His first appearance as bishop, however, is not until 462, at

---

12. See Duchesne, *Fastes* 2.163, and Griffe, *Gaule* 2.288.
13. See chapter 8 above, n.109.
14. The *Chronicle* of Marcellinus Comes misleadingly states under the year 456 (*M.G.H. A.A.* 11.86), "Eucherius Lugdunensis ecclesiae pontifex multa scripsit. . . ."

one of Hilarus' councils in Rome.[15] He probably was ordained, however, some time earlier. At both the council on Mamertus in 463 and the Council of Lyons of c.470, his name and that of Auxanius appear immediately after the name of Veranus of Vence, who was ordained c.451.[16] At the council on Mamertus, moreover, no fewer than ten of the twenty bishops present ranked below Faustus and Auxanius. Unless there had been an exceptionally high rate of episcopal turnover in the years immediately before 463, one would conclude that Faustus, and Auxanius, must have become bishops some time before 460, perhaps c.455. Faustus' ability to prevail over Theodorus of Fréjus just a few years earlier, along with his close ties to his predecessor Maximus, could have been important factors in his election.

Along with establishing approximate dates of ordination for all the otherwise undated bishops in the list, this method also helps to correct many previous mistakes and uncertainties about these bishops' identities and dates of service. It becomes clear, for example, that the Armentarius who was deposed as bishop of Embrun in 439 could not possibly be Armentarius of Antibes, for the latter was in office by 427.[17] Similarly, the Rusticus who aided in the consecration of Ravennius is in exactly the right tenure position to be identified with Rusticus of Narbonne, and no doubt should be expressed about his see.[18]

---

15. See chapter 9, n.20 above.

16. See chapters 8, 10 above.

17. Identity suggested by Griffe, *Gaule* 2.157 n.43, and Langgärtner, *Gallienpolitik* pp.63-64 n.4.

18. As by Langgärtner, *Gallienpolitik* p.79.

THE NAMES IN RAVENNIUS'
LETTER TO LEO

The letter to Leo sponsored by Ravennius in 451/452 presents some special problems. It is headed by the names of Ravennius of Arles, Rusticus of Narbonne, and Venerius of Marseilles. These three names are followed by those of sixteen other bishops, ten of whom were old partisans of Hilary at his councils of 439-442, and twelve of whom appear in either or both of the lists of the consecrators of Ravennius and the supporters of Arles in 449-450. Of these bishops, moreover, there were at least four from Viennensis, two from Narbonensis Secunda, and two from Alpes Maritimae, including Ingenuus, the *de iure* metropolitan whose status still was not recognized. The sees of the remainder of this group of sixteen are not known for certain, although one of them, Sabinus, may be a Spanish bishop of that name who at that time was exiled in Gaul.[1] The bishops of this group whose tenures in office are known all appear in their proper places in all the versions of the list, and there are no obvious inconsistencies in this part of the list.

The rest of the list, however, twenty-five names in all, has striking irregularities about it (see Table 3). Although it does include the names of a few known bishops of recent date of ordination, such as Venantius, Chrysaphius, Fonteius, and Petronius, many of the bishops in this part of the list cannot be identified with any certainty at all, and indeed are otherwise unknown. Another problem with these last twenty-five bishops concerns the ordering of the names, which appear in one order in the addresses of both the Gallic letter to Leo and Leo's

---

1. For Sabinus, see Hyd. *Chron.* 124 s.a.441, "Sabino episcopo de Hispali factione depulso...." and 192a s.a.458, "Sabinus episcopus Hispalensis post annos XX quam certaverat expulsus de Galliis ad propriam redit ecclesiam"; see Thompson, "Roman Spain. Part III" pp.10-11: Sabinus had been an orthodox catholic and was expelled by the Priscillianist party. For the possibility that the Eugenius who subscribed was an exiled African bishop, see Greg. Tur. *H.F.* 2.3 and chapter 8 above, n.91. If these two identifications are correct, Ravennius really, was attempting to get as many signatures as he could.

TABLE 3. *The Final Twenty-Five Names in Ravennius' Letter to Leo**

Addresses	Subscriptions
Chrysaphius (?Narbonensis Prima)	Verus
Fonteius (Vaison)	Helladius
Petronius (Die)	Aetherius
Hydatius (?Tarentaise)	Eulalius
Aetherius	Anemius
Eulalius (?Viviers)	Chrysaphius
Eustathius (?Aoste)	Petronius
Fraternus (?Langres or Glandève)	Fonteius
Victurus (?Le Mans)	Hydatius
Eugenius (?Africa)	Hilarius
Hilarius	Victurus
Verus	Eugenius
Amandus (?Châlons)	Palladius
Gerontius	Fraternus
Proculianus	Amandus
Julianus	Gerontius
Helladius (?Auxerre)	Proculianus
Armentarius (?Auch)	Dynamius
Honoratus (?Lugdunensis Prima)	Julianus
Eparchius (Clermont)	Armentarius
Anemius	Honoratus
Dynamius (Béziers)	Eparchius
Maximus	Eustathius
Venantius	Maximus
Palladius	Venantius

*For sees, see Duchesne, *Fastes* passim.

response of 27 January 452, and in another order in the subscriptions to the Gallic letter.[2]

A number of observations can be made about this variation. For one thing, the two lists of addresses are the same, perhaps reducing the possibility that these lists, at least, were corrupted by scribal error. On the other hand, the names in the subscriptions seem to be grouped roughly according to geographical region, at least as far as can be told based upon the few bishops whose sees are known or can be inferred.[3] This could suggest that rather than everyone meeting to discuss Leo's letter at a single council at Arles, only the first sixteen bishops actually did so, whereas the remainder merely forwarded their subscriptions to one or more copies of the letter which were circulated around Gaul, perhaps after having met at local *conventicula* ("meetings",

2. See the letters "Perlata ad nos" and Leo, "Optassemus quidem."
3. For known sees, see chapter 8 above and appendix "Episcopal Hierarchy" above.

"churches") to discuss it.[4] Then, after the conclusion of the actual meeting held at Arles, the forwarded subscriptions of the bishops who had not attended would have been appended to the lists of those who did.

This reconstruction would help to explain the extraordinary delay in Ravennius' response to Leo. It also would explain the different orders of the names: the last twenty-five or so subscriptions would be in the haphazard order in which they arrived, whereas the address of the Gallic letter represents someone's attempt to put the names into some kind of hierarchical, or other, order.[5] Leo, not knowing any better, then simply copied the names from the address of the Gallic letter.

4. Note the canon of the Council of Orange specifying the use of such forwarded acquiescence (no.28[29], *Corp. chr. lat.* 148.85: "per consensus suos . . . destinandos"); see also Thalassius of Angers' *ex post facto* subscription to the Council of Tours of 461 (ibid.p.148), "hanc definitionem domnorum meorum episcoporum ab ipsis ad me transmissam in civitacula mea relegi, subscripsi atque consensi." Note that Leo merely requested Ravennius to bring his *Epistula* to the attention of the other bishops, viz. "quae per te cupimus ad omnium fratrum et consacerdotum nostrorum notitiam pervenire" ("Diu filios:" *M.G.H. Epist.* 3.21-22): for Ravennius' chancery as the "centro di promulgazione dei documenti ricevuti da Roma," see Silva-Tarouca, "Nuovi Studi" pp. 396-397. Silva-Tarouca (p.394) also represents the universal view that all the bishops who signed did so in person. And Jalland, *Leo* p.137, assumes not only that bishops attended "from the whole of Roman Gaul," but also that they came "even from the now independent Visigothic kingdom," although he cites no specific examples of such persons.

5. The confusion could have been worsened if the latter group of subscriptions were appended on several different slips.

BIBLIOGRAPHY

PRIMARY SOURCES

Ado, *Chron.* and *Mart.* = Ado of Vienne, *Chronicon* and *Martyrologium*: *P.L.* 123.23ff.

Agnell. *Lib. pont. eccl. rav.* = Agnellus of Ravenna, *Liber pontificalis ecclesiae ravennatis*: *M.G.H. Scriptores rerum langobardorum* 263-391.

Agrestius (or Agroecius), *De fide*: K. Smolak ed., *Das Gedicht des Bischofs Agrestius. Eine theologische Lehrepistel aus der Spätantike* (Vienna, 1973).

Agroecius, *Ars de orthographia*: H. Keil ed., *Grammatici latini* 7 (Leipzig, 1880) 113-125.

Ambrose of Milan, *De obitu Valentiniani*: O. Faller ed., *C.S.E.L.* 73 (Vienna, 1955); *P.L.* 16.

Amb. *Epist.* = Ambrose of Milan, *Epistulae*: O. Faller ed., *C.S.E.L.* 82 (Vienna, 1968); *P.L.* 16.913-1342.

Alc. Avit. *Carm.*, *Epist.*, and *Serm.* = Alcimus Ecdicius Avitus, *Carmina*, *Epistulae*, and *Sermones*: R. Peiper ed., *Alcimi Ecdicii Aviti Viennensis episcopi. Opera quae supersunt*, *M.G.H. A.A.* 6.2 (Berlin, 1883).

Aug. *Epist.* = Aurelius Augustinus, bishop of Hippo Regius, *Epistulae*: A. Goldberger ed., *C.S.E.L.* 34, 44, 57-58 (Vienna, 1895-1925); *Epist.** = J. Divjak ed., *Sancti Aureli Augustini opera, Epistolae ex duobus codicibus nuper in lucem prolatae*, *C.S.E.L.* 88 (Vienna, 1981).

Aug. *Cont. Iul. Pel.*, *De corr.*, *De don. persev.*, *De gest. Pel.*, *De grat.*, *De haer.*, *De mor. Man.*, *De praedest.*, *Retract.*, *Serm.* = Aurelius Augustinus, bishop of Hippo Regius, *Contra Iulianum Pelagianum* (*P.L.* 44), *De correptione et gratia* (*P.L.* 44), *De dono perseverantiae* (*P.L.* 44), *De gestis Pelagii* (*C.S.E.L.* 42), *De gratia Christi et de peccato originali* (*C.S.E.L.* 42), *De haeresibus* (*P.L.* 42), *De moribus Manichaeorum* (*P.L.* 42), *De praedestinatione sanctorum* (*P.L.* 45), *Retractiones* (*C.S.E.L.* 36), *Sermones* (*P.L.* 38-39).

Boniface, bishop of Rome, *Epistulae*:
no.3: "Valentinae nos": *P.L.* 20.756-758,
no.12: "Difficile quidem": *P.L.* 20.772-774.

Caes. = Caesarius of Arles: G. Morin ed., *Sancti Caesarii arelatensis, Opera varia. Epistulae, concilia, regulae monasticae, opuscula theologica, testamentum, vita ab eius familiaribus conscripta* (Maretioli, 1942) and *Sermones*, *Corp. chr. lat.* 103-104 (Turnholt, 1953).

Carm. de div. prov.: see Prosper.

Cass. *Coll.* = Johannes Cassianus, *Collationes*: E. Pichery ed., *Jean Cassien,*

Conférences (3 vols.) *Sources chrétiennes* 42, 54, 64 (Paris, 1955-1959); E. Petschenig ed., *C.S.E.L.* 13 (Vienna, 1886).

Cass. *De incarn.* = Johannes Cassianus, *De incarnatione Christi*: M. Petschenig ed., *De incarnatione domini contra Nestorium*, *C.S.E.L.* 17 (Vienna, 1888) 232-391; *P.L.* 50.9-273.

Cass. *Inst.* = Johannes Cassianus, *De institutis coenobiorum*: J.-C. Guy ed., *Jean Cassien, Institutions cénobitiques*, *Sources chrétiennes* 109 (Paris, 1965), M. Petschenig ed., *De institutis coenobiorum et de octo principalium vitiorum remediis*, *C.S.E.L.* 17 (Vienna, 1888) 1-231.

Cass. *Chron.* = Cassiodorus, *Chronica*: T. Mommsen ed., *Cassiodori senatoris, Chronica ad a. DXIX*, *M.G.H. A.A.* 11 = *Chronica minora saec. IV. V. VI. VII.* 2 (Berlin, 1894, repr. Munich, 1981) 109-161.

Celest. *Epist.* = Celestine, bishop of Rome, *Epistulae*:
no.4, "Cuperemus quidem": *P.L.* 50.430-436,
no.21, "Apostolici verba": *P.L.* 50.528-530.

Ceretius of Grenoble, Salonius of Geneva, and Veranus of Vence, *Epist.* "Recensita epistola" = Leo of Rome, *Epist.* 68: *P.L.* 54.887-890.

Chron. gall. 452 = *Chronica gallica anno 452*: T. Mommsen ed., *M.G.H. A.A.* 9 = *Chronica minora saec. IV. V. VI. VII.* 1 (Berlin, 1982, repr. Berlin, 1961) 615-662.

Chron. gall. 511 = *Chronica gallica anno 511*: T. Mommsen ed., *M.G.H. A.A.* 9 = *Chronica minora saec. IV. V. VI. VII.* 1 (Berlin, 1982, repr. Berlin, 1961).

Mamert. Claud. = Mamertus Claudianus, *De statu animae* and *Epistula ad Sapaudum*: A. Engelbrecht ed., *Claudiani Mamerti opera*, *C.S.E.L.* 11 (Vienna, 1885).

C.J. = *Codex Justinianus*: P. Krüger ed., *Corpus iuris civilis*, vol.2, *Codex justinianus* (Berlin, 1954).

C. Th. = *Codex Theodosianus*: T. Mommsen, P. M. Meyer, P. Krüger eds., *Theodosiani libri XVI cum constitutionibus sirmondianis et leges novellae ad Theodosianum pertinentes* (2 vols.) (Berlin, 1905).

Concilia: C. Munier ed., *Concilia Galliae a.314-a.506*, *Corp. chr. lat.* 148 (Turnholt, 1963); C. de Clercq ed., *Concilia Galliae a.511-a.695*, *Corp. chr. lat.* 148A (Turnholt, 1963); C. Munier ed., *Concilia Africae a.345-a.525*, *Corp. chr. lat.* 149 (Turnholt, 1974); J. Sirmond ed., *Concilia antiqua Galliae* vol.1 (Paris, 1629); M. Zelzer ed., *Gesta concili aquileiensis*, *C.S.E.L.* 82 (Vienna, 1982).

Const. *Epist. ad Pat.*, *Epist. ad Cens.*, and *VGerm.* = Constantius of Lyons, *Epistula ad Patientem*, *Epistula ad Censurium*, and *Vita s. Germani episcopi Autissiodorensis*: R. Borius ed., *Constance de Lyon. Vie de saint Germain d'Auxerre*, *Sources chrétiennes* 112 (Paris, 1965); W. Levison ed., *M.G.H. S.R.M.* 7 (Hanover and Leipzig, 1920) 225-283.

Cyprianus Gallus: R. Peiper ed., *Cypriani Galli poetae Heptateuchos*, *C.S.E.L.* 23 (Vienna, 1881).

Dyn. *VMaximi* = Dynamius of Marseilles, *Vita s. Maximi episcopi Reiensis*: *P.L.* 80.31-40.

Ennod. *Carm.*, *Epist.* and *VEpiphanii* = Magnus Felix Ennodius, *Carmina*,

Epistulae and *Vita s. Epifani episcopi Ticinensis ecclesiae*: F. Vogel ed., *Magni Felicis Ennodi. Opera*, *M.G.H. A.A.* 7 (Berlin, 1885); G. de Hartel ed., *C.S.E.L.* 6 (Vienna, 1882); G.M. Cook, *The Life of Saint Epiphanius by Ennodius. A Translation with an Introduction and Commentary* (Washington, 1942).

Ennod. *VAntonii* = Magnus Felix Ennodius, *Vita Antonii monachi Lerinensis*: F. Vogel ed., *M.G.H. A.A.* 7.185-190; *P.L.*63.239-246.

Epist. arel. = *Epistulae arelatenses genuinae*: W. Gundlach ed., *M.G.H. Epist.* 3 (Berlin, 1892) 1-83.

Epist. aust. = *Epistulae austrasicae*: W. Gundlach ed., *M.G.H. Epist.* 3 (Berlin, 1892) 110-153.

Epist. imp. = *Epistulae imperatorum*: O. Guenther ed., *Epistulae imperatorum pontificum aliorum inde ab a. CCCLXVII usque ad a. DLIII datae avellana quae dicitur collectio*, *C.S.E.L.* 35.1-2 (Vienna, 1895-1898).

Epist. "Memores quantum" = Leo of Rome, *Epist.* 65: *P.L.* 54.879-883 = *Epist. arel.* 12: *M.G.H. Epist.* 3.17-20.

Epist. "Perlata ad nos" = Leo of Rome, *Epist.* 99: *Corp. chr. lat.* 148 (Turnholt, 1963) 107-110, *P.L.* 54.966-970.

Euch. *De laud. herem.*, *Form.*, *Instruc.*, *Epist. ad Salv.* = Eucherius of Lyons, *De laude heremi ad Hilarium Lirinensem presbyterum epistula*, *Formulae spiritalis intellegentiae*, *Instructiones ad Salonium*, *Epistula ad Salvium*: C. Wotke, *C.S.E.L.* 31.1 (Vienna, 1894) p.177ff; S. Pricoco ed., *Eucherii. De laude heremi* (Catania, 1965).

Euch. *Epist. ad Valer.* = Eucherius of Lyons, *Epistula paraenetica ad Valerianum cognatum de contemptu mundi et saecularis philosophiae*: *P.L.* 50.701-726.

Euch. *Pass. acaun. mart.* = Eucherius of Lyons, *Passio acaunensium martyrum*: B. Krusch ed., *M.G.H. S.R.M.* 3 (Hanover, 1896) 20-41.

Eutrop. *Epist.* = Eutropius presbyter, *Epistulae*: *P.L.* 30.45-50, 75-104 (= 57.933-958), 188-210, *P.L.S.* 1.529-556.

Faust. *De grat.*, *De spir. sanct.*, *Epist.*, and *Serm.* = Faustus of Riez, *De gratia*, *De spiritu sancto*, *Epistulae*, and *Sermones*: F. Glorie ed., *Eusebius 'Gallicanus', Collectio homiliarum*, *Corp. chr. lat.* 101-101B (Turnholt, 1970–1971); A. Engelbrecht ed., *Fausti Reiensis praeter sermones pseudo-Eusebianos opera*, *C.S.E.L.* 21 (Vienna, 1891); B. Krusch ed., *Fausti aliorumque epistulae ad Ruricium aliosque*, *M.G.H. A.A.* 8 (Berlin, 1887), 265-298.

Faust. *Hom.s.Hon.* = Faustus of Riez, *Homilia in depositione sancti Honorati*: F. Glorie ed., *Corp. chr. lat.* 101A (Turnholt, 1971) 775-780, *P.L.S.* 3.690-693.

Faust. *VMaximi* = Faustus of Riez, *Sermo de sancto Maximo episcopo et abbate*: F. Glorie ed., *Corp. chr. lat.* 101 (Turnholt, 1970) 401-412; S. Gennaro ed. (Catania, 1966) 131ff; *P.L.S.* 3.634-640.

Faustus of Riez, *Sermo de sancta Blandina Lugdunensis*: *P.L.* 50.560.

Fred. *Chron.* = Fredegarius scholasticus, *Chronicarum libri IV*: B. Krusch ed., *M.G.H. S.R.M.* 2 (Berlin, 1888) 1-193.

Gennad. *Lib. eccl. dog.* = Gennadius, presbyter of Marseilles, *Liber ecclesiasticorum dogmatum*: *P.L.* 42.1213-1222, 58.970-1054.

Gennad. *Vir. ill.* = Gennadius, presbyter of Marseilles, *De viris inlustribus*:

E.C. Richardson ed., *Texte und Untersuchungen zur Geschichte der altchrist-lichen Literatur* 14 (Leipzig, 1896); *P.L.* 58.1059-1120.

Gildas, *De excid.* = Gildas Sapiens, *Liber querulus de excidio et conquestu Britanniae*: *M.G.H. A.A.* 13.25-85.

Greg. Tur. *Glor. conf.*, *Glor. mart.*, *Virt. Mart.*, *Virt. Jul.*, and *Vit. pat.* = Georgius Florentius Gregorius of Tours, *Liber in gloria confessorum, Liber in gloria martyrum, De virtutibus sancti Martini episcopi, Liber de passione et virtutibus sancti Juliani martyris*, and *Liber vitae patrum*: B. Krusch ed., *M.G.H. S.R.M.* 1.2 (Hanover, 1885).

Greg. Tur. *H.F.* = Georgius Florentius Gregorius of Tours, *Historia Fran-corum (Libri historiarum X)*: B. Krusch and W. Levison eds., *M.G.H. S.R.M.* 1.1 (Hanover, 1951).

Hil. Arel. *Epist. ad Euch.* = Hilary of Arles, *Epistula ad Eucherium Lugdu-nensem*: C. Wotke ed., *C.S.E.L.* 31 (Vienna, 1894) 197-198.

Hil. Arel. *VHonorati* = Hilary of Arles, *Sermo de vita sancti Honorati*: S. Ca-vallin ed., *Vitae sanctorum Honorati et Hilarii episcoporum arelatensium*, Publications of the New Society of Letters at Lund 40 (Lund, 1952).

Hil. *Epist.* = Hilarus, bishop of Rome, *Epistulae*:
no.4, "Movemur ratione": *P.L.* 50.20-22, Thiel, *Epistulae* no.12, 152-155,
no.5, "Quantum reverentiae" = *Epist. arel.*16: *M.G.H. Epist.* 3.23, Thiel, *Epistulae* no.4, 137-138,
no.6, "Dilectioni meae" = *Epist. arel.*17: *M.G.H. Epist.* 3.24, Thiel, *Epis-tulae* no.6, 139-140,
no.7, "Miramur fraternitatem" = *Epist. arel.*15: *M.G.H. Epist.* 3.22-23, Thiel, *Epistulae* no.7, 140-141,
no.8, "Quamquam notitiam" = *Epist. arel.*18: *M.G.H. Epist.* 3.25-28, Thiel, *Epistulae* no.8, 141-146,
no. 9, "Qualiter contra sedis" = *Epist. arel.*19: *M.G.H. Epist.* 3.28-29, Thiel, *Epistulae* no.9, 146-147,
no.10, "Etsi meminerimus" = *Epist. arel.*20: *M.G.H. Epist.* 3.29-30,Thiel, *Epistulae* no.11, 151-152,
no.11, "Sollicitis admodum" = *Epist. arel.*21: *M.G.H. Epist.* 3.30-32, Thiel, *Epistulae* no.10, 148-151,

Hon. *VHilarii* = Honoratus of Marseilles, *Vita s. Hilarii episcopi Arelatensis*: S. Cavallin ed., *Vitae sanctorum Honorati et Hilarii episcoporum arelaten-sium*, Publications of the New Society of Letters at Lund 40 (Lund, 1952).

Hyd. *Chron.* = Hydatius Lemicus, *Chronica*: A. Tranoy ed., *Hydace: Chro-nique, Sources chrétiennes* 218-219 (Paris, 1974); T. Mommsen ed., *Hydatii Lemici, Continuatio chronicorum hieronymianorum ad a. CCCCLXVIII, M.G.H. A.A.* 11 = *Chronica minora saec. IV. V. VI. VII.* 2 (Berlin, 1894, repr. Munich, 1981) 1-36.

Jer. *Chron.* = Hieronymus, *Chronicon*: R. Helm ed., *Die grieschischen christ-lichen Schriftsteller der ersten Jahrhunderts* 24 = *Eusebius Werke* 7.1-2 (2nd ed.) (Berlin, 1956).

Jer. *Epist.* = Hieronymus, *Epistulae*: J. Labourt ed., *Saint Jérome, Lettres* (8 vols.) (Budé: Paris, 1949-1963); I. Hilberg ed., *C.S.E.L.* 54-56 (Vienna, 1910-1918).

Jer. *Vir. ill.* = Hieronymus, *De viris inlustribus*: E.C. Richardson ed., *Texte und Untersuchungen zur Geschichte der altchristlichen Literatur* 14.1 (Leipzig, 1896) 1-56.

Innoc. *Epist.* = Innocent, bishop of Rome, *Epistulae*:
no.2, "Etsi tibi": *P.L.* 20.468-481,
no.3, "Saepe me": *P.L.* 20.485-494,
no.6, "Consulenti tibi": *P.L.* 20.495-502,
no.24, "Et onus et honor": *P.L.* 20.547-550.

Jord. *Get., Rom.* = Jordanes, *De origine actibusque Getarum* and *De summa temporum vel origine actibusque Romanorum*: T. Mommsen ed., *M.G.H. A.A.* 5.1 (Berlin, 1882).

Isid. *Vir. ill.* = Isidore of Seville, *De viris inlustribus*: *P.L.* 83.1081-1106; Carmen Codoñer Merino ed., *El "De viris illustribus" de Isidoro de Sevilla* (Salamanca, 1964).

Isid. *Etym.* = Isidore of Seville, *Etymologiarum*: W. M. Lindsay ed., *Isidori Hispalensis episcopi. Etymologiarum sive originum libri XX* (2 vols.) (Oxford, 1911).

Leo *Epist.* = Leo, bishop of Rome, *Epistulae*:
no.1, "Relatione sancti": *P.L.* 54.593,
no.4, "Ut nobis gratulationem": *P.L.* 54.640-644,
no.10, "Divinae cultum": *P.L.* 54.628-635,
no.15, "Quam laudabiliter": *P.L.* 54.677-686,
no.28, "Lectis dilectionis": *P.L.* 54.755-782,
no.40, "Justa et rationabilis" = *Epist. arel.*9: *M.G.H. Epist.* 3.15,
no.41, "Provectionem dilectionis" = *Epist. arel.*10: *M.G.H. Epist.* 3.16,
no.42, "Circumspectum te" = *Epist. arel.*11: *M.G.H. Epist.* 3.16-17,
no.66, "Lectis dilectionis" = *Epist. arel.*13: *M.G.H. Epist.* 3.20-21,
no.67, "Diu filios" = *Epist. arel.*14: *M.G.H. Epist.* 3.21-22,
no.68, "Recensita epistola": *P.L.* 54.887-890,
no.96, "Ad praecipuum": *P.L.* 54.945,
no.102, "Optassemus quidem": *A.C.O.* 2.4.53-55, *P.L.* 54.983-988,
no.103, "Impletis per": *A.C.O.* 2.4.155-156, *P.L.* 54.988-991,
no.108, "Sollicitudinis quidem": *P.L.* 54.1011-1014,
no.138, "Cum in omnibus" *P.L.* 54.1101-1102,
no.167, "Epistolas fraternitatis": *P.L.* 54.1195-1209,
"Cum in dei": *P.L.* 20.661,
"Quali pertinacia" (spurious): *P.L.* 54.1237-1238.

Leo, *Serm.* = Leo of Rome, *Sermones*: J. Leclercq, R. Dolle eds., *Leo le Grand. Sermons, Sources chrétiennes* 22, 49, 74 (Paris, 1964-1969).

Leporius: R. Demeulenaere ed., *Leporii. Libellus emendationis*, Corp. chr. lat. 64 (Turnholt, 1985) 95-123.

L.H.F. = *Liber historiae Francorum*: B. Krusch ed., *M.G.H. S.R.M.* 2 (Hanover, 1888) 215ff.

Lupus of Troyes and Euphronius of Autun, *Epist.* "Commonitorium quod": Corp. chr. lat. 148 (Turnholt, 1963) 140-141.

Mar. Avent. *Chron.* = Marius Aventicensis, *Chronica*: T. Mommsen ed., *Marii episcopi aventicensis, Chronica a. CCCCLV-DLXXXI, M.G.H. A.A.*

11 = *Chronica minora saec. IV. V. VI. VII.* 2 (Berlin, 1894, repr. Munich, 1981) 225-239.

Marcel. *Chron.* = Marcellinus Comes, *Chronicon*: T. Mommsen ed., *Marcellini v.c. comitis, Chronicon ad a. DXVIII, M.G.H. A.A.* 11 = *Chronica minora saec. IV. V. VI.* VII. 2 (Berlin, 1894, repr. Munich, 1981) 37-108.

Not. Gall. = *Notitia Galliarum*: T. Mommsen ed., *M.G.H. A.A.* 9 = *Chronica minora saec. IV. V. VI. VII.* 1 (Berlin, 1982, repr. Berlin, 1961) 552-612.

Olymp. = Olympiodorus of Thebes, *Fragmenta*: C. Müller ed., *Fragmenta historicorum graecorum* 4 (Paris, 1851) 57-68.

Orient. *Comm.* = Orientius, *Commonitorium*: R. Ellis ed., *Orientii Carmina, C.S.E.L.* 16 (Vienna, 1886) 191-261.

Oros. = Orosius, *Historia adversum paganos*: C. Zangemeister ed., *Pauli Orosii Historiarum adversum paganos libri VII, C.S.E.L.* 5 (Vienna, 1882) and Orosius, *Commonitorium de errore Priscillianistarum et Origenistarum*: G. Schepss ed., *C.S.E.L.* 18 (Vienna, 1889) 149-157.

Pan. lat. = *Panegyrici latini*: E. Galletier ed., *Panégyriques latins (I-XII)* (2 vols.) (Budé: Paris, 1949-1955).

Pallad. *Dial.* = Palladius, *Dialogi de vita s. Joannis Chrysostomi*: P.R. Coleman-Norton ed. (Cambridge, 1928).

Paul. *Epig.* = Paulinus of Béziers, *Epigramma*: C. Schenkl ed., *C.S.E.L.* 16 (Vienna, 1888) 503-508.

Paul. *VAmbrosii* = Paulinus, deacon of Milan, *Vita s. Ambrosii*: *P.L.* 14.27-46.

Paul. Nol. *Carm.* = Meropius Pontius Paulinus, *Carmina*: G. de Hartel ed., *Sancti Pontii Meropii Paulini Nolani carmina, C.S.E.L.* 30 (Vienna, 1984).

Paul. Nol. *Epist.* = Meropius Pontius Paulinus, *Epistulae*: G. de Hartel ed., *Sancti Pontii Meropii Paulini Nolani Epistulae, C.S.E.L.* 29 (Vienna, 1894).

Paul. Pell. *Euch.* = Paulinus Pellaeus, *Eucharisticos*: C. Moussy ed., *Sources chrétiennes* 209 (Paris, 1974); G. Brandes ed., *Paulini Pellaei Eucharisticos, C.S.E.L.* 16 (Vienna, 1888) 263-334.

Paul. Pet. *Epist. ad Perp.* and *VMartini* = Paulinus of Périgueux, *Epistula ad Perpetuum* and *De vita sancti Martini episcopi libri VI*: M. Petschenig ed., *Paulini Petricordiae quae supersunt, C.S.E.L.* 16 (Vienna, 1888) 1-190.

Philast. *Haeres.* = Philastrius, *Diversae haereseis* or *Liber de omnibus haeresibus*: F. Marx ed., *Sancti Filastrii episcopi Brixiensis Diversarum hereseon liber, C.S.E.L.* 38 (Vienna, 1898); F. Heylen ed., *Filastrii episcopi Brixiensis. Diversarum hereseon libri, Corp. chr. lat.* 9 (Turnholt, 1957) 207-324.

Polem. Silv. *Laterc.* = Polemius Silvius, *Laterculus anni CCCCXLIX* : T. Mommsen ed., *M.G.H. A.A.* 9 = *Chronica minora saec. IV. V. VI. VII.* 1 (Berlin, 1982, repr. Berlin, 1961) 511-559.

Jul. Pom. *Vit. cont.* = Julianus Pomerius, *De vita contemplativa*: *P.L.* 59.415ff.

Praedestinatus sive praedestinatorum haeresis: *P.L.* 53.579-671.

Priscil. *Tract.* = Priscillianus, *Tractatus*: G. Schepss ed., *Priscilliani quae supersunt, maximam partem nuper detexit adiectisque commentariis criticis et indicibus, C.S.E.L.* 18 (Vienna, 1889).

Priscus, fr. = Priscus Panites, *Fragmenta*: F. Bornmann ed., *Prisci Panitae Fragmenta* (Florence, 1979).

Prosp. *Chron.* = Prosper Tiro, *Epitoma chronicon*: T. Mommsen ed., *M.G.H. A.A.* 9 = *Chronica minora saec. IV. V. VI. VII.* 1 (Berlin, 1982, repr. Berlin, 1961) 341-499.

Prosp. *Contr. coll., Epist. ad Ruf.,* = Prosper of Aquitaine, *De grati a dei et libero arbitrio contra collatorem* and *Epistula ad Rufinum de gratia et libero arbitrio*, also *Pro Augustino responsiones ad capitula obiectionum Gallorum calumniantium, Carmen de providentia divina* [?], *Epigrammata in obtrectatorem Augustini, Epitaphium Nestorianae et Pelagianae haereseon, De ingratis, Poema coniugis ad uxorem* [?], *De vocatione omnium gentium*: *P.L.* 51.

Querolus: F. Corsaro ed. (Catania, 1964); R. Peiper ed., *Aulularia sive Querolus Theodosiani aevi comoedia Rutilio dedicata* (Leipzig: Teubner, 1875).

Ruric. *Epist.* = Ruricius, *Epistulae*: A. Engelbrecht ed., *Ruricii epistularum libri duo, C.S.E.L.* 21 (Vienna, 1891) 349-450; B. Krusch ed., *Ruricii epistulae, M.G.H. A.A.* 8 (Berlin, 1887) 299-350.

Rutil. Namat. *De red.* = Rutilius Claudius Namatianus, *De reditu suo*: E. Doblhofer ed., *Rutilius Claudius Namatianus. De reditu suo sive Iter Gallicum* (Heidelberg, 1972); J. Vessereau and F. Préchac eds., *Rutilius Namatianus, Sur son retour* (Budé: Paris, 1933).

Salv. *De gub., Ad eccl.,* and *Epist.* = Salvian of Marseilles, *De gubernatione dei, Ad ecclesiam sive adversus avaritiam*, and *Epistulae*: G. Lagarrigue ed., *Salvien de Marseille. Oeuvres, Sources chrétiennes* 176, 220 (Paris, 1971-1975); F. Pauly ed., *Salviani presbyteri Massiliensis opera omnia, C.S.E.L.* 7 (Vienna, 1883); C. Halm ed., *Salviani presbyteri Massiliensis libri qui supersunt, M.G.H. A.A.* 1.1 (Berlin, 1877).

De sept. ord. eccl. = *De septem ordinibus ecclesiae*: *P.L.* 30.148-161.

Sirm.: see *C. Th.*

Sid. Apoll. *Carm.* and *Epist.* = Sidonius Apollinaris, *Carmina* and *Epistulae*: A. Loyen ed., *Sidoine Apollinaire: Poemes* (Paris, 1960) and vols.2-3, *Sidoine Apollinaire: Lettres* (Paris, 1970); W.B. Anderson, *Sidonius Apollinaris: Poems and Letters I-II* (Loeb: London, 1936-1965); P. Mohr ed., *C. Sollius Apollinaris Sidonius* (Teubner: Leipzig, 1895); C. Leutjohann ed., *Gai Sollii Apollinaris Sidonii epistulae et carmina, M.G.H. A.A.* 8 (Berlin, 1887).

Soc. *Hist.eccl.* = Socrates, *Historia ecclesiastica*: R. Hussey ed. (Oxford, 1853); *P.G.* 67.

Soz. *Hist.eccl.* = Sozomen, *Historia ecclesiastica*, J. Bidez and G.C. Hanson eds., *Die griechischen christlichen Schriftsteller der ersten Jahrhunderts* 50 (Berlin, 1960); *P.G.* 67.

Stat. eccl. ant. = *Statuta ecclesiae antiqua*: C. Munier ed., *Corp. chr. lat.* 148 (Turnholt, 1963) 162-188.

Symm. *Epist.* = Q. Aurelius Symmachus, *Epistulae*: O. Seeck ed., *Q. Aurelii Symmachi quae supersunt, M.G.H. A.A.* 6.1 (Berlin, 1883).

Sulp. Sev. *Chron., Dial., Epist.* and *VMart.* = Sulpicius Severus, *Chronicorum libri II, Dialogi, Epistulae* and *Vita s. Martini episcopi Turonensis*: J. Fontaine ed., *Sulpice Sévère, Vie de saint Martin*, vol.1. *Introduction, texte et traduction* and vols.2-3, *Commentaire et index, Sources chrétiennes* 133-135 (Paris, 1967-1969); C. Halm ed., *Sulpicius Severus, Libri qui supersunt, C.S.E.L.* 1 (Vienna, 1866).

Turribius of Asturias, *Epist.* "Molesta semper" = Leo of Rome, *Epist.* 16: *P.L.* 54.693-695.

Val. *Serm.* and *Epist. ad mon.* = Valerianus of Cimiez, *Homiliae* and *Epistula ad monachos: P.L.* 52.691-758.

Venantius Fortunatus, *Vita s. Albini:* B. Krusch ed., *M.G.H. A.A.* 4.2 (Berlin, 1885, repr. Berlin, 1961) 27-43, and *Vita s. Leobini:* ibid. 73-82 (spurious).

Vict. Aquit. *Curs. pasch.* = Victorius of Aquitania, *Cursus paschalis annorum DXXXII ad Hilarum archidiaconum ecclesiae romanae a. CCCCLVII:* T. Mommsen ed., *M.G.H. A.A.* 9 = *Chronica minora saec. IV. V. VI. VII.* 1 (Berlin, 1982, repr. Berlin, 1961) 667-735.

Vict. Tonn. *Chron.* = Victor Tonnennensis, *Chronica:* T. Mommsen ed., *Victoris episcopi tonnennensis, Chronica a. CCCCXLIV-DLXVII, M.G.H. A.A.* 11 = *Chronica minora saec. IV. V. VI. VII.* 2 (Berlin, 1894, repr. Munich, 1981) 163-206.

Victric. *De laud. sanct.* = Victricius of Rouen, *Liber de laude sanctorum:* R. Demeulenaere ed., *Corp. chr. lat.* 64 (Turnholt, 1985) 53-93; *P.L.* 20.443-458.

Vinc. *Comm.* = Vincentius of Lérins, *Commonitorium seu tractatus Peregrini:* R. Demeulenaere ed., *Vincentii Lerinensis. Commonitorium, Excerpta, Corp. chr. lat.* 64 (Turnholt, 1985) 125-231; R.S. Moxon ed. (Cambridge, 1915); *P.L.* 50.625-686.

Zos. *Epist.* = Zosimus, bishop of Rome, *Epistulae:*
no.1, "Placuit apostolicae" = *Epist. arel.*1: *M.G.H. Epist.* 3.5-6,
no.2, "Magnum pondus" = *Epist. imp.*45: *C.S.E.L.* 35.99-103,
no.3, "Posteaquam a nobis" = *Epist. imp.*46: *C.S.E.L.* 35.103-108,
no.4, "Cum adversus" = *Epist. arel.*2: *M.G.H. Epist.* 3.7-9,
no.5, "Multa contra veterem" = *Epist. arel.*5: *M.G.H. Epist.* 3.11,
no.6, "Mirati admodum" = *Epist. arel.*3: *M.G.H. Epist.* 3.9-10,
no.7, "Quid de Proculi" = *Epist. arel.*4: *M.G.H. Epist.* 3.10-11,
no.9, "Exigit diletio": *P.L.* 20.669-673,
no.10, "Cum et in" = *Epist. arel.*6: *M.G.H. Epist.* 3.12,
no.11, "Non miror" = *Epist. arel.*7: *M.G.H. Epist.* 3.13,
"Licet proxime": Duchesne, *Fastes* 1.101-102 n.2,
"Quamvis patrum": *P.L.* 35.115-117,
"Revelatum est nobis": *P.L.* 20.704.

Saints' Lives

VAbbAcaun. = *Vita abbatum Acaunensium:* B. Krusch ed., *M.G.H. S.R.M.* 7 (Hanover-Leipzig, 1920) 328-335.

VAlbini = *Vita s. Albini episcopi Catalaunensis: A.A.S.S.* September III 85-89.

VAmbrosii: see Paulinus, deacon of Milan.

VAniani = *Vita s. Aniani episcopi Aurelianensis:* B. Krusch ed., *M.G.H. S.R.M.* 3 (Hanover, 1896) 108-117.

VAmbrosii: see Paulinus, deacon of Milan.

VAniani = *Vita S. Aniani episcopi Auretianensis:* B. Krusch ed., *M.G.H. S.R.M.*

VAntonii: see Magnus Felix Ennodius.

VCaesarii: see Caesarius of Arles.

VCaprasii = *Vita s. Caprasii abbatis Lirinensis*: *A.A.S.S.* June I 75-78.
VConsortiae = *Vita s. Consortiae*: *A.A.S.S.* June V 214-217.
VDomitiani = *Vita s. Domitiani*: *A.A.S.S.* July I 44-50.
VEpiphanii: see Magnus Felix Ennodius.
VEutropi = *Vita s. Eutropii episcopi Arausicensis*: P. Varin ed., *Vie de saint Eutrope évêque d'Orange, Bulletin du Comité Historique des Monuments Ecrits de l'Histoire de France* 1(1849) 52-64.
VFelicis = *Vita s. Felicis episcopi Treverensis*: *A.A.S.S.* March III 612-622.
VGermani: see Constantius of Lyons.
VHilarii: see Honoratus of Marseilles.
VHonorati: see Hilary of Arles.
VIohannis = *Vita s. Iohannis abbatis Reomaensis*: B. Krusch ed., *M.G.H. S.R.M.* 3 (Hanover, 1896) 505-517.
VIusti = *Vita Iusti episcopi Lugdunensis*: *A.A.S.S.* Sept. I 373-374.
VLeobini: see Venantius Fortunatus.
VLupi = *Vita s. Lupi episcopi Tricassinae*: B. Krusch ed., *M.G.H. S.R.M.* 7 (Hanover-Leipzig, 1920) 284-302.
VLupicini = *Vita s. Lupicini abbatis*: F. Martine ed., *Vie des pères du Jura*, *Sources chrétiennes* 142 (Paris, 1968) 308-363.
VMarcelli = *Vita s. Marcelli episcopi Deensis*: see F. Dolbeau and G. Kirner in Secondary Sources.
VMarcellini = *Vita s. Marcellini episcopi Ebredunensis*: *A.A.S.S.* April II 749-752.
VMartini: see Sulpicius Severus.
VMaximi: see Dynamius of Marseilles and Faustus of Riez.
VOrientii = *Vita s. Orientii episcopi Ausciensis*: *A.A.S.S.* May I 60-65.
VRomani = *Vita s. sancti Romani abbatis*: F. Martine ed., *Vie des pères du Jura*, *Sources chrétiennes* 142 (Paris, 1968) 242-307.
VViviani = *Vita s. Viviani episcopi Santonensis*: B. Krusch ed., *M.G.H. S.R.M.* 3 (Hanover, 1896) 92-100.

SECONDARY SOURCES

The great number of potentially relevant studies combined with the restrictions of space require that only directly relevant studies be cited. The following list, therefore, usually omits (1) most local studies, (2) most hagiographical studies, (3) most non-Gallic studies, (4) most general histories of the church and times, (5) most discussions of the barbarian settlement, (6) most purely secular studies, and (7) dictionary articles. More specialized relevant works that have been consulted, but may not have found their way into the notes, also are cited here.

Adam, K., *"Causa finita est"* in *Beiträge zur Geschichte des christlichen Altertums und der byzantinischen Literatur. Festgabe Albert Ehrhard*, A. M. Königer, ed. (Bonn-Leipzig, 1922) 1-23 = *Gesammelte Aufsätze zur Dogmengeschichte und Theologie der Gegenwart*, F. Hofmann, ed. (Augsburg, 1936) 216-236.

Aingrain, R., *L'hagiographie, ses sources, ses méthodes, son histoire* (Paris, 1953).

Alfonsi, Luigi, "Il 'De laude eremi' di Eucherio," *Convivium* 36(1968) 361-369.

Allard, P., *Un empereur gaulois au Ve siècle* (Paris, 1904).

——, *St. Sidoine Apollinaire (431-489)* (Paris, 1910).

Alliez, L., *Histoire du monastère de Lérins* (Paris, 1862).

Allmer, A. and Dissard, P., *Musée de Lyon: inscriptions antiques* (Lyon, 1888-94).

Altaner, B., *Patrologie* (2nd ed.) (Freiburg, 1960) = Hilda C. Graef, trans., *Patrology* (New York, 1961).

Anderson, W. B., *Sidonius. Poems and Letters* (London, 1936-65).

Andrieu-Guitrancourt, P., "Essai sur saint Victrice. L'Eglise et la province ecclésiastique de Rouen aux derniers temps gallo-romains," *Année canonique* 114(1970) 1-23.

——, "La vie ascétique à Rouen au temps de saint Victrice," *Mélanges Jules Lebreton II, Recherches de science religieuse* 40(1951-1952) 90-106.

Arnheim, M. T. W., *The Senatorial Aristocracy in the Later Roman Empire* (Oxford, 1972).

Arnold, Carl F., *Caesarius von Arelate und die gallische Kirche seiner Zeit* (Leipzig, 1894).

Arsac, P., "La dignité sénatoriale au Bas-Empire," *Revue historique de droit français et étranger* 47(1969) 198-243.

Auer, J., "Militia Christi. Zur Geschichte eines christlichen Grundbildes," *Geist und Leben* 32(1959) 340-350.

Auerbach, E., *Literary Language and its Public in Late Antiquity and the Middle Ages* (London, 1965).

Babut, E.-Ch., *Le concile de Turin. Essai sur l'histoire des églises provençales au Ve siècle et sur les origines de la monarchie ecclésiastique romaine, 417-450*, Bibliothèque de Fondation Thiers 6 (Paris, 1904).

——, "La date du concile de Turin et le développement de l'autorité pontificale au Ve siècle," *Revue historique* 88(1905) 57-82.

——, "Paulin de Nole et Priscillien," *Revue d'histoire et de littérature religieuse* 1(1910) 40-57.

——, *Priscillien et le Priscillianisme* (Paris, 1908).

——, *Saint Martin de Tours* (2 vols.) (Paris, 1910-12).

Barralis, Vincent, *Chronologia sanctorum* (Lyons, 1613).

Bardy, Gustave, "Copies et éditions au Ve siècle," *Revue des sciences religieuses* 23(1949) 38-52.

——, "L'église et l'enseignement en Occident au cinquième siècle," *Mélanges offerts au R. P. Ferdinand Cavallera* (Toulouse, 1948) 191-214.

——, "L'*Indiculus de haeresibus* du pseudo-Jérome," *Recherches de science religieuse* 19(1929) 385-405.

——, "Les origines des écoles monastiques en Occident," *Sacris erudiri* 7(1953) 86-104.

——, "Les répercussions des controverses théologiques des Ve et VIe siècles dans les églises de Gaule," *Revue d'histoire de l'église de France* 24(1938) 23-46, reprinted as "La répercussion des controverses christologiques en

Occident entre la concile de Chalcédoine et la mort de l'empereur Anastase (451-518)," in A. Grillmeier and H. Bacht, eds., *Das Konzil von Chalkedon* vol.2 (Wurzburg, 1954) 771-789.

Bardy, Gustave, P. de Labriolle, L. Brehier, G. de Plinval, *Histoire de l'église 4. De la mort de Théodose à l'élection de Grégoire le Grand* (A. Fliche, V. Martin, eds.) (Paris, 1948).

Barnes, Timothy D., "Patricii Under Valentinian III," *Phoenix* 29(1975) 155-170.

———, "Who were the Nobility of the Roman Empire?" *Phoenix* 28(1974) 444-449.

Barruol, G., "Un centre érémetique au temps de Cassien dans l'ancien diocèse d'Apt," *Revue des études ligures* 37(1971) 155-171.

Bartrik, C., "L'interpretation théologique de la crise de l'empire romain par Léon le Grand," *Revue d'histoire ecclésiastique* 63(1968) 745-784.

Batiffol, Pierre, "Les églises gallo-romaines et le siège apostolique," *Revue d'histoire de l'église de France* 8(1922) 145-169.

———, *Le siège apostolique (359-441)* (3rd ed.) (Paris, 1924).

Baus, K. and E. Ewig, *Die Reichskirche nach Konstantin dem Grossen. Erst Halfband: Die Kirche von Nikaia bis Chalkedon* (Freiburg, 1973).

Beck, H. G. J., *The Pastoral Care of Souls in South-East France during the Sixth Century* (Rome, 1950).

Bennett, C. E., *New Latin Grammar* (Boston, 1918).

Benoit, Fernand, *L'Abbaye de Saint-Victor et l'Eglise de la Major à Marseille* (Paris, 1966).

———, "Les chapelles triconques paléochrétiennes de la trinité de Lérins et de la Gayole," *Rivista di archeologia cristiana* 25(1949) 129-154.

———, "La crypte en triconque de Theopolis," *Rivista di archeologia cristiana* 27(1951) 69-89.

———, "L'Hilarianum d'Arles et les missions en Bretagne (Ve-VIe siècle)," in G. le Bras, ed., *St. Germain d'Auxerre et son temps* (Auxerre, 1950) 181-189.

Bergmann, Wilhelm, *Studien zu einer kritischen Sichtung der südgallischen Predigtliteratur des 5. und 6. Jahrhunderts* (Leipzig, 1898; repr. Aalen, 1972).

Berthet, M., "L'authenticité de la Vie des Pères du Jura," *Semaine religieuse du diocèse Saint-Claude (Lons-le-Saunier)* 76(1943) 114-117.

Besson, Marius, "Un évêque exégète de Genève au milieu du Ve siècle: Saint Salone," *Anzeiger für schweizerische Geschichte* 9(1902-1905) 252-265.

———, *Monasterium Acaunense. Etudes critiques sur les origines de l'abbaye de Saint-Maurice en Valais* (Friburg, 1913).

Bickerman, E. J., *Chronology of the Ancient World* (London-Southampton, 1968).

Binns, J. W., ed., *Latin Literature of the Fourth Century* (London, 1974).

Birley, A. R., "Magnus Maximus and the Persecution of Heresy," *Bulletin of the John Rylands Library* 66(1983) 13-43.

Blanc, Andre, *La cité de Valence à la fin de l'antiquité* (Paris, 1980).

Blanchet, A., *Carte archéologique de la Gaule romaine* (Paris, 1931).

Bohlin, Torguy, *Die Theologie des Pelagius und ihr Genesis* (Uppsala, 1957).

Bömer, Franz, *Der lateinische Neuplatonismus und Neupythagoreismus und Claudianus Mamertus in Sprache und Philosophie* (Leipzig, 1936).

Bonner, Gerald I., *St. Augustine of Hippo: His Life and Controversies* (Philadelphia, 1963).

Borchardt, C. F. A., *Hilary of Poitiers' Role in the Arian Struggle* (The Hague, 1966).

Boshof, Egon, "Die Rombeziehungen der Trierer Kirche im 4. und beginnenden 5. Jahrhundert," *Annuarium historiae conciliorum* 7(1975) 81-108.

Botte, B., "Le rituel d'ordination des Statuta ecclesiae antiqua," *Recherches de théologie ancienne et médiévale* 11(1939) 223-241.

Bouhot, Jean-Paul, "Le texte du *Sermo de vita sancti Honorati* d'Hilaire d'Arles," *Revue des études augustiniennes* 28(1982) 133-147.

Boyd, William, "The Ecclesiastical Edicts of the Theodosian Code," *Columbia Studies in History, Economics and Public Law* 24(1905) 1-125.

Bratton, Timothy L., *Tours: From Roman Civitas to Merovingian Episcopal Center c.275-650 A.D.* (diss. Bryn Mawr, 1979).

Brehier, L., *La crise de l'Empire romain en 457* (Zagreb, 1929).

————, "Un empereur romain à Brioude, Flavius Eparchius Avitus," *Almanach de Brioude* (1930) 39-55.

Bright, William, *Select Anti-Pelagian Treatises of St. Augustine and the Acts of the Second Council of Orange* (Oxford, 1880).

Brochet, J., *La correspondence de saint Paulin de Nole et de Sulpice Sévère* (Paris, 1906).

Brown, Peter R. L., *Augustine of Hippo. A Biography* (Berkeley, 1967, repr. 1969)

————, *The Cult of the Saints: its Rise and Function in Latin Christianity* (Chicago, 1981).

————, "The Patrons of Pelagius: The Roman Aristocracy between East and West," *Journal of Theological Studies* 21(1970) 56-72.

————, "Pelagius and His Supporters: Aims and Environment," *Journal of Theological Studies* 19(1968) 93-114.

————, "The Rise and Function of the Holy Man in Late Antiquity," *Journal of Roman Studies* 61(1971) 80-101 = *Society and the Holy* 103-152.

————, *Society and the Holy in Late Antiquity* (Berkeley, 1982).

Bruckner, A., *Julian von Eclanum, sein Leben und seine Lehre. Ein Beitrag zur Geschichte des Pelagianismus*, Texte und Untersuchungen zur altchristlichen Literatur 15.3 (Leipzig, 1897).

————, *Quellen zur Geschichte des pelagianischen Streites* (Tübingen, 1906).

Brugière, Marie-Bernadette, *Littérature et droit dans la Gaule du Ve Siècle* (Paris, 1974).

Brunetière, Ferdinand, P. de Labriolle, *Saint Vincent de Lérins* (Paris, 1906).

Buchner, R., *Die Provence in merowingischer Zeit* (Stuttgart, 1933).

Bugiani, C., *L'imperatore Avito* (Pistoia, 1909).

Burckhardt, Max, *Die Briefsammlung des Bischofs Avitus von Vienne (+518)* (Berlin, 1938).

Burkitt, F. C., *The Religion of the Manichees* (Cambridge, 1924).

Bury, J. B., *History of the Later Roman Empire* (2nd ed.) (London, 1923).

Buse, A., *Paulinus, Bischof von Nola und seine Zeit* (Regensburg, 1856).

Buytaert, E., *L'héritage littéraire d'Eusèbe d'Émèse* (Louvain, 1949).

Cameron, Alan, "Rutilius Namatianus, St. Augustine, and the Date of the *De reditu*," *Journal of Roman Studies* 57(1967) 31-39.

Cappuyns, D. M., "L'origine des capitula pseudo-Célestiniens contre le semi-pélagianisme," *Revue bénédictine* 41(1929) 156-170.

―――, "Le premier représentant de l'Augustinisme médiévale. Prosper d'Aquitaine," *Recherches de théologie ancienne et médiévale* 1(1929) 308-337.

Carcopino, Jérôme, "Choses et gens du pays d'Arles," *Revue du lyonnaise* 6(1922) 42-70.

Carette, E., *Les assemblées provinciales de la Gaule romaine* (Paris, 1895).

Carney, T. F., "Prosopography: Payoffs and Pitfalls," *Phoenix* 27(1973) 156-179.

Casey, P. J., "Magnus Maximus in Britain," in *The End of Roman Britain. Papers Arising from a Conference, Durham 1978* (Oxford, 1979) 66-79.

Caspari, C. P., *Briefe, Abhandlungen und Predigten. Aus den zwei letzten Jahrhunderten des kirchlichen Alterthums* (Christiana, 1890; repr. Brussels, 1964).

Cavallin, Samuel, "Die Lobrede des heiligen Hilarius auf das Leben des heiligen Honoratus. Eine textkritische Studie," in *Liber Floridus. Mittellateinische Studien. Festschrift Paul Lehmann* (St. Ottilien, 1950) 83-93.

―――, "Le poète Domnulus. Etude prosopographique," *Sacris erudiri* 7(1955) 49-66.

―――, "Saint Genès le notaire," *Eranos* 43(1945) 150-175.

Chadwick, H. M., "The End of Roman Britain," in N. K. Chadwick ed., *Studies in Early British History* (Cambridge, 1959) 9-20.

―――, *Priscillian of Avila. The Occult and the Charismatic in the Early Church* (Oxford, 1976).

Chadwick, Nora K., "Intellectual Contacts between Britain and Gaul in the Fifth Century," in N. K. Chadwick, ed., *Studies in Early British History* (Cambridge, 1959) 189-263.

―――, *Poetry and Letters in Early Christian Gaul* (London, 1955).

Chadwick, Owen, "Euladius of Arles," *Journal of Theological Studies* 46(1945) 200-205.

―――, *John Cassian* (2nd ed.) (Cambridge, 1968).

Chaffin, Christopher, "Civic Values in Maximus of Turin and his Contemporaries," *Forma Futuri. Studi in Onore di M. Pellegrino* (Padua, 1975) 1041-1053.

Chalon, M., "A propos des inscriptions dédicatoires de l'évêque Rusticus," *Narbonne archéologie et histoire* 1(1973) 223-232.

Chapman, John, *Studies on the Early Papacy* (Port Washington/London, 1971).

Charaux, Augustus, *Tonantius Ferreolus provinciae Galliae praefectus, Imp. Valentiniano III* (Besançon, 1876).

Chastagnol, Andre, "Le diocèse civil d'Aquitaine au Bas-Empire," *Bulletin de la Société Nationale des Antiquaires de France* (1970) 272-292.

―――, "L'évolution de l'ordre sénatorial aux IIIe et IVe siècles de notre ère," *Revue historique* 244(1970) 305-314.

———, "Les modes de recrutement de sénat au IVe siècle après J.-C.," in *Recherches sur les structures sociales dans l'antiquité classique* (Paris, 1970) 187-211.

———, "Notes chronologiques sur l'Histoire Auguste et le Laterculus de Polemius Silvius," *Historia* 4(1955) 173-188.

———, "La prosopographie, méthode de recherche sur l'histoire du Bas-Empire," *Annales, Economie, Societés* 25(1970) 1229-1235.

———, "Le repli sur Arles des services administratifs gaulois en l'an 407 de notre ère," *Revue historique* 249(1973) 23-40.

———, *Le sénat romain sous le règne d'Odoacre* (Bonn, 1966).

———, "Le sénateur Volusien et la conversion d'une famille de l'aristocratie romaine au Bas-Empire," *Revue des études anciennes* 58(1956) 241-253.

Chatillon, F., "Dardanus et Theopolis (409-417)," *Bulletin de la Société d'Etudes Historiques Scientifiques et Littéraires des Hautes-Alpes* 62(1943) 29-151.

———, "Paulin de Périgueux, auteur de la *Vita Martini*, et Sidoine Apollinaire, panégyriste des empereurs," *Revue du moyen âge latine* 23(1967) 5-12.

Chavasse, A., "Le deuxième canon du concile d'Orange de 441. Essai d'exégèse," in *Mélanges E. Podechard* (Lyons, 1945) 103-120.

Chevalier, U., *Etude historique sur la constitution de l'église métropolitaine et primatiale de Vienne en Dauphiné* vol.1 (Vienne, 1922).

Christophe, P., *Cassien et Césaire, prédicateurs de la morale monastique* (Paris, 1969).

Chrysos, Evangelios, "Die angebliche 'Nobilitierung' des Klerus durch Kaiser Konstantin den Grossen," *Historia* 18(1969) 119-129.

———, "Konzilsakten und Konzilsprotokolle vom 4. bis 7. Jahrhundert," *Annuarium historiae conciliorum* 15(1983) 30-40.

Claude, D., "Die Bestellung der Bischöfe im merowingischen Reiche," *Zeitschrift der Savigny-Stiftung für Rechtsgeschichte, Kanonistische Abteilung* (1963) 1-75.

Clerc, M., *Massalia* (Marseilles, 1927-1929).

Cloché, P., "Les élections épiscopales sous les mérovingiens," *Le Moyen-Age* 26(1924-25) 203-254.

Clover, F. M., *Flavius Merobaudes. A Translation and Historical Commentary* (Philadelphia, 1971).

Colin, J., "Les sénateurs d'origine gauloise et les gouverneurs des Gaules," *Latomus* 13(1954) 226-228.

Collingwood, R. G., "The Roman Evacuation of Britain," *Journal of Roman Studies* 12(1922) 74-98.

Collins, Frank, *The Antiquity of the Gallo-Roman Aristocracy during the Fifth Century A.D.* (thesis, Univ. of Virginia, 1974).

Consolino, F. E., "Fra biografia e confessio: la forma letteraria del Sermo de Vita s. Honorati di Ilario d'Arles," *Orpheus* 2(1981) 170-182.

Cooper-Marsdin, A. C., *The History of the Islands of the Lérins* (Cambridge, 1913).

Corbett, John H., "The Saint as Patron in the Work of Gregory of Tours," *Journal of Medieval History* 7(1981) 1-13.

Courcelle, Pierre, *Histoire littéraire des grandes invasions germaniques* (3rd ed.) (Paris, 1964).

———, *Les lettres grecques en Occident* (Paris, 1943).

———, "Nouveaux aspects de la culture lérinienne," *Revue des études latines* 46(1968) 379-409.

———, "Trois diners chez le roi wisigoth d'Aquitaine," *Revue des études anciennes* 49(1947) 169-177.

Coville, Alfred, *Recherches sur l'histoire de Lyon du Vme siècle au IXme siècle (450-800)* (Paris, 1928).

Crabbe, Anna, "Cologne and Serdica," *Journal of Theological Studies* 30(1979) 178-185.

———, "The Invitation List to the Council of Ephesus and Metropolitan Hierarchy in the Fifth Century," *Journal of Theological Studies* 32(1981) 369-400.

Cristiani, Leon, *Lérins et ses fondateurs: Saint Honorat, Saint Hilaire d'Arles, Saint Eucher de Lyon* (S. Wandrille, 1946).

———, *Saint Eucher de Lyon. Du méprise du monde* (Paris, 1950).

Cristo, S., "Some Notes on the Bonifacian-Eulalian Schism," *Aevum* 51(1977) 163-167.

Cunze, O., *Die Geographie des Ptolemaeus* (Berlin, 1923).

Curti, C., *Due commentarii inediti de Salonii ai vangeli di Giovanni e di Matteo* (Turin, 1968).

———, "La 'Passio acaunensium martyrum' di Eucherio di Lione," *Convivium dominicum. Studi sull'eucarestia nei padri della chiesa antica e miscellana patristica* (Catania, 1959) 297-327.

———, *Salonii Commentarii in parabolas Salomonis et in ecclesiasten* (Catania, 1964).

———, *Salonii De evangelio Iohannis, de evangelio Matthaei* (Turin, 1968).

Curtius, E. R., *Europaische Literatur und lateinisches Mittelalter (2nd ed.)* (Bern, 1954).

Czapla, B., *Gennadius als Litterarhistoriker. Ein quellenkritische Untersuchung der Schrift des Gennadius von Marseille "de viris illustribus,"* Kirchengeschichtliche Studien 4.1 (Münster, 1898).

d'Alès, Aldhémar, "Le concile d'Ephèse," *Gregorianum* 12(1931) 201-266.

———, "La fortune du Commonitorium," *Recherches des sciences religieuses* (1936) 334-356.

———, *Priscillien et l'Espagne chrétienne à la fin du IVe siècle* (Paris, 1936).

Dalton, O. M., *The Letters of Sidonius* (Oxford, 1915).

Dauzat, A., *La toponymie française* (Paris, 1939).

Dauzat, A. and Rostaing, Ch., *Dictionnaire étymologique des noms de lieux en France* (Paris, 1963).

de Beausobre, Isaac, *Histoire critique de Manichee et du Manicheisme* (New York, 1979).

de'Cavalieri, Pio Franchi, "S. Genesio di Arelate, s. Ferreolo di Vienna, s. Giuliano di Brivas," *Studi e Testi* 65(1935) 203-229.

Declareuil, J., "Les curies municipales et le clergé au Bas-Empire," *Revue historique du droit française et étranger* 14(1935) 26-53.

de Clercq, V. C., "Ossius of Cordova and the Origins of Priscillianism," *Texte und Untersuchungen zur altchristlichen Literatur* 63 = *Studia patristica* 1(1957) 601-606.

de Coulanges, Fustel, *Histoire des institutions politiques de l'ancienne France* (7 vols., revised by C. Jullian) (Paris, 1924)

Degengardt, F., *Studien zu Iulianus Pomerius* (Eichstatt, 1905).

Dekkers, E. and A. Gaar eds., *Clavis patrum latinorum* (2nd ed.) (Turnhout, 1961).

de Labriolle, Pierre, *Histoire de la littérature latine chrétienne* (Paris, 1947).

de la Broise, R., *Mamerti Claudiani vita eius doctrina de anima hominis* (Paris, 1890).

Delehaye, Hippolyte, *Les passions des martyrs et les genres littéraires* (Brussels, 1921).

————, *Sanctus. Essai sur le culte des saints dans l'antiquité* (Brussels, 1954).

de Leo, Pietro, "Deposizioni vescovili ed ecclesiologia nei sinodi della Gallia premerovingia," *Annuarium historiae conciliorum* 15(1983) 15-29.

de Letter, P., *Prosper of Aquitaine: Defense of St. Augustine* (Westminster and London, 1963).

Demandt, Alexander, "Magister militum," in Pauly-Wissowa-Kroll, *Real-Encyclopädie* Supp. 12(1970) 553-790.

de Manteyer, G., *Les origines chrétiennes de la IIe Narbonnaise, des Alpes-Maritimes et de la Viennoise* (Aix, 1915).

————, "Les origines chrétiennes: Lérins et Jersey, bases insulaires des Gaules au Ve siècle," *Bulletin de la Société d'Etudes Historiques Scientifiques et Littéraires des Hautes-Alpes* 46(1927) 161-179.

de Montauzan, Germain, "Saint-Eucher, évêque de Lyon et l'école de Lérins," *Bulletin historique du diocèse de Lyon* 2(1923) 81-96.

Demougeot, Emilienne, "A propos des interventions du pape Innocent Ier dans la politique séculiere," *Revue historique* 212(1954) 23-38.

————, "Attila et les Gaules," *Bulletin de la Société d'Agriculture, Commerce, Sciences et Arts du Département de la Marne* 73(1958) 7-41.

————, "Constantin III, l'empereur d'Arles," in *Hommage à André Dupont* (Montpellier, 1974) 83-125.

————, *De l'unité à la division l'Empire romain 395-410. Essai sur le gouvernement impérial* (Paris, 1951).

Denkinger, H., *Alcimus Ecdicius Avitus, archévêque de Vienne (460-526) et la destruction de l'arianisme en Gaule* (Geneva, 1890).

de Plinval, Georges, *Pélage, ses écrits, sa vie et sa réforme. Etude d'histoire littéraire et religieuse* (Lausanne, 1943).

Desgranges, H. Legier, *Les Apollinaires. Histoire d'une famille gallo-romaine pendant trois siècles* (Paris, 1937).

Desjardins, Ernest, *Géographie de la Gaule d'après la Table de Peutinger* (Paris, 1869, repr. 1969).

————, *Géographie historique et administratif de la Gaule romaine* vols.3-4 (Paris, 1889-1893).

Dessau, H., *Inscriptiones latinae selectae* vol.1 (Berlin, 1954).

de Vogüé, Adalbert, "Sur la patrie d'Honorat de Lérins, évêque d'Arles," *Revue bénédictine* 88(1978) 290-291.

de Wewer, J., "La xŵpa massaliote d'après les fouilles recentes," *Antiquité classique* 35(1966) 71-117.

Di Capua, Francesco, *Il ritmo prosaico nelle lettere dei papi e nei documenti della cancelleria romana dal IV al XIV secolo* (vol. 1) (Rome, 1937-46).

Diekamp, F., "Eine moderne Titelfälschung," *Römische Quartalschriften* 14(1900) 341-355.

Diesner, H.-J., "Das Buccellariertum von Stilicho und Sarus bis auf Aetius (454/455)," *Klio* 53(1972) 321-350.

Dill, Samuel, *Roman Society in Gaul in the Merovingian Age* (London, 1926).

———, *Roman Society in the Last Century of the Roman Empire* (London, 1899).

Disdier, M.-Th., "Le pélagianisme au Concile d'Ephèse," *Echos d'Orient* 34(1931) 314-333.

Dolbeau, François, "La vie en prose de saint Marcel, évêque de Die. Histoire du texte et édition critique," *Francia* 11(1983) 97-130.

Dollinger, P. ed., *Bibliographie d'histoire des villes de France* (Paris, 1967).

Drinkwater, John F., *Roman Gaul: The Three Provinces, 58 BC-AD 260* (Ithaca, 1983).

Dubois, J., "La composition des anciennes listes épiscopales," *Bulletin de la Société des Antiquaires de France* (1967) 74-104.

———, "Les listes épiscopales témoins de l'organisation ecclésiastique et de la transmission des traditions," *Revue d'histoire de l'église de France* 62(1975) 9-23.

Duchesne, Louis, "La civitas Ricomagensium et l'évêché de Nice," *Mémoires de la Société Nationale des Antiquaires de France* 43(1882) 36-46.

———, "Le concile de Turin," *Revue historique* 87(1905) 278-302.

———, "Concile de Turin ou concile de Tours?" *Comptes rendues de l'Académie des Inscriptions et Belles-Lettres* 35(1891) 369-373.

———, *Fastes épiscopaux de l'ancienne Gaule* (3 vols.) (2nd ed.) (Paris, 1907-15).

Duckett, Eleanor S., *Latin Writers of the Fifth Century* (New York, 1930).

Dufourcq, A., "Rutilius Namatianus contre saint Augustin," *Revue d'histoire et de littérature religieuse* 10(1905) 488-492.

Duprat, E., "Etudes sur les légendes saintes de Provence. S. Trophime d'Arles," *Memoires de l'Institut Historique de Provence* 17(1940) 146-198, 18(1941) 87-125.

Duval, Paul-Marie, *La Gaule jusqu'au milieu du Ve siècle* (Paris, 1971).

Duval, Yves-Marie, "La présentation arienne du concile d'Aquilée de 381," *Revue d'histoire ecclésiastique* 76(1981) 317-331.

Ebel, C., *Transalpine Gaul: The Emergence of a Roman Province* (Mt. Airy, Md., 1976).

Eck, W., "Der Einfluss der konstantinische Wende auf die Auswahl der Bischöfe im 4. und 5. Jahrhundert," *Chiron* 8(1978) 561-585.

Edling, Ernst, *Priscillianus och den äldre Priscillianismen* (Upsala, 1962).

Elg, A., "In Faustum Reiensem adversaria," *Eranos* 42(1944) 24-46.

Emonds, H., "Geistlicher Kriegsdienst. Der Topos der militia spiritualis in der antiken Philosophie," in *Heilige Uberlieferung. Ausschnitte aus der Ge-*

schichte des Mönchtums und des heiligen Kultes. Festschrift I. Herwegen (Münster, 1938) 21-50.

Englebrecht, A., "Beiträge zur Kritik und Erklärung der Briefe des Apollinaris Sidonius, Faustus und Ruricius," *Zeitschrift für die österreichischen Gymnasien* 41(1890) 481-497.

————, *Studien über die Schriften des Bischofes von Reii Faustus* (Vienna, 1889).

————, "Untersuchungen über die Sprache des Claudianus Mamertus," *Sitzungberichte der Wiener Akademie* 110(1885) 423-537.

————, "De vita et scriptis Fausti episcopi Reiensis," *Corpus scriptorum ecclesiasticorum latinorum* 21(1891) v-lxxv.

Ensslin, Wilhelm, "Zum Heermeisteramt des spätrömischen Reiches. III. Der magister utriusque militiae et patricius des 5. Jahrhunderts," *Klio* 24(1931) 467-502.

————, "Valentinians III. Novellen XVII und XVIII von 445. Ein Beitrag zur Stellung von Staat und Kirche," *Zeitschrift der Savigny-Stiftung für Rechtsgeschichte, Romanistische Abteilung* 57(1937) 367-378.

Espérandieu, E., *Inscriptions latines de Gaule (Narbonnaise)* (Paris, 1929).

Evans, Robert, "Pelagius' Veracity at the Synod of Diospolis," in John R. Sommerfeldt ed., *Studies in Medieval Culture* (Kalamazoo, 1964) 71-80.

Ewig, E., "Kaiserliche und apostolische Tradition in mittelalterlichen Trier," *Trierer Zeitschrift* 24-26(1956-1958) 147-186 = *Gesammelte Schriften* 2(1979) 51-90.

————, "Von der Kaiserstadt zur Bischofsstadt. Beobachtungen zur Geschichte von Trier im 5. Jahrhundert," in *Gesammelte Schriften* 2(1979) 33-50.

————, *Spätantikes und fränkisches Gallien. Gesammelte Schriften* (2 vols.) (Munich, 1976-1979).

————, *Trier im Merowingerreich. Civitas, Stadt, Bistum* (Trier, 1954).

Fabre, P., *Saint Paulin de Nole et l'amitié chrétienne* (Paris, 1949).

Ferguson, John, *Pelagius: A Historical and Theological Study* (Cambridge, 1956).

Février, Paul-Albert, "Arles aux IVe et Ve siècle, ville impériale et capitale régionale," *Corsi di cultura sull' arte ravennate et bizantina* 25(1978) 127-158.

————, *Le développement urbain en Provence de l'époque romaine à la fin du XIVe siècle* (Paris, 1964).

————, "The Origin and Growth of the Cities of Southern Gaul to the Third Century A.D.: An Assessment of the Most Recent Archaeological Discoveries," *Journal of Roman Studies* 63(1973) 1-28.

Flint, V. I. J., "The True Author of the Salonii Commentarii in Parabolas Salomonis et in Ecclesiasten," *Recherches de Théologie ancienne et médiévale* 37(1970) 174-186.

Fontaine, Jacques, "L'affaire Priscillien ou l'ère des nouveaux Catilina. Observations sur le 'Sallustianisme' de Sulpice Sévère," in P. T. Brennan ed., *Classica et Iberica. A Festschrift in Honor of the Rev. Joseph M.-F. Marique, S.J.*, (Worcester, Mass., 1975) 355-392.

————, "L'aristocratie occidentale devant le monachisme aux IVème et Vème siècles," *Rivista d'Istoria e Letteratura di Storia Religiosa* 15(1979) 28-53.

————, "L'ascétisme chrétien dans la littérature gallo-romaine d'Hilaire à Cassien," in *Atti de Colloquio sulla Gallia Romana. Accademia Nazionale dei Lincei, 10-11 maggio 1971* (Rome, 1973) 87-115.

————, "Hagiographie et politique, de Sulpice Sévère à Venance Fortunat," *Revue d'histoire de l'église de France* 62(1975) 113-140.

Fortin, E. L., *Christianisme et culture philosophique au cinquième siècle. La querelle de l'âme humaine en Occident* (Paris, 1959).

Fowden, G., "The Pagan Holy Man in Late Antique Society," *Journal of Hellenic Studies* 102(1982) 33-59.

Franses, Desiderius, *Paus Leo de Groote en s. Hilarius van Arles* ('s-Hertogenbosch, 1948).

Frantz, Peter N., *Avitus von Vienne (ca.490-518) als Hierarch und Politiker* (Greifswald, 1908).

Freeman, E. A., *Western Europe in the Fifth Century* (London, 1904).

Frend, W. H. C., "Paulinus of Nola and the Last Century of the Western Empire," *Journal of Roman Studies* 59(1969) 1-11.

Fuhrmann, Horst, "Die Fabel von Papst Leo und Bischof Hilarius," *Archiv für Kulturgeschichte* 43(1961) 125-162.

Gabba, Emilio and Tibiletti, G., "Una signora di Treviri sepolta a Pavia," *Athenaeum* 38(1960) 253-262.

Gaidioz, J., "Saint Prosper d'Aquitaine et le tome à Flavien," *Revue des sciences religieuses* 23(1949) 270-301.

Galtier, P., *Saint Hilaire de Poitiers. Le premier docteur de l'église latine* (Paris, 1960).

Gamber, Kl., "Das Lektionar und Sakramentar des Musaeus von Massilia (+ 461)," *Revue bénédictine* 69(1959) 193-215.

Ganghoffer, R., *L'évolution des institutions municipales en Occident et en Orient au Bas-Empire* (Paris, 1963).

Ganshof, F. L., "Note sur l'élection des évêques dans l'empire romain au IVme et pendant la première moitié du Vme siècle," *Revue internationale des droits de l'antiquité* 4(1950) 467-498.

Ganss, George E., *Saint Peter Chrysologus, Selected Sermons, and Saint Valerian, Homilies* (Washington, 1953).

Gaudemet, Jean, "Aspects de la primauté romains de Ve au XVe siècle," in *La société ecclésiastique dans l'occident médiévale* (Paris, 1980) no.5, 93-101.

————, *Conciles gaulois du IVe siècle* (Paris, 1977).

————, *L'Eglise dans l'Empire Romaine (IVe-Ve siècles)* (Paris, 1958).

————, "Note sur les formes anciennes de l'excommunication," in *La société ecclésiastique dans l'occident médiévale* (Paris, 1980) 64ff.

Gebhardt, H. E., *Die Bedeutung Innozenz I. für die Entwicklung der päpstlichen Gewalt* (Leipzig, 1901).

Gelzer, Matthias, *The Roman Nobility* (2nd ed.) (Oxford, 1969).

Germain, A. C., *De Mamerti Claudiani scriptis et philosophia* (thesis Montpellier, 1840).

Gessel, W., "Germanus von Auxerre (um 378 bis 448). Die Vita des Konstantius von Lyon als homileische Paränese in hagiographischer Form," *Römische Quartalschrift für christliche Altertumskunde und Kirchengeschichte* 65(1970) 1-14.

Gibson, Edgar C. S., *The Works of John Cassian* (New York, 1894).

Gilliard, F. D., "The Apostolicity of Gallic Churches," *Harvard Theological Review* 68(1975) 17-33.

————, "The Senators of Sixth-Century Gaul," *Speculum* 54(1979) 685-697.

Gillmann, F., "Das Institut der Chorbischöfe im Orient," *Veröffentlichungen aus dem Kirchengeschichte* 2.1 (Munich, 1903).

Gioffredo, P., "Saint Valérien, confesseur, évêque de Cimiez," *Nice historique* 38(1935) 154-155, 39(1936) 31-32.

Girardet, Klaus, "Trier 385," *Chiron* 4(1974) 577-608.

Glorie, Fr., "La culture lérinienne (Notes de lecture)," *Sacris erudiri* 19(1969-70) 71-76.

Glorieux, P., *Prénestorianisme en Occident* (Tournai, 1959).

Glover, Terrot R., *Life and Letters in the Fourth Century* (New York, 1901).

Gmelin, U., *Auctoritas, römischer Princeps und päpstlicher Primat* (Berlin-Stuttgart, 1936).

Goffart, Walter, *Barbarians and Romans, A.D. 418-584. The Techniques of Accommodation.* (Princeton, 1980).

Gore, C., *Leo the Great* (New York, 1932).

Gottlieb, Gunther, "Das Konzil von Aquileia (381)," *Annuarium historiae conciliorum* 11(1979) 287-306.

Gottlob, T., *Der abendländische Chorepiskopat* (Bonn, 1928).

Gouilloud, A., *Saint Eucher, Lérins et l'église de Lyon au Ve siècle* (Lyon, 1881).

Graham, A. J., "The Limitations of Prosopography in Roman Imperial History (with special Reference to the Severan Period)," *Aufsteig und Niedergang der antiken Welt* 2.1(1974) 136-157.

Grahn-Hoek, Heike, *Die frankische Oberschicht im 6. Jahrhundert. Studien zu ihrer rechtlichen und politischen Stellung* (Sigmaringen, 1976).

Graus, Frantisek, *Volk, Herrscher und Heiliger im Reich der Merowinger. Studien zur Hagiographie der Merowingerzeit* (Prague, 1965)

Greenslade, S. L., "The Illyrian Churches and the Vicariate of Thessalonica 378-395," *Journal of Theological Studies* 46(1945) 17-30.

Griffe, Elie, "L'apocryphe hiéronymien 'De septem ordinibus ecclesiae,'" *Bulletin de littérature ecclésiastique* 57(1956) 215-224.

————, "La date du concile de Turin (398 ou 417)," *Bulletin de littérature ecclésiastique* 64(1973) 289-295.

————, "L'épiscopat gaulois de 481 à 561. Le choix des évêques," *Bulletin de littérature ecclésiastique* 79(1978) 285-300.

————, "L'épiscopat gaulois et les royautés barbares de 489 à 507," *Bulletin de littérature ecclésiastique* 76(1975) 261-284.

————, *La Gaule chrétienne a l'époque romaine* (3 vols.) (Paris, 1964-65).

————, "Un example de pénitence publique au Ve siècle," *Bulletin de littérature ecclésiastique* 59(1958) 170-175.

————, "L'hagiographie gauloise au Ve siècle. La Vie de saint Germain d'Auxerre," *Bulletin de littérature ecclésiastique* 66(1965) 289-294.

————, "Les origines de l'archiprêtre de district," *Revue d'histoire de l'église de France* 13(1927) 16-50.

————, "Les paroisses rurales de la Gaule," *Le maison-dieu* 36(1953) 33-62,

————, "La pratique religieuse en Gaule au Ve siècle. Saeculares et sancti," *Bulletin de littérature ecclésiastique* 63(1962) 241-267.

————, "La primatie d'Arles et les métropoles d'Aix et d'Embrun au Vme siècle," *Bulletin de littérature ecclésiastique* 51(1950) 65-74.

————, "A propos des origines chrétiennes de la Gaule," *Bulletin de littérature ecclésiastique* 49(1948) 148-159.

————, "Pro Vincentio Lerinensi," *Bulletin de littérature ecclésiastique* 62(1961) 26-32.

Grillmeier, A. and H. Bacht eds., *Das Konzil von Chalkedon. Geschichte und Gegenwart* (2 vols.) (Wurzburg, 1951-1954).

Grosjean, Paul, "Le dernier voyage de s. Germain d'Auxerre," *Analecta bollandiana* 75(1957) 180-185.

————, "Le monastère fondé par Saint Germain à Auxerre," *Analecta bollandiana* 7(1957) 168ff.

————, "Notes chronologiques sur le séjour de Patrice en Gaule," *Analecta bollandiana* 73(1955) 53ff.

————, "Palladius episcopus . . . qui Patricius," *Analecta bollandiana* 70(1952) 317-319.

————, "S. Patrice à Auxerre sous s. Germain," *Analecta bollandiana* 75(1957) 158-185.

————, "La seconde visite de S. Germain d'Auxerre en Grand-Bretagne," *Analecta bollandiana* 75(1957) 174-180.

Gryson, R., "Elections épiscopales en occident au IVe siècle," *Revue d'histoire ecclésiastique* 75(1980) 257-283.

Gugumus, J. E., "Der heilige Germanus von Auxerre und die Anfange des Klosters St. German vor Speyer," in *St. German vor Speyer in Stadt und Bistum* (Speyer, 1957) 11-27.

Gundlach, Wilhelm, "Die Sammlung der Epistolae Austrasicae," *Neues Archiv der Gesellschaft für ältere deutsche Geschichtskunde* 13(1887) 367-387.

————, "Der Streit der Bisthümer Arles und Vienne um den Primatus Galliarum," *Neues Archiv der Gesellschaft für ältere deutsche Geschichtskunde* 14(1888) 251-342, 15(1889) 9-102.

Haarhoff, Theodore, *Schools of Gaul. A Study of Pagan and Christian Education in the Last Century of the Western Empire* (Oxford, 1920).

Haenel, G., *Corpus legum ab imperatoribus romanis ante Justinianum latarum* (Leipzig, 1857).

Hagendahl, Harald, *La correspondance de Ruricius* (Göteborg, 1952).

————, *Von Tertullian zu Cassiodor. Die profane literarische Tradition in dem lateininschen christlichen Schrifttum* (Leiden, 1983).

Hanssens, J. M., "Il concilio di Aquileia del 381 alla luce dei documenti contemporanei," *La Scuola Cattolica* 103(1975) 562-644.

Hanson, R. P. C., "The Church in Fifth-Century Gaul: Evidence from Sidonius Apollinaris," *Journal of Ecclesiastical History* 21(1970) 1-10.

Harmand, L., *Le patronat sur les collectivités publiques des origines au Bas-Empire* (Paris, 1957).

Harries, Jill, "Church and State in the *Notitia Galliarum*," *Journal of Roman Studies* 68(1978) 26-43.

Hartranft, C.D., *The Ecclesiastical History of Sozomen* (New York, 1890).

Haslehurst, R. S. T., *The Works of Fastidius* (London, 1927).

Hassebrauk, G., *Westrom zur Zeit des Aëtius, 425-454* (Braunschweig, 1899).

Hatt, J. J., *Histoire de la Gaule romain (120 avant J.-C.-451 après J.-C.)* (Paris, 1959).

Havet, J., "Questions mérovingiennes. II. Les découvertes de Jérome Vignier," *Bibliothèque de l'Ecole des Chartres* 46(1885) 205-274.

Hefele-Leclercq: see von Hefele

Heinzlemann, Martin, *Bischofsherrschaft in Gallien: Zur Kontinuität römischer Führungsschichten von 4. bis zum 7. Jahrhundert* (Munich, 1976).

————, "Gallische Prosopographie 260-527," *Francia* 10(1982) 531-718.

————, "Neue Aspekte der biographischen und hagiographischen Literatur in der lateinischen Welt (1.-6. Jh.)," *Francia* 1(1973) 27-44.

Held, W., "Die gallische Aristokratie im 4. Jahrhundert hinsichtlich ihrer Siedlungsstandorte und ihrer zentralen Stellung zur römischen Provinzial- bzw. Zentraladministration," *Klio* 58(1976) 121-140.

Hess, H., *The Canons of the Council of Sardica* (Oxford, 1958).

Heurtley, C. A., *The Commonitory of Vincent of Lérins. An Introduction, Translation, and Commentary* (New York, 1894).

Hill, H., "Nobilitas in the Imperial Period," *Historia* 18(1969) 230-250.

Hirschfeld, Otto, "Die Organisation der drei Gallien durch Augustus," *Klio* (1908) 703-743.

Hoare, F. R., *The Western Fathers: Being the Lives of Martin of Tours, Ambrose, Augustine of Hippo, Honoratus of Arles, and Germanus of Auxerre* (New York, 1954).

Hodgkin, T., *Italy and Her Invaders* (5 vols.) (London, 1880-89).

Holder-Egger, Oswald, "Untersuchungen über einige annalistische Quellen zur Geschichte des fünften und sechsten Jahrhunderts," *Neues Archiv der Gesellschaft für ältere deutsche Geschichtskunde* 1(1876) 13-120, 213-368.

Holmes, T. S., *The Origin and Development of the Christian Church in Gaul during the First Six Centuries of the Christian Era* (London, 1911).

Hubert, J., "Evolution de la topographie et de l'aspect des villes de Gaule du Ve au IXe siècle," *Settimane di Studio del Centro Italiano di Studi sull' Alto Medievo* 9(1959) 591-602.

Huegelmeyer, C., *Carmen de ingratis S. Prosperi Aquitani. A Translation with an Introduction and a Commentary* (Washington, 1962).

Hunt, Edmund, *St. Leo the Great. Letters* (New York, 1957).

Instinsky, H. U., "Consensus universorum," *Hermes* 75(1940) 265ff.

Jaffé, P., *Regesta pontificum romanorum* (2nd ed.) (Leipzig, 1885).

Jalland, Trevor G., *The Life and Times of St. Leo the Great* (London/New York, 1941).

————, *The Church and the Papacy. An Historical Study* (London, 1946).

Jauncey, E., *The Doctrine of Grace up to the End of the Pelagian Controversy* (London, 1925).

Jerg, E., *Vir venerabilis. Untersuchungen zur Titulatur der Bischöfe in den ausserkirchlichen Texten der spätantike als Beitrag zur Deutung ihrer öffentlichen Stellung* (Vienna, 1970).

Joannou, Périclès-Pierre, *La législation impériale et la christianisation de l'empire romain (311-476)* (Rome, 1972).

Johnstone, K., "Vortigern and Aetius—A Re-appraisal," *Antiquity* 20(1946) 16-20.

Jones, Arnold H. M., *The Later Roman Empire 284-602. A Social, Economic and Administrative Survey* (Oxford, 1964).

————, "Were Ancient Heresies National and Social Movements in Disguise?" *Journal of Theological Studies* 10(1959) 280-298.

————, Martindale, John R., and Morris, John, *The Prosopography of the Later Roman Empire. Volume I. A.D. 260-395* (Cambridge, 1971).

Jugie, M., *Nestorius et la controverse nestorienne* (Paris, 1912).

Jülicher, A., "Ein gallisches Bischofsschreiben des 6. Jahrhunderts als Zeuge für die Verfassung der Montanistenkirche," *Zeitschrift für Kirchengeschichte* 16(1896) 664-671.

Jullian, Camille, *Histoire de la Gaule* (8 vols.) (Paris, 1920-1926).

Kaden, E.-M., "Die Edikte gegen die Manichäer von Diokletian bis Justinian," in *Festschrift für H. Ewald* (Basel, 1953) 55-68.

Kalff, A. W., *Ps.-Hieronymi De septem ordinibus ecclesiae* (Wurzburg, 1938).

Kaufmann, G., "Rhetorenschulen und Klosterschulen oder heidnische und christliche Kultur in Gallien wahrend des 5. und 6. Jahrhunderts," *Historisches Taschenbuch* 10(1869) 1-94.

Kellett, Frederick W., *Pope Gregory the Great and His Relations with Gaul* (Cambridge, 1889).

Kelly, J. F., "The Gallic Resistance to Eastern Asceticism," *Studia patristica* 17(1982) 506-510.

Kidd, B. J., *Documents Illustrative of the History of the Church to 461*, vol.2 (Oxford, 1922)

————, *A History of the Church to A.D. 461. Volume III. A.D. 408-461* (Oxford, 1922).

Kirner, G., "Due vite inedite di s. Marcello vescovo di Die," *Studi Storici* 9(1900) 289-327.

Kissling, W., *Das Verhältnis zwischen Sacerdotium und Imperium nach den Anschüngen der Päpste von Leo der Grosse bis Gelasius I* (Paderborn, 1921).

Klauser, Theodor, "Bischofe als staatliche Prokuratoren im dritten Jahhundert?," *Jahrbuch für Antike und Christentum* 14(1971) 140-149.

————, *Der Ursprung der bischöflichen Insignien und Ehrenrechte* (Bonn, 1948).

Klein, Richard, *Constantius II und die Christliche Kirche* (Darmstadt, 1977).

Klingshirn, William, "Charity and Power: Caesarius of Arles and the Ransoming of Captives in Sub-Roman Gaul," *Journal of Roman Studies* 75(1985) 183-203.

Koch, Anton, *Der heilige Faustus, Bischof von Riez. Eine dogmengeschichtliche Monographie* (Stuttgart, 1895).

Koch, Hugo, *Vinzenz von Lerin und Gennadius. Ein Beitrag zur Literaturgeschichte des Semipelagianismus*, Texte und Untersuchungen zur Geschichte der altchristlichen Literatur 31.2 (Leipzig, 1907).

———, "Vincentius von Lerinum und Marius Mercator," *Theologische Quartalschrift* 81(1899) 396-434.

Kolon, B., *Die Vita s. Hilarii Arelatensis. Eine eidographische Studie* (Paderborn, 1925).

Krusch, B., "De Fausto episcopo Reiensi," *Monumenta Germaniae historica. Auctores antiquissimi* 8(1887) liv-lxi.

———, "De Ruricio episcopo Lemovicensi," *Monumenta Germaniae historica. Auctores antiquissimi* 8(1887) lxii-lxxx.

Kurth, G., "Les sénateurs en Gaule au VIe siècle," in *Etudes franques* vol.2 (Paris-Brussels, 1919) 97-115.

Labroue, Emilio, "L'école de Périgueux au Ve siècle. Poètes et rhéteurs," *Atti del Congresso Internazionale di Scienze Storiche* 2(1905) 161-174.

Lambaglia, N., *Liguria Romana* (Alassio, 1939).

Lana, I., *Rutilio Namaziano* (Turin, 1961).

Langgärtner, Georg, *Die Gallienpolitik der Päpste im 5. und 6. Jahrhundert. Eine Studie uber den apostolische Vikariat von Arles* (Bonn, 1964).

Lanzoni, Francesco, *Le diocesi d'Italia dalle origini al principio del secolo VII (an. 604)* (Faenza, 1927).

Lapidge, M. and D. Dumville eds., *Gildas: New Approaches* (Woodbridge, 1984).

Larsen, Jakob A. O., "The Position of Provincial Assemblies in the Government and Society of the Late Roman Empire," *Classical Philology* 29(1934) 209-220.

Latouche, R., "Nice et Cimiez (Ve-XIe siècle)," in *Mélanges d'histoire du Moyen-Age offerts à M. Ferdinand Lot* (Paris, 1925) 321-358.

Lauras, A., "Saint Léon le Grand et le manichéisme romain," *Texte und Untersuchungen zur altchristlichen Literatur* 108 = *Studia patristica* 11.2(1972) 203-209.

Le Blant, E., *Inscriptions chrétiennes de la Gaule antérieures au VIIIe siècle* (2 vols.) (Paris, 1856-65).

le Bras, Gabriel and Etienne Gilson eds., *Saint Germain d'Auxerre et son temps* (Auxerre, 1950).

Lebeau, P., "Hérésie et providence chez Salvien," *Nouvelle revue théologique* 85(1963) 160-175.

Lécrivain, Charles, "Note sur la vie de saint Orientius, évêque d'Auch," *Annales du midi* 3(1891) 257-258.

———, "Un épisode inconnu de l'histoire des Wisigoths," *Annales du midi* 1(1889) 47-51.

———, *Le sénat romain depuis Dioclétien à Rome et à Constantinople* (Paris, 1888).

Leeming, B., "The False Decretals, Faustus of Riez and the Pseudo-

Eusebius,"*Texte und Untersuchungen zur altchristlichen Literatur* 64 = *Studia patristica* 2.2(1957) 122-139.

Leglay, M., "Quelques données nouvelles sur les routes des Alpes et leur trafic," in *Actes du colloque international sur les cols des Alpes* (Bourg-en-Bresse, 1969) 121-123.

Lepelley, Claude, "Saint Léon le Grand et l'église maurétanienne: primauté romaine et autonomie africaine au Vème siècle," *Cahiers de Tunisie* 15(1967) 189-204.

Leroy, J.-B., *L'oeuvre oratoire de s. Fauste de Riez. La collection gallicane dite d'Eusèbe d'Emèse* (Strasburg, 1954).

Levillain, L., "La crise des années 507-508 et les rivalités d'influence en Gaule de 508 à 514," in *Mélanges offerts à M. Nicholas Iorga* (Paris, 1933) 537-567.

————, "Saint Trophime, confesseur et métropolitain d'Arles, et la mission des sept en Gaule," *Revue d'histore de l'église de France* 13(1927) 145-189.

Levison, Wilhelm, "Bischof Germanus von Auxerre und die Quellen zu seiner Geschichte," *Neues Archiv der Gesellschaft für ältere deutsche Geschichtskunde* 29(1904) 95-175.

————, "Zur Geschichte des Frankenkönigs Chlodowech," *Bonner Jahrbucher* 103(1898) 42-67.

Liebeschuetz, W., "Did the Pelagian Movement have Social Aims?," *Historia* 12(1963) 227-241.

————, "Pelagian Evidence on the Last Period of Roman Britain?," *Latomus* 26(1967) 436-447.

Lienhard, Joseph T., *Paulinus of Nola and Early Christian Monasticism* (Köln, 1977).

Lippert, W., "Die Verfasserschaft der Canonen gallischer Concilien des V. und VI. Jahrhunderts," *Neues Archiv der Gesellschaft für ältere deutsche Geschichtskunde* 14(1889) 9-58.

Longnon, A., *Géographie de la Gaule au VIe siècle* (Paris, 1878).

————, *Les noms de lieu de la France* (Paris, 1920-29).

Lorenz, R., "Die Anfänge des abendländischen Mönchtums im 4. Jahrhundert," *Zeitschrift für Kirchengeschichte* 77(1966) 1-61.

————, "Der Augustinismus Prospers von Aquitanien," *Zeitschrift für Kirchengeschichte* 73(1963) 217-252.

Lot, Ferdinand, *La Gaule. Les fondements ethniques, sociaux et politiques de la nation française* (Paris, 1947).

————, "La *Vita Viviani* et la domination visigothique en Aquitaine," in *Mélanges Paul Fournier* (Paris, 1929) 467-477.

————, "Vitae, passiones, miracula, translationes sanctorum Galliae (500-1000)," *Archivum latinitatis medii aevi* = *Bulletin du Cange* 14(1939) 181-230, 20(1950) 55-64.

————, "Vitae sanctorum anonymae addendae," *Archivum latinitatis medii aevi* = *Bulletin du Cange* 20(1950) 55-64.

Lotter, Friedrich, "Zu den Anredeformen und ehrenden Epitheta der Bischöfe in Spätantike und frühem Mittelalter," *Deutsches Archiv für Erforschung des Mittelalters* 27(1971) 514-517.

————, "Antonius von Lérins und der Untergang Ufernorikums. Ein Beitrag zur Frage der Bevölkerungskontinuität im Alpen-Donau-Raum,' *Historische Zeitschrift* 212(1971) 265-315.

————, "Designation und angebliches Kooptationsrecht bei Bischofserhebungen," *Zeitschrift der Savigny-Stiftung für Rechtsgeschichte, Kanonistische Abteilung* 59(1973) 112-150.

Louis, R., "La séjour de saint Patrice à Auxerre," in *Mélanges L. Halphen* (Paris, 1951) 447-457.

Loyen, André, "Etudes sur Sidoine Apollinaire," *Revue des études latines* 46(1968) 83-90.

————, "La mère de Faustus de Riez (Sidoine Apollinaire C. XVI, v. 84)," *Bulletin de littérature ecclésiastique* 73(1972) 167-169.

————, "L'oeuvre de Flavius Merobaudes et l'histoire de l'occident de 430 à 450," *Revue des études anciennes* 74(1972) 153-174.

————, *Recherches historiques sur les panégyriques de Sidoine Apollinaire* (Paris, 1942).

————, "Résistants et collaborateurs en Gaule à l'époque des grandes invasions," *Bulletin de l'Association G. Budé* 22(1963) 437-450.

————, "Le rôle de saint Aignan dans la défense d'Orléans," *Comptes rendus de l'Academie des Inscriptions et Belles-Lettres* (1969) 64-74.

————, *Sidoine Apollinaire: Poemes* (Paris, 1960) and vols.2-3, *Sidoine Apollinaire: Lettres* (Paris, 1970)

————, "Sidoine Apollinaire et les derniers éclats de la culture classique dans la Gaule occupée par les Goths," *Settimane di Studio del Centro Italiano di Studi sull' Alto Medievo* 3 (Spoleto, 1956) 265-284.

————, *Sidoine Apollinaire et l'esprit précieux en Gaule aux derniers jours de l'empire* (Paris, 1943).

Luff, S. G., "A Survey of Primitive Monasticism in Central Gaul (c.350-700)," *Downside Review* 70(1952) 180-203.

Lumpe, Adolf, "Zur Geschichte der Wörter *Concilium* und *Synodus* in der antiken christlichen Latinität," *Annuarium historiae conciliorum* 2(1970) 1-21.

————, "Die konziliengeschichtliche Bedeutung des Ennodius," *Annuarium historiae conciliorum* 1(1969) 15-36.

————, "Die Synode von Turin vom Jahre 398," *Annuarium historiae conciliorum* 4(1972) 7-25.

MacDonald, J., "Who Instituted the Papal Vicariate of Thessalonica?," *Texte und Untersuchungen zur altchristlichen Literatur* 79 = *Studia patristica* 4(1961) 478-482.

MacMullen, R., *Enemies of the Roman Order: Treason, Unrest and Alienation in the Empire* (Cambridge, Mass., 1966).

Madoz, P. J., "El concepto de la tradicion en s. Vincente de Lerins," *Analecta gregoriana* 5(1933) 59-89.

————, "¿Contra quién escribo san Vincente de Lerins su Conmonitoria?," *Estudios Ecclesiasticos* (1931) 5-34.

Malcus, B., *Le sénat et l'ordre sénatorial au Bas-Empire* (Lund, 1970).

Malnory, A., *Saint Césaire, évêque d'Arles 503-543* (Paris, 1894).

Manitius, M., *Geschichte der lateinischen Literatur des Mittelalters* (vol. 1) (Munich, 1911).

Mansi, J. D., ed., *Sacrorum conciliorum nova et amplissima collectio*, 31 vols. (Florence-Venice, 1759-1798), reprinted, J. B. Martin, L. Petit eds., 56 vols. (Paris, 1901-1924).

Markus, R. A., "Chronicle and Theology: Prosper of Aquitaine," in C. Holdsworth and T. P. Wiseman eds., *The Inheritance of Historiography 350-900*, Exeter Studies in History 12 (Exeter, 1986) 31-43.

Marrou, Henri-Irénée, "Le dossier épigraphique de l'évêque Rusticus de Narbonne," *Rivista di archeologia cristiana* 3-4(1970) 331-349.

————, "L'épitaphe vaticane du consulaire de Vienne Eventius," *Revue des études anciennes* 54(1952) 326-331.

————, "La fondateur de Saint-Victor de Marseille: Jean Cassien," *Provence historique* 16(1966) 297-308.

————, *Histoire de l'éducation dans l'antiquité* (3rd ed.) (Paris, 1955).

————, "Jean Cassien à Marseille," *Revue du Moyen-Age latiné* 1(1945) 5-26.

————, "Un lieu dit 'Cité de Dieu'," *Augustinus magister* 1(1954) 101-110.

Marschall, W., *Karthago und Rom. Die Stellung der nordafrikanischen Kirche zum apostolischen Stuhl in Rom*, Päpste und Papsttum 1 (Stuttgart, 1971).

Martindale, John R., *Prosopography of the Later Roman Empire. Volume II. A.D.395-527* (Cambridge, 1980).

Mathisen, Ralph W., "Avitus, Italy and the East in A.D. 455-456," *Byzantion* 51(1981) 232-247.

————, *The Ecclesiastical Aristocracy of Fifth-Century Gaul: A Regional Analysis of Family Structure* (diss., University of Wisconsin, 1979: Ann Arbor, 1980).

————, "Emigrants, Exiles, and Survivors: Aristocratic Options in Visigothic Aquitania," *Phoenix* 38(1984) 159-170.

————, "Epistolography, Literary Circles, and Family Ties in Late Roman Gaul," *Transactions of the American Philological Association* 111(1981) 95-109.

————, "The Family of Georgius Florentius Gregorius and the Bishops of Tours," *Mediaevalia et Humanistica* 12(1984) 83-95.

————, "Hilarius, Germanus and Lupus: The Aristocratic Background of the Chelidonius Affair," *Phoenix* 33(1979) 160-169.

————, "The Last Year of Saint Germanus of Auxerre," *Analecta bollandiana* 99(1981) 151-159.

————, "Late Roman Prosopography in the West (A.D.260-640): A Survey of Recent Work," *Medieval Prosopography* 2(1981) 1-12.

————, "Patricians as Diplomats in Late Antiquity," *Byzantinische Zeitschrift* 79(1986) 35-49.

————, "Petronius, Hilarius and Valerianus: Prosopographical Notes on the Conversion of the Roman Aristocracy," *Historia* 30(1981) 106-112.

————, "*PLRE II*: Suggested *Addenda* and *Corrigenda*," *Historia* 31(1982) 364-386.

————, "Resistance and Reconciliation: Majorian and the Gallic Aristocracy after the Fall of Avitus," *Francia* 7(1979) 597-627.

————, "Sidonius on the Reign of Avitus: A Study in Political Prudence," *Transactions of the American Philological Association* 109(1979) 165-171.

————, "The Third Regnal Year of Eparchius Avitus," *Classical Philology* 80(1985) 192-196.

Matthews, John F., *Western Aristocracies and Imperial Court A.D. 364-425* (Oxford, 1975).

Maurin, Jean, "La prosopographie romaine: Perts et profits," *Annales, Economie, Societés* 37(1982) 824-836.

McClure, Judith, "Handbooks against Heresy in the West, from the Late Fourth to the Late Sixth Centuries," *Journal of Theological Studies* 30(1979) 186-197.

McGeachy, John A., *Quintus Aurelius Symmachus and the Senatorial Aristocracy of the West* (Chicago, 1942).

McHugh, M. P., *The Carmen de Providentia Dei, Attributed to Prosper of Aquitaine: A Revised Text with an Introduction* (Washington, 1964).

McShane, Philip, *La romanitas et le pape Léon le Grand. L'apport culturel des institutions impériales à la formation des structures ecclésiastiques* (Tournai/Montreal, 1979).

Mellier, A., *De vita et scriptis s. Eucherii* (Lyons, 1877).

Menna, P., "Illud carmen quod ad coniugem inscribitur divi Paulini Nolani sitne an divi Prosperi Aquitani?" *Latinitas* 10(1962) 208-214.

Meslin, M., *Les Ariens d'Occident 335-430* (Paris, 1967).

————, *Le Commonitorium de saint Vincent de Lérins* (Namur, 1959).

Miller, M., "The Last British Entry in the 'Gallic Chronicles'," *Britannia* 9(1978) 315-318.

Mirot, L., *Manuel de géographie historique de la France* (Paris, 1930).

————, *Les noms de lieu de la France, leur origine* (Paris, 1929).

Molinier, A., "Saint Prosper d'Aquitaine," *Revue historique* 75(1901) 114-116.

Momigliano, A., "Cassiodorus and Italian Culture of his Time," *Proceedings of the British Academy* 41(1955) 207-245.

Mommsen, Theodor, *The Provinces of the Roman Empire*, T. Broughton ed. (Chicago, 1968)

————, "Die Synode von Turin," *Neues Archiv der Gesellschaft für ältere deutsche Geschichtskunde* 17(1892) 187-188 = *Gesammelte Schriften* vol.3 (Berlin, 1965) 582-584.

————, "Zeitzer Ostertafel vom Jahre 447," *Gesammelte Schriften: Historische Schriften* vol.3 (Berlin, 1965) 589-601.

Moreau, J., *Dictionnaire de géographie historique de la Gaule et de la France* (Picard, 1972).

Morel, B., "De invloet van Leporius op Cassianus. Weerlegging van het Nestorianisme," *Bijdragen. Tijdschrift voor Philosophie en Theologie* 21(1960) 31-52.

Moricca, U., "La morte violenta di un fratello di Paolino di Nola," *Didaskaleion* 4(1926) 85-90.

Morin, Germain, "La collection gallicane dite d'Eusèbe d'Emèse et les problèmes qui s'y rattachent," *Zeitschrift für die neutestamentliche Wissenschaft* 35(1935) 92-115.

————, "Castor et Polychronius: un épisode peu connu de l'histoire ecclésiastique des Gaules," *Revue bénédictine* 51(1939) 31-36.

————, "Le destinataire de l'apocryphe hiéronymien *De septem ordinibus ecclesiae*," *Revue d'histoire ecclésiastique* 34(1938) 229-244.

————, *Etudes, textes, découvertes. Contributions à la littérature et à l'histoire des douze premiers siècles* vol.1 (Paris, 1913).

————, "Examen des écrits attribués à Arnobe le Jeune," *Revue bénédictine* 26(1909) 419-432.

————, "Hiérarchie et liturgie dans l'église gallicane au Ve siècle d'apres un écrit restitué à Fauste de Riez," *Revue bénédictine* 8(1891) 97-104.

————, "La lettre-préface du *Comes*, AD CONSTANTIUM, se rapporterait au Lectionaire de Claudien Mamert?," *Revue bénédictine* 30(1913) 228-231.

————, "Le *Liber dogmatum* de Gennade de Marseille et problèmes qui s'y rattachent," *Revue bénédictine* 24(1907) 446-456.

————, "Portion inédit de l'apocryphe hiéronymien 'De septem ordinibus ecclesiae'," *Revue bénédictine* 40(1928) 310-318.

————, "Saint Lazare et saint Maximin. Données nouvelles sur plusieurs personnages de la tradition de Provence," *Memoires de la Société Nationale des Antiquaires de France* 56(1897) 27-51.

————, "Les 'Statuta ecclesiae antiqua', sont-ils de s. Césaire d'Arles?," *Revue bénédictine* 30(1913) 334-442.

————, "De trois ou quatre chapitres qui portent le nom de Gennade à fin de deux catalogues hérésiologiques du Ve siècle," *Revue bénédictine* 24(1907) 451-454.

Moris, H., *L'Abbaye de Lérins, son histoire, ses possessions, ses monuments anciens* (Nice-Paris, 1905).

Morris, John, *The Age of Arthur. A History of the British Isles From 350 to 650* (New York, 1973).

————, "Pelagian Literature," *Journal of Theological Studies* 16(1965) 26-60.

Morrison, Karl, *Tradition and Authority in the Western Church 300-1140* (Princeton, 1969).

Moss, J. R., "The Effects of the Policies of Aetius on the History of Western Europe," *Historia* 22(1973) 711-731.

Muhlberger, Steven A., "The Gallic Chronicle of 452 and its Authority for British Events," *Britannia* 14(1983) 23-33.

————, *Prosper, Hydatius and the Chronicler of 452: Three Chroniclers and Their Significance for Fifth-Century Historiography* (diss. Toronto, 1982).

Mulders, J., "Victricius van Rouaan. Leven en Leer," *Bijdragen. Tijdschrift voor Philosophie en Theologie* 17(1956) 1-25, 18(1957) 19-40, 270-289.

Munier, Ch., "Un canon inédit du XXe concile du Carthage: 'Ut nullus ad Romanam ecclesiam appellare audeat'," *Revue des sciences religieuses* 40(1966) 113-126.

————, *Les Statuta ecclesiae antiqua* (Paris, 1960).

Munz, Peter, "John Cassian," *Journal of Ecclesiastical History* 11(1960) 1-22.

Musumeci, Anna Maria, "La politica ecclesiastica di Valentiniano III," *Siculorum gymnasium* 30(1977) 431-481.

Myres, J. N. L., "Pelagius and the End of Roman Rule in Britain," *Journal of Roman Studies* 50(1960) 21-36.

Nagel, P., *Die Motivierung der Askese in der alten Kirche und der Ursprung des Mönchtums* (Berlin, 1966).

Nagl, Maria Assunta, *Galla Placidia* (Paderborn, 1908).

Nautin, P., "La lettre de Félix III à André de Thessalonique et sa doctrine sur l' église et l'empire," *Revue d'histoire ecclésiastique* 77(1982) 5-34.

Nesselhauf, Herbert, *Die spätrömische Verwaltung der gallisch-germanischen Länder* (Berlin, 1938).

Noethlichs, Karl Leo, *Beamtentum und Dienstvergehen: Zur Staatsverwaltung in der Spätantike* (Wiesbaden, 1981).

———, "Zur Einflussnahme des Staates auf die Entwicklung eines christlichen Klerikerstandes, schicht- und berufsspezifische Bestimmung für der Klerus in 4. und 5. Jahrhundert in den spätantiken Rechtsquellen," *Jahrbuch für Antike und Christentum* 15(1972) 136-153.

———, "Materialien zum Bischofsbild aus den spätantiken Rechtsquellen," *Jahrbuch für Antike und Christentum* 16(1973) 28-59.

Norcock, C. R., "St. Gaudentius of Brescia and the *Tome* of St. Leo," *Journal of Theological Studies* 15(1913-14) 593-596.

O'Donnell, J. Reginald, *Prosper of Aquitaine. Grace and Free Will (De gratia dei)*, The Fathers of the Church vol.7 (New York, 1949) 333-418.

Oehler, Klaus, "Der consensus omnium als Kriterium der Wahrheit in der antiken Philosophie und der Patristik," *Antike und Abendland* 10(1961) 103-129.

Oost, Stewart I., *Galla Placidia Augusta, A Biographical Essay* (Chicago, 1968).

Opelt, I., "Zur literarischen Eigenart von Eucherius' Schrift 'De laude eremi'," *Vigiliae christianae* 22(1968) 198-208.

Otto, W., "Die Nobilität der Kaizerzeit," *Hermes* 51(1916) 73ff.

Palanque, Jean-Rémy, "La date du transfert de la préfecture des Gaules de Trèves à Arles," *Revue des études anciennes* 36(1934) 358-365.

———, *Le diocèse d'Aix-en-Provence* (Paris, 1975).

———, *Le diocèse de Marseille* (Paris, 1967).

———, "Les dissensions des églises des Gaules à la fin du IVe siècle et la date du concile de Turin," *Revue d'histoire de l'église de France* 21(1935) 481-501.

———, "Les évêchés de Narbonnaise Première à l'époque romaine," *Annales de l'Université de Montepellier et de Languedoc méditerranéen-Rouszillon* 1(1943) 177-186.

———, "Les évêchés provençaux à l'époque romaine," *Provence historique* 1(1951) 105-143.

———, "Du nouveau sur la date du transfert de la préfecture des Gaules de Trèves à Arles?" *Provence historique* 23(1973) 29-38.

———, "Les premiers évêques d'Aix-en-Provence," *Analecta bollandiana* 67(1949) 377-383.

———, *Saint Ambroise et l'Empire romain. Contribution à l'histoire des rapports de l'église et de l'état à la fin du quatrième siècle* (Paris, 1933).

Paret, Friedrich, *Priscillianus. Ein Reformator des vierten Jahrhunderts. Eine kirchengeschichtlicher Studie zugleich ein Kommentar zu den erhalten Schriften Priscillians* (Wurzburg, 1891).

Parisot, R., "Des ordinationes 'per saltum,'" *Revue de l'Orient chrétien* 5(1900) 355-369.

Pastorini, A., "Il concetto di tradizione in Giovanni Cassiano e in Vincenzo di Lerino," *Sileno* 1(1975) 37-46.

Pelland, L., S. *Prosperi Aquitani doctrina de praedestinatione et voluntate dei salvifica et eius in Augustinum inflexu* (Montreal, 1936).

Pellegrino, M., *Salviano di Marsiglia. Studio critico.* (Rome, 1946).

Pelletier, Andre, *Vienne gallo-romaine au Bas-Empire, 275-468 ap. J.-C.* (Lyons, 1974).

―――, "Vienne et la réorganisation provinciale de la Gaule au Bas-Empire," *Latomus* 26(1967) 491-498.

Peter, Hermann, *Der Brief in der römischen Litteratur* (Leipzig, 1901).

Pflaum, Hans-Georg, "Quelques réflexions sur l'interprétation prosopographique de l'histoire romaine," *Rheinisches Museum* 115(1972) 318-321.

Pietri, Charles, *Roma christiana. Recherches sur l'église de Rome, son organisation, sa politique, son idéologie de Miltiade à Sixte III (311-440)* (Rome, 1976).

Piganiol, Andre, *L'Empire chrétien (325-395)* (2nd ed.) (Paris, 1972).

Pinchon, R., *Etudes sur l'histoire de la littérature latine dans les Gaules, les derniers écrivains profanes* (Paris, 1906).

Plagnieux, J., "Le grief de complicité entre erreurs nestorienne et pélagienne d'Augustin à Cassien par Prosper d'Aquitaine," *Revue des études augustiniennes* 2(1956) 391-402.

Poupardin, M., "Etude sur les vies des saints fondateurs de Condate," *Le Moyen-Age* 11(1898) 31-48.

Prete, S., *I chronica di Sulpicio Severo* (The Vatican, 1955).

―――, *Pelagio e il Pelagianesimo* (Brescia, 1961).

Pricoco, Salvatore, "Barbari, senso della fine e teologia politica. Su un passo del 'De Contemptu Mundi' di Eucherio di Lione," *Romanobarbarica* 2(1977) 209-229.

―――, *L'isola dei santi. Il cenobio di Lerino e le origini dei monachesimo gallico* (Rome, 1978).

―――, "Modelli di santità a Lerino. L'ideale ascetico nel 'Sermo de Vita Honorati' di Ilario di Arles," *Siculorum Gymnasium* 27(1974) 54-88.

―――, "Studi su Sidonio," *Nuovo Didaskaleion* 15(1965) 71-151.

Prieux, J., *La province romaine des Alpes Cottiennes* (Lyons, 1968).

Prinz, Friedrich, "Die bischöfliche Stadtherrschaft im Frankenreich vom 5. bis zum 7. Jahrhundert," *Historische Zeitschrift* 217(1973) 1-35.

―――, *Frühes Mönchtum im Frankenreich. Kultur und Gesellschaft in Gallien am Beispiel der monastischen Entwicklung (4.-8. Jahrhundert)* (Munich-Vienna, 1965).

―――, *Klerus und Krieg im früheren Mittelalter. Untersuchungen zur Rolle der Kirche beim Aufbau der Königsherrschaft* (Stuttgart, 1971).

Prunel, L., *Saint Germain d'Auxerre (378-448)* (Paris, 1929).

R.-Alföldi, Maria, "Zum Datum der Aufgabe der Residenz Treviri unter Stilicho," *Jahrbuch für Numismatik* 20(1970) 241-249.

Raby, F. J. E., *A History of Secular Latin Poetry in the Middle Ages* (Oxford, 1934).

Rahner, Hugo, *Die gefälschten Päpstbriefe aus dem nachlass von Jérôme Vignier* (Freiburg, 1935).

——, "Leo der Grosse, der Papst des Konzils," in A. Grillmeier and H. Bacht eds., *Das Konzil von Chalkedon* 1 (Wurzburg, 1951) 323-339.

Rampal, A., "Embrun, métropole des Alpes-Maritimes," *Provincia* 10(1930) 211-228.

Rehling, Bernardus, *De Fausti Reiensis epistula tertia. Commentatio historica* (Münster, 1898).

Reindel, K., "Die Bistumorganisation im Alpen-Donau-Raum in der Spätantike und im Frühmittelalter," *Mitteilungen des Instituts für österreichische Geschichtsforschung* 72(1964) 277-310.

Reuter, Timothy ed., *The Medieval Nobility. Studies on the Ruling Classes of France and Germany from the Sixth to the Twelfth Century* (Amsterdam/ New York/Oxford, 1979).

Richards, Jeffrey, *The Popes and the Papacy in the Early Middle Ages 476-752* (London-Boston-Henley, 1979).

Riché, Pierre, *Education et culture dans l'Occident barbare, VIe-VIIIe siècles* (Paris, 1962).

——, "La survivance des écoles publiques en Gaule au Ve siècle," *Le Moyen-Age* 63(1957) 421-436.

Rivet, A., "The Notitia Galliarum: Some Questions," in *Aspects of the Notitia Dignitatum* (London, 1976) 119-141.

Rocquain de Courtemblay, F., "Variations des limites de l'Aquitaine depuis l'an 56 avant J.-C. jusqu'au Ve siècle," *Bibliothèque de l'Ecole des Chartres* 22(1861) 256-271

Roger, M., *L'enseignement des lettres classiques d'Ausone à Alcuin, introduction à l'histoire des écoles carolingiennes* (Paris, 1905).

Rouche, Michel, *L'Aquitaine des Wisigoths aux Arabes, 418-781: Naissance d'une région* (Paris, 1979).

——, "Le changement de nom des cheflieux de cité en Gaule au Bas-Empire," *Mémoires et travaux publiées par la Société Nationale des Antiquaires de France* 84(1969) 47-64.

Rouselle, Aline, "Quelques aspects politiques de l'affaire priscillianiste," *Revue des études anciennes* 83(1981) 85-96.

Rousseau, Philip, *Ascetics, Authority and the Church in the Age of Jerome and Cassian* (Oxford, 1978).

——, "In Search of Sidonius the Bishop," *Historia* 25(1976) 356-377.

——, "The Spiritual Authority of the Monk-Bishop. Eastern Elements in Some Western Hagiography of the Fourth and Fifth Centuries," *Journal of Theological Studies* 22(1971) 388-419.

Roux, J.-M., "Les évêchés provençaux, de la fin de l'époque romaine à l'avènement des Carolingiens (476-751)," *Provence historique* 21(1971) 373-420.

Rusch, William G., *The Later Latin Fathers* (London, 1977).

Rutherford, Hamish, *Sidonius Apollinaris. l'homme politique, l'écrivain, l'évêque. Etude d'une figure gallo-romaine du Ve siècle* (Clermont-Ferrand, 1938).

Saint Martin et son temps. Mémorial du XVIe centénaire des débuts du monachisme en Gaule, 361-1961, Studia Anselmiana 46 (Rome, 1961).

Salles, L., *Hilaire, compagnon de Prosper, sa vie et ses oeuvres* (Paris, 1854).

Schanz, Martin, C. Hosius and G. Krüger, *Geschichte der römischen Litteratur bis zum Gesetzgebungswerk des Kaisers Justinians. Vierter Teil: Die römische Litteratur von Constantin bis zum Gesetzgebungswerk Justinians. Zweite Hälfte: Die Litteratur des fünften und sechsten Jahrhunderts* (Munich, 1920)

Schmëing, K., *Flucht und Werbungssagen in der Legende* (Munster, 1911).

Schmidt, Ludwig, "Das Ende der Römerherrschaft in Gallien (Chlodowech und Syagrius)," *Historisches Jahrbuch* 48(1928) 611-618.

———, *Geschichte der deutschen Stämme bis zum Ausgang der Völkerwanderung.* vol.1 *Die Ostgermanen* and vol.2 *Die Westgermanen* (Munich, 1934-1941).

Schmitz, Hermann J., "Die Rechte der Metropoliten und Bischöfe in Gallien von 4. bis 6. Jahrhundert," *Archiv für katholisches Kirchenrecht* 72(1894) 3-49.

———, "Die Tendenz der Provinzialsynoden in Gallien seit dem 5. Jahrhundert und die römischen Büssbucher," *Archiv für katholisches Kirchengeschichte* 71(1894) 21-33.

Schulze, M., *Die Schrift des Claudianus Mamertus, Presbyter zu Vienne, über das Wesen der Seele* (diss. Leipzig, 1883).

Schuster, Mauriz, "Der religiöse Standpunkt des Rutilius Namatianus," *Philologische Wochenschrift* 45(1925) 713-717.

Schwartz, Eduardus, ed., *Acta conciliorum oecumenicorum. Iussu atque mandato societatis scientiarum argentoratensis* (Berlin, 1965ff).

Seeck, Otto, *Geschichte des Untergangs der antiken Welt* (vol.6) (Stuttgart, 1920).

———, *Regesten der Kaiser und Päpste für die Jahre 311 bis 476 n. Chr.* (Stuttgart, 1919).

Selb, Walter, "Episcopalis audientia von der Zeit Konstantins bis zur Nov. XXXV Valentinians III.," *Zeitschrift der Savigny-Stiftung für Rechtsgeschichte, Romanistische Abteilung* 84(1967) 162-217.

Selle-Hosbach, Karin, *Prosopographie merowingischer Amtsträger in der Zeit von 511 bis 613* (Bonn, 1974).

Sieben, Hermann J., "Der Konzilsbegriff des Vinzenz von Lerin (+ vor 450)," in *Die Konzilsidee der alten Kirche* (Paderborn, 1979) 148-179.

———, "Leo der Grosse (+461) über Konzilien und Lehrprimat des römischen Stuhles," in *Die Konzilsidee der alten Kirche* (Paderborn, 1979) 103-147.

Silva-Tarouca, C., *Collectio thessalonicensis* (Rome, 1937).

———, *S. Leonis Magni epistulae*, Textus et Documenta 9, 15, 20, 23 (Rome, 1932-1937).

———, "Nuovi studi sulle antiche lettere dei papi," *Gregorianum* 12(1931) 3-56, 349-425, 547-598 = (Rome, 1932) (with pages renumbered).

Simonetti, Manlio, "Fausto di Riez e i Macedoniani," *Augustinianum* 17(1977) 333-354.

―――, "Le fonti del *De spiritu sancto* di Fausto di Riez," *Siculorum Gymnasium* 29(1976) 413-425.

Sirago, Vito A., *Galla Placidia e la trasformazione politica dell' Occidente* (Louvain, 1961).

Sitwell, N. H. H., *Roman Roads in Europe* (New York, 1981).

Smolak, Kurt, *Das Gedicht des Bischofs Agrestius. Eine theologische Lehrepistel aus der Spätantike* (Vienna, 1973).

Souter, A., "Cassiodorus' Copy of Eucherius's *Instructiones*," *Journal of Theological Studies* 14(1912-13) 69-72.

―――, "Observations on the Pseudo-Eusebian Collection of Gallican Sermons," *Journal of Theological Studies* 41(1940) 47-57.

―――, "Pelagius' Doctrine in Relation to His Early Life," *Expositor* 1(1915) 180-182.

Speigl, Jakob, "Der Pelagianismus auf dem Konzil von Ephesus," *Annuarium historiae conciliorum* 1(1969) 1-14.

―――, "Zum Problem der Teilnahme von Laien an den Konzilien im kirchlichen Altertum," *Annuarium historiae conciliorum* 10(1978) 241-248.

Stancliffe, Clare, *St. Martin and His Hagiographer. History and Miracle in Sulpicius Severus* (Oxford, 1983).

Stein, Ernst, *Geschichte des spätrömischen Reiches vom römischen zum byzantinischen Staate (284-476 n. Chr.)* (vol.1) (Vienna, 1928), translated by J.-R. Palanque, *Histoire du Bas-Empire. Tome premier. De l'état romaine à l'état byzantine (284-476)* (Paris, 1959, repr. Amsterdam, 1968).

Sternberg, G., "Das Christentum des V. Jahrhundert im Spiegel der Schriften des Salvianus von Massilia," *Theologischen Studien und Kritiken* 82(1909) 29-78, 163-205.

Sterzl, A. G., *Romanus-Christianus-Barbarus. Die germanische Landnahme im Spiegel der Schriften des Salvian von Massalia und Victor von Vita* (Erlangen, 1950).

Stevens, Courtenay E., "Marcus, Gratian, and Constantine," *Athenaeum* 35(1957) 316-347.

―――, *Sidonius Apollinaris and His Age* (Oxford, 1933).

Stockmeier, P., "'Imperium' bei Papst Leo dem Grossen," *Studia patristica* 3(1961) 413-420.

―――, "Leo der Grosse und die Anfänge seines synodalen Tätigeit," *Annuarium historiae conciliorum* 12(1980) 38-46.

―――, "Das Schwert im Dienst der Kirche. Zur Hinrichtung Priszillians in Trier," *Festschrift A. Thomas* (Trier, 1967) 415-428.

Stone, Lawrence, "Prosopography," *Daedalus* 106(1971) 46-79.

Streichhan, F., "Die Anfänge des Vikariats von Thessalonica," *Zeitschrift der Savigny Stiftung für Rechtsgeschichte, Kanonistische Abteilung* 12(1922) 355-384.

Stroheker, Karl F., *Eurich, König der Westgoten* (Stuttgart, 1937).

―――, "Die Senatoren bei Gregor von Tours," *Klio* 34(1942) 293-305.

―――, *Der senatorische Adel im spätantiken Gallien* (Reutlingen, 1948).

Studer, B., "Zur Fräge des westlichen Origenismus," *Texte und Untersuchungen zur altchristlichen Literatur* 94(1966) 270-287.

Sundwall, Johannes, *Weströmische Studien* (Berlin, 1915).

———, *Abhandlungen zur Geschichte des ausgehenden Römertums* (Helsingfors, 1919).

Syme, Ronald, *The Roman Revolution* (Oxford, 1952, repr. Oxford, 1968).

Täckholm, Ulf, "Aetius and the Battle on the Catalaunian Fields," *Opuscula romana* 7(1969) 259-276.

Thiel, Andreas, *Epistolae romanorum pontificum genuinae et quae ad eos scriptae sunt a s. Hilaro usque ad Pelagium II* (Brunsberg, 1867).

Thompson, Edward A., *Attila and the Huns* (Oxford, 1948).

———, "Barbarian Invaders and Roman Collaborators," *Florilegium* 2(1980) 71-87.

———, "A Chronological Note on St. Germanus of Auxerre," *Analecta bollandiana* 75(1957) 135-138.

———, "The End of Roman Spain," parts 1-4 *Nottingham Medieval Studies* 20(1976) 3-28, 21(1977) 3-31, 22(1978) 3-22, 23(1979) 1-21.

———, *Romans and Barbarians. The Decline of the Western Empire* (Madison, 1982).

———, *Saint Germanus of Auxerre and the End of Roman Britain* (Woodbridge, 1984).

———, "Zosimus on the End of Roman Britain," *Antiquity* 30(1956) 162-167.

Thouvenot, R., "Salvien et la ruine de l'Empire romaine," *Mélanges d'archéologie et d'histoire de l'Ecole Française de Rome* 38(1920) 145-163.

Tibiletti, Carlo, "Fausto di Riez nei giudizi della critica," *Augustinianum* 21(1981) 567-587.

———, "Giovanni Cassiano. Formazione e dottrina," *Augustinianum* 17(1977) 355-380.

———, "Libero arbitrio e grazia in Fausto di Riez," *Augustinianum* 19(1979) 259-285.

———, "La salvezza umana in Fausto di Riez," *Orpheus* 1(1980) 371-390.

Tobin, M. D., *The Commonitorium of Orientius* (Washington, 1945).

Travers-Smith, Richard, *The Church in Roman Gaul* (London/New York, n.d. [c.1905]).

Turbessi, G., *Ascetismo e monachesimo prebenedettino* (Rome, 1961).

Turner, C. H., "Arles and Rome: The First Developments of Canon Law in Gaul," *Journal of Theological Studies* 17(1916) 236-247.

———, "The *Liber Ecclesiasticorum Dogmatum* Attributed to Gennadius," *Journal of Theological Studies* 7(1906) 78-99; 8(1907) 103-114.

Twyman, Briggs L., "Aetius and the Aristocracy," *Historia* 19(1970) 480-503.

Ulbrich, H., "Augustins Briefe zur entscheidenden Phase des pelagianischen Streites," *Revue des études augustiniennes* 9(1963) 51-75, 235-238.

Vacandard, E., *Saint Victrice, évêque de Rouen (IVe-Ve siècle)* (2nd ed.) (Paris, 1903).

Valentin, L., *Saint Prosper d'Aquitaine: Etudes sur la littérature latine ecclésiastique au Ve siècle en Gaule* (Paris-Toulouse, 1900).

van Andel, G. K., *The Christian Concept of History in the Chronicle of Sulpicus Severus* (Amsterdam, 1976).

———, "Sulpicius Severus and Origenism," *Vigiliae christianae* 34(1980) 278-287.

Van Dam, Raymond, *Leadership and Community in Late Antique Gaul* (Berkeley, 1985).

van den Eynde, D., "Le deuxième canon du concile d'Orange de 441 sur la chrismation," *Recherches de théologie ancienne et médiévale* 11(1939) 97-109.

van der Lof, L. J., "San Ambrosio de Milán y san Martin de Tours," *Helmantica* 21(1970) 441-450.

van der Straeten, Joseph, "S. Martin, sauveteur de s. Brice," *Analecta bollandiana* 100(1982) 237-241.

Vassili, Lucio, "Il *comes* Agrippino collaboratore di Ricimero," *Athenaeum* 14(1936) 175-180.

Vogel, C., *Introduction aux sources de l'histoire du culte chrétien* (Spoleto, 1966)

———, *Ordinations inconsistantes et caractère inamisible* (Turin, 1978).

Völker, W., "Studien zur päpstlichen Vikariatspolitik im 5. Jahrhundert. I. Die Grundung des Primats von Arles und seine Aufhebung durch Leo I," *Zeitschrift für Kirchengeschichte* 46(1927) 335-380.

Vollmann, B., *Studien zum Priszillianismus. Die Forschung, die Quellen, der fünfzehnte Brief Papst Leos des Grossen*, Kirchengeschichtlich Quellen und Studien 7 (St. Ottillen, 1965).

von Campenhausen, H., *Ambrosius von Mailand als Kirchenpolitiker* (Berlin, 1929).

———, *Die asketische Heimatslosigkeit im altkirchlichen und frümittelaterlichen Mönchtum* (Tübingen, 1930).

von Dobschütz, Ernst, ed., *Das Decretum gelasianum de libris recipiendis et non recipiendis in kritischen Text* (Leipzig, 1912).

von Hähling, R., *Die Religionszegehörigkeit der hohen Amtsträger des römischen Reiches von 325 bis 450* (1978).

von Harnack, A., *Lehrbuch der Dogmengeschichte* (vol. 3) (Tübingen, 1932).

———, *Militia Christi. Die christliche Religion und der Soldatenstand in den ersten drei Jahrhunderten* (Tübingen, 1905; repr. Darmstadt, 1963).

von Hefele, Karl Joseph and H. Leclercq, *Histoire des conciles* (10 vols.) (Paris, 1907-1938).

von Schubert, H., *Die sogenannte Praedestinatus, ein Beitrag zur Geschichte des Pelagianismus*, Texte und Untersuchungen zur altchristlichen Literatur 24.4 (Leipzig, 1903).

Voss, Bernd Reiner, "Berühungen von Hagiographie und Historiographie in der Spätantike," *Frümittelalterliche Studien* 4(1970) 53-69.

Wallace-Hadrill, John M., "Gothia and Romania," *Bulletin of the John Rylands Library* 44(1961) 213-237.

———, *The Long-Haired Kings* (London, 1962)

Walser, Gerold, *Via per Alpes Graias. Beiträge zur Geschichte des Kleinen St. Bernhard-Passes in römischen Zeit*, Historia Einzelschriften 48 (Stuttgart, 1986).

Walsh, P. G., *Letters of St. Paulinus of Nola, Volume I. Letters 1-11* and *Vol-*

ume II. Letters 23-51, Ancient Christian Writers 35-36 (Westminster, Md. and London, 1966-67).

Ward Perkins, J. B., "The Sculpture of Visigothic France," *Archaeologia* 87(1938) 79-128.

Weigel, Gustave, *Faustus of Riez. An Historical Introduction* (Philadelphia, 1938).

Weiss, Jean-Pierre, "L'authenticité de l'oeuvre de Salonius de Genève," *Texte und Untersuchungen zur altchristlichen Literatur* 107 = *Studia patristica* 10.1(1970) 161-167.

————, "Essai de datation du Commentaire sur les Proverbes attribué abusivement à Salonius," *Sacris erudiri* 19(1969-1970) 77-114.

————, "La personnalité de Valérien de Cimiez," *Annales de la Faculté des Lettres et Sciences de Nice* 11(1970) 141-162.

————, "Valérien de Cimiez et Valère de Nice," *Sacris erudiri* 21(1972-73) 109-146.

Wermelinger, Otto, "Das Pelagiusdossier in der Tractoria des Zosimus," *Freiburger Zeitschrift der Philologie und Theologie* 26(1979) 336-368.

————, *Rom und Pelagius. Die theologische Position der römischen Bischöfe im pelagianischen Streit in den Jahren 411 bis 432* (Stuttgart, 1975).

Werner, Karl F., "Le rôle de l'aristocratie dans la christianisation du nordest de la Gaule," *Revue d'histoire de l'église de France* 62(1975) 45-63.

Wes, Martin A., *Das Ende des Kaisertums im Westen des römischen Reiches* (The Hague, 1967).

Wickham, C., *Early Medieval Italy. Central Power and Local Society, 400-1000* (Totowa, N.J., 1981).

Wiener, L., *Commentary to the Germanic Laws and Mediaeval Documents* (Cambridge, Mass., 1915).

Wieruszowski, Helene, "Die Zusammensetzung des gallischen und fränkischen Episkopats bis zum Vertrag von Verdun (843) mit besonderer Berücksichtigung der Nationalität und des Standes," *Bonner Jahrbucher* 127(1922) 1-83.

Wightman, Edith, "Peasants and Potentates: An Investigation of Social Structure and Land Tenure in Roman Gaul," *American Journal of Ancient History* 3(1978) 97-128.

Wilmart, A., "Ad Constantium liber primus de saint Hilaire de Poitiers et les fragments historiques," *Revue bénédictine* 24(1907) 149-179, 219-317.

————, "Les 'fragments historiques' du synode de Béziers de 356," *Revue bénédictine* 25(1908) 225-229.

Wood, I. N., "The End of Roman Britain: Continental Evidence and Parallels," in M. Lapidge and D. Dumville eds., *Gildas: New Approaches*, Studies in Celtic History 5 (Woodbridge-Dover, 1984) 1-25.

Woods, F. H., *The Canons of the Second Council of Orange A.D. 529* (Oxford, 1882).

Woodward, E. L., *Christianity and Nationalism in the Later Roman Empire* (London, 1916).

Wörter, F., *Beiträge zur Dogmengeschichte des Semipelagianismus* (Paderborn, 1898).

Wright, Frederick Adam and T. A. Sinclair, *A History of Later Latin Literature. From the Middle of the Fourth to the End of the Seventeenth Century* (New York, 1931, repr. New York, 1969).

Wuilleumier, P., *L'Administration de la Lyonnaise sous le Haut-Empire* (Paris, 1948).

Zecchini, Guiseppe, *Aezio: L'ultima difesa del'occidente romano*, Richerche e documentazione sull'antichita classica 8 (Bretschneider, 1983).

———, "La politca religiosi di Aezio," *Contributi dell' Istituto di Storia Antica dell' Universita del Sacro Curore* 7 (Milan, 1981) 250-277.

Zeiller, J., "Les églises de Gaule dans la première moitié de Ve siècle," in G. le Bras ed., *Saint Germain et son temps* (Auxerre, 1950) 1-13.

Zeller, Joseph, "Das concilium der Septem Provinciae in Arelate," *Westdeutsche Zeitschrift* 24(1905) 1-19.

Zimmermann, F., "Des Claudianus Mamertus Schrift 'De statu animae libri tres'," *Divus Thomas* 1(1914) 238-256, 332-368, 470-495.

INDEX